The Journal OF THE CENTURY

The Journal OF THE CENTURY

Compiled by Bryan Holme
with the Editors of The Viking Press
and the Ladies' Home Journal.

A Studio Book · The Viking Press · New York

NOTE

All the stories in this book—such as those by Ernest Thompson Seton, Dorothy Parker, Booth Tarkington, Agatha Christie, Rebecca West, Shirley Hazzard, and Truman Capote—are complete and as originally published in the *Journal*. Many of the articles have been abridged so that a more representative collection of work between the 1880s and 1970s (involving more than 350,000 pages) could be used. However, in no case have words been changed. It should be pointed out that most of the time neither the original art work nor the original photographs were available for reproduction purposes, meaning that where duplicates or facsimiles were not procurable engravings had to be made from the printed pages of the magazine, a process apt to bring about moiré effects and a harshness of tone. This risk would not have been taken in some instances had not the material been deemed unique and interesting enough to warrant it.

Copyright © Viking Penguin, Inc., 1976
All rights reserved
First published in 1976 by
The Viking Press
625 Madison Avenue, New York, N.Y.
10022

Published simultaneously in Canada by
The Macmillan Company of Canada
Limited
Text and black-and-white illustrations
printed in U.S.A.
Color illustrations printed in Japan

Page 348 constitutes an extension of
this copyright page

Library of Congress Cataloging in Publication Data

Main entry under title:
The Journal of the century.
    (A Studio book)
    Includes index.
    1. United States—Social conditions—Addresses, essays, lectures. 2. Women—United States—Social conditions—Addresses, essays, lectures. 3. United States—Social life and customs—Addresses, essays, lectures.
I. Holme, Bryan, 1913- II. Viking Press, New York. III. Ladies' home journal.
HN57.J68   309.1'73   76-22767
ISBN 0-670-40941-3

CONTENTS

PREFACE

"Never underestimate the power of a woman" the *Ladies' Home Journal* was the first to say, years and years ago. But never had the magazine underestimated the power of a man either. By keeping a well-appointed editorial eye on his interests as well as on hers, the *Journal* became a family affair, an international institution, in short the most successful magazine of its kind in the world. Which is by way of saying that the interest of *The Journal of the Century* is general, the content varied and not without surprises—the amusing, happy, nostalgic, or just plain fascinating kind of surprises one would hope to encounter while journeying through the magazine's long and glamorous past.

Who, for instance, would expect to find that the *Journal* had "discovered" the young English talent, Rudyard Kipling, in the 1890s, and published his first "Just So" story in 1900; that Theodore Roosevelt, by writing for the magazine in 1905, had established a precedent other Presidents were to follow; or that in 1906 the "ladies" would have thought to resurrect a Robert Burns poem in "auld" Scottish brogue and ask Germany's Richard Strauss to put a tune to it. But they did.

Parlor music—live—remained a popular home entertainment throughout the 1900s and 1910s. So the *Journal*'s editors persuaded the brilliant young Josef Hofmann to answer reader's piano questions monthly, pretty Geraldine Farrar to write for "the girl who wants to sing," and the great Enrico Caruso to set the hearts of the *thé dansant* circuit aflutter with "Love's Torment"—a waltz Richard Barthélemy helped the tenor to compose a few years before the Great War. After that, the young—those who had survived the holocaust—tuned into the "blues" on their crystal "wireless" sets, and danced madly.

By the 1920s the sport of big-name hunting had become a more lackadaisical affair. Increased circulation and higher revenues from advertisers meant that fees for name writers like J. P. Marquand, A. A. Milne, Zane Grey, and Dorothy Parker, and for illustrators of the stature of N. C. Wyeth, Arthur Rackham, Maxfield Parrish, and Norman Rockwell could be made increasingly attractive. This put the editors in a much easier chair. Rather than wooing the distant peacock, the problem now, to judge from a typical star-filled issue of the *Journal,* was one of glorious abundance.

Pavlova, Chaplin, the Fairbanks, Maude Adams, the Barrymores, and the Gish sisters— Lillian and Dorothy—were among the many who descended from aloft to write for the magazine and returned the better off. "The Chaotic Decade," Mary Roberts Rinehart called the 1920s, when skirts went high, the stock market higher, and the price of bootlegged liquor the highest yet, prompting the *Journal* to ask, "Can the Church Take the Place of the Saloon?" and, in another concerned editorial, "Does Jazz Put the Sin in Syncopation?"

But were the 1920s more chaotic than any era since, or even before? The financial debacle that ended the 1920s left the 1930s to swim bravely out of economic gloom into the flames of 1940. But on the way to World War II there were such "ups" as Garbo and Gable and Gershwin, Coward and Christie and Colette—and social security—to balance the "downs." The frustrations of listening to Hitler shout or watching Mussolini strut turned to hope as Winston Churchill and Franklin Delano Roosevelt took their monumental stance in history. What did the *Journal* do besides enlist entertainers like Will Rogers, Beatrice Lillie, and Fanny Brice to help put the world in better perspective? Very typically the magazine reached to the top, signing up the First Lady in one of the biggest morale-building coups of its adventurous career.

"If You Ask Me," Eleanor Roosevelt's column said in bold type at the head of the page, and everyone did; they asked her everything they felt like asking her right on through the 1940s: Were Adam and Eve mere stuff and nonsense? Did she believe in prayer? Who were her favorite men, women? Why wasn't the United States more prepared for World War II? And, what, if she didn't mind one of her readers being so impertinent as to inquire, was the reason for not changing her coiffure?

The *Journal*'s menu was always well-balanced with royal and popular reading. Truth— as with England's prince-then-king charming and Mrs. Wallis Simpson of Baltimore—sometimes proved stranger than a Daphne du Maurier or Rumer Godden plot in fiction. On the other hand, there were always those sensible articles about everything under the sun, from raising a family, to better ways to dress oneself or the salad, to make money, or save it, to sew or plant herbs in the garden, to tell fortunes, add a new ring to the finger or a wing onto the end of the house.

Superficially the fare may have changed, but basically the same self-help texts, the food, flower, and fashion features, the major novels or thought-provoking pieces by the likes of Sherwood Anderson, James Michener, John Gunther, and John Steinbeck continued through to the postwar years, when suddenly everyone who had the money flew abroad instead of crossing the oceans or seas by "steamer," and those who did not stayed home, glued to their newest of toys, the TV set.

Time moved on through the affluent fifties of second houses and swimming pools and the fairy-tale pageantry of Elizabeth II's coronation in London, Grace Kelly's Hollywood abdication to become Princess Grace of Monaco, and George Bernard Shaw's rebirth with *My Fair Lady*, to the mixed sixties when the White House was briefly young with the Kennedys, the Beatles were singing, the hippies swinging, and what else was there left to do but to take off for the moon?

The Journal of the Century is about all these things and so very many more, including unisex, and other happenings of the 1970s. Besides stories—there are ten short but complete ones, the first by Ernest Thompson Seton, two middle ones by Agatha Christie and Rebecca West, and the last by Truman Capote—and features on the arts and household matters, these pages might be said to contain some of the most enduring articles and endearing pictures by which this outrageously successful magazine has marked the passage of time since 1883.

That, incidentally, was the year the Brooklyn Bridge opened. No one has quite dared yet to suggest that the birth of the *Ladies' Home Journal* in its tall, slim format and crowded pages of type had caused the same kind of wonderment, delight, and excitement in its native Philadelphia that the Roeblings' masterpiece had in New York earlier in the year. But like many a Cinderella beginning, once the ball got rolling, everything—as we see—turned to gold.

Bryan Holme

FOREWORD

Women, they say, have a tendency to the personal. Equality may eventually expose this as another sexist myth. Nevertheless, history viewed through the pages of a women's magazine becomes a personalized portrait of changing society and culture; a rich tapestry of daily life, fantasy, and dream that recalls each age's flavor and texture with gentle accuracy. In the case of the *Ladies' Home Journal,* there are other unusual perspectives. For ninety-three years the *Journal,* more than any other magazine in its field, has reached out beyond an absorption in traditional domesticity to offer women an inspiring range of artistic, intellectual, and social stimulation. The *Journal* has always put a high value on women's minds and tastes; the *Journal* has always encouraged women to reach up and out. Add an unflagging devotion to the grand idea, a big-game hunter's instinct for the top names and talents, and a passed-along sense of journalistic daring, and it becomes clear why the *Journal* has remained a major institution in American life.

And who has made and kept it that way? A group largely omitted in the credits for these archives: *the editors.* I wish there had been some way to note on every page which of these passionate architects had created or pursued or perfected the offerings. But editors, alas, usually listen to applause off stage. There have been only nine chief editors of the *Journal* in its history, including myself, and because the Goulds were counted as a team, I am only the second woman on the list.

Which is why I am sensitive to the 1920 statement of *Journal* editor Edward Bok, who said that "the full editorial authority" of a modern magazine could not "safely be entrusted to a woman when one considers how largely executive is the nature of such a position." Mr. Bok, who also disapproved of women's suffrage, redeemed himself in other ways, but I always wonder how he had the courage to neglect the contributions of his own mother-in-law, who started it all.

In 1883 a small weekly called *The Tribune and Farmer* was being published and edited in Philadelphia by Cyrus H. K. Curtis, a man from Maine whose name was later to grace a total publishing empire. One night he showed his wife a new woman's department he intended to start, mostly from secondhand material. Mrs. Curtis thought his efforts unworthy and volunteered to do the column herself under her maiden name, Louisa Knapp. The column grew to a page and in December 1883 became a magazine.

Its name was a matter of accident. "Call it anything you want," said Mr. Curtis. "It's a sort of ladies' journal." Which the printer took literally. But between the "Ladies'" and the "Journal" in the first issue, a drawing of a domestic scene was inserted, with the caption "Home." As readers responded enthusiastically with their subscriptions to the new publication, they referred to it as the "Ladies' Home Journal." And a great moving force in American journalism was born.

Louisa Knapp Curtis continued to edit the *Journal* for six years. When she retired in 1889, its monthly circulation was 440,000. Her successor was a twenty-six-year-old Dutch-born extrovert, Edward Bok, who admittedly knew little about women but eventually married the Curtises' daughter, Mary Louise. Under Bok's editorship, the *Journal* bloomed and flourished. It was he who brought in the greatest authors of his time, introduced Rose O'Neill's kewpies, Kate Greenaway's quaint verses and drawings. He mingled with Presidents and world leaders and invited them to write for the *Journal.* His covers and pages utilized the talents of the best artists of the time: John Singer Sargent, Charles Dana Gibson, Maxfield Parrish, and others. Although nobody could ever call him a feminist, he was outspoken on many other issues, campaigning against the common drinking cup as a source of disease, chiding billboard users and power companies for despoiling the environment, and even taking on the then-taboo subject of VD, despite the shocked protests of subscribers and advertisers.

When Bok retired in 1919, the *Journal* had achieved undisputed leadership among women's magazines, and its circulation was two million. For the next sixteen years, under the editorships of Barton W. Currie (until 1928) and Loring A. Schuler (until 1935), the *Journal* continued to steer the same course, with such additional contributors as F. Scott Fitzgerald, Lytton Strachey, Thomas Hardy, Willa Cather, and Edith Wharton adding to its literary luster.

In July 1935 Bruce and Beatrice Gould became the *Journal* editors and started a new era attuned to the changing pace of the thirties. Their midwestern background and unflagging enthusiasm infused the *Journal* with new spirit, and I am convinced that the fact that Mr. and Mrs. Gould were married collaborators added to their power. Privately and professionally, they brought in another sphere of names: Eleanor Roosevelt, Dorothy Thompson, Ogden Nash, Isak Dinesen. It was the Goulds who focused attention on many relevant new issues of national and international concern, and who introduced such unique features as "Can This Marriage Be Saved?" and "How America Lives," both of which are still to be found in the pages of the *Journal*. (Examples of both are also in this book.)

It was in the time of the Goulds that an advertising agency came up with the slogan for the *Journal:* NEVER UNDERESTIMATE THE POWER OF A WOMAN. Then it was a coy reminder that women were pulling the strings behind the men. Today it is a definitive statement of what women are doing on their own.

When the Goulds left in 1962, they were followed by Curtiss Anderson, and then in 1964 by Davis Thomas. With the April 1965 issue, a young man from Kentucky named John Mack Carter took over the editor's seat. John added his own vitality and sure-handed journalistic flair to the magazine, and a whole battery of new names and authorities: Sylvia Porter, Amy Vanderbilt, Gene Shalit, Dr. Theodore Rubin, and others. John, an innovator, was the first to use a black model on the cover of a mass magazine, and it was he who introduced the "real people" concept to service pages. In 1971 a women's movement demonstration held John Carter (and myself, although I am usually omitted from the accounts) captive in his office for eleven hours, perhaps foreshadowing the day when Edward Bok would be proved wrong. In October 1973, when John Carter left for greater challenges, I became the second woman editor in *Journal* history and decided to add my own convictions and conceptions to the mix . . . largely based on a philosophy that women today are increasingly "multipersonal" in their interests, with longer lives and many more options on how to live them.

There is much in the *Journal* today that carries on where other editors have left off but is adaptive to the new life-styles for women. Because it is a time for female recognition, I am proud to have originated the *Journal* "Women of the Year" awards, which not only appear in the magazine, but also on network TV.

I seem to keep returning to Edward Bok. (His grandson is now president of Harvard, by the way.) But he also wrote: "It is a question . . . whether the day of the woman's magazine, as we have known it, is not passing. Already the day has gone for the woman's magazine built on the old lines which now seem so grotesque and feeble in the light of modern growth."

I think anyone studying this book would argue the point. The *Journal* has come through the shoals of the past with astounding strength and style and relevance.

Which is perhaps the underlying message of this unusual volume, edited with such flair and discernment by Bryan Holme. Television, the computer, and other high-speed electronic technologies may seem to threaten the future of the printed page. But the permanence of the perspective offered in good books and good magazines speaks to a part of us that is uniquely responsive. Experiences and images reach out into our inner life and buried memories. Creativity lives, outdistancing time.

Magazines will never seem "grotesque and feeble" as long as they reflect both their readers' needs and the times in which they are edited. Which is why I trust there will be a second edition of this volume in 2076.

Lenore Hershey, Editor-in-Chief,
Ladies' Home Journal (1973–   )

THE LADIES JOURNAL

AND PRACTICAL HOME HOUSEKEEPER.

FIVE CENTS PER COPY. PHILADELPHIA, DECEMBER, 1883. FIFTY CENTS PER YEAR.

Early Marriages

So long as the cat is left in company with the cream jug the cream will be "absorbed," and so long as young people of both sexes are allowed to meet freely in social intercourse there will be more or less marrying and giving in marriage.

It is greatly to be feared that with the thoughtlessness of youth, the young people will not stop to consider the question of ways and means, nor calmly calculate whether they shall be able to gather sticks in sufficient quantity to keep the matrimonial pot boiling. Tom, with a lover's ardor, will probably forget to inquire, before marriage, whether Jemima is capable of cooking dinner, while Jemima, on her part, is just as likely to be left in blissful ignorance whether Tom has a bank account, outside of his salary, which will ensure there being a dinner to cook as well as a kitchen wherein to cook it.

It is a mistake to say two people can live as cheaply as one; for proof controvertive you have only to ask for rates at any boardinghouse.

For example, Augustus manages to support life quite endurably on his salary of $10 or $15 per week; perhaps even maintains a certain position in society thereon, but he would never dream of asking Augusta to share it. If he did, Augusta with her worldly wisdom, would think him either demented or tipsy. Six dollars a week pays for his bedroom in the respectable boardinghouse which he patronizes, or, perhaps, he rents a small furnished room, and, trusting to occasional invitations to dinner, takes his meals on the European plan. The rest of his salary, with close economy, keeps him in clothes, gloves and cigars, with an occasional theatre ticket and admission to the opera on gala nights. His well-kept dress suit does not often need renewal, and dancing men are always in request at parties.

But what on earth could he do with a wife? Angels and ministers of grace defend us. Where are Augusta's dresses to come from? How is even the board bill for two, instead of one, to be paid? How could they expect "people" to visit them? So he dances on, hoping vainly to find a rich wife, while she, on her part, knows that her duty to herself requires that her husband shall be able to give her at least the luxuries to which she has been accustomed and keeps detrimentals at a safe distance.

Or if they forget themselves so far as to marry, in all probability both of them are miserable, since neither can help looking back with longing eyes to the world whence they have shut themselves by their wedding.

To insure happiness in married life there must be perfect support, thorough sympathy as well as sincere affection between the twain who have been made "one flesh." When there is wealth and to spare, less may answer, for the wedded pair who, while two in heart, must bear the privations of poverty as one, life is hard indeed. While love may not actually "sweeten sugarless tea," it does much to render the cup less nauseous. That woman cannot be altogether unhappy who knows that she is the light of her husband's eyes—that man cannot be utterly discouraged who knows that, come what may, his wife believes in him thoroughly.

While it is not always a safe experiment, a man, if he be worthy the name, will often work the harder, and win success in the face of apparently insurmountable obstacles because he has given hostages to fortune. More than one man has won his laurels chiefly because he could not bear to disappoint the woman whose faith in him might have moved mountains, when, left to himself, he had probably sat down content with a little success.

A good wife is seldom, if ever, a hindrance to a man, and it has passed into a proverb that "marriage either makes or mars a man." "It is not good for man (still less woman) to be alone," and, however willingly single blessedness may have been chosen, there are few in such cases who do not sometimes feel how hard a thing it is to look at happiness through other people's eyes. Still marriage is by no means to be lightly entered into. As a wise old lady used to say, never marry anybody until you are quite sure that you cannot be comfortable without them.

How Girls Deceive Their Parents

The liberty which is permitted to young American girls is something to be proud of, as long as it is not abused; but as soon as it is abused, the boast that our girls are discreet and decorous enough to take care of themselves, and need no chaperone, becomes a glaring absurdity. In such a case a sensible person will begin to understand that English mothers, or even the more rigorous French parents, are in the right. It is beginning to be understood that what is well for some quiet village, where every one is known by name and reputation, is bad for a great metropolis, crowded with strangers, and full of men ever ready to take advantage of ignorance and innocence, or to encourage recklessness and impropriety when manifested by pretty young women.

The other day a friend of mine, riding in one of the city cars, overheard a conversation between a man of mature years and two young girls. These girls, evidently fresh from school, had met the man by chance, and he had been impertinent enough to speak to them. They did not even know his name until he gave them one to call him by. He had invited them to go with him to Coney Island on a certain day, and remarked: "Two being company and three none, he meant to bring a friend as escort for one of the girls." Then the questions arose, How would pa take it? What would ma say? and an arrangement was made which would obviate these difficulties. That evening Rachel would meet one of the men in the street, and take him to Helen's house, and introduce him to Helen's mother as a friend of hers; and on the next evening Helen would bring the other gentleman, whom she had not yet even seen, to Rachel's house, and introduce him to Rachel's parents as her friend. After that the party could be made up, and the parents be none the wiser.

The girls never seemed to think that this proposition was an insult to them and to their parents. They considered it a brilliant idea, and they were peculiarly anxious, as well they might be, to learn all about the "other gentleman." Was he handsome? Would he be well dressed, and full of fun? Whereupon the gallant assured them that he "wouldn't bring any but a real jolly, handsome, nobby fellow, on any account."

After this my friend lost sight of the trio. I do not know whether Rachel and Helen went with the stranger and his "nobby" friend to Coney Island. Perhaps Providence interposed to prevent the excursion. Let us hope that he did, or else those foolish, deceitful girls may have branded their brows with the mark of shame forever.

The Salon of Mrs. Oscar Wilde

Mrs. Wilde and her boy, Cyril.

There is perhaps no house in London where more brilliant and delightful people congregate during the season, and where the talk is sure to be so effervescent, as in the little salon presided over by Mrs. Oscar Wilde. Poets, artists, sculptors, members of Parliament, scientific men, actors and actresses, ladies of high title, men of lofty position, and the gilded youth of the day, gather together around Mrs. Wilde's tea-table, attracted quite as much by the charm of the hostess as by the inimitable wit of her husband.

Hints on Etiquette

One of two things, money or birth, seem to be necessary to maintain a position in fashionable society. In older cities perhaps birth is more essential, but as a rule, money is the golden key that opens all doors. In small towns society cannot be too exclusive and the wealthiest lady in the place may meet her dressmaker or milliner at evening parties. After all there is but one standard by which to judge whether or not a person is worthy to become a member of good society. Is he a gentleman? is she a lady? should be the only question asked. Not that they are well dressed, or handsome, or rich, but do they possess certain qualities, such as kindheartedness, good feeling towards the world in general, repose of manner, dignity, refinement, sincerity, and a character above reproach. But a lady who is in all respects a real lady may chance to be ignorant of certain rules of etiquette.

It is an established decree that a lady receiving calls in her own house, must not introduce two ladies who are residents of the same town. This rule holds good in exclusive society, but will doubtless surprise those who live in country towns, and to many hostesses would seem the height of impoliteness, the visitors, also, feeling that they were treated with discourtesy if not positive rudeness. Circumstances alter cases, and what would be considered proper in strictly fashionable society would perhaps give offense in less formal circles. But there is one important point upon which Americans and English differ. The latter never hesitate to speak to any visitors they may chance to meet at the house of a mutual friend, while Americans maintain their stiffest manner until properly introduced. How embarrassing this formality is to a hostess who does not dare introduce her callers. If they would but exchange a remark or two all would be easy. There is certainly much to be said against promiscuous introductions. How do you know that your friends desire to become acquainted? Certainly no gentleman should be introduced to a lady until her permission has been granted. In making an introduction the gentleman is presented to the lady, as for instance, "Mrs. B. allow me to introduce (or present) Mr. C."

Another rule is that a gentleman who has been introduced to a lady with her consent is at liberty to call upon her or leave his card at her door. Generally people bow formally upon being introduced, but in certain places, perhaps especially in the South, it is the custom to shake hands. In her own house a hostess should certainly shake hands with a person introduced to her.

At a dinner party, a few minutes before dinner, the hostess introduces to a lady the gentleman who is to take her down to dinner, but it is not customary to give further introductions, the guests being at liberty to converse with each other.

A mother is always at liberty to introduce her son or daughter, a husband may introduce his wife, and a wife her husband.

At informal gatherings it is proper to introduce guests, in fact one's own tact and judgement must frequently be the guide.

After a gentleman has been introduced to a lady, should he meet her again, he must wait for her to bow first before claiming her as an acquaintance.

In almost all places it is considered the lady's place to bow first when passing a gentleman friend on the street. On the Continent the gentleman bows first, and this is said to be the custom in some Southern cities. Should the ladies who accompany a gentleman, recognize an acquaintance the gentleman should raise his hat.

When a gentleman is introduced to a lady it is the gentleman's place to open conversation. The one who is introduced should make the first remark.

A gentleman must not shake hands with a lady until she has made the first movement. A married lady should always offer her hand to a stranger brought to her house by a mutual friend.

A first call should be returned within a week. In England the lady highest in rank makes the first call. Here, the oldest resident calls first. If there is no distinction one lady may wait for the other until both are ashamed to take the initiative. As a rule, however, it is well to be slow about calling upon strangers, say one's new neighbors, for it is sometimes difficult to become rid of undesirable acquaintances, and a lady does not wish to slight anyone.

Calls should be made within three days after a dinner, or an entertainment of any kind if it is a first invitation, and within a week after a party or ball, whether you accept the invitation or not.

Between two and six in the afternoon are the hours preferred for making formal calls.

A gentleman when making a call may leave his overcoat or umbrella in the hall but he must take his hat and cane with him into the parlor. If he does not wish to retain these articles in his hands he may place them on the floor near his chair but should not deposit them on any article of furniture in the room.

In Europe, if a gentleman has had himself introduced to a lady, he calls the following day and the call is returned by the gentleman of the house if there is a desire to continue the acquaintance. If, after an introduction, the gentleman does not call not even a bowing acquaintance is continued.

The usual custom here is for the young lady or her mother to invite the gentleman to call, and it would be thought strange for him to do so without an invitation. If a gentleman should bring a friend to call on you it would be polite to invite the stranger to repeat his visit.

There is one more rule that we fear will never meet with much favor in America, and this is that a young lady's mother should always sit with her when she is receiving a call from a gentleman.

1883. Mrs. William K. Vanderbilt as she appeared at her fancy dress ball this spring, celebrating the opening of her new house on Fifth Avenue.

Home Cooking

Original Recipes for Desserts Contributed by The Journal Sisters

ANGEL'S CAKE. Find a tumbler which holds exactly 2¼ gills or 18 tablespoonfuls, (8 tablespoonfuls liquid measure is an accurate enough measure of a gill) 1½ tumblers of granulated sugar, sifted several times before measuring, 1 teaspoonful of cream of tartar sifted in 1 tumbler of flour, no soda, whites of 11 eggs well beaten, and 1½ teaspoonfuls of vanilla. The cake must be mixed in a large flat dish. Beat the eggs

very thoroughly, add easily the sugar, then as lightly as possible, the flour, and lastly, the extract. Bake in a new tin—without greasing. When done, invert the pan on two or three goblets. Let it cool, then with the assistance of a knife it is easily removed. Be sure to ice it.

CHRISTMAS FRUIT CAKE. One pound each of flour, butter and sugar, three pounds each of raisins and currants, one pound of citron, nine eggs, one pint of brandy, half an ounce each of ground cloves, cinnamon, nutmeg and mace. Bake slowly or send it to your baker, who will bake it just right and only charge 25 cents for doing it.

BUTTER SCOTCH. 1 cup of molasses, 1 cup of sugar, ½ cup of butter. Boil until done —trying as for molasses candy.

CHOCOLATE CARAMELS. 1 cup each of grated chocolate, milk, molasses and sugar, a piece of butter size of an egg; boil together until the mixture hardens when dropped into cold water; add vanilla, pour in buttered tins, and mark in squares when nearly cold.

Engraving by George Cruikshank. 1835.

SUGAR KISSES. Whites of 2 eggs, and ¾ lb. of pulverized sugar stirred together until very light. Drop on buttered paper in teaspoonfuls, and bake in quick oven.

SPANISH CREAM. ⅓ box of gelatine dissolved in 1½ pints of milk, boil, then stir in the yolks of 3 eggs, add 3 tablespoonfuls of sugar, boil again. Beat the whites to a stiff froth and stir in after taking the cream from the fire. Flavor with orange and cool slowly.

CREAM PUFFS. 1 cup of hot water, ½ cup of butter, boil together and, while boiling, stir in 1 cup of sifted flour, dry. Take from the stove and stir to a smooth paste, and after this cools stir in 3 eggs (not beaten). Stir it 5 minutes. Drop in tablespoonfuls on a buttered tin and bake in a quick oven 25 minutes, being careful not to open oven door oftener than is absolutely necessary. Makes 12 puffs. Don't let them touch each other in the pan.

For the cream:—1 cup of milk, ½ cup of sugar, 1 egg, 3 tablespoonfuls of flour, flavor with vanilla. When both this and the puffs are cool open the puffs a little way with a sharp knife and fill them with the cream. These never fail to puff.

SQUASH PIE. Steam a Hubbard squash, and when it is done mash it in the colander. To every quart of strained squash add 5 well beaten eggs, 2 quarts of milk, 1 tablespoonful of ground ginger and 1 of cinnamon, salt and sweeten to suit the taste.

ENGLISH PLUM PUDDING. 1 pound each of baker's bread, brown sugar, suet chopped fine, seeded raisins and currants, 1½ pounds of flour, ¼ pound each of candied citron and lemon peel chopped, and 1 ounce of bitter almonds powdered, 1 gill of brandy, 4 eggs, 1 tablespoonful each of ground cloves, cinnamon, and nutmeg. Soak the

bread until soft in milk, work the other ingredients into it, add the flour last. Put into a well buttered mold and boil steadily for 5 hours. Water should be boiling when the pudding is put in. When the pudding is done, put on a pretty flat dish, garnish with smilax, pour alcohol on top of the pudding and light it bringing the pudding on to the table in a flame. Serve the pudding with plain brandy sauce.

Sauces for the Christmas Pudding

1½ cups of sugar, ¾ cup of butter, (light brown sugar is best) rubbed together until they are of a very light foam, then stir in 3 teaspoonfuls of flour and a little vinegar; stir into a pint of boiling water and let it just come to a boil, then grate on nutmeg and serve hot.

1 cup sugar, 1 tablespoonful butter, 1 tablespoonful of flour, 1 coffee cup boiling water. Stir sugar, butter and flour together, then pour on the boiling water and let it cook until it thickens, stirring to keep from burning. Flavor after removing from fire. More butter added will make a richer sauce.

½ cup sugar, ¼ cup butter or less, 1 egg. Flavoring, lemon or vanilla; tablespoonful of flour; beat all together. Pour on boiling water just before serving the pudding, and stir thoroughly. Excellent, almost equal to a custard.

HARD SAUCE. ¼ lb. of sugar, ¼ lb. of butter, ¼ of a nutmeg grated, white of 1 egg. Beat sugar and butter to a cream in a cool place, so that the butter will not oil. Whip whites of eggs to a stiff froth, and mix lightly into the creamed sugar and butter. When done put the sauce into a crystal dish for serving and grate the nutmeg over it.

HOW TO GO ABROAD

Mrs. A. R. Ramsey

If you have before you that most delightful of prospects, a trip to Europe, the first law must be to avoid all superfluous baggage, for in some countries you pay for every pound not carried in the hand. You will therefore save money and trouble, if you dispense with a trunk, using a valise or hand satchel.

Illustrated is a most convenient hand bag, easily made, which will hold all you are likely to need. It is made of waterproof serge, lined with blue silesia,—the edges bound with braid.

Hand bag

If a valise is used it should be of a kind that opens quickly at the demand of custom house officials, for this examination is a nuisance to be suffered at every frontier.

You will find a steamer trunk a great convenience. It may be of the humblest description, even one of those known as "shoe box trunks," and ought not to cost more than $1. It must be small enough to slip under the berth, or sofa, for nothing is more disagreeable than a trunk which must stand in the middle of the stateroom, and against whose corners you are thrown at every lurch of the vessel.

The trunk should contain an old woollen dress, the older and darker the better, since a ship is a dirty place, and there is always something to "rub off" from the fresh paint, oiled brasses, and tarry ropes, besides the innumerable possibilities of being drenched with soup, or hot gravy, if you encounter rough weather.

The trunk should hold, likewise, plenty

Choose a steamer with a reputa-tation for having a "dry-deck."

of wraps, an old winter coat, besides a heavy shawl, to wrap about your fluttering skirts as you sit on deck: a hood, or nubia, to go over your hat in the same breezy place; a woollen wrapper for seasickness; a night dress; knit slippers; underclothing, including flannel shirts and skirts; thick shoes; warm gloves; smelling salts; a little fine brandy or whiskey; some lemons; and a few books—for the ship's library is always most limited in quality and quantity.

The medicines you are most likely to need are arnica, ammonia, ginger, a good diarrhœa mixture, a box of French pills, a roll of court plaster, around a tiny pair of scissors, and a vial of quinine pellets.

Among the minor conveniences you will find most useful a small bag in which to keep scissors, needles, thread, buttons, and shoe fastenings, and you should not fail to provide yourself with a bag to hang *inside* your berth, near the pillow, in which to keep handkerchief, brush and comb, hairpins, watch and trinkets—for, if you are very seasick, you will want to reach all these things without raising your head.

Your regular travelling dress may be worn to the ship, and changed as soon as you are off.

You will be wise if you cover your hat closely with brown paper, and hang it up on a nail, for the sea air takes color and stiffness out of millinery, and woe to the ostrich plumes not thus protected.

Whatever you select for your travelling dress, let it be all wool and of quiet colors; but, in the name of all the proprieties, do have it made simply. Finery in travelling is vulgar, and you will not wish to be one of the Americans whose nationality is at once detected by their elaborate dressing.

Your ulster will go ashore with you, your umbrella and overshoes likewise, with underclothes, some ruching for emergencies, several pairs of good American shoes. Do not fail to provide yourself with soap and candles, and *always carry flannel underwear* —at least skirts and shirts. The differences in climate between a Swiss mountain and an Italian valley are extreme, yet you may experience both in the course of a day. For the warmer climates a prettily made waist of French sateen, or of Foulard silk, will be extremely comfortable with the skirt of your travelling dress.

For table d' hote dinners you will want a little more dress, though simplicity is to be aimed at here also. Black silk, or cashmere, square at the neck, or finished at throat and wrists with fine lace, a knot of ribbon or velvet at the neck, with little or no jewelry, and no showy jet is appropriate.

On all good lines the tables fairly groan under a supply of food as varied as in a first-class hotel; but a box of good prunes is sometimes very acceptable, and a few pint bottles of champagne may be a wise provision, since, in case of violent sickness, iced champagne is sometimes the only thing the stomach will retain.

It is well to choose a steamer having a reputation for a "dry deck," as this will enable you to be out many an hour otherwise spent in a close, almost air-tight cabin. A steamer-chair is a great luxury, but as few steamers carry them, you must provide them for yourself. They cost $2.00 delivered at the ship.

THE MAKING AND SAVING OF MONEY

Henry Clews

It does not require a genius to make money. The accumulation of wealth is, after all, an easy matter. It does not require education, breeding, or gentle manners, and certainly luck has nothing to do with it. Any man or woman may become wealthy. The opportunities for gathering the nimble dollar are very numerous in this country. But there are certain fundamental rules that must be observed.

The first step to acquiring a fortune lies in hard work. I could give you no better advice than that given by Poor Richard, "Save something each day, no manner how little you earn!" Cultivate thrifty habits. Make your toil count for all that you can. Always save some portion of your wages, and then be on the alert for investment. If you do this wisely, your money will begin to accumulate, double, treble.

Keep a bank account.

When you have saved one hundred, or two hundred, or five hundred dollars, look about for a good investment. Do not take up this or that scheme at a venture, but examine it carefully, and if you see your way clear, put your money into it. Real estate is usually a good investment. More money has been made in real estate than you could estimate in a day. A first mortgage is, in nine cases out of ten, safe. But take advice on the subject before you invest. Go to some good conservative man and get his views. I should advise the same course if you should put your money in stocks or bonds, or railway shares.

If your first investment prospers, by careful management, and by always being on the alert, you can increase your fortune by reinvesting your profits.

A man who had only a few hundred dollars left out of a fortune, called one day at a banking house and asked to see the manager, who was a man of conservative mind and fully acquainted with the best and most profitable investments.

Throwing down his roll of bank notes, he said: "Invest this for me. Use your pleasure with it. I'm going to the country for the remainder of the summer. I will leave my address with you, and you can let me know what you do with it."

The man walked out, and was not seen again for many months. His money was judiciously invested on his carte-blanche order, and began to accumulate.

This was an example of a man who more than doubled his savings by simply taking the advice of an experienced and reliable man. And this is not a solitary case.

How did Samuel J. Tilden attain his elevated position and immense fortune?

Simply by the exercise of thrift and industry, together with a certain degree of common sense, the capacity for taking advantage of the chances thrown in his way, and his own smartness for turning them to the best account.

Industry, persevering and untiring, is essential to the accumulation of money. I have myself some little knowledge of the toil attendant upon the amassing of wealth, and I have the highest respect for the man who, in the face of adverse circumstances, turns his pennies into dollars, and his dollars into millions.

The life of Commodore Vanderbilt affords singular scope for reflection on the immense possibility of a great business capacity to amass a large fortune in a few years, especially in this country. From being the possessor of a row-boat on New York Bay, he rose in sixty years to be the proud possessor of $90,000,000. William H. Vanderbilt, his son, obtained $75,000,000 of this, and largely increased the fortune before his death.

It has been truly said that any fool can make money, but it takes a wise man to keep it. William H. Vanderbilt's ability was signally displayed in keeping intact this great fortune, besides adding easily once again as much more to it. I make special mention of Mr. Vanderbilt because he was not a speculator, in the true sense of that term. He was, first and for all time, an investor.

Collis P. Huntington came to New York when a boy of fifteen, without a penny. His father was a farmer and small manufacturer. Collis early showed great shrewdness in business, and unlimited energy and resolution. But success is not usually attained without long and persistent effort, and so Mr. Huntington found to be the case. But after years of hard work his fortune was made, and now he is worth about $30,000,000.

Leland Stanford received an academical education and commenced the study and practice of law. At twenty-eight years of age, a fire wiped out his law library and other property, which led him to the west in search of better fortunes. Here his native shrewdness and energy asserted itself, and soon the dollars began to multiply. Now he is worth from $25,000,000 to $30,000,000.

Darius O. Mills is one of the most notable figures daily seen down town in New York. He was born in a small town on the Hudson River some sixty years ago, and began life in very humble circumstances. His courage was equal to that of a Richelieu, and his caution, conservatism, energy, and industry,

were all fully developed. He has always been dependent on his own exertions, and has fought his way up in life by sheer force of his own keen intelligence and undaunted enterprise. In the battle of life he has achieved signal success. He is worth about $20,000,000.

John W. Mackay was born in the humblest circumstances in Dublin, Ireland, some fifty-five years ago. Coming to this country very early in life, he worked for a time on board ship. During the years that followed, in whatever occupation he engaged, he labored industriously and faithfully. He saved his money, and watched his opportunity, which so very few people do. He is now twenty times a millionaire, and all by reason of hard and continuous effort and thrift.

The wealth of the Astors is remarkable for the way it has been kept intact, and for the steady and considerably rapid augmentation which is continually taking place. The elder Astor made a mint of money out of the fur trade, and would have continued in that business, but he found that investment in real estate was vastly more profitable. The family has steadily adhered to this line of investment through three generations.

George Peabody was a poor Massachusetts boy who, by hard industry, rose to be one of the great millionaires of his day. His fortune at one time exceeded $10,000,000, and during his life-time he gave away more than $7,000,000 to charitable purposes. His millions arose from pennies, by the exercise of thrift, honesty and persevering effort.

Alexander T. Stewart, "the merchant prince," amassed his millions by close attention to business and by the aid of shrewd common sense and thrift. He was reputed to be one of the three wealthiest men in the United States, Commodore Vanderbilt and John Jacob Astor being the other two. He left an estate exceeding $20,000,000.

Peter Cooper had a hard time of it getting an education. He was born in New York, one hundred years ago, and at the age of seventeen was apprenticed to a shoemaker. He tried his hand at several trades, and got together a comfortable fortune of about $6,000,000, through unremitting toil, conscientious devotion to duty, and economical habits.

August Belmont came to New York poor, and lived to be worth some millions. Prudence, acuteness and sagacity, were the instruments by which his wealth was accumulated.

Cyrus W. Field is another apt illustration. He has been termed a locomotive in

PRACTICAL FASHIONS

trousers. The simile serves to convey an idea of the indefatigable energy of the man. His indomitable resolution and his energy of character have placed him high among the distinguished men of the age.

Russell Sage, as a boy, was employed in a village store. His business aptitude early manifested itself, and in six years he bought out his employer. He is one of the largest capitalists in the country, and all his millions have been rolled up by energy and thrift.

John Wanamaker, Chauncey M. Depew, James M. Brown, Anthony Drexel, Moses Taylor, George W. Childs, J. Pierpont Morgan, and a host of others, are men who have fought their way to prominence and affluence by sheer force of integrity, pluck, intelligence and industry.

The lives of all the men mentioned are instances of what can be attained by any boy or man in America. They are eloquent testimony of the truth that industry, perseverance, honesty and thrift can accomplish anything. A man who is wise, careful, and conservative, energetic, persevering and tireless, need have no fear of his future. But there is one other thing. He must have a steady head, one that can weather the rough sea of reverses, from which no life is altogether free, and one that will not become too big when success attends his efforts.

Keep out of the way of speculators. Take your money, whether it be much or little, to one whose reputation will insure you good counsel. Invest your money where the principal is safe and you will get along.

But don't forget the acorns. It is from little acorns that great oaks grow. See that you begin aright early in life. Save your money with regularity. By so doing, you will more than save your money; you will make money.

A "Coming Out" Dress

A Tennis Suit

Child's Play Dress

An "Aunt's" Costume

A Mountaineering Costume

OFF FOR DANCING SCHOOL:

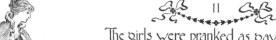

Drawings by Kate Greenaway,   Verses by Laura E. Richards.

These words can be sung to the Elizabethan air :
"To all you ladies now on land," etc.

I

We started off for dancing school,
  My sisters twain and I;
The night was lovely, clear and cool,
  The moon was in the sky.
I wore a gown of sarcenet blue,
And Madge and Kitty had them too,
   For to trip and to skip,
    And to skip and to trip,
And be merry all the glad time through.

II

The girls were pranked as gay and bright
  As peacocks in their pride;
The parson's Rose was all in white,
  Most like an April bride,
Her sister Nell in gown of green,
Good lack! she thought herself a queen,
   For to trip and to skip,
    And to skip and to trip,
And be merry all the glad time through.

III

The lads in corner huddled close,
  Just like a flock of sheep;
    Beneath their lids at Nell and Rose
They scarcely dared to peep.
    But yet, "How fair so e'er they be,"
Methought, "There's one will come for me,
For to trip and to skip,   And to skip and to trip,
    And be merry all the glad time through."

IV

The master tapped his fiddle-bow,
  And bade us rise to dance.
The girls stood perking in a row,
  All waiting for the chance.
And up comes Ned with beck and bow,
  And says "Wilt be my partner now,
For to trip and to skip,
  And to skip and to trip,
And be merry all the glad time through?"

V

I dropped my curtsey wide and deep,
  And gave to Ned my hand.
Pit! pat! my feet the time did keep,
  The while we took our stand.
Then ting! tang! ta! the notes did play,
  And Ned and I set quick away,
For to trip and to skip,
  And to skip and to trip,
And be merry all the glad time through.

VI

Now hop! hop! hop! we all did go,
  A slide and then a bounce.
    And Rose flew by, a wreath of snow,
  And Nell did flaunt and flounce.
"But best," cried Ned, "I like the blue!
And oh, there's none of them all like you,
   For to trip and to skip,
    And to skip and to trip,
    And be merry all the
      glad time
       through!"

THE PHILADELPHIA ASSEMBLY—*in the foyer of the Academy of Music. By Alice Barber Stephens.*

THE MOST ARISTOCRATIC EVENT IN AMERICA

During just one hundred and fifty years the entrance into "society" in Philadelphia has been through the doorway of "The Assembly." The managers of the functions of that annual court of honor have been foremost in regulating the social sovereignty of the city. Nowhere else in the United States is there a dynasty which has held longer or more nearly uninterrupted sway. Indeed, the City Dancing Assembly of Philadelphia was in existence before the aristocracy of Charleston had begun their Cæcilia, and even before the far-famed Almack's was founded as the seventh heaven of the fashionable set in London.

Many of the families who now take part in the Assemblies at the Academy of Music are the descendants of the belles and beaus who danced the minuet in the halls of the State House long before the Revolution.

THE WOMAN IN BUSINESS.

By Alice Barber Stephens.

A $5000 COLONIAL HOUSE

Ralph Adams Cram

Nothing is much better as a model for American domestic work than architecture of the early part of the century.

The accompanying design shows an attempt to restore something of the simplicity characteristic of good Colonial work. The plan is a rectangle, broken only by an open porch in front and a covered porch behind. In the centre is the main entrance hall, nine feet wide, with a curved flight of stairs at the end. Opening from this hall on the right are two rooms of equal size, connecting by means of arches on either side of the chimney. These rooms can be used as double parlors, or one may be used as a library or a reception-room. On the left of the hall is the dining-room. Behind this is a good-sized kitchen, china-closet and the pantry, servants' entrance and stairs.

On the second floor are three large bedrooms and one small one, together with a bath. A portion of the hall at the front of the house is separated from the stairway by a wide arch, and may be used either as a portion of the hall or as a sewing-room. On the third floor are two servants' rooms, a linen-closet, and a large playroom. The cellar extends under half the house, containing the furnace, coal-bins, a cold closet, set tubs and a servants' lavatory.

The exterior is practically a reproduction of an old Colonial house. The walls are to be clap-boarded. The chimneys have been made of considerable size to obtain the dignity so characteristic of the Colonial period. Small chimneys will ruin any design; large chimneys will do much toward dignifying the most trivial travesty of architecture.

The construction contemplated is of the utmost simplicity. The foundations and underpinning are of local split stone. Walls, floors and roofs are lined with sheathing paper, and the walls are fire-stopped with brick at each floor. Inside, the floors of the first story, and of the halls and bath in the second, are of maple, the standing finish—whitewood. The effect, such as it is, is dependent solely on simple lines and quiet detail.

A house built after this plan would cost, in the vicinity of the larger cities of the East, about $5000, including heating and plumbing.

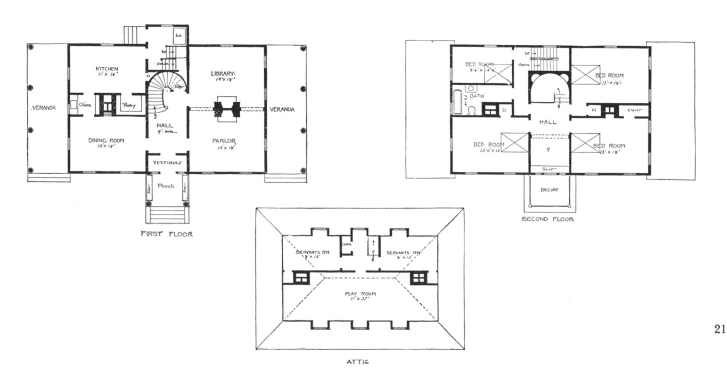

WHAT VICTORIA HAS SEEN

William George Jordan

In June, 1837, Victoria, then a young girl of eighteen, ascended the throne of England. Her sixty years' reign, the longest of any English sovereign, has covered a period of progress and prosperity unequaled in the annals of history. No other sixty years have seen such strides of science, such development in education, such growth in religious tolerance, such strengthening of the bonds between nations, such universal advance toward higher living.

When Victoria was called to the throne the United Kingdom contained 26,000,000 people. To-day it has over 39,000,000. The "wise men" of the time said the nation would go to pieces. They claimed it could never govern its home and colonial possessions. Under Victoria the new territory acquired alone is one-sixth larger than all Europe. To-day Victoria rules over 402,-514,000 people, or twenty-seven per cent. of the population of the globe. Her Empire extends over 11,399,316 square miles, covering twenty-one per cent. of the land of the world.

The United States, at the time of Victoria's coronation, had only 17,000,000 people; to-day it has 70,000,000. All territory west of the Mississippi contained less people than Philadelphia has to-day. The territorial area has increased seventy-five per cent.; National wealth has increased about seventeen hundred per cent.

Australia was important as a penal colony. Its total population in 1837 was 345,000. Now it is over 3,300,000. To-day its trade exceeds that of all Great Britain at the beginning of Victoria's reign. The city of Melbourne then consisted of a church, an inn, three shops, twenty huts and a kangaroo-meat market. It is now Australia's largest city, with 500,000 people.

Africa was an almost unknown territory. In South Africa, Cape Colony alone was known. Victoria has seen one-third of the country brought under civilization by Livingstone, Baker, Stanley, Speke, Du Chaillu, Johnston and a host of other explorers. Plantations, farms and great cities are now on the sites of deserts and forests.

No telephone or telegram carried messages sixty years ago and no submarine cable—not even a foot—lay in the ocean. Electricity was in its infancy. Electric lights, electric power, electric cars, electric bells—the thousand applications of electricity to every-day life belong to the past sixty years.

Great social reforms belong to Queen Victoria's reign. The degrading practice of flogging has been abolished in the armies and navies of America and England. Children are no longer permitted to work in the mines of Britain. Press gangs no longer force men into the service of the Queen's navy. Executions are no longer conducted in public. The treatment of criminals has become humane. Factory laws and building acts make life easier for the poor.

THE QUEEN IN HER CORONATION ROBES, *1837. Painting by Sir George Hayter.*

Trans-Atlantic steamers, making regular trips, did not exist in 1837; now there are over ninety. Steamers in those days were wooden affairs with paddle wheels. The iron steamer with the screw had not yet appeared. The time for a trans-Atlantic trip was then about fourteen days. Now it can be made in five days and a quarter.

Political unity has made great progress in Victoria's reign. She has seen over twenty small States consolidated into the great German Empire. Italy has been a unified kingdom for only twenty-six years. Switzer-land's squabbling cantons were unified into a strong and model republic in 1848.

Medicine and surgery have made wondrous strides. Deaths from amputation have been reduced one-half, the smallpox mortality has been lessened seventy-five per cent. Anæsthetics have made daring surgical operations possible. Many so-called "incurable" diseases have been conquered.

Steel was expensive when Victoria was crowned. The Bessemer process, invented by one of her subjects, caused the price to fall at once from $300 to $30 a ton. The inventor netted $5,000,000 in royalties. In forty years his invention has saved the world one thousand million dollars!

Light and air were taxed when Victoria became England's Queen. The tax on windows brought in £1,000,000 a year to the treasury. Poor people blocked up windows to escape payment.

Street lighting was unknown, except in the large cities. New York could boast of only 300 oil lamps and a few lonely gas lamps. In smaller towns, citizens carried lanterns.

Railways were just beginning. The world's mileage was only 1600 miles; now it is over 420,000. In 1837 twenty miles an hour was good time; now regular trains make over fifty miles an hour.

Running-water in houses did not exist, even for royalty, sixty years ago. In New York rain water was largely used, and most houses had cisterns. The wealthy used water brought in casks from the upper wards of the city.

Slavery existed throughout the world sixty years ago. In the second year of Victoria's reign emancipation was complete in England. Ten years later France and South American republics freed their slaves. Russia and the United States followed in 1863. Brazil declared its slaves free in 1871, Portugal in 1878, and Cuba in 1886.

No snap-shots were taken of the coronation ceremonies. Photography was then unknown. There was no steam heating. Flint and tinder did duty for matches. Plate glass was a luxury undreamed of. Envelopes had not been invented and postage-stamps had not been introduced. Sewing machines had not yet supplanted the needle. Stem-winding watches had not appeared. So it was with hundreds of the necessities of our present life.

The Queen in 1898 during the visit of their Imperial Majesties The Emperor and Empress of Russia at Balmoral Castle. From left to right: Alexandra Feodorovna, baby Grand Duchess Tatiana, Nicholas II, Victoria, and Edward Prince of Wales.

THE BROWNIES AT NEWPORT

By Palmer Cox

WHEN summer brought around the days
So noted for the golden blaze
That soon makes people seek the shade
As through the town they promenade,
Still hoping blessings may bring ease
And rest to those who planted trees,
The Brownies met as evening shade
Was settling on the dewy glade.
Said one: "This is the time of year
When people of some means appear
To weary of their homes in town,
Or work, perhaps, that weighs them down,
And closing up their doors they seek
For pleasure on a mountain peak,
Or turn their steps in haste to reach
The joys found at an ocean beach."
Another said: " We something know
About the sea, for years ago
We proved the trials, less or more,
Of those who venture from the shore,
But all the same there is a charm
About the sea that will disarm
The ready fears that whispering stand,
Saying 'praise the sea, but keep on land,'
So I advise without delay
We start upon our seaward way,

Will always answer like a goad
To start the Brownies on the road,
The miles and leagues that must be crossed,
However rough or well embossed
With stumps and stones, by Brownies bright
Are counted naught but matters light.
And soon the band so bold and spry
The fashionable port drew nigh,
And stood to view the buildings grand
That stretched along the famous strand
Where mingling thousands through the day
Disport themselves as best they may.
But night it was, and they could boast
The right of way, and that's the most
That Brownies care for; well endowed,
Their wants are few, their spirits proud.
Retire betimes, and shut your door,
And they'll not ask a favor more.
Upon themselves be sure they'll wait,
And think it not beneath their state.
They'll find their way to every shelf,
Nor ask your servant nor yourself
To set the table, pass the cake,
Or use the corkscrew for their sake.
Said one: " It's pleasant to abide
In towns where care is laid aside,
Where every thought of morrow lies
In some sport-yielding enterprise.

Here beauty reigns, and rules the hour
While circling subjects own her power.
Here wealth and fashion tread a measure
And life is one sweet draught of pleasure."
Another said: " While here we'll try

Not to a point or shaky pier
Where few convenient things are near,
But to some place of high estate
Where wealthy people congregate,
To study fashions, bathe and pose,
Or ride in traps and tallyhoes."
A little speech, a hint or two
Of pleasures that are ever new

The surf, that now is rolling high,
For if I guess the time aright
We've reached the middle point of night,
And much we Brownies have to do
Ere dons the East its purple hue."
Few minutes passed away before
The band stood on the sandy shore,
Nor did they listen long with care
To hear what waves were saying there.
Some threw their outer clothes aside,
Some as they were rushed in the tide,
And rather than be last to breast
The wave that came with foaming crest

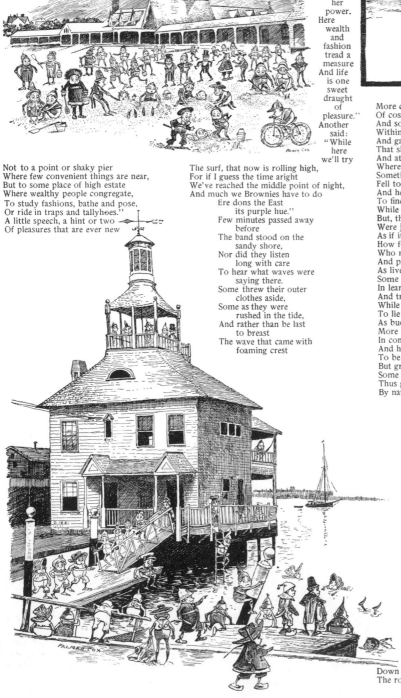

More chanced to find a fair supply
Of costumes that were left to dry,
And soon their tiny forms were lost
Within the garments wrapped and crossed
And gathered to take up the slack
That showed in front and at the back,
And at the sides and feet as well,
Where cloth in great abundance fell.
Sometimes the largest suit on hand
Fell to the smallest in the band,
And here and there he wildly flitted
To find a robe that better fitted,
While others cared not for the size,
But, though enveloped to the eyes,
Were just as pleased that happy hour
As if it fitted like a dower.
How fortunate are Brownie kind
Who make the most of what they find,
And pass along their given way
As lively as the bees in May.
Some spent the time they had on hand
In learning how to boldly stand
And tread the water there with ease,
While more it seemed to greatly please
To lie and float upon the wave
As buoyant as a chip or stave.
More dived so deep they brought their head
In contact with the ocean's bed,
And had they not been fitted out
To be through life well knocked about,
But great mishaps to still survive,
Some scarce had left the place alive.
Thus gifted in a manner high
By nature, well may mortals sigh
And gravely ponder on their fate,
Their slighted race and hampered state.
The band has cause to bless the star
Or planet that shed lustre far
Through empty space and midnight shade,
When they on earth their entrance made.
No bathers fresh from dusty nooks
Where calicoes, or shoes, or books,
Engage their minds from day to day,
Could plunge with such a great display
Of joy into the billows white,
That broke upon the beach that night.
The wave that tries the vessel's side
When rolling on the ocean wide,
Could hardly force the Brownie band
To quit the sport they had on hand.
Down like a fish into the swell
The rogues would soon themselves propel,

There out of sight and sound be lost
To every friend, till wildly tossed
Upon a crested wave they'd rise
To greet the rest with joyful cries.
Could mortals but have gained a peep
At them while in that rolling deep,
They would have been surprised, no doubt,
To see the way they splashed about.
There's not an art to swimmers known
But cunning Brownies make their own.
They swim like dogs, and swim like fish,
And swim like serpents if they wish,
Where using neither hands nor feet
They wriggle through each wave they meet,
In ways would make a person sigh
Who scarce could keep a nose or eye
Above the flood, however fast
His feet and hands through water passed.
Said one: " 'Tis not in rapid strokes
Or kicks behind that Brownie folks

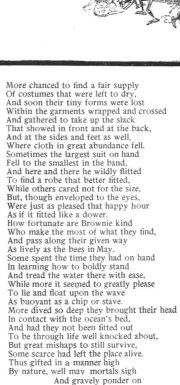

Put all dependence, as you see,
But in peculiar gifts that we
Could freely use if no set rules
Were practiced in the swimming schools."
Another said: " 'Tis not alone
In water that our skill is shown,
But on the skate or wheel as well,
Or prancing horse, as stories tell,
We hold our own in every case,
And far excel the ' human ' race."
Time moves along, though fingers light
May catch at moments in their flight,
Though back the dial's hand we bring
Or check the pendulum's honest swing,
The sun is far beyond our sway
And opens wide the gates of day.
So even Brownies don't neglect
To pay the minutes due respect,
But shape their actions to agree
With time that moves so fast and free.
That night offered many a freak
Of which the Brownies long will speak,
For many a ride and many a run
And swim they had ere sport was done
And they retired from beach and lawn
And roadway at the flush of dawn.

THE AMERICAN GIRL AT HER SPORTS. *By Howard Chandler Christy.*

THE ELEPHANT'S CHILD

Rudyard Kipling

The first of a series of Mr. Kipling's animal stories written especially for the *Journal*.

In the High and Far Off Times the Elephant, oh, Best Beloved, had no trunk. He had only a blackish, bulgy nose, as big as a boot, that he could wriggle about from side to side; but he could not pick up things with it. But there was one Elephant—a new Elephant—an Elephant's Child—who was full of 'satiable curtiosity, and that means he asked ever so many questions. And he lived in Africa, and he filled all Africa with his 'satiable curtiosities. He asked his aunt, the Ostrich, why her tail-feathers grew just so, and she spanked him with her hard, hard claw. He asked his uncle, the Giraffe, what made his skin spotty, and his uncle, the Giraffe, spanked him with his hard, hard hoof. And still he was full of 'satiable curtiosity. He asked his other aunt, the Hippopotamus, why her eyes were red, and she spanked him with her hard, hard hoof; and he asked his other uncle, the Baboon, why melons tasted just so, and his other uncle, the Baboon, spanked him with his hard, hard paw. And still he was full of 'satiable curtiosity. He asked questions about everything that he saw, or heard, or felt, or smelt, or touched, and all his uncles and his aunts spanked him; and still he was full of 'satiable curtiosity.

One fine morning in the middle of the Precession of the Equinoxes this 'satiable Elephant's Child asked a new fine question that he had never asked before. He asked: "What does the Crocodile have for dinner?" Then everybody said "Hush!" in a loud and dretful tone, and they spanked him immediately and directly.

By and by when that was finished, he came upon Kolokolo Bird sitting in the middle of a wait-a-bit thorn and he said: "My father has spanked me and my mother has spanked me; all my aunts and uncles have spanked me for my 'satiable curtiosity; and still I want to know what the Crocodile has for dinner!"

Then Kolokolo Bird said, with a mournful cry: "Go to the banks of the great, gray-green, greasy Limpopo River all set about with fever-trees and find out."

That very next morning when there was nothing left of the Equinoxes, because the Precession had gone by, this 'satiable Elephant's Child took a hundred pounds of bananas, and a hundred pounds of sugar-cane, and seventeen melons, and said to all his families: "Good-by. I am going to the great, gray-green, greasy Limpopo River

all set about with fever-trees to find out what the Crocodile has for dinner." And they all spanked him once more for luck, though he requested them most politely to abstain.

Then he went away, a little warm but not at all astonished, eating melons and throwing the rind about.

He went from Graham's Town to Kimberley, and from Kimberley to Khama's Country, and from Khama's Country he went east by north, eating melons all the time, till at last he came to the banks of the great, gray-green, greasy Limpopo River all set about with fever-trees precisely as Kolokolo Bird had said.

Now you must know and understand, oh, Best Beloved, that till that very week, and day, and hour, and minute, this 'satiable Elephant's Child had never seen a Crocodile and did not know what one was like. It was all his 'satiable curtiosity.

The first thing he found was a Bi-Colored-Python-Rock-Snake curled round a rock.

"'Scuse me," said the Elephant's Child most politely, "but have you seen such a thing as a Crocodile in these promiscuous parts?"

"Have I seen a Crocodile?" said the Bi-Colored-Python-Rock-Snake, in a voice of dretful scorn. "What will you ask me next?"

"'Scuse me," said the Elephant's Child, "but could you kindly tell me what he has for dinner?"

Then the Bi-Colored-Python-Rock-Snake uncoiled himself very quickly from the rock and spanked the Elephant's Child with his hard, hard tail.

"That is odd," said the Elephant's Child, "because my father and my mother, and my uncle and my aunt, not to mention my other aunt, the Hippopotamus, and my other uncle, the Baboon, have all spanked me for my 'satiable curtiosity—and I suppose this is the same thing."

So he said good-by very politely to the Bi-Colored-Python-Rock-Snake, and helped to coil him up on the rock again, and went on, a little warm but not at all astonished, eating melons and throwing the rind about till he trod on what he thought was a log at the very edge of the great, gray-green, greasy Limpopo River all set about with fever-trees.

But it was really the Crocodile, oh, Best Beloved, and the Crocodile winked one eye.

"'Scuse me," said the Elephant's Child most politely, "but do you happen to have seen a Crocodile in these promiscuous parts?"

Then the Crocodile winked the other eye and lifted half his tail out of the mud; and the Elephant's Child stepped back most politely, because he did not wish to be spanked again.

"Come hither, Little One," said the Crocodile. "Why do you ask such things?"

"'Scuse me," said the Elephant's Child most politely, "but my father has spanked me, my mother has spanked me; not to

mention my aunt, the Ostrich, and my uncle, the Giraffe, who can kick ever so hard, as well as my other aunt, the Hippopotamus, and my other uncle, the Baboon, *and* including the Bi-Colored-Python-Rock-Snake just up the bank who spanks harder than any of them; and so, if it's quite all the same to you, I don't want to be spanked any more."

"Come hither, Little One," said the Crocodile, "for I am the Crocodile," and he wept Crocodile tears to show it was quite true.

Then the Elephant's Child grew all

breathless, and panted and kneeled down on the bank and said: "You are the very person I have been looking for all these long days. Will you please tell me what you have for dinner?"

"Come hither, Little One," said the Crocodile, "and I'll whisper."

Then the Elephant's Child, very excited and breathing hard, put his head down close to the Crocodile's musky, tusky mouth, and the Crocodile caught him by his little nose, which up to that very week, day, hour, and minute, was no bigger than a boot, though much more useful.

"I think," said the Crocodile, and he said it between his teeth like this, "I think to-day we will begin with Elephant's Child!"

At this, oh, Best Beloved, the Elephant's Child was much annoyed, and he said, speaking through his nose like this: "Led go! You are hurtig be!"

Then the Bi-Colored-Python-Rock-Snake scuffled down from the bank and said: "My young friend, if you do not now, immediately and instantly, pull as hard as ever you can, it is my opinion that your acquaintance in the large-pattern leather ulster (and by this he meant the Crocodile) will jerk you into yonder limpid stream before you can say Jack Robinson."

This is the way Bi-Colored-Python-Rock-Snakes always talk.

Then the Elephant's Child sat back on his little haunches, and pulled, and pulled, and pulled, and his nose began to stretch. And the Crocodile floundered into the water, making it all creamy with great sweeps of his tail, and *he* pulled, and pulled, and pulled. And the Elephant's Child's nose kept on stretching, and the Elephant's Child spread all his little four legs and pulled, and pulled, and pulled; and his nose kept on stretching, and the Crocodile threshed his tail like an oar, and

he pulled, and pulled, and pulled, and at each pull the Elephant's Child's nose grew longer and longer—and it hurt him hijjus!

Then the Elephant's Child felt his legs slipping, and he said through his nose, which was now nearly five feet long: "This is too buch for be!"

Then the Bi-Colored-Python-Rock-Snake came down from the bank and knotted himself in a double clove-hitch round the Elephant's Child's hind legs and said: "Rash and inexperienced traveler, we will now seriously devote ourselves to a little hard pulling, because if we do not it is my impression that yonder self-propelling man-of-war with the armor-plated upper deck (and by this, oh, Best Beloved, he meant the Crocodile) will permanently vitiate your future career."

That is the way all Bi-Colored-Python-Rock-Snakes talk.

So he pulled, and the Elephant's Child pulled, and the Crocodile pulled, but the Elephant's Child and the Bi-Colored-Python-Rock-Snake pulled hardest; and at last the Crocodile let go of the Elephant's Child's nose with a plop that you could hear all up and down the Limpopo.

Then the Elephant's Child sat down most hard and sudden, but first he was careful to say "Thank you" to the Bi-Colored-Python-Rock-Snake, and next he was kind to his nose and wrapped it all up in cool banana leaves and hung it in the great, gray-green, greasy Limpopo to cool.

"What are you doing that for?" said the Bi-Colored-Python-Rock-Snake.

"'Scuse me," said the Elephant's Child, "but my nose is out of shape and I am waiting for the swelling to go down."

"Then you will have to wait a long time," said the Bi-Colored-Python-Rock-Snake. "Some people do not know what is good for them."

The Elephant's Child sat there three days, waiting for his nose to get well. But it never grew any shorter, and besides it made him squint. For, oh, Best Beloved, you will see and understand that the Crocodile had pulled it out into a really truly trunk same as all Elephants have to-day.

At the end of the third day a fly came and stung him on the shoulder, and instantly he lifted up his trunk and hit that fly dead with the end of it.

"'Vantage number one!" said the Bi-Colored-Python-Rock-Snake. "You couldn't have done that with a mere-smear nose. Try and eat a little now."

Before he thought what he was doing the Elephant's Child put out his trunk and plucked a large bundle of grass, dusted it clean against his fore legs and stuffed it into his own mouth.

"'Vantage number two!" said the Bi-Colored-Python-Rock-Snake. "You couldn't have done that with a mere-smear nose. Don't you think the sun is hot here?"

"It is," said the Elephant's Child, and, before he thought what he was doing, he scooped up a lump of mud from the banks of the great, gray-green, greasy Limpopo and slapped it on his head where it made a cool mud-cap all trickly behind his ears.

"'Vantage number three!" said the Bi-Colored-Python-Rock-Snake. "You couldn't have done that with a mere-smear nose. Now how do you feel about being spanked again?"

"'Scuse me," said the Elephant's Child, "but I should not like it at all."

"How would you like to spank somebody?" said the Bi-Colored-Python-Rock-Snake.

"I should like it very much indeed," said the Elephant's Child.

"Well," said the Bi-Colored-Python-Rock-Snake, "you will find that new nose of yours very useful to spank people with."

"Thank you," said the Elephant's Child, "I'll remember that; and now I think I'll go home to my families, and try it."

So the Elephant's Child went home across Africa frisking and whisking his trunk. When he wanted fruit to eat he pulled it down from a tree, instead of waiting for it to fall as he used to do. When he wanted grass he plucked it up from the ground, instead of going on his knees as he used to do. When the flies bit him he broke off the branch of a tree and used it as a fly-whisk; and he made himself a new, cool, slushy mud-cap whenever the sun was hot. When he felt lonely walking through Africa he sang to himself down his trunk, and the noise was louder than several brass bands. He went especially out of his way to find a Hippopotamus (she was no relation of his), and he spanked her very hard to make sure that the Bi-Colored-Python-Rock-

Snake had spoken the truth about his new trunk. The rest of the time he picked up the melon rinds that he had dropped on his way to the Limpopo—for he was a Tidy Pachyderm.

One dark evening he came back to all his families and he coiled up his trunk and said, "How do you do?" They were very glad to see him and immediately said: "Come here and be spanked for your 'satiable curtiosity.'"

"Pooh," said the Elephant's Child. "I don't think you peoples know anything about spanking, but I do and I'll show you."

Then he uncurled his trunk and knocked two of his brothers head over heels.

"Oh, Bananas!" said they, "where did you learn that trick and what have you done to your nose?"

"I got a new one from the Crocodile on the banks of the great, gray-green, greasy Limpopo River," said the Elephant's Child. "I asked him what he had for dinner and he gave me this to keep."

"It looks very ugly," said the Baboon.

"It does," said the Elephant's Child. "But it's very useful," and he picked up his other uncle, the Baboon, by one leg and hove him into a bees' nest.

Then that bad Elephant's Child spanked all his families for a long time till they were very warm and greatly astonished. He pulled out his Ostrich Aunt's tail-feathers, and he caught his uncle, the Giraffe, by the hind leg and dragged him through a thorn bush; and he shouted at his other aunt, the Hippopotamus, and blew bubbles into her ear when she was sleeping in the water after meals, but he never let any one touch Kolokolo Bird.

In the end things grew so bad that all his families went off one by one to the banks of the great, gray-green, greasy Limpopo River to borrow new noses from the Crocodile. When they came back everything started fair; and ever since that day, oh, Best Beloved, all the Elephants you will ever see, besides all those that you won't, have trunks precisely like the trunk of the 'satiable Elephant's Child.

Henry Ford with Barney Oldfield at the wheel of his "999," which won the Diamond Trophy at the Grosse Point track in 1902.

CHARLES DANA GIBSON

Robert Howard Russell

A "Gibson" Head

Mr. Gibson at his easel. 1902.

The "Every-Day" Girl

The American Girl

a pair of scissors, blunt-pointed so I would not injure myself. I can remember that this accomplishment of mine was a matter of considerable family pride, and I was often called away from my playmates in the back yard to give a reluctant exhibit of my skill with the scissors for the benefit of those callers who strove to please the family by refusing to believe that the paper horses and dogs shown in the drawing-room were my work. I remember one day that a large, stout lady caused us much alarm by saying that her husband, who was a captain in a prominent Boston militia regiment, had a

Young as Charles Dana Gibson is—he is but in his thirty-fifth year—he has been famous and successful for the past ten years, although it is within the latter half of that period that the fullness of artistic reputation has come to him. Yet in his case there has been no exception to the rule, "No royal road to success." He has worked hard, he has known the agony of disappointment, the humiliation of rejection, the bitterness of deferred hope. But manfully he has held on his way, sure of himself, surer of his art; profiting by the salutary discipline of adversity; encouraged by the admiration of his friends; helped also by that candid and impersonal criticism which compels the artist to the best expression of himself. Thus his career, extraordinary as it has been, cannot be pronounced exceptional, save in the rapid ripening of his powers.

His beginning is perhaps best told in his own words:

"The first public exhibition and sale of my work took place in Boston. I was then about six years old, and ever since I could remember I had been able to cut paper pictures of horses, cows, dogs, elephants and tigers from pieces of white note-paper with

man in his company who could cut figures as well as I could. This knowledge that I had a rival in my particular field set me thinking that perhaps the captain's friend made his living by his skill in this line, whereas I had only followed it for amusement; and, being seized for the first time with the desire to make money, I talked the matter over with my brother, and we decided that if a certain little girl playmate up the street approved we would give this new business venture a trial the very next morning."

29

ETHEL BARRYMORE

Gustav Kobbé

Ethel Barrymore is essentially girlish—girlish in her love of pretty clothes; girlish in her enthusiasm for authors, artists and people; girlish in spirits; in her love of fun and pleasure; girlish in her years which have been twenty-three. She is an actress because she cannot help herself, even if she would stay the hand of heredity. Her father, Maurice Barrymore, was an actor; her mother, Georgie Drew Barrymore, was an actress; her brother, Lionel, is an actor. Her uncle, John Drew, is the actor we all know of that name. Her grandmother, the famous Mrs. John Drew, is one whose memory every theatre-goer cherishes; and her grandfather, "John Drew, the elder," was considered the best Irish comedian on the American stage. "I just had to be an actress, don't you see?" laughingly says Miss Barrymore. "What else could I be?"

Charmingly girlish on the stage, she is equally so away from the footlights. She is, practically, the same "off" as "on" the boards. As she dresses in her plays so she dresses in her home—pretty, but simply. "It is the way a dress is cut and made and worn that makes it pretty," she says. "Put good work into the most ordinary material and you have a pretty dress. I know lots of girls who would look perfectly charming if their dresses were more simply made. But they put a lot of fussy things on them, and they spoil their dresses and their own looks."

Miss Barrymore gives her mentality as much attention as her wardrobe. Her home is an apartment on West Fifty-ninth Street, New York City, overlooking Central Park. You can locate it by the cast of the "Winged Victory" in one of the windows of the sitting-room. This and the adjoining music-room, are such abiding-places as one might expect an art-loving girl to have—and I use "art" in its broadest sense. Miss Barrymore is artistic in every fibre.

Her love of music amounts to a passion. Though she did not become a professional pianist, piano-playing still remains one of her greatest diversions. Often when she comes home from the theatre, she sits down at her piano after a light supper and plays. Prominent on her piano is a volume of Brahms. She is familiar with the songs of Richard Strauss. "I saw Richard Strauss at a party in London last summer," she said. "He was sitting there just like an ordinary man listening to what was going on. But I felt as if I were in the presence of a divinity."

On the music-rack of the piano, one day when I visited Miss Barrymore, there was an open score of "Tosca," Puccini's opera. There was music all over the grand piano; on the sitting-room table was a set of Schumann's works—music, music everywhere. "It seems to me," she exclaimed, "that I have more music than any one else in the world. There is all this"—with a wave of the hand that took in both rooms—"and lots more in England."

Just as her enthusiasm for music leads her to hear as much of it as she can, so her love for art takes her to the galleries. She still goes into ecstasy over the Rembrandt which she saw in Glasgow. There, too, she saw Whistler's portrait of Carlyle. A reproduction of his famous portrait of his mother hangs in her apartment. Also conspicuous there is the "Pearl Diver," from the Louvre. "I like it so much," she exclaims, "that I never cared to know who did it!" In sculpture the "Winged Victory" is her special adoration. "It seems to swing through the world," is the way she describes the sense of movement which thrills the beholder.

When she talks about authors Miss Barrymore particularly reflects the enthusiasm of the girl. She "simply adores" George Eliot. She "worships" Robert Louis Stevenson. She has a "tremendous feeling" for Balzac. All around her are books, and she is entertaining as she talks about them. She says she has never met a man who did not recognize himself in "Sentimental Tommy," especially in the Tommy of "Tommy and Grizel." She admires Henry James from his first book to his last. Then she says she thinks his last could have been written in five pages, but is "so glad he preferred to do it in two volumes." She reads much of Turgenev, "the only Russian writer who strikes me as international." But her greatest literary love, "Alice in Wonderland," she takes wherever she goes. "I read 'Alice' every other day," she says "just to keep myself alive."

WOMEN'S CHANCES AS BREADWINNERS

Gleeson White

In the rush toward things artistic to-day, too many persons unfitted for the career adopt the profession of an artist, with a light heart; that, as years roll on, too often grows to be a very heavy one. Before deciding whether one's taste for dabbling in paint or plaster is likely to outlast the necessary drudgery of the first years of study, it is well to be quite sure that not only the will but the power is there. Usually the first efforts of a girl, who shows some knack of handling brush or pencil, are greeted with a chorus of praise; those who know better withhold the sharp criticism the prentice's attempts deserve; while those who do not know insist that with such genius it would be a shame to remain content with mere common-place pursuits. So the victim to circumstances listens greedily to prophecies of future fame and fortune, and decides to become another Rosa Bonheur. In rare cases the decision is right, and both the individual and the world gain thereby. But in the large majority of failures one wishes that some kindly friend could have stayed the waste of time and energy by telling the truth in time.

To decide whether a clever girl has or has not the talent—without which success is impossible, or, at best, dishonorable—is not easy. If she turns to friends and acquaintances, their politeness forbids plain speaking; if she approaches a local teacher, the chances are that the natural eagerness to secure another pupil makes him discern hidden talent where otherwise he would fail to find it. Nor is it easier to obtain valuable advice from a stranger; it is a serious responsibility to stay the career of one who may be great some day; and so, mindful of the romances of unappreciated genius, we all shrink from saying—"You have no shadow of a chance of eminence as an artist; abandon the attempt wholly."

To begin with, there is no royal road to art; genius alone cannot paint a great picture. Knowledge of drawing and anatomy; skill in technique, in brush-work and the laying on of color are all gained only by hard and serious study. To copy good paintings is a help; but nothing replaces the teacher. A serious objection to many art schools is that the level of the class is lowered to avoid showing the utter incompetence of the worst. The first steps are made too easy, and when a spurious facility is gained, the young miss (or master) sallies out to conquer the world. Possibly a dealer buys a few sketches; personal friends offer small commissions, and the student's head is turned. Ignorant of her own want of knowledge—the deepest of all ignorance— she paints daubs that defy every law of art, but attract a certain class of admirers; and so, content with her beginning, goes on to find a younger novice forestalling her, and the appreciation of those worth having, lost forever.

What has been called a "divine discontent" is at once the artist's sorrow and crown. The ideal aimed at must always be far ahead of the result; satisfaction, beyond a certain point, with one's finished work is the deadliest indication of all. If before a great painting a young artist secretly feels she could paint as well, in one case out of a million she may be right; but in the others it is a dead certainty that both the humility of real genius and the genius itself are lacking.

But besides the lack of that supreme talent men call genius, there are other secondary qualities that must be hers who would succeed in art. Of these, a power of steady application, a keen observance of natural facts, a love of nature, and real delight in color and the beauty of things seen as well as things painted, are among the most important; but energy, patience and study can alone make them fruitful.

Difficult as it is to ascertain whether a beginner has solid reason to hope for success, there are a few rough-and-ready tests that, if unflinchingly applied, would weed out the most hopeless incapables. Note first whether the would-be artist is clever at copying, or tries to invent her pictures. If her sketches are full of every technical fault and yet show honest attempts to draw or paint what she sees, there is room for hope. If, however, her pictures are all mere copies of the work of other artists, though done ever so well, they prove nothing; beyond the lower faculty of imitation, that is only a small part of the equipment an artist should have.

Such an one may go to nature and yet paint her scenes after a previously learned formula. If all her sketches—gray days or sunny days, autumn or spring—have a similar chromo-like coloring, it is proof positive that the vision of the real artist has been denied her.

The choice of subjects is another test. A real artist makes everything paintable; the most unpromising scene has its rare moments of beauty and, like the smile on a homely face, may be lovely at times. The amateur is always trying to make pictures; the real artist is satisfied with half a dozen rough lines, if she grasps the essentials of the fact she wishes to note. The study needed is not to be put away with the easel and palette at the art school, but continued always; jotting down stray memoranda in pencil or color, noting the effects of atmosphere and color under every condition. That a course of tuition at a good school of art is essential to success, goes without saying. In default of working in the studio of a first-rate painter—almost impossible in this country—it is the only way.

A table set by Delmonico.

The new summer dresses for girls are things of frills and laces. The shoulders are drooping, the sleeves big, the skirts full, and lace is the trimming par excellence. Original designs by Mrs. Ralston as drawn by Henry Hutt.

Good Taste and Bad Taste

A jardinière of dull green pottery forms the base of this well-designed lamp. A brass font holds the oil, and a good burner is fitted on the jar. The wide-spreading Japanese shade sends a splendid glow of light over a table—and altogether this combination of plain materials shows remarkably good results for a comparatively small outlay of money. The idea is a simple one easily carried out in other harmonious colors.

In sorry contrast is this lamp where the intricacies of the design and the trimmings of the ruffle-shaded lamp indicate that it is intended to be a showy ornament rather than a lamp to be used. In addition to its badly-proportioned outlines and cheap decorations it would be very hard to clean properly. Such a lamp has no permanent value, and it represents a wasted expenditure of time and money.

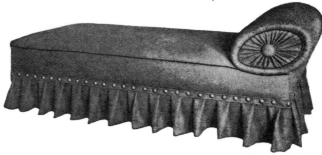

The design of this couch is not particularly objectionable, but the fringe at the base is bad and unsanitary. It is a most effective dust-catcher, and it soon becomes worn and frayed into untidy strings. The large-figured covering is also undesirable.

This unique German couch is original in design and most attractive. The wooden frame should be painted or stained to harmonize with the upholstering, and both should be done in accordance with the prevailing colors of the room.

A beautiful old desk built on the very simplest and plainest lines. When closed it has somewhat the appearance of a chest of drawers. It is of mahogany with an inlaid line of holly-wood. The handles and fittings are of brass. The beauty of the wood is apparent at once, and the eye is grateful for the wonderfully fine sweep of line developed at the base.

In comparison with the desk at left how cheap this looks. There is an attempt at ornament evidently intended to catch the eye. Compare the line of the top back board with any cap-piece in Colonial work and its futility is at once apparent. Then the legs are structurally weak—a flaw that should always be avoided in designing furniture.

A brass bedstead to be commended for its absolute simplicity. Its square posts and spindles in upright lines may seem too rigid for some tastes, but they make for cleanliness and require little care from busy housewives.

This design is most objectionable. Compared with the bed at left it seems almost crazy in construction. It gives one a feeling of discomfort, and constant effort will be needed to keep it presentable in appearance.

A design possessing marked individuality. The pottery urn base and shade harmonize beautifully—both being in dull, soft tones of yellow and white. This lamp is serviceable and easy to move by means of the curved arms on the urn. Its generous dimensions and shape make it a very desirable one for reading or simply to light a room.

Nearly every housemaid has at some time burned her fingers in lifting one of the round globes from a lighted lamp to see if the flame is burning all right; and again, because her fingers are slippery or because she cannot hold it securely, owing to its round, smooth surface, she has dropped it with a crash to the floor. The light which should emanate from this lamp is covered by a globe decorated with unsightly ornaments.

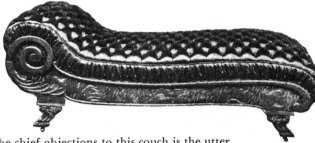

Here is a simple, plain, restful couch that seems to be designed along the lines of common-sense. An inexpensive covering, such as denim, may be used. The broad plaits at the bottom relieve the somewhat severe lines, and they can easily be kept free from dust.

One of the chief objections to this couch is the utter lack of adaptability to any practical use. In looking at it one cannot escape the conviction that it is designed to pitch the would-be occupant on the floor. It suggests exactly the opposite of comfort.

An example of good modern work. This oak desk of Mission design is thoroughly satisfactory, practical and durable. It should, of course, be placed in quiet surroundings. Nothing of the gimcrack variety either in ornaments or in furniture should be near it.

A design which has the appearance of a top division laid on a table for a few moments, awaiting quick removal. There is no unity of effect; consequently the impression is most unpleasant. The details are also lacking in symmetry, and there has been no care for good, sound construction.

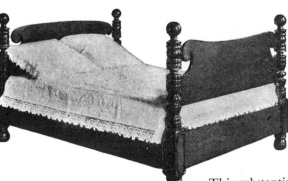

In contrast, this modern Louis XV bed seems unsound in construction, over-ornamented and generally weak and insipid throughout. Such furniture should have no place in any sane American home. It is typical of an artificial period of French history.

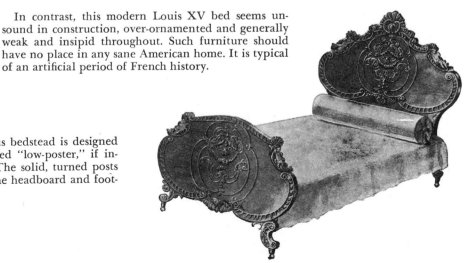

This substantial and generous bedstead is designed on the lines of the old-fashioned "low-poster," if indeed it is not an actual copy. The solid, turned posts are dignified and the lines of the headboard and footboard are most graceful.

ARNAUX, THE HOMING PIGEON

Ernest Thompson Seton

We passed through the side door of the big barn on West Nineteenth Street. The mild smell of the well-kept stable was lost in the sweet odor of the hay as we mounted a ladder and entered the long garret. The south end was walled off, and the familiar "Coo-oo—coo-oo—ooruk—at-a-coo," varied with the "whirr-whirr-whirr" of wings, informed us that we were at the Pigeon-loft.

This was the home of a famous lot of birds, and to-day there was to be a training race among fifty of the youngsters. They had been taken out for short distances with their parents once or twice, then set free to return to the loft. Now for the first time they were to be flown without the old ones. The point of start was Elizabeth, New Jersey. It was a long journey for their first unaided attempt. "But then," the trainer remarked, "that's how we weed out the fools; only the best birds make it, and that's all we want back."

There was another side to the flight. It was to be a race among those that did return. Each of the men about the loft, as well as several neighboring fanciers, were interested in one or another of the Homers. They made up a purse for the winner, and on me, as an unprejudiced outsider, devolved the important duty of deciding which should take the stakes. Not the first bird *back,* but the first bird *into the loft,* was to win; for a bird that returns to his neighborhood merely, without first reporting at home, is of little use as a letter-carrier.

The Homing Pigeon used to be called the Carrier because it carried messages; but here I found the name Carrier restricted to the show-bird, the creature with grotesquely developed wattles and leg-feathers; the one that carries the messages is now called the Homer, or Homing Pigeon—the bird that always comes home. These Pigeons are not of any special color, nor have they any of the fancy adornments of the kind that figure in bird-shows. They are not bred for style, but for speed and for their mental gifts. They must be true to their home, and able to return to it without fail. The sense of direction is now believed to be located in the bony labyrinth of the ear. There is no creature with finer sense of locality and direction than a good Homer, and the only visible proof of it is the great bulge on each side of the head over the ears—that, and the superb wings that complete his equipment to obey the noble impulse of home love. And now the mental and physical gifts of the last lot of young birds were to be put to test.

Although there were plenty of witnesses I thought it best to close all but one of the Pigeon doors, and stand ready to shut that behind the first arrival.

I shall never forget the sensations of that day. I had been warned: "They start at 12, they should be here at 12:30; but look out! they come like a whirlwind. You hardly see them till they're in."

We were ranged along the inside of the loft, each with an eye to a crack or a partly-closed Pigeon door, anxiously scanning the southwestern horizon, when some one shouted: "Look out—here they come!" Like a white cloud they burst into view, low skimming over the city roofs, around a great chimney pile, and in two seconds after first being seen they were back. The flash of white, the rush of pinions, were all so sudden, so short, that, though preparing, I was unprepared. I was at the only open door. A whistling arrow of blue shot in, lashed my face with its pinions, and passed.

I had hardly time to drop the little door as a yell burst from the men: "Arnaux! Arnaux! I told you he would. Oh, he's a darling, only three months old and a winner—he's a little darling!" and Arnaux's owner danced, more for joy in his bird than in the purse he had won.

The men sat or kneeled, watching him in positive reverence as he gulped a quantity of water, then turned to the food-trough.

"Look at that eye, those wings; and did you ever see such a breast; oh, but he's the real grit!" so his owner prattled to the silent ones whose birds had been defeated.

That was the beginning of Arnaux's exploits. Best of fifty birds from a good loft, his future was bright with promise.

He was invested with the silver anklet of the Sacred Order of the High Homer. It bore his number, 2590 C, a number which to-day means much to all men in the world of the Homing Pigeon.

In that first flight from Elizabeth only forty birds had returned. It is usually so. Some were weak and got left behind, some were foolish and strayed. By this simple process of flight selection the Pigeon owners kept improving their stock. Of the ten, five were seen no more, but five returned later that day, not all at once, but straggling in. The last of the loiterers was a big, lubberly blue Pigeon. The man in the loft at the time called: "Here comes that old sap-headed blue that Jaky was betting on. I didn't suppose he would come back, and I didn't care, neither, for it's my belief he has a streak of Pouter."

The Big Blue, also called "Corner-box," from the nest where he was hatched, had shown remarkable vigor from the first. Though all were about the same age he had grown faster than the others, was bigger, and incidentally handsomer, though the fanciers cared little for that. He seemed fully aware of his importance and early showed a disposition to bully his smaller cousins. His owner prophesied great things of him, but in Billy's mind grave doubts arose over the length of his neck, the size of his crop, his carriage, and his oversize. "A bird can't make time pushing a bag of wind ahead of him; them long legs is dead weight, an' a neck like that ain't got no gimp in it," Billy would grunt disparagingly as he cleaned out the loft of a morning.

The training of the birds went on after this at regular times. The distance of the start from home was "jumped" twenty-five or thirty miles farther each day, and its direction changed, till the Homers knew the country for one hundred and fifty miles around New York. The original fifty birds dwindled to twenty, for the rigid process weeds out not only the weak and foolish but also those who may have temporary ailments or accidents, or who may make the mistake of overeating at the beginning. There were many fine birds in the flock, broad-breasted, bright-eyed, long-winged creatures, made for swiftest flight, for high, unconscious emprise: for these were destined to be messengers in the service of man in times of serious need. Their colors were motley, white, blue or brown. They wore no uniform, but each and all of the chosen remnant had the brilliant eye and the bulging ears of the finest Homer blood—and best and choicest of all, nearly always first among them was little Arnaux. He had not much to distinguish him when at rest, for now all of the band had the silver anklet; but in the air it was that Arnaux showed his make, and when the opening of the hamper gave the order, "Start," it was Arnaux that first got under way, soared to the height deemed needful to exclude all local influences, divined the road to home and took it, pausing not for food, drink or company.

Notwithstanding Billy's evil forecasts the Big Blue of the Corner-box was one of the chosen twenty. He was often late in return—he never was first—and sometimes when he came back some hours behind the rest it was plain that he was neither hungry nor thirsty, sure signs that he was a loiterer by the way. Still, he had come back, and now he wore on his ankle, like the rest, the sacred badge, and a number from the roll of possible fame. Billy despised him, set him in poor contrast with Arnaux; but his owner would reply: "Give him a chance—'soon ripe, soon rotten,' an' I always notice the best bird is the slowest to show up at first."

Before a year little Arnaux had made a record. The hardest of all work is over sea, for there is no chance of aid from landmarks, and the hardest of all times at sea is a fog, for then even the sun is blotted out, and there is nothing whatever for guidance. With memory, sight and sound unavailable, the Homer has one thing left, and herein is his great strength: the inborn sense of direction. There is only one thing that can destroy this, and that is fear, hence the necessity of a stout little heart between those noble wings.

Arnaux, with two of his order in course of training, had been shipped on an ocean steamer bound for Europe. They were to be released out of sight of land, but a heavy fog set in and forbade their start. The steamer took them on, the intention being to send them back on the next vessel. When ten hours out the engine broke down, the fog settled dense over the sea, and the vessel was adrift and helpless as a log. She could only whistle for assistance, and so far as results were concerned the captain might as well have wig-wagged. Then the Pigeons were thought of. Starback, 2592 C, was first selected. A message for help was written on waterproof paper, rolled up and lashed to his tail-feathers on the under side. He was thrown into the air and disappeared. Half an hour later a second, the Big Blue Corner-box, 2600 C, was freighted with a message. He flew up, but almost immediately returned, and alighted on the rigging. He was the picture of Pigeon fear; nothing would induce him to leave the ship. He was so terrorized that he was easily caught and ignominiously thrust back into the coop.

Now the third was brought out—a small, chunky bird. The shipmen did not know him, but they noted down from his anklet his name and number—Arnaux, 2590 C. It meant nothing to them, but the officer who held him noted that his heart did not beat so wildly as had done that of the last bird. The message was taken from the Big Blue. It ran: "Ten A.M., Tuesday. We broke our shaft two hundred and ten miles out from New York; we are drifting helplessly in the fog. Send out a tug as soon as possible. We are whistling one long, followed at once by one short, every sixty seconds. (Signed) The Captain."

This was rolled up, wrapped in waterproof film, addressed to the steamship company, and lashed to the under side of Arnaux's middle tail-feather.

When thrown into the air he circled around the ship, then around again higher, then again higher in a wider circle, and he was lost to view; and still higher till quite out of sight and feeling of the ship and above the fog. Shut out now from the use of all his senses but one, he gave himself up to that. Strong in him it was, and untrammeled of that murderous despot, *Fear*. True as a needle to the pole went Arnaux

now, no hesitation, no doubts; within one minute of leaving the coop he was speeding straight as a ray of light for the loft where he was born, the only place on earth where he could be made content.

That afternoon Billy was on duty when the whistle of fast wings was heard, a blue flyer flashed into the loft and made for the water-trough. He was gulping down mouthful after mouthful when Billy gasped: "Why, Arnaux, it's you—you beauty." Then, with the quick habit of the Pigeon man, he pulled out his watch and marked the time, 2:40 P.M. A glance showed the tie-string on the tail. He shut the door, and dropped the catching-net quickly over Arnaux's head. A minute later he had the roll in his hand; in two minutes he was

speeding to the office of the company, for there was a fat tip in view. There he learned that Arnaux had made the two hundred and ten miles in fog, over sea, in four hours and forty minutes, and within one hour the needful help had set out for the steamer.

Two hundred and ten miles in fog over sea in four hours and forty minutes! This was a noble record. It was duly inscribed in the rolls of the Homing Club. Arnaux was held while the secretary with rubber stamp and indelible ink printed on the first snowy primary of his right wing the record of the feat, with the date and reference number.

Starback, the second bird, never was heard of again. No doubt he perished at sea.

Blue Corner-box came back on the tug.

That was the beginning of Arnaux's fame, his first public record, but others came fast, and several curious scenes were enacted in that old Pigeon-loft, with Arnaux as the central figure. One day a carriage drove up to the stable, a white-haired gentleman got out, climbed the dirty stairs, and sat all morning in the loft with Billy. Peering from his gold-rimmed glasses first at a lot of papers, next across the roofs of the city, watching, waiting, for what? News from a little place not forty miles away. News of greatest weight to him —tidings that would make or break him, tidings that must reach him before they

could be telegraphed: a telegram meant at least an hour's delay at each end. What was faster than that for forty miles? In those days there was but one thing: a high-class Homer. Money would count for nothing if he could win. The best, the very best, at any price, he must have, and Arnaux, with seven indelible records on his wings, was the chosen messenger. An hour went by, another, and a third was begun, when with whistle of wings the blue meteor flashed into the loft. Billy slammed the door and caught him. Deftly he snipped the threads and handed the roll to the banker. The old man turned deathly pale, fumbled it open, then his color came back. "Thank God!" he gasped, and then went speeding to his office, master of the situation. Little Arnaux had saved him.

The banker wanted to buy the Homer, feeling in a vague way that he ought to honor and cherish him; but Billy was very clear about it. "What's the good? You can't buy a Homer's heart. You could keep him a prisoner, that's all, but nothing on earth could make him forsake the old loft where he was hatched."

So Arnaux stayed at 211 West Nineteenth Street. But the banker did not forget.

There is in our country a class of miscreants who think a flying Pigeon is fair game, because he is probably far from home, or they shoot him because it is hard to fix the crime. Many a noble Homer, speeding with a life-or-death message, has been shot down by one of these wretches and remorselessly made into a potpie. Arnaux's brother, Arnolf, with three fine records on his wings, was thus murdered in the act of bearing a hasty summons for the doctor. As he fell dying at the gunner's feet his superb wings, spread out, displayed his list of victories. The silver badge on his leg was there, and the gunner was smitten with remorse. He had the message sent on, and he returned the dead bird to the Homing Club, saying that he "found it." The owner came to see him, the gunner broke down under cross-examination, and was forced to admit that he himself had shot the Homer, but did so in behalf of a poor sick neighbor who craved a Pigeon pie.

There were tears in the wrath of the Pigeon man. "My bird, my beautiful Arnolf! Twenty times he has brought vital messages, three times has he made records, twice has he saved human lives; and you'd shoot him for a potpie! I could punish you under the law, but I have no heart for such a poor revenge. I only ask you this: if ever you have a sick neighbor who wants a Pigeon pie come to us: we'll freely supply him with pie-breed squabs; but if you have a trace of manhood about you you will never, never again shoot, or allow others to shoot, our noble and priceless messengers."

This took place while the banker was in touch with the loft, while his heart was warm for the Pigeons. He was a man of influence, and the Pigeon protection legislation at Albany was the immediate fruit of Arnaux's exploit.

Billy had never liked the Corner-box Blue (2600 C). Notwithstanding the fact that he still continued in the ranks of the silver badge, Billy believed he was poor stuff. The steamer incident seemed to prove him a coward; he certainly was a bully.

One morning when Billy went in there was a row. Two Pigeons, a large and a small, were alternately clenching and sparring all over the floor, feathers were flying, there was dust and commotion everywhere. As soon as they were separated Billy found the little one was Arnaux and the big one was the Corner-box Blue. Arnaux had made a good fight, but was overmatched, for the Big Blue was half as heavy again.

It was soon very clear what they had fought over—a pretty little lady Pigeon of the bluest Homing blood. The Big Blue cock had kept up a state of bad feeling by his bullying, but it was the Little Lady that had made them close in mortal combat, and Billy, not having authority to wring the Big Blue's neck, decided to interfere as far as he could in behalf of his favorite Arnaux.

Pigeon marriages are arranged somewhat like those of mankind. Propinquity is the first thing; force the pair together for a time, and let Nature take its course. So Billy locked Arnaux and the Little Lady up together in a separate apartment for two weeks, and to make doubly sure he locked the Big Blue up with an Available Lady in another apartment for two weeks.

Things turned out just as was expected. The Little Lady surrendered to Arnaux and the Available Lady to the Big Blue. Two nests were begun and everything shaped for a "lived happily ever after." But the Big Blue was very big and handsome. He could blow out his crop, and strut in the sun, and make rainbows all around his neck in a way that might turn the heart of the staidest Homerine.

Arnaux, though sturdily built, was small, and, except for his brilliant eyes, not especially good-looking. Moreover, he was often away on important business, and the Big Blue had nothing to do but stay around the loft and display his unlettered wings.

It is the very proper custom of moralists to point to the Pigeon for an example of love and constancy. But alas! there are exceptions. Vice is not by any means limited to the human race.

At the outset Arnaux's wife had been deeply impressed with the Big Blue, and now that Arnaux was absent the dreadful thing took place.

Arnaux returned from Boston one day to find that the Big Blue, while he retained his own Available Lady in the corner box, had also annexed the box and wife that belonged to himself, and a desperate battle followed. The only spectators were the two wives, and they maintained an indifferent aloofness. Arnaux fought with his famous wings, but they were none the better weapons because they now bore twenty records. His beak and feet were small, as became his blood, and his brave little heart could not make up for his lack of weight. The battle went against him. His wife sat unconcernedly in the nest as though it were not her affair, and Arnaux might have been killed but for the timely arrival of Billy. He was savage enough to wring the Blue bird's neck, but the bully escaped from the loft in time. Billy took tender care of Arnaux for a few days. At the end of a week he was well, and in ten days he was again on the road. Meanwhile he had evidently forgiven his faithless wife, for without any apparent feeling he took up his nesting as before.

That month Arnaux made two new records. He brought a message ten miles in eight minutes, and he came from Boston in four hours. Every moment of the way he had been impelled by the master passion of home-love. But it was a poor home-coming, if his wife figured in his thoughts at all, for he found her again flirting with the Big Blue cock. Tired as he was, the duel was renewed, and again would have been to a finish but for Billy's interference. He separated the fighters, then shut the Blue up in a coop, determined to get rid of him.

Meanwhile the "All-Age Sweepstakes Handicap" from Chicago to New York was on: a race of one thousand miles. Arnaux had been entered six months before. His forfeit money was up, and, notwithstanding his domestic complications, his friends felt that he must not fail to appear.

The birds were shipped by train to Chicago and liberated at intervals according to their handicap, and the last of the "start" was Arnaux. They lost no time, and outside of Chicago several of the prime racers joined by common impulse, and the racing flock went through the air on the same invisible track. A Homer may make a straight line when following his general sense of direction, but when following a familiar back track he sticks to the well-remembered landmarks. Most of the birds had been trained by way of Cleveland. Arnaux knew the Cleveland route, but he also knew the way by Detroit, and soon after leaving Lake Michigan he took the straight line for Detroit. Thus he caught up in his handicap and had the advantage of many miles. Detroit, Buffalo, Rochester, with their familiar towers and chimneys, faded behind him, and Syracuse was near at hand. It was now late afternoon, six hundred miles in twelve hours he had flown, and was undoubtedly leading the race; but the usual thirst of the flyer had attacked him. Skimming over the city roofs he saw a flock of Pigeons about their home, and descending from his high course in two or three great circles, he followed the ingoing Pigeons to the loft, drank greedily at the strange trough, as he had often done before, and as every Pigeon lover hospitably expects the messengers to do. The owner of the loft was there, and noted the strange bird. He stepped quietly up where he could inspect him. One of his own Pigeons made momentary opposition to the stranger, and Arnaux, sparring sidewise with an open wing in Pigeon style, displayed the long array of printed records. The man was a fancier. He started, pulled the string that shut the flying door, and in a few minutes Arnaux was his prisoner.

The robber spread the much-inscribed wings, read record after record, and glancing at the silver badge—it should have been gold—he read his name: "Arnaux!" then he exclaimed: "Arnaux! Arnaux! Oh, I've heard of you, you little beauty, and it's glad I am to trap you." He snipped the message from his tail, unrolled it, and read: "Arnaux left Chicago at 4 A.M., scratched in the Any-Age Sweepstakes for New York."

"Six hundred miles in twelve hours! By the powers, that's a record-breaker," and the Pigeon-stealer gently, almost reverently, put the fluttering bird back into a padded cage. "Well," he added, "I know it's no use trying to make you stay, but I can breed from you and have some of your strain."

So Arnaux was shut up in a large and comfortable loft with several other prisoners. The man, though a thief, was a lover of Homers. He gave his captive everything that could insure his comfort and safety. For three months he left him in that loft. At first Arnaux did nothing all day but walk up and down the wire screen, looking high and low for means of escape, but in the fourth month he seemed to have abandoned the attempt, and the watchful jailer began the second part of his scheme. He introduced a coy young lady Pigeon, but it did not seem to answer; Arnaux was not even civil to her. After a time the jailer removed the female, and Arnaux was left in solitary confinement for a month. Now a different female was brought in, but with no better luck, and thus it went on for a year, different charmers being introduced. Arnaux either violently repelled them or was scornfully indifferent, and at times the old longing to get away came back with twofold power, so that he darted up and down the wire front or dashed with all his force against it. When the storied feathers of his wings began to moult his jailer saved them as precious things, and as each new feather came he reproduced on it the story of its owner's fame.

Two years had gone slowly by, and the jailer at length put Arnaux in a new loft with a new lady Pigeon. By chance she closely resembled the faithless one at home. Arnaux actually seemed to heed this latest one. Once the jailer thought he saw his famous prisoner paying some slight attention to the charmer, and yes! he surely saw her preparing a nest. Then, assuming that they had reached a final understanding, the jailer for the first time opened the outlet, and Arnaux was free. Did he hang around in doubt, did he hesitate? No, not for one moment. As soon as the drop of the door left open the way he shot through, he spread those wonderful blazoned wings, and with no second thought for the latest Circe sprang from the hated prison loft—away and away.

We have no means of looking into the Pigeon mind; we may go wrong in conjuring up for it deep thoughts of love and welcome home; but we are safe in this, we cannot too strongly paint, we cannot too highly praise and glorify, that wonderful God-implanted, mankind-fostered home-love that glows unquenchably in this noble bird. Call it what you like, a mere instinct deliberately constructed by man for his selfish ends, explain it away if you will, dissect it, misname it, and it still is there, in overwhelming, imperishable master-power as long as the brave little heart and wings can beat.

Home, sweet home. Never had mankind a deeper love of home than had Arnaux. The trials and sorrows of the old Pigeon-loft were forgotten in that all-dominating force of his nature. Not years of prison bars, not later loves nor fear of death, could down its power; and Arnaux, had the gift of song been his, must surely have sung as sings a hero in his highest joy, when he sprang from the "lighting" board up, circling free, soaring, up, up, in widening, heightening circles of ashy blue, in the blue, flashing those many-lettered wings of white, till they seemed like jets of fire —up, and on, driven by that home-love, faithful to his only home and to his faithless love; closing his eyes, they say; closing his ears, they tell; shutting his mind, we all believe—to nearer things, to two years of his life, to one-half of his prime—but soaring in the blue, retiring, as a saint might do, into his inner self, giving himself up to that inmost guide. He was the captain of the ship, but the pilot, the chart and compass all were that deep-implanted instinct. One thousand feet above the trees the inscrutable whisper came, and Arnaux, in arrowy swiftness now, was pointing for the south-southeast. The little flashes of white fire on each side were lost in the low sky, and the reverent robber of Syracuse saw Arnaux never more.

The fast express was steaming down the valley. It was far ahead, but Arnaux overtook and passed it, as the Wild Duck passes the swimming Muskrat. High in the valleys he went, low over the hills of Chenango, where the pines were combing the breezes. Out from his oak-tree eyrie a Hawk came wheeling and sailing, silent, for he had marked the flyer and meant him for his prey. Arnaux turned neither right nor left, nor raised nor lowered his flight, nor lost a wing-beat. The Hawk was in waiting in the gap ahead, and Arnaux passed him, even as a Deer in his prime may pass by a Bear in his pathway. Home! home! was the only burning thought, the blinding impulse.

Beat—beat—beat—those flashing pinions went with speed unslacked on the now familiar road. In an hour the Catskills were at hand. In two hours he was passing over them. Old friendly places, swiftly coming now, lent more force to his wings. Home! home! was the silent song that his heart was singing. Like the traveler dying of thirst who sees the palm trees far ahead, his brilliant eyes took in the distant smoke of Manhattan.

Out from the crest of the Catskills there launched a Falcon. Swiftest of the race of rapine, proud of his strength, proud of his wings, he rejoiced in a worthy prey. Many and many a Pigeon had been borne to his nest, and riding the wind he came, swooping, reserving his strength, awaiting the proper time. Oh, how well he knew the very moment. Down—down like a flashing javelin: no Wild Duck, no Hawk could elude him, for this was a Falcon. Turn back now, oh, Homer, and save yourself: go around the dangerous hills. Did he turn? Not a whit, for this was Arnaux. Home! home! home! was his only thought. For the danger he merely added to his speed, and the Peregrine stooped: stooped at what?—a flashing of color—a twinkling of whiteness—and went back empty; while Arnaux cleft the air of the valley as a stone from a sling, to be lost—a white-winged bird—a spot with flashing halo— and quickly, a speck in the offing. On down the valley of the Hudson, the well-known highway—for two years he had not seen it! Now he dropped low, as the noon breeze came forth and ruffled the river below him.

Home! home! home! and the towers of a city are coming into view! Home! home! past the great spider bridge of Poughkeepsie, skimming, skirting the river banks. Low now by the bank as the wind arose. Low, alas! too low! What fiend was it tempted a gunner in June to lurk on that hill by the margin? What devil directed his gaze to the twinkling of white that came from the blue to the northward? Oh, Arnaux, Arnaux, skimming low, forget not the gunner of old! Too low, too low you are clearing that hill. Too low—*too late!* Flash—bang! and the death hail has reached him; reached, maimed, but not downed him. Out of the beating pinions broken feathers printed with records go

fluttering earthward. The "nought" of his sea record is gone: not two hundred and ten, but twenty-one miles, it now reads. Oh, shameful pillage! A dark stain appears on his bosom, but Arnaux keeps on. Home, homeward bound. The danger is past in an instant. Home, homeward he steers, straight as before, but the wonderful speed is diminished; not a mile a minute now; and the wind makes undue sounds in his tattered pinions. The stain in his breast tells of broken force, but on, straight on, he flies. Home, home is in sight, and the pain in his breast is forgotten. The tall towers of the city are in clear view of his farseeing eye as he skims by the high cliffs of Jersey. On—on—the pinion may flag, the eye may darken, but the home-love is stronger and stronger.

Under the tall Palisades, where, screened from the wind, he passed, over the spar-

kling water, over the trees, under the Peregrines' eyrie, under the pirates' castle where the great, grim Peregrines lurked, peering like black-masked highwaymen, and marked the oncoming Pigeon. Arnaux knew them of old. Many a message was lying undelivered in that nest, many a record-bearing plume had fluttered away from its fastness. But Arnaux had faced them before, and now he came as before— on, onward, swift, but not as he had been —the deadly gun had sapped his force, had lowered his speed. On, on—and the Peregrines, biding their time, went forth like two bow-bolts; strong and lightning swift, they went against one weak and wearied.

Why tell of the race that followed? Why paint the despair of a brave little heart in sight of the home he had craved in vain? In a minute all was over. The Peregrines screeched in their triumph. Screeching and sailing they swung to their eyrie, and the prey in their claws was the body, the last of the bright little Arnaux. There, on the rocks, the beaks and claws of the bandits were red with the life of the hero. Torn asunder were those splendid wings, and their records were scattered unnoticed. In sun and in storm they lay till the killers themselves were killed and their stronghold rifled. And none knew the fate of the matchless dove till deep in the rubbish of that pirate-nest the avenger found, among others of its kind, a silver ring, the sacred badge of the High Homer, and read upon it the pregnant inscription:

ARNAUX, 2590 C

THE HONEST AMERICAN MARRIAGE

Grover Cleveland

We have fallen upon a time in our national life when it is well for us to look to the simplicity of our homes. Of course it will not do to inveigh indiscriminately and in wholesale fashion against our country's legitimate advance, which has greatly increased the comforts and reasonable luxury of our domestic life. Our plea should be for the subordination of all this to a standard of simplicity which will safeguard the integrity of the home, without curtailing the greater comfort or decent luxury of latter-day changes.

Many of us remember an earlier and better simplicity. We knew in our young days the old well with its oaken bucket and its awkward sweep, the brick oven and its savory smells of pies and cakes, the big fireplace with its crane and pot-hooks supporting simmering pots and singing kettles, the tallow candle with its safe and sufficient light not yet under the ban of optical science, and the apple-paring bees and husking bees with their love-making and courtships. Those of us who have enjoyed these advantages should not be proud nor arrogant because of our good fortune. Those who have been born to later scenes are not at fault if they have missed the incidents that naturally give simplicity to home enjoyments. Perhaps, if we are parents, we shall find on self-examination that we ourselves have so far drifted with the current of present conditions that the old simplicity we knew is becoming a sentimental recollection, still dear to us, but whose absence from the lives of our children we are strangely willing to permit. We will not acknowledge that we have abandoned our faith in the saving grace of simple homes; but pride beguiles so easily that many parents, whose success in accumulating riches and gaining social prominence had its root in early home simplicity, yield to the vortex of wealth's senseless display, and attempt to cajole themselves by the shallow persuasion that their own purse-proud self-glorification will pass current for an effort to make life more comfortable and easy for their children. Thus it lamentably happens that the lessons of simplicity learned by parents in early life are lost to their children, and thus too frequently the sons become useless drones in the community, and the daughters frivolously betray the mission of true womanhood.

If this dangerous backsliding on the part of parents were to be characterized in words, it could not be more charitably defined than as a willingness to permit their children to begin the task of life at the point which they themselves struggled long to reach. What is the real meaning of this? It means that though the father started upon his life of manhood with strong hands and rugged determination, and with the woman he loved at his side, the son will begin with an abundance of money, but with no determination or purpose, unless it be to marry conveniently a woman whose money and lack of serious purpose will supplement his own. It means that though the mother, guided by pure and simple love, became the happy, cheerful partner and helper of the man with strong hands and rugged determination, and though in the surroundings of their simple home she became the mother of his children, her daughter must forget these things and learn that the chief purpose of her life is marriage—not necessarily a marriage of love, but by all means one called fitting or eligible—which being interpreted frequently signifies that she and her prospective wealth are in cold blood to be put on exhibition as prizes in the lottery of fortune-hunting. Dead love lives in thousands of the palaces of the rich; loveless and wrecked lives are thickly strewn along the coast of perverted matrimony, and the scandals of divorce, and their frequent sequel of indecent predetermined remarriage, constantly offend the moral sense of right-minded people.

It is almost inconceivable that any one with judgment can fail to see how simplicity befits the beautiful and honorable marriage God has ordained. Because it is of God no decree of fashion and no social exaction can control it except to its hurt. Because it is the beginning of a life of unreserved heart-to-heart confidences, and a commingling in simple faith and love of all that human goodness in man or woman can give, it cannot thrive under submission to arbitrary or extraneous interference; and because it is the entrance upon responsibilities which make or mar life and destiny, and upon joys that should not turn to tears, it can be happily guided only by the intuitive virtue and unselfish love of the man and woman who have pledged their troth.

In our plea for simplicity in the things that belong to the marriage relation we can hardly claim that in this day and generation the outer incidents attending it should be of the same primitive sort as those attending the marriage of our parents and grandparents. Perhaps we ought not to expect that the marriage presents of today should be on the same scale as the chest of drawers, the dining-table, the comfortables and quilts, the crockery and furniture, and the other articles useful in home-building which our grandmothers gave our mothers on their wedding days. But this does not oblige us to concede that either these homely gifts, with the loving solicitude that made them doubly dear, or the joyfully-tearful congratulations of near relatives and friends, are well exchanged for the many costly gifts and the formal atmosphere of modern wedding days. It is to be hoped that matters have not gone so far that it will be considered in bad taste to suggest that the notoriety of columns of newspaper gabble, and bad pictures of the bride and bridegroom scattered broadcast for the delectation of the curious and gaping crowd, are somewhat discordant with the retiring impressiveness which is the fitting accompaniment of a young woman's wedding time. And may not an old-fashioned man be excused if he feels a slight shock when he learns that extravagant and bewildering collections of marriage gifts are sometimes guarded by detectives during their inspection by wedding guests?

A deluge of costly wedding gifts—some capable of expensive usefulness and more that are merely ornamental—cannot be the best preparation for the experiment of home-building and the joys it insures to the newly wed. Besides, it invites them to the dangerous indulgence of extravagant tastes through their desire to live on a scale fitting the use of things given them as marriage presents much more expensive than they would have purchased for themselves.

It may be said that these protests amount only to officious and querulous interference with questions that can safely be left to take care of themselves. Such a charge is justified or not according to the view that may be taken of the importance to our people and our country of the matters discussed, and the correctness of the statements made.

I know that the inner consciousness of thousands of my countrymen will second the appeal I have made for greater simplicity in living, and for more real home-building throughout our land. And I am sure I shall not be misinterpreted by the youths and maidens, upon whom the care of our institutions and the integrity of our homes must soon devolve, when I earnestly assure them that honor and usefulness, dutiful living and the highest joys of life will always be found in honest, consistent American simplicity.

A WINTER SERVICE AT CHURCH.   *By W. L. Taylor.*

JAPANESE AND WESTERN WAYS OF ARRANGING FLOWERS

Gazo Foudji

The day lily, a most graceful flower, shows to special advantage arranged in the Japanese way.

How much prettier is the Japanese arrangement of these hydrangeas and irises, where the beauty of each particular flower is brought out.

Japanese and western ways of arranging cut flowers are quite different, as the pictures on these pages show. There are two pictures given of each arrangement of vase and flowers, the one on the right being Japanese.

In Europe and America people seem to try to get all they can in a vase, massing the flowers, and do not seem to realize that a flower showing its long stem and its beautiful foliage is much more effective than when it is set down low in a vase.

On the other hand, the Japanese are particular to arrange their flowers very carefully. They select the one that has the longest stem, and trim off the superfluous leaves and the stem if necessary. This flower is then placed at the top. Then they pick out the flowers for the second position, treating them in the same way, and lastly those for third place, which are generally draped gracefully over the sides of the vase. This way of arranging the flowers is called by the Japanese "Ben chi jin," meaning God, universe and man.

By arranging them in this way, according to their general attractiveness, each flower shows its color and beauty without detracting from the others in the vase.

The flat arrangement of pansies by Americans does not show anything like the beauty of the free and natural style of the Japanese.

These two ways of arranging daffodils are in marked contrast: the American style is so flat, the Japanese so much more effective.

These wild roses and vines are most gracefully arranged by the Japanese, while the American group is not nearly so picturesque in effect.

The Japanese arrange their national flower, the chrysanthemum, as if it were growing. In the American style the flower looks cramped.

How beautiful peonies look when they are artistically grouped, with their foliage hanging gracefully over a vase, as the Japanese arrange them.

These fleurs-de-lis are other flowers which show marked contrast in their arrangement—the American style being massed, and the Japanese showing each flower together with its beautiful leaves.

Here we have two vases of the iris. The Japanese use the foliage of this flower, which is extremely graceful. The American arrangement is stiff and inartistic.

Roses are much more effective if they are not grouped too closely. The difference in the American and Japanese methods of placing roses in a bowl is shown quite plainly here.

The Japanese know how to bring out all the beauty of the anemone. What a great difference there is in these two styles of arranging the flowers.

MY GRANDFATHER AS AN ACTOR

Charles Dickens

Charles Dickens
From a Portrait by Sol Eytinge, Junior

My father always held to the belief that the history of the time spent by Nicholas Nickleby with Mr. Vincent Crummles was as much my grandfather's autobiography as anything he wrote in "David Copperfield."

Although Charles Dickens never chose the stage as a career, that he was a fine actor was proved by his readings. And that he combined with his dramatic power a marvelous capacity for stage management was shown by the many amateur performances he organized at various times. Every line of character suited my grandfather equally well: from old-fashioned farce to the lightest of light comedies and thence to the most intense melodrama; from the tremendous force of the murder of Nancy to the Buzfuz speech; from the pathos of Paul Dombey to the humor of Mrs. Gamp —it was all the same.

What the stage lost is best expressed by a remark a stage manager made during some amateur theatricals at The Haymarket: "Ah, Mr. Dickens, it was a sad loss to the public when you took to writing!"

As for his power as a stage manager, Forster wrote: "Greatly as his acting contributed to the success of the night, this was nothing to the service he had rendered as a manager. He was the life and soul of the entire affair. He took everything on himself and did the whole of it without effort. He was stage director, very often stage carpenter, scene manager, property man, prompter and bandmaster. He adjusted scenes, assisted carpenters, invented costumes, devised playbills, wrote out calls."

In November 1850, at Lord Lytton's seat at Knebworth, the foundations were laid for some of the best-known theatricals organized by my grandfather. After three private performances of Ben Jonson's "Every Man in His Humour," the question came up as to whether it would be possible to create a fund to make such benefits permanent. The result was the formation of "The Guild of Literature and Art." A

new comedy was to be written by Sir Edward Bulwer Lytton, and a farce by my grandfather, which, however, owing to pressure of work, was never written. A new farce by Mark Lemon, added to by my grandfather, was substituted. The Duke of Devonshire offered Devonshire House for the first presentation, and defrayed all expenses. "Not so Bad as We Seem" was played for the first time at Devonshire House on May 16, 1851, before the Queen and the Prince Consort and as large an audience as the place could hold. It was one of those theatrical absurdities in which the characters disguise themselves and deceive other people, in a way which could happen only in stageland; and in it my grandfather played a touch-and-go barrister, a deaf sexton, a "boots," an invalid, a pedestrian, and an old woman.

Perhaps the most celebrated theatricals managed by my grandfather were those that took place at Tavistock House. In 1854 he produced a version of "Tom Thumb." This met with such success that the next year saw a more ambitious production, in Planché's "Fortunio." In both of these my grandfather acted, besides doing everybody's work in the course of preparation. He revised and adapted the plays, selected and arranged the music, chose and altered the costumes, wrote the new incidental songs, invented all the stage business and taught all the performers their parts. He himself played the Ghost of Gaffer Thumb (with a song) and Baron Dunover, the impecunious father of the three heroines in "Fortunio."

But bigger things were to come. In Wilkie Collins's drama, "The Lighthouse," my grandfather displayed that melodramatic intensity which his readings afterward brought before the public. Other chief parts in the production were taken by Wilkie Collins, Mark Lemon, my late aunt, Miss Mamie Dickens, and my great-aunt, Miss Hogarth. My grandfather composed a prologue, which he himself delivered:

A story of those rocks where doomed ships come
To cast their wrecks upon the steps of home,
Where solitary men the long year through—
The wind their music and the brine their view—
Warn mariners to shun the beacon light;
A story of those rocks is here tonight.
Eddystone Lighthouse, in its ancient form;
Ere he who built it wished for the great storm
That shivered it to nothing; once again,
Behold outgleaming on the angry main!
Within it are three men; to these repair
In our frail bark of fancy, swift as air!
They are but shadows, as the rower grim
Took none but shadows in his boat with him.
So be ye shades, and, for a little space,
The real world a dream without a trace.
Return is easy. It will have ye back
Too soon to the old, dusty, beaten track;

For but one hour forget it. Billows rise,
Blow winds, fall rain; be black, ye midnight skies,
And you who watch the light, arise! arise!

At the cue, "billows rise," a storm was let loose with all the correct theatrical appliances, including a sheet of iron for the rattle of thunder, and an assortment of cannon balls to roll about to simulate the shaking of the lighthouse as it was struck by waves. My father was in charge of this storm, which went on, at intervals, all through the first act. It had to come on exactly at the right word, and the director of the elements had an anxious time. He could always tell by the look of my grandfather's shoulders at rehearsal, as he sat on stage with his back to him, that he was ready for the smallest mistake, whereupon there would immediately come the peremptory cry of "Stop," which pulled everybody up with a round turn.

In 1857 the theatricals at Tavistock House reached their climax with the production of Wilkie Collins's "Frozen Deep." Rehearsals went on for something like three months, three or four times a week.

In the last act, in a demented condition, my grandfather had to rush off stage, and my father and three or four others had to stop him. He gave them notice early in rehearsals that he meant fighting in earnest, and they soon found he meant it. He went at it with such determination they really did have to fight, and my father, being leader of the attacking party, and bearing the brunt of the first onslaught, was tossed in all directions, and was black and blue several times before the first performance.

The play was given some three or four times at Tavistock House. There was also a private performance at the Gallery of Illustration before the Queen and the Prince Consort, accompanied by the Princess Royal and the Crown Prince of Prussia, just engaged to be married. My grandfather wrote: "My gracious sovereign was so pleased that she sent round begging me to go and see her and accept her thanks. I replied that I was in my farce dress, and must beg to be excused. Whereupon she sent again, saying that the dress couldn't be so ridiculous as that, and repeating the request. I sent my duty in reply, but again hoped Her Majesty would have the kindness to excuse my presenting myself in a costume and appearance that were not my own."

The opportunity of presenting himself in his own dress did not occur until the year of his death. At that interview, thirteen years after the performance of "Frozen Deep," Her Majesty spoke of the deep impression made on her by his acting, and, when he stated that the piece had not been very successful on the public stage, she said it did not surprise her, as it had no longer the advantage of his performance in it.

"Frozen Deep" was the last appearance of my grandfather as an actor in the ordinary sense, but after appearances as a reader in the cause of charity he started reading his own books in public.

His first appearance in this character was on April 29, 1858, at Saint Martin's Hall, in London. How wonderful those readings were, and into what a success they grew, are matters of history, but, unfortunately, they did have a distinct bearing upon the premature close of my grandfather's life. They must be said to have hastened his death, even if not actually brought it about.

The first two series, 1858–1859 and 1861–1863, did no particular harm. But in the early part of 1865 he was ill. Perfect rest was necessary, but not taken. In 1867 my grandfather paid his second visit to America, and after his return came the new reading, that of the Sikes and Nancy murder. At this time my father happened to be alone with my grandfather at Gadshill. He was at work one day in the library,

supposing my grandfather to be in the Swiss chalet across the road. Presently my father heard a noise as if a tremendous row were going on outside, as if two people were engaged in a violent quarrel. It being a country infested with tramps, he looked upon the disturbance at first as merely one of the usual domestic incidents of some tramp beating his wife, as was quite the common custom, and he gave it hardly a moment's attention. Presently the noise came again, worse than before, and he thought it necessary to ascertain what was going on. Stepping out of the house on to the lawn at the back, there, at the other end of the meadow, was my grandfather, striding up and down, gesticulating violently, and, in the character of Bill Sikes, murdering Nancy as brutally as possible.

After dinner he told my grandfather what he had seen and had a private reading all to himself. His verdict was: "The finest thing I have ever heard, but don't do it." There was other opposition, but to no avail. Nothing could stop my grandfather. The series commenced with the murder of Nancy added to the program, and went on until Nature stepped in and brought the

series to a sudden close in April 1869. My grandfather had made what bade fair to be his last appearance as a reader and actor. The enforced rest brought about some improvement, but there was to be a farewell series of twelve readings at Saint James's Hall, and my father had no doubt whatever that that farewell series completed the work which the murder reading had begun. My grandfather's doctor told my father: "I have had steps put up against the side of the platform, Charley. You must be there every night, and if you see your father falter in the least you must run up and catch him, and bring him off to me, or, by Heaven, he'll die before them all."

What my father felt during those readings may be imagined, but, strangely enough, he said, he remembered well that, toward the end, on the night of March 15, 1870, he thought he had never heard my grandfather read the "Christmas Carol" and "The Trial from Pickwick" so well and with so little effort, and almost felt inclined to hope against hope that things had not really been so bad as the doctors had supposed. But it was not to be, and on the ninth day of June, 1870, my grandfather made his last appearance on any stage.

"A Dream of Dickens"—from a painting by R. W. Buss, left unfinished at his death. The novelist appears in his Gadshill Study, surrounded by his best-known characters.

THE CLOSING CHORD.   *By Henry Hutt.*

A New Song by Richard Strauss

A Setting of Robert Burns's Poem, "John Anderson My Jo."

By Henry Hutt

What the Old Grandfather's Clock   Take-Your-Time   Courtship as it
Seemed to Say: Take-Your-Time
      Take-Your-Time

Was and Is

What the Modern Little French Clock
Seems to Say:

Get Together
Get Together
Get Together

MY FIRST DAYS IN PARIS

Lilian Bell

It was a fortunate thing that I went to London first, and had my first great astonishment there. It broke Paris to me gently.

For a month I have been in this city of limited republicanism; this extraordinary

"His inexpressible manner of raising his hat."

example of outward beauty and inward uncleanness; this bewildering cosmopolis of cheap luxuries and expensive necessities; this curious city of contradictions, where you might eat your breakfast from the streets—they are so clean—but where you must close your eyes to the spectacles of the curbstones; this beautiful, whited sepulchre, where exists the unwritten law, "Commit any offense you will, provided you submerge it in poetry and flowers"; this exponent of outward observances, where a gentleman will deliberately push you into the street if he wishes to pass you in a crowd, but where his action is condoned by his inexpressible manner of raising his hat to you, and the heartfelt sincerity of his apology; where one man will run a mile to restore a lost franc, but if you ask him to change a gold piece he will steal five; where your eyes are ravished with the beauty, and the greenness, and the smoothness and apparent ease of living of all its inhabitants; where your mind is filled with the pictures, the music, the art, the general atmosphere of culture and wit; where the cooking is so good but so elusive, and where the shops are so bewitching that you have spent your last dollar without thinking, and you are obliged to cable for a new letter of credit from home before you know it—this is Paris.

Paris is very educational. I can imagine its influence broadening some people so much that their own country could never be ample enough to cover them again. It

is amusing, it is fascinating, it is exciting, it is corrupting. The French must be the most curious people on earth. How could even Heavenly ingenuity create a more uncommon or bewildering contradiction and combination? Make up your mind that they are as simple as children when you see their innocent picnicking along the boulevards and in the parks with their whole families, yet you dare not trust yourself to hear what they are saying. Believe that they are cynical, and *fin de siècle,* and skeptical of all women when you hear two men talk, and the next day you hear that one of them has shot himself on the grave of his sweetheart. Believe that politeness is the ruling characteristic of the country because a man kisses your hand when he takes leave of you. But marry him, and no insult is too low for him to heap upon you. Believe that the French men are sympathetic because they laugh and cry openly at the theatre. But appeal to their chivalry, and they will rescue you from one discomfort only to offer you a worse. The French have sentimentality, but not sentiment. They have gallantry, but not chivalry. They have vanity, but not pride. They have religion, but not morality. They are a combination of the wildest extravagance and the strictest parsimony. They cultivate the ground so close to the railroad tracks that the trains almost run over their roses, and yet they leave a Place de la Concorde in the heart of the city.

I often blush for the cheap Americans with loud voices and provincial speech, and general commonness, whom one meets over here; but with all their faults they cannot approach the vulgarities at table which I have seen in Paris. In all America we have no such vulgar institution as their mouth wash—an affair resembling a two-part finger-bowl, with the water in a cup in the middle. At fashionable tables, men and women in gorgeous clothes, who speak four or five languages, actually rinse their mouths and gargle at the table, and then slop the water thus used back into these bowls. The first time I saw this I do assure you I would not have been more astonished if the next course had been stomach pumps.

And as for the toothpick habit! Let no one ever tell me that that atrocity is American! Here it goes with every course, and without the pretended decency of holding one's *serviette* before one's mouth, which, in my opinion, is a mere affectation.

But the most shameless thing in all Europe is the marriage question. To talk with intelligent men and women, who know the secret history of all the famous international marriages, as well as the high, contracting parties, who will relate the

price paid for the husband, and who the intermediary was, and how much commission he or she received, is to make you turn faint and sick at the mere thought, especially if you happen to come from a country where they once fought to abolish the buying and selling of human beings. But our black slaves were above buying and selling themselves or their children. It remains for civilized Europe of our time to do this, and the highest and proudest of her people at that.

It is not so shocking to read about it in glittering generalities. I thought it a pity that Frenchmen never married without a *dot.* But when it comes to meeting the people who had thus bargained, and the moment their gorgeous lace and satin backs were turned to hear some one say, "You are always so interested in that sort of thing, have you heard what a scandal was caused by the marriage of those two?"—then it ceases to be history; then it becomes almost a family affair.

"How could a marriage between two unattached young people cause a scandal?" I asked.

"Oh, the bride's mother refused to pay the commission to the intermediary," was the airy reply. "It came near getting into the papers."

At the Jubilee garden party at Lady Munson's I saw the most beautiful French girl I have seen in Paris. She was superb. In America she would have been a radiant, a triumphant, beauty, and probably would have acquired the insolent manners of some of our spoiled beauties. Instead, she was modest, even timid-looking, except for her queenly carriage. Her gown was a dream, and a dream of a dress at a Paris garden party means something.

"What a tearing beauty!" I said to my companion. "Who is she?"

"Yes, poor girl," he said. "She is the daughter of the Comtesse N——. One of the prettiest girls in Paris. Not a sou, however; consequently she will never marry. She will probably go into a convent."

"But why? Why won't she marry? Why aren't all the men crazy about her? Why don't *you* marry her?"

"Marry a girl without a *dot?* Thank you, mademoiselle. I am an expense to myself. My wife must not be an additional incumbrance."

"But surely," I said, "somebody will want to marry her, if no nobleman will."

"Ah, yes, but she is of noble blood, and she must not marry beneath her. No one in her own class will marry her, so"—a shrug —"the convent! See, her chances are quite gone. She has been out five years now."

I could have cried.

THE
AMERICAN GIRL
IN FRANCE.
By Harrison Fisher.

MOTHER. *A scene from the new story by Kathleen Norris. Illustration by F. C. Yohn.*

TWENTY-SIX WAYS

In the spring, when eggs become more plentiful and reasonable in price, we plan to use them more freely in the serving of our meals. To do this we need to know different ways in which to prepare them. On this page are a number of ways which I think you may like. One of the favorite ways of cooking eggs, yet one with which the inexperienced housekeeper often fails, is poaching. A much easier method, which

Eggs à la Goldenrod

1 Cupful of Rice
4 Hard-Boiled Eggs
2 Tablespoonfuls of Butter
2 Tablespoonfuls of Flour
1 Cupful of Milk
1 Level Teaspoonful of Salt
A Dash of White Pepper
A Dash of Paprika

WASH the rice and boil for twenty-five minutes. Drain, blanch, spread it on a platter, and sprinkle it with one teaspoonful of salt. Make a sauce of butter, flour and milk. Chop the whites of the eggs very fine and add to the sauce. Pour the cream sauce on the rice. Garnish the rice with grated egg yolks, parsley and paprika.

Eggs Valenciennes

4 Eggs
1 Cupful of Strained Tomatoes
1 Cupful of Boiled Rice
4 Tablespoonfuls of Cheese
1 Teaspoonful of Salt
⅛ Teaspoonful of White Pepper
¼ Teaspoonful of Grated Nutmeg
A Dash of Paprika

PUT the tomatoes into a saucepan; add the rice; when hot, add the grated cheese, stirring until heated through; then add the salt, pepper and nutmeg. Brush an earthenware dish with a little melted butter, and make a border of the rice, tomatoes and cheese; into the center break the four eggs. Season, place in a hot oven for four or five minutes or until it is done to suit the taste. Sprinkle with chopped parsley.

Baked Eggs in Rice With Tomato Sauce

1 Cupful of Rice
1 Cupful of Tomato Sauce
4 Eggs
2 Teaspoonfuls of Salt

WASH and boil the rice; dust with one teaspoonful of salt, spread on a hot platter, and with the back of a spoon make four places, each to hold one egg. Dust with salt and pepper, place in the oven for five minutes, remove, and cover with the sauce.

Rice and Eggs

1 Cupful of Cold Boiled Rice
4 Eggs
1 Teaspoonful of Butter
4 Tablespoonfuls of Cold Water
1 Tablespoonful of Finely Chopped Parsley or Chives
½ Teaspoonful of Salt

PUT the butter into a frying pan; when melted pour in the rice, and stir until heated through. Break the eggs into a bowl; add the water, and beat until well mixed; then add the salt, and pour over the hot rice; stir until the eggs are set and firm. Serve on a hot platter, sprinkled with the parsley or chives and dusted with paprika. A little grated onion adds to this dish.

Daisy Eggs

6 Eggs
6 Rounds of Toasted Bread
½ Cupful of Milk
½ Teaspoonful of Salt
Pepper

BUTTER the toast and put it on a platter or plate which can be put into the oven. Separate the eggs, leaving each yolk separate in a small dish; beat the whites until light; pile the whites on the buttered toasted bread. With the back of a spoon make places in the white of egg and put a yolk in each; place in a hot oven for three minutes or until the eggs are set or baked to your liking. Dust with salt and

pepper. Serve at once. This makes a very appetizing dish.

Coral Eggs

1 Cupful of Stewed Tomato
3 Eggs
½ Teaspoonful of Salt
1 Teaspoonful of Sugar
A Dash of Pepper
1 Teaspoonful of Parsley
1 Teaspoonful of Grated Onion

PUT the stewed tomato in a small saucepan over the fire; then add the seasonings. Beat the eggs until they are well mixed; pour them into the hot tomato, stir until the egg is set, or firm. Serve this on four rounds of toasted bread.

Daffodil Eggs With Spinach Border

8 Small Rounds of Toast
2 Cupfuls of Creamed Spinach
4 Hard-Boiled Eggs
½ Teaspoonful of Salt
A Dash of White Pepper

PLACE small rounds of toasted bread on a hot platter; on each put a tablespoonful of creamed spinach, covering the bread. Cut the whites of four hard-boiled eggs into small pieces and put through a fruit press, or chop fine. Cover the spinach with the whites of eggs. The yolks are grated and sprinkled over the top; add salt and pepper; warm in oven. Garnish with parsley.

Progressive Eggs

6 Hard-Boiled Eggs
6 Thin Slices of Toasted Bread
2 Cupfuls of Milk
4 Tablespoonfuls of Butter
4 Tablespoonfuls of Flour
1 Tablespoonful of Onion Juice
1 Teaspoonful of Salt
Pepper

MAKE the cream sauce as usual. Chop the whites of the eggs fine, and add to half of the cream sauce; rub five yolks through a strainer, and add to other half of cream sauce; place the toasted bread on hot platter, pile the whites in the center, and the yolks, in sauce, around the toast. Grate the sixth yolk over all, and garnish with parsley.

Eggs and Mushrooms

1 Cupful of Mushrooms
4 Eggs
2 Tablespoonfuls of Butter
2 Tablespoonfuls of Flour
1 Cupful of Milk
1 Teaspoonful of Salt
¼ Teaspoonful of White Pepper
4 Rounds of Toasted Bread
1 Tablespoonful of Caramel

PREPARE the cream sauce as usual. Chop the mushrooms, and add. Boil slowly for fifteen minutes; add salt, pepper and caramel. Pour the mushroom sauce on the toasted bread, and on each piece of toast break an egg. Put in a hot oven for six minutes before serving. Garnish with watercress, and serve.

Celestial Omelet

4 Eggs
1 Tablespoonful of Red Jelly
1 Cupful of Orange Sauce
½ Cupful of Whipped Cream
½ Teaspoonful of Salt
1 Tablespoonful of Drippings

MIX the omelet as usual. Have the drippings hot; pour in the omelet, and put it over a moderate fire until the bottom is set. Spread with orange sauce, fold, and serve on a hot platter, with whipped cream and jelly.

Orange Sauce: Mix one teaspoonful of cornstarch with a little water, one well-beaten egg, one teaspoonful of lemon juice, three tablespoonfuls of orange juice, three tablespoonfuls of sugar and a pinch of salt; add to three-quarters of a cupful of boiling water, and boil for three minutes.

Omelet Flavored With Dried Beef

4 Eggs
2 Tablespoonfuls of Dried Beef
1 Teaspoonful of Drippings
4 Tablespoonfuls of Cold Water
A Little Onion Juice
A Pinch of Salt

BEAT the eggs and water until light; add onion juice and salt. Heat the drippings; add eggs; shake pan while frying; when set, add the dried beef, which has been broken into fine pieces and heated. Double the omleet, and serve.

Rice Omelet

1 Cupful of Cold Boiled Rice
1 Tablespoonful of Drippings
3 Tablespoonfuls of Cut Onion
3 Eggs
½ Teaspoonful of Salt
Pepper

PUT bacon drippings into a frying pan; fry the onion until tender but do not brown, stirring all the time; add the rice to heat through. Beat the eggs with three tablespoonfuls of cold water until light; add the salt and pepper; pour over the hot rice. Shake the pan constantly; raise the edges so the soft part will run underneath. When set and firm, sprinkle with parsley, and double over. Serve on a hot platter.

Savory Omelet

6 Eggs
2 Tablespoonfuls of Grated Onion
1 Cupful of Creamed Vegetable
1 Tablespoonful of Drippings
2 Tablespoonfuls of Chives, Scullion Tops or Parsley
1 Teaspoonful of Salt
A Pinch of White Pepper

SEPARATE the eggs, and beat the whites until light; then beat the yolks with a quarter of a cupful of cold water, salt, pepper, chives or scullion tops; add the yolks to the whites, stir lightly until well mixed; pour into a hot pan, in which the oil, or drippings, and onion have been heated; keep over a slow fire until bottom is set (try by raising with knife). If the oven is hot put the omelet in for from three to five minutes to dry the top; if not, cover the omelet and leave on a slow fire, shaking the pan until set. Spread one side with creamed vegetable; fold over omelet. Garnish.

Spanish Omelet

4 Eggs
2 Cupfuls of Strained Tomatoes
½ Cupful of Finely Cut Onion
2 Tablespoonfuls of Drippings or Oil
2 Tablespoonfuls of Green Pepper
1 Tablespoonful of Cut Parsley
1 Teaspoonful of Salt
1 Tablespoonful of Flour

SEPARATE the eggs; beat the whites until dry, then the yolks, adding four tablespoonfuls of milk or water; add the well-beaten yolks to the whites, and mix lightly. Have a large pan hot, put in the oil, pour in the egg mixture, and place over a slow fire; cook until set. If the oven is hot put the omelet in; otherwise leave the pan on a slow fire, and cover for a few minutes; it will puff up and cook through. Cover the omelet with sauce, double over, put on platter, and pour the rest of the sauce around.

Sauce: Put one tablespoonful of oil, or drippings, into a pan; add the onion, and boil for a few minutes; then add the tomatoes, salt and green peppers; boil for five minutes; add the flour, which has been mixed with a little cold water. Half a cupful of chopped mushrooms may be added if desired, or a little spice.

Baked Eggs With Cheese Sauce

4 Eggs
1 Tablespoonful of Grated Cheese
2 Tablespoonfuls of Butter
2 Tablespoonfuls of Flour
1 Cupful of Milk
1 Teaspoonful of Salt

BRUSH an earthenware dish with a little butter; break into the dish the four eggs, cover the mixture with cream sauce, and sprinkle it with one tablespoonful of grated American cheese. Bake in a hot oven for twelve minutes.

Cream Sauce: Melt the butter; add the flour; mix well, and add the cold milk slowly, stirring until smooth and creamy; add the salt, a little pepper, and boil for two minutes.

Escalloped Eggs

4 Hard-Boiled Eggs
2 Cupfuls of Cold Boiled Ham
1 Cupful of Cream Sauce
2 Cupfuls of Bread Crumbs
2 Tablespoonfuls of Milk

MAKE the cream sauce as usual. Brush a casserole dish with bacon drippings, or butter; cover the bottom with one-third of the bread crumbs; cut two eggs into rounds, and place on the crumbs; cover with half of the ham and half of the cream sauce; add half of the remaining bread crumbs, the other two eggs sliced, the rest of the cream sauce, ham and the bread crumbs, which have been moistened with the milk. Bake in moderate oven for twenty minutes.

Steamed Eggs Flavored With Ham

4 Tablespoonfuls of Cold Boiled Ham
4 Eggs
2 Teaspoonfuls of Drippings
1 Teaspoonful of Salt
Paprika

BRUSH an earthenware dish or four custard cups with bacon drippings; put a tablespoonful of ham into each cup, or the four tablespoonfuls into the bottom of the dish. Break the eggs on the ham, being careful not to break the yolks. Sprinkle with salt and a little paprika. Place the dish or the cups in a pan of boiling water; cover, and boil for five minutes, or until the egg is set. Serve at once.

Deviled-Egg-Paste Sandwiches

4 Hard-Boiled Eggs
2 Teaspoonfuls of Mustard
1 Teaspoonful of Salt
2 Teaspoonfuls of Vinegar
2 Teaspoonfuls of Melted Butter
A Dash of Paprika
A Dash of White Pepper
A Dash of Cayenne Pepper

CUT the eggs in halves and remove the yolks with a silver fork; powder the yolks; add the mustard, salt, white pepper, Cayenne pepper, paprika and vinegar; mix well; add the melted butter (or olive oil). Chop the whites very fine; mix all together, and, if not thin enough to spread, add a little more vinegar. Spread on thinly sliced bread from which the crust has been removed.

Eggs Harrison

3 Hard-Boiled Eggs
3 Medium-Sized Potatoes
2 Tablespoonfuls of Butter
2 Tablespoonfuls of Flour
1 Cupful of Milk
1 Teaspoonful of Salt
1 Teaspoonful of Onion Juice
⅛ Teaspoonful of White Pepper
1 Tablespoonful of Parsley

BOIL the potatoes; when tender drain, and break apart with a fork. The hard-boiled eggs are cut crosswise, added to the potatoes, covered with the cream sauce, and served. Sprinkle with parsley.

Egg Salad

Lettuce Leaves
4 Hard-Boiled Eggs
French or Mayonnaise Dressing

WASH and clean the lettuce breaking it into pieces. Make a bed of lettuce in the salad bowl; shred the whites of eggs very fine and put on top of the lettuce. Mash the yolks through a fruit press, or strainer. Put the yolks one inch around the edge, and heap the remainder in the center. Cover with dressing. Garnish with slices of pepper.

Shirred Eggs Flavored With Bacon

BRUSH ramekins, or custard cups, with drippings; put in one tablespoonful of finely cut bacon which has been fried until nearly done; break one egg into each cup. Bake in a moderate oven until as firm as desired. Serve at once.

Egg Cutlet, Tomato Sauce

4 Hard-Cooked Eggs
1 Cupful of Milk
1 Tablespoonful of Butter
2 Tablespoonfuls of Flour
1 Teaspoonful of Onion Juice
1 Tablespoonful of Parsley
A Dash of White Pepper
A Dash of Paprika
½ Teaspoonful of Salt

FIRST chop the whites of the eggs fine, and add to the cream sauce; add seasonings and mashed yolks; spread on a platter and cool. When firm take up one tablespoonful in floured hands and shape into oblongs two inches by two inches and one inch thick, making the ends rounded. Dip in egg beaten with one tablespoonful of cold milk, and then in bread crumbs; fry in deep fat. Serve hot with tomato sauce.

Deviled Eggs

4 Hard-Boiled Eggs
1 Teaspoonful of Mustard
1 Tablespoonful of Butter or Olive Oil
1 Tablespoonful of Vinegar
1 Tablespoonful of Cut Parsley
A Dash of Cayenne Pepper
A Dash of Paprika
1 Teaspoonful of Salt

CUT the hard-boiled eggs into halves, lengthwise; remove the yolks, being careful not to break the whites. Powder the yolks with a silver fork; then add the mustard, salt, paprika, Cayenne pepper and vinegar mixed together; add the butter, or olive oil, or half a cupful of mayonnaise; mix until smooth, and fill into the whites; rough the tops with a fork. Serve on a bed of lettuce.

Eggs, Rice and Tomato Sauce

4 Eggs
2 Cupfuls of Tomatoes
½ Cupful of Cut Mushrooms
1 Tablespoonful of Flour
2 Tablespoonfuls of Drippings
2 Tablespoonfuls of Peppers
2 Tablespoonfuls of Pimientos
2 Tablespoonfuls of Cut Onion
2 Teaspoonfuls of Salt

THE onion should be cooked in the drippings until tender; add the tomatoes, and boil for five minutes; rub through a strainer; add the pimientos, peppers and mushrooms; salt, and boil for ten minutes. Add the flour, mixed with cold water, and pour into a baking dish; open the eggs carefully, put into the sauce, and bake until firm. Garnish with a border of boiled rice.

THAT I SERVE EGGS — Anna B. Scott

in the end, when served at the table, gives an egg that tastes about the same, is steaming. Break one or two eggs into ramekins or sauce dishes, which have been brushed with butter, and place them in a shallow pan in which there are two or three inches of boiling water. Cover the pan and cook for from three to five minutes. Sprinkle with salt, and serve in the dishes in which the eggs were steamed.

A Spring Dish of Eggs, Rice and Spinach

BOIL and blanch a cupful of rice and heap it on the center of a platter. With the back of a spoon make places for as many eggs as you wish to serve. Break each egg carefully into its place, and season. Place spinach, cooked and seasoned, around the edge of the rice. Bake until the eggs are as firm as you like them.

Eggs in Bread Cases Garnished With Bacon and Parsley

Eggs, Rice and Tomato Sauce

EGGS IN BREAD CASES: Cut slices of bread two inches thick from a large loaf; with a sharp knife cut out the centers, leaving an opening in each slice large enough for one egg. Brown in the oven. Immerse quickly in hot salted water, place in a pan, drop eggs in the centers, and bake until firm.

FASHIONS

Although extravagantly luxurious there is a certain broad simplicity in the use of furs on the new coats—little fussy bands and ornaments are lacking, fur borders and trimmings have assumed wider and greater proportions. Even the animal scarfs are emerging plumper, looking alarmingly life-like in asserting their part in the general display of lavishness.

Unique in the fur sets is the one in the lowermost corner, a "Samson" fox, combining the rare and unusual markings of a cross between the brilliant red and the dark silver fox. Barrel-shape is the muff, made of a whole skin with tail, head and paw trimmings.

With fur being used in such big applications for coats, it is but sparsely used for hats, except in the case of small turbans in military style, which are practically un-trimmed and almost always made of short-haired fur like dyed muskrat, generally termed Hudson seal, or beaver or nutria.

Distinction is achieved by hats of rich velvets, in plain tones or rich tapestry color-ings, hatter's plush or beaver cloth. Mi-nute ostrich tips, long straggling feathers, small curious ornaments, appliquéd fruit and flowers, and fur bandings and ribbon bows reproduce delightfully old-fashioned effects in trimming.

THE YOUNG GIRL'S SUMMER DRESS.

Selected by
GERALDINE
FARRAR.

*It is quite evident
from her charming
choice of design
that, notwithstand-
ing her world-wide
experiences, Miss
Farrar is still thor-
oughly in sympathy
with the American
girl and her clothes
problem.*

*These attractive
dresses, each in its
special place, will ac-
centuate most plea-
santly a young girl's
charming personal-
ity and figure. Surely
one cannot do better
than take Miss
Farrar's selection in
its entirety for one's
summer frocks.*

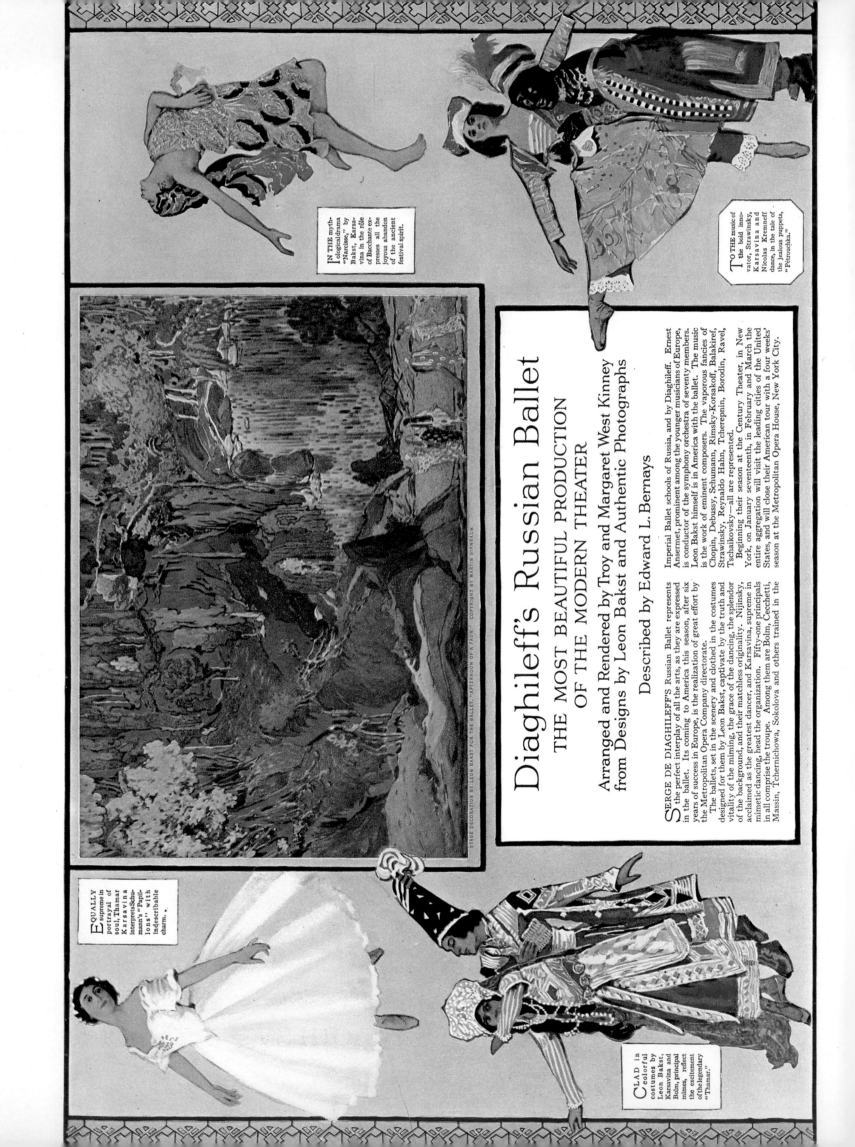

IN THE mythological drama "Narcisse," by Bakst, Karsavina in the rôle of Bacchante expresses all the joyous abandon of the ancient festival spirit.

TO THE music of the bold innovator, Strawinsky, Karsavina and Nicolas Krennieff dance, in the tale of the jealous puppets, "Pétrouchka."

EQUALLY supreme in portrayal of soul, Thamar Karsavina interprets Schumann's "Papillons" with indescribable charm.

CLAD in colorful costumes by Leon Bakst, Karsavina and Bolm, principal mimes, reflect the excitement of the legendary "Thamar."

STAGE DECORATION BY LEON BAKST FOR THE BALLET, "AFTERNOON OF A FAUN." COPYRIGHT BY MARTIN BIRNBAUM

Diaghileff's Russian Ballet

THE MOST BEAUTIFUL PRODUCTION OF THE MODERN THEATER

Arranged and Rendered by Troy and Margaret West Kinney from Designs by Leon Bakst and Authentic Photographs

Described by Edward L. Bernays

SERGE DE DIAGHILEFF'S Russian Ballet represents the perfect interplay of all the arts, as they are expressed in the ballet. Its coming to America this season, after six years of success in Europe, is the realization of great effort by the Metropolitan Opera Company directorate.

The ballets, set in the scenery and clothed in the costumes designed for them by Leon Bakst, captivate by the truth and vitality of the miming, the grace of the dancing, the splendor of the background, and their matchless originality. Nijinsky, acclaimed as the greatest dancer, and Karsavina, supreme in mimetic dancing, head the organization. Fifty-one principals in all comprise the troupe. Among them are Bolm, Cecchetti, Massin, Tchernichowa, Sokolova and others trained in the

Imperial Ballet schools of Russia, and by Diaghileff. Ernest Ansermet, prominent among the younger musicians of Europe, is conductor of the symphony orchestra of seventy members. Leon Bakst himself is in America with the ballet. The music is the work of eminent composers. The vaporous fancies of Chopin, Debussy, Schumann, Rimsky-Korsakoff, Balakiref, Strawinsky, Reynaldo Hahn, Tcherepnin, Borodin, Ravel, Tschaikovsky—all are represented.

Beginning their season at the Century Theater, in New York, on January seventeenth, in February and March the entire aggregation will visit the leading cities of the United States, and will close their American tour with a four weeks' season at the Metropolitan Opera House, New York City.

EXOTIC Orientalism is concentrated in this pose and costume of Karsavina in Bakst's masterpiece, "Scheherazade," the story of a sultan's harem.

NIJINSKY as the specter and Karsavina as the shy and pensive girl in "Le Spectre de la Rose" bring before us, most realistically, the immaterial.

THE weird new scenery and costumes in "L'Oiseau de Feu," "The Firebird," were designed by Leon Bakst; the music was written by Strawinsky. Karsavina and Bolm, in this fantastic tale of sorcery, endow their parts with a superhuman character.

IN THIS pantomime ballet Karsavina and Nijinsky, greatest dancer of his generation, dance together to the music of Schumann's "Carnaval."

BOLM assumes that demand virility, quickness, force. He combines these qualities in his portrayal of the bowman in the Russian "Prince Igor."

THESE pictures of the principals of Serge de Diaghileff's Russian Ballet bring out the full splendor of the Bakst costumes and suggest the spectacular settings which serve these dancers as a background. They convey, as well as can be conveyed by print, some idea of what London has called "The Glory of the Russian Ballet," and what Parisians have looked forward to each spring as their *saison Russe*. Short of actual flesh and blood, the striking pictures of these artists, who appear in ballets as varied as the music which accompanies them, show most vividly why the ballet has been universally termed "the greatest artistic sensation of the twentieth century."

Children's Cut-Out Paper Parties

Of the Stories They Love Best—"Alice in Wonderland"

By Helen Pettes and Julia Greene

Little Alice

Alice's Pink and White Dress

The Rabbit's Coat

The White Rabbit

The Cook

Alice's Hat

Alice's Blue Dress

The Duchess Holding the Baby

The Rabbit's Hat

The Cook's Cap

The Cheshire Cat

The Duchess's Headdress

The Queen of Hearts

The Frog Footman

The Cook's Stove

The Fish Footman

The King of Hearts

The Gryphon

The Mock Turtle

The Hatter's Hat

In this Style 10/6

The Dodo

The Hatter

Cut along dotted lines in each hat and slip the doll's head into these slits. By mounting objects on paper or thin cardboard they will last longer, and by pasting a strip of thin cardboard at the back, slightly bent to form easel, they can be made to stand.

WHAT THE PRESIDENT CAN DO AND WHAT HE CANNOT DO

William Howard Taft

There is a class of people who think that the President can do everything, that he ought to regulate everybody and everything —that is, to regulate other people, not themselves. These persons visit the President with responsibility for everything that is done and that is not done. If poverty prevails where in their judgment it should not prevail the President is responsible. If other people are richer than they ought to be the President is responsible. They clothe him with absolute power and yet the minute he begins to exercise, to their discomfort, the power he really has, they resent it with all the vociferousness of one oppressed by the most absolute tyrant.

I have been introduced to audiences many times in such words as "I have the honor to present to you the greatest ruler in the world! Greater than any monarch in Europe, he exercises a power that he derives from the people." It is true that there are some monarchs who do not have the power that the President has. The King of England used to have it; under the Constitution in England, he still has the veto power, but the exercise of that power would destroy the dynasty. He, therefore, does not exercise it, and it has not been exercised for more than a century in England.

The President of the United States has the veto power. He can say to Congress, or to the house in which the bill originated, "I return this bill with my objections," and then unless two-thirds of each of the houses, two-thirds of those present constituting a quorum, vote to pass the bill notwithstanding the objections of the President, the bill fails to become a law. That is a very great power. When the President exercises this power he is generally denounced by the members of Congress as a tyrant who is introducing kingly prerogative and saying to the representatives of the people, "Your will shall not be law." The truth is, instead of being a kingly prerogative, it is the institution of a republic, this veto power of the Chief Executive, because it is only in a republic that it can be safely exercised. The Constitution says that a bill shall become a law by being passed by one house and then by the other, and shall then be submitted to the President for signature. If he does not approve the bill he shall withhold his signature and return the bill to the house in which it originated, stating his objections. There is a Constitutional duty. He takes the oath to observe the Constitution. He is just as much a representative of the people as any member of the House or any member of the Senate, whether he comes from Oregon or Massachusetts. The truth is he is more of a representative in the sense that he represents more people than any one member of either the House or the Senate, and generally he is in such a position, having been elected by the whole people, that he parts with his local prejudices and does represent them.

Another important form of power that belongs to the President is that which comes to him as Commander-in-Chief of the Army and Navy. Many who hear of this title that belongs to the President think of fuss and feathers; of shoulder straps and of guns and swords. And, while the President never meets an enemy, and he may not know one end of a gun from the other, he is nevertheless the man who orders and directs what the army shall do. But wherever the United States law is resisted by violence, wherever the decrees of a United States Court are so resisted, and the Court calls upon the President to enforce its decrees, it is the business of the President to see that this is done, and if his United States marshals are unable to do it he may call upon the army to do so.

There is another power that the President has that is very great: he has to receive all foreign Ambassadors. That seems a very simple thing. It seems to entail upon him only the duty of being in the White House and having somebody there to take a card and bring in the Ambassador. That is all that appears on the face of the Constitution, but that power gives the President all the functions there are, except two, to direct the International relations of the Government.

Professor Taft working at his desk at Yale University.

THE WHITE HOUSE. *Watercolor by C. Durand Chapman.*

Congress has the right to declare war, therefore the President cannot declare war; and the President may not make a treaty without the consent of two-thirds of the Senate, and in that respect his power is limited. If the treaty is not consented to by two-thirds of the Senate then the treaty fails. But all correspondence with foreign governments is carried on by the President. He initiates all treaties. The President may listen to a resolution of the House or a resolution of the Senate asking him to make a treaty, and they may pass such a resolution, but he is not obliged to make such a treaty or to initiate it as they request it.

From the fact that the President is directed by the Constitution to receive Ambassadors, it falls on him to recognize foreign governments. He has to consider all the claims that are made as to whether we have been doing something unjust to foreigners, and he has to present all the claims of our people against foreign governments. The power with respect to the International relations that the President exercises without control is as important as the others that I have mentioned.

Now the power that bothers the President more than any other that he has is that of the appointment of persons to office. I believe, of course, that the President of the United States ought to appoint the chief officers of the Government. He ought to appoint the Judges of the courts. He ought to appoint the Cabinet officers because they represent him; they carry out what he wishes and they advise him. He ought to appoint the Ambassadors and the Ministers. The great Generals of the army and the general officers he ought to appoint. But these are about all he ought to appoint. Under the Constitution he is required to appoint these chief officers, and to appoint with the consent of the Senate, and to appoint all other officers whom Congress says he shall appoint, with the consent of the Senate or without, as Congress shall say. And what is the result? The President has to appoint postmasters, collectors of internal revenue, collectors of customs and customs inspectors, and all sorts of officers running to the hundred thousand, and they have to be confirmed by the Senate. Congress can take that power away from the Senate of confirming and say, "The President shall appoint," and then the President can put those officers under the Civil Service Reform provision, that is, put them in the Classified Service. That is what ought to be done. The action of the President in respect to all minor offices ought practically to be nothing more than a formal acquiescence in a system which prevails in other well-governed countries, by which the selection and promotion of all officers are by examination, and their tenure is for life. The President would not then be bothered, as he is now, with having to exercise an arbitrary discretion enabling him, if he choose, to use the offices for political purposes, and involving him in controversies that interfere with his effectiveness as the Chief Executive officer of the nation. Congressmen think that to control or influence these appointments contributes to their political power in the district. But it does not in the end, because if the Congressman appoints a postmaster it is very true, as the saying is, that it makes one ingrate and twenty enemies. If Congressmen only knew what was good for them they would get rid of this patronage. I recommended to Congress four times that they take away the requirement that the Senate shall confirm and then let me put them in the Civil Service, but they would not have it so.

The fact is that what the United States Government is attempting to do today requires the services of the best experts in each line, and if we change, as we now do, the men who hold those offices every four years with the political complexion of the Administration, we lose the benefit of experience, we lose the benefit of the disinterested devotion to the public service that a life tenure brings about, and we deprive the public service of its attractiveness for the many whose services would be valuable, but who, because of the uncertainty of tenure in the Government service, decline to accept positions of responsibility in it.

I speak whereof I know when I say it injures the dignity and the usefulness of a President to be bothered about the preference to be given to candidates for post-offices, for collectors of customs, collectors of internal revenue all over this country. One of the most aggravating features of his present duties is this constant attention that he has to pay to the visits of Representatives and Senators in regard to the local patronage. He ought not to have anything to do with such offices at all.

There is another power and a wide power that the President of the United States has: the power of pardoning those who are in prison for violating the laws of the United States. The President may exercise this power after a crime is committed and before any trial begins; may exercise it before the man is arrested. The power of pardons in States has been abused by Governors, but I have never heard that any President had called down on himself just criticism for his use of this great and merciful instrument.

What a great many people have in mind when they speak of what the President of the United States can do, however, is not the powers I have tried to explain, but they have in mind that what the President does goes, like kissing, by favor. Now the Presidency actually offers but few opportunities for discretion of that sort. The responsibility of the office is so heavy, the earnest desire by the man who fills the place to deserve the approval of his countrymen by doing the thing that is best for the country is so strong, and the recognition of just popular criticism is so controlling, that it is difficult for me, for example, who have been through four years of the Presidency, to remember more than half a dozen personal favors that I was able to confer.

The assassination of three Presidents has

led Congress to provide that the Chief of the Secret Service shall furnish protection to the President as he moves about, either in Washington or in the country at large. So when you go about the country while you are President you have three or four men wherever you go. You get the feeling that you are not being protected, but that you are yourself under surveillance, that you are in a way under the control of your guards and that they are afraid you are going to escape. It is not pleasant, and yet you need them to protect you against the jostling and the curiosity that bring people up close to you to shake hands and to manifest in every way their interest in you. Mothers want their children to shake hands with you so that they shall remember it, as they do. They remember it a great deal longer than a good many important things that they ought not to forget.

These Secret Service men are gentlemanly men—they are men that are highly paid. They are experts in determining the men who are dangerous. It is not the man who has determined to kill the President, made up his mind as a sane person to kill him, and is willing to sacrifice his life in order to accomplish the purpose, that they are there to guard against, because such a man can kill the President, if there be such

a man, because the President must show himself in such a way and must come near enough a crowd, so that if a man puts himself where he is willing to be taken and hanged, it is hardly possible for escape. But the presence of a President in a community excites a great many excitable persons, persons who are not fully calm, and they begin to think about it and it goes over and over again in their heads. That is the kind of people that it is wise to protect the President against.

Perhaps it is too much to say, but I almost feel that if there had been as great watching, as great expert attention at the time, the question whether Mr. McKinley would have been exposed as he was is doubtful in my mind.

I would like to say a word to every boy who hears, and every man or woman who reads these words as to his or her relation to the President of the United States:

The President of the United States is your Chief. You are an American, and he represents America and the United States. He is the man whom the people have put at the head of the Government, and for the time being he embodies the sovereignty of the United States. He is entitled, therefore, to your support and to your respect. The trouble about our present condition is that

we are losing respect for authority. We are getting into the thought that every man knows as much as everybody else, whether he be old or young.

Now it is not necessary for any of us to give up the independence of our thought, our mind, but we have no right to assume that we know it all until we have made investigations, and taken into consideration the fact that we are not as old as Methuselah, and that we are in a situation where we have got to learn something. That is the case with respect to the President. He is put at the head of the Government by the people. He represents the dignity and the majesty of the people, and while you may differ with some of his policies, while you may think that his assistants are not all that they ought to be, nevertheless he represents for you your country. Therefore do not allow yourself by flippant references even to think that he is not worthy of your respect. Believe that he is doing the best he can, and that he feels much more deeply than you can possibly feel the responsibility and the burden of that responsibility, and is much more anxious than you can possibly be that things shall come out all right, and that what he does shall inure to the benefit of the people.

Illustration by Alice Barber Stephens for MOTHER CAREY'S CHICKENS *by Kate Douglas Wiggin.*

MY PAST, MY PRESENT,

MY HEALTH

Sarah Bernhardt

When I am asked what the difference is between the past and the present with regard to my emotions—my sensations—I can truthfully say that I find none. My emotions are as lively, my tears as warm, my laugh is as hearty, as they were forty years ago.

My belief is that one should determine to live one's life without fear of death. The saddest of the cares by which humanity in general is ridden seems to me the fear of death. One sees men and women, as years follow upon years, yielding to the idea that the end is near and that it is no longer worth while to struggle.

That is a mistake—a grievous mistake. Every minute brings its joy: every hour brings its sorrow. One must make the most of the former and wage war against the latter.

The secret of strength is to be always on the defensive. One must say to one's self that life is a long battle. Illness, sorrow, trouble, accident, death, lie in ambush at every turn of the road. One must go armed against all those enemies, fear none of them, stop for none of them, but walk ahead, armed with faith, cheerfulness and will.

One must know how to *will*—always, and in spite of all. *Quand même* (In spite of all) has been my motto since the age of nine, and I have been faithful to it. I have fought with time and been stronger than time. I have striven with illness and conquered it. I have battled with death and repulsed it—requesting it to come back later. That is the secret of my youth.

Some one asked me once if I consider woman inferior to man. It is a delicate question; I have always believed that the natural constitution of woman is inferior to that of man. She is subject by the misfortune of her sex to ailments which give her nerves a temporary predominance over her brain. She is subject to maternity, and, while carrying her child, is not wholly responsible for her actions.

An amiable suffragette said to me not long ago: "But there are queens!" Certainly there are queens, but they have not chosen women for their ministers or chamberlains. Queens have chambermaids, but not maids in the Chamber of Deputies.

No! a thousand times no! Let woman not go into politics. Woman's part in the world is fine enough; little luster would be gained for it by descending to the base intrigues of politics.

That women should be lawyers I understand. That there should be woman doctors I admit. Had the medical schools been open to women when I was sixteen I might possibly have devoted myself to little children.

Let women claim the right to vote if they choose. I cannot see why it should be denied them, for the weaknesses of their sex can in no way affect their judgment upon a worthy man or a rascal. And as women are generally more patriotic than men their vote would certainly be more honest than the votes of certain men.

It is better to be nobly remembered than nobly born.
—RUSKIN

I am convinced, however, that if, for example, Joan of Arc were now living she would not be a suffragette. She would be a sweet and simple countrywoman, and her mysterious power would remain unknown, having no opportunity to manifest itself. She would, perhaps, be one of those humble and modest Sisters of Mercy who heroically go forth to die in far lands, poetic torches of faith whose pure light leaves in the heart a deeper and surer trace than is left in the flesh by bullets and bayonets!

The case of Joan of Arc was not one of hysteria, as certain writers have asserted. It was a case of faith.

"If you had faith, if you had perfect faith,
And said unto that mountain: 'Walk, huge rock!'
Mount Gerizim, obedient, would walk!"

says Jesus in "The Woman of Samaria," by Edmond Rostand.

Joan of Arc had faith—not in herself, but in her voices. And this faith upheld her in prison, where, outworn with privations and want of air, she found strength to answer that tribunal composed of rhetoricians, theologians and heads of universities. And she confounded them by her admirably logical answers. They would twist her words and make them inadmissible. Exhausted, panting, she would return to the contest, and, in her untutored and childlike language, reject the meaning they endeavored to impose upon such and such of her expressions.

She communicated her faith to the rough warriors surrounding her, because they could feel throbbing in the breast of that peasant love of her fellow-man, love of her country, love for her "Celestial Ladies."

Joan of Arc was aflame with faith and love, and drew all after her by the magic of a luminous hope.

Now as to the oft-asked question whether, personally, I have a system of health by which I live. I have none—or rather, I have one. But it is execrable according to doctors. I eat little and often. I forget the hour of meals. I am never in bed before three o'clock in the morning. I take baths too hot. I drink water too cold. On days when there is an afternoon and an evening performance I stand for eight hours, never finding a minute to sit. I sleep well, and I adore sleep. I never rise before ten o'clock. By way of airing I go from the hotel to the theater, and from the theater back to the hotel: that is all.

For ten months of the year I do not walk: then, suddenly, at my summer home in Belle-Île, I walk two or three miles. For ten months of the year I have no outdoor life whatever: at Belle-Île I am from six o'clock in the morning until eight o'clock at night in the open air, playing lawn tennis three hours at a time; or I go hunting or fishing.

Such is my health system.

But—I advise no one to adopt it!

Miss Bernhardt as "Joan of Arc."

LOVE'S TORMENT

Enrico Caruso and Richard Barthèlemy

PIANO QUESTIONS

Answered by Josef Hofmann

Playing in Correct Time

I have studied music diligently for four years, but cannot play evenly or in correct time. My teacher has tried with the metronome, but this has had no effect. Can you tell me what is wrong with me and what the cure is?   M. C.

Mr. W. F. Apthorp cites the case of a boy who had not enough sense of rhythm to keep step in marching, and was, therefore, excused from participating in the boys' military drill; but it is the only case he (or I) ever heard of. In all other cases I found bad time-keeping due to a weakness of the musical will, or, which was more frequently the case, to an inclination to negligence. Whichever is the case with you, the metronome will only help you to be on time at certain intervals; what you play between the beats of the metronome may still be uneven. Try to play each hand separately and divide again the parts each hand has to play. Endeavor thus to play each part in time and to hear each part rhythmically. Your imaginative hearing of rhythmical sounds will impel your fingers to reproduce them. Are you quite sure that you did not leave the cure of your weakness altogether to your teacher?

A Matter of Ear Training

I have been much puzzled by this phrase from Gottschalk's "Last Hope," as the modulations seem very harsh to me. Is it correct as it stands?
L. E.

Are you sure that in performing the passage you played the chords correctly and, above all, clearly? Have you not blurred their purity by unnecessary pedaling? I see nothing unusual, much less anything harsh, in these chords, and I advise you to familiarize yourself with more compositions of merit. They would soon train your ear to become receptive of select harmonies, so as not to get startled by a simple chord of the ninth.

The Effect of a Piano's Action

Is a piano with a stiff action detrimental to a person's touch, and why?   STUDENT.

A piano must be responsive. If by "stiff action" you mean a heavy action this would not interfere so much with your musical development as it might injure your hands. If, however, by "stiff action" you mean one that is unresponsive to the various dynamic degrees of your touch this would surely be detrimental to your musical development, as it would prevent you from producing color variety on the piano, which is one of the chief means of expression and in importance equal to the "rubato." Color in the domain of touch is what the "rubato" is in the province of tempo and rhythm.

Varying the Playing of Mordents

In Chopin's First Impromptu (opus 29) is the first note of the mordent struck with the first note of the bass, or is the mordent all played before the bass note is sounded at all?
A. B. K.

DRAWN BY JOHN R. NEILL

In a (comparatively speaking) modern piece like this it may not be amiss to vary the execution of the mordent here and there, for it is so often repeated. According to Philip Emanuel Bach the normal way is to start the mordent simultaneously with the bass note. The other ways must, therefore, be regarded as variations of or deviations from the normal.

Improving Sight Reading

Will the study of sight singing improve my reading at sight on the piano? I have a great deal of difficulty in reading and cannot do it at all well.   PERPLEXED.

If your difficulty does not arise from a general slowness of visual perception—which your oculist could determine and perhaps cure, as it may have to do with the power of accommodation of your eyes—it may lie in the polyphonic structure of the music you try to read. It is, of course, more difficult to read many parts at once than only one part, because of the greater complexity. Begin by reading each part (or "voice") separately, as you do in sight singing. While playing the second part try inwardly to hear also the first, and so on. I think that thus you will gradually overcome at the same time the difficulty of transmitting the mental impressions to your fingers.

Schumann's "Träumerei"

Please explain the fingering of this phrase from Schumann's "Träumerei." I find it very difficult to make the necessary reach. Why are the "Träumerei" and the "Romance in A minor" often published together? Are they not separate compositions?   KATHARINE.

In the right hand play the chord A and G with the thumb. In the left hand if you cannot reach the stretch to strike the chord promptly roll it a little and use the pedal.

The "Romance in A minor" has neither an organic nor any other connection with the "Träumerei." They are played in succession in orchestral arrangements, probably because each of the pieces is too short to make it worth while to set so large an apparatus as an orchestra in motion.

Playing Arrangements

In playing orchestral music for the piano is the best effect produced by four hands or are eight hands (two pianos) better still? In arranging from a score would two equally competent musicians produce substantially the same piano parts?   IGNORANT.

It depends upon which element of the reproduction you lay the greatest stress. If it is unity of tone quality one piano would be better because two pianos are rarely of exactly the same tone quality. If, however, you aim at the most nearly complete reproduction of all the parts that make up an orchestral work, I should say the more hands the better.

Replying to your second question, I would remind you that two musicians, though they be ever so much alike in good musicianship, are always two different personalities. I doubt if their work would be exactly the same.

When the Time Meter Changes

In the following passage should the measure in 3-4 time be hurried so as to give it just the same duration as those in 2-4, or should it receive an extra beat?   G. P.

It is difficult to say, when I do not know the composition and when the absence of the title and of the composer's name made it impossible for me to look it up. However, a change of time meter does not imply a change of speed in the time beats unless it is especially indicated.

Practicing Accentuation

In Litolff's "Spinning Song" are the sextolets true or false? By this I mean do you accent "one," "three" and "five," or only "one" and "four"?   ALMIRA.

It depends upon the melody, and as this changes from triplets to couplets, and vice versa, so (in practice) must your accentuation change. When you have acquired a technical command of the piece you should gradually lessen the accentuation until it disappears altogether.

Acquiring a Sense of Rhythm

Is a knowledge of higher mathematics of any help in mastering rhythm?   P. K.

Mathematics is a purely intellectual and therefore unemotional acquisition, while musical rhythm is an utterance of human, musical impulse. Musical rhythm is not to be confounded with metronomical time beats, which are mechanical. Musical rhythm is closely connected with the action of the heart, which is varyingly affected by our feelings and emotions. Hence we may link musical rhythm with human pulse beats, which are subject to variations, while the metronomical time beat is the throb of a machine and does not vary. If you will read good poetry aloud, emphasizing the meter, it will help you much more than will mathematics.

Playing Broken Chords

Is the wrist movement the best way in which to play broken chords?   E. H.

The wrist movement is a good way to play chords, but it is by no means the only way, for chords occur in so many different combinations with other things as to require a variety of manner of playing them. It is impossible to generalize this matter.

Changing Hands in Playing a Melody

How shall I play these two measures from a Barcarolle of Rubinstein? I am unable to play all the notes, and I do not know with which hand to play the melody in the first measures.
C. M.

In the first measure the melody is played by the left hand in the second, third and fourth eighths; at the fifth eighth the right hand takes it up again. You must connect the notes so as not to betray the fact that all the notes were not played by the same hand. As to the chords, they should be very soft. The one in the left hand is probably the only one of which you cannot play all the notes; if you roll it slightly you will find it easy enough, especially if you take the pedal just for that chord.

Why the 2/2 Signature is Used

I have been told that there is no difference between 2/2 and 4/4 time. Is this true?
MYRA KEAT.

Since one half equals two quarters and two halves equal four quarters—as you are aware, no doubt—the equation is self-evident. The reason why a composer employs the time signature of 2/2 instead of 4/4 lies in the circumstance that he may have the intention of varying the subdivisions of his half notes, and, instead of the usual two quarters to a half note, he may wish to use quarter-triplets, which would be awkward to count in 4/4 time.

Subdividing a Measure

What is the correct way to count this measure?
READER.

The last note of the left hand ought to be a quarter note. As a half note it is either a misprint or you made a mistake in copying. Divide the six quarter beats of the measure into twelve eighths and play the left hand on 1, 5, 7 and 11, while the right hand must strike at all the even beats, thus: 2, 4, 6, 8, etc.

A Theme Continued Over Two Measures

How is this measure in Kuhlau's Sonatina, opus 55, No. 3, to be counted? This copy is from the Steingraeber edition. ADMIRER.

The editor has used a dotted line here instead of a bar to intimate that in spite of the eighth rest the subject does not end there, but the next measure is an integral part of it. In other words, the little theme occupies not one but two measures. You should therefore regard the eighth rest not as a period (.) but as a comma (,).

The Time of Mendelssohn's "Spring Song"

How do you advise the playing of Mendelssohn's "Spring Song"? One teacher tells me to play it slowly, with much expression, and another says to play it fast and lightly. EDITH.

I would advise playing it slowly and lightly. The "Spring Song" is a graceful and lyric composition, and music of this kind is not intended to be played rapidly.

A "Motive" and its Relation to a Theme

How shall I explain to my pupils what is meant by a "motive"? H. C.

A theme is always a complex sentence, such as this, which is interspersed with several commas; possibly, also, with a semicolon, before it concludes with a period point. A motive may be likened to those parts of this sentence that are between the various punctuation marks. Thus the theme of Beethoven's Andante in F comprises eight measures, but the motive, the germ which develops into a theme, occupies only three eighths, two in the first measure and one preceding it. This motive is at once reiterated two degrees lower and differently harmonized.

How to Tell a Tie From a Slur

In Lemoine's Études Enfantines, opus 37, No. 3, in the second measure of the following excerpt are the two B's tied together or is the sign a slur? Please say how a slur can be distinguished from a tie where the notes are the same. M. L.

This is undoubtedly meant to be a tie. When two consecutive notes of the same pitch are connected by a curved line we call the line a tie; if the notes differ from each other in pitch we call it a slur. Where in spite of a tie the second note is intended to be struck again it is usually supplied with either a dot or a dash. Are you sure that you have a good edition of the Lemoine Études?

A Player's Discretion in Interpreting

To what extent is a performer allowed to use his discretion in the rendition of an instrumental selection? M. K.

Rubinstein said: "Play exactly what is written; not less in quantity or quality. If, after that, you have something of your own—and of equal merit—to add, you may do so, but not before." I recommend his advice to you. It is good.

Playing a Trill in a False Movement

How shall I play the following trill which occurs so frequently in the first movement of Beethoven's Sonata, opus 2, No. 3?

Also, in the cadenza near the end of the movement, is the duration of the trill on the D left to the discretion of the player? WINNIE.

I offer this manner of executing this trill as a suggestion, not as dogma. In the brisk motion of this movement it seems hardly advisable to attempt the playing of a larger number of notes in the trill. In the cadenza the length of the trill is left to your pleasure and good taste, although the fact that Beethoven made it a half note should be of some guidance to you.

A Strong Body Necessary to Good Playing

I have completed the Kohler "First Book" and Heller's "Twenty-Five Melodious Studies," but my progress is slow. I cannot play anything at the right speed, yet my fingers are weak rather than stiff. Kindly tell me how I can strengthen them. ELLA.

Let me illustrate your case by an automobile. To make it run faster you have to increase the power. The weakness of your fingers prevents you from playing at high speed, and this weakness of the fingers is, I fear, due to a general feebleness of your muscular system. As long as the body and arms are weak the fingers cannot acquire strength. Yet strength is necessary for any quick motion, whether by a human being, an automobile or any other moving mechanism.

Acquiring a Loose Wrist

How can I best and soonest acquire an entirely loose wrist and what studies will help me most? LOUISE.

Practice wrist octaves with a light touch, reaching at most only a mezzoforte. Keep the wrist low in a hanging condition, and watch well that it does not stiffen. As soon as you feel the slightest approach to a stiffening stop playing and rest until the free circulation of the blood from the arm into the hand (and return) is fully reëstablished. The closer you watch this particular matter of stiffening the sooner you will experience an increase of endurance and strength. Do not be alarmed if you should, in the beginning, have to stop after every few minutes; the period of continuous playing will soon lengthen.

The Elementary Study of the Classics

Please suggest a list of the easiest classics suitable for a pianist who has not much time to practice but who is anxious to become familiar with some good music. E. D.

There are a number of collections of classic pieces published in which all sorts of "facilitations" are resorted to. I do not, of course, approve of such editions; but if you wish to use them you can obtain them at any large music publishing house.

The Evolution of the Piano

What books shall I read to gain the best idea of the predecessors of the piano and the development of the present-day instrument? Also how can I learn the various styles of composition of the great masters? I desire this information for teaching purposes, so that my pupils shall play more intelligently. JULIA.

You will find a concise but complete account of the evolution of the piano in Baltzell's "History of Music," beginning at page 236. I think this book will also inform you as to the styles of the great masters, as far as it is possible to give such information. The best way to understand the characteristics of style in the works of the masters is, of course, to study the works themselves.

The Close of Chopin's D-Flat Waltz

I do not see how these last four measures of Chopin's waltz in D flat can be played in correct time. HESTON.

Why not? In the first two of the measures quoted can you not play three notes to a beat and lessen your speed in the next measure so that two notes fill the beat? Keep counting aloud your 1, 2, 3, and let your playing be governed by your counting, instead of the reverse, as I suspect you to have done if you have counted at all. Besides, you may accelerate the run a little and make up for it by a slight retard in the last but one measure.

Compositions for Study Without a Teacher

Please suggest some compositions which I can study alone. I have advanced under instruction so that I play Chopin's Sonata, opus 35, the Ballade in G minor, and the Fantasie in F minor. M. S.

Beethoven, Sonata Appassionata; Schumann, Carneval; Mendelssohn, Variations Sérieuses; Brahms, Ballades and Rhapsodies; Tschaikowski, Variations, opus 19; MacDowell, Suite in E minor; Sternberg, Impromptu in D flat and Concert Étude, opus 103; Schütt, Carneval Mignon; Schytté, Bourrasque de Neige.

How Much of This Do You Want Your Daughter to Share?

An Editorial in Pictures

THE pictures on this page are from photographs taken at the "bathing hour," on various public beaches that dot the Atlantic Coast from Cape May to Cape Ann. They accurately indicate the free-and-easy familiarity that is continuous on these great midsummer playgrounds from the opening of the season to its close.

Are the situations shown such as you would wish your daughter to have a share in, such as you would even care to have your daughter see? Where do you think such easy familiarity between the sexes—between the *young* of the sexes—leads? Nowhere, do you say? Would you be willing for your daughter to take the chance of such familiarity, leading—no-where? Yet that is precisely the chance thousands of American parents do take when they permit their daughters unrestricted indulgence in the "attractions" of our public bathing beaches.

THE GIRL WHO WANTS TO SING

Geraldine Farrar

A great many people have the idea that an opera singer is a happy and carefree person who appears on the stage once or twice a week and has a joyous time there displaying her talents, with nothing to do for the rest of the time but lie upon the proverbial bed of roses.

This is hardly a true picture. At least it is not a true picture in my case—and, being an apostle of individuality, I can only recount my own experience without attempting to speculate outside of it. From the viewpoint of the average woman I am a slave to duty, always rebellious at the routine, fearful of ills and minor cares that might compromise a night's performance, more or less of a solitary student, seldom happy with my results, and not always a blessing to my family when I have "nerves." How can any one be happy in the ordinary pleasant human way when she subordinates every consideration to that of an overwhelming ambition which it takes all her energies, physical and mental, to sustain?

If you take your work as seriously as you ought you are never at rest, for your whole career depends on watchfulness. I never have any peace in this regard, for after all I have experienced I feel my ambition growing stronger when it feeds on achievement. My ambition? Well, to develop my powers as near to their peculiar ripeness as can be before they are taken away from me. It is such a little time! I know one does not reach perfection; it is not within the possibilities of human beings to do so, I suppose. But the fiery ambition and active mind will permit of no rest.

The appeal of the artist to the public is such a fragile thing! Today you appear, tomorrow you are forgotten. Sincerity is the all-important keynote in all this. Give of yourself! Spare nothing! It is better, in my opinion, to have a lazy voice than an inactive mind. With an agile mind and a mediocre instrument I can still give more of my soul than the mere warbler, fortunate in her lung capacity and dazzling roulades. Give of your emotions, your feelings, yourself—and your listeners will rise to greet your message. In this I have never spared myself. As soon as you begin to reserve and calculate, coldness will begin to creep in and you lose your power over your audience. All depends on the artist's geniality, spontaneity and generosity of emotion. Be lavish and give! It is the most exquisite tribute to feel your public's interest when you do so.

This point suggests a very vital question for girls, who are aspirants for operatic honors, to ask themselves: "Have I such a combination?" If they have not I doubt if they will be entirely successful. That is not a thing which the early music lessons will let them know with any certainty.

Now just what can I say to the great army of girls who are thinking of becoming professional singers? I believe there is nothing to be said to them, for the reason that among the mass which ought to be dissuaded for their own good there will be two or three who are destined to be successful. They will make their way on that mysterious quality which we call individuality, and there is no living person—not even the aspirant herself—who can tell whether any single case is one where the needed gift has been vouchsafed until her trial before an audience. These, the more talented ones, the more venturesome souls—will survive many bitter tests, and there is nothing for them to do but go ahead and learn their own lesson. Nobody can do it for them.

If I have succeeded in persuading a few that a good voice is but one asset among many more important qualities I shall think I have done a good thing.

That is why I object to putting myself in the position of judging an unknown singer and advising whether she should be given the means to persevere. I could never know the depth and quality of her gifts. It hurts to have to tell a young, pretty girl with a good voice that you do not think she ought to take up singing professionally, and besides, she very seldom will believe or thank you for an adverse criticism. The singing teachers, to my mind, are those who should direct young students, not the singer who knows only her own particular talents and cultivates them in her own individual way.

Many letters come to me from women who want to go into opera, and some of them are pitiful. What are you going to do when a woman writes you that she is sure she has a voice, but that she is married to a man who does not sympathize with her ambitions, and that she has children? The operatic stage is no place for a discontented married woman if she takes the matter seriously. She will have to give up the idea either of being a singer or of making a home.

One's whole energy must be concentrated in one's career. How can a woman advance in it if she has such family cares to consider? You must give yourself up altogether to keeping yourself in proper condition, regardless of other people's wants. All depends on two little sensitive vocal cords, nerves, moods, a turn of the public, anything, good or ill. You must slave all winter when you are singing, and work all summer getting ready to be in a condition to slave again the following winter. Where's the time to sing lullabies and figure out the grocery bills?

The price of being an opera singer is constant slavery, constant grind, and the denial of everything that makes the usual run of womankind's happiness: friends, family ties, society, sports, and all the touches that make up the happiest part of ordinary human life.

Then there is the physical side. For the singer it is a strict matter of business to keep in the most perfect condition of health. If you have ever heard the audience murmur when it is announced that some favorite singer will not appear because of indisposition you will realize what this means. For the public a cold is a regrettable incident; for us, a tragedy.

Ordinarily I would be called a strong girl, with a strong constitution and general good health. As the opera season opens, however, and this life on the nerves starts, it is an unceasing effort to keep up to the proper physical condition. During one week there were three nights when I could not sleep at all because my nerves refused to allow me to get the proper grip on myself. Very frequently there comes a period when I cannot eat properly. An idea evades one, and until the inspiration comes there is no middle road of content or regulated existence. Then there are always rehearsals, studying at home, your routine daily work and a hundred other things to keep you from the ordinary life of a healthy person, not to mention the nervous fatigue. For me exercise is just so much energy lost from a performance, so I take and advocate none.

I hope I have given some idea of what it means to arrive as an opera singer and strive to remain on the shaky pinnacle. I hope, too, I have demonstrated that the voice is but a valuable card of admission in conjunction with much else to Opera Land, which may entitle you to gaze at what you think are its wonders, but gives uncertain promises whether you will be allowed to participate.

My sympathies are with the girls who were born with that same certainty that I had, because neither you nor I nor their friends—least of all the girls themselves—will know, until they have gone through many hard moments with the required combination of grit, aptitude, strong individuality and much self-confidence, if the achievement is worth all it demands. It means work, and work, and work, and a cool head, sacrifices, discouragements often, and a firm belief in one's self.

Geraldine Farrar as Caterina Hübscher and Pasquale Amato as Napoleon in Giordano's new opera, "Mme. Sans-Gêne."

The lady had been getting fairly accurate transcripts of every letter the big munitions men dictated on international business, which she delivered to her "superiors" in this country.

THE WOMAN AS A WAR SPY

Anonymous

It is an axiom among intelligence bureaus of the various European governments that "a *white* man is worse than useless as a spy and that a straight woman is more dangerous than a bomb."

Napoleon held that all spies were by nature traitors. He would employ as spies only men whose lives had been soiled, or who had something criminal in their past, which he could use as a curb bit on their every move. Frederick the Great has been called the father of the entire modern spy system, with its ugly spawn working in the slime of the underworld like the tentacled devilfish which fouls the waters where it floats to hide its approach. He boasted that, for every cook he employed, he had a hundred spies; and he was inclined to use as spies only criminals. If he could detect a young officer in some grave fault—tied up in gambling debts, involved in some matrimonial disgrace, misusing official funds—that youth was a marked man for the great monarch's first choice when he added to his collection of spies.

Unfortunately this system has come down to the practice of contemporaneous intelligence bureaus and has extended its tentacles to embrace many decent men in its foul waters. Men who would be blackballed from social clubs as bounders if they habitually lied have boasted in this war how they set this, that or the other "yarn" afloat to mislead the enemy; and men who in social or business life would not harm the meanest employee, or defraud him of a cent, have in this war received and obeyed orders to commit arson, murder, assassination, and to throw the blame on some poor tool.

Not only has the system seized on guilt in past records to enforce obedience to still deeper guilt, but it has put temptation in the way of young officers, who would not otherwise commit crimes, to compel them to carry out some sinister purpose at which ordinary decency might balk.

For instance, this record of a Polish intrigue, the time and place of which cannot be given: it was observed of a young Polish officer serving in a Bavarian regiment that he was growing dissipated. It was also observed that he was showing symptoms of a fatal disease—democracy, sympathy with Polish aspirations for freedom. His Polish sympathies were ascribed to his friendship with an elderly Polish patriot. The patriot had a flighty daughter of the type to balance continuously tiptoe on the edge of the forbidden, not from innate folly in herself, but "to keep people guessing."

Some sinister eye "higher up" playing chess with human motives for pawns had the young officer billeted in the patriot's house—a very excellent and benevolent plan, as you doubtless guess, to throw two friends with secret leanings toward democracy together in one household! "A white man" or a "straight woman" would have been afraid of that arrangement for fear the younger man would not report plans on the part of the patriot; but enters across the chessboard—Flighty Daughter balancing tiptoe on the edge of folly "to keep people guessing"; and the unseen Master Player smiles beneath all his stately gravity. Daughter and officer run off in a clandestine marriage.

Not knowing she was betraying freedom, and never dreaming for a moment that she had done exactly what his superiors guessed

From a painting by Howard Giles.

she would, the bride revealed all her father's plans, all his pecuniary embarrassment, all his associates, which, of course, went straight up to headquarters as the Master Player had guessed it would. What pressure was brought to bear I do not know; but the young patriot lost all his aspirations for democracy; and the elder patriot suddenly became patriotically pro-German and financially prosperous. No, he was not bought! He signed a note or something to an obliging friend who had advanced him money. After that he obeyed orders.

This girl was not a spy; but she accomplished what ten spies could not have done; and she didn't know she did it. The incident is somewhat analogous to those hostesses who, in the summer of 1916, welcomed to their homes officers of foreign submarines which we now know were carrying in their holds parts of submarines to be put together at an American base near Panama. This base has since been suppressed. The hostesses had no idea that their hospitality was being used to cloak covert attacks on this country. They did for the enemy what no spy could do.

It is in this way—and I think, I may add, almost entirely in this way—that many American women have been used as tools in the present war. Women of spotless reputation and sincerity to the very marrow gave of their names and reputations in pacifist movements, financed by a foreign power to keep this country in a state of unpreparedness. But where American women have acted as unconscious tools, quite otherwise has been the situation with the host of foreign adventuresses who have flocked to this country like crows to a cornfield.

Early in the war orders for munitions were chaotic in the United States. Two representatives from the same government would be in the same field competing against each other. Two men would be bidding for the same lot of copper, running up the price—for the same bunch of horses, for the same wheat, the same ships. I know of a case where three different agents were bidding for a line of ships against one another for the same government, with the result that ships which had been chartered at $30,000 a year formerly suddenly commanded $75,000 a month; and when the home government sent out inspectors to check this riot run mad, the inspectors were dogged night and day by agents of the enemy to countermand or confuse the orders, or to bribe the venial, or mislead the fools.

There were two or three well-known midnight dance resorts in New York, classed as fashionable and respectable too, where these shadows were caught with drugs enough on their persons to keep an inspector drunk or befuddled for weeks. Some of the shadows were men. Many were women; so the home governments finally each selected a very big man, indeed, to come out and inspect the inspectors and reduce confusion to order.

It looked for a moment as if war secrets could no longer be extracted from the "drug"-drunk inspectors or "dance"-drunk young purchasing agents; so the Master Player, higher up—the unseen hand that shifts the human chess pawns and guesses what the interplay of basest motives will be—moved a queen forward on the boards. (I don't mean a real empress. There was a real empress used later; and I'll tell that story too.) I mean a queen of that curious half world where people of good birth and position sell themselves to such work from motives which "white people" can't fathom. This woman was beautiful. She had social position of a kind in Berlin, Munich, Vienna. That is, she knew emperors and princes and officers, but not many empresses, princesses, officers' wives. She wasn't what you would call a woman's woman. She was distinctively a man's woman. She did not lack means. She knew too well what was over the edge. She affected the coy and the feminine and the artless. She was a well-known figure in opera boxes and fashionable hotel tea rooms. She was ultra-exclusive. She wore no jewels. There was not a flash about her, but there was an ambiguous distinction that drew all eyes wherever she went.

Well, she chanced—purely chanced—to come across on the same steamer as the big functionaries sent out to straighten the inspectors. (I confess here, I am disguising things because I have to.) It was very easy

The things most people want to know about are usually none of their business.   G. B. SHAW

on deck "to bump" into an acquaintance with the secretaries and attachés of the big men. In vain she tried her artless dodges to bump into the functionaries themselves. They were adamantine icebergs. They literally did not see her because they were so intent on the terrible gravity of their own position. She was a signpost to them; and if she spelled anything it was possibly—danger.

Now the particular intelligence bureau for which this siren served is known to pay very liberal salaries in advance; but it pays still more liberal bonuses for results. Though the artless emissary could not "bump" into the big munitions men, by the time the steamer had bumped into New York piers the woman had bumped one of the secretaries stonily senseless. She took an elaborate suite of rooms in the same hotel as the munitions men. It was easy to hold cozy little afternoon teas for two in her apartments. She was a personage of such distinction that the secretaries were conscious of a rarefied social atmosphere every time they shook hands with her.

I don't believe an American boy would have come a fall so easily; for I don't believe the average American boy eats and sleeps and dreams with hopes of "a leg up" socially. He doesn't want "a leg up" socially till he has the means to sustain it; but your old-country boy thinks of a rung up the social ladder as an American boy thinks of a promotion on his job. How it was dis-

covered I don't know; but it was discovered that for three months the lady had been getting fairly accurate transcripts of every letter the big munitions men dictated on international business, which she delivered to her "superiors" in this country.

Now, there may be a law to punish for betraying military secrets; but there is no law, or method, either, so far as I know, to prevent a pair of artless ears hearing the foolish babbling of an infatuated young donkey. A picture of the lady was sent to America. She was recognized as one of the cleverest and most unscrupulous women spies in the service of Berlin.

In this case the Master Player calculated amiss as to the big men's motives; but he got his results through a foolish secretary, who probably to this day does not know that he betrayed Allied secrets to Germany.

The question is sometimes asked what the difference is between secret-service work and spy work. Both work under intelligence bureaus; and probably, to the Master Player, there is no difference; but to the workers themselves the difference is that between a good sporting dog and a skunk. A military man for military ends seeks military information, as Kitchener did when he disguised himself as a peddler and went among the Arabs' tents. If he had been caught he would have stood up like a man and taken his medicine before a firing squad, as countless men have taken their medicine in this war, but he did not betray those Arabs among whom he went in disguise. He did not put poison in their wells. He did not run off with a man's daughter or wife and then throw her to the dogs. He did not blacken other people's reputations to cover his own doings.

A secret-service man is an emissary for his government. A spy is a scavenger out to pick garbage from the ash can and then throw it where it will stick to advantage. One is a soldier of chance. The other is a sneak protecting himself as the devilfish does—by emitting a poison; or as the skunk does—by poisoning the atmosphere; and there are all sorts of gradations between the two extremes.

Most of us would say, without a moment's hesitation, that if the officer of a foreign power came here and studied forts and mapped our harbors and got a line on all our munitions—if we were big enough fools to let him—he would not be transgressing the code of a gentleman; but if the officer came here and laid the plots that drowned one hundred American citizens while eating bread at our tables, most of us would say he was not only a spy of the most despicable type, but a human hyena unfit to live; and no wonder decent men, pushed to the limit by the new code of dishonor, have threatened suicide rather than obey orders. There were 8000 spies in Belgium before the war broke out. There were 15,000 by August of 1914 in France. How many there are in this country no one knows; but, judging by the pay roll, quite as many as in either Belgium or France.

I have spoken of the "unconscious use" of women. I mean unknown to the actors themselves. Perhaps the most tragic example of this in the present war is the Russian Empress. The Empress was German by birth and naturally in her sym-

Illustration by C. H. Taffs

pathies. Her sister's husband had been assassinated in Moscow; and it was not surprising her feelings ran against the radicals. Then in the midst of the great affliction of her son's deformity came the monk, Rasputin, who seemed to heal the boy. A lady in waiting had brought Rasputin to the court. How could the Empress know that both the lady in waiting and the monk were paid agents of a foreign power doing all that money and intrigue could do to trade the poor Russian peasant soldiers into certain slaughter before the German hosts?

How was this done? Supplies were delayed or diverted going to the front. Rifles were sent without shells. Shells were sent without rifles; and, when England rushed shiploads of supplies in by Archangel, orders from the Russian Government held the British ships so long they were frozen in the water and sent back in spring without so much as ballast—this at a time when the whole world was threatened with starvation for lack of ships.

Do you wonder the Russian soldiers threw down their arms and wept with rage? Whole trainloads of guns came to them which would not fire a shot. Do you wonder that, for the first time in history, the Russian soldiers refused to support the government? Was not all this the result of incompetent bureaucracy rather than spies?

Naturally if anyone had caught the *grande dame* in the act she would have been strangled or murdered. Five hundred thousand shells of large caliber went from America to the Russian front which would not fire a shot. They were examined. They were all filled defectively. They had been inspected and passed. When the inspection had been traced it led up to a man acting quite independently of the Embassy. He was very intimate with and seemed to take orders from a *grande dame* who represented herself as close to Russian officialdom.

She was the invisible link between Berlin and a Russian shell order in America. Who was the invisible link between an inspector appointed by the Imperial Government of Russia and the Russian *dame* who was from Berlin?

That the Empress was utterly unconscious of the machinations going on under her native-born sympathies did not minimize the tragedy. Plots of this kind cost her the crown and the loyalty of the army. Rasputin was assassinated, and the woman who had stood sponsor for him in the court was either assassinated or committed suicide; and with her died secrets which Berlin will never tell. In this case there was no money motive. Nor could the powers of darkness themselves offer any social ascendancy or power to a monk and a woman who were already the power behind the throne.

One wonders what strange perversity of judgment or heart leads any woman into this underworld of intrigue and crime. But in the criminal type of spy you always find this motiveless intrigue a ruling, consuming passion. It is not the upstart's liking to dabble his fingers in the pie of the big world's affairs. It is the evil passion for intrigue for its own sake; and it is not confined to court circles or to Russia.

We may thank our stars "we are not as other men are" and that petticoat intrigue and backstairs diplomacy can never dangle the fate of our nation in a light woman's lap; but when the lid is pried off all the devious secrecy with which the whole world is being gagged in the war, we shall be rudely shocked out of some of our smug complacency. There have been times in the last three years when action vital to the victory of freedom has been clouded, or diverted and confused, because a light fool, out for what she called "a good time," passed the word to an adventuress, out for profits in Wall Street from ambassadorial secrets; and the adventuress in turn passed the word through a renegade spy down to the drab underworld, who take toll of lust and crime; and the ships sailing out were bombed; or the harbors were set on fire; or the factories were blown up. And the Master Hand manipulating the puppets on the wire was back in Berlin.

But just now, for some inscrutable reason, these things must not be told, and our old-fashioned open diplomacy is gradually giving place to star-chamber secrecy.

I do not know whether it is an extenuation or not that most of the women soiling their hands with such work have not realized to what ends they were working, but when the page of history comes to be turned it will not make any fairer reading than the worst records of Napoleon's sleuth Schulmeister, or of Frederick the Great's uncanny hyena Stieber. Only in our time the dirty work seems to have enlisted the services of higher-class men and women.

BREAKFAST   *From a painting by William M. Paxton.*

The day has come when America is privileged
to spend her blood and her might for the principles that gave her birth and happiness and the peace
that she has treasured. God helping her, she can
do no other.

Woodrow Wilson

Painting by Gayle Porter

THE DOG THAT SAVED
A REGIMENT

It happened in the Argonne. A regiment was cut off from its support. The telephone was knocked to pieces. To get aid it was needful to send word to the supporting column, three miles away and out of sight over a low ridge. The cut-off regiment was surrounded by its foes. It could hold out but a few minutes longer. No human courier could hope to traverse one-tenth of that three thousand yards of open ground without being blown to atoms or riddled with bullets.

A dispatch, telling of the regiment's plight, was tied to the neck of a young collie. The colonel lifted the dog over the top of the trench. Every eye in the regiment watched him sweep away toward the distant ridge. It was three miles to the supporting column—three thousand yards of it raked with the German fire. The collie set off like a streak of golden light. He ran as gayly as if his master and his home waited for him, instead of death.

The enemy sharpshooters blazed into action at the first glimpse of him, all along the line, taking pot shots at that collie. For over two thousand yards he sped along, close to earth, his gold-and-white body whizzing through the shell-shaken air like a catapult. He cleared craters in his stride, he hurdled groups of dead. He ran as unerringly straight, toward that ridge, as a crow could have flown. And all the time the bullets were *spatting* in to the rocky earth in front of him and behind him and over his back. It was a glorious race with death!

When he was within five hundred yards of the ridge a groan went up from the whole fascinated regiment. The collie had leaped high in air and had come crashing to the ground a squirming, huddled heap.

But, on the instant, the groan changed to a hysterical cheer. For the dog was up again!

Reeling, staggering, lurching, bleeding—stumbling along as no animal does unless he is mortally wounded—the collie continued his journey. And the sharpshooters redoubled their efforts to get him. On he lurched, still in a straight line, and with such speed as his mighty will power could inject into his stricken body.

As he neared the summit of the ridge, and was outlined against the skyline, another bullet—or more than one—found him. He collapsed, helpless; and lay still.

But presently he was not lying still any longer. He was moving. He could not stand.

The last shot had hit him somewhere in the spine. But he could still crawl along, by means of his forelegs and his splendid will. And over the ridge he wriggled his way.

He crawled up to the general to whom he had been sent; and died as his nose touched the general's outstretched hand.

He had saved a whole regiment. And he had lost nothing but his own life.

Painting by Frank E. Schoonover

HOW TWENTY MARINES
TOOK BOURESCHES

June 6, 1918, saw one of the most spectacular bits of fighting that occurred during the Bellau offensive. Two hundred and fifty Marines, facing a terrific machine-gun fire, charged across this wheat field. The wheat, nearly waist high and still very green and dotted with poppies, was their only protection. Of this number only 20 were left to take Bouresches, held by 300 Germans.

79

THEIRS IS THE JOB TO KEEP
BOTH "OVER THERE" AND "OVER HERE"
JUST NOW THEY ARE HEROICALLY IMPERSONATING

You Remember it, the Dear Old Singing Team of "Variety," as it Was Called Before They Brought it Into the Parlor as "Vaudeville." The Song Began: "While Strolling Through the Park One Day"

If We Were to Do This in Front of a Real Audience Instead of Just the Camera Man, it Would be Pathetic, So Many of the Folks Would be in Tears Over Memory of Their Lost Youth

But Even for the Camera We Had to Rehearse the Stunt. Our Evenings Were Spent in This Way. We Began Our Rehearsals in a House, but Later Moved Into a Remote Tent at the Request of Neighbors Without Sentiment

My Little Friend on My Left Could Not Convey Such an Impression of Pleased Dignity Coupled With Complete Self-Confidence if He Tried a Week, or Even Longer

Honesty Compels Me to Confess That in This Part of Our Imitation I Resorted to Camouflage. Still Mine Was a Real Hat; My Little Friend's Was Not. More Honesty Compels the Disclosure That His Was Painted on the Negative After the Picture Was Taken. Thus are We Often Deceived Even by Those We Love

I Have Always Believed That I Could Sing Tenor, and Still Believe it in Spite of the Arguments the Little Person at the Piano Has Put Forth to Upset My Faith. You Yourself Shall Judge Just as Soon as the Talking-Machine Attachment to Moving Pictures is Perfected. At That Time, However, I Shall, in Person, be Far Away

THE WORLD SAFE FOR SMILES

THEY ARE SOLDIERS OF HAPPINESS

AN OLD-FASHIONED VAUDEVILLE SINGING TEAM

And This Dear Old Interpolation When One of the Artists Asks the Other a Question Fraught With Humor, and When the Other Replies the First Smites Him in the Countenance With a Folded Newspaper

Now We're Off Again. The End of the Chorus of "While Strolling Through the Park One Day" Always Concluded With This Posture. A Very High Order of Talent is Required to Do This and Still Live

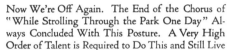

And Then the Partners in Those Dear Old Teams, After Singing "While Strolling Through the Park One Day" Across the Country and Back, Would Return to This, the Art of Their Youth, Wherein They Excelled All Others

This is My Page and I Insist Upon Giving My Well-Known Impersonation of Napoleon Before We Proceed With Our Performance as Planned

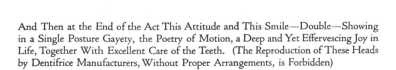

And Then at the End of the Act This Attitude and This Smile—Double—Showing in a Single Posture Gayety, the Poetry of Motion, a Deep and Yet Effervescing Joy in Life, Together With Excellent Care of the Teeth. (The Reproduction of These Heads by Dentifrice Manufacturers, Without Proper Arrangements, is Forbidden)

And Even We, in All Probability, Should Have Had to Revert to the Shining Profession Illustrated Above, Had Not a Humanitarian Inventor Perfected the Moving-Picture Machine, Rendering Possible Our Embalmment, So to Speak, in Celluloid, for Generations Yet Unborn. On Behalf of My Imitative Associate and Myself, I Thank You

(Signed) *Charlie Chaplin*
(Approved) *Douglas Fairbanks*

Jane Cowl in "Smilin' Through."

HOW I KEPT MYSELF

FROM BEING A FAILURE

Jane Cowl

My formula for progress is one word: "dissatisfaction." I mean dissatisfaction with myself. This dissatisfaction with myself began early in life with my first theatrical engagement when I was given a start with but a single line to speak. Mr. David Belasco evidently agreed with me, for when rehearsals began he came to me and said:

"Jane Cowl, you can't be heard in the first row. If you can't do better than that we'll have to take the part away from you."

I felt as though my career had stopped before it had begun. There was only one thing to do. That was to make them hear me in the last row of the gallery even if I had to shriek. They could hear me all over the theater after that. Then three lines were put into my part to encourage me.

This was my first lesson. The following season, however, there was nothing in the way of a part in the plays about to be produced.

This led to the second important decision of my life: whether I was to remain with Mr. Belasco or take a part offered me by another manager; whether I was to look to the future instead of the present.

I made up my mind that to stay around and watch how other actresses were trained would be an education for me. And stay I did.

My next experience was one with David Warfield, in "The Grand Army Man." The only part that was open to me was that of an old woman of sixty-five with less than half a dozen lines to speak. My friends advised me against taking it, but I took it.

Many an actor has sacrificed the big chance of the future for the needs of the present. And vanity, the desire to keep up appearances, has a great deal to do with the decision to take a better job now, get more money now, and lose the chance that looms in the future.

After several seasons I came to the conclusion that something was wrong with me. I had never lost my fears. I had learned a great deal in the theatrical world, but I needed mental training. I realized that if men and women fail to study outside of their particular profession or trade, their minds are naturally bound to be lopsided. So I set aside a definite amount for education and took up courses at Columbia University.

For two years I continued on the stage and went to Columbia at the same time. At the end of that time I felt that I had at least a more or less good groundwork of philosophy, economics and advanced history. To aid in my professional work I also studied the drama and literature.

Then I realized that what I needed was variety of experience, so as soon as my season closed I accepted an engagement as leading woman of a stock company in New Jersey. Thirteen performances a week!

When the curtain went down on the evening play it did not mean an end to the day's work, for there were lines to learn, and I usually studied until I fell asleep from sheer exhaustion. Finally my doctor predicted a breakdown if I persisted in going on. It was a question of sticking or of quitting. I determined that, as we usually live through almost everything, I would stick.

I now began to realize that the first importance to an actress is to be healthy in order to stand the strain of important rôles. I took up gymnasium work in winter and horseback riding and cycling in summer, and these have been of immense value to me.

Then came the desire to write a play.

"Daybreak" was the first of my plays written with Jane Murfin. The idea of doing something different so as not to be a "one-part" actress inspired the writing of "Lilac Time," the most successful of the plays we have written.

It seemed as though the only opportunities I had to get away from a single type of stage figure had to be created by myself. And these opportunities came about simply because of my old trouble: dissatisfaction with myself.

Whoever it was who said "Don't wait for opportunities—create them" put a great deal of philosophy into a small space. And it seems to me, from my experience thus far, that dissatisfaction of the individual with himself is the best possible lever for one who wants to rise.

VERNON AND IRENE CASTLE

All the rage in ballrooms these days is "The Castle Fox Trot." Everyone is doing it. Here the popular couple demonstrate Step Number One of their creation. "Most important," says Mr. Castle, "in taking the slow steps is to remember that the stride should be as long as possible."

When transatlantic flying becomes the vogue this is how you will travel to London.

GOING TO EUROPE IN 1925

Waldemar Kaempffert

You walk into the offices of the Transatlantic Airplane Company one day in 1925. "One ticket for next Saturday's flying boat to Plymouth," you say.

The clerk at the counter looks you over with an appraising eye. "Please step this way."

You follow him.

"Step on the scales, please. One hundred and sixty-five pounds," he reads off.

"At this season of the year the rate is five dollars a pound," he tells you. "Your fare will be eight hundred and twenty-five dollars. Luggage, two dollars a pound extra. Each passenger may take not more than twenty pounds."

It was driven home in 1919 that fuel-carrying capacity is all-important when the Atlantic is crossed on the wing. Only so many pounds of fuel and so many pounds of letters, baggage, food and humanity can be taken on board the transatlantic flyer. There is always "room for one more" even on the smallest steamship. Not on a flying machine. The pilot must reckon not in terms of passengers but in terms of weight.

The fare charged will be based on the initial cost of the machine, depreciation, repairs and the thousand-and-one items that business men consider. Airplanes are notoriously short-lived. A transatlantic flyer is good for not more than two years at the most of strenuous Atlantic service. Those purring engines of hers, thoroughly overhauled at the end of every voyage, are taken out at the end of three hundred hours to

be supplanted by others. It costs fully thirty-five thousand dollars a year to keep a huge oceanic airplane in condition, even though her original cost is under one hundred thousand dollars.

The ticket that you buy entitles you to seat No. 5 in the flying boat Seagull. True, the Atlantic Ocean was first crossed in a single flight by Alcock in a machine that started from the ground and landed on the ground. But after Hawker dropped into the sea, aëronautical engineers decided that it would be criminal to fly across the ocean with ten or fifteen precious lives in a craft that would sink if it ever had to descend midway between America and Europe.

So free is the Seagull from retarding obstructions that she seems curiously naked in comparison with the lumbering machines of 1919. Everything is inclosed in a beautiful, clean hull. You step aboard. Here in the bow is the compartment for the navigators, who are as completely inclosed as if they were seated in a limousine.

Behind the navigators' compartment are the passenger accommodations. What a contrast with the cold, cramped quarters of the first transatlantic flyers! This is as luxurious as a little drawing-room. The foremost interior decorator of America designed the color scheme. He overlooked nothing—not even electric sidelights and an oval Colonial mirror.

A Japanese shows you to your seat. The company engaged him as steward and cook

because he is small—ounces must be reckoned with on a flying machine.

You miss the spaciousness of the fast, luxurious transatlantic steamship. There is just this one cabin, perhaps twenty-five feet long and seven feet wide. There are no staterooms. But what about sleeping? You don't sleep in a parlor car when you journey by rail in the daytime. Why should you sleep in the air while the sun is shining?

The Seagull could cross the Atlantic in ten hours. But her owners are hard-headed business men. They are not trying to realize age-old poetic dreams—they are bent on making each voyage pay.

How can the Transatlantic Airplane Company make money if the Seagull is to fill her tanks with thousands of pounds of fuel in order to carry only one or two passengers? She must carry as little fuel and as many passengers as possible if the Transatlantic Airplane Company is to declare any dividends. And what if she does fly by way of the Azores? What if you do spend the night on Flores or in Lisbon? You will reach England in less than thirty-six hours.

The passenger cabin is not nearly so noisy as a railway parlor car. You sit in a cabin luxuriously padded to deaden the thunder of the engines; your nerves are not racked by one-tenth of the noise and vibration that the pioneer Atlantic voyagers had to endure. The Seagull is flying at top speed now, imagine it, two hundred miles an hour.

ANNABEL LEE.

W. L. Taylor's illustration for the poem by Edgar Allan Poe.

A FLORENTINE FETE.
By
Maxfield Parrish.

One of the seventeen murals of youths and maidens in gala dress especially designed by Maxfield Parrish for the new girls' dining-room of The Ladies' Home Journal in Philadelphia. All is happiness and beauty, everybody young.

THE GREEN DOOR
*Illustration by
Arthur Rackham
for the new story by
A. A. Milne.*

THE BATTLE HYMN OF THE REPUBLIC

Julia Ward Howe

In the late autumn of the year 1861 I visited Washington in company with my husband, Doctor Howe, and a party of friends, among whom were Governor and Mrs. Andrew, Mr. and Mrs. E. P. Whipple, and my dear pastor, Rev. James Freeman Clarke. The journey was one of vivid, even romantic interest. We were about to see the grim Demon of War, face to face, and long before we reached the city his presence made itself felt in the blaze of fires along the road, where sat or stood our pickets, guarding the road on which we traveled.

One day we drove out to attend a review of troops, appointed to take place at some distance from the city. In the carriage with me were James Freeman Clarke and Mr. and Mrs. Whipple. The day was fine, and everything promised well, but a sudden surprise on the part of the enemy interrupted the proceedings before they were well begun. A small body of our men had been surrounded and cut off from their companions, reënforcements were sent to their assistance, and the expected pageant was necessarily given up. The troops who were to have taken part in it were ordered back to their quarters, and we also turned our horses' heads homeward. For a long distance the foot soldiers nearly filled the road. They were before and behind, and we were obliged to drive very slowly. We presently began to sing some of the well-known songs of the war, and among them,

John Brown's body lies a-moldering in the
    grave.

This seemed to please the soldiers, who cried, "Good for you," and themselves took up the strain. Mr. Clarke said to me: "You ought to write some new words to that tune." I replied that I had often wished to do so.

In spite of the excitement of the day, I went to bed and slept as usual, but awoke next morning in the gray of the early dawn, and to my astonishment found that the wished-for lines were arranging themselves in my brain. I lay quite still until the last verse had completed itself in my thoughts, then hastily arose, saying to myself: "I shall lose this if I don't write it down immediately." I searched for a sheet of paper and an old stump of a pen which I had had the night before, and began to scrawl the lines almost without looking, as I had learned to do by often scratching down verses in the darkened room where my little children were sleeping. Having completed this, I lay down again and fell asleep.

The poem was published soon after this time in the Atlantic Monthly. It first came prominently into notice when Chaplain McCabe, newly released from Libby Prison, gave a lecture in Washington, and in the course of it told how he and his fellow prisoners, having somehow become possessed of a copy of the "Battle Hymn," sang it with a will in their prison, on receiving surreptitious tidings of a Union victory.

A Facsimile of Two Verses From the First Draft of Mrs. Julia Ward Howe's Famous Hymn

"I Searched for a Sheet of Paper and an Old Stump of a Pen, and Began to Scrawl the Lines Almost Without Looking"

MAKING A HOME ON A FARM

A Farmer's Wife

What does making a home on a farm mean? What do you, the farmer's wife, get out of it as wife, mother, home maker, that would cause you to prefer it to any other life that might have been open to you?

I have been asked to answer these questions, and I may as well start out by saying I get so much that, if I had my life to live over again, this is what I should choose, because life for the farmer's wife can be as happy and successful as any other life open to the ordinary woman who must work for what she has, and with certain pleasures and satisfactions thrown in that the city woman never has.

The farmer's wife is no exception to the rule that you get out of life what you put in, you get what you give.

Farmer and wife are partners literally from the ground up, intimately associated in all their work both inside and outside the house in a way that few other husbands and wives have to be. Some women say they don't care to know anything about their husbands' business so long as the money comes in. That attitude in a farmer's wife would be ruinous. To be a success, their work must go hand in hand. There can be no operations, business secrets or dealings that one of the partners does not understand and knows nothing about. Everything in their daily lives is an open book between them.

On a dairy-and-trucking farm, such as ours, much of what one begins the other finishes, as for instance the rhubarb and asparagus which the man cuts and the wife bunches for market; and even the work she does not do herself, such as the plowing and mowing, she must know about, when it comes and how long it will take, if extra help is to be hired for it and fed in the house, and all the rest.

Partnership from the ground up also means the farm is *ours*. Our land is ours, the home is ours, and all the work we put into improvements is ours. When you step outside your door, you have your own good brown earth and green grass under your feet. Nothing can take it away from us as long as we pay the taxes.

It gave me such a feeling of security, besides pride and ambition to do my best in helping to push ahead and build up the farm until we were financially independent. For that reason it seems to me that the word "ours" is the foundation stone of any real success in farming, the word that bridges you over discouragements, the word that keeps you working for the future.

When I married, my husband took over

his father's farm and I had to go to live with his parents. It was that, or not marry him. I rebelled against it some at first, but as it turned out, that was the only way we could have built up the farm and made it pay. If you have a dairy-and-trucking farm and a family of children, it takes two women in the house to keep things going, and unless you have one of the older generation or a sister living with you and looking after one or two branches of the work, you have to hire outside help—or kill yourself. That's all there is to it.

Of course, I don't know how it is on some of the big Western farms. I am speaking of an Eastern Pennsylvania farm running fifteen or twenty cows, a hundred or more chickens, fruits and vegetables, with stuff going to market all the time, milk, butter, eggs, every day, and the fruits and vegetables in their season—what you might call the average farm on which you expect

to raise almost everything you eat, and to make enough profit to pay for the other things and the clothes, and lay by something every year for your old age.

And remember, the farmer intends to have plenty of everything. He wants plenty of feed for the stock he keeps, and he wants plenty of food on his own table. Nothing makes a hearty, hungry man so mad as to sit down to a meal of little fancy dabs of this and that, with the butter rolled up in little marbles the size of a robin's egg. He wants to see a pound of butter on at once, a quart pitcher of cream, fried eggs by the platterful, bread by the loaf, and everything else to match. If he doesn't, it means that things aren't going right with the business of the farm.

Perhaps if he had to lay his money on the counter for every mouthful he ate he would go slower. But coming right off his own ground the way it does, the food seems more as if he got it for nothing, so he says, "Give me plenty." This means plenty of work to keep two women busy all the time, one indoors, the other in and out, helping with everything.

Take the milking as one of the chores that pretty generally falls to the woman on the farm—there's not much poetry to it when you have to do it twice a day, every day of the week, at a certain time, rain or shine, winter and summer, year in, year out! The milking is one of the big questions to the women on the farm that you'll always find them discussing whenever two or three are gathered together. Should you or shouldn't you, ought you or oughtn't you, will you or won't you do the milking? Some women hate it so much they positively won't, no matter what happens; but I have known a few that like it better than almost any other work on the farm.

When we say milking, we don't mean one or two cows kept for your own use— that's nothing anybody could object to— we mean fifteen, eighteen, twenty or even thirty cows, night and morning, and all to be done by hand, and the milk served on a route. For more than twenty years, excepting six weeks before and after the babies came, I was up every morning at half past two on week days, three on Sundays, and milking fifteen, eighteen—sometimes as many as twenty-two cows before breakfast and again before supper.

As fast as I milked, my husband carried the pails down to the springhouse and cooled the milk, put it into the cans, skimmed last night's milk for the cream we sold, brought up the skimmed milk for the pigs and cottage cheese, fed and watered the stock while I was in the house cooking his breakfast, and was away by six o'clock every day of the week, and half past on Sundays.

That springhouse was our pride, and I kept it looking like a lily, inside and out. Oh, yes, of course I did the whitewashing! But then, it doesn't have to be done very often, and it's one of the pleasures you get on the farm, seeing something like that coming out so fresh and sweet-smelling after its bath, the water sparkling in the cooling troughs, and bright pans filled with milk and rich yellow cream. It encourages you to keep the rest of the place looking just as nice to go with it.

Clean milk pays, too, but it means work for the farmer's wife. My husband was serving about 400 quarts of milk and ten of cream on the daily average, and all of it had to go into pans and cans which I had to wash with my own hands. I wouldn't have been ashamed to have the Queen of England walk into my springhouse any day of the week and see it just as it was.

You don't think of your home on a farm as just the space inside four walls—the feeling of home spreads out all round, into the garden, the orchards, the henhouses, the barn, the springhouse, because you are all the time helping to produce live things in those places and make them grow, and they or their products are all the time coming back into your kitchen from orchard, garden, barn or henhouse as part of the things you handle and prepare for meals or market every day.

Little chores like tying up 1000 bunches of rhubarb and 150 bunches of asparagus a week always fell to my share. The men don't like bothering with such small things; it means so much sorting to get the bunches all the same size, as they must be if you want to keep up your trade. Rhubarb and asparagus came along in April—150 bunches of rhubarb and twenty-five to thirty-five of asparagus a day. Rhubarb isn't much trouble, but asparagus is, because the tips are so apt to break off if you handle it carelessly; besides, you have to watch it all the time in the bed and cut it almost on the minute, it grows up so fast. Leave it out a few hours on a hot day, and it has grown too tall and leafy to sell.

Both crops ran about six weeks, and then came the beets—at least a thousand bunches a week right along for a month—with carrots, radishes and young onions whenever we raised enough to sell. So taking them all together, the bunches I tied and got ready footed up to about 15,000 every year.

All this work kept right on every day of the week, for growing things don't rest on Sundays, and must be picked and prepared for Monday's market, the cows milked, the stock and chickens fed, eggs gathered and sorted and boxed, dinner cooked and cleared away—the biggest dinner of the week, too, with company always to be expected in the summer if you have any friends living in the city. Only the heavy work, such as plowing and harrowing, stops for the day's rest; the chores never do.

Once in a while we had a chance to go to church, generally in the winter, and we always took one day off in the summer to go somewhere on a sort of a picnic, the whole family together.

Perhaps you are asking how I ever got time to sleep. I didn't! Nine o'clock was as early as I ever got to bed—which wasn't often except in winter—but ten o'clock more nearly hit it for early. Eleven, twelve, half past, and even one in summer, to be up again at half past two, was what I counted on.

If you find a farm prospering, the buildings in repair, everything kept up and increasing from year to year, you will find in the house a woman who loves the farm animals. They are all her pets. She has names for every one down to the last little pig in the litter; the colts follow her about in the fields; the cows come running when she calls them; the hens want to roost on her shoulders.

But if you see a farm where everything is running behind and going downhill, you'll be sure to find in the house a woman who takes no interest in the stock and probably dislikes animals—or no woman at all. When a woman feels that way she might as well quit trying to be a farmer's wife.

A farmer needs encouragement sometimes more than he needs a good loaf of bread, and if the wife can't give it to him, I don't know where else he could go for it. He may see a whole crop he has been counting on destroyed in a few hours by an insect pest, or rabbits, or beaten to the ground by hail storm; or the season may be so backward that he cannot get his land plowed and planted in time to raise the earliest vegetables that would sell the best; or the frost takes his late ones before he can realize a cent on them; or there comes a big drought and he loses half his hay or corn, and all he made on his vegetables goes to buying enough feed to winter his stock. Weather is the one thing you can never get away from on the farm.

The kind of encouragement that keeps a man pushing ahead every day in spite of the weather comes mainly from his wife's interest in everything about the place, and the feeling that she is with him in everything and appreciates his difficulties, his efforts and his successes.

I suppose it is partly the feeling of having so much depending on you to make the home, and partly the feeling of having all outdoors for your home, that makes you care so much less about furnishings, fixings and ornaments.

After you have milked eighteen cows, cooked and cleared away the breakfast for ten people, made the beds, seen to getting the children clean and ready for school, tended to the baby, made up and baked the batch of bread you set to rise last night, besides a dozen pies, a couple of loaves of cake and a pudding, prepared the meat and vegetables for dinner, churned and worked up ten to fifteen pounds of butter, made up the sour milk into cottage cheese, scalded the churn and twenty-five to thirty-five milk tins and sundries, fed the hens and the pigs, finished getting dinner, eating it and washing up after it, and stood up to your pile of four hundred to five hundred

We built a fine house and retired with enough saved up for comfort for the rest of our lives.

asparagus and seven hundred to eight hundred rhubarb stalks to be sorted and tied up, and finally got that all done about three o'clock without a single minute's rest since half past two except the half hour while you were eating your dinner—well, take my word for it, you aren't hankering for the pleasure of roaming the house with a broom and dust cloth taking care of furniture and ornaments!

Making a home on a farm means that your hands are never empty, but your life is full of interest because there is always something new on the farm, every day, every season; something growing or blooming, or being born or hatched. There is something always coming to you, and you enjoy a thousand little pleasures from these new things and the quiet happiness and satisfaction of accomplishing what you undertake and being free and beholden to nobody for the bread you eat.

WE HAVE COME TO STAY

Charles Chaplin

The motion picture has come to stay. It is a recognized medium of art, though it has seldom been exploited in that way. It has shown great possibilities of providing a cheap and almost universal amusement, and it has demonstrated that it can do certain things better than the stage.

But the motion-picture producers must turn to more serious work. The picture drama that we have had so plentifully provided for us in the past must be altered. That little sweetie of a heroine must go. So, too, must the eternal triangle of husband, wife and lover. There have been too many commonplace happy endings arrived at, not by any process of clear or logical thinking but simply because it has been thought that virtue must triumph if the box office is to do a big business. I do not deliberately want tragedy, nor do I disparage the story that turns out prettily, but the motion-picture drama of today has no other problem, once we are introduced to the heroine, than that this same young thing shall receive the just reward of her goodness four or five reels later.

All this has ceased to be entertaining. It seems to me that the successful picture will henceforth depend upon more actual action, construction and "business." Now "business," to those of us who work in the theater or the studios, means that certain something that the performer does in a scene that is entertaining apart from its connection in the building up of the story. If the script or story calls for a character lighting his pipe, so that later the house may be set on fire, some directors will merely call upon the actor at the right time to light that pipe. A more inspired director will make the lighting of the pipe interesting or individual in itself so that it seems natural and characteristic, and so that it will not appear to have been done merely because of possible importance later. All greatly successful motion pictures and most successful plays are full of these little incidents which make for the naturalness and the humor of the entertainment.

No public is more loyal than the motion-picture public, except the regular clientele of the English music halls. There the tried performers, so long as they keep up their acts, always make the biggest hits, and the newcomers are compelled to struggle and to be very good indeed in order to command any attention.

In the pictures the newcomer has much to defeat. I remember my own beginning in those early days of the movies. About nine years ago I appeared for the first time in what was thought to be a very funny comedy. I had seen the picture a number of times, but I was anxious to know how it would go before an audience, so I went into a picture theater.

All around me I heard my work being compared with that of another comedian. "Who's that gink?" "Aw, he's no good." "He thinks he's funny."

It is not wholly a question of loyalty to the known performer. The person who is familiar to the audience has an advantage from the start. The public is not tired of old faces. It is tired of the old faces in the old material. It would have even greater apathy for new faces in the old material.

A great many actors and critics have insisted that there never can be good acting on the screen because that certain coöperation, that electrical something or vibration or understanding that exists between the audience and the performer is missing.

The mere fact that a man is an actor presupposes that he has some imagination and the sense of how a thing should be played. When a thing is perfectly played, regardless of whether the audience is a small one or the whole world, the creative artist must know that he is acting the scene correctly.

In acting before the camera there is more than an audience. The actor has a sense of importance of the thing that is grinding away, recording, perhaps immortalizing, his gesture at the very moment of inspiration. There are many actors who rehearse extraordinarily well when they go over scenes before the actual photographing, but when the command "Camera!" is given, their acting is much less good. This unquestionably is due to a subconscious knowledge or fear or sense of the importance of the thing. What is to be done cannot be undone easily. Things often seem funny or good in the rehearsal, and when later seen in the projection room I often wonder why anyone allowed them to be photographed. I have never, for my own part, been so nervous before an audience as I have been before the cameras.

Conveying thought on the stage is simpler than on the screen. This is due to the natural pauses or spaces that come between speeches. On the stage, when a character speaks a line such as "I want that," and another replies "You can't have it," the meaning is not only clear but the attention is readily focused on the characters speaking in turn.

As the movies developed there came into being what are called spoken titles. These are merely printed words of dialogue. The expression on the actor's face is supposed to indicate the speaker and his thought. The problem is to attract attention to him, and then after an interval to the character who has the answering line, such as "You can't have it."

On the screen this cannot be accomplished by doing what the newspaper cartoons and comics do, that is to print a balloon of words floating out of the mouth of the comic figures.

The spoken titles besides being most difficult to act correctly will always be inferior to the voice, but in spite of the difficulties I see nothing wrong with the film as a medium of artistic expression.

It is not easy to sustain character on the screen. Here and there you will discover a good bit, but all too seldom. I do not know whether the difficulty in acting for the screen is due to the fact that there are too many scenes or because the inspiration is lost in the delays that come up in the photographing of the story. For my own part, I do not believe that I have ever sustained a character through an entire picture, and the one that I am working on now is my ninety-eighth.

What too often passes for acting on the screen is a matter of make-up. We have too many make-up or what I call crêpe-hair artists. They can put on a beard and wear a wig, but that is as far as they go in the assumption of a character. Sometimes a muscle working in the face is recorded by the camera, and this is acclaimed as acting.

The hastily assumed externals, which mean so much to the impersonation of

A new portrait of Mr. Chaplin by James Abbe.

character in the theater, are useless on the screen. As a boy of seventeen I played old men in touring companies in the English provinces—old colonels and such. This was done chiefly by throaty voice and labored walk—and a great deal of make-up. On the screen obviously there is no voice, and the labored walk would merely burn up footage.

The crêpe-hair bad actor has an emotional sister who is very tiresome and always commonplace. Her assets are quivering eyelids, glycerine tears and a chest which heaves up and down. She faces the camera for a long scene and fights with her back against the wall, as her sister in the theater used to do.

Emotion in the pictures does not come from the close-up of a face in action. It is a matter of construction. When the crippled boy drops his crutches in The Miracle Man and runs up the path, the audience felt a certain emotional tenseness. No tears were on the screen.

Jackie Coogan in "Circus Days."

Before I had anything to do with the pictures I was just as ignorant as the ordinary person about procedure and construction in the making of the film. I believed that it was the usual thing to have a sequence of scenes, and that these were taken in order and developed and then projected. I did not know that a reel of about a thousand feet was made up of a hundred scenes averaging ten feet each and that these were put together and rearranged and edited and cut until the finished product is thought ready for the theater.

Nor did I know that for a finished reel of a thousand feet, ten thousand feet of film might have been taken and the best bits of this put together.

Most of the people who make pictures, it seems to me, make the mistake of wanting too much plot. The scenario writer and the director build and rebuild, criss-cross and dove-tail and lay so many pipes in preparation for the plot or a situation that when the time for it arrives there is an anti-climax.

I feel certain that it is better to begin with a casual or a general idea. In my own work I have found that an elaborate plot is not necessary—just a slim structure or a sequence of scenes which will enable me to create a great deal of action and business which will entertain the audience apart from the story that is to be developed. A plot is of no importance to me unless it does suggest these opportunities.

I was looking over some old notes the other day, the notes from which The Kid, my most successful picture, was made. There was only one idea, and that was that the character I play in all my pictures was somehow to be made responsible for a child who is to get into all sorts of mischief and especially into a fight with a larger boy whose father is to be a great bruiser. This father was to demand that, if his boy is licked, I fight him. In my original plan for the story I had some indication of the nice feeling of comradeship which resulted in the picture, but there was originally no idea of parenthood or of any of the things which made the appeal when the picture was finished. These things developed as we began to work and naturally grew out of what we were doing.

One of the important things in the construction of a play is providing effective entrances for the leading characters. In a revival of Sherlock Holmes, in London, I played Billy the page in Holmes' Baker Street apartment. All the characters in the first act did nothing except talk about the great detective and his marvelous powers. William Gillette, who wrote the play and was the star, knew that it was far more effective to come on toward the end of the act after there had been a good deal of preparation, and that any audience would be more ready to accept Holmes' greatness after they had heard the other characters talk about him.

It is much easier for a comedian to get an effective entrance than it is for the leading character in a drama. It seems to me that the entrance in The Kid was very effective. First came a succession of melodramatic scenes, and since the spectator knew from my association with the picture that it was a comedy, he was naturally led to wonder all during this melodrama what the possible connection could be and just how the child that I adopt from the ash can could possibly get to the back alley where I am discovered.

In The Mark of Zorro, Zorro, the part played by Douglas Fairbanks, comes into the story effectively and legitimately. In a tavern a number of soldiers are talking about this good-bad man who commits crimes to relieve the oppressed. A boasting sergeant tells the others just what he will do when he comes face to face with this Zorro. The door is thrown open and a

masked figure enters. It is Zorro, and he soon proves that everything that has been said of him is true.

But these considerations are really not my worries, for the making of comedy does not entail quite the same search for material. Ideas of comedy are pretty much the same and have been for centuries.

The comedy that lives is the robust comedy that keeps its feet on the ground. The too sweet and too vague comedy loses its point too often and is not long popular. Buffoonery does not die. It has come to us from the classics. There is slapstick in the comedy of Shakespeare and Molière.

Screen comedy used to put a great deal of reliance upon the chase, the throwing of food and the tragedy of the banana skin. Because of the presence of these things, many theater-goers felt somewhat superior to the robustness of our humor.

When I wanted to get more repression into my work I found there was little enthusiasm.

In a comedy called Making a Living, I stood on a street corner and borrowed some money from another character. When this was projected the scene got a laugh, but no one connected with the making of it thought the material of any use whatever. It was much more comic to knock over an apple cart or to fall into some mortar or to knock a man off a ladder.

One of my earliest sure-fire methods of obtaining a comic situation was to let dignity collapse. This of course is much the same as throwing food or beating a man. I also found that to quarrel with a man bigger than myself, as in Easy Street, was certain to make for humor. The triumph of the mite over the mighty was sure to be sympathetic. It is the old idea of the under dog, or of David and Goliath.

In those days I was just as flippant about the films as the rest. We took a picture a week. We would start out with a company made up as a policeman, a sailor, a big man, a girl, a nursemaid or any other perfectly familiar or labeled characters. We had no particular idea of what we were going to do, and we would go to the park and just sort of let a picture happen.

Frequently visitors want to see the making of a comedy, because they think that the whole thing will be a great lark. I always feel self-conscious when visitors are present, because I know they are going to be disappointed. The taking of a comedy is such a laborious, tedious proceeding, far more so than the taking of an ordinary drama.

People often ask me, since my pictures are comedies, why I cannot tell a score of amusing things that happen during the taking of a comedy—of Shoulder Arms, of Easy Street—and I always refer these inquirers to members of my company or to my manager. It is not funny to me. During the taking of a picture I have no sense of humor.

1920. Mary Pickford and Douglas Fairbanks back in New York after a triumphant tour of Europe.

About one-third of our people are responsible for most of the extravagance and waste.

THRIFT AND AMERICAN WOMEN

Herbert Hoover

It is as imperative to-day as it was during the war, even more so, that we should practice thrift in all its forms—more so because, in fact, it seems that the world is yet farther on the economic down grade that began in 1914 and also because we do not have now the social control that prevailed during the war. When production was regulated to national advantage and when waste was checked both by law and by public sentiment, there was less danger than there is in the present conditions. A menacing factor to-day is the moral let-down. I speak of this not from a religious but from an engineering or scientific standpoint. Whatever the consequences of moral letdown may be in another or future world, their consequences here and now are sufficient to engage our attention.

Every one of us should cut our extravagance and waste. We should eliminate every unnecessary expense. We should save every possible five-cent piece, even though it is worth no more than a postage stamp. We should put our savings into savings banks or into government or other securities or into such strictly useful investments as homes and farms. Money that is wasted is destroyed as if cast into a fire, and the evil results are not confined to the individual waster and his or her family, but are, in fact, spread throughout society. This is the crime and damage done by waste.

Now of course it is difficult and sometimes almost impossible to define waste with exactitude and most of us take refuge in this fact and in the easy interpretation of a liberal conscience. We can see our neighbor's waste pretty clearly, but we cannot see our own. Still, though it is difficult to define specifically, we know there is a boundary somewhere between proper economy and waste, even as there is a boundary somewhere between the water of the Atlantic Ocean and the Gulf Stream.

It would be futile for me to attempt to specify in any detail what constitutes waste or extravagance, yet a few suggestions may tend to clarify ideas on the subject. Take the matter of clothing. What proportion of our expenditure in this direction is dictated by need of warmth and comfort and what proportion by the requirement of style? A minority, we know, are one hundred per cent influenced by style; it is the only consideration that governs.

Then there are those who are fifty per cent governed by style and the rest by utility, and so on down or up. Of course circumstances alter cases, and there is limited justification for the style factor, as in the case of men and women who travel or engage in business or public life and who

97

have not sufficient eminence or philosophy to disregard public canons or superstitions. It is also a tradition that people must "doll up" for holidays and social occasions. There is perhaps a certain justifiable latitude for young folks who are in the period of courtship and must decorate themselves to enhance their natural charms. It is quite possible to be economical in clothes and yet to be suitably appareled, for each person to have a Sunday or holiday outfit besides working or office costumes without crossing the border of extravagance or doing national harm.

Much has been said and written about silk shirts and silk stockings. I will not condemn the use of these articles, but if those who wear silk stockings could see the millions of people in Europe who have no stockings at all and indeed no shoes, they would take less satisfaction in the sheen and pattern of their costly hose. And if those who wear silk shirts could visualize the millions who lack shirts of the cheapest material, they too would feel differently. This is not a moral, religious or brotherly-love proposition—at least not from the standpoint of my argument—but an economic proposition of enlightened self-interest. If we spend our resources on silk and luxuries and thereby heighten the world shortage of necessities, we hasten the day of catastrophe for all mankind. One pair of silk stockings is a venial lapse and one superfluous hat is a trifle, but all these lapses and trifles added together may be enough to stagger the world.

About one-third of our people are responsible for most of the extravagance and waste in this country. It is a heavy responsibility that they bear, not only for direct economic damage to our common interest but for the creation and maintenance of class feeling because of their conduct. If we could convert this one-third to simple living, the problem would be solved.

It is the one-third who are guilty of extravagant eating and drinking in public places. They spend $200,000 every night in New York City alone on restaurant suppers, according to an estimate that seems reasonable. The whole nation spends at least a million dollars a day or three hundred and sixty-five million dollars a year in superfluous eating at hotels and restaurants. In fact, you could safely multiply this figure by five; and the annual total is more than the normal cost of running the entire Government of the United States. These are not meals required for nourishment, but absolutely useless and indeed physically harmful indulgence.

Again it is the one-third who are mostly responsible for the waste involved in the use of jewelry, on which so many millions of dollars are being spent. We are now obtaining a great many diamonds, other precious stones and articles of ornament from Europe. This brings me to an important point. America sends to Europe shiploads of useful commodities, such as foodstuffs and machinery and cotton. She gets back in return a wheelbarrow load of diamonds and jewelry!

Of course I do not mean to say that we should not do business with or help Europe; quite the contrary. Merely I wish to point out that this particular form of trade or barter is not wise.

Doubtless our craze for jewelry to-day has a shadow of justification, like that of the corresponding craze among Europeans. People think that diamonds are a good investment at a time when Liberty Bonds and practically all other securities and even money itself are depreciating in value. But this is a great and childish fallacy. If persisted in a lot of people will find themselves owning a handful of precious stones just as worthless as are the titles of many former monarchs of Europe.

In the same class with jewelry are perfumes, which are now so largely imported and used. There was recently advertised a bargain sale of perfume in which several bottles of choice quality were marked down from about $65 to only $54 apiece. No doubt there is somewhere in nature or art a legitimate place for perfume, but the thought occurs that hitherto the American people have managed to do very well with the minimum of perfumery. In fact, someone has remarked that the fundamental difference between Europe and America is that while they believe in perfume we pin our faith to bathtubs.

The press has reported that the greatest sales of fur ever known have occurred in the United States this year and that we are, or will be, the fur center of the world. In this connection an inquiring mind might ask whether reports from the weather bureau indicate that our climate is changing and that our winters have become so much colder as to require the use of fur

garments more extensively. I do not believe the climate has changed or that winters are colder. Furthermore, I understand that an increasing proportion of furs is worn, not as a protection against cold, but apparently as an insulation against heat in summer.

However that may be, the fact remains that it is poor national economy to exchange money or useful commodities and services for articles of wear whose function is more showy than useful. Those who take long rides in automobiles during cold weather in the way of business, such as doctors and traveling men, are entitled to protect themselves with the skins of animals. People who live in the states along the Canadian border have a legitimate excuse for furs. We who live in a moderate climate might as well be decent and let the people in the cold regions have our share of the furs.

The installment system of credit for clothes and furniture is a direct cause of a great deal of extravagance, for it lures its victims with the idea of small occasional payments of which the total is almost never comprehended.

Why single out American women to bear with an essay on thrift? Why not go after American men? Of course the men need it, and probably a lot more in many respects than the women. But to make a special address on this subject to American women is really to pay them a high compliment as indicating that they are very largely the guardians of the American pocketbook. They are, in fact, to a great extent the treasurers of the United States and they jointly handle every year far more cash than does the gentleman at Washington who supervises the national purse. It is true that not every woman in this country signs her husband's checks or has a free and equal partnership in his bank accounts.

Nevertheless, even though she may work on the traditional allowance for household expenses, she may be, in fact, the financial

Remedies for Cooking Disasters

By Mary Hamilton Talbot

"HASTE makes waste" is perhaps truer in the work in the kitchen than any other place in the house, for it is almost always hurry which causes most of the kitchen troubles—it is invariably this which makes the custard curdle, the soup too salty, the gravy lumpy. When such things happen the unknowing housewife too often throws away the apparently spoiled food, which she might have saved had she known the best method of restoring it to palatability.

IF IN your hurry in preparing boiled custard you have not taken the time to allow the milk to scald in the double boiler, but have used an ordinary saucepan and the intense heat has caused it to curdle, do not waste time wishing you had not taken the chance, but turn the custard quickly into a cold bowl and beat it vigorously with an egg beater. As a rule this treatment will make it "come" again; if it does not, however, take a level tablespoonful of cornstarch, moisten it with cold water, add it to the custard and place in the double boiler just long enough to cook the cornstarch, and strain. You will save eggs and milk—too expensive to waste.

IT USUALLY happens that the soup is abnormally salty the night there is a particular guest for dinner. Of course you cannot remove the salt, but if you will add a grated raw potato and cook a short time longer you will find the potato has absorbed the excess salt. Have you ever tried adding a teaspoonful of vinegar to the pea or bean soup which seemed too thin? It thickens up at once and one cannot detect even the slightest taste of the vinegar.

MANY of us have been at our wit's end when trying to mold croquettes, and do what we would they proved too soft. If this should happen take a teaspoonful of granulated gelatin, soak it in a very little cold water a few minutes, dissolve it over hot water and add to the croquette mixture, then pop into the ice box to chill, and when the gelatin has had time enough to harden you will find you can mold the croquettes without any further trouble. You will notice, too, that they are far better than if they had been very stiff without the gelatin, for the latter melts with the cooking heat and makes the croquettes nice and creamy inside. Never try to cook your croquettes in a shallow pan with just a little fat in it if you find that your supply of cooking fat is low; they will be grease-soaked and unfit to eat. Instead, put them in the oven after they have been prepared as for frying, and bake them.

IF YOU find the cream has soured, or there is not enough for the breakfast or dinner coffee, whip an egg very light, divide it among the coffee cups and pour the coffee over it. The resulting beverage is so delicious the absence of the cream will not be missed. An egg will also save the situation if the cream refuses to whip. Add the white of an egg to the cream, let both get chilled thoroughly, then try again, and you will have no further trouble. An egg will again come to the rescue if you have planned to have fried ham with cream gravy and the milk is spilled at the last moment. Make the gravy with water and add the yolk of an egg, beaten, season with a bit of parsley if you have it, and you will perhaps be glad the milk was spilled.

THE frying of potatoes is such a convenient way to serve left-over potatoes for luncheon. Because it is a left-over, however, the supply is usually limited, so when company unexpectedly drops in for luncheon, there often does not seem to be enough to serve. If this should happen, do not set aside your good fried potatoes, but add to them some stale bread cut into small dice after removing the crusts. Add some more good drippings or cooking fat, season well, and cook, turning frequently until the whole is nicely browned. You will find that the bread blends admirably with the potatoes. If you have at hand a green pepper, chop it and add it to the potatoes with the bread cubes.

IF YOU find the butter crock is empty when you go to season the vegetables for dinner, you can substitute cream and the fat in it will answer just as well as that in the butter for flavoring the dinner vegetable. As there is no salt in the cream, a little more of it will need to be added than when the butter is used. If, perchance, the cream bottle is empty, and the cream from the top of the milk bottle has been used, add some good unsalted vegetable fat or oil and plenty of salt.

MAYONNAISE has a way of curdling at the most inopportune time, when one is in a hurry, and it is usually the hurry which causes it, for the oil is added too fast; or it may be the ingredients are too warm. However, there is no use in beating and thinking it may get smooth; it won't. Take another egg yolk, put it in a dry, cold bowl, and add the curdled mixture a little at a time, as the oil should have been added in the first place, and, when it is well beaten in, proceed with the fresh oil.

manager of the whole establishment. She may not only rule and regulate expenditure within the home, but may extend her influence, consciously or unconsciously, to all the affairs of the family and its so-called head. Even a husband and father may learn the lessons of thrift taught in his home by a wise helpmeet.

Thrift at home shames a man who needs shaming and it stimulates to greater exertion the man who has been working along at half speed. It is this sort of home thrift to which a great many men refer when they say: "I owe everything to my wife." No man ever said that he was inspired to succeed or gained anything by the lavish expenditures of the woman he married. No monument was ever put up to a wife praising her as a reckless and prodigal spender. No writer of proverbs from the time of Solomon to ours has considered it feasible to celebrate favorably the wasteful housekeeper.

If the women of America see their opportunity and their duty and act upon them, civilization will be their debtor.

Mary Pickford in a frock especially designed for her by Lanvin of Paris.

CAN THE CHURCH TAKE THE PLACE OF THE SALOON?

James H. Snowdon

It really began more than a century ago when Benjamin Rush of Philadelphia, a high medical authority and signer of the Declaration of Independence, lifted his influential voice against strong drink and gave an impulse to the cause of temperance that started it toward victory. At first the doctrine of prohibition and even of personal abstinence found little favor in a day when the use of liquor was common among all classes, including ministers, and the Whisky Rebellion in Western Pennsylvania was a proof of how deeply this custom was entrenched in the habits of the people.

But the work of education got started and went on with persistence and increasing purpose and power. In time it got into the pulpits and schools and newspapers; temperance societies were formed, and temperance voices and agencies multiplied. From time to time waves of pledge-signing and other means of temperance reform swept over the country, and seemed to promise swift results, if not final triumph. But such movements usually were emotional waves that quickly subsided, although the sea never receded quite to the old level.

Before the Civil War, Maine and seven other states enacted constitutional prohibition, but these were temporary victories, and the Civil War set the temperance cause back. The tide began to rise again soon after the war and slowly made headway with more permanent gains. A notable point was passed when, on December 5, 1887, the Supreme Court of the United States upheld the constitutionality of prohibition. Ten years later the movement began to make rapid gains in the South, and before the outbreak of the Great War the Anti-Saloon League set 1920 as the date by which national constitutional prohibition would be achieved. The Great War had the effect of accelerating the movement, and in 1919 the victory was won.

But no sooner is one question settled than another and perhaps several others start up in its place. The saloon is gone, but it has left a vacancy which must be filled, for society abhors a vacuum as much as nature is said to do, and something must take its place. The saloon fulfilled a function in society, or it never would have existed so long and grown into such a deep-rooted and widespread institution.

The first and fundamental service of the saloon was to supply men with intoxicating beverages that would gratify their appetite and produce a state of exhilaration; in extreme cases this exhilaration passed by degrees into intoxication. In our complex civilization, with its toil and weariness and excitement and depression, men feel the need of and easily acquire a craving for stimulating and intoxicating beverages, and this wide, deep desire was the enormous demand which the saloon inevitably came forward to supply.

But the saloon became a breeding-ground of drunkenness and vice and crime, a prolific cause of poverty, a burden on all legitimate business, and a heavy tax on the state. These social damages and scandals multiplied and accumulated until they aroused public sentiment and conscience and organized opposition against the institution in such volume and force as swept it away as a dam is carried away by a flood.

Yet strange as it may appear to some people, the saloon was not wholly evil, for a pure evil is self-destructive and cannot long endure. This ugly thing had another side of a better nature and use than that which condemned and abolished it, and this was its function as a meeting place, a room of light and warmth where men met on the common ground of good fellowship. Men who were weary with toil and jaded in their interests and who had few attractions in their uncongenial homes or no homes at all, and loiterers drifting around the streets could enter through a door lightly swinging on its hinges into a brightly lit and warm saloon, perhaps with the additional allurements of music and possibly with singing and dancing, and find welcome change and relief and good cheer.

The social nature is strong in men and is bound to find some way of gratification. There are peculiar affinities and ties that bind men together in social intercourse, and if this craving is shut off from satisfaction in one direction it will find and force its way out through some other channel. The abolition of the saloon has taken away one of these centers and means of social fellowship among men, and something should be found that will afford new means of gratification that are free from the temptations and vices of the old.

The question now arises: Can the church supply this new need? More than any other single agency it was the church that put the saloon out of business. Are the churches willing only to destroy and not to build, to deprive men of one means of enjoyment without supplying them with another? Having shown their destructive power in abolishing the saloon, is it not now up to them to be equally constructive in furnishing some better thing?

What is the church for? What is its primary work? Church people themselves, including ministers, would hardly be able to agree on an answer that would cover the whole ground of the church; for the church, like any organized institution, has various objects or aspects of its work. But it will be generally agreed that the primary and fundamental object of the Christian church is to supply the religious nature and needs of people with the appropriate means of satisfaction and activity; to worship God, to work out the glory of God in peace and good will among men; to teach religious faith and service to the young and to spread them among men; in a word, the object of the church is to build the kingdom of God in the world.

The religious nature of man creates all religious doctrines and ordinances and institutions, as the seed in the soil creates the harvest. The Bible and the priest and the church did not make religion, but religion made them.

The church is the only institution that has a spire pointing toward the sky, a finger feeling after the Infinite and Eternal. The church must therefore first give itself to this, its primary work, and not be expected to permit itself to be drawn off into unrelated fields of service, however useful and worthy they may be.

One reason for the existence of the saloon was the low intellectual and social and moral life of its visitors and victims, and whatever elevates these men will deliver them from the bondage of the saloon into a purer and freer life. A partial answer to the question is the institutional church equipped in its building and appointments for offering the very attractions of a social nature that were found in a saloon with additional advantages. Many have a special building or parish house for such work, and others find room for it in the church building proper. A large room, well-lighted and heated, furnished with tables and chairs, newspapers and magazines and books, games and other forms of amusement, is opened to all men and boys for rest and recreation and fellowship. There may also be a gymnasium and a swimming pool. Night classes may be held in which courses of instruction in various subjects are given, and lectures and concerts are held. Various kinds of clubs for men and boys are organized. There may also be a dining room where coffee and sandwiches are often furnished, and occasionally a dinner is given.

The church cannot take the place of the saloon in all respects. Some men do not want to live a decent and wholesome life and will refuse to be drawn into clean social centers. Church people must expect to meet with some discouragement in their best endeavors to solve this problem.

Nevertheless, prohibition has come to stay. Having swept the saloon out of our social order, if we do not fill the vacancy with some better social service, seven devils worse than the first will come back and take its place. This is the challenge that the church has created for itself. Having destroyed the saloon, it must now make the loss good, or its own condemnation will be swift and sure. It is up to the leaders and members of the church to see their duty and do it.

QUEER ANIMALS OUTSIDE THE ZOO

Mabel Detwiler Miller

The Thermos Bottle

The Airplane

The Piano Player

The Submarine

The Trolley Car

The Telephone

The Alarm Clock

The Missing-Dollar Bird

The Automobile

THE UNSPEAKABLE
GENTLEMAN
Illustration
by Arthur I. Keller
for the story by
J. P. Marquand

THE CALL OF THE
CAÑON
Illustration
by H. R. Ballinger
for Zane Grey's
new tale of the West

"Then, with a thrill that I never again shall know, I saw the buffalo stumble, stagger a second and fall headlong."

In these days of the scarcity and government protection of the buffalo, it must be borne in mind that in the days of Buffalo Bill, about which his widow, Louisa Frederici Cody, now speaks, the bison roamed the Western plains by the thousands and buffalo meat was the food of the plainsmen.

"I remember," she says, "the day my husband jokingly remarked: 'You can't very well go on being Mrs. Buffalo Bill without being able to say that you killed a buffalo.' To his surprise I answered, 'If you can . . . then I can too.' "

The next day the family turned up to lead a hunting party—some twenty miles east of Fort Sheridan where buffalo was plentiful. Buffalo Bill had strapped Arta, their daughter, to Louisa's lap "to take part in the festivities too."

"At the sight of the herd," Louisa remembers, "a thrill went through me; but,

strangely enough, it was not the thrill of fear. I suppose there is something about the hunt which gets into one's blood. For years I had lived in the atmosphere of it, hearing about the exciting adventures and the zest of it without absorbing it. But now I was on the edge of that excitement myself.

" 'You're sure you're not afraid?' Bill asked quickly.

" 'Absolutely not,' I replied. He rode close to me and leaned and kissed Arta and myself.

"My heart was pounding like a trip-hammer. The whole world was hazy—except for those plunging buffalo, upon which my every attention was centered. I knew what to do, and as one of the charging creatures came close I clutched my revolver and aimed. With a thrill that I never again shall know, I saw the buffalo stumble, stagger a second and fall headlong. . . ."

HUNTING
WITH
BUFFALO BILL

DOES JAZZ PUT THE SIN IN SYNCOPATION?

Anne Shaw Faulkner

The correct position to be taken in dancing.

We have all been taught to believe that "music soothes the savage breast," but we have never stopped to consider that an entirely different type of music might invoke savage instincts.

Never in the history of our land have there been such immoral conditions, and in surveys made by many organizations, the blame is laid on jazz and its evil influence on the young. Never before have such outrageous dances been permitted in private as well as public ballrooms, and never has there been such a strange combination of tone and rhythm as that produced by the dance orchestras of to-day.

If this music is in any way responsible for the immoral acts which can be traced to these dances, then it is high time that the question should be raised: "Can music ever be an influence for evil?"

To-day, the first great rebellion against jazz music and such dances as the "toddle" and the "shimmy" comes from the dancing masters themselves. The National Dancing Masters' Association, at their last session, adopted this rule: "Don't permit vulgar cheap jazz music to be played. Such music almost forces dancers to use jerky half-steps, and invites immoral variations, for, after

all, what is dancing but an interpretation of music?"

Many people classify under the title of "jazz" all music in syncopated rhythm, whether it be the ragtime of the American Negro or the csardas ·of the Slavic people. Yet there is a vast difference between syncopation and jazz.

The Encyclopaedia Britannica sums up syncopation as "the rhythmic method of tying two beats of the same note into one tone in such a way as to displace the accent." This curious rhythmic accent on the short beat is found in its most highly developed and intense forms among the folk of Slavic countries. It was also the natural expression of the American Negroes, used by them as the accompaniment for their bizarre dances and cakewalks. Negro ragtime, it must be frankly acknowledged, is one of the most important and distinctively characteristic expressions to be found in our native music. Many of the greatest compositions by American composers have been influenced by ragtime. Like all other phases of syncopation, ragtime quickens the pulse, it excites, it stimulates; but. it does not destroy.

Jazz is neither a definite form nor a type of rhythm; it is rather a *method* employed by the interpreter. Familiar hymn tunes can be jazzed until their original melodies are hardly recognizable. Jazz does for harmony what the accented syncopation of ragtime does for rhythm. In ragtime the rhythm is thrown out of joint, as it were, thus distorting the melody; in jazz exactly the same thing is done to the harmony. The melodic line is disjointed and disconnected by the accenting of the partial instead of the simple tone, and the same effect is produced on the melody and harmony which is noticed in syncopated rhythm. The combination of syncopation and the use of these inharmonic partial tones produces a strange, weird effect, which has been designated "jazz."

The jazz orchestra uses only those instruments which can produce partial, inharmonic tones more readily than simple tones—such as the saxophone, the clarinet and the trombone, which share honors with the percussion instruments that accent syncopated rhythm. The combination of the syncopated rhythm, accentuated by the constant use of the partial tones sounding off-pitch, has put syncopation too off-key. Thus the three simple elements of music—rhythm, melody and harmony—have been put out of tune with each other.

Jazz originally was the accompaniment of the voodoo dancer, stimulating the half-

crazed barbarian to the vilest deeds. The weird chant, accompanied by the syncopated rhythm, also been employed by other barbaric people to stimulate brutality and sensuality.

The human organism responds to musical vibrations. What instincts then are aroused by jazz? Certainly not deeds of valor or martial courage.

This posture scarcely commends the modern dance to the discriminating.

In a recent letter to the author, Dr. Henry van Dyke says of jazz: "As I understand it, it is not music at all. It is merely an irritation of the nerves of hearing, a sensual teasing of the strings of physical passion. Its fault lies not in syncopation, for that is a legitimate device when sparingly used. But 'jazz' is an unmitigated cacophony, a combination of disagreeable sounds in complicated discords, a willful ugliness and a deliberate vulgarity."

Never have we more needed the help and inspiration which good music can give. The General Federation of Women's Clubs has taken for its motto: "To Make Good Music Popular, and Popular Music Good." Let *us* carry out this motto in every home.

Rudolph Valentino with his wife Natacha Rambova.

THE MAN AND HIS CLOTHES

John Chapman Hilder

There are times in the affairs of almost every man when he must forswear the comfort and ease of ordinary clothes and array himself in the trappings of formality. And gosh, how the average man dreads it!

If you have a husband there is little I can tell you about the masculine state of mind when it is confronted with the necessity of climbing into the royal regalia.

You know how it is. You cough gently once or twice, as a signal that you are about to broach a painful subject; you sit on the arm of his chair and slowly but firmly draw the evening paper out of his nervous fingers. Not quite sure what choice morsel of news you are going to launch at him but very certain that he is going to be given medicine of some sort, he raises a wary eye and grins apprehensively. When he is thoroughly on the defensive you begin, somewhat like this:

"Henry, dear, I wish it might have been any night *except* to-night, because I know you must have had a hard day, but the Blenkinsops are having a little bridge party and I'm afraid ———"

Evening dress should be devoid of all fancy touches.

"Oh, golly," groans Henry. "Can't you get George to take you? George loves that kind of thing. Besides, I haven't got any shirts."

"I'm sorry," you murmur, "but I'm afraid you must go. Mrs. Blenkinsop is counting on you to be her partner. She said only this morning, in the butcher's—when I told her how tired and busy you'd been lately—she said it would ruin her party if you couldn't be there. I tried my best to get you out of it, you see, but she wouldn't hear of it and so I bought you some new shirts and—*please* get ready as soon as you can."

With a wry grimace Henry surrenders. For half an hour you hear him stomping about, talking in undertones to his collar and his tie, communing more or less vigorously with his shirt studs and condemning the man who first invented the stovepipe hat. And you smile to yourself because you know very well that, deep down inside, Henry rather fancies himself in full dress; that at some time during the Blenkinsop séance you will catch him admiring himself in the long mirror by the side of the hatstand.

The aversion of the male toward formal clothes springs partly from laziness and partly from hypocrisy.

It seems to me that the sensible attitude to adopt toward evening dress and the cutaway is this: "Formal clothes are the survival of a tradition. They do not differ from everyday things in any useful way. They are a convention. They are considered as either a social passport or as the uniform of a head waiter. By adhering very closely to the best and most conventional standard of tastes in my choice of dress clothes and their appurtenances, I can get

The cutaway has supplanted the stately frock coat.

the utmost social and commercial value out of wearing them and at the same time minimize my resemblance to a head waiter. I will therefore take the trouble to find out what constitutes formal dress as it ought to be and, having secured this information, which will probably not change radically during my natural life, I will conscientiously apply it with as little fuss as possible."

A dinner jacket should fit like a well-cut sack coat.

UNMATCHING
THE DINING-ROOM FURNITURE
Ethel Davis Seal

Today, in the 1920's, it is no longer at all necessary to spend fabulous sums for a suite of Adam, Queen Anne or some other period reproductions because one's neighbors and friends have set such a pace. Reproductions have grown prohibitive in price, except perhaps those spurious offshoots no one of discernment is tempted into acquiring simply because they are of moderate cost a full set.

We have glimpsed dining rooms furnished with treasures from the Old World; we have felt the spell of a Louis commode in blue, fawn and gold, used with an old mahogany Chippendale sideboard and Chinese ladderbacks to realize the delight of unmatching the dining-room furniture, even on a much more humble scale.

As a nucleus around which to build a quaint unmatched dining room, nothing is more charming than a drop-leaf table. Gate-legs come in a variety of styles and prices, from large to small ones of mahogany or walnut to those of nondescript wood waiting to be transformed by paint. The latter are admitted into the class of fine furniture when accented by fine lines and posies upon a ground of decorative blue, green or black.

With a drop-leaf table the quainter type of chair should be used, such as the ladderback or Windsor. When the price of a buffet is prohibitive or the dining room is too small, a chest of drawers is a possible alternative with a picture hung over it.

The dining room below has ivory walls and putty color and jade-green furniture. The chest and china cupboard are putty outside, jade inside, the drawers knobbed in black. Putty-colored chairs were drawn up to a jade green table, on a black rug with green band. At the windowside (reflected in the mirror) drapes and valance of jade contrast with curtains of pale orchid mull.

Unmatched pieces may always be given a related effect with paint. To be very modern, try a dull Chinese red for quaintly shaped things, lining them with black and

Ivory walls, putty color and jade-green furniture, with a note of lavender in curtains and china.

The furniture is dull Chinese red, lined with black and decorated outside with black and gold.

Drawings by Marion Dismant

Unmatched mahogany furniture in a color scheme of blue and ivory, developing the popular colonial spirit. The rug is blue and black and cream, and there are a few notes of yellow in the bowls of fruit and the rush seats of the ladder-back chairs.

decorating them outside with black and gold. This has been tried with great effect in the dining room (extreme left) with the diamond-paned lattice window, against softly toned gray walls. While the furniture is originally of the cottage type, the rich treatment greatly enhances its value. The curtains are of printed linen with a black ground and a design of Chinese red, blue and old gold.

Above is an unmatched dining room in the colonial spirit, with a color scheme of blue, ivory and mahogany. On the brown floor is a rug of blue, black and cream. The walls and woodwork are ivory; the buffet and the lowboy (used for the serving table), the table and chairs are of mahogany, matching in color if unmatched in type. The corner closet is ivory, the Canton china blue, and the curtains predominantly blue and lavender.

COOKERY AT A GLANCE

A. Louise Andrea

All recipes for any one kind of food are similar in essentials, but differ in details. The cookery card on the next two pages will show you the variations at a glance. When you want to cook fish, make a salad dressing or a sauce, a glance at this card will show you what ingredients you will need and the method of putting them together.

The abbreviations used throughout are these: **T** means 1 level *table*spoonful; **t** means 1 level *tea*spoonful; **C** means 1 level *cup*ful, using the standard half-pint measuring cup.

Meat and Fish Soups

Kind and Base Ingredients	How Prepared	Seasonings and Flavorings	Liquid	Cooking	Method	Thickener	Garnishing and Serving
BOUILLON. 6 pounds beef from round, 2 pounds marrowbone	Cut meat into small pieces. Brown one-third in marrow. Put balance in soup kettle. Crack all bones. Add browned meat	4 cloves, 18 peppercorns, ½ bay leaf, 2 sprigs thyme, 3 sprays parsley, ½ C each of diced carrot, onion, turnips and celery, ¼ C sliced leeks. Salt. Pepper	3 quarts cold water	7 hours at simmering temperature	Strain, cool, remove fat. Add 1 beaten egg white and crushed shell for each quart. Stir. Boil 2 minutes, simmer 10 minutes. Strain through cheesecloth	.....	Plain or with a garnish of fancy-cut vegetables cooked tender in stock. Or with any kind of tiny soup dumplings
CONSOMMÉ. 3 pounds veal shank, body of uncooked chicken, (breast and legs saved for other dishes), giblets and cleaned feet, 3 pounds beef shin	Cut meat into small pieces. Brown ½ in marrow. Crack bones. Place all meat and bone in kettle	½ C each diced onion, turnip, carrot, celery, 2 cloves, 18 peppercorns, 4 sprays parsley, 2 sprigs thyme, ½ blade mace, ½ bay leaf	3 quarts cold water	4 to 5 hours at simmering temperature	Strain, cool, remove fat. Add 1 beaten egg white and crushed shell for each quart. Stir. Boil 2 minutes, then simmer 10 minutes. Strain through cheesecloth	.....	Plain or with some finely cut pieces of cooked veal or chicken, or with fancy-cut vegetables or soup dumplings
OXTAIL. 1 oxtail	Cut into small pieces	2 T each minced onion, carrot, raw ham, 1 T parsley, stirred over fire for 15 minutes in 3 T butter. Salt. Pepper	3 pints brown stock	1 hour at simmering temperature	Strain	1½ T each of butter and flour rubbed to a paste	Meat cut from oxtail
STOCK FROM COOKED MEATS. Bones from roast turkey, chicken, beef, lamb, etc.; leftover gravy	Crack bones; add any tough ends of meat	2 T each minced onion, carrot, celery, 6 peppercorns, 2 cloves, ½ blade mace, 2 sprays parsley. Salt. Pepper	Cold water to well cover meat and bones	2 to 3 hours at simmering temperature	Strain	.....	Meat diced or 1 T each of cooked peas, diced celery, or carrots cut in fancy shapes
FISH STOCK. Head, tail, skin, bones, and flesh on bones of cod or haddock	....	1 T each minced carrot and onion, 1 clove, 6 peppercorns. Salt. Pepper	Cold water to cover	½ hour at simmering temperature	Strain	.....	Plain, or with minced parsley

METHOD: Place bone and meat (prepared as directed) in kettle, cover with liquid. Let stand half an hour, place over fire, bring slowly to boiling point, simmer two-thirds of cooking time; season, complete cooking time. Strain, clarify, and add thickener when designated.

Broiled Steaks and Chops

Kind and Cut	Cooking Method	Serve With — Potatoes	Serve With — Other Vegetables	Gravy or Sauce	Garnish and Service
FLANK STEAK. Cut across grain in several pieces	Broil steaks one inch thick 4 minutes for rare; 5 minutes for medium rare; 6½ minutes for well done	Au gratin, or Hashed	Sautéed eggplant, stuffed peppers, grilled onions	Melted Butter Sauce	Bacon curls and parsley
ROUND STEAK. Cut from top of round, 1 inch thick		Croquettes or Sweet-potato glacé	Baked macaroni and cheese, stuffed tomatoes, buttered carrots	*Seasoning or Maître d'hôtel Butter	Watercress
SIRLOIN STEAK. Cut from middle and first cut of loin, 1¼ inches thick		French fried or Baked	Baked squash, fried sliced tomato, creamed parsnip	Maître d'hôtel Butter	Parsley
HAMBURGER STEAK. Cut from lower round and chop with 2 ounces of suet to 1 pound of meat. Add minced ½ clove, garlic and ½ t of onion juice	Mold in cakes 1 inch thick; 6 to 8 minutes	Lyonnaise, Creamed, or Baked	Buttered carrots, stewed tomatoes, fried onions	Maître d'hôtel Butter or Tomato Sauce	Parsley
LAMB CHOPS. From loin, 1 inch thick	Broil one-inch-thick chops 5 minutes for rare	Balls, Chips, or Hashed brown	Asparagus tips, buttered peas, buttered Limas, Brussels sprouts, cauliflower	Bearnaise Sauce, or Seasoning Butter	Arrange chops on bed of watercress
MUTTON CHOPS. From loin, 1 to 2 inches thick	Broil very thick chops, 15 to 20 minutes	Croquettes, Hashed, or Au gratin	Creamed turnips, buttered beets, spinach en croustades, stuffed onions	Seasoning Butter	Broiled ½ kidney, and bacon. Watercress
PORK CHOPS. From loin, cut 4 to a pound	Broil 8 to 10 minutes until well done	Fried sweet potatoes, Plain or Parsley	Brussels sprouts, cauliflower croquettes, creamed cabbage, apple sauce	Seasoning Butter	Fried-apple rings

METHOD: Wipe steaks and chops with a clean, damp cloth; cook on greased broiler rack under gas flame or over clear coals, turning often to sear. When done remove to hot platter and serve with sauce, seasoning butter or gravy.
* SEASONING BUTTER: To each person allow half a tablespoonful of butter, an eighth of a teaspoonful of salt and two dashes of pepper. Cream and spread on both sides of lean meat. When steaks or chops are to be served with a sauce use salt and pepper.

Cream Soups

Kind and Base Material	Hot Liquid	Thicken With — Flour	Thicken With — Butter	Seasonings and Flavorings	Garnishings
ASPARAGUS. 1 can	2 C milk, 4 C white stock	4 T	4 T	Salt and pepper	Asparagus tips
CAULIFLOWER. One	2 C milk, 4 C water in which cauliflower boiled	4 T	4 T	1 stalk celery, salt and pepper	Flowerettes dipped in grated cheese
CELERY. Three C minced	2 C white stock, 3 C milk	3 T	2 T	2 slices onion, salt and pepper	Slices of cooked celery
LETTUCE. Two heads	2 C water, 1 C milk	2½ T	2 T	Salt and pepper and dash of nutmeg	Hard-boiled egg yolk put through sieve
POTATO. 4 Cooked and sieved	4 C milk	2 T	3 T	3 slices onion, salt and pepper	1 t chopped parsley
SPINACH. 2 quarts	2 C milk, 4 C white stock	5 T	4 T	Salt, pepper and 1 blade mace	Croutons
TOMATO. ⅔ can Cooked with seasonings; add soda, stir and sieve.	4 C milk. Cook, with thickener, in double boiler	4 T	5 T	¼ t soda, 1 t chopped onion, salt and pepper	One T whipped cream on each service

METHOD: Cook base materials and seasonings tender in stock or water. Reserve, if any, base materials for garnish. Press balance through sieve. Rub flour and butter together; add to milk and heat in double boiler; add the sieved mixture and bring to boiling. Garnish and serve.

Fried and Sautéed Meats

Kind and Cut	Cook With	Season With	Method of Cooking	Gravy or Sauce	Serve With — Potatoes	Serve With — Other Vegetables	Garnish
VEAL CUTLET. From leg, ½ inch thick	Boil until tender; drain; dip in egg, then crumbs	Salt, pepper, 1 T lemon juice	Fry in deep fat until browned	Brown flour and butter; add Veal stock, seasoning and lemon juice	Balls, Escalloped, Pimiento, or Sweet-potato glacé	Buttered carrots, stewed tomatoes, creamed turnips	Fried parsley
BACON. ⅛ inch thick, rind removed	.....	......	Place in cold pan on slow fire until crisp, turning often	....	Cakes, Grilled Sweet potatoes, Lyonnaise, or Hashed	Creamed spinach, Brussels sprouts, boiled cabbage	Triangles of toast, edges dipped in paprika
PORK TENDERLOIN. Split, pound with cleaver to flatten	......	Salt and pepper, a pinch of sage	In pan, 20 minutes, with minced fat pork	Pan gravy, thickened with flour	Mashed, Au gratin, or Sweet-potato glacé	Corn fritters, fried-apple rings, fried bananas	Watercress and bacon curls
HAM. Sliced, ½ inch thick	Cold water; bring to boil; drain, to freshen	Pepper	In pan, 10 minutes	Add flour, then milk, to fat in pan. Stir until thick	Mashed, Sweet-potato glacé or cakes	Spinach, grilled eggplant, hot slaw	Parsley

METHOD: Season meat, dust with flour where directed, and place in frying pan, with two tablespoonfuls of melted drippings. Have fire hot to sear so that juices are retained. Reduce heat and cook until tender. When serving with a thickened sauce, pour this on heated platter, then arrange the meat on sauce; where the sauce is a thin one, pour over the meat before serving.

Roasted Meats

Kind and Preparation for Oven	Approx. Time to Cook	Style of Potatoes	Garnish With	Sauce or Gravy	Other Accompaniments
LEG OF LAMB. Remove caul, season with salt and pepper, place on rack, dredge with flour	1½ hours	Boiled sweet, Mashed, or Parsley	Watercress	Mint sauce	Squash, cauliflower, peas, mushrooms, eggplant, baked tomatoes, currant jelly.
MUTTON. Season with salt and pepper, place meat on rack in pan and dredge with flour	1¼ to 1½ hours	Boiled white, or buttered balls	Watercress	Caper sauce	Turnips, parsnips, stringless beans, kohl-rabi, currant jelly
*SHORT RIBS OF BEEF. Slice 1 onion, 1 carrot, 1 small turnip, ½ green pepper. Mix and lay in roaster. Place meat on top. Salt and pepper	Until nicely browned	Hashed, Lyonnaise, Baked, Au gratin, or Pimiento	Parsley	Brown gravy made from pan	Corn fritters, stuffed tomatoes, stuffed peppers, spinach
LOIN OF PORK. Salt and pepper, lay in pan, cover top with slices of raw onion, carrot and apple. Add 1 pint of boiling water	15 minutes per pound	Mashed white, Baked sweet, or Lyonnaise	Fried-apple rings	Gravy made from pan	Corn (Creole style), spinach, beets, cauliflower, gooseberry or apple sauce
RIB ROAST. Season with salt and pepper. Place meat on rack in roasting pan, with skin side down, dredge with flour. Turn meat once	For a rare roast allow 12 minutes per pound; well done, 16 minutes	Mashed, Au gratin, Baked, or Sweet-potato glacé	Parsley, or watercress	Plate gravy or gravy made from pan	Corn pudding, baked squash, creamed spinach, baked egg plant, stuffed tomatoes, currant or quince jelly

METHOD: Wipe all meat with clean, damp cloth. Have oven hot at first to sear surface, reduce heat and baste every fifteen minutes with liquid in pan. If necessary add boiling water. When done, remove meat, pour off fat, add flour and boiling water and stir until thickened.
* When meat is browned, place in another pan; add flour and 1 pint of boiling water to vegetables, and stir until slightly thickened. Strain over the meat and simmer until tender.

Boiled, Baked and Fried Fish

Kind	How Prepared	Liquid and Seasonings	Approximate Cooking Time	Serve With: Potatoes	Serve With: Sauce and Garnish
Boiled Cod	4 pounds fresh, cut in one piece. Wash in cold water	3 quarts cold water, 1 onion, sliced, 2½ T salt, ½ C mild vinegar, 10 peppercorns, 2 cloves, 3 sprays parsley	25 to 30 minutes, depending upon thickness	Plain boiled, mashed, or buttered balls	Egg or mustard. Garnish with parsley
Boiled Salmon	2½ to 3 pounds fresh	2½ quarts cold water, 1 onion, sliced, 1 carrot, sliced, 5 peppercorns, 1 clove, 3 sprays parsley, ½ C mild vinegar, 2 T salt	25 to 30 minutes, depending upon thickness	Boiled or buttered balls	Oyster or hollandaise. Garnish with parsley
Baked Bluefish	3½ to 4 pounds, stuffed* and sewed	½ C melted butter, ½ C boiling water, mixed. Salt, pepper	40 to 50 minutes in hot oven	Hashed browned or au gratin	Shrimp or cucumber. Garnish with parsley and lemon slices
Baked Haddock	4 pounds, stuffed* and sewed	½ C water, 1 T lemon juice, 2 T melted butter. Salt, pepper	1 hour in hot oven	Creamed, au gratin, or parsley	Mustard or egg. Garnish with parsley and lemon slices
Fried Smelts.	1½ pounds, clean, wash and dry	Salt, pepper	5 to 6 minutes	Lyonnaise, buttered balls, or hashed brown	Cucumber or tartare. Garnish with cress and lemon slices
Fried Codfish Steak	2½ pounds, cut one inch thick. Remove bone	Salt, pepper	5 to 6 minutes	Buttered balls, baked, or plain boiled	Mustard. Garnish with parsley
Fried Fresh Mackerel	Clean, split, remove head and tail. Wash and dry	Salt, pepper	8 to 10 minutes	Baked or French fried	Economy hollandaise. Garnish with parsley and lemon sections
Fried Fillets	Cut fish into 6 or 8 fillets	Salt and pepper, and sprinkle with lemon juice	3 to 4 minutes	French fried	Tartare, lobster, or shrimp. Garnish with parsley

METHOD: *Boiled*—Add seasonings to liquid and boil for ten minutes. Place fish in cheesecloth or on rack; place in boiling liquid; bring to boil again and *simmer* until fish is done. *Baked*—Place seasoned, stuffed fish on greased cheesecloth or rack; place in oven in dripping pan; baste every ten minutes with liquid. *Fried*—Season prepared fish, dip in flour, then beaten egg and crumbs, and fry in hot oil, or in half lard and half butter, deep enough to nearly cover.

* Fish Stuffing: Mix together one cupful of soft crumbs, four tablespoonfuls of melted butter, a quarter of a teaspoonful of scraped onion, with salt and pepper, and hot water to soften.

Salad Dressings

(Fish, Meat, Vegetable and Fruit Salads)

Kind	Oils and Eggs	Vinegar or Lemon Juice	Seasonings	Added Ingredients	Serve With Following Salads
French Dressing	4 T olive oil	2 T red-wine vinegar	1 clove garlic, cut, ½ t salt, ⅛ t white pepper, dash paprika	....	Green vegetables
Curry	6 T olive oil	3 T mild vinegar	½ t curry paste, ½ t salt, dash paprika	....	Chicken, egg and some vegetables
Russian	1 yolk, ¾ C olive oil	1 T lemon juice, 1 T vinegar	½ t salt, ⅛ t pepper, ½ t English mustard	½ green pepper, chopped, 3 T chili sauce, 1 T piccalilli, 1 t scraped onion	Lettuce, endive or vegetable macédoine
Roquefort	6 T olive oil	2 T mild vinegar	½ t salt, ¼ t paprika	⅓ C Roquefort cheese, creamed, 1 T heavy cream	Lettuce, tomato, cucumber, vegetable macédoine
Mayonnaise	2 yolks, 1½ C olive oil	2 T lemon juice, 2 T mild vinegar	1 t salt, ¼ t white pepper, 1 t English mustard	....	Chicken, salmon, vegetable, fruit
Fruit Mayonnaise	1 yolk, ¾ C olive oil	2 T lemon juice	½ t salt, ½ t English mustard, dash paprika	2 T juice from canned pineapple, 1 T orange juice, ¼ C cream, whipped	Fruit and lettuce
Thousand Island	1 yolk, ¾ C olive oil	2 T lemon juice	½ t salt, ½ t English mustard, dash cayenne, dash white pepper	1 T green pepper, minced, 1 T pimiento minced, 1 T chili sauce, 1 t grated horse-radish	Vegetable and meat
Tartare	2 yolks, ¾ C olive oil	1 T mild vinegar, 1 T lemon juice	½ t salt, ½ t English mustard, dash cayenne	½ T each chopped capers, gherkins and parsley	Fish
Cucumber	2 yolks, ¾ C olive oil	2 T lemon juice	¾ t salt, ½ t English mustard, dash paprika	1 C diced cucumber, drained, ¼ C cream, whipped	Salmon salad

French Dressing Style: Place seasonings, vinegar, lemon juice and oil in bottle; cork, and shake vigorously. Place in ice box to chill. When ready to serve remove garlic; add ingredients in "Added Ingredients" column. Use, as soon as mixed, with salad.

Mayonnaise Style: Place seasonings in round-bottom bowl, with yolks and one teaspoonful of vinegar or lemon juice. Mix thoroughly; then add a tablespoonful of oil, and begin beating with a Dover egg beater. As the dressing thickens, add half a teaspoonful of vinegar or lemon juice. Continue beating until all the oil and acid have been added. It is not necessary to have ingredients chilled; the temperature of the room is preferable. But it *is* necessary that each addition of oil and acid be thoroughly blended in the dressing before adding more. That is the secret of a successful mayonnaise dressing. When the mayonnaise is made, chill; add ingredients in "Added Ingredients" column, and use as soon as prepared.

Hot Fish Sauces

Kind	Butter	Thickener	Liquid	Seasonings	Base Materials	Serve With
*Cucumber	6 T, creamed	Yolks of three eggs	⅔ C boiling water	½ t lemon juice, dash nutmeg, salt and pepper	1 cucumber, seeds removed and finely cut, 1 t vinegar	Broiled swordfish, broiled pompano, lobster timbale, fried shad roe
Egg	4 T	3 T flour	1½ C milk	Salt and pepper, 1 T lemon juice	2 hard-boiled eggs, whites finely chopped, yolks pressed through sieve	Baked haddock, boiled fresh cod, boiled salmon
Lobster	4 T	4 T flour	2½ C water	Salt and pepper, 1½ t lemon juice	1 C boiled lobster meat, cut small. Leave claws in even-cut pieces	Baked halibut, halibut croquettes, boiled (white) fish
Mustard	5 T	3 T flour, yolk of one egg	1½ C cold water	Salt, dash of nutmeg, 1 T lemon juice	1 T mixed mustard	Baked haddock, baked cod
Oyster	2 T	2 T flour	1 C strained oyster liquor and water	1 t tomato catchup or table sauce, salt and pepper	1 C oysters. Remove muscle, bring to boil in strained oyster liquor, drain and chop. Save liquor	Boiled cod, boiled salmon
†Shrimp	4 T	Yolk of one egg, 3 T flour	1¼ C milk	Salt and pepper, 1 T lemon juice	½ C shrimps cut into small pieces	Baked bluefish, fish timbales, boiled (white) fish
Economy Hollandaise	2 T	2 T flour, yolk of one egg	¾ C milk	Salt and paprika, 1 t lemon juice	....	Fried codfish steak

METHOD: Melt butter; add flour; cook for two minutes; then add liquid, yolk (where given) and seasonings. Strain; add base materials; reheat.

* Cucumber: Cream butter; stir in yolks, one at a time. Stir over boiling water until thick; add liquid slowly, and seasoning; when creamy, take from fire and add cucumber.

† Shrimp: Prepare as directed in general directions; stir in yolk just before removing from fire.

Hot Vegetable and Meat Sauces

Kind	Butter	Thickener	Base Material and Liquids	Chopped Ingredients	Seasonings	Serve With
Butter	3 T	2 T flour	1 C water in which vegetables were boiled	....	Salt, pepper and grating of nutmeg	Boiled cucumbers, vegetable marrow, asparagus, Jerusalem artichokes, Lima beans, etc.
Curry	3 T	2 T flour	2 t curry powder, 1 C water in which vegetables were boiled, ¼ C cream	2 T each onion and carrot, ½ small apple cooked tender in butter	1 minced gherkin, salt and pepper	Carrots, Lima beans, macédoine of cooked vegetables (peas, Lima beans, carrots, turnips, string beans, corn cut from cob)
Gratin	2 T	2 T flour	½ C grated cheese, 1 C hot milk	....	Salt and pepper, dash of paprika	Asparagus, cauliflower, potato marbles
*Hollandaise	4 T	Yolks of two eggs	2 T mild vinegar, ½ C thin white sauce	1 shallot	1 t lemon juice, ½ bay leaf, 5 peppercorns	Asparagus, celery, cauliflower, potatoes
Onion	2 T	2 T flour	1 onion, chopped, boiled tender and drained, 1 C milk	....	Salt, pepper, paprika	Boiled turnips, new potatoes, vegetable marrow, cucumbers
Parsley	3 T	2 T flour	2 t minced parsley, 1 C milk	....	Salt, pepper, 1 t lemon juice	New potatoes, vegetable marrow, summer squash, onions, turnips
†Tomato	3 T bacon drippings	2 T flour	1½ C liquid from canned tomatoes	1 small onion, ½ green pepper, 3 hot Italian peppers	Salt, pepper, pinch of soda, ½ bay leaf	Spaghetti, egg timbales, cucumbers, rice, okra, mushrooms
Béchamel	5 T	4 T flour	2 C hot milk	1 slice onion, 2 slices carrot	1 clove, 10 peppercorns, ½ bay leaf, nutmeg, salt, pepper	Chicken
‡Béarnaise	8 T	Yolks of four eggs	3 T boiling water, 4 T tarragon vinegar	2 T shallots, 1 bouillon cube	6 crushed peppercorns, salt and pepper	Steak, sweetbreads
‖Brown	2 T (browned)	3 T flour (browned)	1 C hot brown stock	1 t parsley, 1 T onion	Salt and pepper, 1 t kitchen bouquet	Beef, calf's liver
Caper	5 T	2 T flour	1½ T capers, 1 C hot milk	....	½ T vinegar, salt and pepper	Mutton
Horse-radish	3 T	2 T flour	⅛ C grated horse-radish, 1 C hot milk	....	Salt and pepper, ½ t sugar	Cold chicken, fillet of beef, boiled beef
Milk	3 T	3 T flour	1½ C hot milk	....	Salt and pepper	Broiled ham

METHOD: Melt butter; add chopped ingredients; sauté for five minutes; add flour; cook for two minutes; add liquid, seasonings, stir until thick; strain; add base material; reheat.

* Hollandaise: Cook minced shallot, peppercorns and bay leaf in vinegar until nearly dry. Add white sauce and, when boiling, add yolks. Stir thoroughly and strain. Add butter gradually and lemon juice last.

† Tomato: Minced vegetables are cooked in butter for five minutes, then proceed as above.

‡ Béarnaise: Cook shallots, peppercorns and vinegar until nearly dry. Cool; add yolks, and stir. Set pan over hot water, add butter gradually, stirring until melted; then add bouillon cube dissolved in boiling water, and stir until sauce thickens. Serve at once.

‖ Add eight canned mushrooms, sliced, and half a cupful of mushroom liquor to brown sauce for steak or fillet.

THE MIRACLE

Booth Tarkington

The happiest man I have ever known may be seen almost any day in the year by motorists who pass through our village. No matter what the weather, he will be found in the square, engaged in being cheerful, for he has no other occupation. When it rains hard or snows with northeasterly vehemence, he will take inadequate shelter in the doorway of one of the small shops, or lean close against the wall of the post office, which is a building of only one story, so that its eaves may be used by imaginative people as about half of an umbrella. But rain squalls, rough winds and snow and sleet have no effect upon this happy man's high spirits. He laughs as gayly when rain pours as when the sun shines.

A few years ago, in an accident, he lost most of his fine front teeth; and not long after that his right leg had to be cut off as the result of another injury; moreover, he is what people call "tongue-tied" to an extent that prevents him from making himself understood except by gestures and the queerest of vocal gobblings. Nevertheless, he has always been able to laugh—laughter is the one human expression in which he was naturally as proficient as other people, and there he has made himself more than the equal of the rest of us. He laughs better than we do. He has nothing except a package of bad cigarettes, and some old clothes which he keeps as neat as he can, but he has made his merriment into a talent. He stands all day in the square, crippled, defective, eagerly watching everything, delighted with the waddlings of a wet pigeon, and plainly he finds the world beautiful and leads a jolly life. Many people think him an "idiot"; but often when I see him I think of something an awed young writer heard a great man say, one night, years ago.

The great man was Mark Twain, and another great man sat beside him at a small supper party to which the awed young writer had been invited. The other was Mr. Howells, and the two were talking of the nature of the state of mind—and body, perhaps—that we call happiness. Mark Twain settled the question finally to the perfect satisfaction and agreement of his old friend sitting beside him. "Happiness," Mark Twain said, "is merely a person's unconsciousness of troubles that he really has."

This was dismaying to the young listener, for at that time it was not fashionable for youth to appear pessimistic; and he dared to suggest a variation upon the theme. Mightn't unhappiness be merely a person's unconsciousness of blessings that he really

had? But Mark Twain said "No," and became more explicit. "The young jackass hard at work in the cornfield looks over the fence at the old jackass on pension in the meadow, with nothing to do; and the young jackass envies him his leisure, and thinks there isn't anything in the world harder than to be a young jackass; and the old jackass in the meadow looks over the fence at the young jackass at work, and envies him his youth and power; and the old jackass is sure there isn't anything in the world more unpleasant than being an old jackass. Each of them is really miserable, and knows it; and if either of them could be happy for a minute or two it would be because something distracted his attention from his own wretched condition."

In his own way Mark Twain meant what he said; but of course he was only playing—amusing himself and Mr. Howells at supper; and the theme he chose is, in fact, capable of many plausible variations. You may say that our happy man in the village square is happy because he is unaware of his actually pathetic condition, or you well may doubt that his condition is pathetic, since obviously he is happy. He is happy because he was born a merry spirit and has never made any plans of his own that he would like to substitute for the system governing the universe.

Carlyle said of the lady who remarked that she accepted the universe as it is, "Gad! She'd better!" And most of us think we agree with him, but in practice are not always equal to so plain a bit of wisdom. Far from "accepting the universe as it is," many of us are but little resigned to it, and really believe our lives to be not much more than a disjointed series of chance calamities, with intervals of "good times" scattered haphazard between the "bad times"—and the end oblivion after a final agony!

For man has not long risen a little out of the ageless muck that scientists believe to be his origin. Reckoning in the time of astronomers and geologists, man is a new creature; is yet imperfectly developed, and has not long been able to wonder about certain things that never bothered the heads of his relatives and ancestors, the "lower animals." He is so far from comprehending whence he came and where he is to go that it might fairly be said that such questions have only begun to puzzle him since he learned how to make a fire. But, having made a fire, he straightway made fire his servant; that is to say, he unchained a vast power and used it, but never became

---

Farewell
to an Old Room

By L. M. MONTGOMERY
Author of Anne of Green Gables, Etc.

IN THE gold of sunset bloom
I must leave my old, old room,
Bid good-by and shut the door
Never to repass it more.
Tender things my lips would say
To it ere I go away,
For this room has seemed to be
In itself a friend to me.

Here I knew how sweet was sleep—
Sweeter still to lie in deep
Wakefulness of joy that came
Touched with youth's enchanted flame;
Lovely laughter has been here,
Moonlit dreaming, very dear,
And the waking rapture when
Morn came dancing up the glen.

Here I sought to make me fair,
Looped and coaxed and bound my hair,
Slipped the sheen of kissing silk
Over shoulders white as milk,
Loved myself because I knew,
Seeing, *he* would love me, too,
Waited at this window—so—
For a hurrying step below.

Here have I aforetime lain
Cheek to cheek with biting pain;
Death came here one shuddering day,
Looked on me, but went away;
Good and evil, rest and strife,
All the wonderment of life,
All its lavish pageantry
Here have been a part of me.

So I say good-by with tears
To my room of happy years,
And if she who comes to stay
Here when I have gone away
Be a girl, I leave her, too,
All the fairy dreams I knew,
All my fancies, all the hosts
Of my little friendly ghosts.

May she have, as I have had,
Many things to make her glad,
Beckoning sunshine, singing showers,
Long, serene, contented hours,
Muted wind in boughs of fir,
Nights that will be kind to her,
And a room that still will be
Friend, as it has been to me.

CHRISTMAS.   *By Gertrude A. Kay.*

its master, for the true master of fire must be a law that existed before either fire or man. So, when man built certain fires to serve him, but did not treat them in wise accordance with the law that is the true master of fire, these fires burned his huts and his children; and he sat and lamented, and reproached some gods he had made in his own image; and he said that his luck was bad. Nevertheless, he might as well have thought that here was a hint for him to try to understand the law, and to "accept the universe as it is."

We found out how to make fires, and with fires we made other dangerous servants, using them not only to get us our food and our garments and our dwellings, but to disrupt the mountains that stood in our way and to bear us up in flight upon the whirlwind. We built great cities and made "new diseases" for ourselves thereby; we flew in the air and will fly out of it, some day, to the moon and to the planets; there is no end to what we will to do and shall do. With his frail body, a polyp three-quarters water, bursting and perishing upon the slightest squeezing or puncturing, man rides the hurricane and essays to harness the earthquake. Naturally there are "accidents."

We know that laws govern ourselves and govern those dangerous servants of ours, "the forces of Nature," but we know these laws so little that we are continually changing our minds about them. Every new generation offers a new opinion upon the

old laws, and discovers new laws that will be repealed by a newer generation. And we are still children of the night when we puzzle our heads over that greatest of all questions: Whence come we, Whither go we, and Why? We know nothing—and yet we ride the hurricane!

Misfortunes fall upon us inexplicably, and often with so little warning that they seem to leap treacherously out of blue and promising skies. We find life teaching us to be wary, to be never unready for terrible surprises. Even in the safest of civilizations, when we part with a friend for half an hour we cannot be sure of ever seeing him again. Motor cars and trolley cars move at such speeds that one of them may run him down; an elevator may fall with him; a loosened signboard may crush his head; a killing bit of wire may touch him; a coal-hole may lie open in his way; he may be stifled in a subway tunnel; he may "pick up a germ" on a crowded corner; he may be shot by a bandit running away from the police; he may be suffocated because a janitor has left some rags in a cupboard. We know that all these things happen to other people every day, and we can never know when it may be our friend's "turn" for one of them to happen to him—or our own for one of them to happen to us. We seem to walk perilously among deadly chances; we are, for our own little while, survivors, but survivors always in danger and often in pain.

How, then, can we know any happiness

that is not the happiness of ignorance, the happiness of a dreamer unawakened? Where, anywhere in the wilderness through which humanity straggles, trying vaguely to form itself into an onward-marching brotherhood, is there a token that we may go forward with a little confidence and even be merry, sometimes, with a good understanding as well as a light heart? Was ever a token shown to us on a promise made to us?

He who can truly read the New Testament and honestly say "No" has a mind too vehemently agnostic, I think, to be practical; for the miracle of the token and the promise is in that Book. If Jesus Christ was a god, the miracle is established; and if He was only a man, then it is proved by what He said and did, and by His life and death, that a man can be a god, and the miracle of the token and the promise is none the less established.

So came Christmas into the world, and we keep Christmas rightly by being merry, for Christmas is our remembrance that we have had a sign. In the light of the Christmas stars we know that we do not walk altogether among shadows, and that our happiness can rightfully be more than ignorance. That is why we move the stars indoors to shine from a Tree, and it is why we say to one another

MERRY *Christmas!*

Opposite: BEFORE THE CURTAIN RISES. *By Henry Raleigh.*

ETCHING BY Z. P. NIKOLAKI

THE EDUCATION OF GLORIA

Dorothy Parker

With her delicate precision of utterance, which makes a time-worn adage sound as if it were being said for the first time, Mrs. Tomlinson has always affirmed that it is all in the way one starts. Guided by that admirable precept, she gave her only daughter a send-off in the right direction by naming her Gloria. It was, you see, at that period when the first families were still leaning toward the more fanciful names for their female offspring. Had Gloria deferred her arrival for a decade or so, she would have found that those appellations which once gained favor only in farm circles had come strongly into vogue as being "deliciously quaint," and she would doubtless have gone through life as an Ann, a Jane, a Nancy or an Ellen. As it was, at the time of her advent young mothers showed their knowledge of the fashionable thing by letting themselves go in the selection of poetical names for their

little ones. For quite some while, indeed, Mrs. Tomlinson was rather strongly inclined toward Consuelo; however, there was an appropriately exalted, almost a regal sound about Gloria, which Consuelo was felt to lack. So Gloria was the irrevocable decision.

At seventeen Gloria is, as everyone concedes, a sweet, dear girl. It is virtually impossible to give a more striking word-picture of her than that which is drawn by that single arresting phrase, in which all her social peers sum her up. More, even before she became a sweet, dear girl she was a sweet, dear child. She was congenitally equipped with a restfully uninquiring mind, an amiable submissiveness of spirit, a readily formative point of view. It was as if some generous fairy, acting under the explicit instructions of Gloria's mother, had endowed the infant with those three priceless gifts at her christening.

Certainly, her offspring's pleasing plasticity of temperament has been a great comfort to Mrs. Tomlinson. There never was a child, it is safe to say, who responded any more gratifyingly to her bringing up. Gloria's entire existence is a prolonged credit to her home training; pardonable indeed is the pride which Mrs. Tomlinson takes in the living results of her handiwork. Of course, if one wanted to be that way about it, one might hint that, had Fate directed the stork to deposit Gloria upon some less imposing hearthstone, her almost excessively amenable nature would have rendered her equally susceptible to whatever system she would have there encountered. But that, as Mrs. Tomlinson herself would be among the first to point out, is emphatically neither here nor there. The ever-present fact is that Gloria is the model daughter of a zealous mother. She is the perfect outcome of her mother's ef-

116

ficient methods of twig-bending.

Now that Gloria has been brought practically to the verge of womanhood, Mrs. Tomlinson, while in no way relaxing her vigilance, gives herself over to the cosily restful feeling that she need never have a moment's fear for her daughter's future. There will never be any danger of her developing into one of those frightful democratic women, for which her mother daily returns appropriate thanks to an indulgent Providence; Gloria will never succumb to any current notion to concern herself with community betterment, which would necessitate her mingling almost freely with her inferiors and thus spoiling them completely. Hastily, lest any misinterpretation set in, it must be explained that Mrs. Tomlinson is no rigid reactionary who would insist upon confining her daughter's activities to the home; as she frequently declaims, if she does pride herself upon one thing more than another, it is her broad-mindedness. Certain concessions must be made, she generously admits, to the restlessness of modern times and the craving of the modern woman to take active part in non-domestic affairs. And Mrs. Tomlinson would never let it be implied that her daughter was a moment short of being thoroughly up to date. If Gloria should want to interest herself in a little indirect charitable work, accomplished by means of various festivals to raise money for deserving causes, Mrs. Tomlinson would never be the one to urge against it. Indeed, she would even go so far as to advocate it, provided that there were impressive enough names on the committee in charge.

Any less exclusive interest, Mrs. Tomlinson feels snugly secure, will never hold Gloria's attention. Her early training has given her so firm a foundation as to preclude all danger of possible bourgeois leanings. In fact, the veriest stranger has only to observe Gloria for a few brief moments, even at her present more or less tender age, to be utterly convinced that throughout her lifetime she will never fail unhesitatingly to do the thing that is being done by the best people.

Provided that one were on such intimate terms as to feel free to ask, and also provided that she would unbend sufficiently to reply, Mrs. Tomlinson would doubtless attribute her success in the up-bringing of her daughter to the fact that she has never allowed Gloria to lose sight of the lofty social estate to which it has pleased Heaven to call her. And, indeed, no one is better fitted to impress this upon a plastic mind than is Mrs. Tomlinson. In her rating, it is the one really important thing in life; position, to her way of thinking, is nine-tenths of the law. Her entire life is neatly arranged in accordance with the demands exacted by her social standing. It absorbs her whole attention and requires her unceasing care, just as do all newly acquired and somewhat uncertain possessions.

It is Mrs. Tomlinson's social position, as her friends so well know, which supplies the major part of her repertory of conversational topics. It ranks next to her good breeding as a subject for continuous discourse and self-congratulation. This latter topic she injects into the talk on all occasions, almost as if there were some danger that it might be overlooked were not attention expressly directed to it; it is doubtful, in fact, if anywhere else, outside the cattle countries, the phrase "good breeding" is employed so often as it is in Mrs. Tomlinson's conversation.

So, thanks to her mother's publicity work, Gloria has had every opportunity to realize her inherited place among the elect. She was taught the importance of social position at her mother's knee, and it has for her the sacredness that always surrounds subjects there acquired. In the charming intimacy of mother-and-daughter talks together, Gloria learned that she must always be an aristocrat to the tips of her fingers, and must strive to associate only with those whose aristocracy went to like extents. Yet, it was stressed, it was her duty always to be charitable, and so, should she encounter those with hearts of gold and with safe-deposit vaults heaped with the same pleasant material, she need not set the limit quite so far as the finger tips.

In connection with this same injunction to be always graciously charitable, she must try to be kind to the middle classes—*noblesse oblige*, as her mother concisely put it, for Mrs. Tomlinson has long employed French phrases to convey her more exalted thoughts. Gloria has never forgotten those tender, hushed talks in the rosy glow of the nursery firelight.

It was really surprising to see how quickly Gloria learned, even as a tiny child. There were times, positively, when her mother feared that her intelligence was almost abnormal, and thought seriously of asking the doctor if she were not in need of a good, strengthening tonic with plenty of iron in it. It was in her powers of observation that she was so precocious.

At an amazingly early age she could distinguish, in a single glance at the frocks worn by her little playmates, which were trimmed with real lace and which boasted either base imitation or—what her sharp little brain even then decided to be worse—no lace at all. It was as if, in her infant mind, she graded her tiny comrades accordingly. It was pretty to see how happily she played with those of the first class; how cunningly she ordered about the members of the second group; how contentedly she played alone, rather than join in the diversions of what might have been called Grade C. It was on such occasions as these that Mrs. Tomlinson, although understandably worried that the little one's intellect was over-developed, felt her heart swell with loving pride and knew that in her child she lived again.

It was remarkable how Gloria escaped those unfortunate affiliations which so often mar an otherwise impeccable childhood. There are few of us who have not, buried away in our dark pasts, the memory of some juvenile friendship with the neighboring janitor's child, some devoted affection for the progeny of the local tradespeople. Gloria widely averted all such associations. Chicken pox did not pass her by, and measles claimed her for its own, but from democracy, that far more insidious ailment of childhood, she was utterly immune. Obediently she would cleave only to the playfellows whom her mother classed under the narrow heading of "really nice children." At dancing school, for instance, Gloria bestowed her dances only upon those little boys who came in their father's automobiles. Prospective partners who walked from their homes or who arrived *via* the street car, even though they might be much smoother dancers and have far more dashingly mischievous personalities, would almost invariably find that Gloria's dances were otherwise disposed of. Mrs. Tomlinson would sit in state in the space reserved for admiring mothers, with her manner which made a throne of any chair she chanced to occupy, and beam indulgently upon this childish by-play.

Undoubtedly, a leading factor in Gloria's training has been that perhaps greatest of educational forces, example. She has had her mother ever before her, a self-confessed pattern of the more exclusive virtues. Gloria had but to observe and then to imitate and, as you might say, there she was.

Think, for instance, of the indelible effect upon her mind of that living lesson in correct deportment toward the large portion of humanity rated by her mother as socially beneath her. Mrs. Tomlinson has long been passionately absorbed in the welfare of the lower classes; there are times, really, when those close to her almost fear that her unceasing solicitude for the masses —with which generous word she sweepingly covers all servants, sales persons, tradespeople, and employees in general—will wear her out. One has only to overhear the briefest excerpt from her conversation to realize how deep is her concern for them. It is not too much to say that her life is spent in the constant dread that they may be spoiled; that, carried away by some ill-advised leniency on the part of their betters, they may forget their lowly station and even lose their fitting servility of demeanor. Mrs. Tomlinson early felt the call to combat this; she has consecrated the major part of her existence to the end of keeping the lower classes in their proper place.

Such devotion to an espoused cause requires, of course, incessant activity, but Mrs. Tomlinson gives it ungrudgingly. It is her consuming interest, almost her hobby; when she speaks of it her voice soars free above the forgotten fetters of gentle modulation, and the red surges surprisingly to her patricianly pallid countenance, even, in fact, to her statuesque neck and aristocratically set ears. In her excitement she frequently overlooks chances to work in her favorite *"noblesse oblige,"* although the subject presents admirable opportunities for its display.

Naturally, she has drilled her only daughter not only to assist her in this mighty work but to carry it pluckily on after Mrs. Tomlinson has passed impressively over into that section of the Great Beyond which is reserved for the most exclusive people.

And Gloria has proved a singularly able recruit to the cause. From her earliest years she showed herself to be exceptionally happy at reproducing her mother's attitude toward social inferiors. The true precocity of this feat of impersonation can be appreciated only when one comprehends the lavish scale on which it had to be performed; for, it must be understood, under the general term of inferiors Mrs. Tomlinson lists practically the entire known population of the globe. She excepts only those fortunate few whom, on the score of birth, breeding, or bank account, she can conscientiously claim as equals.

It would indeed be a lesson to the lax to observe the ceaseless care with which Mrs. Tomlinson has labored to keep her only child from contact with any save those few. It would almost seem as if she feared that Gloria's bloom of aristocracy was so delicate that it could not be guaranteed not to rub off in mingling with coarser beings. But, in this imperfect world, it is impossible for things to work out without ever a hitch; into each life, as one of the more heavily bearded poets has so adroitly worded it, some rain must fall. There have been times when, despite every care, Gloria has been hurled into the very midst of the *bourgeoisie*, to use one of her mother's milder names for them. The family motors have been out of commission, the more plebeian taxicabs have obstinately refused to answer to call, in short, a malicious fate has expressly arranged things so that Gloria has been forced to employ a common street car.

But her deportment, even in such a trying position, has been one hundred per cent patrician. Packed in though she may be with as many of the masses as the car will hold, her bearing is a testimonial to her upbringing. The casual observer, doubtless, would gather that she was giving an impersonation of Marie Antoinette on her way to the guillotine; but it is really nothing so far-fetched as that. It is simply faithful emulation of her mother's demeanor in similar circumstances.

With like care has Gloria followed her mother's formula in direct dealings with inferiors. When compelled to meet those of whose social standing she is by no means sure, she accurately copies Mrs. Tomlinson's wearily aloof inattention; when addressing servants or shop girls, she gives an admirable imitation of her mother's gracious patronage, yet commanding power, the exquisitely balanced medium between the manner of a Lady Bountiful toward her protégés and that of a lion tamer toward his charges. The impression which Gloria has so early made by the use of these methods is but additional proof of the perfection of her working model.

From her mother Gloria has picked up a neat turn of phrase which lends her conversation that individuality so much to be desired. Mrs. Tomlinson has a way of making the fortunate words that she employs signify much more than they do in vulgar usage. The word "nobody," for example—she has invested that noun with a meaning almost entirely the opposite of what it has heretofore conveyed. With her, it has come to be synonymous with "anybody"—anybody, that is, of no social importance, for there is that stigma attached to the word as she uses it. To hear the lofty contempt with which she scathingly disposes of some unfortunate as "a nobody" is to realize that to the fullest.

Oddly enough, the word "everybody," as employed by Mrs. Tomlinson, has a whimsically reversed meaning. When she speaks of what "everybody" says, where "everybody" goes, what "everybody" wears, she refers to the exclusive little band of her peers. These two common nouns, although her use of them renders them anything but common, appear with almost monotonous frequency in Mrs. Tomlinson's discourse; with their aid she classifies the whole world. One would say, having once heard Mrs. Tomlinson utter the words, that no one else could do them equal justice. But one's opinion would soon change on hearing Gloria use them, for she can invest them with equal meaning and apply them just as unerringly.

Of course the most important part of Gloria's education has been the home influence. But Mrs. Tomlinson is too efficient a mother not to realize the importance of correct scholastic training, and her daughter has enjoyed the inestimable privilege of an impeccable school life. In her extreme youth Gloria attended a neighboring school, presided over by an austere and highly unmarried personage, last remnant of an aristocratic family whose fortune had, unfortunately, petered out shortly before her advent.

The attendance at this institution was limited to a selectly small number of miniature ladies and gentlemen, and Mrs. Tomlinson had always the soothing assurance that daily, from nine-thirty until one o'clock, her offspring was absorbing learn-

Drawing by
Hanna Klingbers

ing of the most exclusive little seekers after knowledge. The *grande dame* who ruled the school was firm, almost fanatic, in her belief that the youthful mind should not be overtaxed, and she carried out this admirable idea to an extraordinarily successful degree. In her several years at this academy Gloria acquired a firm foundation in the three r's—reading, 'riting and rhythmic dancing.

The finishing touches to her daughter's education Mrs. Tomlinson regarded as so important, so vital, really, that she planned for them years in advance. Scarcely had she heard the welcome words "It's a girl" before she was making arrangements to enter the infant's name upon the waiting list of a most exclusive finishing school, one attended solely by the daughters of the best, or, at any rate, the most affluent, families. This is one of the features that adds so much to the school's prestige—this ceremony of entering the would-be pupil's name as shortly after birth as possible, if she hopes to round out her education there.

So at this school Gloria, at seventeen, is being finished—which is putting it mildly. It has proved satisfactory in every way to her mother; she has never needed to worry lest Gloria, during these impressionable years, should fall under the influence of upstart associates. Gloria's schoolmates are all surprisingly like herself, all the progeny of mothers surprisingly like Mrs. Tomlinson, although, of course, this last must be a mere surface resemblance, for it does not seem quite plausible that other mothers are so highly efficient.

At any rate, Mrs. Tomlinson concedes that the process of finishing Gloria is going along spendidly. With her graduation only one short year away Gloria would have to work out twelve times seven for you with a pencil and paper, and she is almost touchingly open to suggestion as to whom the war of 1812 was with; but she has had an unparalleled opportunity to make firm friends of the most important of the girls in her class, and she has assured her inclusion in all their future social activities. And that, as Mrs. Tomlinson says, is the main thing.

There are those less-accomplished mothers who are sometimes tormented with the fear that their daughters may make unfortunate marriages. But no such distressing thoughts crash in upon the placid meditations of Mrs. Tomlinson. She knows that with the perfectly trained Gloria nothing can go wrong. Other girls, who have not had the advantage of such careful upbringing, may marry socially obscure or even poor young men, with some hysterical notion of making their way together; but not so a girl of Gloria's high ideals. When the right time comes—and it is fairly safe to say that Mrs. Tomlinson will be the judge of that—Mrs. Tomlinson knows that she can trust her own little Gloria to follow the dictates of her mother's heart.

Indeed sometimes, in the poppy-laden quiet of the twilight, Mrs. Tomlinson dreams proud dreams of one day starting Gloria's little ones in the right direction, just as she started her own daughter.

For, as she so often affirms, it is all in the way that one starts.

Miss Billie Burke

HOW THE ROCKEFELLERS GIVE MILLIONS

M. A. DeWolfe Howe

It was not until the industrial development following the Civil War got into its full swing that vast fortunes began to accumulate in private hands, and individuals had to ask themselves what in the world they could do with their embarrassing riches.

Even before the time of Mr. John D. Rockefeller, Sr., others must have found themselves in the dilemma he recognized when he wrote: "These rich men we read about in the newspapers cannot get personal returns beyond a well-defined limit for their expenditures. They cannot gratify the pleasures of the palate beyond very moderate bounds, since they cannot purchase a good digestion; they cannot lavish very much money on fine raiment for themselves or their families without suffering from public ridicule; and in their homes they cannot go much beyond the comforts of the less wealthy without involving them in more pain than pleasure. As I study wealthy men, I can see but one way in which they can secure a real equivalent for money spent, and that is to cultivate a taste for giving where the money may produce an effect which will be a lasting gratification."

In a book, Random Reminiscences of Men and Events, which the older John D. Rockefeller published in 1909, he devotes one chapter to The Difficult Art of Getting, and another to The Difficult Art of Giving. He is an authority on both of these arts, and there is nothing to suggest that he regards one as more difficult than the other. The precedents for going wrong in the art of giving are many in number.

In America the wise Ben Franklin created what seemed in his lifetime a generous and well-devised fund for the benefit of apprentices a century later–when apprentices had ceased to exist. A mayor of St. Louis in 1857 willed a considerable sum, now, in 1925, nearly a million dollars, to the relief of "worthy and distressed travelers and emigrants" on their way to establish bona fide homes in the West. It never occurred to him that St. Louis would change from a terminus to a way station. And in Pennsylvania there was the woman who left an estate and one hundred thousand dollars "to establish a home for superannuated Presbyterian clergymen above the age of seventy who do not use tobacco." It was held at first that the wives of these blameless gentlemen could not be admitted to the home, but when its occupants dwindled to one a court ruling lifted the embargo on both wives and weed. It is no wonder that public sentiment in recent

years has favored the extension of the Community Trust idea, embodied only a little more than ten years ago in the Cleveland Foundation and already operative in about fifty American cities, under a carefully devised plan for devoting the income from benevolent trusts to the changing needs of mankind. But that is a different story from that of the largest foundations established by individuals.

In these the penalties of going wrong are even more serious than in the disposition of moderate fortunes. Because Mr. Rockefeller has justified his faith that "the same energy and thought should be expended in the proper and effective use of money when acquired as was exerted in the earning of it," because he has seen the realization of the hope he has "always indulged . . . that during my life I should be able to help establish efficiency in giving so that wealth may be of greater use to the present and future generations," his work in these directions is chosen for special scrutiny. He and his son are today the chief exponents of the "difficult art" of applying the highest intelligence to the useful expenditure of wealth almost unlimited.

Nobody ever listened himself out of a job.   CALVIN COOLIDGE

Born in Richford, Tioga County, New York, July 8, 1839, John D. Rockefeller was primarily fortunate in his parents. His father, William Avery Rockefeller, of Huguenot and Yankee descent, was a physician and business man of energy, thrift and piety. His mother, Eliza Davison Rockefeller, combined a strong religious faith with a stern sense of discipline.

When he was fourteen the family moved to Cleveland, and the boy began to keep a little account book, now proudly preserved and designated "Ledger A." It records his first meager earnings of fifty dollars for three months of service at the end of 1855 as an assistant bookkeeper in a forwarding and commission house, and an advance to twenty-five dollars a month at the beginning of 1856. Then in a year came an annual salary of five hundred dollars followed by an offer of seven hundred dollars, which the young clerk refused because he thought he was worth eight. But he had already begun to save, and through borrowing a thousand dollars from his father at the current rate of 10 per cent was able to join in 1858 with a young Englishman, Morris

B. Clark, in establishing the commission house of Clark and Rockefeller.

But Ledger A is as significant on the giving as on the getting side. It shows, for example, the systematic giving of one cent a week to the Sunday school in the days of the scantiest income. In the five months from November, 1855, to April, 1856, it appears that young Rockefeller gave away in all five dollars and fifty-eight cents. When he was nearing sixty he summarized these revelations of Ledger A in saying: "In one month I gave to foreign missions, ten cents; to the Mite Society, fifty cents, and there is also a contribution to the Five Points Mission. I was not living then in New York, but I suppose that I felt that it was in need of help. Then to the venerable teacher of my class I gave thirty-five cents to make him a present. To the poor people of the church I gave ten cents at this time, and in January and February following I gave ten cents more, and a further ten cents to the foreign mission."

These items would be quite unimportant but for their illustration of a principle stated by Mr. Rockefeller himself: "It is a mistake for a man who wishes for happiness and to help others to think that he will wait until he has a fortune before giving away money to deserving objects." Another article of his creed appears in the same discussion of Ledger A: "I believe it is a religious duty to get all the money you can, fairly and honestly; to keep all you can, and to give away all you can."

This identification of religious and financial duty is illustrated by the fact that when Mr. Rockefeller describes the part he bore in collecting funds to pay off the mortgage on a Baptist mission church in Cleveland, at about the time of his election at seventeen or eighteen as one of its trustees, he declares: "My first ambition to earn more money was aroused by this and similar undertakings in which I was constantly engaged." Nor was his work for his church by any means confined to money raising. For many years—the very years in which he was building up his fortune—he served as superintendent of the Sunday school of the Euclid Avenue Baptist Church. It was a Cleveland friend and neighbor who wrote of him at this time: "From the first he has won the love of the children by his sympathy, kindness, and his interest in their welfare. No picnic ever would be satisfactory to them without his presence."

The image of the Standard Oil Company, uniting in 1870 the oil interests with which Mr. Rockefeller began to identify himself in 1865, and grown at the beginning of the present century to an unexampled stature of wealth and power, was still the image of a ruthless monster, bitted and reined by an equally ruthless man. In a world of competition neither man nor organization can become supremely successful without leaving beside the pathway of advance a broken line of defeated figures, suffering from wrongs either real or imaginary, or both.

John D. Rockefeller, Sr., is today, in 1925, in his eighty-sixth year, John D. Rockefeller, Jr., in his fifty-second. It is a new world in which the younger man has grown up. If the older has come to look on many things in a new light, that is the light to which the changes in social, industrial and religious conditions in America have accustomed the younger man ever since he began to assume his enormous responsibilities. In the form of wealth and of the powers, excellent or tyrannous, which it enables its possessor to exercise, these responsibilities now rest primarily upon him. He has been called "a new kind of millionaire," and the definition is apt, for, finding himself in control of resources which from their very abundance attach to the word "money" an entirely unfamiliar meaning, he has made it his chief concern to see that they shall be used to the greatest possible advantage of his fellow creatures.

The new world in which he is living is notorious for the chasm between the older and younger generations. Many of the old sanctions and safeguards of existence are believed to have disappeared. The spectacle of the Rockefellers, father and son, contradicts this belief. The essentials of a strong religious faith, with the Christian grace of giving at its core, have obviously been transmitted from the one to the other. They have both been Sunday-school teachers, to the confusion of those with a different standard of relative values; they have both made incalculable contributions to the development of American industry. The one instituted, the other is actively concerned with the benevolent trusts that bear their name.

Until the full personal story can be told the development of the present scheme for distributing vast and steadily increasing funds cannot be followed in detail. Certain principles, however, became clear to Mr. Rockefeller and his advisers as early as the eighties. Among them were the careful preliminary study of the object to be helped, that there may be no doubt of its worthiness; the giving of a portion rather than the whole of the sum desired, that others may be stimulated to a contributory and continuing interest in it; and the policy, after giving to an object of proved value, of trusting the expenditure of the sums so bestowed entirely to those who are responsible for the institution or cause that has been helped.

Another important point of policy has been the avoidance of objects, social, political, religious, of which the influence upon the public is in any way open to question. The causes of general education and health are obviously causes from which an entire people may expect to profit. Yet, says the Annual Report of the Rockefeller Founda-

tion for 1917, there are things which a foundation "cannot successfully or wisely do; such as, for example, give money to make loans to individuals, or invest in securities which have a philanthropic rather than a business basis, or assist in securing patents, or aid altruistic movements which involve private profit. It must also refrain from supporting propaganda which seek to influence public opinion about the social order and political proposals, however disinterested and important these may be."

The Rockefeller Institute for Medical Research, founded in 1901, was the first of the existing bodies to be organized. Its purposes, as defined in its charter from the state of New York, is "to conduct, assist, and encourage investigations in the sciences and arts of hygiene, medicine, and surgery, and allied subjects, in the nature

and causes of disease and the methods of its prevention and to make knowledge relating to these various treatments, and subjects available for the protection of the health of the public and the improved treatment of disease and injury."

Mr. Rockefeller first committed himself to it only to the extent of pledging two hundred thousand dollars, payable in ten annual installments. With no more definite assurance than this, the men of science who began to work at the Institute bore notable witness in so doing to their faith in its pur-

JOHN D. ROCKEFELLER—*by John Singer Sargent.*

poses. As time went on Mr. Rockefeller steadily enlarged the resources of the Institute, so that it now occupies spacious laboratory and hospital buildings of its own, overlooking the East River in New York City, and has established a Department of Animal Pathology in laboratory and animal buildings at Princeton.

A year after the establishment of the Rockefeller Institute for Medical Research the General Education Board was planned. Incorporated by an Act of Congress on January 19, 1903, it took for its object "the promotion of education within the United States, without distinction of race, sex, or creed," and was authorized to pursue these ends by a great variety of means.

Mr. Rockefeller's first gift to the endowment—ten million dollars—was to support an inquiry into the educational needs of the Southern people. It is significant that the Board recognized the need of a better economic condition in the South before it would be possible to support an adequate school system, as it should be supported, by local taxation. Accordingly an educational campaign of farm demonstrations was undertaken, and state, national and county authorities have coöpeiated in it to the advantage of large agricultural districts. Successive gifts of Mr. Rockefeller to the Board have brought its resources to nearly one hundred and thirty million dollars.

When Mr. Rockefeller gave some twenty million to the Board in 1919 for the advancement of medical education his words about it were, "the income to be used currently and the principal to be expended within the next fifty years." Of itself the Board has said: "In due time, its objects will have been achieved; and problems will have emerged. The General Education Board will then have ceased to exist. The statesmen and benefactors of the next age will invent the organizations and provide the means then requisite."

Without waiting for the next age to arrive, it became evident in a little more than ten years that, beyond advanced researches in the field of medical science and beyond the furthering of education in America only, there were important objects which could be helped in accordance with the general Rockefeller plan of assistance. To the Rockefeller Institute for Medical Research and the General Education Board a new organization was added—The Rockefeller Foundation chartered under the laws of the State of New York, May 14, 1913, "to promote the well-being of mankind throughout the world." Within about a year Mr. Rockefeller had placed in the hands of its trustees the sum of one hundred million dollars, since increased to approximately one hundred and sixty-five million.

At first a few obligations were imposed by Mr. Rockefeller, but in 1919 he removed them all so that the trustees are now entirely free to expend both principal and interest as they wish. At first the appropriations were somewhat miscellaneous in character, as on behalf of the Interstate Palisades Park on the Hudson and the National Bird Sanctuary in Louisiana. The advantage of such flexibility appeared especially in wartime, when, beginning with Belgian relief, the Foundation appropriated over twenty-two million dollars for the alleviation of human suffering, due to the war, in Europe.

About each department an astonishing tale of performance could be told.

The International Health Board, which in 1915 took over the work begun five years before by the Rockefeller Sanitary Commission for the Eradication of Hookworm, has made a world-wide extension of its effort to demonstrate the possibility of vast economic and educational progress simply by conquering a disease which has rendered whole peoples backward. This work is now carried forward by local and national authorities.

The China Medical Board is maintaining, to name but one of its many undertakings, the Peking Union Medical College, in which the effort to bring from the West to the East the best results of medical science, is most highly exemplified. The Division of Medical Education, besides forwarding higher medical studies in the United States, has carried the work to Canada, Brazil and also to Europe, especially in London, Edinburgh, Oxford, Cambridge and Brussels. The International Health Board of the Foundation has helped to create or strengthen Schools of Public Health at Johns Hopkins, Harvard, the University of Toronto and in London. The millions applied to these objects have been matched by other millions expended in all parts of the world.

Nor is this list of Rockefeller benefactions yet complete. In memory of Mrs. John D. Rockefeller, who died in 1915 after a lifetime of intense sympathy with her husband's philanthropic enterprises, especially on behalf of the South and the negro race, the Laura Spelman Rockefeller Memorial was established in 1918, with a fund of approximately seventy-five million dollars. In 1912 the Bureau of Social Hygiene for "the study, amelioration and prevention of those social conditions, crimes and diseases which adversely affect the well-being of society," was established by Mr. John D. Rockefeller, Jr. And in 1923 the International Education Board was founded by this inheritor of the traditions and impulses of both his parents.

It is a new thing in the world to give more than half a billion dollars from a single fortune to objects in which its possessors believe. It is a new thing to put into the processes of giving the thought which has gone into the distribution of millions of income from the "benevolent trusts" which bear the Rockefeller name. These things are of a significance which matches their newness.

And as these are all new things, so are they distinctively American things. What governments and public subscriptions have done abroad—as in the establishment of the Pasteur Institute in Paris—individuals of great wealth have had the humanitarian and civic spirit to do in the United States.

Not for any pride of leadership, but to serve mankind throughout the world, America is now confronted as never before with the opportunity to add to the sum of human happiness by extending the boundaries of human knowledge and by quickening the human spirit.

Such agencies as the Rockefeller endowments are already contributing, directly and indirectly, to this end. Indirectly they are doing much more—in demonstrating to men and women of wealth that, when their own immediate needs and those of their families are met, there are the needs of mankind to be considered, and that in meeting them the deepest incentives and rewards for success are to be found. The Rockefellers have not worn their hearts on their sleeves for all to read their inmost promptings. But there are many and valid tokens that what they have demonstrated is what they have lived—and it is of good omen that a democracy has been the scene of it all.

From THE WOODLAND SCHOOL *by Harrison Cady.*

Paris Says Straight Coats

And Decrees Odd Sleeves in Frocks

From Drecoll's fall and winter opening comes the coat of brown duvetyn, trimmed with marmot, which has been sketched at the extreme left below. The slightly circular flounce set on at a very low waistline is a new thought in construction, which has been used also on some of this season's capes. In this instance the flounce flares over a band of marmot which edges the bottom of the coat. The Suzanne Talbot hat is of dull red velvet with black beads.

Reversible wraps have appealed strongly to Parisian fancy, and the reason is quite clear when one considers the delightful Molyneux cape, sketched second from the left below. Ermine, or white rabbit, is combined with seal for the side which is shown; the reverse is of black broadcloth, with a collar of ermine and seal rosettes just like the band about the cape.

By trimming gray wool corduroy with dyed gray rabbit, as sketched at the left, Drecoll obtains a coat that is noticeably smart and at the same time is wearable. The tam-o'-shanter turban with its coque pompon is of putty-colored velvet—velvet being as good for hats this winter as for frocks. Suzanne Talbot is the designer. Three-piece suits, with the coats of seven-eighths length, still lead in favor for matrons' wear. At the left, Renée tops the simplest of soft, supple, black-cloth chemise dresses with a coat of matching cloth trimmed with monkey fur. Placing the fur band slightly above the hem and having it extend only across the front of the coat gives the apron effect, which is so much to be desired this winter. The good-looking hat is of black felt cloth. Peach-colored poplin is the medium chosen by Madeleine, the designer of Drecoll's, to illustrate the charm of the new waistline in the afternoon frock at the left above. It is made over a brown duvetyn underskirt which blends smartly with the deep band of beaver edging the circular overskirt and serves to emphasize the new slanting line of the waist. Of interest also are the oddly shaped sleeves.

Lanvin uses most effectively black jet embroidery on white crêpe, as sketched in the center above. The skirt overlaps on the left side and a band of embroidery runs halfway to the waist. All of Lanvin's collection showed the influence of Italy and the moyen âge. As in this case, embroidery, even on the most modern of frocks, suggests the medieval and ecclesiastical. By dropping the shoulder line, and then filling in about the neck with the jet embroidery, she gives the off-shoulder effect that is so good this season, yet obtains a frock that is entirely appropriate for afternoon wear. Many of the new topcoats have the absolutely straight lines of the green gaberdine sketched directly above. Worth, who is the designer, makes the collar and cuffs of beaver and combines tan and green silk with gold metal thread in the embroidery. The delightful hat was made by Lanvin of black satin with a roll of metal brocade embroidered in jet.

Torre-Bevans

INTERPRETATIONS

Anna Pavlova

My life's ambition crystallized when I was somewhere between five and six years old. One day my mother took me, as a special holiday treat—Christmas, it was, if I remember rightly—to a performance of the imperial ballet in Petrograd. That day Brianza, then ballerina of the imperial ballet, danced the Sleeping Beauty by Tschaikovsky. I was entranced. The unfolding of this familiar tale by the ballet was fairy stuff indeed, doings possible only to elfin people. Brianza was a graceful, exquisite magnet for my eyes. They followed her unblinking.

At the conclusion of the ballet I turned to my mother and announced with calm intenseness, "Some day I shall be Brianza. I am going to dance like that."

My mother stared down a moment, startled, at the audacious scrap clutching her hand, and then laughed good-naturedly and promptly forgot the whole matter.

But I did not forget. The memory of that lovely, lovely princess seethed and bubbled in my mind until it brewed a pretty determination. I was going to be the ballerina of the imperial ballet. If one was the ballerina, then for a brief hour one might be the lovely princess. It was a reward not lightly to be scoffed at. It never entered my mind that there were easier goals to gain than that of the principal dancer of the imperial ballet. For me it was the lovely princess or nothing. As well break my neck leaping to the stars as live safely, cloddishly, stepping over a broomstick.

So at nine years I began my campaign. I quietly announced my intention of attending the Imperial School of Dancing. No one was unduly exercised or even seemed to hear me. But when I found dignified statement of fact had no effect, I resorted to violent methods. I teased, I tormented, I begged. I loosed storms of tears, tantrums and temper upon a harassed household. I laid siege to my mother's resistance and vanquished it, and at ten years of age I entered the Imperial School of Dancing. I remained there seven years, the allotted term of training demanded of our dancers, and then became automatically a member of the imperial ballet.

In order to understand the Imperial School one must know something of its tradition. There is a belief among some people that the quality, the excellence of Russian dancing is due to the fact that it is Russian; that only to the Russian is given the true genius of the dance. I am often asked to confirm this opinion. And that of course is impossible.

Russian dancing as we know it today, that particular interpretative style conceived, born and developed in the Imperial School at Petrograd, is not basically Russian; it is French. A strongly Russianized, acclimatized French, I admit, but still French.

About one hundred and fifty years ago the Empress Elizabeth, daughter of Peter the Great, having already sponsored Italian opera and French drama in Russia, looked about for another muse to subsidize. Her generosity pounced upon the dance. And the result was a permanent school for dancing in Russia, the Imperial School.

The first step taken by this great patroness of the arts toward establishing the Imperial Conservatory was to request the French Government to send her someone able to help her in the foundation of such a school. They dealt more than well with her and sent her the great Didelot. Being very sane and practical and wise in art patronage she gave him carte blanche. With unlimited funds, power and influence as his henchmen, and without hindrance from a patroness' whims or caprices, Didelot planned and inaugurated his school.

Thus, in truth, the Imperial School as it was founded by Didelot at the behest of the Empress Elizabeth was nothing more or less than a French school housed in Russia. But French it did not remain. The Russian temperament quickly absorbed the Latin, nationalized it, colored it with the Slavic emotionalism, until in the end Didelot's school was uniquely and completely Russian.

Didelot was dictator of the Imperial School for many, many years. At length his extreme age made his responsibilities too great a burden, and he called from France another compatriot, Saint Leon, and appointed him director of the institution founded by the Empress Elizabeth. Saint Leon ruled the school according to the precepts of his predecessor for fifty years. Then came M. Petipa, my master, who conscientiously built upon the foundation of Didelot and Saint Leon. Thus for almost one hundred and fifty years three men, whose views, theory and practice were identical, molded the Ballet Russe. Is it at all remarkable that they built up a tradition that became as inviolable as the law of the Medes and Persians? To their glory be it said that that tradition was no stupid, pedantic thing, but a fine welding of the brightness, the delicate deftness, the vivacity of the French to the passion, the melancholy and the emotionalism of the Russian.

Then, too, it was an outrageously flexible tradition. M. Petipa was never known to teach its doctrines twice in exactly the same way. I studied with him every day for seven years, and coached with him at intervals for years after that, and never once did he repeat himself in a lesson. Basically he adhered to formula; that, naturally, was inescapable; that was tradition. For example, during my study of Giselle he explained to me in elaborate detail just how Taglioni, who was ballerina of the imperial ballet about 1830 and one of his first pupils, danced it. Here was a handing down of tradition indeed!

But subtly, in those fine points that really make the interpretation, my eighty-five-year-old master, as keen and quick and despotic as the day he took the reins from Saint Leon, flung tradition to the bleak Russian winds. The interpretation of Giselle that I fashioned under his tutelage was as remote from the one he built with Taglioni more than half a century before as the earth is from the stars.

This illimitable variability of interpretation in the dance is, incidentally, one of its greatest joys and dangers. The musician has

Anna Pavlova in "Dragonfly."

notes, the actor has words, the dancer—a mood. The music student, even under the instruction of a charlatan, has at least the accuracy of the page of music to guide him. The embryo thespian has his definite lines to speak; some sense, some honest substance, despite wrong teaching or his own shortcomings, must come of his work. But the dancer! A little exaggeration, a trivial lack of coördination in the muscles, and you have a clown, a scarecrow, a grotesquerie. And the ballet master is responsible always! It rests with him whether you will be a dancer of beauty and a joy forever, or an automaton at whose cavortings the gods shall hold their sides and laugh. And to M. Petipa and the Imperial School I make grateful obeisance that I am—Pavlova.

I learned my art under as nearly perfect conditions as are ever found on this earth. The Russian ballet owes its subtle perfection of detail, its greatness, its rank to the fact that it is made up of dancers who from the day they went to live in the dormitories of the Imperial School saw nothing—were surrounded by nothing—but beauty—beauty!—and the highest standards physically, morally, mentally and spiritually.

From the very hour of my ninth year that my mother gave me into the keeping of the Imperial School to the time I began my world wanderings I never saw a badly painted, cheap or stupid picture; I never read an ill written, tawdry or trashy book; I never saw acting that was not of the finest; I never attended an ill-made play or a badly sung opera; I never ate a badly cooked or ill-chosen meal; I never slept in a poorly ventilated room; I neither worked nor played too long; I never witnessed gross manners, heard vicious talk or was threatened, bullied or cowed after the usual adult fashion. My general education, from mathematics and languages to science, came to me from the finest teachers procurable. The special training in dancing was in the hands of M. Petipa and his associates.

Neither religiously was I neglected. Those who are accustomed to thinking that all of us of the world of mimes are moral pagans, learn with amazement of a quaint little chapel that was an integral part of the Imperial School. There, every Saturday and Sunday morning, I went reverently with my comrades and learned the gospel according to the Orthodox Church.

With such strict training it was impossible for the students at the Imperial School to take life other than reverently. The greatest simplicity, the most old-fashioned ideals were instilled into us. Kindliness and goodness surrounded us. Many of the artists intermarried, until the school became actually almost one family. And we married for keeps. The years that I have been Victor Dandre's wife will attest to that. Scandal the hall mark, and newspaper notoriety the accolade of the artist, were unknown to us.

Until I left Russia on the first of my tours, I never dreamed that in the public mind the life of an artist is usually put down as synonymous with a life of personal degradation. It seemed unbelievable to me, like some ghastly joke, that when people encountered in my travels spoke of a girl becoming a dancer, they used the same tone they would have whispered of her entrance into the oldest profession in the world. At the imperial conservatory we were as guarded, as cherished, as protected, as any child trained in a convent. And amazing as it may seem, when the gay, colorful, ecstatic nature of our profession is considered, there was a severity, a simplicity about our daily thought and living that was almost Quakerish. We were taught that we were dedicated to art, body, mind and soul; we grew up with the conviction that art was very close to God and therefore very

sacred; and for us to commit any act that would degrade or defile that art would have been as much profanation to us as to have gone marauding in a sanctuary.

Along with the most careful mental, spiritual and artistic training, we fortunate inmates of the imperial conservatory received the finest medical attention. No child was permitted to get up on the toes until it was known that his little ankles and legs were strong enough and ready. After I had been in the imperial conservatory about two years I began to be used in such imperial ballets or operas as required children. One of the tremendous events in my life at this time was when I assumed the role of a lotus bud at a most elaborate entertainment given by the czar in honor of the kaiser at Peterhof, the royal palace outside of Petrograd which was built by Catherine the Great. That the Russian court was the most luxurious of the modern world was legend, but this fête, given by the czar for his German cousin, was my first complete view of how thoroughly gorgeous this court could be.

Upon the completion of the allotted seven years of my study at the imperial conservatory I became, automatically, a member of the imperial ballet.

Like an army, the imperial ballet had its rank and file and its leaders. At first one was merely among the corps de ballet present. One was a leaf or a bud or a flower petal fluttering or swaying or drifting about the stage with dozens of one's kind, as the occasion demanded.

Then, if one fluttered or swayed or drifted diligently enough, the czar, at the recommendation of the director of the imperial theater, promoted one from the ranks. The ecstasy of that moment when a dancer ceased to be atmosphere and became an individual! The feeling of delicious importance that dizzied one as one stepped forward from one's fellows to do one's special bit—for the first time!

After about three years of graded promotions, one becomes a coryphee or leader of the ballet. And then, in due course of time, if the gods are kind and the director a man of discernment (!), one reaches the last honor, the final glory. One becomes a ballerina. That is the usual procedure. However, I had never been a stickler for customs, so instead of waiting meekly three years to become a coryphee, I routed precedent and promotions and became a ballerina in two. It saved so much time!

After I had been ballerina three years, I made my first tour. This was also the first exodus of a ballerina from her home land in the history of the imperial ballet. Hitherto the ballet had been regarded as entertainers extraordinary and exclusively of the Russian nobility, and as such were not to be contaminated by contact with alien people and ways.

In consequence, no one outside of Russia knew anything of Russian dancing or even of its existence, with the exception of those few who occasionally visited Moscow and Petrograd. When our tour was first suggested, it met a terrible thundering of disapproval. But the clamor was stilled by some secret and adroit diplomacy, and permission was given us to undertake the pilgrimage.

QUEEN MARY
by
Sir William Llewellyn R. A.

This beautiful portrait of Queen Mary was painted for the United Service Club in London by Sir William Llewellyn, R. A. The Queen immediately pronounced it her favorite of all the many portraits of her and had a copy of it made which now hangs in Buckingham Palace.

KEWPIEVILLE

Rose O'Neill

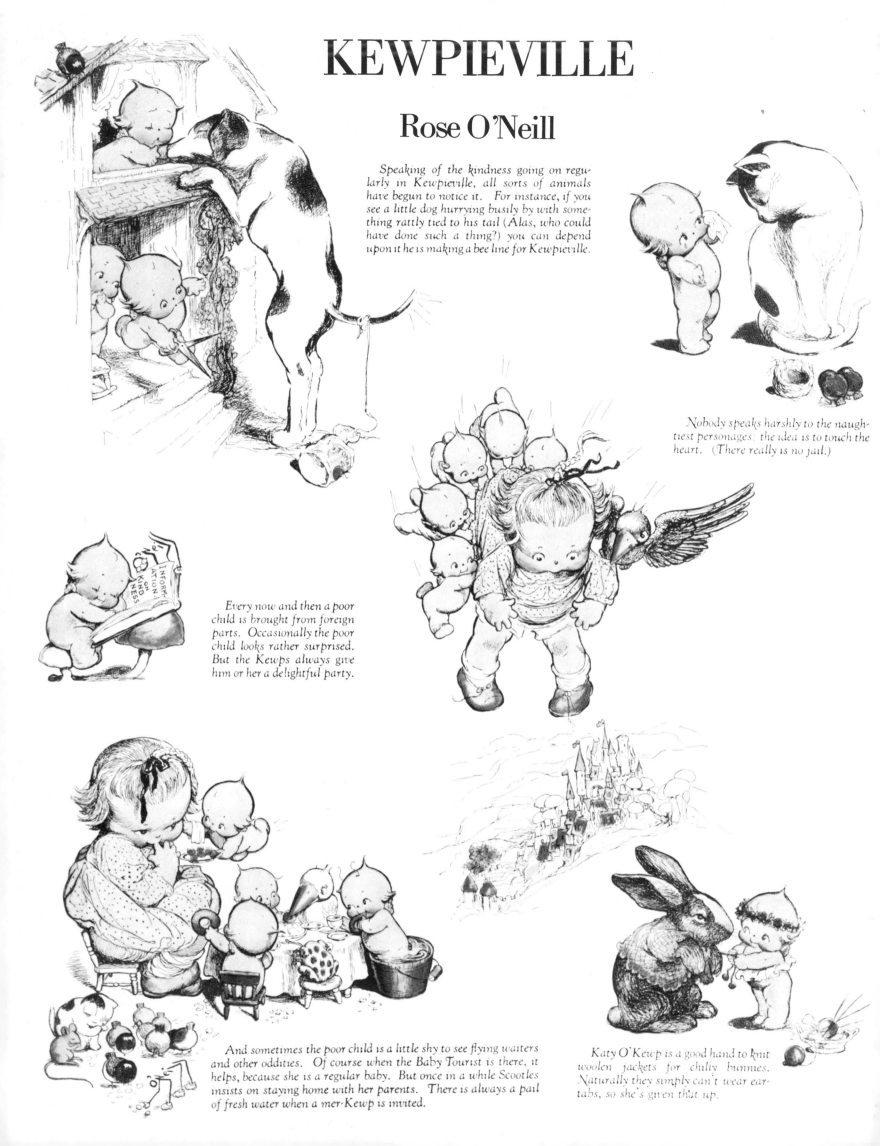

Speaking of the kindness going on regularly in Kewpieville, all sorts of animals have begun to notice it. For instance, if you see a little dog hurrying busily by with something rattly tied to his tail (Alas, who could have done such a thing?) you can depend upon it he is making a bee line for Kewpieville.

Nobody speaks harshly to the naughtiest personages; the idea is to touch the heart. (There really is no jail.)

Every now and then a poor child is brought from foreign parts. Occasionally the poor child looks rather surprised. But the Kewps always give him or her a delightful party.

And sometimes the poor child is a little shy to see flying waiters and other oddities. Of course when the Baby Tourist is there, it helps, because she is a regular baby. But once in a while Scootles insists on staying home with her parents. There is always a pail of fresh water when a mer-Kewp is invited.

Katy O'Kewp is a good hand to knit woolen jackets for chilly bunnies. Naturally they simply can't wear eartabs, so she's given that up.

GOOD NIGHT, COLUMBINE. *Painting by W. E. Webster.*

THE STAY-AT-HOMES.   By Norman Rockwell.

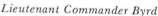

Lieutenant Commander Byrd

THIS HERO BUSINESS

Lieutenant Commander Richard E. Byrd

At nine o'clock on the morning of May 9, 1926, Floyd Bennett and I circled the North Pole in our plane. For the first time in history that grim goal was seen from the air. On the way north we gazed on several hundred thousands of square miles of unexplored territory. This flight will always be the great thrill of my life. But strange to say, my greatest discovery came on my return home.

We arrived at New York on the morning of June 22, 1926. We were met by the mayor's official tug, the Macom, on board of which were several official welcoming committees, a delegation from Congress, a regiment of newspaper reporters, and enough photographers to man a battleship.

For half an hour I was tossed about like a leaf in a storm. Then a friend cornered

me. I could see he was laboring under high tension.

He spoke feverishly:

"We arrive at the Battery at noon. You will be presented with a medal and the keys to the city at twelve-fifteen. You will make two speeches in reply. At lunch you will make another speech. At four-thirty-two we leave for Washington. On arrival you will be met by a committee of welcome. Twenty minutes later President Coolidge will present you with a gold medal. You will make a speech ——"

"But I'm not a speech maker," I protested. My friend seemed to grind his teeth. "Makes not the slightest difference," he snapped. "You are now a national hero."

What did this mean? I realized that an adventure like our polar flight aroused

great public interest. I knew before I left that there would be a certain amount of risk in crossing the polar ice, just as there is in any flight over an unknown terrain. I had gumption enough to see that such a stunt is great stuff for the publicity hounds. But my idea of a national hero was somebody like George Washington or John J. Pershing. They had held the safety of our country in their hands. They had suffered the agony of long campaigns. They had led armies to victory against a public enemy.

I hadn't done anything so valiant. Nor did Bobby Jones, or Gertrude Ederle, who came after me.

"Yes, they are national heroes, too," admitted a newspaperman whom I queried about this curiously American phenomenon.

133

"But what is a national hero, and why?" I persisted.

"Oh, someone who's worth two columns and a front-page streamer, fireboats and a basket of medals," came the cynical reply.

But I wasn't satisfied; not when I thought of the thousands of American citizens who had grasped my hand since my return; and of the tens of thousands of jubilant letters and telegrams that had reached me.

No, there was something more, something deeper.

The first inkling of the greatest discovery in my life came in Washington just before I faced the President and a large audience of distinguished diplomats. I had never spoken before so august an assemblage. To rehearse some of the thoughts that crowded my mind, I managed to sneak away for a few moments in the stage wings of the giant auditorium where the ceremony was being held. I stood in a little bare alcove glancing over my notes. Suddenly a door

Gay Costumes for

Small Masqueraders

Pierrette

Pierrot

Bo-Peep

behind me opened, then softly closed. I turned. Facing me stood a little white-haired lady in black bonnet and gown. Despite the age in her face, her eyes were brown and bright. They looked into mine unblinking.

"You are Commander Byrd?" she asked.

"Yes, madam."

She came a step forward in a sudden wistful eagerness. "And you reached the North Pole?"

"There seems to be no doubt of it."

Her lips parted as if to speak again. But before she could utter a word an abrupt change came over her. She gave a quick sigh, almost a sob. Her mouth trembled. She thrust out one hand as if to touch me. Her eyes dimmed and filled. Then she cried out:

"Oh, I'm so glad!" Before I could stop her she was gone.

I heard a step behind me. "All right, Byrd." The same irritating whiplash of necessity that notoriety brings. "The President is arriving. You will have to go on the stage at once."

I went on the stage. But the mystery of the little lady in black clung to me. I espied her in the audience. I managed to inquire about her during a lull in the ponderous proceedings of the evening.

"Poor thing," whispered my informant. "She's had a tough break in life. Lost her husband twenty years ago. Brought up two fine boys on what she could make herself. Lost both of them in the World War. Now she's all alone."

In a flash of understanding I knew something of the answer to my question: What is a national hero?

I was a hero to that sad little mother, but not in the way the word is usually used. No doubt she admired us for having succeeded. Probably the story of it all gave her daily newspaper a fresh flavor. Possibly she speculated over what it felt like to fly. But those weren't the things that made her seek me out and face me first-hand with her tears of gladness.

What that mother saw in me was the living memory of her husband and sons. They had been brave men. I later learned they had been adventurous. They were the kind who would have liked to have flown to the North Pole. They were fine, keen, courageous men. And if they were all that to the passing acquaintance who retailed their virtues to me, what demigods must they have been to that little white-haired lady of the brown eyes and black bonnet.

To her I was the living flesh she so longed to touch. I, she knew, was son and husband. Wife and mother of mine would sit out there among a great throng and listen while the President of the United States extolled my virtues, even as she might have sat and listened had Fate been equally generous to her.

It may sound incredible, but in that moment of understanding my philosophy of life changed. I had been human in my home-coming. The thrill of a grand public welcome had well-nigh swept me off my feet, though I had felt humble and more or less undeserving of such recognition. I had had to pinch myself every now and then to see if it were all true. I had felt like a man who had unexpectedly reached a mountain

top and finds a gorgeous panorama spread before his eyes. I had wanted to throw my hat in the air and shout, "Gosh, but this is great!"

Now, in a trice, another man's mother had wiped away my smug acceptance of unexpected fame.

My memory sprang back to Annapolis days. I recalled the first time I marched down the town street as color bearer. The band was playing. As I passed, men uncovered, ladies applauded, children waved their hands. I was stirred by this show of admiration. Pride filled and warmed me. I seemed walking on the air. I felt brave, superior, triumphant. Then, with a thump, came the truth. I blushed right out in

public. People weren't saluting and cheering me. They were saluting the Stars and Stripes which I carried.

Exactly that was happening now. The cheers and the handclaps, the waving hats and flags, the music and the speeches, weren't really meant for me any more now than that boyhood morning in Annapolis when I marched at the head of the procession holding aloft the flag of my country. The banner I carried now wasn't so visible, nor easily painted. It didn't in its symbolism depict the stormy history of a people. It never would stir a nation to righteous indignation against an invader. It couldn't be nailed to the mast of a sinking ship.

No, my banner was none of these. My banner—I was the banner. In me and my single success people saw success that might have been their own. In me mothers saw their sons, wives their husbands, sisters their brothers. In me men saw what they might have done had they had the chance. In me youth saw ambition realized.

In me America for the moment dramatized that superb world-conquering fire which is American spirit.

For the moment I seemed to have caught up the banner of American progress and carried it a few steps onward.

For the moment I appeared to typify to them the spirit of America.

This was my discovery.

It was great to think that, even for these precious moments, I was destined to carry the banner aloft!

Was I proud? Insufferably so. Vainglorious? Never. But humble, grateful. There were a half hundred members of our expedition who deserved equally with me to carry that banner.

The Land of Nod

FROM A CHILD'S GARDEN OF VERSES, BY ROBERT LOUIS STEVENSON

Illustrated by H. Willebeek Le Mair

FROM breakfast on through all the day
At home among my friends I stay,
But every night I go abroad
Afar into the land of Nod.

All by myself I have to go,
With none to tell me what to do—
All alone beside the streams
And up the mountain-sides of dreams.

The strangest things are there for me,
Both things to eat and things to see,
And many frightening sights abroad
Till morning in the land of Nod.

Try as I like to find the way,
I never can get back by day,
Nor can remember plain and clear
The curious music that I hear.

By permission of Charles Scribner's Sons

PLAYING HAMLET IN LONDON

John Barrymore

My Hamlet was not put on in London until I had been through two years of the greatest disappointment. I had a very good company lined up, but I could not get a theater. Everyone I went to see was most cordial and kind, but no one had faith

The duel scene.

enough to help me. I could not altogether blame the lessees and managers of the London theaters, because Shakspere has not been particularly successful in the recent years in the West End. The plays of Shakspere are constantly and very beautifully played at the Old Vic, which, as I remember, is more North than West.

I was always embarrassed at being turned down, but I became slightly hardened to it. I persisted because I was encouraged by the flattering success that I had had in America as Hamlet. Finally, after two years of negotiations that came to nothing, I met Frederick Harrison, who owns the Haymarket Theater. He agreed to let me rent

the house for six weeks. Half of the money for the production was raised in London; the other half I put up myself. Had it not been successful, I stood to lose twenty-five thousand dollars. No one could have been more gracious or more interested than Mr.

Harrison was. At the end of the six weeks he postponed his own production of a new A. A. Milne play in order that Hamlet might run three weeks more. I was particularly delighted to have the Haymarket Theater, not only because it is the best in London, but because in this theater my father played many years ago. I never went into the stage door without smiling over a story that I had heard so often. The stage entrance is in a cul-de-sac street, and there is only one way in. One night my father and Charles Brookfield, who was, a few years ago, the play censor in England, were leaving the theater together. My father espied two bailiffs approaching and antic-

ipated that they were for him, as they were. There being no other way out of the street, my father grabbed hold of the more athletic appearing of the two, and then shouted to Brookfield: "Run, Barry, run." There was nothing for Brookfield to do but to oblige by running, and when he had been given sufficient time for a getaway my father, as Brookfield, apologized good-naturedly to the bailiff that he had detained. The other one made a feeble effort to follow Brookfield, who jumped into a cab and disappeared.

The rehearsals of Hamlet were more fun than anything I ever have done. I had wanted to put it on in London so much, and one crashing disappointment after another merely made me keener to do so. There was another pleasure for me, and that was because I was doing the whole thing myself. In London I had no producer or director.

This added responsibility was really a delight, as there was such a splendid sense of collaboration and helpfulness everywhere. The company, including Miss Constance Collier, who was the Queen, Fay Compton Ophelia, and Herbert Waring Polonius, was interested extraordinarily by the way in which the production was staged; this was quite new for Shakspere in London.

Finally the first night. The man in front of the house, who was diplomatic, courteous and dressed in evening clothes, as the business people of the English theaters always are, came back to me several times to tell me about the audience. His enthusiasm was so whole-hearted. "Of course, you know," he said, "Mr. Shaw is in the house." Next he came back to tell me: "With the greatest difficulty we just found two seats for Mr. Masefield." The effect of this upon a fairly nervous American in London, who is about to appear in the best play that England has produced, can well be imagined. But the man from the front of the house kept on. He told me of the arrival of Dunsany, Maugham, Mary Anderson, that beloved actress of Shaksperean rôles, the Asquiths, Sir Anthony Hope Hawkins, Henry Arthur Jones, Pontius Pilate, Paul of Tarsus and the Pope. Somehow, it did not add to my scare, for one had the same sense of detachment, I imagine, that one would feel on the route to the guillotine.

I powdered the beads of sweat off the forehead and sauntered onto the stage smoking a cigarette. I wanted to put up a bluff of casualness to the other members of the company. It was much worse for me,

"On the darkened stage I sat waiting for the curtain to go up."

playing Hamlet under my own management and direction in a new country, but I understood that they were apprehensive and I appreciated their reason for being so. There had only been time for one full dress rehearsal with the scenery, and it was complicated for persons not accustomed to it. Many of the entrances and exits were made by the steps that lead up to the massive arch which formed the permanent background of the entire production. I did the best I could to encourage them. I think this is the best performance I have ever given. No other make-believe that I have accomplished has been so authentic, I am sure, as my simulated calmness that night. Then came my own first scene. I threw my cigarette away and on the darkened stage I sat waiting for the curtain to go up. Those seconds that I sat there are reasonably unforgettable.

At the end of the engagement of nine weeks, Hamlet closed. The run could not be extended because some of the cast were under contract to appear in other plays. The last night I look back to as the pleasantest I have ever spent in the theater. There was enthusiasm all through the play, and at the end, when I stood with the company to acknowledge the applause, there were cries of "Come back." After the play I gave a party on the stage of the theater for the entire company and everyone connected with the Haymarket Theater. The charwomen and cleaners sat upon the steps of Elsinore and drank Cointreau, thinking, I'm afraid, that it wasn't very good gin.

A few days after Hamlet was produced in London, I received the following letter from G. Bernard Shaw:

22nd February, 1925.

My dear Mr. Barrymore: I have to thank you for inviting me—and in such kind terms too—to your first performance of Hamlet in London; and I am glad you had no reason to complain of your reception, or, on the whole, of your press. Everyone felt that the occasion was one of extraordinary interest; and so far as your personality was concerned they were not disappointed.

I doubt, however, whether you have been able to follow the course of Shakespearean production in England during the last fifteen years or so enough to realize the audacity of your handling of the play. When I last saw it performed at Stratford-on-Avon, practically the entire play was given in three hours and three quarters, with one interval of ten minutes; and it made the time pass without the least tedium, though the cast was not in any way remarkable. On Thursday last you played five minutes longer with the play cut to ribbons, even to the breath-bereaving extremity of cutting out the recorders, which is rather like playing King John without little Arthur.

You saved, say, an hour and a half on Shakespear by the cutting, and filled it up with an interpolated drama of your own in dumb show. This was a pretty daring thing to do. In modern shop plays, without characters or anything but the commonest dialogue, the actor has to supply everything but the mere story, getting in the psychology between the lines, and presenting in his own person the fascinating hero whom the author has been unable to create.

He is not substituting something of his own for something of the author's: he is filling up a void and doing the author's work for him. And the author ought to be extremely obliged to him.

But to try this method on Shakespear is to take on an appalling responsibility and put up a staggering pretension. Shakespear, with all his shortcomings, was a very great playwright; and the actor who undertakes to improve his plays undertakes thereby to excel to an extraordinary degree in two professions in both of which the highest success is extremely rare. Shakespear himself, though by no means a modest man, did not pretend to be able to play Hamlet as well as write it; he was content to do a recitation in the dark as the ghost. But you have ventured not only to act Hamlet, but to discard about a third of Shakespear's script and substitute stuff of your own, and that, too, without the help of dialogue. Instead of giving what is called a reading of Hamlet, you say, in effect, "I am not going to read Hamlet at all: I am going to leave it out. But see what I give you in exchange!"

Such an enterprise must justify itself by its effect on the public. You discard the recorders as hackneyed back chat, and the scene with the king after the death of Polonius, with such speeches as "How all occasions do inform against me!" as obsolete junk, and offer instead a demonstration of that very modern discovery called the Oedipus complex, thereby adding a really incestuous motive on Hamlet's part to the merely conventional incest of a marriage (now legal in England) with a deceased husband's brother. You change Hamlet and Ophelia into Romeo and Juliet. As producer, you allow Laertes and Ophelia to hug each other as lovers instead of lecturing and squabbling like hectoring big brother and little sister: another complex!

Now your success in this must depend on whether the play invented by Barrymore on the Shakespear foundation is as gripping as the Shakespear play, and whether your dumb show can hold an audience as a straightforward reading of Shakespear's rhetoric can. I await the decision with interest.

My own opinion is, of course, that of an author. I write plays that play for three hours and a half even with instantaneous changes and only one short interval. There is no time for silences or pauses: the actor must play on the line and not between the lines, and must do nine-tenths of his acting with his voice. Hamlet—Shakespear's Hamlet—can be done from end to end in four hours in that way; and it never flags nor bores. Done in any other way Shakespear is the worst of bores, because he has to be chopped into a mere cold stew. I prefer my way. I wish you would try it, and concentrate on acting rather than on authorship, at which, believe me, Shakespear can write your head off. But that may be vicarious professional jealousy on my part.

I did not dare to say all this to Mrs. Barrymore on the night. It was chilly enough for her without a coat in the stalls without any cold water from

Yours perhaps too candidly,
G. BERNARD SHAW.

TRAINING OF AN ACTRESS

Laurette Taylor's Views

If I am to suggest a few simple principles that may guide or encourage the gentle feet of youth turned stagewards, I would ask: Have they a sound education? Or do they wish to add to the appalling ignorance of the young people of the American stage, some of whom can hardly read a word of three syllables? Have they the natural gift for the stage, and are they seeking earnestly to express it rather than to become famous or notorious overnight? Have they the physical requirements to play many parts? And—most important of all, in my mind—can they stand up to the physical and nervous work, which is very punishing at times?

I cannot overemphasize the importance of a proper understanding of and approach to "the job." The mental attitude toward the stage and one's work upon it has, I believe, determined many a successful stage career. Approach all your work reverently,

Laurette Taylor

and do it well. Continue your training and your self-imposed lessons throughout all your work.

With our aspirations almost fulfilled, we find the hardest training—and a very definite daily physical grind is required in the days of our success. We *must* keep fit.

The elusive quality of success is one of the most discouraging factors of professional life. But I have almost overcome that by trying honestly to satisfy my own standard. I have tried to do a better job in each play.

Discontent with one's work is, in my judgment, a degree of ambition. Do not have an ultimate goal. Hitch your wagon to the highest, and keep your chin up and your face to the stars. Success has spoiled many a great artist.

Above all, try to retain that most evanescent quality of all, simplicity. Simplicity of thought and feeling is a natural stage of perfection. The real art of the stage should consist in acquiring experience without losing simplicity. And don't be afraid to call yourself and to feel yourself an artist. Be an aristocrat of your own sphere, instead of breaking your heart and your talent by trying to climb into another.

Dressing the Children

For Better or for Worse

Bridge the age beyond babyhood with the close-fitting type of suit above, rather than the one below which makes the same little boy appear thin and top-heavy.

The young hopeful who is plump should wear short, straight trousers and narrow-collared blouses; not the fussy, baggy clothes which disfigure the child below.

Short hair and short skirts indubitably belong to the little girl. They make all the difference in the world in the three above and below, who are identical in size, posture and face.

TORRE BEVANS

RAINING
CATS AND
DOGS
By
Oliver Herford.

FRENCH ACE HAILS LINDBERGH

Paul Tarascon

Charles Lindbergh

Note: This brief appreciation of Colonel Charles Lindbergh and his epoch-making flight from New York to Paris on May 21 [1927] in the monoplane, The Spirit of St. Louis, was written in Paris for the Ladies' Home Journal by Capitaine Paul Tarascon, the greatest French aviator after Nungesser, only a few hours after the event. Tarascon was to have flown to New York last year with Coli, but their plane crashed before the take-off. The article and the accompanying sketches by Guy Arnoux were rushed to America on the first steamer.

Voila! The great dream that has burned within me for three whole years has suddenly, with a swoop of wings, entered into the marvelous realm of reality. And this modern knight is a mere boy of twenty-five!

Another had realized my dream, yet I was happy—for is he not one of us?

This boy, whom they tried to tell us was an utter madman, has proved that he is a "born bird" and not a "flying fool." He prepared his tremendous exploit meticulously: he had assembled complete data of every kind; his famous Spiry magnetic compass, which comes as near as possible to perfection, his second "compas de contrôle" and his "navigraphe," constituted the essential navigation instruments. And if Fortune, indispensable even to the most foreseeing, favored him, one must recognize the fact that he helped Fortune considerably. This young hero—loved by his gods—deserved to succeed. His machine was remarkable, but its pilot got the utmost from it, like a young virtuoso who draws from

Although I had ardently longed for the success of the bird from America, my heart was too full of the thought of my poor friends Nungesser and Coli not to beat with fear.

What a relief when at last the silhouette of the silver bird burst into the luminous shafts of the great searchlights that pierced the enveloping darkness. I felt the terrific surge of enthusiasm that swept the people of Paris poignantly at first, then with a sort of frenzy.

his instrument the quintessence of harmony.

After this fantastic exploit, one that had daunted my unfortunate comrade Coli and myself for so many months, there is but one gesture left for us, his brothers in France—to hurl into the sky of America the greeting that the heroic American boy came to bring to the land of France, where the blood of the sons of both countries has been gloriously intermingled in the defense of Liberty—the great ideal of two great people.

THE LITTLE DONKEYS WITH THE CRIMSON SADDLES. *Illustration by James Preston for Hugh Walpole's new story.*

SWAN SONG. *Illustration by Henry Raleigh for John Galsworthy's novel.*

CONSTANCE AND CONSTANCY. *Illustration by Henry Raleigh for the story by Booth Tarkington.*

I KNOW A NEW GAME

Kathleen Norris

Games have taken the table—and every other place—by storm. When you go to a dinner party nowadays, in the writing, play acting, singing, painting and newspaper sets of any big city, the black coffee is hardly gulped before the games begin.

Well-managed games—and they do take management—will turn the stiffest group of strangers into friends in the course of two or three hours and transform the dullest and most hopeless of dinners into a memorable event.

Everyone likes games, although contradictorily enough many persons rather shudder away from the thought of games. "Oh, let's not be intellectual," they plead feebly. "I'm no good at it; I'm hopeless at guessing and statistics!"

And perhaps those very persons are the ones who rank highest when the actual tests begin. Mousy little women exhibit a strange quickness with figures and a strange retentive memory of dates and names, while their blustering confident partners fail completely.

There are scores of games, some popular with one sort of group, some with another. They vary constantly, and they must vary. Nothing spoils a game more than inflexibility; some patient voice reiterating "Well, we always played it *this* way!" can kill any game. No game ought to be played too long; two or three times at most.

Of the table games perhaps the simplest, for children, is merely to observe "I can see something beginning with *s*." Even six and seven year olds can play this game; it was a little girl of seven who varied it one day by saying, "I can see something in this room that has two colors, two materials and two kingdoms."

Then there is the old riming game: "I know something that rimes with bread."

The answer must be descriptive, as "Is it a part of the body?" or "Is it a fine string for sewing?" Here again the immediate educational value to children is apparent, for even the smallest of them soon begins to show ingenuity in describing words, and mere infants will soon be asking, "Is it the past tense of say?" or "Is it slang for a banquet?" in a way that amazes uninitiated elders.

Then there is an insulting and hilarious game called You Have a Face. Every player in turn makes this simple remark to his right-hand neighbor; the neighbor naturally asks "What kind of face?" A letter having previously been selected, the player must now mention a face beginning with that letter. A repetition puts him out, while a

"You know that fight about the word 'lurid' last night? Well, I've got the dictionary right open here beside me."

too farfetched face is ruled out and he is given another chance. With the letter *p*, for example, the faces might be pale, peaked, pretty, pallid, pinched, puffy or pathetic—but not Pullman, piny, packed or personal.

The old game of Ghosts is also good at the table. Words are spelled, a letter to a person, and the object is to avoid adding a letter which completes a word four or more letters in length. When such a word is spelled out the player who adds its last letter becomes a "ghost" and is eliminated from the contest, while the next player begins a new word. If the ghost can persuade some active player to speak to him, however, he is reinstated and the other forfeits his place. A player may always challenge the word being spelled when his turn comes to supply a letter; and if the latest player is bluffing and cannot mention a bona-fide word as the one he has in mind he goes out, the challenger remaining in the game. The play finally narrows down to a lone survivor. There are variations of Ghosts. Choose your own.

There are infinite variations to geography games. Merely naming towns, rivers and countries beginning with some selected letter is one of them; another is to have each player in turn name a country beginning with the last letter of the one just mentioned—America, Afghanistan, Netherlands, Spain and so on. A similar game is to name widely advertised products whose names begin with a certain letter or with all the letters in alphabetical order—no letter being finished until nobody at the table can think of another name. The famous ask-me-another type of game is easily playable at the table if any person begins suddenly with "I know a great historical character—a woman whose name begins with *J.*" The answer may be Judith, Jeanne d'Arc, Jane Grey or Jezebel; and it becomes the turn of whoever guesses right to launch his own query in any field he chooses.

GREEN CHRISTMAS. *Illustration by Pruett Carter for the story by Stephen Vincent Benét.*

Fastidious Artemis

Song to a Lady

By WILLIAM ROSE BENÉT

HUNTRESS in the far wood, beyond and beyond,
   I have heard your horn winding and your
      hounds respond.
You fled with silver sandals, but you turned at the
      kill.
Sudden in the clearing, your heart stood still.

Sudden in the clearing, you were witched by a bird;
A note from a feathered throat you and I heard.
You were stilled to a statue, you were tranced in
      dismay.
Arrows rained about you from the golden day.

Huntress, you are questing beyond the mortal bounds.
Your hounds bay the quarry, but they are not earthly
      hounds.
Sudden you are stricken by a change of the moon,
By a hare in the quicken, by a wild bird's tune.

You kneel with your quiver to the earth's distress.
You halt and hark forever to the sky's silentness.
Where the stag has started you cast aside the quest—
And you, O noble-hearted, I gather to my breast!

Motor games are by no means absorbing only to children; grown-ups will find themselves playing them with all the younger generation's zest. Alphabets from advertising signs make one—the party being divided into two groups, each taking one side of the road. Similarly, to count roads to left and right can become a frenzied contest. Poker hands on passing licenses is perhaps a rather adult amusement for children, but one that they can share.

The best of all motor games is to count licenses from other states and countries. An arbitrary number must be selected at the beginning of the trip, say sixteen. The game is to find sixteen of these alien licenses.

There is an infinitely superior type of game that must be played by a fireside circle or that calls for pencils and paper. Dividing a company into two sides, putting them in separate rooms, giving each a card, with some long word like "self-determined" written on it, and seeing which side can find the greater number of five-letter or longer words contained in the big word fills a whole hour. I know no name for it. Proper names are prohibited.

Hanging the Fool consists in the selection by one person of any word in the language—a five or six letter word is best, because there is real science to finding it. Long words are too easy, and three and four letter words involve sheer guesswork. The company has nine guesses at letters; they first ascertain the vowels and then consult one another as to consonants. If they guess a correct letter the giver of the word must say so and tell them how it is placed. Nine mistaken guesses end—and lose—the game. For example: One player says, "I have a six-letter word." The group asks, after consultation, "Is 'e' in it?" "Yes, 'e' is the last letter." They all draw six blanks, and place "e" in the last. They then chance a, u, i, or o, knowing that this word must have another vowel. If an "o" is placed in the second space, they then can speculate as to exactly how many words have those two letters in that position—bottle, jostle, coddle, boggle—it is to be noted that there are surprisingly few, and then to ask "l" would be safe. Good players, by the way, never lose this game, if the word has five letters or more. Correct guesses do not count; the nine points scored are on incorrect guesses only.

A hysterical game is Stammering. In its simple description there is no hint of the stupefied helplessness of the player and the convulsions of mirth it causes the listeners. To play it one person keeps time with a watch; on the commencing second of a minute another of the group springs a letter of the alphabet on the selected victim. All he has to do is say all the words he can think of beginning with that letter in the space of sixty seconds. But strangely, he becomes petrified and cannot think at all. I once heard a really brilliant woman produce only six words. She said "them, they, those, that, the——" rapidly, then fell to musing, after which she hesitatingly added "thesis" and was back at "those" when her minute was up. The score is kept by one person, the watch by another; vowels and difficult letters like *z*, *q* and *v* must not be given.

Who Am I? is an amusing game and easy to play. One player leaves the room, and the others select some well-known figure—Mussolini, Billy Sunday, Anne Boleyn or Noah. The exile returns and asks everyone in turn, "Who am I?" The answer must be as true, yet as misleading, as possible.

Adverbs is another game whose quality cannot be captured by a written description. While one person is out of the room the others decide on an adverb—say, "simperingly" or "significantly." When he returns he questions them one after another, and they answer in the manner indicated. To see gentle little women being "ferocious" and large men being "flirtatious" is incredibly diverting.

Circumstantial Evidence is a game that needs a little rehearsing and preparation, but it is well worth working for. A simple little scene, usually containing a murder, must be worked out in advance by the hostess and a few confederates. The guests are seated as for a play, and the action takes place, occupying only about five minutes. Then papers and pencils are distributed, and twenty-five questions are asked and answered by number.

These questions must not all be the obvious ones, but some may be easy. They would run something like this: What was the girl doing when the action began? What was the maid's name? What fruit was on the dish? How do you know what city the action took place in? How many times did the telephone bell ring? What change had the older woman made in her costume when she returned? From what person did her letter come? What had delayed the little boy on his way home?

False clews must be planted here and there in the play, so that while everyone is trying desperately to remember some bi-

zarre detail another escapes notice. To speak of the Left Bank, the Loop, the Golden Gate, the Third Avenue Elevated, of course, places a city. The fact that a daughter came home in the subway would supply a clew for the question as to whether her family was rich.

Under the simple yet impressive name of Murder, another good game is easily introduced. The leader of the group states merely, in commencement, "I am accused of the murder of Mary Brown." Mary Brown may be his employer, his fiancée, or any person present or not present. A judge

The luxury of vacationing in Europe in the new Cadillac convertible.

is appointed to hear the evidence, and everyone is cross-examined in turn by the defendant. He asks as rapidly as he can, "Why did I do it? When? Where? How? At what time of what day of what year? Who saw it? What was her testimony? When did you hear of it?"

There must be real evidence in answer. No one is allowed to say "I don't know anything about it." Everyone must know something about it, and the accused man is acquitted as soon as evidence is contradictory. For example, if someone has testified that it was a snowy day it is enough to have some other person later say that he was going swimming. If the motive for deliberate murder has first been stated as jealousy later evidence that it was accident, that it was impulse or that the police could find no motive will acquit. In one of these games a wood fire had been described in the murder chamber, and later the method of murder was mentioned as "turning on the gas while the victim was asleep"—which obviously threw out the evidence. While only the defendant cross-examines, any player who notices a discrepancy can say "Discharged!" and call attention to it; whereupon the judge accepts or refuses it.

Twenty Questions and Proverbs are two good old stand-bys, excellent for variety. Sardines has one great drawback—it all but breaks up the home. In the pitch darkness necessary to Sardines glasses crash ominously on pantry shelves, telephones bang on the floor, ink drips eerily out of sight, and long-forgotten jig-saw puzzles rain down from obscure shelves. But for sheer fun —— In Sardines one person hides in a perfectly dark house. He may hide in a spot that would be perfectly visible in daylight, lie comfortably along a ceiling beam, or stand on a mantel with a candlestick artfully placed before each foot, to deceive exploring fingers.

The first person to find him huddles or dangles or crouches closely against him and also remains silent and hidden—and the third likewise; so that finally a few terrified stragglers return from the search of other rooms to receive no answer to their panicky calls and to realize that close beside them somewhere, in the maddening blackness, some dozen forms are all strangling, laughing, panting together.

Finally, I confess a weakness for charades, the prettiest of all games. Charades are really little plays, with everyone in the family entitled to play his favorite part. They sound formidable and old-fashioned, but they are simple; and the delicious youthful faces disguised with mustaches, the small girls as Red Cross nurses and the inverted sofa conveying Washington into a frozen Delaware do make pictures that last forever in the maternal heart.

A development of the old charade is to have all the little syllable acts performed as consecutive acts in one play; as, for instance, if the word were "inundate" the first scene would be weary travelers arriving at a supposed hostelry, the second the hospitable sisters welcoming them, the third a discussion of their telegram and a misunderstanding as to the time of arrival, and the final, completed picturization, a flood that swept travelers, nuns and convent ignominiously across the carpet.

Insuring Well-Tailored

How to Solve the Common Problems They Present:

Drawings by Mary Cornwell

Correct (above) and incorrect ways of treating windows in rooms with high ceilings.

Have you ever entered a room, after a short absence, to find that its entire personality has changed? You were amazed at this miracle. But, when you began to investigate the reason for all this change, you were even more surprised to find that it is only the draperies that were different. Here, with a few deft touches, a clever person had changed the entire appearance of the room.

We are, therefore, quite correct in giving first consideration to the treatment of the windows. The money we expend in their behalf is never lost when well used. In planning draperies one does not need to change completely the fabric, for often with a few dollars and a few hours we can perform a marvelous transformation with old materials.

One often encounters problems in changing the furnishings of a room, or in moving from one place to another. We find that the room is too dark or too light, or that it lacks character and dignity. It may have windows that are too small or too large, too high or too low; and they may be unevenly spaced. Before making any changes one should first consider a few factors.

The first consideration is the color scheme. We must consider the location and light of the room, as well as the certainty of our color choice harmonizing with the furnishings that are already there. Let us first think about the influence of the room's location upon our color scheme.

Windows

By Lewis R. Hastings

If your room has a cold and bare feeling —perhaps it faces the north—you should select warm colors. Such colors are found in the many different tones of yellow, orange and red. If the variety of warm colors that you use is not too great, the result will be cozy and livable. The overuse of these colors will result in a most exciting and disturbing interior. Should the room face the south, or if it has an abundance of heat, we should choose such colors as greens, blues and blue-violets.

In selecting colors we must remember that rooms which have little sunlight should have light or pale colors, and rooms with quantities of light should have dark or heavy colors. This will overcome either that soggy or dazzling effect we feel in rooms too dark or too light to be really comfortable.

It is true, of course, that the colors which we use in our draperies are somewhat limited by the colors already existing in the room. There must be compatibility between these.

Draperies should never be obviously things apart from the rest of the decorative scheme—that is, they should not "stand off" from the wall as a special decorative feature in the room, but their coloring should be repeated about the room in different places.

The problem of a large center window with radiator, as shown in small illustration, is happily solved in treatment above.

This repetition, or echoing, of the color will probably be found in the pictures, vases, upholstery, rugs and lamps. This ties the color of the draperies into the rest of the composition. One way to insure the compatibility we are discussing is to select a suitable color that exists in some of the objects in the room. Using this as a basis for your color scheme, you can build up a harmony that will be consistent and delightful.

Two treatments for more formal drawing or living room windows are shown in these illustrations.

Here the drapery is drawn back at one side of the window, allowing both light and air to enter the room.

THE CHAOTIC DECADE:
THE 1920's

Mary Roberts Rinehart

Already it is difficult to look back to the beginning of this queer chaotic decade. Women will remember that dresses were long ten years ago, and men that Prohibition had just gone into effect. Hostesses will recall a society vainly seeking to formalize itself once more after the war, and a younger generation will not have forgotten the attempts to bring it to heel after two years of comparative freedom of action.

None of them, men or women, readjusted easily. At the end of ten years, some of them have not yet found themselves again. We discover them wandering from city to city, eternally restless, eternally unfit. Or we find them back in the old environment, either listless and defeated, or seeking by any means in their power to recapture the old thrill, the drama which is gone.

Nor was this true only of the men and women whose lives had been radically altered by the war. It was true of the entire American people. The excitement had buoyed them, stimulated them; under it many of them had given money and effort, had sacrificed themselves cheerfully. But in return they had been given a vast, incredibly dramatic interest.

With the sudden withdrawal of that interest they suffered from a sense of defeat and anticlimax. Daily lives became dull and humdrum once more. And what is more important, life seemed even more stale and uneventful, by comparison, than it had ever been.

For those first postwar years, it may be said that the whole people were mentally below normal. And national depressions of this type are not matters of a day or a week. Life was stale, business conditions uncertain; to dullness was added anxiety. And as if at the very beginning to threaten the result of the experiment, in those low days came Prohibition.

The result was obvious. Precipitated suddenly, amounting to confiscation of vast properties founded in good faith, Prohibition came to a depressed people at the worst possible time for their cheerful acceptance of it.

The immediate result was a low-minded people, anxious by any means to return even temporarily to the normal, and the immediate organization of competent underground bootlegging machinery to enable them to do so.

Also, since only the so-called "hard" liquors could be transported by underground methods, the further result was that only the habit-forming whiskies and gins were available.

One of the first significant social changes of the decade was the substitution of the cocktail as a pick-up, for the glass of wine and a cracker of previous years. That this cocktail was unlawful does not enter into this discussion; what does enter is the drink for the jolt, instead of the mild stimulant.

But there were other changes. For some years before the war many of the old re-

strictions as to the mingling of the sexes had been abandoned, and properly so. This new relationship had been healthy, open and companionable.

With the first days of the war, however, the bars began to go down, and promiscuous mixing of the sexes took place. Why not? Who could tell whether these boys would ever come back or not? Make them happy. Be good to them.

But they were only boys, many of them, men in uniform but children in experience; and among them naturally was the fixed percentage who could not be trusted. The

letting down of the bars sometimes went to rather terrible lengths. Nor were the men alone responsible. And even the most fatuous optimist cannot fail to recognize that letting down such bars is a vastly different thing to putting them up again.

The free and easy manners of wartime had been comfortable. They required no effort. Metaphorically, the American man had taken off his dinner jacket and his women folk their stays. Later of course women were to do this literally, but not at first. There was rather a bad time when young women, in order to have dancing partners, began to park their stays in automobiles or in the dressing rooms at balls. Only now, after ten years, is there an attempt to return to the decorums and even some of the decencies of fastidious living.

The cult of sex is a totally different thing from its honest recognition. Honest recognition is neither prurient nor salacious; but the cult of sex is both. It is a failure to recognize this difference which has made the usual censorship of books and plays so absurd, so that even that proud matter, the conceiving and bearing of a child, is made somehow shameful.

But side by side with this movement toward honest knowledge in sex matters have come its exploiters during this past decade. They have debased it, made it decadent and even degenerate. It is fortunate that to the average American, neither subtle nor degenerate himself, much of its true significance has been lost.

Following the cult of sex, or accompanying it, comes invariably the cult of the body, the woman body. This may be camouflaged as the quest for beauty, or it may amount to exhibitionism. But in its final analysis it is a part of the exploitation of sex.

Perhaps beauty is its own excuse, and we need not cavil at nudity. But the amount of beauty revealed by the skirt to the knee or above it was rather offset by its ugliness. For one revelation of beauty there were a hundred knock-kneed and bowlegged women whose contribution was negligible. At the same time, under the guise of beauty or honesty or both, the practically unclothed woman began to creep into the public prints, onto the stage and into the moving pictures, where, exaggerated into enormous proportions, her nudity is inescapable.

So, one thing leading to another during the past decade, an idealistic and rather simple and direct-minded people found it-

Fred and Adele Astaire try out a new step.

self, while making magnanimous gestures against war and achieving real and solid progress in many directions, rather heading toward the gutter in others.

Along with the general awakening, however, comes the professional reformer. He believes that the bad may be legislated into being good, and he sets up his own arbitrary standards of right and wrong.

To the moralist the Ten Commandments are all the law and the prophets; to the Christian the virtues are the virtues of the spirit, charity and loving kindness.

So the end of this strange decade has seen the moralist-reformer going to absurd lengths in his futile endeavor to impose reform from without instead of from within the individual.

A flagrant example of this has been the extension of the power of censorship. A law originally designed only to prevent the manufacture or import of pornographic material has been extended to cover a greatly enlarged field. Books otherwise doomed to a small group of readers, or to die practically unread at all, have thus been advertised into large sales. Literary classics, long unsuspected, have had their hidden wantonness revealed. Honest writers, writing for the adult mind, have been haled into court because their honesty might contribute to the forbidden knowledge of youth.

Why should youth be forbidden knowledge? It is its only safe ground. And this same censorship, which has reduced the

A Yale Lock.

footage in a moving-picture kiss and the uses of beds in all pictures to deathbed scenes and similar innocuous episodes, still permits unclothed women both on the stage and on the screen!

But the reformer is at his worst in his endeavor to enforce Prohibition. So strangely has this warped our judgment that the killing of men, women and even children for the manufacture and sale of contraband liquors is not only condoned, it is greeted with cheers, in one of our

houses of Congress, only three weeks before a bootlegger is arrested on the steps of the Capitol in Washington.

The drug trade goes on, and no one yet has shot a peddler of dope because of his trade. The gangster goes his way, often doped to the killing point, and no great wave of nation-wide indignation puts him out of existence. Only the bootlegger is friendless; the very people who make his business possible ignore him in trouble.

At the same time that these things were going on other social changes were taking place. Partly because of fashion and partly because of necessity, the old-fashioned womanly woman showed a tendency to disappear. And with her went the protective male, the "strong man" of prewar days.

In society, as in fiction, during the past decade, his place has been largely usurped by dancing youths and playfellows. The strong man has retired, out of life and out of fiction, to his club, where he probably prefers to be, anyhow.

Now that the pendulum has swung again, he may emerge. We may even find him in fiction—which reflects current life with fair accuracy—and thus ending the literary vogue of the male introvert, the decadent and the weakling in favor of something more robust.

However, more interesting and more important than what has happened to men and women during the past decade is what has happened to the children, and by children I mean adolescent youth. To say

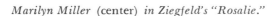

Marilyn Miller (center) *in Ziegfeld's "Rosalie."*

1929. Fanny Brice is wed to Billy Rose, husband number three, by New York's Mayor, Jimmy Walker.

that they have not been influenced in their most formative period by the example of their elders would be ridiculous. But to claim that anything hopelessly grave has destroyed them is even more absurd.

The true revolt of youth is not necessarily a revolt against law and order or the essential decencies, but a determination to assert himself as self-thinking, self-acting, self-controlling.

As a matter of fact, children fail their parents rather less than parents fail their children. And this has been particularly true in recent years. The movement of women from homes has not been entirely economic, and the so-called free woman is more free today than ever before. And never was amusement outside the home so cheap and so accessible, or sophistication so available, to the child. Home ties, to say the least, have been considerably stretched.

At the same time has come this sophistication of the children, and with it its inevitable discoveries; the infallible has become fallible, maturity has its weaknesses. Respect for age as age dies, and this sophisticated youth surveys its world with eyes shrewd with knowledge and unsoftened by experience.

Fortunate is the parent who can bear this cool survey, this calm appraisal! The old hypocrisies in which he clothed himself have been stripped away. His pride is hurt, his illusion of grandeur is gone. He wails that he does not understand this new generation, but what he means is that this new generation understands him.

We Test Our Readers' Recipes

STUFFED BAKED HAM. Clean the ham well. If it is covered with mold use a stiff brush and scrub it off. Put in a large boiler, cover with cold water and add an onion sliced, two bay leaves, two tablespoonfuls of vinegar and a cupful of brown sugar. Bring to a boil and simmer slowly, allowing twenty minutes to the pound. Let the ham cool in its own liquor. Then remove the skin and the small bone below the joint, which will break off and slip out easily. If you wish to, cut the ham open along the inside and take out the whole bone. Also make holes through the meat with a wooden skewer. Make the stuffing, enough for a six to eight pound ham, as follows:

1 Quart of Fine Crumbs	1 Tablespoonful of Chopped Parsley
1 Tablespoonful of Mustard	1 Small Chili Pepper, Chopped
2 Tablespoonfuls of Sugar	2 Egg Yolks, Beaten
2 Teaspoonfuls of Salt	3 Cupfuls—about—of Thin Cream or Top Milk
1 Teaspoonful of Celery Seed	
¾ Cupful—about—of Melted Butter or Margarine	

USE beaten biscuit crumbs if they are available; if not, fine bread crumbs will do nicely. Mix the dry ingredients and combine with the egg yolks, cream and butter. Use slightly more or less of the cream and the butter to make the mixture a good stuffing consistency. Pack it into the opening left by removing the bone and into the skewer holes and spread a layer of it all over the outside of the ham. Brush with the egg whites, just slightly beaten, place on a greased rack in the roasting pan and bake in a quick oven until the crust is brown—450° F.—for fifty minutes. Serve with a cream gravy made as you would make white sauce, substituting all or part ham fat for butter.

Mrs. F. D., Kingston Springs, Tenn.

Simplified Candied Sweets

5 Sweet Potatoes	½ Cupful of Granulated Sugar
4 Tablespoonfuls of Water	1 Teaspoonful of Salt
1 Tablespoonful of Lard or Butter	

PARE and quarter the five sweet potatoes or enough to fill a good-sized frying pan. Add the water and shake the sugar and salt over them, then add the lard or butter. Cook covered until the potatoes are soft, then remove cover and the liquid will have cooked down enough so they will brown. Turn often so they will

---

A Midwinter Dinner

Clear Tomato Bouillon	Croutons
Stuffed Baked Ham	Cream Gravy
Simplified Candied Sweets	Carrots Lyonnaise
Hot Biscuits	Mustard Pickle
Dublin Salad	
Prune Nut Pudding	Cup Cakes

---

be equally glazed and browned on all sides. If a gas stove is used the pan is best put over an iron lid or asbestos pad to keep the heat very even and low. It takes about thirty-five minutes to soften the potatoes and ten to brown them.

Miss E. G. G., Philadelphia, Pa.

Carrots Lyonnaise

12 Small Carrots	4 Tablespoonfuls of Butter
1 Onion	¾ Teaspoonful of Salt
4 Large Outer Leaves of Lettuce	¼ Teaspoonful of Pepper

WASH and scrub the carrots well and without scraping them cut in very thin slices. Melt the butter, add the carrots, the onion sliced, and the lettuce shredded. Cover and cook slowly for twenty minutes, stirring frequently to prevent its sticking. At the end of this time add a cupful of boiling water together with the salt and pepper and cook for a few minutes longer until the vegetables are tender and the water absorbed.

Mrs. G. A. E., Morro Bay, Cal.

Dublin Salad

TO ONE and a half cupfuls of leftover mashed potatoes add two tablespoonfuls of melted butter, one and a half tablespoonfuls of vinegar, two tablespoonfuls of minced parsley, one teaspoonful of scraped onion and one-half teaspoonful of salt. Mix all together well, roll into marble sized balls and chill. Serve three in a nest of lettuce—use what is left from the head needed for the Carrots Lyonnaise—and cover with boiled dressing.

Mrs. G. F. P., Kansas City, Mo.

Prune Nut Pudding

1 Pound of Prunes	4 Teaspoonfuls of Cornstarch
¾ Pound of Sugar	Juice of One Orange
½ Teaspoonful of Cinnamon	½ Cupful of Nut Meats
¼ Teaspoonful of Cloves	2 Egg Whites

SOAK, cook the prunes and remove pits. Simmer them five minutes in two cups of the water in which they cooked, with the sugar and spices. Add the cornstarch first moistened with cold water and the orange juice. Cook stirring for fifteen minutes. Mix in the nuts chopped, let cool a little, then fold in the stiffly beaten egg whites. Turn into a mold and chill.

Mrs. L. G. H., Sandwich, Ont., Can.

Worth   Doucet   Cheruit   Louiseboulanger

BEHIND THE SEAMS

*With the Women of Paris
Who Dress the Women of the World*

Janet Flanner

For women, Paris is the fashion arbiter of the world. American matrons, five thousand miles distant from the Rue Royale, are no less influenced by its dress decisions than brides in the immediate *banlieus* of the capital of France.

Twice a year international styles are stabilized by collections shown in the Parisian salons of certain dressmakers. They are the Frenchwomen who, often not Parisiennes themselves, dominate all Parisiennes. They are, in short, the fashion leaders of the world—not the smart women who wear smart clothes, but the women who design the smart clothes for the smart women to wear.

What are they like, *ces grandes couturières?* Do they dress well? What is their appearance, what are their tastes?

Chanel, Parisian dominator of de luxe fashion, is a peasant from the Auvergne. She dislikes society, has no small talk and still speaks urban French with a country accent. She is slender, is entering her forties, uses no make-up, her throat is tall, her head is small. She looks like a model swan. She was one of the first women to bob her hair. As it was never clipped short and is still worn to the same full length, she now has the air of being one of the first women to wear it long.

She opened her career as a milliner in one room of what is today her vast establishment in the Rue Cambon. She now owns a château in Normandy, a villa near Monte Carlo, and various other properties which she does not use.

She started her riches by launching *le genre pauvre*—by popularizing for rich women the simple woolen sweaters and scarfs of poor workmen. Recognizing the futility of her wearing or successfully creating the complicated class-conscious fripperies fashionable women once affected, she designed a new type of clothes which were so simple, so linear, so intelligently foolproof that a factory hand would look chic in them and only a rich woman could afford to. Chanel, as she states bluntly, has no interest in dressing the masses.

In a mechanical age, she invented garments which were small mechanical perfections, regardless of who wore them, as an impeccable motor car remains impeccable no matter who rides inside. This was and is her stated ideal: That the flawlessly well-dressed woman is so well dressed that no one notices she is well dressed.

As a result, Chanel was denied entrance one night to the Casino at Cannes; the doorman claimed she was not sufficiently

Chanel

chic. When informed that she was the greatest couturière in Paris, he said: "Well, she doesn't look like it anyway." This must have been Chanel's greatest theoretic triumph.

No one sees her except her friends—Jean Cocteau, the writer, and the artists Sert, Christian Bérard and Picasso, who regards her as one of the few women in Europe worth knowing.

By day she wears the inevitable sweater, coat, skirt and hat, all beige. At night she wears those uncopiable simple black gowns she has perfected and which she unjustly calls her frocks for *"deux sous."* Her jewels are illustrious. Around her throat she wears an armada of pearls, all Oriental and of all colors. On her wrists are chains of multicolored stones, all precious, and all, for her pleasure, set to look like imitations. Their air of being gewgaws satisfies her peasant instinct for gay trumpery which, to be perfect, she knows should at any rate look inexpensive.

Nicole Groult is perhaps the most worldly and native of the women dressmakers. She was born in Paris and was daughter to the intelligent, esteemed Veuve

Poiret, sister to the great couturier Paul Poiret, who has been playwright, actor, painter besides, to Mme. Germaine Poiret, who has been poet and dressmaker, and to Madame Boivin, excellent designer of jewels. Talent, professionalism and the Parisian viewpoint were therefore indigenous to her.

Like her brother, Paul Poiret, she conceives garments only in terms of her own personality. Both believe that in previous incarnations they were Orientals, he a Persian, she an Egyptian, and both royal.

She is a civilized and modern woman who likes the pleasure of spending the money she earns. She has a collection of shoes which runs into the half hundreds. In Cairo, where she spends her winters, in one morning she has bought a dozen pairs of mules in the souks.

During past seasons in which Paris fashion has lowered the waist to what in any country is the hip, Madame Groult remained tactful but truculent. Her clothes continued to indicate the waistline at the waist—where Venus wore it as a girdle, warriors as a belt, cooks as an apron string, where, in fact, Nature placed it. A normal indented waistline is classically a sign of youth.

In the past seventy-five years four British have dared to come to Paris to make clothes for Parisiennes. It is presumed that they did this rather than take up the profession of sending coals to Newcastle.

The first was Worth, originator of the present house, invited over by the Empress Eugénie—an invitation the Second Empire considered unnatural, unpatriotic and a scandal. The second was Lucille, the third was Capt. Edward Molyneux, and the fourth is Elspeth Champcommunal.

A few seasons ago she came to Paris without a penny, rented a magnificent eighteenth-century mansion in the Rue Penthièvre, called on Picasso, invited his favorite pupil, the Spanish Pruna, to decorate the rooms, hired cutters, fitters, bought some needles and pins and opened her doors as a dressmaker.

In a twelvemonth she had done business that touched six figures, in two years had established her house as one of the most important small establishments in Paris and in three years had made a tennis frock for Suzanne Lenglen.

Before these victories she passed a peaceful childhood in Scotland as a preliminary to being a violinist in England, a sculptor in Paris. Her French husband, killed the first Monday of the war, was a member of the famous cubist painting group with Derain and Léger.

Many couturières design on paper. Madame Champcommunal works on the flesh, with pins and scissors instead of chisel. She usually adjusts a model to five different mannequins' coloring and form before she decides a gown is serviceable to a general public and capable of representing a composite taste.

By day she fancies the drooping largish hats always popular among her compatriots and, when she has time to have them made, the elegant printed-chiffon gowns known by Londoners as Ascot frocks. Caring nothing for jewels, she satisfies her taste for decoration in exquisite shoes, commanding them to her measure in Italy. She has a passion for gloves and can order and lose as many as thirty pairs in the course of a month.

Mme Lanvin

Her generosity is her greatest extravagance. She will give away in a moment what it has taken her hours to acquire. She is tall, blond, blue-eyed, introspective, shy; like most shy people, she is honest, incapable of flattery. She likes spring weather, philosophy and good conversation, dislikes ostentation and substitutes, and is fond of garden flowers.

Mme. Jeanne Lanvin is the dean of the great couturières of Paris. She is the only one who has long hair, still works eight hours a day, as in her youth, is indifferent to public life and is an admitted elegant sixty.

Herself a woman of the nineteenth century and admiring fabrics and forms of even earlier periods, by her preference and position she popularized frocks which in the fifties and sixties were hailed as the *dernier cri* and in this generation of electricity are more respectfully known as *robes de style*.

In an age of athleticism, no petticoats and political freedom for women, she

pulled the past forward. She saved the full long skirts of our grandmothers from the museum by wrapping them by night around their granddaughters' dancing ankles.

She is a type of old-fashioned French business woman disappearing from the ranks of Parisian dressmakers today. She enters her office in the Rue du Faubourg-St.-Honoré punctually at ten, goes to her private room, where, according to the season, she designs, dictates, selects materials, and sees no clients. At noon she returns to lunch in her home in the Rue Barbet-de-Jouy, quiet white street of hidden gardens and departed aristocrats. At two she returns to her office, where she designs or dictates or selects materials, and sees no clients. Work over for the day, she goes home at eight to dine.

Years ago she started her business on a thousand francs. It is her boast that she has never borrowed one sou. Like those who do not borrow, she is not lavish, is not extravagant. Her purchases and pleasures are not ephemeral, now that she has a fortune at their disposal.

She is a self-made woman and she buys only what she feels is permanent—magnificent diamonds, which she is constantly having reset, canvases by Renoir, and good food, which to a hearty French gourmet, as she is, probably is the most permanent pleasure of all.

Occasionally she attends a good theater for its first night. Her establishment is represented at the Opéra at its annual Bal de la Couture. And once a year, in person, Madame Lanvin attends the races.

The short lamé jackets which of late have had such a vogue were originally her idea and personal property. She is a connoisseur of old brocades and she is, being a Frenchwoman, susceptible to drafts; the lamé jackets were the result. Made to satisfy her pleasure in fine stiff fabrics and possibly to prevent her sneezing, she created a comfortable house garment for herself which chic women the world over wore in public.

She maintains her own dye works, her own perfume laboratories. From them comes her special scent made for her use alone—a characteristic and elegant Cologne water, flavored with thyme.

Louise Boulanger is the last of the great dressmakers who can pin up a hem. She is the only one who sees her clients, advising them "Madame, that frock is becoming to you," or "Madame, that frock is not becoming to you." She is the only one who, in the midst of all the details and duties incumbent upon her as head of a great house, supervises the fittings of the gowns it makes, explaining, "That's perfect," and how; or "That's wrong," and where.

In winter in her workrooms Madame Boulanger wears a magnificent working smock of white lamb fur. Her jewels were at one time like no one else's—precious floral set pieces with leaves of emerald or jade and buds of pink stones, a fashion patronized in its origin by her.

Interested in dressmaking, she is interested even in the making of her own clothes. She is therefore an exception and perhaps the best-dressed dressmaker in Paris—a plump, perfectly gowned woman in her forties, mother of a married daughter; her skin is pale, her hair black, her voice dominant, her teeth dazzlingly white and her smile ravishes the beholder.

Her taste in clothes is feminine. She wears gowns of black, beige, gray—erudite colors; her success in her appearance is never ignorant. Her hats are of simplicity and felt.

As an individual, Madame Boulanger, being talented, is temperamental. Here is the privilege of absent-mindedness; unable

Madame Boulanger

to remember any of her employes' names, her constant cry of *"Jeune fille,"* being generic, brings every young woman of her staff to her door; she may not recognize on her own staircase someone with whom she has conversed for an hour not an hour before. The only thing she unfailingly recognizes is her work—what is right with it, what is wrong with it, and the many shrewd ideas that lie in between.

"When someone says to me, 'I saw Madame So-and-So, wearing a beautiful frock,' I know something was the matter with it. When I hear someone say, 'I saw Madame So-and-So, looking beautiful,' I know the frock was perfect. When a gown is perfect no one notices it; one sees only the woman inside."

FAIT EXPRÈS

Gabrielle Chanel

Although the mode, lest it become drab and colorless, sometimes takes on a form which ends by being ridiculous, one of the essential principles of fashion is simplicity. Too great an emphasis put on line, on color or on ornament leads to eccentricity and hinders *élégance*. I use the French word, for the English, elegance, does not carry quite the same fullness of meaning. The complete costume—uniformity—replaces the dress. Must we conclude inevitably from this that women are not to be permitted any latitude for fantasy? How can a woman express her own personality, make the impress of her personal charm and her individual style felt, if, because of a desire to be inconspicuous, she is reduced to wearing a kind of uniform—a uniform of which even the details of cut and material are subject to strict rules?

It is not to be conspicuous, not from a sort of brazen immodesty, that a woman adopts certain designs, certain colors, certain ornaments, but in order to adapt herself to circumstances while sacrificing to them neither her comfort nor her individual taste.

There again, as in all creative work, it is important to think first to what use the mode is to be put, for it is from this harmony between the useful and the beautiful that elegance springs. "How becoming that is!" will not be said of a dress if it has not first been *fait exprès*, specially made. And by specially made we mean appropriate for its purpose.

Suitability

Every circumstance of life, every hour of the day, each season, each age, suggests a suitable *toilette*. There are dresses for the theater, for the restaurant. These are worn not only for oneself but for the many people who look at them. There are other gowns suitable for the privacy of the home, or for formal occasions, and still others for the open air, seashore, golf or tennis.

How should one dress for dining out in a restaurant? Just as it is normal that a smart woman should allow herself a certain initiative and daring in what she wears in her own home or among her intimate friends—just so, it is strange and abnormal to see women exhibit themselves in public almost naked, only one table away from perfect strangers, laying themselves open to the cynical judgment of men of perhaps a completely different *milieu*.

I devoutly hope that little by little women will begin to give to a public place, where different strata of society mingle, the true character that it should have, by wearing hats and dresses which can give no one the illusion of a false intimacy.

Informal dresses should be quiet but allow the wearer more freedom of choice. This type of dress requires great taste in choosing; for is there anything more ridiculous and more opposed to true informality than to have the air of being dressed for a costume ball or the theater? The surprise awakened by such a costume in the first few moments changes rapidly into uneasiness, and constraint follows.

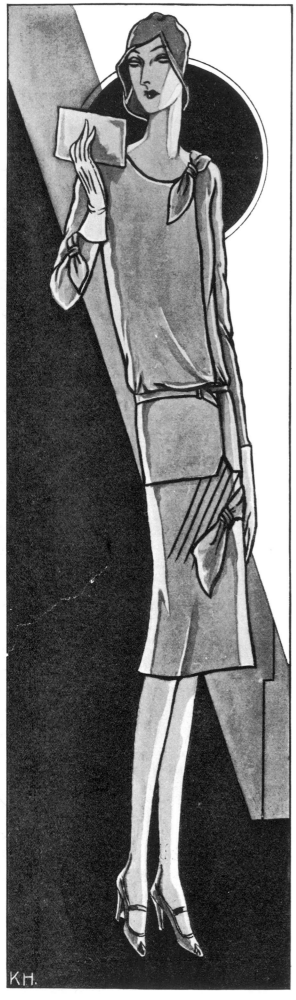

In public the rule is arbitrary. It seems to me inadmissible that women should not show clearly and precisely in a hotel or restaurant that they do not wish to make a sudden startling sensation aided and abetted by clouds of smoke, by music and by alcohol, but rather to have each table sheltered by an invisible screen of good taste, thanks to which dining out will take on once more an aspect that it should never have lost.

In the open air your true *élégante* takes inspiration from both the season and the scene which is to be her background; she must give an impression not of "prettiness" but of comfort.

On the golf course, for instance, she must avoid all overdressing and all studio elegance; you do not play in order to be looked at but for the pleasure of the sport itself. Nothing is more ridiculous on a golf course than a dress in a complicated elaborate design made of a loud material. Choose materials that are durable first and foremost, and that resist sun and rain. Shoes and gloves should be sensible and mannish. The best shoe for sport will gain immeasurably in smartness from being made of simple heavy leather. It will lose it in the exact proportion that ornaments, stitching, fringe and arabesques are added; not to mention the objectionable shiny new look that is fatal to all true *chic*.

Elegance

Finally, if you use perfume, keep away from heavy oriental scents with a base of musk, for nothing is so inappropriate to grass and trees. What could be better than to limit oneself to the fragrance of leather and Scotch wool?

At tennis, the dress should be chosen with an eye to the vigorous movements necessary to the game. Elegance will consist much more in a well-proportioned balance of line than in decorative detail.

It seems to me that tennis players ought always to wear white. The only vivid colors permitted on a tennis court should be a skin bronzed and reddened by exercise. These magnificent natural tints ought to be enhanced by a judicious choice of whites; for white offers a wide diversity of shades. White materials that have a bluish cast like snow accent the grace of brunettes, but blondes are at their best in a creamy tint which contrasts with the whiteness of their skins, even if they are very lightly sunburned.

As for sea bathing, the basis of all elegance is boldly to disclose the natural perfections or imperfections of the feminine form and to suppress all subterfuges of the mode. Don't wear picture hats or picturesque costumes. Don't wear materials that water makes transparent and clinging; nor rubber ribbons, nor flowers. Do not attract attention by such vulgar means, but be at your ease, be comfortable, swim and splash, wrap yourself up in a thick bathrobe and do not try to confuse your seashore background with a scene from musical comedy.

If good taste demands a place for everything and everything in its place, the mode must also adapt itself to the rhythmic beat of life. Each age has its pleasures and each its own particular fashions.

Modern Women

It is self-evident that women's lives have doubled, even tripled, their rhythm. Life no longer resembles the passive existence of our great-grandmothers. Woman nowadays plays her true rôle; she has developed enormously, thanks to hygiene and exercise which assure her a second youth, not so blooming perhaps as the first, but more striking and lasting. A woman with white or gray hair, with a fresh complexion, neat, well groomed, has her praises sung. On the other hand is there any spectacle more painful than that of old women who have lost their figures, dyed their hair and shortened their skirts to show legs that are too fat or too thin, smoking, strutting and dancing like ridiculous clowns?

Once for each age, according to an unchanging code, there were certain colors, forms and materials. There were young girls' dresses, mature women's dresses and old women's dresses. Now that is finished. Young girls have lost the reserve, the timidity, the simplicity of attitude that they think of now as fetters, but which on the contrary gave them a mysterious prestige.

Thus each hour of the day, each month, each age, and not as æsthetes say "according to each mood," there is a corresponding line, a style—dashing or reserved—a shade or a color. For taste does not shut itself up in rigid laws. It is as mobile as life itself; it is made up of a thousand nothings that women must sense if they are not to burn their candle at both ends or be lost in a disorder which shakes them to their profoundest depths.

THE HAPPY HOSTESS

Beatrice Lillie

I've never been able to see why a hostess shouldn't enjoy her own parties and feel at least as festive as her guests. If she can't do it spontaneously, she might make believe that she has just walked in on someone else's party and hasn't a care in the world.

I never feel like giving a party unless I'm sure I'm going to enjoy it. For one's guests' sake, if for no other reason, why wander about with that harassed look that suggests trouble in the kitchen or measles in the nursery?

Of course, there's often cause for the party giver to look about her with the glassy eye of despair as she sees the wrong people bunched together. I've frequently noticed how guests show infallible judgment in picking their opposites. The fire-eating major is sure to find the only pacifist present; and the stone-deaf duchess is apt to fasten on the bright young man with ideas that he feels must be heard.

This is where the tactful hostess should refrain from showing concern. If the guests refuse to mix, she can always turn her back and let them fight it out. Interference may make them resentful, since some people love a party row. I do myself. It's so good for the circulation. But even when the fur doesn't fly, there's something diabolically willful about a party. It either goes or it doesn't, and the hostess can scarcely be held responsible for the turn it takes. Her choice of guests may be perfect; her buffet superb; but the party can still fall flat. When this happens, she should never rush about, openly anxious, trying to puff life into a sagging crowd. Much better let the balloon collapse, say good-by to one's guests with a nimble handshake and go whistling to bed.

A good hostess must develop an insidious technique in putting a party over. If she's wise she'll do what she likes and let everyone else alone. I do condemn the hostess who regiments her guests into antics they loathe, like competing in guessing games so difficult that they are shown up as morons; or dragging them out to play tennis, when it's the one game at which they don't shine. It's disastrous to exert compulsion on a crowd assembled for pleasure.

I don't care for large parties. I feel lost when I walk into a room and see swarms of faces I don't recognize. It's worse still if the hostess tries to introduce one all round. I prefer to say hello to the first person I see and amble about as the spirit moves me. The English method of letting introductions go hang is a little less appalling than the thorough technique developed in America. I let my guests do pretty much as they like about getting to know one an-

A photo of Beatrice Lillie taken ten years ago in the show that made her a star overnight—"Charlot's Revue of 1924."

other, although the chances are that they are all old friends. I also like to arrive quite late at a party, even my own. Once I practically didn't get there at all. That proved to be one of the best parties I ever gave. Nobody missed me, which just goes to show that the hostess isn't nearly so important as she imagines herself to be.

Spontaneous parties are nearly always the best. I like to waken in the morning with the feeling that it's a good day for a party, and then call up my friends. When they haven't had time to think about it, they arrive in a more expectant frame of mind. I can't begin to count the number of parties I've given in this casual way.

My first impressions of being a hostess were picked up from my mother at the age of five. We were a somewhat musical family, known as the Lillie trio: mother, sister Muriel and dear little Bea, who wore braids then—very ducky—and poured water on the guests from a balcony at one of the Wednesday soirees.

We were so addicted to musicales and entertaining our friends with songs and poetic gestures that I grew up with the conviction that a hostess must always do more than merely feed her guests. It became quite the natural thing for me to do my turn at a party.

Then we migrated to Britain and I started my theatrical career in earnest. After that, parties came thick and fast, so that I soon absorbed a number of ideas on how a hostess could best avoid being bored at her own parties. One thing I learned was never to repeat any sort of practical joke. Guests are often touchy about having their hair disarranged, or finding trick frogs tucked underneath sofa cushions.

A hostess can have a superb time if her friends happen to be people of talent. What hostess couldn't make a party go with Noel Coward or Cole Porter at her piano, Clifton Webb dancing on her floor or Fannie Brice improvising with a shawl muffling her head?

If a hostess can sing or dance or do splits or card tricks, I see no reason why she shouldn't be part of the show. I've known women who could lift a party with their marvelous stories; and others who knew how to draw out their guests, a rare gift in the party giver. Of course, this must be done with finesse. For instance, the professional is unlikely to suffer from stage fright, but he may feel acute resentment if called on in a peremptory way to be the life of the party. I know this from my own experience. If someone invites me to a party and suggests that I do some entertaining, I'm apt to arrive in a balky frame of mind; but if the thing had never been mentioned, I should undoubtedly have started anyway. I always find it wonderful fun to make people laugh. Once I have started I feel so stimulated that I can go on from one piece of fooling to another.

I've tried most of the party games, starting long ago with pinning the tail on the donkey, down through the cryptogram-anagram era to the present time, when I sometimes launch my yacht game if things seem to be getting a little dull.

You say to your guests, "I'm giving a party on my yacht and I want you all to come. But you can't climb aboard unless you guess the two things I want you to bring." You decide what the gifts should be. The sillier the better. A parrot and a pea shooter, perhaps. The guests must then discover what is in your mind. You can give them a little help by saying that the two gifts begin with the same initials as somebody's name. It's a variation of the old parlor game where you went out of the room while everyone concentrated deeply on something in sight, and then you came in and guessed what it was.

Refreshments are most important to any party, and here's where a hostess should study the tastes of her guests.

There are sure to be gourmets as well as wits, and sometimes the two are one. The evening's success may lurk in the goose liver and champagne if it doesn't hide around the corner among the potted palms.

It's a great mistake to break up groups that are having a good time. I simply cannot cheer for anyone who catches me in the middle of my latest joke and whizzes me off to meet someone who has just come in from the West.

My favorite parties by all odds are the after-the-theater kind and country week ends, and beach parties. Absolutely one of the best parties I ever had anything to do with was given on the rocks at Antibes. It had quite a Lorelei touch. The piano was moored on a rock and the guests sat on adjacent rocks, the waves lapping at their feet. The stars shone down on us. It was lovely to sit above the water and sing, then plunge into the waves and clamber back to one's rock again.

Surroundings can help a lot. A hostess has much on her side when the moon shines through palm trees, or her guests can wander in scented gardens. One of the best parties I gave—and it was entirely spontaneous—was at the Villa d'Este. It was a gorgeous night—moonlight, the scent of mimosa coming from the gardens, Como a rippled sheet of silver. I walked out on the balcony and began to sing, and before I knew what was happening people had gathered on the terrace steps. I went on and on, for the night was divine, and I liked that uninvited audience.

A good party is a good party, no matter where you give it. I've had as much fun at some of my crowded dressing-room parties as in lush settings. True, there wasn't room to move, but we laughed and stumbled over one another and had a very good time indeed, for it's *people* who make the party, not a tropical moon.

At the moment we seem to be having a wave of novelty parties, rather than the formal masquerade. I like those easygoing gatherings with jungle settings where one can wear pajamas, a grass skirt or some rags and tatters, and call oneself dressed.

But whether her party is a masquerade or not, a hostess should give careful thought to her dress. Her party can be spoiled by an unbecoming dress, a poor coiffure or an unmanageable train. In fact, a train is something I no longer recommend since I wore one at a recent party and as a result of it had a pretty delirious night. You can have fun once with a train, but never again, and a hostess doesn't dare let herself be stepped on too often. I do much better with a fan.

I always dress quickly for my parties, possibly the result of my stage changes. It helps if one doesn't have to bother much about one's hair. Since I had it cropped some summers ago after a cruise on Lord Beaverbrook's yacht, it's been the simplest thing to get ready. I prefer white or black frocks and the plainer the cut the better. I usually wear a string of pearls.

One should always send one's guests away from a party with the feeling that they have been well sustained to the last. For now, as always, the hostess must feed the hungry, listen to the bore and rescue the wallflower—although one rarely sees the dear girls any longer who used to pine on the gilded chairs while their smarter sisters mowed down the stag line. I believe they're practically an extinct species. And in time perhaps the party bore will follow them to oblivion. Meanwhile, let the hostess rejoice at her own party, so that her guests may enjoy it too.

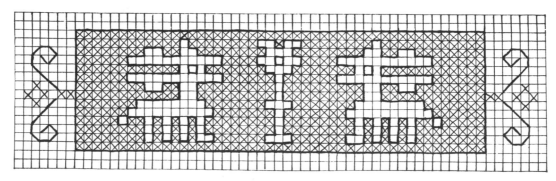

Design for cross-stitch.

MUSIC BY GERSHWIN

Isaac Goldberg

What is he like, this unseen presence of the Broadway play, whose very name is enough to lift the hearers from their chairs?

George Gershwin is as simple, as unaffected, as modest and as charming a youth as one would desire to meet. There is nothing about him that is forbidding. He wears his unprecedented celebrity as lightly as if it were a cane—that cane which one can hear swinging so jauntily in the opening rhythms of An American in Paris.

He is above medium height. He is of athletic build; not too spare however. He is dark-complexioned with dark eyes to match. His smile is almost cryptic; it is not an affirmation, but a question. Indeed, it is this quality in his whole make-up that lends him a particular, unobtrusive charm. Let there be no mistake: the composer of Concerto in F, of the Jazz Preludes, of The Man I Love is not a shrinking violet. But he has something of the humility which every instinctive artist must possess. His modesty is not a mask for swollen self-esteem.

The man has, too, that psychological rarity, the saving grace of self-knowledge. His is one of the most objective mentalities that I have encountered, and this, in a young man whose success has been so rapid, so phenomenal, is doubly rare. Listen to his popular music, dance to it, play it, and you soon discover that it is almost devoid of sentimentality. It has been one of his functions, in fact, to lift popular song up from the bogs of sentimental slush in which it had been shamelessly wallowing since the days of the Spanish-American War. There are no romantic didos in Gershwin's tunes. Rarely, as in the first version of the Concerto, does he overwrite. Even his longer pieces are as spare as his muscles. Something urban and at the same time open-airy inheres in them. It is the essential simplicity, the directness, the honesty translated into tone.

"I feel," he once said to me, "that I was meant for hard, physical work, to chop down trees, to use my muscles. This composing is indoor labor, much of it, and it takes it out of a fellow like me. Do you know, I could write reams of ballads now, full of sad sobs and moony languors. But it wouldn't be me. And later, when I'd get over my blues, I'd play them over and feel that they were written by somebody else. When I'm in my normal mood the tunes come dripping off my fingers. And they're lively tunes, full of outdoor pep."

Gershwin, composer of some of the best "blues" we have, doesn't write them when he himself is blue. He waits. Between the sob ballad and the blues lies a world of difference; the one is more or less perfunctory, while the other reaches many of us where we live. The blues that glorifies the second half of the Rhapsody in Blue is, literally and figuratively, true blue. It is from a Gershwin who may be over his blues, but from a Gershwin that still feels them vibrating through his being.

The composer of the music to so many of White's Scandals, to Tip Toes, Oh, Kay, Funny Face, Strike Up the Band, Girl Crazy (his latest hit) and other tuneful memories is not only modest but he is intellectually nervous, keyed ever to concert pitch. The quality appears almost at the very beginning of his career and remains with him in his greatest triumphs. It is not only an element of his personality; it infuses his writing.

Gershwin is something like Alibi Ike in Ring Lardner's story of that apologetic baseball player, who, whenever he slammed out a three-bagger, instead of rejoicing with his team-mates, sadly reflected how nearly it had been a home run. It is amusing to listen to a sober conversation between George and his brother, Ira Gershwin, who has written so many clever lines for George's musical comedies.

"I know," George will say. "You may be right. But I maintain that a composer needs to understand all the intricacies of counterpoint and orchestration. When I see what Mozart had accomplished in his childhood, and what Brahms and ——"

"Yes, yes," interposes the more practical Ira. "But it's every composer for himself, and for the special talents that he has. If you went ahead and became self-conscious with your writing, and packed it full of counterpoint and all those other things I know nothing about, you might achieve a certain academic standard, but you'd kill everything spontaneous in your gifts."

George, for a moment, looks worried. "I don't know," he mutters, at once convinced and unconvinced. From the tone of the brothers' voices, you would gather that they

are discussing a nearly hopeless failure. George, still shaking his head, gets up, moves automatically toward the piano, strikes a few chords, and before you know it they are executing a number from a forthcoming operetta. Ira knows all his words by heart; George's fingers dance over

George Gershwin

the black and white while he sings too, through the fragrance of the omnipresent cigar.

He loves to play his music, and other people's music too. He does not require to be coaxed. This is his conversation; this is the way George Gershwin talks to you.

RAISING A FAMILY

Elizabeth Cook

If it's a choice between a Sunday dress and a ping-pong set, get the ping-pong set.

I wonder just what do we mean by patience. Susie, aged almost three, comes into the kitchen with two cups. She has filled one of them in the bathroom and, being a sociable creature, she wants to do her pouring in a place where there is something going on. On most of these occasions mother has been an understanding companion. She has even put down paper on the chair seat and supplied the little cloth for wiping up the inevitable spills.

But this is a bad morning. The telephone rings constantly, the cake has fallen, papa has been politely sedate about nothing in particular and the domestic atmosphere is turgid. It is a saintly mother indeed who doesn't long to snatch up those cups, turn Susie over, or otherwise work off her personal feelings on friend daughter.

Then, ah, then, my friends, we summon that old lady, Patience. After all, a cake is only a cake, but a child unjustly treated is a tragedy. Let the telephone ring. Susie is more important than a dozen telephone calls.

Isn't there a verse in the Bible about agreeing with one's adversary quickly? To do this, look at the matter from Susie's point of view. There is nothing so beautiful as water sliding down through the air from cup to cup. And if you hold the cup and feel that you are the master of this mystery, what a thrill!

If you can show this wonder to mother and feel that you have struck a spark of understanding in her, how satisfying this all is. If mother shows the right spirit, she is laying the foundations for that lovely thing which later on we call the "confidence of the child."

Children are like streams of running water themselves. You can't push them

aside with an impatient hand. They go on their way, regardless, and you can either enjoy their experiments, direct them as wisely and lovingly as you know how, or else get left on the bank.

P. S. Should children be allowed to pour in the first place? Certainly, and to measure sugar and coffee in spoons for their mothers, and to carry books and dishes. They should run the egg beater too! Live with 'em. It may be a trifle inconvenient at the moment, but the dividends make compound interest look pale.

It it's a choice between a Sunday dress and a ping-pong set, get the ping-pong set. Spend the most money for the things children use oftenest and get the most good from. Substitutes for the old-style slipper and trips to the woodshed are roller skates, tennis rackets, footballs, basket balls, skis, home duties, Camp Fire, Girl Scouts, Boy Scouts, 4-H clubs, Sunday schools, books, music and dancing lessons, a pool table at home, things to ride, things to climb, like stepladders, big blocks, baseball bats. Also a good umpire, preferably the parent.

A natural child wants lots of interesting things to do. He likes to do real things too.

Years ago I knew a child who sat on the roof and held shingle nails for her father, who made terrible apple pies that were eaten and praised by her family, who learned to make wonderful bread when she was only ten, who planted potatoes that the family really needed. Perhaps her efforts were bungling, but when her folks criticized her "the quality of mercy was not strained."

She was an eager, rebelling child, and so her mother taught her how to hemstitch in order that she might learn patience. Her mother told her about the nuns sitting in-

side their stone walls in their gardens as they, too, learned patience, and to this day the child never picks up a needle without hearing that far-off note of convent bells. This child remembers scrubbing the kitchen floor three times before it suited the mistress of ceremonies and, far from resenting it, she says daily grateful prayers for the habit of thorough work. Children recognize sincerity in anything and they respect and remember it.

People who give children no creative work and then complain of their behavior are like people who stand a horse between the shafts without putting on any harness and then kick the poor brute because he doesn't pull the wagon. I firmly believe in creative work as a builder of discipline, a means of forming a good attitude toward living.

Let children bake cookies and make candy, let them arrange their own rooms. If this means tacking up unhemmed muslin squares with crayola pictures, think of the impressionistic school and be polite. If the child's taste runs to collection of sick clocks, keep your eyes open for more sick clocks. Let the children plan, dig and plant gardens.

When one of my children was nine, he made out an elaborate plan to aid me in my day's housework. Did I tell him to mind his own affairs? Certainly not. I let him help me carry out the plan and he admitted at the end of the day that there was more to it than he had thought. He then started making budgets for himself!

There are so many things a mother can do to bring this creative feeling to the fore. Have the children write letters, fix play houses, print a home newspaper, have the privilege of arranging the living room for a

Menus for Entertaining the Bride

week. Let them make pop stands and racers.

The other day while I was talking to a visitor, a little nine-year-old neighbor boy burst into our presence with a bunch of goldenrod. He hadn't knocked, his shirt tail was out, his hair stuck up and his face was smudged. A tooth was out, but his eye was bright and blue. "I picked it myself," he said. "It's for you. It's pretty, ain't it? You can have it."

I could see my guest shiver.

"My, what a dreadful child," she said. "Does he always break in on you this way?"

I thought of another boy who knocks, takes off his hat and stands till he is told to sit. When his mother has friends in for bridge, he and his sisters are paraded in formation and do their social tricks. Yet these children did the neighborhood a favor by moving away.

Social graces do not come easily to a natural child. Of the two, I infinitely prefer the bearer of the goldenrod. He was sincere, he appreciated beauty, he wanted to share it and he never did a mean trick behind my back. The substance of good conduct must be considered as well as its form.

A child misbehaves for one of the same reasons that an adult does: He isn't using his powers and he hasn't conquered his environment. In fact, he never will completely. None of us does. Else there'd be no more inventions. Life is a big dish of ice cream and lots of us don't have any spoon. A child who has a talent for music is a better-behaved child if he is having a chance to develop that love of beautiful melody. The child with a talent for the dance is a better-behaved child if she has a chance to work out these rhythms.

If the children in a family become increasingly happy, ambitious, healthy and mentally independent as they pass from one year of childhood to the next, the mother need not fear any criticism of her methods. In the news dispatches from Moscow there is quoted the troubles of the commissariat of education. Says the dispatch: "A uniform solution of the baby problem is being sought now for all the communes." Hello, Russia! A whole lot of us got to this stage before you did!

And no matter how we solve it, some friend, relative or neighbor is going to see our fatal errors and think that modern mothers ought to stay home more. In our neighborhood we are thought to be either intensely Victorian or futuristic. It all depends on what situation we are caught in. We are so old style that we like to be spoken to respectfully by our children, but our daughters are at liberty to put on shorts and do chest rolls on the roof if they wish.

After listening to a young orator rehearse a floor talk, helping another to make his cowlick lie down, being invited to inspect a radio diagram in the magazine, giving a stern little lecture on how bad manners at home are lots worse than bad manners away from home and various other things not listed in any book on homemaking, there is frequently little time for intensive housework. But my home is alive!

Breakfast

VARIEGATED COLORS
Variegated Tulips, Purple and Blue Candles, Pottery Flower Bowl

FRUIT AURORA
Fresh Pineapple Wedges, Unhulled Strawberries and a Cone of Confectioners' Sugar, Arranged in Triangular Form

EGGS À LA PRINTEMPS
An Oval Piece of Broiled Ham on a Slice of Toast, Under Stalks of Buttered Fresh Asparagus, Topped With a Poached Egg

BUTTERED TOAST *or* **CREAMED NEW POTATOES**

TOASTED ENGLISH MUFFINS
or
CORNMEAL MUFFINS WITH MARMALADE
or
ENGLISH MARMALADE GRIDDLE CAKES
Tiers of Griddle Cakes Put Together With Marmalade and Cut Layer-Cake Fashion

COFFEE

Dinner

GOLD AND SILVER
Killarney Roses, Silver or Gold Candles, Silver Flower Bowl

CLAM BOUILLON
Garnished With Oyster Crabs, and Whipped Cream Sprinkled With Nutmeg
TOASTED OYSTER CRACKERS

BROILED SPRING CHICKEN
DUCHESS POTATO ROSES **RASPBERRY SAUCE**
BUTTERED NEW GREEN PEAS *or* **LIMA BEANS**

BRIDAL JELLY SALAD
Ordinary Gelatin Salad, Whipped, and Shredded Ripe Olives and Celery Folded in Before Molding
CRIMPED-EDGE CRACKERS

FRENCH VANILLA ICE CREAM ON ANGEL FOOD CAKE
With
FRESH PINEAPPLE *or* **BUTTERSCOTCH SAUCE**

AFTER-DINNER COFFEE

Luncheon

GREEN AND WHITE
Lilies of the Valley With Asparagus Fern, Green Candles and Crystal Glass Flower Bowl

MINTED PEARS
Canned Pears Dipped in Lime Juice and Sprinkled With Chopped Mint
or
AVOCADO COCKTAIL
Half Grapefruit With Alternate Sections Replaced With Slices of Avocado and Center Filled With Chopped Green Olives

BROILED QUAIL ON TOAST
or
LONG ISLAND DUCKLING
CONTINENTAL SAUCE **STEAMED RICE**

FRENCH ARTICHOKE SALAD WITH FRENCH DRESSING

MERINGUE GLACÉ MADE WITH PISTACHIO ICE CREAM
or
BAKED ALASKA
PEPPERMINT WAFERS DECORATED WITH TINY WEDDING BELLS
SALTED ALMONDS

TEA *or* **COFFEE**

Supper

YELLOW AND LAVENDER
Jonquils With Lavender and White Sweet Peas, Lavender Candles, Colored Glass Flower Bowl

HORS D'ŒUVRES
Herring on Slices of Hard-Cooked Egg, Wafer-Thin Slices of Rolled Smoked Sturgeon on a Sliver of Dill Pickle, a Circle of Sliced Chicken Breast Garnished With a Diamond-Shaped Piece of Cervelat Sausage

TONGUE MOUSSE LOAF
BUTTERED NEW POTATO BALLS **HUNGARIAN MUSTARD SAUCE**
ASPARAGUS TIPS IN DRAWN-BUTTER SAUCE
HOT BISCUIT

FLAGEOLET SALAD IN ROMAINE STALKS
or
HEARTS OF PALM SALAD

BLUSHING FLUFF
Whipped Cream and Egg White Folded Into Stewed Rhubarb
or
STRAWBERRY ICE-CREAM

COFFEE

Reception

SPRING COLORS
Delphinium, Shasta Daisies and Pink Roses
POULET AUX OLIVES
Chicken Breast Creamed With Celery and Pimiento-Filled Ripe Olives
PICKLED WATERMELON RIND **HOT SCONES**
FROZEN PEAR GLACÉ
MACAROONS **COCONUT KISSES**
PINK FONDANT-DIPPED PEPPERMINT CREAMS
RECEPTION CHOCOLATE
or
COFFEE

AND SO YOU ARE IN LOVE!

Dorothy Dix

And so you are in love!

Nothing remarkable about that. It is Nature taking its regular course, for, in a manner of speaking, every woman is in love from the time she ceases sticking out her tongue at the little boy who lives next door and wondering why God encumbered the earth with a grubby creature who shies rocks at cats and doesn't play dolls, until the undertaker folds her hands over a heart that has had as many tenants as a hotel for transients. The theme song of girlhood is the chorus of the old Florodora sextette: "I must love somebody and it might as well be you." So eager is every girl to love and be loved, so overflowing is she with sentiment, that she spends her adolescence embroidering with her imagination a beautiful cloak of romance that she is ready to fling around the first boy who comes along.

This causes her to fall into many and grievous errors, and only too often to believe that a lad is her Fairy Prince who never, himself, dreamed of posing in such a rôle, and who has none of the attributes of royalty save such as she has endowed him with in her fancy. And when she finds out her mistake, sometimes it breaks her heart, and sometimes it breaks the heart of a good, honest, commonplace man who never understands why he has been deposed from the throne.

Most women's memories are filled with the sweet and shadowy ghosts of the men they thought they loved. There was the college sheik. There was the dashing young officer and the daring aviator, with their hypnotic brass buttons. There was the soulful matinée idol with the dreamy eyes and the killing line of love-making. There was the football hero, and a dozen others whose pictures, at one time or another, occupied the silver frames on their dressing tables, and who filled their thoughts by day and their dreams by night, yet whose names they have now forgotten.

Nor do many women ever meet their first sweethearts after the lapse of years without offering up fervent thanksgivings to heaven for merciful deliverance.

So when a girl tells me that she is in love, I always want to implore her to try to be sure of herself, to examine her own heart dispassionately and, at least, attempt to make a correct diagnosis of her own case.

None of us know why we love, or why we cease to love. Even Solomon, whose explorations into the tender passion were numerous and sincere, declared in despair, at the last, that the way of a man with a maid was past all finding out. So love defies analysis, just as it laughs to scorn every effort to regulate our hearts or control our affections.

Every day we see men who are such beauty worshipers that we would think that no female short of a movie star could fire their fancies, fall in love with girls who have saleratus-biscuit complexions and pug noses and skimmed-milk eyes.

Just because you've fallen in love with the dimple is no reason for marrying the whole girl.
W. C. FIELDS

We behold highly cultured, intellectual men enamored of girls who haven't a thimbleful of brains and who never read anything but the society news and the beauty chats in the newspapers.

We see tenderly reared girls fall in love with hopeless derelicts, with drunkards, with brutes, with ne'er-do-wells, with men who are out of their class morally and mentally as well as socially, and we shake our heads and wonder why.

But neither we nor they can give any explanation of the phenomenon. They only know that for some strange reason that is beyond their fathoming some particular man or woman is the one to whom his or her heart goes out; that he or she is the one with power to thrill them and to flood their souls with a joy and fill their lives with a completeness that no other human being can do.

Primarily, of course, this is sex attraction, but although physical appeal is a part of love, there is more to it than that. There is something that lasts after passion has died of satiety. Something that fuses even the antagonistic qualities in a man and woman into a tie that binds. Something that makes men and women such comrades that they never tire of each other. Something that robs sacrifice of its bitterness and makes toil a sacred delight because done for each other. Something that glorifies homely, ordinary men and women in each other's sight so that they never see each other as they are, but only as they exist in each other's imaginations.

That is this strange thing we call love, and the catch about it is that there are no signs and symbols by which we may recognize it at sight in others, or even know whether we are experiencing it ourselves or not; no hall marks upon it by which we are enabled to tell the genuine from the spurious.

No wonder that a young girl confronted with the love problem is bewildered. No wonder that she does not know her own heart and is uncertain whether the feeling she has for some youth is a deathless passion or a passing fancy. No wonder she goes plucking the daisies of her thoughts, sighing, "He loves me, he loves me not. I love him, I love him not." Yet, ironically enough, her happiness and well-being in life depend upon her getting the right answer.

When a girl is in love she is always preoccupied with the state of the man's affections, and is always asking him: "Do you love me?" "Are you absolutely, utterly sure that you will never cease to love me?" "Are you certain that you will never change and grow tired of me?"

If she were wiser she would take the man's love for granted, since in marrying her and assuming her board bill and shopping ticket for life he is giving a proof of it strong enough to draw money on at the bank, and she would devote her time to probing into her own heart and making sure of the temperature of her own affections.

For, contrary to the generally accepted theory, it is much more important for a woman to be madly in love with her husband than it is for him to be wildly in love with her. A man has his business, his career, a million outside interests to distract and amuse him. He can get along comfortably enough on a modicum of affection and a lukewarm liking for his Maria, but a woman's whole existence is centered in her love life. She is always miserably discontented and unhappy unless she is so romantically devoted to her husband that he fills the universe for her and she is kept on her tiptoes always trying to please him.

Hence, the very first test that every girl should apply to love is to ask herself whether she cares enough for a man to be willing to wear her last year's hat and dowdy clothes just to be with him; whether she can cook and wash and scrub and find them exciting occupations if done for him; whether her love is strong enough to stand living in a kitchenette apartment and sleuthing around to find cut-rate butcher-shops without its losing its glamour.

Another test that every girl who thinks herself in love should apply to the man who looks like a Romeo to her is the intelligence test. Especially the conversational test. Has he any line of talk except soft talk? Can he keep a modern, educated woman interested and amused during thirty or forty years of tête-à-têtes?

Illustration by John La-Gatta for BUSINESS WOMEN IN LOVE, *a story by Faith Baldwin.*

More love is bored to death than is killed in any other way, and more women are driven to seek affinities because they are married to men who never have an idea except about the stock market or the grocery trade or the baseball score.

And so a girl does well to stop the love-making long enough to find out whether her Tom, Dick or Harry ever reads anything or has any thoughts outside of his business, and whether he would make a gay and entertaining life companion, or would make her yawn her head off.

And still another test that a girl should apply to love is whether it is built on respect or pity. A man appears to be able to look down on his wife and still love her, but a woman has to look up to her husband if she is going to keep in love with him.

True, we see women stick to husbands they fish out of the gutter. We see women work and support lazy trifling husbands. We see women cling to men who disgrace them, but that is just the mother complex in them. It is not the kind of love that a woman should have for her mate, and in her heart every woman has a secret contempt for the man who is a weakling.

As for a girl being able to tell whether a man is in love with her or not, that is an impossibility. She can only believe as much of his impassioned vows as her credulity will permit, and keep her weather eye out to see how he treats her; whether he puts her happiness and pleasure before his own; whether he is considerate of her; whether he tries to protect her, even against himself, or whether he is jealous and tyrannical and loves himself so much better than he ever will any woman that his wife will never be more than a household convenience to him.

In these days when an ever-increasing number of men are loath to burden themselves with the support of a family, girls are continually assailed with free-love propaganda. They are told over and over again that marriage kills love, and that there is something particularly romantic and beautiful and enduring in love under the rose, and that an illicit love affair has about it some illusive aroma that vanishes in a conventional respectable marriage.

Nothing could be farther from the truth than this, as a survey of one's friends and acquaintances will amply prove. All of us know many marriages in which the devotion of a husband and wife has endured for twenty or thirty, often even for fifty years, but very few can point to a liaison that has lasted even ten years. The thing that kills love is not marriage itself. It is the clash of different temperaments. It is little meannesses, little stupidities, selfishness, the lack of generosity, the lack of understanding and sympathy that come about when a man and woman live in daily companionship, whether they are married or unmarried.

Love nests have just as many thorns in them as the domestic coop has; nor do the little birds in them agree any more harmoniously than do those in the regulation barnyard.

Indeed, so far from marriage having a sinister effect upon love, it is its greatest protector and bulwark. For the husband and wife have the strongest of all ties, a common interest. They are working out their fortune together; they rise or fall together; they are building up a home and a position in society together, and, above all, they have the mutual love of their children and their ambition in their children's future.

Possibly the most dangerous enemy of love is jealousy, and the married couple is far less prone to this than are those men and women whose only hold upon each other is a fancy that may change at any minute. From the nature of their circumstances these are always bound to be filled with fear and suspicion, always looking for someone younger and more beautiful, someone newer, fresher, to dawn upon their horizon and snare away the mate who is forever seeking a new sensation and who knows no law but his or her desire.

Any girl to whom a man proposes an illicit relationship instead of honorable marriage is forewarned that he already has it in his mind to leave her when he wearies of her, and that he has no intention whatever of being faithful to her. Life itself stacks the cards against her because time inevitably robs her of her beauty, familiarity makes of her a twice-told tale that has lost the allure of novelty, and when these are gone she has not the legal claim of matrimony or the power of conventions to hold her recreant lover.

And particularly would I warn girls against falling in love with married men. This is a danger to which every business girl is inevitably exposed, because she is bound to be brought in contact with men who are more worldly-wise, more sophisticated, more intelligent, more polished, more interesting, and who have more money to spend than the boys of her own age. Also propinquity does its deadly work in the office even more effectually than it does out of it, and a girl who is associated day after day with a charming and interesting man is very apt to get romantic fancies in her head about him unless she is indeed a wise virgin who leaves her heart parked at home when she comes to work.

Occasionally the married man is a conscienceless villain who deliberately sets out to win a girl's love just because it flatters his vanity. Sometimes an unhappily married man steals a girl's love because he is starving for the affection his wife does not give him. Very often the married man is entirely blameless and never even suspects that the girl has idealized him into her romantic hero.

But however it happens, it is always a tragedy. For if the girl takes her happiness she does it by wrecking a home and robbing a wife of her husband, and children of their father, and if she does not she knows all the pangs of the cruelest jealousy on earth and all the anguish and bitterness of hopeless love.

It is often said that modern girls do not love with the passionate abandon that their foremothers did, that they are hardboiled and little given to sentiment, but this is not true. The human heart does not change, nor the love of a maid for a man. Certainly women do not die of blighted love, or pine away in a green and yellow melancholy over faithless loves, as was the fashion in the dear, dead, Victorian days, but just as many girls as ever give up good jobs and good homes to marry impecunious youths who have nothing to give them but love. Just as many girls are going without lunch to buy towels for their hope chests as ever. Just as many girls think the chip diamond in their engagement ring is more precious than the Kohinoor. Just as many girls are seeing the embodiment of every manly virtue and charm in some perfectly commonplace young chap.

For love is the same, world without end. It is always the same wonderful and beautiful and foolish and wise mystery that no one can explain, but every girl who tells you with shining eyes that she is in love is glimpsing Paradise.

The Sub Deb

SING a song of sixpence,
A pocket full of rye,
Four and twenty blackbirds
Baked in a pie.
When the pie was opened,
The birds began to sing;
Wasn't that a dainty dish
To set before the King?

The King was in his countinghouse
Counting out his money;
The Queen was in the parlor
Eating bread and honey;
The maid was in the garden,
Hanging out the clothes,
When down came a blackbird
And snapped off her nose.

AS MY Uncle Kipling (who wrote The Jungle Book) said, when I asked him about blackbirds:

Nine are the Laws of the Hedgerow
Which Mavis the Song Thrush wrote.
For blackbirds baked in a pie crust
This is the law they quote:
That the blackbird nearest the egg cup
Is the one which must give the note.

So that the other blackbirds know whether to start on B, or D, which is very important when singing. I very much wanted to tell you why the cook always puts an egg cup in a pie, but when I asked her about it, why, she just said that they always did.

What Really Happened

By A. A. MILNE

Illustrated by E. H. Shepard

THERE was an old woman who lived in a shoe,
She had so many children she didn't know what to do.
She gave them some broth without any bread,
And she whipped them all soundly and put them to bed.

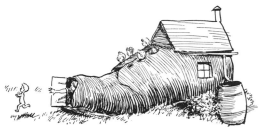

SO THEY say. But I don't believe it. What really happened was this:

There was an old woman who lived in a shoe,
And the whole of her family lived in it too.
She had sixty five sons and a dear little daughter,
And she soaped them by sixes in lavender water.
And when she had rinsed them, their six little faces
Would dry through the holes which were made for the laces.
There were times when she thought, "It would sooner be done,
If I'd sixty-five daughters and one little son."

Because she thought that the girls wouldn't have got so dirty as the boys. But I expect they would.

THERE was an old woman tossed up in a basket
Nineteen times as high as the moon;
Where she was going I couldn't ask it,
For in her hand she carried a broom.

"Old woman, old woman, old woman," quoth I,
"Oh, whither, oh, whither, oh, whither so high?"
"I'm brushing the cobwebs off the sky."
"Shall I go with you?" "Yes, by and by."

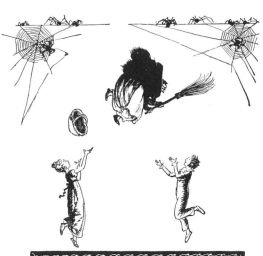

WHEN Uncle Grumphiter heard this, he sat down to multiply the height of the moon (which is six figures in a row, but I've forgotten what they are)—to multiply all this by nineteen! If it had been ten, I should have helped him, but as it was nineteen, which is a very unfriendly number, I just sat down and waited for him to finish . . . and after I had sharpened his pencil twice, and got him another piece of paper, he began throwing things away and saying crossly, "Well, anyhow, it's impossible." So now we shall never know how high she went. But if she was tossed by a Bull, and the Bull was a friend-and-relation of the Cow who jumped over the moon, then I don't think it's as impossible as Uncle Grumphiter says, because it shows they were That Sort of Animal.

ANYTHING CAN HAPPEN

IN HOLLYWOOD

Robert Taylor

There is a suspense about being in Hollywood which I doubt if one finds in any other city. Anything may happen! You are unknown today. Perhaps you will be reading your name in the newspapers tomorrow. Of course, if anyone had told me I should be receiving more than one thousand letters a day within a year, I should have laughed at him. And yet I should have known it might happen. No matter how discouraged you become, that curious sense of adventure does not leave you.

My first test was a trial one with Evalyn Knapp, directed by Harry Bucquet, specialist in the supervising of tests. There is nothing more cold or unfriendly than a test stage. The elaborate detail of a regular set is missing. The realism is not there. One camera, a few lights, a few odd pieces of furniture. This was a drawing-room scene, written especially for a test by a test-script writer. I was in full evening dress. You know how a man feels walking into a restaurant in tails at high noon? Evening dress requires a proper background.

Miss Knapp entered from one side; I came from the other. "Hello"—my first word for the screen was supposed to be nonchalant. I was about as nonchalant as a condemned man saying his last word before walking to the scaffold. "It's a beautiful evening," I added as we sat upon a bench. You could just see the evening—a backdrop with a red moon in a cheap vaudeville theater.

I was a dramatic coach teaching a girl the technique of love-making. The climax was when my play acting was supposed to become the real thing. I had been instructing the girl; I found myself in love with her. I wondered why Mr. Bucquet suddenly left the set at this point. He didn't wish to hurt my feelings.

My excitement was pathetic. I telephoned the studio before nine o'clock the next morning. Three days later there was a report. Mr. Bucquet's secretary said, "I hate to tell you, but the camera went haywire. Everything's blurred. The action's all right, only you can't see it."

That was my luckiest break. Because my test blew up, I had passed my first examination of importance.

Loaned to Fox for my first picture: Handy Andy, with Will Rogers! My feeling was one of keen disappointment. Why couldn't I make my first picture in my own studio? Wasn't I good enough to work where I had been trained?

I know now all actors feel that way at one time or another. Clark Gable admits he

Robert Taylor

objected to being "farmed out" to Columbia for It Happened One Night. He even told director Frank Capra he didn't want to do it. Yet he won the Motion Picture Academy award for it! A studio is a busy place and its executives do not often stop to explain the reasons for their actions. I should have known. I had wanted to get away from Nebraska to learn how other people lived and worked. I did learn much from working at Fox. I had never been off my own lot. I was unknown at home.

At Fox, I was a guest. I became a personality. My name had been changed. Anyone knows that S. Arlington Brough could not go into lights over a theater, if it should deserve to get there. The studio had suggested Geoffrey Taylor. I had kicked about that, knowing I would be called Geof. Robert meant Bob, which was common but comfortable. A new name, a new place to

work—a feeling of self-confidence. When Will Rogers patted my back or threw his arm around my shoulders, I straightened and wondered what the fellows back home would think if they could see it! And people did talk to me at this studio. Even Janet Gaynor and Warner Baxter! I began to have the feeling I have today about a studio, it is a big campus where everyone knows you and you know everyone; a place in which you work, but where you also have fun. You see, I had a recommendation at Fox: I was that "new guy, Robert Taylor, loaned to us by Metro." My studio was my letter of introduction into the fraternal organization of another lot.

The first day on a motion-picture set is terrible. Even though you have been trained for six months and have actually worked in trial productions—both on the stage and on sets—yet there is so much you do not know. You have been taught that relaxation is the secret, and you find yourself as tense as a well-tuned violin string. You stumble against your own make-up table, one of those light dressing-room tables placed on the set so you may give a last dash of powder to your face before you go before the cameras. You feel perspiration seeping through the powder. You know you may not be needed for hours, but you cannot leave because you are "on call." Relaxation? You never heard the word—you must do something. Count sheep? Now, young fellow, you are in pictures! This is your first picture. You don't know much yet; you'd better study what's going on about you. Can you name the equipment being used on this production? Do you know the titles of the men scurrying around you? Probably not. Although you have been instructed, you realize only experience can teach you.

You would expect your eye to travel first to the director. Mine didn't. I hunted and found the property man. He's easy to locate because of the leather belt around his waist. Between this leather belt and his "props box" he carries everything which may be needed, from a clothesbrush to buttons to match the buttons on the suits of the actors. As it happened, Mr. Rogers lost a button during the making of this picture. He didn't notice it, but the prop boy did and was sewing one in its place before Mr. Rogers realized what had happened. Suppose I am smoking a cigarette. It's three-quarters gone when the scene is over. I begin a rehearsal for the next scene. When the actual shooting starts, the property boy bounces over, removes my new cigarette and hands me one which is three-quarters smoked. The moment I have finished the first shot, he has jumped to his box and cut a cigarette to the proper length. I use the words "bounce" and "jump" because I have never seen a property man who has not developed his own peculiar gait, intended, I suppose, to accelerate action.

When I was a student I had been taken on a tour of the studio, and the most amazing sight to me had been the props. "Animate" and "inanimate" properties are the two general classifications. One moves—the other doesn't. If a director wants a duck that can walk, flap its wings and wipe its feet at the same time, he calls the head of the animate property department. Of course, there is no such animal anywhere but in the movies. However, one has been made within a week in the mechanical shop. Anything can happen in Hollywood—and does. The inanimate properties are equally startling. Our guide told us there are eighteen hundred real antiques in that department, and there are scouts continually hunting for antiques, as there are for actors. The hand-property department! Here we saw everything which can be moved by hand: telephones, crutches, suitcases, pie plates, communion cups, mirrors, surgical scalpels, wax flowers—I have never seen such a collection, not even in the largest department store in the world. Speaking of flowers, each studio has its florist's shop. If Norma Shearer is to wear orchids in a scene, six corsages are ready. The scene may take all day and the flowers must be fresh for each shot.

Janet Gaynor

I did not work that first day. I doubt if there is anything more nerve-racking than not to work your first day on your first picture. It is true that Mr. Rogers held us up with his lines. He could not memorize accurately, but he could ad-lib more quickly and humorously than any other actor I have seen. One scene in an entire day!

When I went home, more tired and nervous than if I had worked, I knew one thing for certain: a motion-picture actor who decides his genius is responsible for a successful motion picture is crazy. Every

time I now find myself getting excited about my achievements—which anyone might do when it takes half an hour to get from the lobby of your hotel to your suite because of the women crowding the lobby, as they did during my recent first visit to New York City—I remember that first day with Will Rogers.

Men do not stumble over mountains, but over molehills.
CONFUCIUS

Despite this lesson, I was terrible when I went to work the next morning. I had only two lines and I flunked them. Forgot. Stammered. Stood on the balls of my feet. In other words, I went rigid. I was frightened. I still am on the first day of a picture. Somehow, everything you know runs right away from you. You see, I was thinking of myself, the one thing an actor must not do.

Myrna Loy

Norma Shearer

But when I returned to my own studio, I found my status had changed. I had made a picture! I had worked on another lot. I wasn't just a schoolboy. There were tests made of me for pictures. I was cast in Buried Loot, the first of the "crime doesn't pay" series. This was a short, but I had the lead. My first role of importance. Again I didn't realize it, but the studio had shown its wisdom. This short was all action. Action pictures do not require so much repression as drama. I could still mug a little.

When a studio commences to advertise you, you know opportunity lies not too far ahead. And when the publicity department begins to pay you serious attention—then watch out. Fame is beckoning a finger. It may be a weak gesture, but it is a gesture.

Naturally, I did not see the letters which came in from Society Doctor, in which I played my first important role. I could only guess the results had not been negative when Howard Strickling, Western publicity director, sent for me.

This interview frightened me as had few others. While going to school, I had heard weird tales of this department. If a fellow made a success, the publicity boys would tie him to their apron strings and become dictatorial mammas! They would write our life stories, tell us what girls we could see, what time to get up and retire. Mr. Strickling talked on two subjects: (1) I was to be careful about getting into scrapes or situations which might injure my reputation. If I did get into trouble, such as being arrested for speeding, I was to report immediately to him, so the department would know the truth before a highly colored pic-

Irene Dunne

ture could be printed in the papers. A motion-picture actor was always news. He could not help that. There was no sense in resenting it. Even small fame was a responsibility and one should do his best to live up to it. (2) I was to tell my life story to one of his writers. I was to tell the truth. And I was to continue to tell the men of his department anything of interest which might happen to me from day to day.

The publicity department sorts out the writers who see us. There are careless

Joan Crawford

Clark Gable

Jean Harlow

ing. Dad was asking for mother. "I'm lonely," he'd say, and she'd go down and spend the rest of the day with him. She visited me while I was at Pomona. After two days she was ill. Seriously so, with a high temperature. I secretly wired dad and he came out. The moment he walked into that room she was well; didn't even remember she'd been ill. They were married twenty-five years, and if they spoke a cross word, I didn't hear it. I do not want divorce; I want marriage—the wholesome beauty of the real thing. And I cannot change that story for publicity purposes.

The path leading to motion-picture recognition is lonely and difficult; the one I am traveling now is definitely hazardous. Ten pictures in a year! The studio has a method of building fame exactly as it has of training actors. I had received recognition in one picture, Society Doctor. The next step was to cast me with famous names. A small part in West Point of the Air, with Wallace Beery. No matter how small the part, the Beery following would see me. Then—to playing opposite the ladies. Two program pictures, or inexpensive productions: Times Square Lady, with Virginia Bruce; Murder in the Fleet, with Jean Parker. Then a big picture, one which cost much money and was entitled to a big publicity campaign: Broadway Melody of 1936, with Eleanor Powell.

Because of this bit of luck, Universal borrowed me to play opposite Irene Dunne in Magnificent Obsession. Again, loaning me to Universal for such an important picture was shrewd showmanship. Not only would I play in houses under a different management in this country, but Universal is acknowledged to have the best foreign release for its product. This meant a definite build-up for my name in foreign countries. My reward for not doing a "flop" with Miss Dunne was playing the boy friend to Janet Gaynor in Small Town Girl. This picture pushed my fan mail to the point where I had to hire two secretaries. My latest star is Joan Crawford—I am opposite her in The Gorgeous Hussy. And now I do His Brother's Wife, with Barbara Stanwyck, and then Camille, with Garbo. When a fellow plays opposite Garbo, he's become a leading man in capital letters. Of course, there are still Norma Shearer and Myrna Loy. I'd like to play with them too.

I said this path is hazardous. Of course it is. Fame is always dangerous—especially fame which comes so quickly. You don't know what to do with it. The public liked that boy it saw in that first picture. If he changes, the public may not like the new fellow.

Do I want stardom? It's a lot easier to be Greta Garbo's leading man. If Camille fails, she'll be blamed. If I am a star and a picture is not good, I am to blame. That's the public's viewpoint.

The best thing I can do, as I see it, is to remember the boy who lived in Nebraska. He wanted adventure. He has it. He likes it. But he must not forget: Anything can happen in Hollywood. One can get out much more quickly than he can get in. My father owned several farms in Nebraska. I am holding on to them.

writers, as there are careless stenographers. If I say I admire a certain actress, that does not mean I am in love with her or going to marry her. But a careless writer may misquote me so I embarrass the actress and myself.

The favorite question of fan-magazine interviewers seems to be, "What do you think of marriage?" My mother and dad made it pretty difficult for me when it comes to marriage. Although dad had a nurse in his office, the telephone would ring at home at ten o'clock almost every morn-

Greta Garbo

RECIPES FOR SUCCESSFUL DINING

Elsie De Wolfe

Since food, like fashion, changes with the times, the standard of food in our day is very different from the prewar standard of lavish hospitality. Today, good taste in food is just the reverse of lavish; it is stamped with the same restraint as that shown by a dress worn at dinner in 1934, compared with a dress worn at dinner in 1900.

In my philosophy, the perfect meal is the short meal. Naturally, one presupposes in a short meal that the few dishes served are perfection and served generously. The short meal must have a perfectly balanced menu: one simple dish and one richer one.

As to the decoration of your table, never have high flower vases or things that obstruct the view of the 'beautiful woman across the table, or prevent the witticism of the clever man who is your opposite from reaching you except by dodging to one side or the other.

A very successful decoration I have used in Paris is a cloth of silver, with a crystal ship, all its glass sails and its pennants set and flying and mirrored in a sheet of glass. Added to this are two rock-crystal birds and four rock-crystal candlesticks. At Christmastime, in 1931, I had a table of gold, hoping that it might in some way draw us all back to the old gold standard again. The gold-lamé tablecloth, old white china and many yellow roses proved a great success.

For summer decorations I like what I call the *curé's* garden decoration, where all the flowers are put together and make multicolored bouquets—rose and yellow and white and blue and red, as if they had just been plucked from the herbaceous borders.

I am a great believer in using the plant of the moment, just as I like the vegetable or the fruit or game in season. Cyclamen in bunches of rose and white, and garden lilies when they come in June, cut short and massed together in white or silver jardinières, are lovely, so are nasturtiums, massed in silver cups.

There is a lovely white table to be made with any interesting white pieces that one may possess. Then there are lovely feather flowers that one can use all winter. Mine are dogwood blossoms made of white feathers on brown branches—very beautiful.

But the first thing to learn is to keep your table decoration low, low, low.

There are other rules that add to the success of a dinner. I wonder if you have the same:

Do you have a menu in which there is one simple dish for those who diet, and one rich dish for those who don't?

Are your dishes in the short meal presented the second time as hot as when first served?

Do you serve coffee at the table at the psychological moment when your guests are relaxed and happy, and when good conversation flows? Do not interrupt it by taking them into the drawing-room, where the thread of what might have been interesting is broken. This is not a rule.

And now for some of my favorite recipes, and at the end a few menus as well:

RICE TRIANON. Boil rice in a well-seasoned bouillon. After rice is boiled mix in small cooked "elbow" macaroni, little green peas and green string beans cut into dice and stewed in butter, ham and tongue also cut into small dice, Swiss or Parmesan cheese grated, and a purée of tomatoes. Put all in a mold, sprinkle with grated cheese on top and brown well in oven.

SUZETTE PANCAKES. Make thin round pancakes about six inches in diameter. Mix ¼ pound of powdered sugar with ¼ pound of butter and the grated rind of an orange. Mix a little curaçao liqueur to make a thick paste. Put a teaspoonful of this paste in the center of the pancake, and fold over. Immediately before serving place the folded pancakes in a chafing dish, with melted butter and powdered sugar, pour over a glass of brandy or rum, and set aflame. Serve immediately.

CREAMED HADDOCK. Soak for twelve hours the fillets of haddock in milk diluted one-half by water. Then boil in milk and water (also half milk and half water). At the moment when they commence to boil, put the saucepan to the side of the fire and allow to simmer slowly for three-quarters of an hour. Make a cream sauce and add to it thick fresh cream. Place the fillets of haddock on a platter and dress with the cream sauce. Serve apart, with this dish, small plain boiled potatoes.

INDIAN RICE. Put the required quantity of rice to boil in cold water, and boil for ten minutes commencing from the moment of boiling. Rinse in cold water, and place in the oven for a short time so that each kernel of rice is separate and not sticky.

KIDNEYS ALI-BAB (with credit to Ali-Bab's well-known cookbook). Brown in a saucepan veal kidneys, cut into pieces, in very hot butter. As soon as they have lost their raw red color, set aflame with a glass of brandy. When the flame has died pour over a glass of sherry wine. Add cut-up mushrooms and cook for ten minutes. Then add thick fresh cream and grated horseradish to taste. Bring to a boil and serve at once.

EGGS CARLOS (recipe by Princesse Guy de Faucigny-Lucinge, Paris). Boil rice in a well-seasoned bouillon. Place on serving platter in a mound in the center of the dish and garnish around with fried eggs (fried on both sides, and kept small and round as possible), small whole grilled tomatoes, fried whole bananas and strips of fried bacon.

COLD STUFFED EGGS. Cook until hard the quantity of eggs required. Remove the shells and cut into quarters. Take out the yellows, leaving the white quarters intact. To every 6 eggs, mix into the yellows ½ teaspoonful of anchovy paste and 1 teaspoonful of butter, and work until completely smooth. Season with salt, pepper and a dash of Cayenne pepper. Fill the white quarters of the eggs with this paste and reshape to original form. Serve on a bed of crisp young lettuce leaves or water cress.

ROAST DUCK WITH ORANGES. Roast the duck in the oven in the regular way, until it is a good brown and well done. Prepare in good time the foundation of the sauce, which takes four hours to cook, as follows: Take the giblets, carrots, onions, a bouquet of spices, and brown all in butter, powdering over the whole some flour. Wet with a good bouillon—sufficient to make the quantity of sauce required. Add cut-up mushrooms, peel of some truffles, and cook for four hours. Then pass through a fine sieve, and add the rind of an orange which has been cut into very fine narrow strips and brought to a boil in a little water. Once the duck is roasted, moisten the brown remaining in the roasting pan with the juice of an orange and a little curaçao liqueur. Add this to the above sauce and pour over the duck, serving the rest of the gravy in a sauce bowl apart. Garnish the platter with fresh oranges in slices cut in the shape of the natural orange sections, from which all skin has been removed, and which have been heated.

CREAM OF GREEN PEA SOUP. Boil fresh green peas in salted water (select the peas that are as green as possible) and pass through a fine sieve. Put this purée in a saucepan with the water in which the peas were boiled, and at the moment before

Marlene Dietrich

serving add to it the yellows of eggs, fresh cream and fresh butter. Serve apart fried bread croutons.

FRIED TOMATOES AND COURGETTES. Remove the skins of the tomatoes, slice into pieces the shape of orange sections (not in rounds). Peel the courgettes and cut into slices of the same shape as the tomatoes. Roll the pieces in fresh bread crumbs, season well with salt and pepper and fry in plenty of butter until soft and well done.

NOTE: Courgette is a vegetable found in France, and is very similar to the cucumber. This dish is equally good when made with cucumbers.

FLAMING CHERRIES. Take a bottle of very best conserved red cherries. Heat well. Add

hours. Dry well, fold over each fillet and place in a buttered dish. Sprinkle lightly over with salt and poach in a short bouillon in the oven for about ten minutes. Prepare a cream sauce made with the bouillon of fish and thickened with the yellow of eggs. Prepare apart a dish of fried tomatoes and cucumbers. Arrange the fillets of sole on a long platter, making a circle around the dish. Dress over the sole the cream sauce and garnish with thin slices of truffles. Place a mound of the fried tomatoes and cucumbers in the center of the platter—not dressing these with the cream sauce.

ALSATIAN SOUP. Make a good consommé, and serve separately young tender cabbage prepared as follows: Boil the cabbage in salted water, drain well and rinse with fresh

grated cheese. Put in the oven—not too hot an oven—for one hour. Serve first the cabbage, and then the consommé.

DEVILED MUSHROOMS. Wash and clean fresh mushrooms. Fry whole in butter to which have been added a little lemon juice and ½ cupful of water, salt and pepper. When cold cut into thin slices and fry again in butter, sprinkle well over with chopped shallots and parsley, and add a little thick fresh cream. Prepare slices of toast, butter the toast and place the slices of fried mushrooms carefully on the toast, so that they overlap each other. Pour over a sauce Hollandaise which has been highly seasoned with dry English mustard, paprika and plenty of Cayenne pepper. Brown in the oven and serve very hot.

HOLLANDAISE SAUCE. Put the yellow of 3 eggs in a small saucepan, add salt, pepper, 3 tablespoonfuls of water and 1 ounce of butter. Place in a double boiler and cook until it begins to thicken. Remove to a slower fire and add ½ pound of butter, bit by bit, whipping strongly constantly, and replacing from time to time over a hotter fire.

CHICKEN LOAF (recipe by Mrs. Amos N. Barron). Remove the flesh from a fowl weighing 4 pounds. Add 1½ pounds of veal and 1 pound of fresh pork. If pork is lean add ¼ pound of bacon. Pass all through a meat chopper. Add 4 crackers rolled fine, 5 eggs well beaten, 1 or 2 tablespoonfuls of chili peppers chopped very fine, ⅓ cupful of cream, ¼ teaspoonful of ground mace or nutmeg, and salt to taste. Mix all together very thoroughly, then shape into a long loaf. Put thin slices of fat pork in a baking dish; upon these place the roll of meat. Slice 2 or 3 truffles very thin, ¼ cupful of blanched almonds, and press into the loaf. (Some almonds may be put in when the loaf is mixed.) Place salt pork on top of loaf and bake in a hot oven for fifteen minutes. Lower heat and cook for two hours. Can be served hot or cold.

MARBURY ROLLS (credit for this recipe is given to Miss Elisabeth Marbury). Take very fresh sandwich bread. Cut into very thin slices. Butter the slices. Fry bacon and chop very fine. Then put a little roll of the chopped bacon in the middle of the slice of bread, sprinkle over grated Parmesan cheese and finely chopped parsley. Sprinkle a generous quantity of paprika and a very small dash of Cayenne pepper. Roll like a cigarette and hold together with a wooden toothpick. Put on a tin platter and grill in the oven. Grill until nicely browned and serve hot.

A cloth of silver, with a crystal ship, all its glass sails set and pennants flying, mirrored in a sheet of glass.

a large wineglass of brandy, set aflame. When flame has died add a small glass of kirsch liqueur. Serve hot with vanilla ice cream.

FILLETS OF SOLE CARMEN. Soak the fillets of sole in half water and half milk for two

boiling water. Then chop the cabbage, butter an earthenware baking dish, put in a layer of cabbage, a little consommé, a layer of fine bread crumbs and grated Swiss cheese, and continue in this way layer after layer until your dish is full, finishing with the top layer of the bread crumbs and

CHESTER CAKES. Four ounces of flour; 3 ounces of grated Chester cheese; a little salt; a good pinch of Cayenne pepper. Place the flour on a board, and work in the buttered and grated cheese, then the salt and Cayenne pepper. Roll with rolling pin one time only, until it is very thin. Cut with biscuit cutter in rounds about two inches in diameter. Place on a buttered baking tin and bake in a moderate oven. Can be served hot or cold according to taste.

Some of my favorite luncheon menus are:

Caviar
Braised Chicken With Bacon
Hearts of Artichokes With Asparagus Tips
Cold Virginia Ham
Mimosa Salad
Savarin of Fruit

Fish Cakes With Bacon
Ragout of Spring Lamb
Blancmange With Orange Sauce

Baked Chicken With Noodles
Spring Salad
Caramel Apples

Cold Stuffed Eggs
Smoked Beef Tongue, Cumberland Sauce
Rice   Buttered Green Peas
Macedoine of Fresh Fruit

And finally, here are four sure menus for dinner:

Princess Consommé
Creamed Lobster
Roast Duck With Oranges
Lettuce Salad
Pineapple Ice Cream

Pilaf of Fillets of Sole
Roast Leg of Lamb
Macedoine of Vegetables
Cold Asparagus, French Dressing
Vanilla Cup Cream
Compote of Plums

Oyster Soup
Spoon Duck   Potato Chips
Truffle Salad
Purée of Water Cress
Banana Parfait

Consommé Vert-Pres
Mousse of Sole Hollandaise
Roast Chicken Piemontaise
Buttered Green Peas
Macedoine of Fresh Fruit With Kirsch
Macaroons

Dorothy Lathrop

SOME TESTS USED BY HENRI CARPENTIER IN BUYING FOOD

APPLES—Split the stem. If it is soft and sappy, it is a fresh apple probably tree-ripened.

PEACHES—Choose fragrant ones. Peaches with beautiful skins and no odor are usually tasteless.

GRAPEFRUIT—Those with unblemished, thin skins are most desirable. If there are black spots where the fruit was attached to the stem, beware.

COFFEE—The crack in the bean should be almost invisible. If widely spread, the flavor and aroma will be diminished.

STRING BEANS—Fresh string beans have solid stems. Avoid those of anaemic pallor.

CARROTS—Should be firm and the tender green portion near the leaves cover only a narrow margin. If the green has spread, the vegetable is overgrown and probably tough.

CABBAGE—Young and tender cabbage has closely packed leaves and only slight odor. Watch out for splits. They indicate worms at the center.

SWEET POTATOES—Select those with smooth skins. If there are little rootlets attached, the sweet potato will be fibrous and unpalatable.

BROCCOLI—Take that which has short, crisp stems.

TURNIPS—Test with finger nail. If incision does not fill with liquid, the turnip will be stringy.

SPINACH—Select straight leaves of deep green hue. Curved leaves mean overgrowth.

RADISHES—The center leaves should be small and the flesh crisp.

LETTUCE—Should be firm and crisp. If it has been plunged in water to revive it, the inside will be soft.

MUSHROOMS—Raise the skin. The flesh should be white. If it is dark, the mushroom is spoiled.

PEAS—Press finger nail into pod. If sap does not appear in the wound, the peas are not fresh.

EGGPLANT—The stem and segments should be firmly attached to the skin; the pulp and seeds white. If the segments have begun to detach themselves, the plant has started to spoil and the inside will be spotted with black.

CAULIFLOWER—Flesh should be tightly packed and white. When it has spread, another and unsavory growth has begun.

ASPARAGUS—Stem should be smooth near the cut and pink-white in color. The top should be tightly folded. If leaves have already formed, the asparagus has lost much of its savor.

CHICKEN—A young and tender chicken is soft to the touch at the breast bone and second leg joint; if those places feel tough the chicken is old.

PORK—Meat should be very white, with plenty of fat.

BEEF—Beef should be streaked with fat.

LAMB—Look for meat of a delicate pinkness. Lamb that is red in color is of poor quality.

FISH—Eyes should be brilliant and tongue moist. The fish should be very slippery, not sticky.

OYSTERS, CLAMS—Rap the shells together. If they sound like stones the inhabitants are alive and edible.

Edith Wharton

A BACKWARD GLANCE

Edith Wharton

How describe the old New York to which I came back as a little girl? To me it meant chiefly my father's library, since now for the first time I had my fill of books. Out-of-doors, in the mean monotonous streets, without architecture, without great churches or palaces, or any visible memorials of a historic past, what could New York offer to a child whose eyes had been filled from babyhood with shapes of immortal beauty and immemorial significance? One of the most depressing impressions of my childhood is my recollection of the intolerable ugliness of New York, of its untended streets and its narrow houses, so lacking in external dignity, so crammed with smug and suffocating upholstery. How could I understand that people who had seen Rome and Seville, Paris and London, could come back to live contentedly between Washington Square and the Central Park?

What, above all, I could not guess was that this little low-studded rectangular New York, cursed with its universal chocolate-colored coating of the most hideous stone ever quarried, this cramped horizontal grid-iron of a town without towers, porticoes, fountains or perspectives, hidebound in its deadly uniformity of mean ugliness, would fifty years later be as much a vanished city as Atlantis or the lowest layer of Schliemann's Troy, or that the social organization which that prosaic setting had slowly secreted would have been swept into oblivion with the rest. Nothing but the Atlantis fate of old New York, the New York which had slowly but continuously developed from the early seventeenth century to my own childhood, makes that childhood worth recalling now.

The group to which we belonged was composed of families to whom a middling prosperity had come, usually by the rapid rise in value of inherited real estate, and none of whom, apparently, aspired to be more than moderately well off. I never in my early life came in contact with the gold fever in any form, and when I hear that nowadays in New York business life is so strenuous that men and women never meet socially before the dinner hour, I remember the delightful week-day luncheons of my early married years, where the men were as numerous as the women, and where one of the first rules of conversation was the one early instilled in me by my mother: "Never talk about money, and think about it as little as possible."

The *bon-vivant* side of old New York life was represented in the family by my father, who had inherited a serious tradition of good cooking. I doubt whether my mother, if left to herself, would have been much interested in the pleasures of the table. My father's Dutch blood probably accounted for his gastronomic enthusiasm; his mother, who was a Schermerhorn, was reputed to have the best cook in New York. But to know about good cooking was a part of every young wife's equipment, and my mother's favorite cookery books (Francatelli's and Mrs. Leslie's) are thickly interleaved with sheets of yellowing note paper, on which, in a script of ethereal elegance, she records the composition of "Mrs. Joshua Jones' scalloped oysters with cream," "Aunt Fanny Gallatin's fried chicken," "William Edgar's punch," and the special recipes of our two famous Negro cooks, Mary Johnson and Susan Minneman.

These great artists stand out, picturesquely turbaned and earringed, from a Snyderslike background of game, fish and

Once more Helen Hayes plays a queen on Broadway—now in Laurence Housman's "Victoria Regina."

vegetables transformed into a succession of succulent repasts by their indefatigable blue-nailed hands. Mary Johnson, a gaunt towering woman of a rich bronzy black, with golden hoops in her ears, and crisp African crinkles restrained by the most vividly patterned kerchiefs; Susan Minneman, a small smiling mulatto, more quietly attired, but as great a cook as her predecessor.

Ah, what artists they both were! How simple yet sure were their methods—the mere perfection of broiling, roasting and basting—and what an unexampled wealth of material, vegetable and animal, their genius had to draw upon! Who will ever again taste anything in the whole range of gastronomy to equal their corned beef, their boiled turkeys with stewed celery and oyster sauce, their fried chickens, broiled redheads, corn fritters, stewed tomatoes, rice griddle cakes, strawberry shortcake and vanilla ices?

I am now enumerating only our daily fare, that from which even my tender years did not exclude me; but when my parents "gave a dinner," and terrapin and canvasback ducks, or (in their season) broiled Spanish mackerel, soft-shelled crabs with a mayonnaise of celery, and peach-fed Virginia hams cooked in champagne (I am no doubt confusing all the seasons in this allegoric evocation of their riches), Lima beans in cream, corn soufflés and salads of oyster crabs, poured in their varied succulence from Mary Johnson's lifted cornucopia—ah, then, the *gourmet* of that long-lost day, when cream was cream and butter, butter, and coffee, coffee, and meat fresh every day, and game hung just for the proper number of hours, might lean back in his chair and murmur, "Fate cannot harm me," over his cup of Mocha and glass of Chartreuse.

I have wandered far from my father's library. Though it had the leading share in my development, I have let myself be drawn from it to other forms of nutriment; but the library calls me back, and I pause on its threshold, averting my eyes from the tall oak mantelpiece with a shelf supported on the heads of vizored knights, and looking at the rows of comely bindings and familiar names.

The library was a small room containing probably not more than seven or eight hundred volumes; but, small as it was, it seems to me, as I look back, that it included the essentials. The principal historians were Plutarch, Macaulay, Prescott, Parkman, Froude, Carlyle, Lamartine, Thiers; the diaries and letters included Evelyn, Pepys, White of Selborne, Cowper, Mme. de Sévigné, Fanny Burney, Moore, the journals of the Misses Berry; the poetical works (in addition to several anthologies, such as Knight's Half Hours with the Best Authors and Lamb's precious selections from the Elizabethan dramatists) were those of Homer (in Pope's and Lord Derby's versions), Milton, Herbert, Pope, Cowper, Gray, Thomson, Byron, Moore, Scott, Burns, Wordsworth, Campbell, Coleridge, Shelley (I wonder how or why?), Longfellow, Mrs. Hemans and Mrs. Browning—though not as yet the writer described in one of the anthologies of the period as "The husband of Elizabeth Barrett, and

himself no mean poet." He was to come later, as a present from my sister-in-law, and to be one of the awakeners of my childhood.

Among the French poets were Corneille, Racine, La Fontaine and Victor Hugo; though, oddly enough, of Lamartine the poet there was not a page, nor yet of Chénier, Vigny or Musset. Among French prose classics there were, of course, Sainte-Beuve's Lundis—stimulating fare for a young mind—Sévigné the inexhaustible, Augustin Thierry and Philarète Chasles.

Art, history and criticism were represented by Lacroix's big volumes, so richly and exquisitely illustrated, on art, architecture and costume in the Middle Ages, by Schliemann's Ilios and Troja, by Gwilt's Encyclopædia of Architecture, by Kugler, Mrs. Jameson, P. G. Hamerton and the Ruskin of Modern Painters and the Seven Lamps, together with an anthology (appropriately bound in purple cloth) of all his purplest patches; to which my father, for my benefit, added Stones of Venice and Mornings in Florence, when we returned to Europe and the too-short days of our joint sightseeing began.

In philosophy, I can recall little but Victor Cousin and Coleridge (The Friend and Aids to Reflection); among essayists, besides Addison, there were Lamb and Macaulay; in the way of travel, I remember

chiefly Arctic explorations. As for fiction, after the eighteenth-century classics, Miss Burney and Scott, of course, led the list; but mysteriously enough, Richardson was lacking, save for an abridged version of Clarissa Harlowe (a masterly performance, as I remember it).

Though living authors were remote, the dead were my most living companions. I was a healthy little girl who loved riding, swimming and romping; yet no children of my own age, and none even among the nearest of my grown-ups, were as close to me as the voices that spoke from books.

At this stage my mother's decree against novel reading did me good service. A little girl to whom the Old Testament, the Apocalypse and the Elizabethan dramatists were open could not long pine for Whyte-Melville, or even Rhoda Broughton. Ah, the long music-drunken hours on that library floor, with Isaiah and the Song of Solomon and the Book of Esther, and Modern Painters, and Augustin Thierry's Merovingians, and Knight's Half Hours, and that rich mine of music, Dana's Household Book of Poetry! Presently kind friends began to endow me with a little library of my own, and I was reading Faust and Wilhelm Meister, Men and Women and Dramatis Personæ, in the intervals between The Broken Heart, The Duchess of Malfi, Phèdre and Andromaque. But I remember most intensely one golden birthday when, my mother having despairingly asked our old friend, Mr. North, at Scribner's, "what she could give the child," I woke to find beside my bed Buxton Forman's great edition of Keats and Shelley!

It would be an exaggeration to say that by the time I was seventeen I had read every book in my father's library; but I believe I had looked into them all. Those I devoured first were the poets and the few literary critics—foremost, of course, Sainte-Beuve. Ruskin woke in me memories of the Italy I had never forgotten or ceased to pine for; and Freeman's delightful Subject and Neighbor Lands of Venice, Mrs. Jameson's amiable volumes and Kugler's Handbook of Italian Painting gave a firmer outline to my dreams.

But the works which made the strongest impression on me—doubtless because they fed a part of my awakening intelligence that no one had thought of providing for—were two shabby volumes unearthed among my brother's college textbooks. One was a good abridgment of Sir William Hamilton's History of Philosophy, and the other an obscure work called Coppée's Elements of Logic. This first introduction to the machinery of thinking literally intoxicated me; it was as if it had supplied the bony structure about which my vague gelatinous musings could cling and take shape. Until I read Darwin and Pascal, those two books ranked foremost among my Awakeners.

In a day when such store was set on youthful innocence, my mother chose a singular way of preserving mine when she deprived me of the Victorian novelists but made me free of the Old Testament and the Elizabethans. It is not likely that her plan was premeditated; but had it been, she could not have shown more insight. The glory of those great pages dazzled me, and

---

Home Again
By
LOUIS UNTERMEYER

THIS is the house,
  Reared on no earthly floors,
Where you (and you alone) can rouse
  The echo that endures.

Where the low sill
  And the high roof repeat
New tidings of each syllable
  Sung by your homing feet.

Where swallows cut
  An arc no bird designed,
And moons blown off the eaves are but
  White bubbles of the mind.

Where the young trees,
  Transparent as your thought,
Cluster like children at your knees
  To see what you have brought.

And the whole house
  Blossoms with unseen doors.
The hearth takes root; the lintel grows. . . .
  Reclaim it. It is yours.

their high themes purged my imagination. I cannot recall ever trying to puzzle out allusions which in tamer garb might have roused my curiosity.

I have no idea of defending the sheltered education against that which expounds physiological mysteries in the nursery; I am not sure which method is better. My only point is that great literature does not excite furtive curiosities in normally constituted children; and I can give a comic proof in the fact that, though The White Devil, Faust and Swinburne's Poems and Ballads were among my early storybooks, all I knew about adultery—against which we were warned every week in church—was that those who "committed" it were penalized by having to pay higher fares in traveling; an explanation arrived at by my once seeing on a ferryboat the sign, "Adults, 50 cents; children, 25 cents."

This ferment of reading awoke again my old story-telling fever; but now I wanted to write and not to improvise. My first attempt —at the age of eleven—was a novel, which opened as follows: " 'Oh, how do you do, Mrs. Brown?' said Mrs. Tompkins. 'If only I had known you were going to call I should have tidied up the drawing-room.' " Timorously I submitted this to my mother, and never shall I forget the sudden drop of my creative frenzy when she returned it with the icy comment: "Drawing-rooms are always tidy."

This rebuff, so crushing to a would-be novelist of manners, woke me rudely from my dream of writing fiction; and as an alternative I took to poetry. For some reason it was not deemed necessary to encourage my attempts by supplying me with foolscap, and I was driven to begging for the wrappings of the parcels delivered at the house. After a while it was tacitly understood that they belonged to me, and I always had a provision of wrapping paper in my room. It never occurred to me to fold the sheets and cut them into pages, and I used to spread them out on the floor and travel over them on my hands and knees, building up long parallel columns of blank verse headed: "Scene: A Venetian Palace," or "Dramatis Personæ" (which I never knew how to pronounce).

My dear governess, seeing my perplexity over the structure of English verse, gave me a work called Quackenbos's Rhetoric, which warned one not to speak of the oyster as a "succulent bivalve," and pointed out that even Shakspere was wrong when he made Hamlet "take arms against a sea of troubles." Mr. Quackenbos disposed of the delicate problems of English metric by squeezing them into the classic categories, so that Milton was supposed to have written in "iambic pentameters"; all superfluous syllables were got rid of by an elision and an apostrophe.

Always respectful of the rules of the game, I tried to cabin my Muse within these bounds, and once when, in a moment of unheard-of audacity, I sent a poem to a newspaper (I think The World) I wrote to the editor apologizing for the fact that my meter was "irregular," but adding firmly that, though I was only a little girl, I wished this irregularity to be preserved, as it was "intentional." The editor published the poem, and wrote back politely that he

had no objection to irregular meters himself; and thereafter I breathed more freely.

My poetic experiments, however, were destined to meet with the same discouragement as my fiction. Having vainly attempted a tragedy in five acts, I turned my mind to short lyrics, which I poured out with a lamentable facility. My brother showed some of these to one of his friends, an amiable and cultivated youth named Allen Thorndike Rice, who afterward became the owner and editor of The North American Review. Allen Rice very kindly sent the poems to the aged Longfellow, to whom his mother's family were related; and on the bard's recommendation my babblings were actually printed in the Atlantic Monthly.

Happily, this experiment was not repeated; and any undue pride I might have felt in it was speedily dashed by my young patron's remarking to me one day:

"You know, writing lyrics won't lead you anywhere. What you want to do is to write an epic. All the great poets have written epics. Homer—Milton—Byron. Why don't you try your hand at an epic like Don Juan?"

This was hard saying to a dreamy girl of fifteen, and I shrank back into my secret

retreat, convinced that I was unfitted to be either a poet or a novelist. I did, indeed, attempt another novel, and carried this one to its close; but it was destined for the private enjoyment of a girl friend, and was never exposed to the garish light of print. It exists to this day, written in a thick copy book, with a title page inscribed Fast and Loose, and an epigraph from Owen Meredith's Lucile:

*Let Woman beware
How she plays fast and loose with human
   despair,
And the storm in Man's heart.*

Title and epigraph were terrifyingly exemplified in the tale, but it closed on a note of mournful resignation: "And every year when April comes the violets bloom again on Georgie's grave."

After this supreme effort I withdrew to secret communion with the Muse. I continued to cover vast expanses of wrapping paper with prose and verse, but the dream of a literary career, momentarily shadowed forth by my one miraculous adventure, soon faded into unreality. How could I ever have supposed I could be an author? I had never even seen one in the flesh!

Will Rogers: "All I know is what I read in the papers."

THIS MAN ROOSEVELT

Milton MacKaye

Franklin D. Roosevelt, after three and a half tempestuous years of office, faces the electorate again. He is at the strident moment the nation's emotional storm center. Roosevelt, as partisans and opponents alike agree, is no ordinary nominee; he is unique in his generation for the passions he arouses. No President since Lincoln has been so fanatically and devoutly admired—and so fanatically and devoutly hated.

One faction is quite sure that his reelection means the country's ruin; the other is equally sure that he is the only man who can hold the structure together and prevent a mortal collapse. And both, with a hysteria unusual in American affairs, are convinced that Armageddon is indeed at hand.

It is highly probable that both are wrong. Politics is a legend maker, and legends rarely mirror with accuracy the measure of a man. There are many myths about Roosevelt. They have, of course, changed character since, a white and glittering Deliverer, he took office during the eventful March of 1933. But even in the midst of the general acclaim of his first full year there were some muttering voices.

They said, and most people have forgotten it now, that Roosevelt was not his own man. There was one legend that frail, wispy Louis Howe—an odd choice for a sinister figure—was the Rasputin of the Administration. There was another that Rex Tugwell was the master. There was still another that Mrs. Roosevelt—busy then, as now, going up in airplanes and down in coal mines—was the power behind the throne. On the basis of the legend of Mrs.

Roosevelt's omnipotence, an apocryphal story arose which the President in friendly gatherings has been heard, with disarming merriment, to tell upon himself. The story goes like this:

A New Deal orator was eulogizing Roosevelt before a crowd of enthusiastic Democrats. In the vast and cheering auditorium there was one stubbornly alien voice. When the speaker first referred to "our peerless leader," the voice bellowed: "I don't like him!" A few moments later the speaker brought the house down by calling Roosevelt "the greatest President since Cleveland." The lone voice called out: "I don't like him!" The address drew to a close. The speaker concluded: "And now, my friends, I must say to you that I cannot but believe that the man who has led us through these trials and tribulations of state with such unerring judgment is, and must be, guided by some Higher Power." There was a moment of reverent silence, broken finally by the raucous voice from the audience: "I don't like her either."

There seems to be little doubt that Roosevelt is his own man, that he must stand or fall as such.

The nation's emotional storm center.

Few men emerge unchanged from the presidency. There are cares and responsibilities unmatched in private enterprise. Wilson collapsed before the end of his term. Harding died in office. Coolidge, careful always of health and rest, lived a very few years beyond his retirement.

Roosevelt, by choice as well as necessity, has assumed burdens of work unequaled before his time. Yet, at the age of fifty-four, and after three and a half years in the White House, he shows no evidences of fatigue or ebbing energy. His handsome face is more deeply lined, he is heavier—perhaps because he no longer exercises so regularly in the White House swimming pool—his hair is grayer, but physicians and friends agree that he is in perfect health.

It is significant that a public once conscious of the fact has almost forgotten that the President is a physically disabled man. Even the people around him forget it. For, with a fortitude that even his bitterest enemy must admire, he triumphed over invalidism and lived his life as he had intended before a plunge into the icy waters off the New Brunswick coast brought on the paralysis which cost him the use of his legs. Few men manage to achieve normal lives after such catastrophe; Roosevelt resumed an interrupted career and, with deliberate intent, aimed himself for the presidency.

Perhaps the greatest tribute of all to Roosevelt is that a commentator may speak of his disability without self-consciousness. The fact that he is to a considerable extent the prisoner of a chair has something to do with his enormous capacity for work. Roosevelt doesn't play golf or tennis, he doesn't ride, he rarely goes to the theater; people must come to him.

Roosevelt's average day is a man crusher. It begins between eight and eight-thirty o'clock, when breakfast and newspapers are brought to his bed. His breakfast is almost always the same: orange juice, scrambled eggs, toast and coffee. Breakfast over, and his dressing gown pulled about him, the conferences begin. One is only certain to find one or all of his three secretaries. Marvin McIntyre arrives to discuss the day's appointments; Steve Early, who has charge of press relations, appears to discuss the wording of a public statement or speech; Miss Marguerite Le Hand, the private secretary whom he calls "Missy," makes sure that he catches up with important private correspondence. Henry Morgenthau, Jr., Secretary of the Treasury, and his next-door neighbor at Hyde Park, New York, often puts in an appearance, and during a congressional session Senator Joe Robinson, Senator Robert Wagner or Postmaster General Farley may be summoned.

At ten o'clock the President rises, shaves and, unless his valet is especially careful, dresses himself in anything he finds at hand.

*No President since Lincoln has been so fanatically and
devoutly admired—and so fanatically and devoutly hated.*

The President is quite indifferent to clothes. He likes comfort; he chooses soft collars for every possible occasion. He looks handsome in a dinner jacket, but his favorite costume is the cotton hat, Oxford shirt and duck trousers he wears fishing.

Roosevelt usually appears at the executive offices of the White House at about eleven. He is pushed there in a wheel chair and lifts himself with his stroke-oar shoulders to the chair behind his desk. He rarely leaves until late afternoon. Luncheon is served at the desk, often with one or two guests, and appointments continue in swift succession until the sun disappears below the Potomac. Once dinner is over—provided that it is not one of those gold-plate affairs of state—Roosevelt retires to thresh out the bulk of his work. This is the time

that he selects to dictate the ideas for his speeches and state papers; this is the time during which he formulates policies, and reads the digest of reports of the multifarious agencies of government. And this also is almost the only time when he may be alone. It is twelve-thirty or one o'clock before he goes to bed.

The President's humor is usually good-natured, but there are times when, under exasperating circumstances, it takes on a sharp quality of irony. During the early months of the NRA and the efforts to straighten out bankrupt enterprises, a retired textile manufacturer was a frequent visitor at the executive offices. He always brought with him a new economic plan. One day the manufacturer appeared with an inked-in chart which encompassed the

NRA, the AAA and all the other alphabetical agencies.

"Mr. President," he said, "I've decided that what you need is a co-ordinator."

The President was interested. "Whom would you suggest for the job?" he asked.

The manufacturer pondered. "Well," he said, "you need a man who can get along with the press, and who is tactful enough to be popular with congressmen; a man thoroughly grounded in economics and history and law, who is conservative enough to be *persona grata* with Business and liberal enough to appeal to Labor."

The President waved his cigarette holder. "I know just the man," he said, "but I'm afraid we can't get him."

"Who is that?"

"God Almighty," he said.

WOMEN'S PLACE IN POLITICS

Viscountess Astor, M.P.

I am often asked why I went into politics. A great many of the things I care most about are at the mercy of politics—for instance, the health and living conditions of small children, and the labour conditions of juveniles—but when I look right down into my thought I see that what sent me into politics was something deeper than that: My belief and trust in women, and the sense that they have never yet had a chance to give their full contribution to the world's affairs. Care for children, and for all social questions, is just a part of this. What helped to put me into public life, and especially what keeps me there, is my strong feeling that the world needs women in its political life.

It is true that women voters have a past, but it is a short one—twenty years in twenty centuries. We need not go back twenty centuries—it's too long. We know that women must have had a great influence on their husbands and sons, and there have been famous queens and powerful princesses and even more powerful courtesans who have had great influence on the fate of countries. But the influence of women expressed and made effective by the power of the vote is quite a new thing in the world.

There is nothing in women's past that they want to go back to, so of course they want to go forward. What inspires them, I am sure, is the longing to make a new and much better world for their children to live in, something fairer and safer than the one they were born into; safer for their sons, so that they need not be shot by machine guns, and fairer for their daughters, so that they may have a chance to develop the best that is in them. Women who feel like this do not want dictators; what they want is freedom in a civilised community.

I have thought a lot about what civilisation is. It is a word we use freely, but we do not all mean the same thing by it. For my part I think it means more than just mechanical progress. We want that kind of progress, of course, and no one has more cause to be grateful for modern inventions than women. But I feel that mechanisation, like patriotism, is not enough. We must have something better than both of these if we are to be civilised. The machine must be our servant and not our master; and as for patriotism, it must never lead us to war. So my idea of civilisation includes machines

which help human life, but not those which destroy it, and patriotism which is of a higher and better sort than the old fierce fighting kind.

I am certain that the love of country is so deep in most people that there is no need

Viscountess Astor

to bang and boom about it. We do not need to wave flags in order to work up our love for our native land, and the thing we ought to preach and stimulate is the impulse to be of service to mankind. Unless we can get hold of that feeling I do not believe we can be of any substantial service to our own country, because the whole world is so tied together now that you only help your own nation if you are ready to help others, nor can you injure one without injuring all.

I am not a sloppy pacifist. I know that nations differ, just as our children differ. I know that it would be well worth giving up one's life for freedom, in the right sense of the word, and I know that you cannot treat all countries alike, or, perhaps unfortunately, trust all governments equally. In that respect nations are like a tradesman's customers. He cannot serve them all alike; some of them just *won't* buy the things they need, but *will* have dangerous drugs and firearms and poisons instead. But all the same I repeat that we have *got* to build a world in which war has no place.

I am a very ordinary woman, and ordinary women know how to face facts. I believe that they are the most practical people in the world, and that is why I think they will be able to face all these international facts, and find a way. Somehow, without being sloppy pacifists, and without shutting our eyes to realities, we women have got to deal with this question of war, *and make an end of it.*

BRITAIN'S BIGGEST SHOW

Britain's biggest show will soon be put on again—unless, as sometimes happens with the best-laid plans of mice and men, something unlooked-for at this writing upsets the coronational applecart. Performances are quite rare. The last one was held in 1911. Before that there was one in 1902. But it was almost 100 years ago when the youthful Victoria was proclaimed ruler of the British Empire. Her great-grandson, Edward VIII, will be crowned in Westminster Abbey on Wednesday, May 12, 1937. From Buckingham Palace, on that day, a glittering coach will make its slow progress down the Mall toward the Abbey, and then, after a four-hour ceremony, the Archbishop of Canterbury or some other high church official will place a jeweled crown on the head of the King. This is the supreme moment; an instant later God Save the King will crash through the ancient gothic arches of Westminster. Meanwhile for a year, at least, tens of thousands of British men and women will have been profiting pleasantly from the trade boom which a coronation brings.

H. F. PRINGLE

ST. EDWARD'S IMPERIAL STAFF ORB

The FLAGON

The SALT CELLAR

The TANKARD

The AMPULLA

The GLOVES

The SPURS

TEMPORAL SCEPTRE

SWORD OF MERCY

His Majesty EDWARD VIII

VISCOUNT

BARON

MARQUIS

DUKE

EARL

DINNER FOR THRESHERS. *By Grant Wood. Because of its simplicity of composition, the faithful rendering of characters and incidentals*

DINNER FOR THRESHERS

Ann Batchelder

Native food, like native art, needs no apology—when it bears the unmistakable touch of the master's hand.

It would be to no one's surprise if these threshers, painted in Grant Wood's native Iowa, had sat down to a hearty dinner of fried chicken and salt pork and cream gravy, baked potatoes and cole slaw and corn on the cob—great platters passed and passed again. Such is the dinner I like to think these hearty appetites are being fed.

And for dessert, after a hard day's work in the fields, what could be more suited than apple dumplings, light as gossamer, sweetened with maple syrup and swimming in country cream, or blackberry pie, running over with purple juices, the crust just leaf on leaf, and warm from the sun where they've been in the pantry window since morning.

FRIED SALT PORK. Old-time fried salt pork with cream gravy has a pull that does not lessen as the years go rolling by.

To do this, slice the pork thin. Take off the rind and slash one edge of the slices so the slices won't curl up as they fry. "Freshen" the pork a little; that is, either soak it in cold water or parboil it a few minutes, as it is pretty salty, you know.

Dry the slices thoroughly in a cloth. Mix an equal quantity of flour and fine corn meal and dip each slice in this. Fry in a hot frying pan until brown and crisp.

CREAM GRAVY. Blend well 2 tablespoons of the pork fat with 2 tablespoons of flour. Add ½ cup of milk and ½ cup of cream and cook in a double boiler, stirring all the time, until smooth and creamy and guiltless of a single lump. Season with a very little salt but fairly high with pepper. Serve with the fried pork and chicken.

COLESLAW. This is an old favorite; and if the cabbage is sliced to the thinnest of shreds and is made almost brittle with crispness and is dressed with an old-fashioned "biled" dressing, it's one of those things that are good most anywhere any time. Shred tender green cabbage into a bowl of ice water and let it stand until it is very crisp. Drain and dry it in a towel. Mix it well with the dressing and toss it in a bowl.

BOILED DRESSING. Mix together ½ teaspoon of salt, 2 tablespoons of flour, a "dash" of cayenne, 1 teaspoon of mustard and 1 tablespoon of sugar. Beat 1 egg slightly and add to dry ingredients, then add slowly ¾ cup of milk, ¼ cup of vinegar and 2 tablespoons of butter. Cook in a double boiler, stirring pretty constantly, until the dressing begins to thicken. Take from the fire, beat hard with an egg beater, strain and cool before using it.

Now, this is an old-timer and the kind that mother used to make. But let me tell you something. You may walk right into a grocery store and tell your man the type of salad dressing you want, whether mayonnaise or the boiled kind, and he will set out a jar that will fill the bill and be just what you wish for coleslaw or whatever.

and its general warm humanness, this great work by an outstanding portrayer of the American scene created a sensation when it was first exhibited.

But be sure to tell him—else how can he guess what you're up to!

BLACKBERRY PIE. It is my notion that the blackberries should be put into the crust uncooked. There are two ways of looking at this, but why go into that? So then, line a pie plate with a good pastry. Mix about 1 cup of sugar with 2 tablespoons of flour and mix this into the berries. If they are *wild* blackberries—and how I hope they are —you may use a little less sugar, for the wild blackberry has absorbed and become one with summer at its sweetest—with sun and dew and the fragrance of some hidden secrets of leaf and bud and blossom.

HAVE IT FULL. Fill the pie heaping full of the berries, then add a few more for good measure. Fit over the upper crust, pressing the edges firmly together with a fork. Wet the lower edge with cold water first. Remember? Dot that pie with little dabs of butter, sprinkle it lightly with ice water and put it into an oven at 475° F. and let it bake at that high heat until the crust is set. Then lower the oven to 375° and finish the baking. Slowly the released juice from those elegant berries will seep up through the vents you have cut or pricked in the top crust of your pie, but that only makes it more desirable. And it's more than threshers that will go for such a pie!

APPLE DUMPLINGS. If blackberries are

scarce make up a batch of baking powder-biscuit dough; that is, sift together 2 cups of flour, 4 teaspoons of baking powder, 1 teaspoon of salt. Work in 3 tablespoons of shortening. Add ¾ to 1 cup of milk, gradually, now, to get a dough that can be rolled out—no more. Roll it out on a floured board to about one quarter inch thick. Cut sour apples into eighths. Put the apples in the center of the rolled-out dough, cover with sugar and a dash of salt. Then sprinkle lightly with cinnamon and nutmeg. Bring the dough up around the apples and press the edges together. Put the dumpling into a greased mold, and have the mold large enough so the dumpling won't fill it more than two thirds full. Here's where you allow for expansion.

Set the mold on a rack in a kettle of hot water, letting the water come halfway up the mold—no higher. Keep the water boiling and add more as it boils away. Keep the mold covered and the kettle covered and steam the dumpling about one and one half hours. Serve with foamy or hard sauce, or, better, with maple syrup and cream.

HOMINY CROQUETTES. These are good when you don't want potatoes, and they go so well with meat that it's probable you will like to make them often.

To 1 cup of cold boiled hominy add 1 tablespoon of melted butter and beat hard. The hominy is the fine-grained kind. Then add gradually 1 cup of milk, beating as you add, until the mixture is light and soft. Add

2 teaspoons of sugar, then 1 egg, well beaten. Make the mixture into balls, dip each one in beaten egg, then in fine cracker crumbs and fry in deep fat. Drain on paper towels and serve very hot.

SCALLOPED OYSTERS. This is a two-layer scallop, and I find that is deep enough. But you will decide that, for it depends on the number of oyster lovers at the table.

For 1 pint of oysters allow 1 cup of fine cracker crumbs and ½ cup of bread crumbs. Mix together with ½ cup of melted butter. Cover a deep pie plate with a layer of crumbs, then a layer of oysters, season with salt and pepper and about 2 tablespoons of oyster liquor. Add 1 tablespoon of cream. Add another layer of crumbs, one more of oysters and the last and top layer of crumbs. Dot with butter and bake in an oven at 450° for about thirty minutes.

APPLE TAPIOCA PUDDING. An old stand-by, and one of the best, is this pudding, when eaten hot with plenty of good rich cream. Cook ½ cup of quick-cooking tapioca in 2½ cups of boiling water until the tapioca is transparent. Add a little salt while tapioca is cooking and do the tapioca in a double boiler.

Pare and core 6 or 8 sour apples and fit them into a greased deep baking dish. Fill the cores with sugar and sprinkle lightly with cinnamon and nutmeg. Pour the cooked tapioca over the apples and bake in an oven at 350° until the apples are soft.

Photograph by Edward Steichen.

IN WHAT DO WE BELIEVE?

Dorothy Thompson

The decade of the 1930's has been fateful for history. In it, the Soviet state, based upon a theory of history unique in application, and upon a conception of property at odds with what prevails elsewhere, has solidified itself for the first time in a written constitution. What is happening there is bound vastly to influence the whole world for a long time to come.

In Germany, an awakened national will, fed ever since the war on a sense of humiliation and injustice, broke out in this decade in a revolution which has not only overthrown the parliamentary state but has established the nation on a conception of racial solidarity and totalitarianism, which extends into every phase of life and thought. In its political and economic organization, Germany has closely followed Italy, which made the change in the twenties.

Both Russian Communism and international Fascism are messianic and imperial. They seek to propagate their ideas abroad, either by grandiose propaganda or by direct interference in behalf of similarly minded groups in countries other than their own, or, in the case of the Fascist states, by military action. The reason these experiments abroad influence our thought and produce unrest is that they are affirmative. The people, or those who speak for them, in Russia, Germany and Italy know very definitely what they believe, and what they intend to do. They are going somewhere. It is possible that these nations are going to war or to their own destruction. Or it is possible that Russia will survive and the other systems not, or vice versa. But, for the moment, they represent in the world aggressive affirmation of something.

The reason why the democratic nations are so weak is that they do not know with even a degree of definiteness what they believe, and what they want to do. Their political and economic behavior is habit, and hardly more. Their attitudes and actions have no clear philosophical foundation. We still speak of "Liberty" and "Democracy," but every second American, like every second Englishman and Frenchman, has a different idea of what "liberty" and "democracy" mean.

Many people thought that when President Roosevelt was elected in 1933 we, too, had made a revolution of sorts, and that the New Deal meant a fundamental change in American life. But when we look thoughtfully at what we have done, it is impossible to believe that anything of the kind has happened. The process of disintegrating

confidence in what existed before has gone a long way farther, under the many experiments we have undertaken, but nothing has emerged to reintegrate the public faith. There is hardly an institution of our life in which the ordinary man retains undiminished belief. He doubts the integrity of our banking system; he has been taught to regard industrialists as "economic royalists"; he has seen the two houses of Congress capitulate in a manner unique in

DRAWING BY PERRY BARLOW   **THE SLEEPWALKERS**

their history and develop no distinguished leadership. He is divided in his feelings about the Supreme Court.

Even the ignorant man senses and feels that an epoch in American life is over. He no longer has faith in the shibboleths which dominated our country in the long period from the Civil War, through the Great War, to the Depression. The talk of rugged individualism leaves him cold, because he has experienced that economic catastrophes

can occur to him which he is powerless to avert or overcome.

A realization is dawning that nothing fundamental is being done to revive the promise of American life. The New Deal has enormously increased the sense of awareness; it has contributed radically to the breakdown of confidence in the forms and procedures of yesterday. But it has offered us no comprehensible picture of a future in which we can believe. We have

not had a revival or a conversion—to use evangelical terms—we have just had a Christmas party for the other side of the railroad tracks, with a general distribution of governmental largess and a redistribution of privileges. We have laid no firm foundations under social justice, so it seems to me that if democracy is to become again a proud word, then this nation must redefine its whole attitude toward the things it is supposed to live by.

Color and crystal combine to set the note for an August luncheon.

HOW DOES YOUR GARDEN GROW?

Agatha Christie

Hercule Poirot arranged his letters in a neat pile in front of him. He picked up the topmost letter, studied the address for a moment, then neatly slit the back of the envelope with a little paper knife that he kept on the breakfast table for that express purpose and extracted the contents. Inside was yet another envelope, carefully sealed with purple wax and marked "Private and Confidential."

Hercule Poirot's eyebrows rose a little on his egg-shaped head. He murmured, *"Patience! Nous allon arriver!"* and once more brought the little paper knife into play. This time the envelope yielded a letter—written in a rather shaky and spiky handwriting. Several words were heavily underlined.

Hercule Poirot unfolded it and read. The letter was headed once again "Private and Confidential." On the right-hand side was the address—Rosebank, Charman's Green, Bucks—and the date—March twenty-first.

Dear M. Poirot: I have been recommended to you by an old and valued friend of mine who knows the *worry* and *distress* I have been in lately. Not that this friend knows the actual *circumstances*—those I have kept *entirely* to myself—the matter being strictly private. My friend assures me that you are *discretion* itself—and that there will be no fear of my being involved in a *police* matter which, if my suspicions should prove correct, I should *very much dislike*. But it is of course possible that I am *entirely* mistaken. I do not feel myself clear-headed enough nowadays—suffering as I do from insomnia and the result of a severe illness last winter—to investigate things for myself. I have neither the *means* nor the *ability.* On the other hand, I must reiterate once more that this is a very delicate family matter and that for many reasons I may want the *whole thing hushed up.* If I am once assured of the *facts,* I can deal with the matter myself and should prefer to do so. I hope that I have made myself clear on this point. If you will undertake this investigation, perhaps you will let me know to the above address?

Yours very truly,
AMELIA BARROWBY.

Poirot read the letter through twice. Again his eyebrows rose slightly. Then he placed it on one side and proceeded to the next envelope in the pile.

At ten o'clock precisely he entered the room where Miss Lemon, his confidential secretary, sat awaiting her instructions for the day. Miss Lemon was forty-eight and of unprepossessing appearance. Her general effect was that of a lot of bones flung together at random. She had a passion for order almost equaling that of Poirot himself; and though capable of thinking, she never thought unless told to do so.

Poirot handed her the morning correspondence. "Have the goodness, mademoiselle, to write refusals couched in correct terms to all of these."

Miss Lemon ran an eye over the various letters, scribbling in turn a hieroglyphic on each of them. These marks were legible to her alone and were in a code of her own: "Soft soap"; "slap in the face"; "purr purr"; "curt"; and so on. Having done this, she nodded and looked up for further instructions.

Poirot handed her Amelia Barrowby's letter. She extracted it from its double envelope, read it through and looked up inquiringly.

"Yes, M. Poirot?" Her pencil hovered—ready—over her shorthand pad.

"What is your opinion of that letter, Miss Lemon?"

With a slight frown Miss Lemon put down the pencil and read through the letter again.

The contents of a letter meant nothing to Miss Lemon except from the point of view of composing an adequate reply. Very occasionally her employer appealed to her human, as opposed to her official, capacities. It slightly annoyed Miss Lemon when he did so—she was very nearly the perfect machine, completely and gloriously uninterested in all human affairs. Her real passion in life was the perfection of a filing system beside which all other filing systems should sink into oblivion. She dreamed of such a system at night. Nevertheless, Miss Lemon was perfectly capable of intelligence on purely human matters, as Hercule Poirot well knew.

"Well?" he demanded.

"Old lady," said Miss Lemon. "Got the wind up pretty badly."

"Ah! The wind rises in her, you think?"

Miss Lemon, who considered that Poirot had been long enough in Great Britain to understand its slang terms, did not reply. She took a brief look at the double envelope.

"Very hush-hush," she said. "And tells you nothing at all."

"Yes," said Hercule Poirot. "I observed that."

Miss Lemon's hand hung once more hopefully over the shorthand pad. This time Hercule Poirot responded.

"Tell her I will do myself the honor to call upon her at any time she suggests, unless she prefers to consult me here. Do not type the letter—write it by hand."

"Yes, M. Poirot."

Poirot produced more correspondence. "These are bills."

Miss Lemon's efficient hands sorted them quickly. "I'll pay all but these two."

"Why those two? There is no error in them."

"They are firms you've only just begun to deal with. It looks bad to pay too promptly when you've just opened an account—looks as though you were working up to get some credit later on."

"Ah!" murmured Poirot. "I bow to your superior knowledge of the British tradesman."

"There's nothing much I don't know about them," said Miss Lemon grimly.

The letter to Miss Amelia Barrowby was duly written and sent, but no reply was forthcoming. Perhaps, thought Hercule Poirot, the old lady had unraveled her mystery herself. Yet he felt a shade of surprise that in that case she should not have written a courteous word to say that his services were no longer required.

It was five days later when Miss Lemon, after receiving her morning's instructions, said, "That Miss Barrowby we wrote to—no wonder there's been no answer. She's dead."

Hercule Poirot said very softly, "Ah—dead." It sounded not so much like a question as an answer.

Opening her handbag, Miss Lemon produced a newspaper cutting. "I saw it in the tube and tore it out."

Just registering in his mind approval of the fact that, though Miss Lemon used the word "tore," she had neatly cut the entry out with scissors, Poirot read the announcement taken from the Births, Deaths and Marriages in the Morning Post: "On March 26th—suddenly—at Rosebank, Charman's Green, Amelia Jane Barrowby, in her seventy-third year. No flowers, by request."

Poirot read it over. He murmured under his breath, "Suddenly." Then he said briskly, "If you will be so obliging as to take a letter, Miss Lemon?"

The pencil hovered. Miss Lemon, her mind dwelling on the intricacies of the filing system, took down in rapid and correct shorthand:

Dear Miss Barrowby: I have received no reply from you, but as I shall be in the neighborhood of Charman's Green on Friday, I will call upon you on that day and discuss more fully the matter you mentioned to me in your letter.

Yours, etc.

"Type this letter, please; and if it is posted at once, it should get to Charman's Green tonight."

On the following morning a letter in a black-edged envelope arrived by the second post:

Dear Sir: In reply to your letter my aunt, Miss Barrowby, passed away on the twenty-sixth, so the matter you speak of is no longer of importance.

Yours truly,
MARY DELAFONTAINE.

Poirot smiled to himself. "No longer of importance. . . . Ah—that is what we shall see. *En avant*—to Charman's Green."

Rosebank was a house that seemed likely to live up to its name, which is more than can be said for most houses of its class and character.

Hercule Poirot paused as he walked up the path to the front door and looked ap-

provingly at the neatly planned beds on either side of him. Rose trees that promised a good harvest later in the year, and at present daffodils, early tulips, blue hyacinths—the last bed was partly edged with shells.

Poirot murmured to himself, "How does it go, the English rhyme the children sing?

"Mistress Mary, quite contrary,
How does your garden grow?
With cockle-shells, and silver bells,
And pretty maids all in a row."

"Not a row, perhaps," he considered, "but here is at least one pretty maid to make the little rhyme come right."

The front door had opened and a neat little maid in cap and apron was looking somewhat dubiously at the spectacle of a heavily mustached foreign gentleman talking aloud to himself in the front garden. She was, as Poirot had noted, a very pretty little maid, with round blue eyes and rosy cheeks.

Poirot raised his hat with courtesy and addressed her: "Pardon, but does a Miss Amelia Barrowby live here?"

The little maid gasped and her eyes grew rounder. "Oh, sir, didn't you know? She's

dead. Ever so sudden it was. Tuesday night."

She hesitated, divided between two strong instincts: the first, distrust of a foreigner; the second, the pleasurable enjoyment of her class in dwelling on the subject of illness and death.

"You amaze me," said Hercule Poirot, not very truthfully. "I had an appointment with the lady for today. However, I can perhaps see the other lady who lives here."

The little maid seemed slightly doubtful. "The mistress? Well, you could see her, perhaps, but I don't know whether she'll be seeing anyone or not."

"She will see me," said Poirot, and handed her a card.

The authority of his tone had its effect. The rosy-cheeked maid fell back and ushered Poirot into a sitting room on the right of the hall. Then, card in hand, she departed to summon her mistress.

Hercule Poirot looked round him. The room was a perfectly conventional drawing room—oatmeal-colored paper with a frieze round the top, indeterminate cretonnes, rose-colored cushions and curtains, a good many china knickknacks and ornaments. There was nothing in the room that stood out, that announced a definite personality.

Suddenly Poirot, who was very sensitive, felt eyes watching him. He wheeled round. A girl was standing in the entrance of the French window—a small, sallow girl, with very black hair and suspicious eyes.

She came in, and as Poirot made a little bow she burst out abruptly, "Why have you come?"

Poirot did not reply. He merely raised his eyebrows.

"You are not a lawyer—no?" Her English was good, but not for a minute would anyone have taken her to be English.

"Why should I be a lawyer, mademoiselle?"

The girl stared at him sullenly. "I thought you might be. I thought you had come perhaps to say that she did not know what she was doing. I have heard of such things—the not due influence; that is what they call it, no? But that is not right. She wanted me to have the money, and I shall have it. If it is needful I shall have a lawyer of my own. The money is mine. She wrote it down so, and so it shall be." She looked ugly, her chin thrust out, her eyes gleaming.

The door opened and a tall woman entered and said, "Katrina."

The girl shrank, flushed, muttered something and went out through the window.

Poirot turned to face the newcomer who had so effectually dealt with the situation by uttering a single word. There had been authority in her voice, and contempt and a shade of well-bred irony. He realized at once that this was the owner of the house, Mary Delafontaine.

"M. Poirot? I wrote to you. You cannot have received my letter."

"Alas, I have been away from London."

"Oh, I see; that explains it. I must introduce myself. My name is Delafontaine. This is my husband. Miss Barrowby was my aunt."

Mr. Delafontaine had entered so quietly that his arrival had passed unnoticed. He was a tall man with grizzled hair and an in-

THE DEAR MAN

"*Why don't you just buy something like that you've been wearing?*"

determinate manner. He had a nervous way of fingering his chin. He looked often toward his wife, and it was plain that he expected her to take the lead in any conversation.

"I much regret that I intrude in the midst of your bereavement," said Hercule Poirot.

"I quite realize that it is not your fault," said Mrs. Delafontaine. "My aunt died on Tuesday evening. It was quite unexpected."

"Most unexpected," said Mr. Delafontaine. "Great blow." His eyes watched the window where the foreign girl had disappeared.

"I apologize," said Hercule Poirot. "And I withdraw." He moved a step toward the door.

"Half a sec," said Mr. Delafontaine. "You —er—had an appointment with Aunt Amelia, you say?"

"Parfaitement."

"Perhaps you will tell us about it," said his wife. "If there is anything we can do ——"

"It was of a private nature," said Poirot. "I am a detective," he added simply.

Mr. Delafontaine knocked over a little china figure he was handling. His wife looked puzzled.

"A detective? And you had an appointment with auntie? But how extraordinary!" She stared at him. "Can't you tell us a little more, M. Poirot? It—it seems quite fantastic."

Poirot was silent for a moment. He chose his words with care.

"It is difficult for me, madame, to know what to do."

"Look here," said Mr. Delafontaine. "She didn't mention Russians, did she?"

"Russians?"

"Yes, you know—Bolshies, Reds, all that sort of thing."

"Don't be absurd, Henry," said his wife. Mr. Delafontaine collapsed. "Sorry—sorry—I just wondered."

Mary Delafontaine looked frankly at Poirot. Her eyes were very blue—the color of forget-me-nots. "If you can tell us anything, M. Poirot, I should be glad if you would do so. I can assure you that I have a —a reason for asking."

Mr. Delafontaine looked alarmed. "Be careful, old girl—you know there may be nothing in it."

Again his wife quelled him with a glance. "Well, M. Poirot?"

Slowly, gravely, Hercule Poirot shook his head. He shook it with visible regret, but he shook it. "At present, madame," he said, "I fear I must say nothing."

He bowed, picked up his hat and moved to the door. Mary Delafontaine came with him into the hall. On the doorstep he paused and looked at her.

"You are fond of your garden, I think, madame?"

"I? Yes, I spend a lot of time gardening."

"Je vous fais mes compliments."

He bowed once more and strode down to the gate. As he passed out of it and turned to the right he glanced back and registered two impressions—a sallow face watching him from a first-floor window, and a man of erect and soldierly carriage pacing up and down on the opposite site of the street.

Hercule Poirot nodded to himself. *"Définitivement,"* he said. "There is a mouse in this hole! What move must the cat make now?"

His decision took him to the nearest post office. Here he put through a couple of telephone calls. The result seemed to be satisfactory. He bent his steps to Charman's Green police station, where he inquired for Inspector Sims.

Inspector Sims was a big, burly man with a hearty manner. "M. Poirot?" he inquired. "I thought so. I've just this minute had a telephone call through from the chief constable about you. He said you'd be dropping in. Come into my office."

The door shut, the inspector waved Poirot to one chair, settled himself in another, and turned a gaze of acute inquiry upon his visitor.

"You're very quick onto the mark, M. Poirot. Come to see us about this Rosebank case almost before we know it is a case. What put you onto it?"

Poirot drew out the letter he had received and handed it to the inspector. The latter read it with some interest.

"Interesting," he said. "The trouble is, it might mean so many things. Pity she couldn't have been a little more explicit. It would have helped us now."

"Or there might have been no need for help."

"You mean?"

"She might have been alive."

"You go as far as that, do you? H'm—I'm not sure you're wrong."

"I pray of you, inspector, recount to me the facts. I know nothing at all."

"That's easily done. Old lady was taken bad after dinner on Tuesday night. Very alarming. Convulsions—spasms—what not. They sent for the doctor. By the time he arrived she was dead. Idea was she'd died of a fit. Well, he didn't much like the look of things. He hemmed and hawed and put it with a bit of soft sawder, but he made it clear that he couldn't give a death certificate. And as far as the family go, that's where the matter stands. They're awaiting the result of the postmortem. We've got a bit farther. The doctor gave us the tip right away—he and the police surgeon did the autopsy together—and the result is in no doubt whatever. The old lady died of a large dose of strychnine."

"Aha!"

"That's right. Very nasty bit of work. Point is, who gave it to her? It must have been administered very shortly before death. First idea was it was given to her in her food at dinner—but, frankly, that seems to be a washout. They had artichoke soup, served from a tureen, fish pie and apple tart."

"'They' being?"

"Miss Barrowby, Mr. Delafontaine and Mrs. Delafontaine. Miss Barrowby had a kind of nurse-attendant—a half Russian girl —but she didn't eat with the family. She had the remains as they came out from the dining room. There's a maid, but it was her night out. She left the soup on the stove and the fish pie in the oven, and the apple tart was cold. All three of them ate the same thing—and, apart from that, I don't think you could get strychnine down any-

one's throat that way. Stuff's as bitter as gall. The doctor told me you could taste it in a solution of one in a thousand, or something like that."

"Coffee?"

"Coffee's more like it, but the old lady never took coffee."

"I see your point. Yes, it seems an insuperable difficulty. What did she drink at the meal?"

"Water."

"Worse and worse."

"Bit of a teaser, isn't it?"

"She had money, the old lady?"

"Very well to do, I imagine. Of course, we haven't got exact details yet. The Delafontaines are pretty badly off, from what I can make out. The old lady helped with the upkeep of the house."

Poirot smiled a little. He said, "So you suspect the Delafontaines. Which of them?"

"I don't exactly say I suspect either of them in particular. But there it is; they're her only near relations, and her death brings them a tidy sum of money, I've no doubt. We all know what human nature is!"

"Sometimes inhuman—yes, that is very true. And there was nothing else the old lady ate or drank?"

"Well, as a matter of fact ——"

"Ah, *voilà!* I felt that you had something, as you say, up your sleeve—the soup, the fish pie, the apple tart—a *bêtise!* Now we come to the hub of the affair."

"I don't know about that. But as a matter of fact, the old girl took a cachet before meals. You know, not a pill or a tablet; one of those rice-paper things with a powder inside. Some perfectly harmless thing for the digestion."

"Admirable. Nothing is easier than to fill a cachet with strychnine and substitute it for one of the others. It slips down the throat with a drink of water and is not tasted."

"That's all right. The trouble is, the girl gave it to her."

"The Russian girl?"

"Yes. Katrina Rieger. She was a kind of lady-help, nurse-companion to Miss Barrowby. Fairly ordered about by her, too, I gather. Fetch this, fetch that, fetch the other, rub my back, pour out my medicine, run round to the chemist—all that sort of business. You know how it is with these old women—they mean to be kind, but what they need is a sort of black slave!"

Poirot smiled.

"And there you are, you see," continued Inspector Sims. "It doesn't fit in what you might call nicely. Why should the girl poison her? Miss Barrowby dies and now the girl will be out of a job, and jobs aren't so easy to find—she's not trained or anything."

"Still," suggested Poirot, "if the box of cachets was left about, anyone in the house might have the opportunity."

"Naturally we're onto that, M. Poirot. I don't mind telling you we're making our inquiries—quiet like, if you understand me. When the prescription was last made up, where it was usually kept; patience and a lot of spade work—that's what will do the trick in the end. And then there's Miss Barrowby's solicitor. I'm having an interview with him tomorrow. And the bank

Continued on page 190.

For the answers to "Who Are They Now?", turn to page 196.

Who are They Now?

Although the photographs were taken when these now-very-famous people were much younger, you may be able to find a clue to their identity in the facts, or even in the faces.

1. Taken about 1895. Sportsman, traveler, served eighteen months in France during World War; took important position; now retired.

2. Taken about 1914. Has figured prominently in a recent romance; will no doubt assume a title connected in part with the South Seas.

3. Taken about 1883. Devoted to sailing, deep-sea fishing, motoring; a winning personality, his popularity was for some time in dispute.

4. Taken about 1885. (Right) A Swiss citizen and a fine amateur violinist, whose works, though profound, have made him famous.

5. Taken about 1890. A music lover and amateur painter whose dictates have created in his country a fashionable color in men's wear.

6. Taken about 1890. Once a worker in the oil fields, he rose from comparative obscurity to command the attention of a nation.

7. Taken about 1906. One of the great favorites in her field, and now on regular occasions a queenly figure in a democratic country.

8. Taken about 1912. He has known both brilliant fame and bitter tragedy; has been recognized for his researches in vital science.

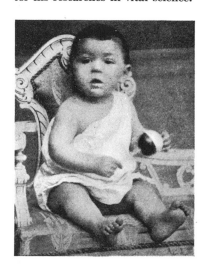

9. Taken about 1917. Known to millions of admirers for his debonair behavior in various vehicles and also for his sartorial perfection.

10. Taken about 1906. The wife of a well-known ex-publisher, whose exploits have made her the leading lady in her very lofty profession.

11. Taken about 1916. Even if we say right out that this young lady is now a leading film star, we wonder if you can guess her name.

12. Taken about 1906. This young man, in full view of thousands, recently pulled one of the biggest surprises in the history of his profession.

manager. There's a lot to be done still."

Poirot rose. "A little favor, Inspector Sims; you will send me a little word how the affair marches. I would esteem it a great favor. Here is my telephone number."

"Why, certainly, M. Poirot. Two heads are better than one; and, besides, you ought to be in on this, having had that letter and all."

"You are too amiable, inspector." Politely, Poirot shook hands and took his leave.

He was called to the telephone on the following afternoon. "Is that M. Poirot? Inspector Sims here. Things are beginning to sit up and look pretty in that little matter you and I know of."

"In verity? Tell me, I pray of you."

"Well, here's item No. 1—and a pretty big item. Miss B. left a small legacy to her niece and everything else to K. In consideration of her great kindness and attention—that's the way it was put. That alters the complexion of things."

A picture rose swiftly in Poirot's mind. A sullen face and a passionate voice saying, "The money is mine. She wrote it down and so it shall be." The legacy would not come as a surprise to Katrina—she knew about it beforehand.

"Item No. 2," continued the voice of Inspector Sims. "Nobody but K. handled that cachet."

"You can be sure of that?"

"The girl herself doesn't deny it. What do you think of that?"

"Extremely interesting."

"We only want one thing more—evidence of how the strychnine came into her possession. That oughtn't to be difficult."

"But so far you haven't been successful?"

"I've barely started. The inquest was only this morning."

"What happened at it?"

"Adjourned for a week."

"And the young lady—K.?"

"I'm detaining her on suspicion. Don't want to run any risks. She might have some funny friends in the country who'd try to get her out of it."

"No," said Poirot. "I do not think she has any friends."

"Really? What makes you say that, M. Poirot?"

"It is just an idea of mine. There were no other 'items,' as you call them?"

"Nothing that's strictly relevant. Miss B. seems to have been monkeying about a bit with her shares lately—must have dropped quite a tidy sum. It's rather a funny business, one way and another, but I don't see how it affects the main issue—not at present, that is."

"No, perhaps you are right. Well, my best thanks to you. It was most amiable of you to ring me up."

"Not at all. I'm a man of my word. I could see you were interested. Who knows, you may be able to give me a helping hand before the end."

"That would give me great pleasure. It might help you, for instance, if I could lay my hand on a friend of the girl Katrina."

"I thought you said she hadn't got any friends?" said Inspector Sims, surprised.

"I was wrong," said Hercule Poirot. "She has one."

Before the inspector could ask a further question, Poirot had rung off.

With a serious face he wandered into the room where Miss Lemon sat at her typewriter. She raised her hands from the keys at her employer's approach and looked at him inquiringly.

"I want you," said Poirot, "to figure to yourself a little history."

Miss Lemon dropped her hands into her lap in a resigned manner. She enjoyed typing, paying bills, filing papers and entering up engagements. To be asked to imagine herself in hypothetical situations bored her very much, but she accepted it as a disagreeable part of a duty.

"You are a Russian girl," began Poirot.

"Yes," said Miss Lemon, looking intensely British.

"You are alone and friendless in this country. You have reasons for not wishing to return to Russia. You are employed as a kind of drudge, nurse-attendant and companion to an old lady. You are meek and uncomplaining."

"Yes," said Miss Lemon obediently, but entirely failing to see herself being meek to any old lady under the sun.

"The old lady takes a fancy to you. She decides to leave her money to you. She tells you so." Poirot paused.

Miss Lemon said "Yes," again.

"And then the old lady finds out something; perhaps it is a matter of money—she may find that you have not been honest with her. Or it might be more grave still—a medicine that tasted different, some food that disagreed. Anyway, she begins to suspect you of something and she writes to a very famous detective—enfin, to the most famous detective—me! I am to call upon her shortly. And then, as you say, the dripping will be in the fire. The great thing is to act quickly. And so—before the great detective arrives—the old lady is dead. And the money comes to you. . . . Tell me, does that seem to you reasonable?"

"Quite reasonable," said Miss Lemon. "Quite reasonable for a Russian, that is. Personally, I should never take a post as a companion. I like my duties clearly defined. And of course I should not dream of murdering anyone."

Poirot sighed. "How I miss my friend Hastings. He had such an imagination. Such a romantic mind! It is true that he always imagined wrong—but that in itself was a guide."

Miss Lemon was silent. She had heard about Captain Hastings before, and was not interested. She looked longingly at the typewritten sheet in front of her.

"So it seems to you reasonable," mused Poirot.

"Doesn't it to you?"

"I am almost afraid it does," sighed Poirot.

The telephone rang and Miss Lemon went out of the room to answer it. She came back to say, "It's Inspector Sims again."

Poirot hurried to the instrument. " 'Allo, 'allo; what is that you say?"

Sims repeated his statement. "We've found a packet of strychnine in the girl's bedroom—tucked underneath the mattress. The sergeant's just come in with the news. That about clinches it, I think."

"Yes," said Poirot, "I think that clinches

it." His voice had changed. It rang with sudden confidence.

When he had rung off, he sat down at his writing table and arranged the objects on it in a mechanical manner. He murmured to himself, "There was something wrong. I felt it—no, not felt. It must have been something I saw. En avant, the little gray cells. Ponder—reflect. Was everything logical and in order? The girl—her anxiety about the money; Mme. Delafontaine; her husband—his suggestion of Russians—imbecile, but he is an imbecile; the room; the garden—ah! Yes, the garden."

He sat up very stiff. The green light shone in his eyes. He sprang up and went into the adjoining room.

"Miss Lemon, will you have the kindness to leave what you are doing and make an investigation for me?"

"An investigation, M. Poirot? I'm afraid I'm not very good ——"

Poirot interrupted her. "You said one day that you knew all about tradesmen."

"Certainly I do," said Miss Lemon with confidence.

"Then the matter is simple. You are to go to Charman's Green and you are to discover a fishmonger."

"A fishmonger?" asked Miss Lemon, surprised.

"Precisely. The fishmonger who supplied Rosebank with fish. When you have found him you will ask him a certain question."

He handed her a slip of paper. Miss Lemon took it, noted its contents without interest, then nodded and slipped the lid on her typewriter.

"We will go to Charman's Green together," said Poirot. "You to the fishmonger and I to the police station. It will take us but half an hour from Baker Street."

On arrival at his destination, he was greeted by the surprised Inspector Sims. "Well, this is quick work, M. Poirot. I was talking to you on the phone only an hour ago."

"I have a request to make of you; that you allow me to see this girl Katrina—what is her name?"

"Katrina Rieger. Well, I don't suppose there is any objection to that."

The girl Katrina looked even more sallow and sullen than ever.

Poirot spoke to her very gently. "Mademoiselle, I want you to believe that I am not your enemy. I want you to tell me the truth."

Her eyes snapped defiantly. "I have told the truth. To everyone I have told the truth! If the old lady was poisoned, it was not I who poisoned her. It is all a mistake. You wish to prevent me having the money." Her voice was rasping. She looked, he thought, like a miserable little cornered rat.

"Tell me about this cachet, mademoiselle," M. Poirot went on. "Did no one handle it but you?"

"I have said so, have I not? They were made up at the chemist's that afternoon. I brought them back with me in my bag—that was just before supper. I opened the box and gave Miss Barrowby one with a glass of water."

"No one touched them but you?"

"No." A cornered rat—with courage!

"And Miss Barrowby had for supper only what we have been told. The soup, the fish pie, the tart?"

"Yes." A hopeless "yes"—dark, smoldering eyes that saw no light anywhere.

Poirot patted her shoulder. "Be of good courage, mademoiselle. There may yet be freedom—yes, and money—a life of ease."

She looked at him suspiciously.

As he went out Sims said to him, "I didn't quite get what you said through the telephone—something about the girl having a friend."

"She has one. Me!" said Hercule Poirot, and had left the police station before the inspector could pull his wits together.

At the Green Cat tearooms, Miss Lemon did not keep her employer waiting. She went straight to the point.

"The man's name is Rudge, in the High Street, and you were quite right. A dozen and a half exactly. I've made a note of what he said." She handed it to him.

"Arrr." It was a deep, rich sound like the purr of a cat.

Hercule Poirot betook himself to Rosebank. As he stood in the front garden, the sun setting behind him, Mary Delafontaine came out to him.

"M. Poirot?" Her voice sounded surprised. "You have come back?"

"Yes, I have come back." He paused and then said, "When I first came here, madame, the children's nursery rhyme came into my head:

"Mistress Mary, quite contrary,
How does your garden grow?
With cockle-shells, and silver bells,
And pretty maids all in a row.

"Only they are not *cockle* shells, are they, madame? They are *oyster* shells." His hand pointed.

He heard her catch her breath and then stay very still. Her eyes asked a question.

He nodded. "*Mais oui,* I know! The maid left the dinner ready—she will swear and Katrina will swear that that is all you had. Only you and your husband know that you brought back a dozen and a half oysters—a little treat *pour la bonne tante.* So easy to put the strychnine in an oyster. It is swallowed—*comme ça!* But there remain the shells—they must not go in the bucket. The maid would see them. And so you thought of making an edging of them to a bed. But there were not enough—the edging is not complete. The effect is bad—it spoils the symmetry of the otherwise charming garden. Those few oyster shells struck an alien note—they displeased my eye on my first visit."

Mary Delafontaine said, "I suppose you guessed from the letter. I knew she had written—but I didn't know how much she'd said."

Poirot answered evasively, "I knew at least that it was a family matter. If it had been a question of Katrina there would

have been no point in hushing things up. I understand that you or your husband handled Miss Barrowby's securities to your own profit, and that she found out ——"

Mary Delafontaine nodded. "We've done it for years—a little here and there. I never realized she was sharp enough to find out. And then I learned she had sent for a detective; and I found out, too, that she was leaving her money to Katrina—that miserable little creature!"

"And so the strychnine was put in Katrina's bedroom? I comprehend. You save yourself and your husband from what I may discover, and you saddle an innocent child with murder. Had you no pity, madame?"

Mary Delafontaine shrugged her shoulders—her blue forget-me-not eyes looked into Poirot's. He remembered the perfection of her acting the first day he had come and the bungling attempts of her husband. A woman above the average—but inhuman.

She said, "Pity? For that miserable intriguing little rat?" Her contempt rang out.

Hercule Poirot said slowly, "I think, madame, that you have cared in your life for two things only. One is your husband."

He saw her lips tremble.

"And the other—is your garden."

He looked round him. His glance seemed to apologize to the flowers for that which he had done and was about to do.

THE KENNEDYS IN LONDON

At 14 Princes Gate, in London—the American embassy—a big American family is making itself at home. The eleven Kennedys—mother, father and nine children—have moved in, and since their arrival the six-story house facing Hyde Park has been something more than the official residence of the American ambassador. The house echoes with phonograph records, quick footsteps and young American voices. A family-group picture is in the study, along with the portrait of George Washington. The room is lighted with American lamps. There are schoolboys playing ball in the back yard, otherwise known as the gardens. A case of soft drinks is in the icebox.

Seated (from left to right) are: Eunice, Jean, Edward, on the lap of his father Joseph P. Kennedy, Patricia and Kathleen; and standing: Rosemary, Robert, John, Mrs. Kennedy and Joseph Jr.

HAVE YOU
AN INFERIORITY COMPLEX?

Charles A. Drake, Ph.D.

THIS IS WHERE A WATCHBIRD WAS BUT

HE HAD TO GO WAY DOWN HERE TO WATCH A BASHFUL.

THIS IS A WATCHBIRD WATCHING YOU

THIS IS A BASHFUL

By Munro Leaf

BASHFULS are so shy that they all have stiff necks. Whenever they see somebody for the first time, they look down at their shoes. Most people never know whether a Bashful has a face or not. All anybody can see is the top of its foolish head.

WERE YOU A **BASHFUL** THIS MONTH?

5. Are you self-conscious when meeting important people?
6. Can you say "no" to salesmen and canvassers?
7. Do you usually talk matters over with others before making an important decision?
8. Do many other persons strongly influence your actions?
9. Can you express your views in public before a group your own age?
10. Are you thrown into confusion when your husband makes a social blunder?
11. Are you deeply hurt by unfair criticism?
12. Do you have severe fits of depression?
13. Do salespeople in stores take advantage of your timidity?
14. Do you often contradict people on statements you know to be wrong?
15. Do you feel self-conscious when wearing new clothing that is in good style and taste?
16. Are you disappointed if you are not praised for the things you do well?
17. Does the thought of some social blunder you have made cause you pain?
18. Do you have times when everything seems to go wrong?
19. Do you have to force yourself to go to an interview in a strange office?
20. Do you often envy the people who seem to be more fortunate than you?
21. Do you think that you have an unusually severe inferiority complex?
22. Do you compromise or back down when there is a difference of opinion with another person?
23. Can you converse with ease when you know people are eavesdropping?
24. Are you emphatic in expressing your likes and dislikes?
25. Do you feel handicapped by your appearance in realizing your ambitions?

How much self-confidence have you? How much self-confidence do your friends think you have? Here is a test that will tell you what your tendencies are. Rate yourself first, and then get several friends to rate you without giving them an inkling as to how you have rated yourself. If you agree you are probably right. If you don't agree *you* are probably wrong. Traits you are sure you possess may not be apparent to others. For example, you may feel nervous and ill at ease in the presence of important people, yet to observers you may appear to be utterly calm and well poised. Your fear of the impression you are making is completely imaginary.

A careful analysis of your answers, one by one, should be of great help in planning a course of action to overcome the deficiencies and to modify the traits that may be too strong. But you must have a firm determination to change them. You are never too old to make such changes. Each successful attempt to say "no" to the sales clerk who is about to wrap up the goods you do not want strengthens your ability to say "no" in other similar situations.

This test is based on similar tests given by psychologists to determine personality characteristics. Can you take it?

Write YES or NO after each of the following questions

1. Do you usually start a conversation instead of waiting for others to start it?
2. Are you usually shy with strangers?
3. Do you join readily in stunts and games at a party?
4. Do you frequently wonder what impression you are making on the others in a group?

Scoring Key

Give yourself 4 points for each of your answers that corresponds to the following:

1. Yes	7. No	13. No	19. No
2. No	8. No	14. Yes	20. No
3. Yes	9. Yes	15. No	21. No
4. No	10. No	16. No	22. No
5. No	11. No	17. No	23. Yes
6. Yes	12. No	18. No	24. Yes
			25. No

SCORE IN POINTS	DEGREE OF SELF-CONFIDENCE
76 to 100 . .	Excessive
60 to 72 . .	Strong
44 to 56 . .	Moderate
32 to 40 . .	Inferiority Complex
0 to 28 . .	Extreme Inferiority Complex

Scene from ALL THIS AND HEAVEN TOO *by Rachel Field. Illustration by Roy Spreter.*

GIVE AND TAKE

The Hollywood make-up boys give **Katharine Hepburn** the gold star for beauty discipline. When she first arrived in Hollywood her "horse laugh" (showing all her gums) had them stumped. One said, "If you practiced making faces that would exercise those muscles around your mouth, you could control your smile so it would never go above the gum line."

For a year and a half Katy made faces at herself in every moment she could snatch. Her control is so perfect now she couldn't smile wrong if she tried.

Hepburn with James Stewart in
"The Philadelphia Story."

Probably more people will read Wuthering Heights in the months to come than in any year since this "most enthralling love story in the English language was written," says **Alexander Woollcott**. **Laurence Olivier** plays the tempestuous Heathcliffe opposite **Merle Oberon**'s Cathy in the screen version of the **Emily Brontë** classic.

Bette Davis

"How can I become an actress?" To this question, perpetually asked, *Bette Davis* says, "I don't know. You work; you take advantage of every break; people are kind to you and help you, or they are arrogant and petty; walk-ons grow into bits and bits into important minor roles. Suddenly you realize you are an actress and you exclaim, with as much surprise as satisfaction, I've done it. As to a concrete answer, I cannot give it. But believe me, if I could, I would."

In a recent poll the JOURNAL discovered that 79 percent of America's married men are happier than bachelors, and 90 percent

feel that married women should not hold jobs after marriage. A majority of 59 percent also declared that they preferred brunettes to blondes.

Shirley Temple recently gave a party for grown-ups in New York. The guests felt the strain of being entertained until the self-assured nine-year-old celebrity visited each table in turn, putting everyone at ease.

A new role for Broadway comedian **Bob Hope**—Master of Ceremonies of NBC's popular Sunday evening show, The Rippling Rhythm Revue. Bob will be bringing his new heckler-in-chief, Honeychile.

Shirley Gives a Party.

Hedy Lamarr

Olivier and Oberon

Bob Hope

Talullah Bankhead in Lillian Hellman's "The Little Foxes."

Maybe you've always been curious, like **Wilhela Cushman,** to know what other women are fussy about, and what they want for their birthdays. Anyhow, she decided one day to ask the first six well-known women she saw; and here is what they said: *Hattie Carnegie:* "My hair and my fingernails; and as for my birthday, I've never had one as long as I can remember." . . .

Judy Garland: "I'm not fussy about anything; and I want a Cadillac." . . . *Helen Wills Moody:* "Getting up in the morning and going to bed at night; and I want a stone house on the sea about a hundred miles south of Monterey." . . . *Tallulah Bankhead:* "I'm fit to be tied when people keep me waiting; and for a birthday present, I want the play I'm in, The Little Foxes, to still be standing them up." . . . *Lulu,* the famous English lady clown: "My job's to be funny, not fussy; and all I want is a wireless set." . . . *Clare Boothe Luce:* "I can't keep from picking pieces of thread and lint up off the carpet; and for my birthday I want a billion dollars in tax-exempt bonds—or if that is impractical, an old-fashioned roll-top desk."

A lifelong desire of **Noel Coward** and the **Lunts** was fulfilled when the curtain went up on the New York production of Mr. Coward's Design for Living. In London the leading roles are played by **Rex Harrison, Diana Wynyard** and **Anton Walbrook.**

Eternal Triangle, Inc.: Alfred Lunt, Noel Coward, and Lynn Fontanne.

THE ART OF LOVE

André Maurois

"It is easier to die for a woman one loves than to live with her." Byron

They tell the story in London of an old gentleman who, buying a book for his daughter, asked timidly of the saleswoman:
"No sex in it, I hope?"
"Oh, no, sir," she answered, "it's a love story."

The joke is full of meaning. To be sure, like all jokes, it exaggerates a real truth. Every love story leans heavily on the instinct of sex. But the miracle of human love lies in the fact that upon a very simple instinct, desire, are built edifices of the most complex and delicate feelings.

The birth of love is, like all other births, the work of Nature. It is later that the art of love comes in. In his treatise on love, Stendhal has a wonderful description of the birth of that emotion. I shall follow the essential outlines of his description, but supplement them with certain personal observations.

1. Every love begins with an impact caused either by admiration or by some accident which reveals an understanding or gives birth to a desire.

2. The impact having drawn the attention to a person, absence then becomes more favorable to love. It is this process which Stendhal calls *crystallization,* by which he means that to the lover the absent sweetheart is like those bits of wood which, left for a few days in the salt mines of Salzburg, are covered with glittering crystals and thus seem to be transformed into precious gems. By crystallization, the beloved is changed into a different being—one superior to his real self.

And this is why Proust says that love is subjective; that we love not real beings but those whom we ourselves create. This is not true when the admiration is more realistic; there is no such thing as crystallization of a genuine diamond. But there are very few diamonds without a defect.

3. From the moment of the first crystallization, a second meeting may take place without imperiling love, because our emotion will be such that we shall no longer see the real person, even when he is right before our very eyes.

4. So long as things remain in this condition, love gives nothing but happiness; but no fire burns without feeding, and that growing flame would quickly die out if a breath of hope, however faint, did not revive it. In the matter of encouraging signals, love is not exacting. A glance, a pressure of the hand, a lively remark stimulate it immediately.

The Kiss

By Walter de la Mare

Now, in the drouth of life,
  I've tasted this:
The thoughtless euthanasia
  Of a kiss.

And what is that but in
  An instant's beat
Two souls in flesh confined
  In freedom meet?

From those strange windows
  Called the eyes there looks
A heart athirst
  For heaven's water brooks.

The hands tell secrets;
  And a lifted brow
Asks, "O lost stranger,
  Art thou with me now?"

All stumbling words are dumb;
  The heart stands still,
Pauses; and then, alas, resumes
  The inevitable.

---

5. When these signals are unmistakable and continued, mutual love develops, and nothing is more beautiful; but in my opinion certainty and security kill romance. For many men and women, love, in its beginning, thrives on doubt, or rather on alternate encouragement and withdrawal.

6. The result of this seems to be that coquetry—that is, deliberate playing of a game that consists of offering allurement, withdrawing it, then offering it again—seems well adapted to arouse love and to keep it burning.

7. But continued coquetry kills love. Madame Récamier, a famous and for a long time an invincible coquette, deciding to make herself loved by Benjamin Constant, really succeeded in bringing it about. "Dare," she tells him, and immediately hope makes a child of that mature man. *I am not loved,* he thinks, *but I amuse her.* From the moment he becomes aware of the game, he suffers. *I had never known a coquette. What a plague!* A little later, *How I hate her!* Then decrystallization set in. *Heavens, I give up. Thanks to her, I have spent a hellish day. She is a harebrained woman, frothy, without memory, understanding or loyalty.*

Thus the coquette may go too far. If she intersperses in her severities enough hope as not to kill the patient, this cruel game is quite stimulating. Is it necessary to play it? It seems to me the better type of men and women relinquish the advantages which coquetry would give them. There is a quality of grandeur in saying, "I know that in confessing my love to you I am putting myself at your mercy; but I want to do it."

Is it possible to make oneself loved? And first, is it necessary? Is it not easier, if love does not respond to love, to exact of it at least its pleasures? It was thus in primitive or ancient civilizations. In those days if a man wanted a woman, he kidnaped her; a couple was formed; the captive woman was at the mercy of the warrior. It quite often happened that she came to love him because he had chosen her, because he was her master, or simply because he was kind to her. In other times, power and money played the role previously played by force. It is less easy to love a man for his fortune than for his courage, for wealth is not a quality of the man himself. However, Zeus, father of the gods, disguised in a shower of gold, still makes his way to Danaë's heart.

To sensitive souls, these servile loves bring little happiness. We don't want to be mastered; we want to be chosen. The beautiful ladies of the harem do not make themselves loved merely because they are prisoners. But, inversely, neither do the lax beauties on our present-day bathing beaches make themselves loved because they are so emancipated. Too much liberty builds transparent walls of an invisible harem around droves of compliant women. Romantic love would have the woman, without being inaccessible, lead a life

Who Are They Now?

(Names of persons shown on p. 189)

1, Duke of Windsor; 2, Princess Juliana, of Holland; 3, President Roosevelt; 4, Dr. Albert Einstein; 5, Reichsführer Adolf Hitler; 6, Ex-Governor Alfred M. Landon; 7, Helen Hayes; 8, Charles A. Lindbergh; 9, Robert Montgomery; 10, Amelia Earhart; 11, Jean Harlow; 12, Max Schmeling.

Photo by Philippe Halsman.

*"The minute one begins to examine one's life, to discover
what makes it good, one speaks of love."—Jessamyn West.*

within limits somewhat narrowed by reverence and decorum. These are the conditions which, admirably fulfilled in the Middle Ages, gave birth to chivalry.

If a young man loves an actress he has seen only on the stage, he endows her with the spiritual perfections which her voice and her face express, and which doubtless she herself does not possess. Because he has known her in some role created by a great playwright, he attributes to her the poetic charm of the heroine she represents. Because he has gazed on her only under the flattering lights of the theater, he is unaware of her wrinkles and her years. And since he has never shared her life, he knows nothing of her fits of bad temper or her egotism. "It is easier," says Byron, "to die

197

for a woman one loves than to live with her."

The combination of courtesies, techniques and artifices by which lovers try to please is called courtship. Let me indicate a few of the customary methods of wooing, by going from the lowest, common to all species, up to the noblest, which characterize mankind.

(A) ORNAMENT. The object of ornament is to draw attention to him or to her who wears it. Just as the firefly, by lighting itself in the night, indicates to those of its kind a proffered love, so women, by the beauty or daring of their clothes, offer themselves to the attention of men.

(B) SKILLFULNESS. One way to please is to do what one does, no matter what it is, better than anyone else. Everyone in love tries to show his skill in some line. The exercise of this skill takes various forms. Some birds dive before the beloved one, and from the bottom of the ponds bring back grasses which they offer her in homage.

"What are you going to look for in the east?"

"Glory, so that I may make myself loved," Chateaubriand replied. And from that plunge into the Mediterranean he brought back to Madame de Noailles some immortal verses.

Almost all musicians have transformed their sorrows and their longings into exquisite harmonies. The tennis player pleases by the perfection of his backhand, the chauffeur by his skillful turns, the ballet dancer by her clever toework.

The need of security, very strong in women, attracts the weakest of them to the man who, by his strength and power, seems to promise them a safe prop. In time of war they count the scalps of the necklace; in peacetime they seek genius, wealth. For a man in love, gifts are a means of declaring his power. Penguins and bankers offer to their loved ones stones more or less brilliant. From the moment they choose their man, swallows and women begin to think of the nest.

(C) PRAISE. Nearly all love poems are built on praise or lamentation. The lament may touch but it soon bores. Praise pleases because almost all men and women, even the proudest, suffer from some form of inferiority complex. The most beautiful doubts her wit; the strongest-minded, her charm. It is delightful to point out to a person a thousand qualities which he has but is unaware of, or regards as negligible. Some timid, unhappy women faint under the heat of admiration, like flowers in the sun. As for men, their hunger for praise knows no bounds. Plain women have made themselves loved because they were adepts at praise. One praises people, not for their evident qualities, which they know they have, but for those they think they have not. The famous novelist will listen lackadaisically while you praise his novels, but he will suddenly brighten up if you talk enthusiastically to him of a certain essay (one of his failures) or of the warmth in his voice.

(D) FEMININE COURTSHIP. A woman has her own ways of love-making. For a long time she leaned heavily on the legend that it was she who waited for the man to choose her. That was true only in appearance. "The woman waits for the man," says Bernard Shaw, "in the same sense as the spider waits for the fly."

For the woman, the art of love must be at the same time a recreation, an encouragement and a support. Consider the conquest of Louis XIV by Madame de Maintenon. Never did an undertaking seem more hopeless. Madame de Maintenon was no longer young; she came in contact with the king only in her capacity of governess to the children of Madame de Montespan, very beautiful, and the ruler of the king's will. Now, not only did the humble and mature woman snatch Louis from her brilliant rival; but more than that, she did what Madame de Montespan had not even dared to hope for: she got herself married to him.

What was her secret? The first was that to the king, beginning to tire of his mistress' rages, she seemed an angel of peace. Men put up for a time with the fits of temper or the jealousies of a much-loved woman. Some of them like emotional storms just as they like storms at sea. But for the most part they are peace-loving creatures.

Second secret of Madame de Maintenon: Every night the king used to assemble his ministers in her presence, and she would listen to the reports of their work without saying a word. But if the king questioned her, she showed by some pointed suggestion that she had followed, understood, weighed and had her own opinion. This was immensely clever on her part, for the man worthy of the name loves his work more than anything else in the world, even more than the woman he loves.

(E) CULTURE. It is the birds themselves that sing and dive into the water; crabs do their own amorous gymnastics in the puddles. But men have made themselves fascinating and skillful by proxy. Instead of composing his own poem, the lover reads those of Baudelaire to his sweetheart. The pianist, hoping for her favor, plays Chopin to her. The master's genius gushes forth upon his admirers and interpreters. The emotions the master engenders, being associated with experiences, enrich a picture and make memories more beautiful. An art shared allows a love to be maintained at a level above excitement and frenzy.

(F) OPINIONS IN COMMON. Whatever the religious faith may be, the political opinion, or belief in the necessity and beauty of work, similar creeds reinforce love tremendously. For a person who thinks passionately it is exceedingly difficult to love someone who does not, in some degree, share his beliefs; for if "love is joy accompanied by the idea of apparent reason," that love will of necessity be thwarted by painful disagreement. All work done with love is delightful; but work and love combined is of all things in this world the most delightful. Thus are born those wonderful households of scientists, artists, preachers, pioneers who are married couples and at the same time partners.

Here all courtship is futile; it is replaced by perfect communion.

After a short or long courtship, skillful or simple, love is born. But the rate of infant mortality is high in the country of love. To raise the child calls for unremitting care. Novelty, the most powerful of attractions, is also the most perishable. At the beginning each lover has a thousand things to learn about the other. Everyone has carried over from his youth memories, scenes, songs, stories which, mingled with caresses, make the first leisurely days enchanting. Alas, the stock of memories spends itself, and soon the stories, once so refreshing, seem monotonous and stale. How many men and women become more brilliant the moment they are no longer in the company of their partners! For then they say without embarrassment what they have already said too often. Look around at the couples seated at restaurant tables. The duration of their silences is too often in proportion to the length of time they have lived together.

This is true, of course, only when they are without imagination. For in love, imagination means that companions keep their love perpetually refreshed. Whoever really loves finds perfect pleasure in wandering every day through the thoughts of the loved one.

When a person has charm, he has it always; and charm never wearies. Every act, every word delights us. Even old age does not change people. A beautiful face grows old beautifully, and we like to rediscover under white hair the expression and the smile we loved when the hair was brown or blond.

Is there a technique to be learned: how not to bore? The great secret lies in being natural. Every strained position is painful to hold; and moreover, it is not beautiful. Hence wise lovers are those who try to keep their mates perfectly natural. There are men who aspire to mold a woman, to impose tastes, ideas upon her. How foolish! If she is so very different from what we are able to love, then let us not love her. But if we have chosen her, let her develop in her own way, freely. In friendship as in love, we go back with pleasure only to those with whom we can be ourselves, with no restraint and no deception.

A few rules for the art of not boring should be observed by both sexes. The first is to show in love's intimacies as much politeness as at the first meeting. For well-bred persons courtesy is not incompatible with naturalness. One may say anything if it is said with kindness, and it would be a strange confusion to think of frankness as brutality. The second rule is to keep a sense of humor in every situation. Then we shall be able to laugh at ourselves when we see how childish most disagreements are. The third is to hold jealousies within reasonable bounds; that is to say, to avoid complacence on the one hand and suspicion on the other, for both are offensive. The fourth is to let absence permit a new crystallization. When one is in love or married, vacations have their dangers; but if they are short and interrupted by letters they play a useful part. Finally, the last and most essential rule is to remain romantic. "Why, having won her, keep on making love to her? . . . Because just being mine, she is not or ever will be mine."

Just as genuine holiness lies less in

ecstasy and vexation of spirit than in humility, gentleness and kindness, so very great loves are recognized not by overwhelming attacks of desire but by the complete and lasting understandings of daily life.

The glorious festivals of desire such as happy lovers may know are like those lovely summer days when the heat of the sun bathes us with listlessness and bliss; when the sky is so pure we cannot imagine it would ever be dimmed; when in the upland the humblest village, transfigured by light, becomes a magic illusion. Those beautiful days—the enchanted memories they leave us, and the hope of knowing similar ones—are necessary to give us strength and courage to bear the months of storm. But since neither summer nor desire may continue beyond its natural time, we should teach ourselves to love also gray days, autumn fogs and the long nights of winter.

We know that marvelous feeling—confidence. In the presence of one person at least we may, during every moment of every day, raise the heavy visor of our armor and fearlessly reveal our deepest selves.

Confidence is so assuring and so precious that, like desire, it gives charm to the least important actions. When they were young, that man and that woman longed for a moment alone for an embrace; now they want it in order to share a secret. The hour of the walk has become as precious to them as formerly the hour of courtship. Now words are not necessary to their understanding. They think the same thoughts at the same time. Each of them suffers in a physical way the spiritual anxieties of the other. Each one would be ready to give his life for the other, who knows it.

How is it possible to describe the life of a happy married couple in the autumn of their love? How show that the god remains always the god even if he has assumed mortal face? The symphony of happiness, orchestrated by a genius, may be sublime; a mediocre musician is helped out by the violence of the storm. The soaring notes of the Parsifal overture, which lift the listener's soul beyond itself; the Béatitudes of César Franck, the Requiem of Fauré evoke better than words what may be the marvelous recurrence, the natural and powerful crescendo of an indestructible understanding. And if I have cited a requiem mass, it is only because the idea of death is the only dissonant note in these too perfect loves.

But death itself is powerless against the deepest love. One day when I was in Spain I met an old peasant woman who said to me:

"Oh, I—I have nothing to complain of. To be sure, I have had trouble in my life; but when I was twenty I loved a young man —he loved me—we married. Then after a few weeks he died. Just the same, I had had my share, and for fifty years I have lived on that memory."

A mighty consolation, that—to be able in hours of solitude and suffering to call up at least one perfect memory! Because of a love without a shadow, because of bright, sweet pictures with which that love furnishes thoughts and dreams; because of the works of great artists, and of religious faith, the man is a part of something which surpasses him. From the swift clash of instincts bursts forth a divine spark.

How? I think it is in vain that I have tried to tell you. "Love has need of poets, not analysts." The final word about the art of love is not to be found in Stendhal, as Stendhal himself said, but in Mozart. Go to a concert, listen to those pure notes, those ravishing harmonies; and if your love then seems to you confused, bitter, discordant, it is because you are still ignorant of the art of love. But if you recognize in your feelings that same perfection, that same marvelous understanding, that same sublime satisfaction with themes beyond all discord, then you are living in one of those rare experiences worthy to be lived—a great love.

ENGLAND'S EX-KING AND HIS DUCHESS IN VENICE

After two years of marriage, the tension lines have almost disappeared from Windsor's pink-and-white countenance. The Duchess, on her part, has added a few becoming pounds. To friends, His Royal Highness speaks proudly of "my wife"; she calls her husband David; he calls her Wallis; and according to their intimates, they are still very much in love.

Atlanta in flames.

GONE WITH THE WIND

Henry F. Pringle

In the fall of 1938, a girl named Vivien Leigh, who had appeared in a few English pictures and who had achieved considerable success on the English stage, decided to spend a vacation in America.

She visited New York and then the Pacific Coast. While there, she took a busman's holiday in Hollywood and met, among other notables, Myron Selznick, David's brother and one of the most successful agents in the business.

Myron took Miss Leigh out to lunch. He noticed that she was dark and small, that her waist was extremely slender. He must have been startled when he looked at her eyes, for they were exactly the shade of green described by Margaret Mitchell as the color of Scarlett O'Hara's eyes.

Selznick gave no hint of what was in his mind at the luncheon. He asked, though, whether she would care to witness the "burning of Atlanta" on his brother's lot that night. For work on Gone With the Wind had started even though a Scarlett had not been chosen. Motion pictures are more often made backward than not. In this case, Atlanta had to be burned before it could be built. Old sets were to be turned into a vast conflagration, and in their place would be erected the streets and houses of Atlanta.

When Miss Leigh and Myron Selznick arrived, flames were already leaping two hundred feet in the sky. Watching them, with his staff, was David Selznick. Myron guided Miss Leigh toward him.

"David," he said softly, "I want you to meet Scarlett O'Hara."

The executives of Selznick Pictures discovered two things, to their consternation: first, that nearly every actress in the land,

200

Vivien Leigh (Scarlett O'Hara) with Clark Gable (Rhett Butler) and, below, with Leslie Howard (Ashley Wilkes).

known or unknown, and every girl with yearnings to be an actress wanted to be Scarlett; their second discovery was that an incredible number of movie fans were threatening to boycott pictures in general, unless their casting demands were met. On the other hand, some comfort was to be found in the fact that all American womanhood—and a percentage of American manhood—was united in nominating Clark Gable for Rhett Butler. Selznick simply had to get Gable, a fact well known to Metro-Goldwyn-Mayer, who have him under contract. He had to pay through the nose for this ideal Rhett Butler: a share of the profits and a distribution agreement with Metro was the price. In return, Metro put up about $1,000,000 of the total cost, and the deal was concluded.

It had been sensibly concluded, from the start, that an indication of Southern speech, rather than exaggerated honeychile tones, would be used. Being a skilled actress, who knows how to use her voice, Miss Leigh rarely had trouble in speaking as Scarlett must have spoken. But after one scene she walked off the set with Leslie Howard, who is also English and who plays Ashley Wilkes. They rested for a few minutes, drank a soft drink and talked together. Then they returned and went on with the next sequence.

"Cut!" called the director.

"What's the matter?" asked Miss Leigh.

"You sound like a couple of actors who have just arrived from London," he told them.

It was true. After that they avoided the contagion of conversing together while they worked.

A statistic or two may be relevant to show the complexities of a picture like Gone With the Wind. Walter Plunkett, in charge of designing the costumes, made 400 individual wardrobe sketches after touring the South and studying in London and Paris, too, for information on feminine styles of seventy-five years ago. He supervised the making of 5000 dresses for stars, principals and extras.

A problem of equal magnitude was the sets. In all, 200 were designed and 90 built.

A section of Atlanta with 53 buildings was erected. The railroad station was reproduced, as was Tara Hall, where the O'Haras lived. Exact breakdown figures for a big production are never released by the film companies. A fairly accurate guess, however, would be that the sets for Gone With the Wind cost $340,000, the wardrobe $150,000, the cast $350,000 and the extras $110,000. This far from totals the $3,700,000 which was spent, of course. The biggest item of all was for overhead—which, on a Selznick picture, is fantastically large. Next, perhaps, came the cost of preparing the script.

January 26, 1939 was the first day on which Vivien Leigh began her portrayal of Scarlett O'Hara. By July most of the shooting was over. But shooting a motion picture is, at best, but half the task. Equally important is the cutting. It is universally agreed in motion-picture circles that David Selznick is little short of a genius in the technical process of cutting a film. The chances, then, for Gone With the Wind look good.

Maureen O'Hara in dotted-Swiss party dress, an exclusive adaptation from "Gone With the Wind"; beading, narrow velvet ribbon.

Claudette Colbert, in a navy-and-white dotted-Swiss organdy afternoon dress with white embroidered organdy frill collar and cuffs and ribbon run through beading.

MAKING MARRIAGE WORK

Clifford R. Adams

That Other Woman

Just how many divorces grow out of triangles is not definitely known, but the proportion is not less than a third; it may be as high as half. In the story of the Cranes, a single episode from my files, we find the basic factors underlying most triangle situations.

First, there is always some serious dissatisfaction in the marriage.

After eleven years, Helen Crane would have said her marriage was happy, and Jim, her husband, wouldn't have called it unhappy. They had a comfortable home, two attractive young sons, and Jim, at thirty-four, had already attained a top executive post.

But the atmosphere of partnership and sharing was lacking from the home. Servants ran the house, while Helen devoted herself to social activities; a maid even arranged the flowers. If Jim called to tell Helen of some business development, she was out, playing bridge or golf. When he came home exhausted by his wartime duties, Helen was too busy with outside activities to provide the companionship he needed. Jim came to feel that his chief role in the family was to pay the bills.

Because he has more opportunity to meet another person, the husband is more likely to get entangled than the wife.

Jim had frequent necessary business contacts with Ruth, an attractive young advertising woman. Over a period of time, she and Jim found they had many things in common besides their work, and business came to be an excuse for being together.

Jim had no desire to break up his marriage, and he recognized the danger. Without mentioning Ruth, he told Helen of his misgivings; and at his insistence, they worked out a definite program for putting more into their marriage.

The plan worked well at first. But Helen gradually began to suspect that another woman was involved, and a few inquiries strengthened her suspicions.

Sooner or later, the wife is almost sure to learn of the existence of "another woman"; on her reaction to the knowledge depends the hope of preserving a worth-while marriage.

At this point, Helen still had a chance to save her marriage. Another woman can seldom cause real trouble unless the husband is already dissatisfied. If Helen had accepted this fact; if, instead of blaming Ruth, she had recognized her own failures and made a sincere effort to improve, she might still be Jim's wife—and on a sounder basis than before. Instead, vengeful and self-righteous, Helen sought outside interference to oust Ruth and punish Jim. Armed with evidence obtained for her by a detective, she went to Jim's boss, demanding that he lecture Jim, and replace Ruth with a man. Jim's boss refused, and Helen confronted Jim with her evidence. Unable to forgive her spying, Jim asked for a divorce. Helen refused, then, after months of bitter quarreling, finally agreed.

Though the settlement stripped Jim of every dollar, he and Ruth are now happily building a new life together. Helen, lonely and embittered, is looking for another husband. But she has still to learn that it is a wife's obligation—and her privilege—to create a happy home for her husband, just as it is the husband's obligation to earn a living for the family.

What can a wife do to minimize the possibility of a broken home?

Here, if ever, is a situation where prevention is more important than cure. Long before any friction arises, a wife with insight knows that things aren't going well. She realizes that the happiness of the marriage and the home depends primarily on her. She makes the home as comfortable and inviting as she knows how; she improves her appearance; she becomes more attentive to her husband, and tries to create an atmosphere of partnership.

She looks for the cause of the tension. Whether it be sexual maladjustment, money worries or inadequate companionship, she seeks out the basic problem, and makes every effort to improve the situation.

If a third person comes on the scene, she tries even harder. This is no time for crying, accusations and running to relatives. Instead of blaming her husband or her rival, she tries to make herself and her home more attractive to him. Doing this isn't easy, but—if she wants her husband—she does it.

As never before, she is patient, cheerful, affectionate. Time is her ally, and she makes the most of it. She takes him off the defensive. He has no grounds for divorce. There are no excuses he can give their friends or his boss for leaving his wife. You can be sure he will think twice before taking further steps.

She may still lose her husband. But this way she has a real chance of keeping him; and if the crisis can be weathered, the marriage may be happier than ever before.

"Want to see pop faint?"

LONDON DURING AN AIR RAID

Ruth J. Drummond

At seven P.M. I reported for duty at the air-raid shelter I had been sent to. It was the end of the harassing day I had spent walking about the East End of London, viewing the results of a senseless bombing of small city homes and shops. I found that people were already settled in the shelter and others, as the invariable siren warning wailed out, came hurrying from near-by houses, carrying blankets and pillows and a miscellany of bedcoverings and rugs. Old, young, middle-aged laughed and greeted one another as they streamed in.

I found a capable, pleasant-faced woman on duty as first-aid worker and she gave me a brief idea of what to do to assist her. "There may be a few minor mishaps—nose bleeds, fainting fits, stomach-aches or cramps—to attend to. These please report to me at once—anything more serious we tell the wardens posted above and they send for an ambulance. Any cases of hysteria or panic you must calm as best you can. Are you nervous?"

I looked at her steadily. "No! Not a bit."

She nodded. "Good! You'll need all your nerves. And don't forget—it's never bombs that we hear, but *always* our own guns."

She looked at me meaningly, then went to discover the cause of a child's cries, and I turned and walked slowly back along the underground shelter and started my new job of shelter marshal and hostess by greeting the people I passed and repassed. Something like this: To a pathetic-looking old couple sitting together with blankets wrapped round them and up to their chins, "Good evening!" A smile. "Wise people, to come here right away and get a good seat. Good way to cheat the Jerries—they hope to make you stay awake, don't they!" I inwardly murmur a far-from-complimentary description of the raiders as I look at the old lady's round but lined cheeks and tired blue eyes. They look like the old couple from a Shirley Temple film I saw recently about a bluebird.

Next to them sit a young husband and wife. The girl clings to the man's arm and I see that she is very lovely. "There ought to be a beauty competition round here!" I say, and the husband beams with pride.

"We've been bombed twice out of our home, but we've started over again for a third time. Wonder if the roof will still be on when we go back tomorrow morning," he says; and as I move on an impudent youth asks me if I'll tuck him into bed—which I do with mock gravity, to the delight of the others, the bed being a six-foot length of the long narrow bench he is sitting on.

Next to him an elderly woman with a strained face momentarily relaxes at the laughter and, as a loud explosion overhead comes to our ears, gazes upward with an ex-

pression of white anger. "Guns are busy tonight!" I venture, but she stares at me stonily.

Another woman explains to me: "Her daughter's house was bombed while her daughter and a little girl, that would be her granddaughter, were in it. They were found in the wreckage by the rescue squad—the mother still holding the child's hand. The child was dead. 'I knew when she died! I knew when she died!' the mother kept exclaiming. Holding her hand, even if she couldn't see her, I suppose she would. It was some time before help could reach them. They were both completely buried in wreckage. Do you wonder the old lady looks so sad? The poor thing! I thought you'd better know. The raider dived suddenly out of a cloud. Oh, yes! Her daughter is over the shock now. She shows a wonderful courage."

I looked again at the woman's unresponsive face and felt sick horror at the tale I had heard. What can one say to the grandmother of that child who sat in a little chair holding her mother's hand and then was crushed to death by the demolition of her home by an unheralded raider? "I knew when she died!"—further comment is useless.

I went on my way and found two small boys of eight and nine, brothers, playing cards for pieces of shrapnel and bomb splinters carefully picked up during the day. A jagged little pile of metal—fit stakes in a game played by two of our children under such conditions. Their mother—a stout, comfortable woman in her late forties—smiled tolerantly at her sons as I watched the game. "They're good boys! Don't give me any trouble! You'll see how soundly they'll sleep when they lie down for the night. Sleep through anything, they would!" There was going on outside a very inferno of sound. The children played on, ignored it.

Roughly speaking, the shelter was at least eight feet underground and about eight feet wide. It ran in zigzags. Its top raised some feet aboveground, and inside it must have been ten to fifteen feet high. Benches ran along each side and the people sat or lay on these, according to the number in the shelter and the space available. Light and water and sanitary arrangements were laid on. It was built for three hundred and fifty people but, I was told, had accommodated five hundred. The people felt perfectly safe inside it and come regularly from near-by streets; there were also some strangers who had been in the vicinity when the sirens sounded.

After one tour I returned to where I started from and found the first-aid worker preparing to depart. "I'm just going over to a near-by shelter to answer a call to a heart-attack case. If I'm wanted, put on this tin hat and service coat and come for me—the wardens up above will direct you—but I'll be back soon." And she was gone. I felt horribly nervous and very much alone, but attempted to look very competent and cool.

One of the younger group came to me and asked, "May we dance, please? The phonograph is under the first-aid box—it belongs to Mrs. —— [the first-aid worker], but we bring our own records."

I looked at her in astonishment. "Dance? Why, yes—I suppose so!" *Dance!* I thought.

The girl went on: "You see, we don't disturb those wanting to sleep because we keep to the corner of the shelter farthest away from them. The glee singers have another zigzag to themselves, and you'll notice those who want to sleep are in the portion nearest to here. It seemed the best arrangement. The lady you are here in place of thought it up."

So the dancing began and the glee singers began and Hitler was forgotten as distant strains of dance music could be heard between the "My bonny lies over the ocean!" and Shenandoah and Home, Sweet Home efforts of the community singers. Most of the old people and all the children slept, and later everything was quiet in the shelter as one by one the younger people tired and curled up on the benches. Shrapnel and heaven knows what rattled by like hail over us from time to time, and enemy planes continually hovered, withdrew before the fearful and deafening barrage our guns put up and then returned to hover again overhead.

The first-aid worker came back and we talked together in low tones. "I've an arrangement with a near-by house for hot water, should we want it. I always bring my own kettle of sterilized water with me. It's all very rough and ready, but adequate. After all, this is a state of emergency," she told me.

At periods I walked through the shelter, which was lit by dim lights, and sorrowed in my heart that British people should have to put up with such a state of affairs. Once a warden accompanied me and, finding one man comfortably taking up most of the floor space right in the path between the benches, he wrote a note saying, "I didn't like to wake you, but you are not allowed to sleep where we must walk. Move as soon as you awaken," left it by his hand. We picked our way over his recumbent form and marveled at his snores. Outside, a seven-hour bombing attack continued with unabated vigor.

Once I put on the tin hat and went to one of the entrances to the shelter to see a glare in the sky. "It's the docks again," the nurse explained. "And they say just now one bomb fell quite close to here. A church has been destroyed ——" Something struck my hat and fell to the ground. I hastily retired and later was given a piece of metal as a souvenir. "I believe it was the one that hit you; I picked it up where you had been standing. Now you see why you were told to wear a tin hat! You'd have got a nasty wound and been dead if you hadn't," I was told.

Twice we had "all clears" and each time the raid recommenced. The people in the shelters ignored the all clears. One man snorted contemptuously as he sought for an easier position to lie in—"Think we pay any attention to that? We know better! They'll be back shortly and in the meantime *we stay here.*" No one moved till dawn and then, as the final all clear sounded, they roused in ones and twos and, picking up their bedding, went home. "See you tonight!" they shouted to one another as they dispersed. No! London's spirit is unbreakable. The men and women, and what children still remain there, are superb. I don't think Hitler reckoned on this.

Winston Churchill, Sir Kingsley Wood and party pick their way through debris in south-west London.

THE FRONT LINE IS IN OUR HEARTS

Robert E. Sherwood

There are, in warfare, *limited* objectives and *unlimited* objectives. Thus, in 1918, when our American troops moved into the Argonne, their limited objective was the occupation of that strategic forest; their unlimited objective was to make the world safe for democracy. Our fighting men achieved the first objective—and it was not their fault that they failed to gain the other.

I believe that this larger failure has obsessed us ever since 1919 with a corroding sense of frustration. For I believe that Americans never have been and never will be satisfied with the attainment of limited objectives.

I believe that our war aims now should be summed up in the statement:

"We shall settle for nothing less than a strong system of world peace and world justice which will endure not just for a quarter of a century but for as many centuries as the boundless imagination of man can conceive."

That is a tall order—yes; but it is not a new order, nor an un-American one. On Christmas night, in 1776, a small force of American troops, inadequately equipped but brilliantly led and possessed of a mighty spirit, crossed the Delaware River. Their limited objective was the occupation of strategic positions at Trenton, New Jersey; their unlimited objective had been stated six months previously in these words:

"We hold these truths to be self-evident, that all men are created equal, that they are endowed by their Creator with certain inalienable Rights, that among these are Life, Liberty and the pursuit of Happiness. That to secure these rights, Governments are instituted among Men, deriving their just powers from the consent of the governed."

Washington's army gained all its objectives, limited and unlimited. The full extent of their victory was realized in the enactment of the Constitution of the United States, which secured "the blessings of liberty to ourselves and our posterity."

There were sweeping statements in the Declaration and the Constitution—but they were not made lightly and they were not fought for lightly and they have not been worked for lightly by succeeding generations of Americans.

Eighty-five years after the Declaration, Abraham Lincoln gave his own interpretation of it. He was speaking in the Independence Hall, in Philadelphia, on Washington's Birthday, a few days before his first inauguration as President, a few weeks before the firing on Fort Sumter. Deeply conscious of the solemnity of the occasion, he spoke of "the wisdom, the patriotism, the devotion to principle, from which sprang the institutions under which we live." He spoke of the great "principle or idea" which had kept this Union so long together, and he said:

"It was not the mere matter of separation of the colonies from the motherland, but that sentiment in the Declaration of Independence which gave liberty not alone to the people of this country, but hope to all the world, for all future time."

Another sweeping statement—but we Americans believe in that sentiment and that hope, or we believe in nothing.

Now—in 1941—we hear the President of the United States say that we will accept only a world consecrated to "freedom of speech—freedom of worship—freedom from want—freedom from fear."

Can we achieve such a world merely by producing vast quantities of ships, planes, tanks, guns and fighting men? Obviously not. We can achieve it only if we are wise enough to know that ours is the greatest opportunity of all time, and, if we are

Sketch by Bill Mauldin.

AU CLAIR DE LA LUNE

BY STRUTHERS BURT

This has destroyed,
Made wrong,
Made impossible
So much the slow centuries have
    implanted in our hearts.
This has turned black the sunshine
    of five hundred years.
No longer now at dusk can one bear
    the songs of France,
Nor the kind minstrelsy that flowed
    along the Rhine;
The children do no dance upon the
    bridge at Avignon,
Pierrot's moon is candle to the dead.

O gay and gallant France, you have
    ruined our music;
O summer-nodding Rhine, you have
    spoiled our song.
Only the English tongue, like some
    lost lark,
Sings in the growing danger to the
    dark.

spiritually strong enough, to seize that opportunity.

I believe we may derive wisdom and spiritual strength from realization of our sacred heritage. The sum of that heritage is told to us in the long, heroic story of the fight for human freedom.

The story began, probably, in the primordial jungle, when the first ape man first managed to straighten up and stand on his own two feet. We don't know about that. But we do know that in the first chapter of the Book of Genesis—the oldest Book known to man—it is written: "So God created man in his own image, in the image of God created he him; male and female created he them." And at the end of that chapter it is written: "And God saw every thing that he had made, and, behold, it was very good."

In these old scriptural words is the fundamental conception of the dignity, the essential virtue of individual man. Herein is the divine assurance that man possesses, within his own immortal spirit, the glory and the power, creative and recreative, which give him the right to acknowledge no master other than his God.

This is the substance of the democratic faith: the faith whose divine light guided the people of Israel out of bondage; the faith which flamed in eternal splendor in Athens in the Golden Age of Pericles; the faith which shone forth in the star over Bethlehem, in Judea.

In the dark centuries that followed the

Crucifixion, that light was a tiny, flickering flame, tended by a few disciples among the tortured Jews and Greeks. But the power of that flame was greater than the power of Imperial Rome. The light spread throughout the crumbling empire and through the barbarian lands of the Gauls and the Teutons.

Early in the thirteenth century after Christ, the English enacted the first great charter of freedom. "To no one will we sell, deny, or delay right or justice" was the revolutionary pronouncement of Magna Charta, in an age when it had seemed incredible that there could ever be recognized any right other than the divine right of kings.

From that time on, Englishmen asserted and established one right after another: trial by jury, habeas corpus, religious freedom, freedom of speech, freedom of assembly, representative government.

It was the suppression of one of these rights which impelled English men and women of strong convictions to leave their homeland and settle here in New England.

It was the suppression of other essential rights by a tyrannous king which compelled the drawing up and signing of the Declaration of Independence.

There are now quibblers among us who say that we cannot enforce our principles of freedom upon alien peoples—and we must therefore sit back and permit a transient tyrant named Hitler to enforce his principles of slavery.

We free Americans do not have to enforce our principles at the point of a gun. Thanks to our own example, these principles are now cherished by the overwhelming majority of the human race.

Four nations today are the avowed enemies of freedom: Germany, Italy, the Soviet Union and Japan. The leadership of each of these nations is a small group which seized power by force or conspiracy or both. Hitler, Mussolini, Stalin and the Japanese war lords were not chosen by vote of the people. They remain in power only by arbitrary, ruthless suppression of the true voice of the people.

Granted that the human race as a whole wants freedom with justice—and peace—it is still insisted by the timid quibblers that neither we nor the British have the right to administer these blessings because our own records are unclean. They tell us to look at what we have done in the Philippines and Central America, and what the British have done in Ireland and India.

Very well, let us look at these unpleasant subjects. Whatever our past crimes, it is obvious that enlightened public opinion in both countries has increasingly demanded atonement. Imperialism is not popular with the masses of Americans and Britons. Settlement of the Philippine, Irish and Indian problems would be closer to solution if new and more ferocious threats of imperialism had not arisen.

Quezon in the Philippines, De Valera in Ireland, Gandhi and Nehru in India have all suffered under American and British rule. But they have not been prevented from pleading their cause to their own peoples and to all the world. How long would they be able to continue their fight for freedom if they and their people were

to fall under the domination of the Japanese, the Nazis or the Communists?

The present power of Hitler, Stalin, Mussolini and the Japanese war lords was created by want and by fear. The seizure and consolidation of this power could have been achieved only in a time of economic crisis and only at the expense of people whose will was paralyzed by poverty and by terror of the future. We in the United States must acknowledge our share of the blame for that paralysis. We must not make the same mistake again; we must never delude ourselves into another attempt at economic isolationism. Only we have the power and the wealth and the world influence to insure reciprocal trade for all peoples, and an equable distribution of the world's supply of food and raw materials.

When we establish our determination to use our power and wealth and influence for these purposes, we shall conquer Nazism, Fascism, Communism and all other forms of aggressive imperialism. The survival of these evils today, in all parts of the world, is due to the lingering fear that the United States will not have the will or the wisdom to give its enormous services to mankind in the promotion of a just peace.

We have already taken tangible, constitutional steps to dispel that fear. The foreign policy of President Roosevelt and Secretary Hull has been enacted by Congress in the Lend-Lease Law. That policy

formally recognizes the existence of a family of nations whom we are pledged to aid and support—and, significantly, no limit has been placed upon the size of that family. This is a historic advance of incalculable importance.

In the last days of his great life, Benjamin Franklin said: "God grant that not only the love of liberty but a thorough knowledge of the rights of man may pervade all the nations of the earth, so that a philosopher may set his foot anywhere on its surface and say: 'This is my country!' "

Ben Franklin and Abe Lincoln. These two men were the supremely representative Americans. In them were magnified our

Avowed enemy of freedom—Adolf Hitler.

greatest national qualities: high idealism and plain common sense, Yankee shrewdness and adventurous courage, earthy humor and deep faith. By using these qualities, and using them to the limit, we can help to fulfill the transcendent hope of freedom for all men, for all future time. It is given to us, of this generation, to achieve real peace—if not for ourselves, for our children. It is given to us to reassert the right of man to live as the image of God.

The front line in this war is in no system of trenches and concrete fortifications; it can be drawn on no map of continents or islands or oceans. The front line is in the hearts and minds of all of us, of all races, who are determined to go forward in the ways of freedom and justice.

OVER THERE

John Steinbeck

The Army bus rattles over the rough road and through a patch of woods. In the distance there are a few squat brown buildings and a flagstaff flying the American flag. This is a bomber station. England is littered with them. Probably no more than twenty-five Flying Fortresses live here, and they are so spread out that you do not see them at once. A raider might get one of them, but he would not be likely to get more than one.

No attempt is made to camouflage the buildings or the planes—it doesn't work and it's just a lot of work. Air protection and dispersal do work. Barbed wire is strung along the road, coils of it, and in front of the administrative building there is a gate with a sentry box.

The bus pulls to a stop near the gate and the men jump down, adjusting their gas masks at their sides. The crews walk slowly to their barracks.

The room is long and narrow and unpainted. Against each side wall are iron double-decker bunks, alternating with clothes lockers. Each bunk is carefully made, and to the foot of each are hung a helmet and a gas mask. On the walls are pin-up girls—big-breasted blondes in languorous attitudes, child faces, parted shiny lips and sleepy eyes, which doubtless mean passion, but always the same girls.

The crew of the Mary Ruth have their bunks on the right-hand side of the room. They have had these bunks only a few weeks. A Fortress was shot down and the bunks were emptied. It is strange to sleep in the bed of a man who was at breakfast with you and now is dead or a prisoner hundreds of miles away. His clothes are in the locker, to be picked up and put away. His helmet is to be taken off the foot of the bunk and yours put there. You leave his pin-up girls where they are. Why change them? Yours would be the same girls.

The crew did not name or come over in the Mary Ruth. On the nose of the ship her name is written, and under it "Memories of Mobile." But this crew does not know who Mary Ruth was, or what memories are celebrated. She was named when they got her, and they would not think of changing her name. In some way it would be bad luck.

A rumor has swept through the airfields that some powerful group in America has protested about the names of the ships, and that an order is about to be issued removing these names and substituting the names of towns and rivers. It is to be hoped that this is not true. Change the name of Bomb

Boogie to St. Louis, or Mary Ruth of Mobile Memories to Wichita, or the Volga Virgin to Davenport, and you will have injured the ship. Sometimes the crew will wait a long time before naming a ship. The name must be perfect and must be approved by every member of the crew. There is enough dullness in the war as it is.

It is a bad night in the barracks, such a night as does not happen very often. Nerves are a little thin and no one is sleepy. The tail gunner of the other outfit in the room gets down from his upper bunk and begins rooting about on the floor.

"What's the matter?" the man on the lower bunk asks.

"I lost my medallion," the tail gunner says.

Everyone gets up and looks. They move the double-decker bunk out from the wall. They empty all the shoes. They look behind the steel lockers. They insist that the gunner go through all his pockets. It isn't a good thing for a man to lose his medallion. The uneasiness creeps all through the room. It takes the channel of being funny. They tell jokes; they rag one

---

---

another: "What size shoes you wear, Brown? I get them if you conk out." The thing runs bitterly through the room.

And then the jokes stop. There are many little things you do when you go out on a mission. You leave the things that are to be sent home if you have an accident. You leave them under your pillow—your photographs and the letter you wrote and your ring. And you don't make up your bunk. That must be left unmade so that you can slip right in when you get back. You go out clean-shaven, too, because you are coming back, and you make dates for that night because then you must come back to keep your date. You project your mind into the future and the things you are going to do then.

In the barracks they tell of presentiments they have heard about. There was the radioman who one morning folded his bedding neatly on his cot and put his pillow on top. And he folded his clothing into a neat parcel and cleared his locker. He had never done anything like that before. And sure enough, he was shot down that day.

The tail gunner still hasn't found his medallion. He has gone through his pockets over and over again. The brutal talk goes on until one voice says, "Shut up. It's after midnight. We've got to get some sleep."

The lights are turned out. It is quiet in the room, and then there is a step, and then a great clatter. A new arrival trying to get to his bunk in the dark has stumbled over the gun rack. The room breaks into loud curses. They tell him where he came from and where they hope he will go. It is a fine, noisy outburst, and the tension goes out of the room. The evil thing has gone.

You are conscious, lying in your bunk, of a droning sound that goes on and on. It is the Royal Air Force going out for night bombing again. Hundreds of Lancasters, with hundreds of tons of bombs. And when they come back, you will go out.

The barrack room is very silent. From a corner comes a light snore. Someone is talking in his sleep. First a sentence mumbled, and then, "Helen, let's go in the Ferris wheel now."

There is secret sound from the far wall, and then a tiny clink of metal. The tail gunner is still feeling through his pockets for his medallion.

In the barracks, a brilliant white light flashes on, jerking you out of sleep. The crew struggle sleepily out of their bunks and into clothes. It is 2:30 A.M. Outside the daylight is beginning to come. The crew grope their way through sleepiness and the semidarkness to the guarded door, and each goes in as he is recognized by the guard.

Inside there are rows of benches in front of a large white screen, which fills one wall. The lights go out and from a projector an aerial photograph is projected onto the screen. It is remarkably clear. It shows streets and factories and a winding river and docks and submarine pens. An Intelligence officer stands beside the screen and he holds a long pointer in his hand. He begins without preliminary.

"Here is where you are going," he says, and he names a German city. "Now this squadron will come in from this direction" —the pointer traces the road, making a black shadow on the screen. The pointer stops at three long narrow buildings, side by side. "This is your target. They make small engine parts here. Knock it out." He mentions times, and as he does a sergeant marks the times on a blackboard. "Stand-by at such a time, take-off at such a time, rendezvous at such a time. You will be over your target at such a time, and you should be back here by such a time." It is all on

Along the Thames. The Prime Minister and Mrs. Churchill inspect docks severely damaged during one of London's worst raids.

the minute—5:32 and 9:43. The incredible job of getting so many ships to a given point at a given time means almost split-second timing. "Good luck and good hunting." The lights flood on. The pictured city disappears.

A chaplain comes to the front of the room. "All Catholics gather at the back of the room," he says.

The crews straggle across the way to the mess hall and fill their plates and their cups, stewed fruit and scrambled eggs and bacon and cereal and coffee.

The Mary Ruth's crew is almost gay. All the tension is broken now, for there is work and flying to be done, not waiting. The tail gunner says, "If anything should happen today, I want to go on record that I had prunes for breakfast."

They eat hurriedly and then file out, washing their dishes and cups in soapy water and then rinsing them in big caldrons near the door.

Dressing is a long and complicated business. The men strip to the skin. Next to their skins they put on long light woolen underwear. Over that they slip on what looks like long, light-blue colored underwear, but these are the heated suits. They come low on the ankles and far down on the wrists, and from the waists of these suits protrude electric plugs. The suit, between two layers of fabric, is threaded with electric wires which will carry heat when the plug is connected to the heat outlet on the ship.

Over the heated suit goes the brown coverall. Last come thick, fleece-lined heated boots and gloves which also have plugs for the heat unit. Next goes on the Mae West, the orange rubber life preserver, which can be inflated in a moment. Then comes the parachute with its heavy canvas straps over the shoulders and between the legs. And last the helmet with the throat speaker and the earphones attached. During the process the men have got bigger and bigger as layer on layer of equipment is put on. They walk stiffly, like artificial men.

They dress very carefully, for an exposed place or a disconnected suit can cause a bad frostbite at 30,000 feet. It is dreadfully cold up there.

It is daylight now and a cold wind is blowing. The men go back to the armament room and pick up their guns. A truck is waiting for them. They stow the guns carefully on the floor and then stiffly hoist themselves in. The truck drives away along the deserted runway. Now you can see the ships set here and there on the field. A little group of men is collected under the wings of each one.

"There she is," the ball-turret man says. "I wonder if they got her nose repaired." It was the Mary Ruth that got her nose smashed by cartridge cases from a ship ahead.

The truck draws up right under the nose of the great ship. The crew piles out and each man lifts his gun down tenderly. They go into the ship. The guns must be mounted and carefully tested. Ammunition must be checked and the guns loaded. It all takes time. That's why the men were awakened so long before the take-off time. A thousand things must be set before the take-off.

A jeep drives up, carrying the officers—Brown, Quenin, Gliley and Feerick. They spill a number of little square packets on the ground, one for each man. Captain Brown distributes them. They contain money of the countries near the target, concentrated food and maps. Brown says, "Now, if we should get into any trouble, don't go in the direction of —— because the people haven't been very friendly there. Go toward —— you'll find plenty of help there." The men take the packets and slip them in pockets below the knees in their coveralls.

The sun is just below the horizon now, and there are fine pink puff clouds all over the sky. The captain looks at his watch. "I guess we better get going," he says.

The other Brown, the tail gunner, runs over. He hands over two rings, a cameo and another. "I forgot to leave these," he says. "Will you put them under my pillow?"

The crew scramble to their places and the door is slammed and locked. The captain waves from his high perch. His window sits right over the ship's name—Mary Ruth, Memories of Mobile. The engines turn over

and catch one at a time and roar as they warm up.

And now, from all over the field, come the bursting roars of starting engines. Along the runway the first ship whips out and gathers speed and takes the air, and behind her comes another, and behind, another, until the flying line of ships stretches away to the north. For a little while the squadron has disappeared, but in a few minutes back they come over the field, but this time they are not in a line. They have gained altitude and are flying in a tight formation. They go roaring over the field and they have hardly passed when another squadron from another field comes over, and then another and another. They will rendezvous at a given point, the squadrons from many fields, and when the whole force has gathered there will be perhaps a hundred of the great ships flying in V's and in V's of V's, each protecting itself and the others by its position. And this great flight is going south like geese in the fall.

When the mission has gone the ground crews stand about looking lonesome. This ground crew will be nervous and anxious until the ships come home. And if the Mary Ruth should fail to return they will go into a kind of sullen wordless mourning. They have been working all night. Now they pile on a tractor to ride back to the hangar to get a cup of coffee in the mess hall.

In the barracks it is very quiet; the beds are unmade, their blankets hanging over the sides of the iron bunks. The pin-up girls look a little haggard in their sequin gowns. The family pictures are on the tops of the steel lockers. A clock ticking sounds strident. The rings go under Brown's pillow.

The crews own a number of small dogs. These dogs, most of which are of ambiguous breed, belong to no one man. The ship usually owns one, and the crew is very proud of him. Now these dogs wander disconsolately about the field.

The morning passes slowly. The squadron was due over the target at 9:52. It was due home at 12:43. As 9:50 comes and passes, you have the ships in your mind. Now the flak has come up at them. Perhaps now a swarm of fighters has hurled itself at them. Now they are making the run for home, keeping the formation tight, climbing, climbing to avoid the flak. It is 10 o'clock—they should be started back; 10:20—they should be seeing the ocean by now.

Beside the No. 1 hangar there is a little mound of earth covered with short, heavy grass. At 12:15 the ground men begin to congregate on it and sweat out the homecoming. A small dog, which might be a gray Scottie if his ears didn't hang down and his tail bend the wrong way, comes to sit on the little mound. He stretches out and puts his whiskery muzzle on his outstretched paws. He does not close his eyes, and his ears twitch. All the ground crews are there now, waiting for their ships. It is the longest set of minutes imaginable.

Suddenly the little dog raises his head. His body begins to tremble all over. The crew chief looks down at the dog and then aims his field glasses to the south. "Can't see anything yet," he says. The little dog continues to shudder, and a high whine comes from him.

And here they come. You can just see the dots far to the south. The formation is good, but one ship flies alone and ahead. "Can you see her number? Who is she?" The lead ship drops altitude and comes in straight for the field. From her side two little rockets break, a red one and a white one. The ambulance—they call it the meat wagon—starts down the runway. There is a hurt man on that ship.

The main formation comes over the field and each ship peels to circle for a landing, but the lone ship drops and the wheels strike the ground and the Fortress lands like a great bug on the runway. But the moment her wheels are on the ground, there is a sharp, crying bark and a streak of gray. The little dog seems hardly to touch the ground. He streaks across the field toward the landed ship. He knows his own ship. One by one the Fortresses land and the ground crews check off the numbers as they land. Mary Ruth is there.

Only one ship is missing and she landed farther south, with short fuel tanks. There is a great sigh of relief on the mound. The mission is over.

THE "OTHER WOMAN"

Seymour Winslow

There must be, thought Janet, two distinct ways of falling in love. There was certainly such a thing as falling in love at first sight, since she had seen it happen to several girls. And then there was what you might call delayed-action love. It was like malaria: you didn't know you had it until it just curled you up.

The way she had fallen in love with Mr. Cooper was clearly delayed-action. Definitely it wasn't first sight, since she remembered very well her first sight of Mr. Cooper. It had been four years ago when she was ten years old and Mr. and Mrs. Cooper had moved into the house next door. She distinctly recalled thinking that he was nice-looking, but that was absolutely all—until a certain overwhelming moment just the other day.

Janet would never forget that moment. It was impossible to describe her sensations, although she had spent hours trying to find words for them. It came down to something like a combination of being knocked loopy by an unexpectedly big wave at the beach and the all-over feeling of utter happiness that arrives just as you finish your second straight cola.

She remembered vividly the moment in which love had come to her. She was in the lawn swing, shelling peas. Mr. Cooper, beyond the hedge, was trimming the grass with a sheep shears at the edges of his zinnia bed. Janet had glanced at him now and then, not feeling in love with him at all, but rather admiring the neatness with which he did things, when Mrs. Cooper, from somewhere inside the house, called, "Andy, where are you?" It wasn't so much calling as it was just plain yelling.

Mrs. Cooper was always yelling at her husband, and she always started her yelling from somewhere deep inside the house—instead of looking out a window to find out where he was and then speaking to him in an ordinary voice like a reasonable being.

To make his voice reach her, Mr. Cooper naturally had to yell back. He yelled, "Here I am. What do you want?"

From the depths, but closer to a window, Mrs. Cooper shrieked, "Where is here, for heaven's sake? Don't be such a dope."

"Out back," he shouted, keeping on with his work.

Janet was swept by a feeling of aching pity for Mr. Cooper, working away in the hot sun and being screeched at and called names by his wife, for whom he was always doing kind things like going on errands and brushing car seats before she got in. Janet wondered how he ever could have married such a woman.

Mrs. Cooper came to an upper back window. Mr. Cooper stood up, clicking his shears. "What's all the racket about?" he asked.

"Racket! Listen, clod, the racket is about those library books you forgot to take back."

"Oh, I just forgot them, I guess."

"You quarter-wit! Well, just take 'em back now. And get me some new ones."

"Can't you do it?" he called. "I don't know what new ones you want."

> All I know I got from an atlas.
> —HENDRIK WILLEM VAN LOON.
>
> My fortune came not from the mustard people eat but from the amount they leave on their plates.
> —JEREMIAH COLMAN, British mustard king.
>
> One half of knowing what you want is knowing what you must give up before you get it.
> —SIDNEY HOWARD.
>
> Be pretty if you can, be witty if you must, be agreeable if it kills you.
> —ELSIE DE WOLFE.

There was no answer. As Janet watched Mr. Cooper's imploring face raised to the deserted window, she wanted to rush to him, to take his hand, to comfort him, to tell him she loved him. Yes, that was the instant in which she knew she loved him. That feeling of the big wave and the two colas had come to her. Mr. Cooper tossed his shears to the grass in a gesture of lonely friendlessness that wrung Janet's heart. She almost ran into the kitchen.

Her mother said briskly, "Well! All done, Jan?"

Janet wondered that her mother couldn't see that she had been overtaken by one of the great shattering experiences of life. Surely her face must show that she was in love. It should even show that hers was a tragic love. That she was in love with a married man!

"Mother, I want to ask you something," she said. "Do you believe in divorce?"

"Well," her mother said, "I could wish there were a lot less of it. But I suppose it's justifiable sometimes, when two people get to hating each other, when their marriage is all washed up and they're leading a cat-and-dog life."

It occurred to Janet that this was exactly the kind of life that Mr. and Mrs. Cooper led. She called him names like "leather-puss" and "jug-ears." She yelled at him.

Sometimes he yelled, too, of course, but only because she started it.

"You mean like Mr. and Mrs. Cooper, mother?"

"Of course not!" her mother said. "The Coopers are crazy about each other! What an idea!"

"But, mother, she yells at him so!"

"That doesn't necessarily mean anything. Janet, you're way beyond your depth. Andy and Bess Cooper are—well, sort of the shouting type. It's a form of heartiness. What you think of as noisy wrangling is—oh, call it affectionate roughhouse. But you wouldn't comprehend that. Now do hurry with those peas, Janet."

Janet hurried with them in dignified silence. The wonderful feeling of the big wave and the two colas was proof against misunderstanding and rebuff. And it came back, more wonderful than ever, that afternoon when, coming out of the Cooky Jar, her mouth full of macaroon, she almost crashed into Mr. Cooper, who was hurrying toward his car. Over his armful of packages he said "Hi, hello," and smiled at her. She had never seen him smile as brightly as that at his wife.

Janet swallowed and said "Hi," wishing she dared say "Hi, Mr. Cooper darling," since that was the way she felt.

"Want a lift home?" he said. He held the car door open for her.

Janet hadn't intended to go home for quite a while, but she got in. Mr. Cooper stowed his packages, climbed in and started off.

"Lucky we met," he said. "I wouldn't have been downtown this afternoon except for a couple of things Bess forgot to get."

Janet could imagine the scene that led up to his trip—bellowing and name-calling on Mrs. Cooper's side, patience, courtesy and unhappiness on his. She sent quick, admiring glances at his profile. It touched her to see how carefree he looked when he was out of reach of Mrs. Cooper's voice.

He made a turn into easier traffic. "Well, how's school? Where are you now?"

"Second-year high," Janet was obliged to tell him. "It's all extremely juvenile—the studies, I mean." She laughed lightly at the absurdity of her being in high school.

"It wasn't for me," Mr. Cooper said. "All I could do to get through second year. But maybe that was because Bess joined the class that year."

So the savage Mrs. Cooper had been at high school with him. Undoubtedly, Janet thought, one of the basic troubles with their marriage was that they were almost the same age. Preparing for the agony his reply might bring her, she said, "Were you in love with her then?"

"Just bugs about her. Hard for me to believe now how completely dizzy I was."

It was plainly an admission of how his feelings had changed. Janet wanted to reach over and touch his hand to show him that she understood.

"Do you think that if a person marries somebody they fall in love with when they're in second-year high ——" So much depended on his answer that she couldn't finish the question. That didn't matter, though, because he guessed the rest of it. She could tell by the chivalrous way he pretended to misunderstand.

"I see. You've been falling in love yourself and you're wondering if it will last, the way it has with Bess and me. Well"—he turned into his driveway; Janet couldn't see his face, but she knew from the tight sound of his voice that he was choosing his words very carefully—"well, Bess is still my best girl and I'm still the guy that carries her books, but I'm afraid we're the exception and not the rule. Don't let our good luck make you feel too sure that this boy you think you're in love with now will be the guy you want to be married to, ten years from now." He got out and began collecting his packages.

Janet found voice enough to say, "Thanks for the lift."

If only there were some way to tell him that she recognized his magnificent loyalty to his wife, his knightly attempt to pretend that he still loved her. It was a noble thing to do, the noblest thing a man could do. Mr. Cooper was the finest man in the world. Janet loved him and would always love him. She would never marry anyone else. Perhaps on her deathbed she would dictate a will leaving the large fortune she would then have to Mr. Cooper's oldest grandchild. The boy—he would be a boy and the image of his grandfather—would never know why she had bequeathed him her estate. Her eyes filled with tears at the sweet sad thought.

But there was one thing she could do for Mr. Cooper now. Something almost as noble, in its way, as Mr. Cooper's splendid loyalty to the unworthy woman he had married. She could try to make his life a little happier by pleading with Mrs. Cooper to change her ways, if only a little, so that Mr. Cooper might be able, sometimes, to half believe that she still cared for him.

Mrs. Cooper was on the lawn, looking for four-leaf clovers. Janet, the lump in her throat almost choking her, walked over to her. "Hello, Jan," Mrs. Cooper said. "How's the girl?"

"Mrs. Cooper," Janet said, "I want to tell you something. It's about Mr. Cooper."

"What's that awful man been up to now? Waking you at dawn by tuning up that old car, I bet."

"Oh, no," Janet said. "It's nothing he's done. It's more about—well, the sort of person he is. About his—his sensitiveness."

From an upstairs window Mr. Cooper shouted, "Hey, Bess, what did you do with my old sweater? And don't tell me you gave it away or I'll lam you—but good!"

Mrs. Cooper yelled back, "It's in the hall closet, you lunk." She turned to Janet. "That man is something. What were you saying about his sensitivity? It must be a very recent development, but go on."

Illustration by Andrew Loomis for A. J. Cronin's
THE KEYS OF THE KINGDOM

"Well, maybe I mean his romanticism. Sensitivity and romanticism both. I can't help but think—in fact, I'm sure—that he'd respond so quickly to—to affection."

Mrs. Cooper's eyes opened wide. "Merciful heaven," she said. "How can you be sure of such a thing, Janet?"

Janet hurried to say, "Only through observation and from knowing him very well, of course, and feeling very close to him, in a way. I mean from understanding his nature so well, knowing him to be such a fine person. Mrs. Cooper," she said in a rush, "I'm sure he cares for you, or at least he *could* care for you again—in spite of everything."

Mrs. Cooper stared blankly for a moment. Then she said, gently and seriously, "I hope you're right, Jan. Do you really think he's—disappointed in his marriage?"

"I'm afraid I have to say yes to that, Mrs. Cooper. But I don't think it's too late, even now."

"I hope not," Mrs. Cooper said soberly. She put an arm across Janet's shoulders and they paced the walk together. "What do you think I ought to do, Janet?"

Janet felt warm with gratefulness toward Mrs. Cooper for making her task less difficult. She said, "Well, Mr. Cooper is so hurt, so awfully wounded—you can see it in his face—when he's spoken to sharply and sometimes even shouted at. Oh, I know I'm being awfully fresh to say these things and you'll never forgive me, but ——"

"Go right on, Jan. I think you're sweet."

"Well, I know he feels it terribly when he's called names like 'dopey' and 'foghead' and especially so loud that other people can hear. Mrs. Cooper, you still do love him a little, don't you? Even if not as much as when he used to carry your schoolbooks?"

"Somewhat differently perhaps, Jan. It's not easy to explain. But I wouldn't hurt him for anything."

"He's one of the grandest men in the world," Janet said.

"And you're one of the nicest girls in the world," Mrs. Cooper said. She glanced toward the house. "I'm afraid I have to go in now. But I'm remembering everything you've said." She kissed Janet and went in, hurrying a little.

Janet went home. She sat in the swing, making it rock gently and trying to remember whether there had been a piece of pie left over from dinner. It was almost dark now. A light came on in the Cooper kitchen. Janet could see Mr. and Mrs. Cooper facing each other in the center of the room. Mrs. Cooper was telling him something that interested him and he was listening intently, his mouth slightly open. When Mrs. Cooper stopped talking they stood looking at each other for a moment and then they both laughed together in a way so fond and intimate that Janet could interpret it only as complete reconciliation. Then still laughing, they fell into each other's arms.

Janet looked away from the window. She felt the exaltation that comes only to those who, through love, and at a great personal sacrifice, bring a happier life to others. There had been a piece of pie left over, she remembered, and she hopped out of the swing to go and get it.

Life with father was difficult, but never dull. At left: Dorothy Stickney and Howard Lindsay in the Broadway production of "Life with Father"; at right: Lillian Gish and Percy Waram in one of the touring companies of Clarence Day's hit.

LINE A DAY

Ann Batchelder

1 Now "the frost is on the pumpkin" and winter is on the way. Pity is that it comes too early and stays too long, like unexpected company on washday.

2 Times change, and customs too. Skirts may go up or down, but with a refrigerator fit to be raided and a good salad bowl you can be ready for anything.

3 Asparagus is never really out of season when you can get those elegant green or white tips frosted or in cans. Try a scallop. Slice four hard-cooked eggs and add to a can of drained asparagus. Mix with a light cream sauce. Season with salt and pepper, cover with crumbs and grated cheese and bake.

4 If it's pleasing family and guests you're after, serve creamed shrimp, crab or tuna fish on hot waffles. Wonderful for Sunday-night supper.

5 Carrots and onions are almost confections when you glaze them with honey. Glaze is made with about four tablespoons of butter or margarine and one-fourth cup of honey. Turn the vegetables as they glaze. And cook them till tender before you glaze.

6 From an old cookbook: "When you have made Bologna Sausages, keep them in ashes. That of vine twigs is best for them." Millie, gather those twigs, and be quick about it!

7 Custards and creams and such love a combination flavor. Orange and vanilla, for instance. Arm in arm they go along.

8 Observation: Fear has kept more people from being artists than failure ever did. That goes for the art of cooking too.

9 When you make a chocolate or lemon pie, go easy on the cornstarch ballast. Let 'er tremble at the knife!

10 Frankfurters are news again. Put a dozen in the frying pan, add half a cup of chili sauce, half a cup of water and two teaspoons of prepared mustard. Simmer for twenty minutes. Potato salad on the side.

THANKSGIVING.

By Doris Lee.

11 From the canners who spend their days over the soup kettles comes this: "Try our black bean and our potato soup and don't say we've been asleep on the job." It's a date!

12 Know about that deviled something-or-other sauce for cabbage and kindred things? Add to one-fourth cup of butter or margarine, a little prepared mustard, a mere trace of Worcestershire sauce, salt to suit and a dash of cayenne.

13 Apples are definitely our stand-by. Baked with honey, they're divine. With brown sugar, a sweet distinction. Along with sausages, a perfect breakfast. Could you ask for more?

14 Apples ought to bake slowly. And if the skins burst, so much the better. Personally, I like them cold. Don't have to get up so early, either. Well-cooked apples is the rule for pies too.

15 November ushers in the pie season as Christmas the tinsel tussle. Don't forget mincemeat and the cranberry-and-raisin business. These are fall styles.

16 Hot boiled rice is the prop over which you may profitably serve cold roast chicken or turkey. Sautéed and sauced with a jar of currant jelly—melted, of course.

17 Lemon jelly is one of my favorite dishes. So clear, so sparkling, so refreshing and as simple as a hook and eye. Ever cut squares of fruit cake and "set" it in the jelly?

18 Scotch woodcock is so called because it is neither Scotch nor bird. Just a Welsh rabbit made with tomato soup and cheese.

19 Rice muffins, split, spread with butter or margarine and filled with raspberry jam, aren't bad on a blue Monday.

20 Who was it raised his voice to say, "Because I like salt I don't wish to be drowned in brine"? A strong hint to all us old seasoners. Reminder: Always taste first.

21 Mixed grills you meet everywhere. A good one is sausage, mushrooms, lamb chop and spaghetti with tomato sauce. All on one plate and dishwashing cut in two!

22 When you make creamed codfish (the salt kind is what I mean), don't forget at the last moment to add a beaten egg. What a difference an egg can make!

23 Why anyone should "season" anything so delicate and distinctive as an oyster with highly spiced sauces, I don't know. Is there debate from the audience?

24 And now that oysters are just about everywhere, after their long absence, let's have a two-layer scallop, and add a little cream.

25 News note: The time is coming when you will get Maine rock crab in cans. The little fellers are up against it after all these years.

26 One of the nice points about tomato juice is that you can do any number of things with it. There's that cold cooked cauliflower in tomato aspic—just an example.

27 Something else that's as new as baby's first tooth. It's a vegetable named celtuce, and how the folks who induce new vegetables to make good have worked over it. A combined celery and lettuce. Goes for both and you'll love it. Tip you off in time when it's ready.

28 The baking-powder biscuit is as versatile as a one-man band. Look at those chicken shortcakes, fruit ones and meat pies. Just for one more time take biscuit, split, fill with orange marmalade and cover with whipped cream and grated chocolate. They'll get you places.

29 If you have any stuffing left over from that turkey, slice it, fry it and let it bolster up the irrepressible scrambled eggs. Good.

30 And here we are again at the end of another month. Go by fast, don't they? Have the kind of Thanksgiving I wish for you all. If you do it will be the best one ever. ANN.

215

Menu

Clam Consommé

Baked Ham, Apricots Piquante

Asparagus, Cheese Sauce

Avocado-Salad Ring

Lovers' Knots

Sweetheart Mold

Salted Nuts

Demitasse   Mints

All Out For Sentiment ♥

These cupids' arrows pierce a heart,
But oh, it is not mine.
He that receives a lover's dart
Is my true valentine.

IT IS only too true that terrible things lurk, like unfriendly ghosts, around our corners, and war, the most terrible of all, has come to torment us; but, while wars come and go, one thing is sure—love goes on forever. Sentiment is immortal. The lovers' own special saint's day—Valentine's—will, I'm sure, still touch the heart and stir the pulses just as it always has done. That's why the fourteenth of February is marked in red on the calendars. And the mails are full of secret tokens, lace paper and silver arrows. All in honor of that oldest of human emotions and the sentiment that sweeps over the heartstrings as a breeze does over the muted strings of an aeolian harp in the sweetness of a summer evening.

Lace and ribbons, hearts and flowers— these are the trappings and trade-marks of the real valentine, and the declarations of despairing love are not half so despairing as they sound. More in the nature of trial balloons, I guess, to see just where the senders stand in the affections, fickle or otherwise, of pined-for boy and girl.

Some of the old valentines are priceless treasures now, and a collector's dream if ever there was one. I kept my first one a good long while, but it grew more yellowed and fragile as the years gathered dust, and somehow, somewhere it vanished from sight and, like a perfumed ghost, became only a memory. Something lost to me forever.

And now we are having just as lovely ones, delicate and frail, and as romantic as a tryst in the moonlight, beside the garden stile.

Illustration by Coby Whitmore for JASON AND THE CRIMSON FLEET *by Paul Ernst.*

Fresh Out of Tonsils

BY OGDEN NASH

I never thought I'd be sitting here telling about my operation, but I myself got told about it in advance so thoroughly and in such relentless detail by explicit friends and relatives that I feel entitled to this minor retaliation.

The whole thing started by my being born too soon, so that I was detonsiled somewhere around 1908 or 1909. I am sorry I cannot remember the name of the man in white, as I should dearly love to drop in on him some evening and kick him in the slats; I figure he'd be past seventy now and I could handle him with one hand tied to a pair of brass knuckles.

You who were detonsiled around 1908 or 1909 have doubtless guessed already what I am bitten by. Others must wait agog for the denouement, which is reasonably certain to be an anticlimax. At this time I will only hint that I shoved my two children under the knife in front of me to see what happened, and got just what I deserved for it.

I first realized that I was in trouble about two years ago, when I began to run a daily fever of just under a hundred. Nothing else was wrong; my only symptoms were a constant surplus moisture, an antipathy to work and a feeling that I was either going to fall down or float away by the time I reached the seventh tee. I didn't really mind cutting down my work, but that meant I couldn't afford golf, and I was feeling too low even to play the golf that I couldn't afford. In addition to this, everybody kept telling me that I had never looked better. This was true, except for the gruesome rash on my feet and ankles, which they couldn't see, as I am seldom to be found without my shoes, socks and trousers.

My children went first

I placed myself in the hands of a series of gentlemen whom I shall designate simply as Doctor Kildare, Doctor Christian, Doctor Ehrlich, Doctor Watson, Doctor Huer and Doctor I. Q., who tested for everything from Malta fever to vultures gnawing at the liver. The tests are sort of fun, if you turn your head away when they siphon off the blood, and don't mind that ramrod they run up your nose to see if your brain's done yet.

By the time I reached Doctor Valley, I had worked my way back across the continent to my own snug little castle just below Mason and Dixon's line. As soon as I said "ah" for him, I could tell that the game was nearly up.

"What about these tonsils?" he asked delightedly.

"What tonsils?" was my riposte.

"Your tonsils," he said.

"I don't know what about my tonsils," I said. "They were taken out in 1908 or 1909, and I haven't kept in touch with them."

"You just think you had them out," he said with an admirable blend of glee and professional reserve. "They didn't really take them out in those days; they just snared the ends."

1908

This was appalling. All I know about snares is that poachers go around snaring rabbits with them; I began to wonder if my parents had accidentally called in a poacher instead of a doctor. With the 1909 telephone service, the error was a possible one. But poacher or doctor, I am sure that all will sympathize with my designs on his slats.

I'm afraid I indulged in a pretty tantrum in Doctor Valley's office. I insisted that I had no tonsils, and that if I did have tonsils they had been planted on me, and that anyway I wouldn't have anything that I did have taken out. But his quiet confidence was chilling when he said he'd leave it up to Doctor Dartley, the tonsil man.

Doctor Dartley looked down my throat and didn't say much; just "Oh, boy." But I begged so hard that he and Valley said well, maybe I might try having a tooth out and see if that helped; so I had a tooth out, thus missing the match race between Challedon and Kayak II, and two months later I was perfectly well except for a steady low fever, a constant surplus moisture, an increased antipathy to work and a tendency to curl up with a good dose of aspirin when anybody asked me to play golf. Oh yes, and a rough tongue from trying to convince myself that my new tooth had been properly installed.

At this point any ordinary patient would

have tossed in the towel and climbed meekly onto the operating table, but two pregnant lines kept jingling through my mind:

A tonsillectomy
Is a pain in the neck to me.

I was not beaten yet. After all, my tonsils might drop off of their own accord. After pondering this possibility for a while, I came to the conclusion that of course they would drop off; indeed, in a day or two I was sure that they had. I went to Doctor Dartley and put it to him flatly that since my tonsils had already dropped off, there was no further need for surgery. But he said that they hadn't dropped off, and we were dead-locked again.

I suppose I would today be swallowing through a throat snared but still unscarred if my two daughters, Eight and Six, hadn't developed tonsillitis. My wife was in bed with a sore throat, something which she isn't supposed to have any more since she had her tonsils out five years ago, so after the trip to Doctor Dartley it was up to me to explain to them that the first Saturday after school closed they would meet a nice man who would let them blow up a big balloon and then they would go to sleep, and when they woke up, their nasty old tonsils would be gone. Six faced the prospect placidly, but Eight was skeptical; it became apparent that the balloon story had been punctured by indignant veterans in the second grade. I dismissed the balloon and dwelt on the freezers of ice cream that would follow the cozy little nap. I described the operation in terms that might have applied to a free trip to a candy store run by Donald Duck in the center ring of the circus. That was my mistake.

"If it's so much fun," said Eight, "why don't you have yours out too?"

With Doctor Dartley's eye on me, I was trapped, but I could still strike back. "All right," I said, "I will. But you've got to have yours out first."

Thus it was that the first Saturday after school closed found me in a hospital room, accompanied by my wife, the children's grandmother and the children's grandfather. We were waiting for Six to come down from the operating room; which was, incidentally, a complicated bit of transportation involving much rerouting, as for reasons of policy she had to be kept out of the sight of Eight on her way up.

The children's grandfather recollected the day he had his adenoids out. He had walked back home from the doctor's office. But that was only adenoids, he explained. Take tonsils, now ——

Fortunately, my wife and I here got the summons to accompany Eight. Upstairs, Doctor Dartley joined us. Six was fine, he assured us. Nevertheless, Eight quietly but firmly informed him that she was scared. Doctor Dartley is a sensible man. "Everybody who comes into this room is scared," he said; "it's only the brave ones who admit it." That seemed to cheer her more than my assurance that if Doctor Dartley didn't do a good job on her, I wouldn't let him handle my operation. We were shooed out after that, and went down to see how Six was coming on, but they wouldn't let us in; she was fine, just fine, they told us, but not yet a sight fit for a parent's eyes. It's been my experience that everybody in a hospital is fine, just fine, right up to the second he stops breathing.

Back in the waiting room, the children's grandfather was saving the story of his tonsillectomy; it seems he had walked home from that, too, but shouldn't have. The children's grandmother said he couldn't have walked home from it; that when she had her tonsils out it hurt worse than when her appendix burst.

Then Doctor Dartley dropped in to say the girls were fine, but they'd have pretty sore throats for about three days. "Yours, of course," he told me, "will be a good deal sorer, being an adult; it's going to be close on two weeks before you're fit for human companionship."

My first glimpse of the children as they began to sit up, take pained notice and be sick was not heartening; it not only harassed my paternal affection, but it made my throat hurt. But they weren't mad at me; I drew some consolation from that.

With my own martyrdom only five days distant, I plied the girls with questions; I begged them to tell me that they felt no discomfort; I was eager for reassurance straight from the trial horse's throat. But Six's only words for forty-eight hours were weak demands for more basins, and Eight wouldn't speak at all until just before she was taken home, when she said her throat hurt the badliest she ever dreamed of.

Meanwhile, I was pleased by the number of friends who dropped by to inquire about the children, until it occurred to me that they were the particular friends who had had their own tonsils out within the past few years, plus one dear old lady who wanted me to know of her Cousin Eustace's hemorrhage. It seems he was doing fine, just fine, until the hemorrhage. I didn't mind the story of my friends' individual agonies so much, but I resented the way they had of looking at my throat and laughing.

Came the breakfastless dawn, marked by the sympathetic sorrow of the children at my departure. In painfully husky whispers they passed on to me the information that they knew it was going to be much badder for me than it had been for them.

At the hospital it was a severe blow to learn that they weren't going to let me blow up the balloon, but planned to knock me out in my room instead with a pair of teensy pink capsules. I suppose Doctor Dartley knew he'd never get me upstairs conscious.

I swallowed the pills and waited for something to happen. Nothing did, except that the children's grandfather began to whistle, but this was probably only a coincidence.

I wasn't sleepy at all, and was rather surprised to find myself in an elevator, lying on an ironing board on wheels. I remember greeting Doctor Dartley and triumphantly taunting him about his ineffective capsules; I remember asking him if I was as valorous as my daughters; I remember a funny smell; and I particularly remember my relief at sitting down in the Bedevere Bar with Doctor Dartley and Doctor Valley. I told them I ought to be in the operating room, but they said I was too tough to anesthetize, and they had run out of ether. The only course left, they said, was to ply me with juleps until unconsciousness engulfed me. I said I should think that would be bad for my heart, but they said, "Who is the doctor, you or us, have another julep." So I did, and unconsciousness did engulf me. Although Doctor Dartley and Doctor Valley both swear that none of us left the operating room, you know how these doctors stick together. For myself, I can only say that since that morning I have been ashamed to enter the Bedevere Bar.

Everyone was awfully good to me when I woke up, but frankly, I didn't care. Who was the mad tyrant who would that everybody in the world had but one neck, that he might sever it at a blow? Though muzzy with the receding fumes of ether, I was able to improve on his wish: I woulded the world had but one throat, and myself a pair of scissors. Nail scissors, preferably, and slightly nicked.

Doctor Dartley sought to cheer me by saying that he had seldom seen such terrible tonsils, a statement I was not prepared to swallow, especially at a time when I could only swallow water with the assistance of two codeines and a shot in the arm. Besides, who has ever heard of a doctor taking out a pair of tonsils and examining them and saying, "Gee, what a healthy pair of tonsils; we should never have taken them out, let's sew them in again and apologize"? No, I was firm in the conviction that if I had my good old tonsils back, and they were hanging down my chin like a beard, I'd let them hang.

A visit from the children and their grandparents did little to weaken this conviction. The conversation, in which I did not join, turned to a discussion of convalescence, particularly its more painful periods. This was the third day of mine. I felt that I had touched bottom; as there was no imaginable way for my throat to feel worse, I was looking with dim hope for some relief on the morrow. Six and Eight were all right; they agreed that the third day was the awfulest, but their grandparents snorted at this. The third day, said the children's grandfather, was just the beginning; if you want to know what a *real* sore throat is, just wait for the fifth day. The children's grandmother gently corrected him: he must be thinking of appendicitis, she said; with tonsils, the discomfort did not reach its climax until the tenth day, sometimes the eleventh. This little chat was as refreshing as a bowl of shredded wheat with a dash of Tabasco.

As it turned out, by the dreaded tenth day I was able to swallow anything up to a fingernail without flinching, and at the end of three weeks it seemed that Doctor Dartley had been right after all. I don't necessarily give him credit for the gradual disappearance of my forbidding rash; he and the dermatologist must settle that between them. But I can now shake hands with people without their drying their hands on their trousers afterward; I speed each morning to my work like a comet to whatever comets speed at; and my game of golf must be seen to be disbelieved. In a word, I'm fine, just fine!

I've got only one bone to pick with Doctor Dartley. While I was asleep, the son of a gun stole my adenoids.

IF YOU ASK ME

Eleanor Roosevelt

The first lady answers questions from her readers.

Who do you think are the three greatest men of all time?

Christ. Aside from Him, it would be hard to name any others, because for different reasons men have been outstanding and valuable at different times; but I think it is almost impossible to pick out, in the history of the world we know, three men who have served the world above all others.

What are the first two things you would ask for if you were making a personal Christmas list?

Peace, and a realization on the part of the people of the world that we have to work together to keep the world at peace in the future.

Do you ever lose your temper?

Occasionally, but not in the way one usually thinks of as losing one's temper. I become cold and silent, and I regret to say that my children recognize this and say, "Look out, ma's mad."

Do you think that it is wise to teach children that all men are created equal?

It is wise, I think, to teach children that intrinsically every human being has the same value before his Maker, but that the moment a child enters the world he is conditioned by his surroundings and that, therefore, there is inequality of opportunity and of development. Therefore, we as individuals should always try to recognize the actual worth of a human being as such and, where opportunities have not been present, make allowances and work toward a world where every individual may have the chance to develop his abilities to the greatest possible extent.

How many children do you think make up the ideal size family?

As many as a mother and father really want.

Except in the matter of anesthetics, do you think the world any better place than it was when you were young?

Yes, I do think the world is a better place than it was when I was young. There are

Eleanor Roosevelt

more people in it who are conscious of the inequalities and injustices of our social setup and who are making an effort to bring these questions out in the open so that the public may become conscious of them and some better solutions be found. Education reaches more people, and there are more enjoyments possible in consequence. Besides anesthetics, many other discoveries and inventions make life easier and pleasanter for human beings.

Should we discourage children from playing war games?

We might wish to discourage them, but it would be utterly useless at the present time, so we might as well give in gracefully and try to see that when war games are played they teach the lessons which we wish our children to learn—fair play, magnanimity in victory, courage in defeat and no hatred of peoples.

As a Jew I have often been puzzled what to answer when confronted with a request for either my nationality or my religion. Since I was born here, my nation is America, and I do not follow the doctrines

of any religion. Yet I am considered deceptive by some in replying "American" to my nationality and "None" to my religion. What do you, as an American and a Christian, think my response should be, and in what manner do you consider me to be a Jew?

As I understand it, to be a Jew is to belong to the Jewish religion; the term has nothing whatever to do with a racial background. If you want to be completely honest, you would naturally say, "I am an American, born in this country. My parents [or grandparents, as the case may be] came from such and such a country. I belong to no religion, but my parents were of the Jewish faith."

What is your greatest fear?

My greatest fear has always been that I would be afraid—afraid physically or mentally or morally—and allow myself to be influenced by fear instead of by my honest convictions.

Being a hairdresser, it has often puzzled me why a modern woman, such as you, has never changed her hair style. Do you have any particular reason for not having a new hair-do?

I have changed my hair style several times, perhaps not often enough. In any case, when you reach my age, if you can find anything which is moderately becoming, it is better to leave it alone and care less about being in the fashion and more about being inconspicuous!

Whom do you consider the three greatest women of all times, and why?

Florence Nightingale is one of the greatest women in history because she contributed a new conception of one of the purposes to which women should dedicate themselves.

I imagine Mme. Curie, because she demonstrated that a woman's brain has as much ability for scientific research as a man's, and that a woman can be as steadfast in purpose and as self-denying in her work, will always be considered great.

Harriet Beecher Stowe, because she had the heart to understand a great social problem and all its implications, and the courage to use her ability as a writer to bring it home to the conscience of the people as a whole, seems to me another great woman.

ALL THIS, AND HEAVEN TOO

By Phyllis McGinley

Princess Elizabeth of England, at seventeen, is slim with a girlish figure. She is keen on dancing, her lively eyes are blue, and her hair has become brunet with a natural wave.
—News item from the New York Times.

Elizabeth of England,
    Going on eighteen,
Was born to be a princess, bound to
    be a queen,
And poets have been telling us since
    history's dawn
How harried lies the head that a
    crown rests on.
It's a fate ill-fated, it is worse than
    death.
But I can't walk weeping for
    Elizabeth,
For she lives in a castle with quite
    extensive yards;
She waltzes with the laddies in the
    Grenadier Guards;
She rates a salutation from the whole
    Royal Navy,
And her hair is reported
    To be naturally wavy.

Ah, there, Betty!
    Yoohoo, Bess!
Thrones are confetti,
    More or less.
But I taste of despair
    And I wake up surly
When I think how your hair
    Is naturally curly.

Elizabeth of England
    Is burdened down with glory,
But there's something to be added to
    her sad, small story:
For her eyes are blue and her ways
    are simple;
She owns a yacht and a nice deep
    dimple;
The handsomest of regiments has
    tapped her for a mascot;
She's invited to the races when
    they're running them at Ascot;
And yearly on her birthday, while
    flags unfurl,
She's presented by her papa with a
    big matched pearl.
Her lines are laid in modified
    clover
And she's just seventeen
    Or a little bit over.

Ah, there, Betty!
    I've this to say:
A diadem is petty,
    You can take it away.
But the cross of a queen
    I would gladly bear,
To be going on eighteen
    With a wave in my hair.

I have used these three women simply as symbols of the development of new phases in women's experience. I doubt if any human beings, just by themselves, are very important; but when they start a new trend of thought and action, they are apt to symbolize for their contemporaries and for the future a new idea, and therefore they become important.

Do you think people of different religions should marry if parents object?

I think this is a very personal question and only the two people concerned can decide. Some married people adhere to different religions and still live happily together all their lives. Others find that a difference in religion becomes a bone of contention and one or the other member of the family usually gives in. I really think that parents who take it upon themselves to object so much that they attempt to keep the young people from marrying, are assuming a heavy burden of responsibility. Parents may not think a difference in religion is conducive to happiness, but religion is personal and only the individuals themselves can decide such a weighty matter.

Do you believe in the power of prayer?

Certainly, but the prayer must be an honest act of faith, and must be devoid of personal selfishness.

Do you ever give to beggars on the street? If so, how do you justify it?

Yes, I do occasionally give to beggars on the street. When I lived in my own home I made it a point to take people home to feed them rather than to give them money, and then to help them in any way possible to get a job if that was what they needed. Now that is impossible. However, when I see someone who looks fairly desperate, I would rather give money, on the chance of sometimes giving unwisely, than to withhold it from some one person who might need a helping hand and who deserves it.

Upon what basis do you say "We know the Adam and Eve story is not true"?

On the basis of science. In one way, of course, the Adam and Eve story is true as an allegory, but when taught without interpretation, as many children learn it, it is not true.

How would you teach the story of Adam and Eve to children, since you regard it as a myth? How can you reject parts of the Bible and accept others? Does your belief in the story of Adam and Eve as an allegory interfere with your faith in Jesus as the world's Redeemer?

I would teach the story of Adam and Eve as an allegory. It is difficult to accept the entire Old Testament in any other way. The story of Adam and Eve does not in any way affect my belief in the beauty and divine inspiration of Christ's life.

What is your favorite quotation?

"But it would make such a nice scoop if you'd only tell me, Franklin."

The thirteenth chapter of First Corinthians:
"Charity suffereth long, and is kind; charity envieth not; charity vaunteth not itself, is not puffed up.
"Doth not behave itself unseemly, seeketh not her own, is not easily provoked, thinketh no evil;
"Rejoiceth not in iniquity, but rejoiceth in the truth;
"Beareth all things, believeth all things, hopeth all things, endureth all things.
"Charity never faileth. . . .
"And now abideth faith, hope, charity, these three; but the greatest of these is charity."

Do you think a marriage should take place between two people who are well matched in every respect except that the woman has had a better education than the man and knows more about cultural things than he does?

I see no reason why a marriage should not be entirely happy, even if the woman has had opportunities for education in certain fields which the man may lack. "Education" is a curious term. Real education is possible of achievement with comparatively few cultural advantages.

If a woman has real appreciation of the worth of her man as an individual, she will make whatever advantages she has serve his purposes. She will never make him feel in any way inferior, because she will know that fundamentally real education is knowledge that is not acquired from books alone, or from a background which has been richer in opportunity for certain kinds of culture, but depends on the ability to think clearly and to understand men and events.

Why wasn't the United States more prepared for war?

Because after the last war we made up

our minds that we were never going to have another war. We taught our children at home and on the college campuses that war never settled affairs of state to anyone's satisfaction. We thoroughly convinced our young people of this, and they in turn convinced a great part of the country that we would never again have a period of war. Therefore, as we watched the rest of the world go to war, we simply insisted that staying at peace was something which we decided for ourselves and which had no relationship to the decisions of the rest of the world. Taking this attitude and feeling so secure, we quite naturally sent to Congress people who held the same opinion, and we upheld them in these opinions and would listen to no others.

What is the best way to help a young girl suddenly grown tall to overcome her feeling of awkwardness?

To talk about it very little; to watch her health so that she has good posture and does not suffer from weakness because of her sudden growth; to have her taught to dance well; and to see that she gets an opportunity to take part in athletics and to meet with young people freely.

When you met Winston Churchill face to face during his recent visit to the White House, what was your first reaction?

My first reaction to the Prime Minister was that I was meeting a personality who seemed oddly familiar, and that this was quite evidently a man of parts, lovable as well as impressive.

"What a perfectly darling outfit!"

FASCINATING FORTIES

Gloria Swanson

"Fascinating" is the word for Gloria Swanson. You called her that twenty years ago if you were old enough to go to the movies. You'd call her that today if you should meet her, because she has the same vivid quality. She is a wise woman who has learned her style and maintained it. If you are in your forties, as she is—or if you are a small piquant type younger or older than she—you'll profit by her tactics. She is not continually searching for the new and different. She finds a dress or coat or suit that is right for her, has it made in several colors and fabrics, changes it with flowers, jewelry or hats, wears it several seasons. She has her own ideas of design, works them out with her dressmaker, Madame Valentina. The scarf dress on this page is one of her pets. She has it in black and brown, ties the scarf a different way every time she wears it. The finger-tip collarless jacket goes for day or night; the full-length coat has the same adaptable quality. Utter simplicity—absence of trimming, collars, buttons —makes her clothes right for a small figure; makes them suitable and economical for any woman. Her wardrobe is based on black, varied with colors. In hats, she lets her fancy play, loves the gayest styles.

In her new picture, "Father Takes a Wife," as in her private life, she is frankly her own age. She has the perfection of posture that all little women ought to cultivate—to make the most of their inches. She is well groomed, but not obviously so—wears her hair simply, does not make the mistake of too much jewelry. She moves with freedom and grace, and her feet and ankles are a dream! She has a married daughter, two younger children, a business in New York, and her renewed career in the movies. She is current fashion—a busy, fascinating woman of today.

HISTORIC HOUSES

Photo: Pratt.

INGHAM MANOR near New Hope, Pennsylvania, is Bucks County architecture at its best. Built of what people call "tailored" stone carefully cut and laid, its flat-arched windows and doorway, and its flanking wings at lower level, are signs of its pre-Revolutionary period, when stone houses began to replace the log cabins of the locality's earliest settlers.

Richard Pratt

WHIPPLE HOUSE in Ipswich, Massachusetts, is one of New England's seventeenth–century Colonial gems. The "overhang" construction of the east side of the house (shown in the photograph opposite) and the diamond-paned windows show the colonists' liking for Elizabethan traditions. The room (in the second photograph) was added as a kitchen in 1670. Early American ladderback chairs face the widespread fireplace with its customary accouterments.

KENMORE, Fredericksburg, Virginia. Few houses from Colonial times are filled with such a wealth of original features and furnishings which beautifully belong. Dominating the Great Room (above) are the Horns of Plenty ceiling and plaster overmantel plaque. The latter depicts an Aesop fable suggested by George Washington, who stayed here with his sister Betty Lewis and her husband Colonel Fielding Lewis. The Lewises built the house in 1752.

ANDALUSIA, the famous Biddle estate outside Philadelphia, is a prime example of Greek Revival architecture. Indoors (as seen in the parlor at left), Regency furnishings predominate. The marble mantel comes from Italy, the chandelier from France.

THE WILLIAM GIBBES HOUSE, built about 1779, is one of the handsomest houses in Charleston, South Carolina. The dazzling yellow and gold Adams style ballroom (opposite) with its rich plasterwork and neoclassic ornamentation is furnished, appropriately, with Louis XV and Louis XVI pieces.

ART FOR ALL TO SEE

Emily Genauer

It's "Next Week—Picasso" on the billboards of America these days instead of "Next Week—East Lynne." Art shows are touring the country the way theatrical troupes used to, hitting the little towns as well as the big ones, playing engagements in museums, galleries, schools, women's clubs—and taking to the road again.

Last year no fewer than fifty million Americans saw them, according to a published report by **Francis Henry Taylor,** director of New York's Metropolitan Museum of Art. They didn't find any road-company casts either. Paintings are no prima donnas. They don't mind tedious train trips and hurried packing. They shine as brightly for the school children of Duluth as for the professional art critics of New York.

PIERRE AUGUSTE RENOIR

1841–1919

A Girl With a Watering Can, *painted in 1876, is one of the most popular pictures in the National Gallery. It is evocative of sunlight and childhood, springtime and the breath of flowers, images and sensations which are in themselves attractive. But these are not enough. To be great, a painting must have more than charm of subject matter; it must have certain aesthetic values as well. In the case of A Girl With a Watering Can these values consist largely in the relationship of figure and landscape, in the way the two are fused by an ingenious repetition of colors and a consistent treatment of detail. The whole picture is made up of a web of brilliantly colored brush strokes, which from a distance is seen to be a child, roses, grass, a garden path. The little girl seems to merge with her surroundings, to become one with the variegated tones of nature. This creates a mysterious sense of interrelation, as though one substance permeated humanity, vegetation and earth. . . .*

"I arrange my subject as I want it," Renoir once said, *"and then I go ahead and paint it like a child." He loved bright colors, joyous and pretty human beings, and nature drenched in sunshine.*
—JOHN WALKER, *Chief Curator, National Gallery of Art, Washington*

Now the curtain is rising on a new art season. Its impresarios are the young and energetic museum directors from Dallas, Iowa City, Chicago, San Diego, who months ago converged on artists' studios, dealers' galleries and public museums in New York, even on those of Paris, London and South America, to round up the paintings, sculpture, drawings and prints they considered good enough for the folks back home to see and enjoy.

What they selected is spread out over America right now. In Chicago there is a special show of masterpieces by three great English artists, **Hogarth, Constable** and **Turner,** sent all the way from London to make their first American appearance in the Windy City's famed Art Institute. And as if that weren't treat enough, the institute has also brought to Chicago the exhibition of art by **Marc Chagall,** one of the world's most celebrated living artists, direct from New York's Museum of Modern Art, where it drew 3500 people opening night, the museum's record for a première.

In Austin, Texas, are paintings by the great nineteenth-century American master, **Thomas Eakins,** fresh from showings in Philadelphia, his home town, and New York. In Bloomington, Indiana, and in Iowa City, Iowa, are prints by the Frenchman, **Georges Rouault,** another top modernist whose pictures are cherished by museums the world over (and bring five-figure prices). The dignified little Museum of Fine Arts in Worcester, Massachusetts, has been transformed into a Pacific atoll by its new exhibition, "Art of the South Seas."

These are only a handful of the art shows which are filling America's 2000 museums at the moment. Next month they will have changed places, puss-in-the-corner fashion. If a specific show you'd like to see is someplace a thousand miles off right now, keep your eye peeled for it. There's a good chance it will turn up in your local museum before long.

Your "eye peeled"? Curious figure of speech. Like "walking on air," or "time flies," or "sitting on top of the world." Our literature even more than our daily speech is peppered with metaphor. In the Bible the Psalmist sings of "the wings of the morning," and of floods that "clap their hands."

All of which puzzles the bushy-haired pixyish **Marc Chagall** deeply. Fifty-seven now, the Russian-born painter who lived for many years in Paris before his arrival in America a few years ago, wonders why people will accept fantasy in the theater, in their daily speech, in the ballet, in poetry, even in their prayers, and bristle like porcupines when they find it in art. Why does he paint cows flying through the air, they demand, houses upside down, angels playing violins, winged clocks? And, innocently and honestly, Chagall, looking like a rotund Harpo Marx, replies, "Because I love them."

Why he loves them, however, is a little more complicated. If you like jigsaw puzzles you can piece out of his own past the source of each of his dream-world symbols. That man on the roof, for instance, who recurs so often in his brilliant-hued canvases. In his autobiography he tells of how his grandfather disappeared one night from a holiday celebration, and how the family found him at last, seated on the roof, refreshing himself in the cool night air and chewing a carrot. That figure who persistently wanders over village roof tops, staff in hand. Has he his origin in the artist's consciousness of his race and its eternal wanderings?

Those lovers embracing somewhere in the vicinity of the moon. It is his own beautiful romance, a tribute to his wife, who died suddenly in 1944. From the year of their marriage in 1915, on each of their wedding anniversaries and birthdays, Chagall had painted lovers—embracing under a huge bouquet, floating on air, riding a rooster or a donkey over the roofs of Paris.

They're at the Chicago Art Institute now, the floating lovers, the violin-playing cows, the upside-down houses; a distillation of Russian folklore, Paris modernism and a great and incorrigibly romantic heart.

The Herron Institute in Indianapolis is right now host to an exhibition of the work of perhaps the greatest woman artist of the twentieth century. She was **Käthe Kollwitz** who, after being a thorn in the side of German officialdom for a half century, died in poverty a year ago in a small town in the German Harz Mountains. The Nazis had driven her there from her home in Berlin, and forbidden her to work. But just before she died, seventy-eight and blind, she had the joy of knowing they were vanquished.

Art's not even satisfied to take trains everywhere these days. Now it's taking to the air, and for exhibition purposes, if you please, not just transportation.

The American Air Export and Import Company has acquired for the planes of its Flamingo Fleet reproductions of paintings owned by the Museum of Modern Art.

They were selected "to illustrate the various schools and influences directing the art of today," the company says, the idea being that air travelers might very enjoyably and profitably spend their hours aloft examining the twenty-four reproductions of works by **Dali, Matisse, Rouault, Renoir, Max Weber, Miró, Léger, Edward Hopper** and others, which will be carried in portfolios on each ship.

Ordinarily articulate persons have been left wordless attempting to describe Yvette Guilbert. She was a famous Parisian entertainer at the turn of the century, forerunner of all the present-day *diseuses* who mutter torch songs into night-club microphones. *She* didn't have much of a voice either. And she certainly wasn't beautiful, to judge from her pictures. She was tall and thin and rather awkward. Still she wowed

them, as the Broadway boys say, when she walked out in her elegant gowns and her inevitable long gloves, and started to sing.

If Guilbert can be called the grandma of night-club entertainers, then it may be said that one of her offspring resembles her. It's Hildegarde, of course, of the long gloves, handsome clothes, vivid personality. Perhaps there's no connection between this and the fact that recently Hildegarde walked into a New York art gallery and bought a series of lithographs of Yvette Guilbert made by **Toulouse-Lautrec,** one of the great figures in modern French art.

Hildegarde says it's coincidence, and that she is an art collector from way back, owning work by **Picasso, Manet** and a host of living Americans from **Thomas Benton** to **Raphael Soyer.** They're hung all over her six-room apartment in a New York hotel.

They're even stacked in corners and piled on tables.

You may see the Toulouse-Lautrec portraits of Yvette Guilbert in a show which is touring the country now, and stopping over, for November, at the California Palace of the Legion of Honor, in San Francisco. A large exhibition of his oils and prints is also hung at the Wildenstein galleries, in New York.

Toulouse was a strange figure. His full name was Count Henri de Toulouse-Lautrec-Monfa, and he came of a family that could trace its noble blood all the way back to Charlemagne. But he was a four-foot dwarf, crippled by a series of childhood bone accidents from which he never properly recovered. There is a story told of how he forgot his drawing pencil at a café table one night, and a derisive patron called after him, "You have forgotten your walking stick!"

He had a large head, thick lips, a black beard, flashing dark eyes. The pity and the ridicule of the women of his own set he could not endure. So he frequented the cabarets and cafés of Paris, where the entertainers were not so choosy, where his name and his money commanded respect, and where he could lose himself in music, dancing and drink.

And in his art. He painted all the singers and the dancers, the sordid nameless ones who did their sensuous *dances du ventre* on the street corners of Paris, and the glittering celebrities, like Guilbert, Cissie Loftus and Anna Held. He created a gallery of night-life characters incomparably vivid, brilliantly colorful—and not a little tragic. He drank increasingly, and his mind and health were shattered. In 1901, at the age of thirty-seven, he went home to the family château and died.

William Hogarth, eighteenth-century Englishman whose most important pictures have been loaned by London's National Gallery to the exhibition of his work now at the Chicago Art Institute, was another artist who liked his night life. Only he claimed to be a moralist, and he painted the series of pictures called Harlot's Progress, Rake's Progress and Marriage à la Mode to show that the wages of sin is death and virtue triumphs in the end.

One can't be too harsh with Hogarth. It was the depravity of London life he was railing against really, its social evils, the condition of its insane asylums, the filth of its streets. These messages he subtly incorporated into the paintings which he did allegedly exhorting young people to lives of purity. Their sensational subject got them the widest possible distribution.

Back in the '60's in Philadelphia, the Pennsylvania Academy of Art ruled that all nude female models posing in the "life" class had to wear masks to conceal their identity. **Thomas Eakins** was a student there at the time, and a charcoal drawing of one of the masked models which he made in 1868, when he was twenty-four, hangs now in the College of Fine Arts of the University of Texas, Austin, Texas, part of a large exhibition of his work touring the country to commemorate the recent hundredth anniversary of his birth.

The nude sits with one leg tucked under

Courtesy Pierre Matisse Gallery

"The Bride and Groom of the Eiffel Tower" again presents Chagall's well-known "floating lovers," perhaps a symbol of his own romance.

In the late nineteenth century, the truth put on canvas was intolerable. Eakins insisted on telling it.

her, with every crease and line of her plump relaxed body recorded most realistically—and covering her face, from hairline to chin, a heavy black veil.

It was like Eakins to have drawn the nude with such fidelity, up to and including her mask. He is the greatest realist in the history of American painting. But he found, in his own day of sentimental idealization in art, that realism was as intolerable and confounding to large portions of the public as interpretive, imaginative, fantastic painting is today.

A great many Philadelphians who didn't know they were thereby cheating themselves of immortality refused to accept the realistic portraits he executed of them. As a contemporary painter put it in explaining his own reluctance to sit for Eakins, "He would bring out all the traits of my character that I have been trying to hide from the public for years."

Yvette Guilbert was the Hildegarde of Paris café society at the turn of the century. Men find it hard to describe her. Toulouse-Lautrec does it in lithograph (at left).

William Hogarth fought the depravity of eighteenth century London beneath a neat camouflage of allegory. Above: one of his pictures from London's National Gallery.

ASK ANY WOMAN

Marcelene Cox

The kind of party the daughters are attending seems to be determined by one thing: whether or not they're wearing hose.

Heredity may be the Cellophane wrapper around a child which environment fails to penetrate.

Love and kindness are something you feel in a house just as you do soap and water in a hospital.

When parents do not agree as to discipline, a child is in the same strategic position as a choir member placed between a singer who always starts just ahead of the beat and one who always starts just behind the beat.

She never had a thing to say, but thought she ought to say something anyway.

Example of heroes-are-not-born-but-made: Boy: "You know something, mother? Every day I'm getting tougher to beat up."

A parent who never listens to the end of what his child has to tell deserves to lose the child's confidence.

His face accomplished in a crowd what one good piece of furniture does in a room.

The highest arts should always give the appearance of ease, including the art of housekeeping.

In child raising as in chess, the game may be won by making a move contrary to what is anticipated. Example: Tell a child he has to stay awake until ten o'clock and note how soon his eyelids flutter.

As we grow older we discover that the truths our parents stressed are still fundamental.

No parent should spend all his time in the garden of a child's life digging up weeds; there's always the danger of scratching out flowers not above ground.

Illustration by Al Parker for KINFOLK *by Pearl S. Buck.*

WHAT

IS

CIVILIZATION?

Will Durant

"I thank the gods," said Plato, "that I was born a Greek and not a barbarian, a man and not a woman, and in the days of Socrates."

Even a philosopher's thinking is two thirds prejudice. The Greeks called all non-Greeks *barbaroi,* probably meaning babblers, people of uncouth speech. The word was flagrantly unjust, for Egyptian, Babylonian, Hebrew and Persian were highly developed languages in Plato's days. The "barbarian," knowing the zest of cool air on the naked body, sleeping under the stars and living under the sun, earning or making his bread with the toil of his hands, unhampered by laws and unspeeded by machines, innocent of cities or factories, dispensing with books but loving song and dance, educating his children fondly to a hundred useful skills, and killing in a thousand years as many men as a civilized person can kill in a day—such a "barbarian" might reasonably laugh at "civilization," and dismiss it as the prejudice of all prejudices, the conceit of all conceits.

Every nation has exaggerated the splendor of its own culture, and has underestimated that of others. Every vigorous people thinks itself the chosen people. This collective egotism is as necessary as individual egotism.

We of the United States are no exception to the rule of national conceit. We have our excuses: our democracy has given us for a century more liberty than any other people has ever enjoyed; our economic system has produced wealth more abundantly, and distributed it more widely, than any other system or country in history; our educational system has opened the doors of opportunity to every mind in every rank—almost; our freedom of thought and speech, of press and worship has withstood all assaults of obscurantism and bigotry; and the zest and camaraderie of our life come like an electric charge to any people that makes contact with American youth.

And yet—our economic system normally leaves a substantial minority of our people

in poverty and slums; our democracy is tarnished with occasional corruption, incompetence and waste; our educational system gives us more skill than wisdom, more cleverness than character; our freedom has a string on it, and does not deter us from racial discrimination and hostility; we lead the semicivilized world in divorce

Drawing by James Thurber

and crime; our music is barbarous, our art (except architecture) is mere groping, our literature has deteriorated since Emerson. We destroy historic cities, architectural masterpieces and noncombatant populations with indiscriminate air raids, and kill 60,000 men, women and children at one blow. We love our civilization, and our enemies call us Huns.

Civilization is order and freedom promoting cultural activity.

Order is civilization's first law, and the mother of freedom, as chaos is civilization's

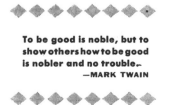

To be good is noble, but to show others how to be good is nobler and no trouble.
—MARK TWAIN

last travail, and the mother of dictatorship.

Four forms of order are needed for civilization: biological, political, economic, moral.

Biologically: there must be order in the relations of the sexes and the generations. The family—which is the biological nucleus of civilization—pursues this aim through marriage and parental care. Marriage is an unnatural institution, whose original purpose was to secure economically an economic helpmate, but whose modern purpose is to channel within orderly limits unreasoning impulses that might otherwise tear a society to pieces. A low birth rate marks a high civilization. Public services of health and sanitation, by lessening illness and mortality, are a major contribution to civilization.

Politically: there must be protection for life, labor, enterprise and property, and for the society as a whole. Primitively the tribe and the clan achieved this through kinship rule and custom; usually in civilization it is accomplished by the state through regional government and laws. Since internal disorder or external attack may destroy a state, we must reckon a police force and an army as indispensable appurtenances of civilization.

Economically: there must be order in the production and distribution of desirable goods; in their secure transport—the history of civilization is in one aspect the history of the wheel; in their provident storage and safe exchange; in the provision of capital to finance these operations; and in the relations of the groups or classes of men and women engaged in these operations.

Morally: a civilization requires order in the conduct and relations of men. Civilization is artificial; the order it entails runs counter to our most powerful impulses. Our individualistic instincts of acquisition and pugnacity, our racial instinct of indiscriminate mating, are stronger than our social inclinations to associate and imitate and conform; these last must be encouraged, the others must be controlled, to ensure the order that makes civilization possible.

Here again the family is the nucleus of civilization. Parental discipline and fraternal strife smooth the projecting corners of the ego. Hence the grievous opposition of young and old: the old must transmit the moral code of the group, the young must attack it with an innovating, liberating passion in which the errors occasionally number less than the trials. The old provide stabilizing heredity, the young offer adaptive variation. The conflict is costly, everlasting and beneficent.

Religion plays a vital role: it warns the rampant ego of a surveillant unforgetting deity, and of eternal punishments; charms it with holy examples and the promise of endless rewards; and fortifies the unwelcome moral code by ascribing it to God Himself.

The compulsion of law generates habits of obedience, which may continue when compulsion ceases or is concealed; conscience is the deposit of a Mississippi of prohibitions. Meanwhile the heavy hand of custom clamps an order upon the soul; rebellion flares as ability seeks room and place, and subsides as place is found; the man of thirty accepts custom as the congealed wisdom of the group. Only twenty years knows more than twenty centuries.

Civilization begins with order, grows with liberty, declines with license and dies with chaos. The great ages of culture have been periods of liberty or license: Periclean Greece, late Republican and early Imperial Rome, Renaissance Italy and France, Elizabethan England. The best condition for a cultural flowering is a conjunction of wealth and freedom, varied trade and the unhindered movement of men and ideas.

Cultural activity is not the sole goal of order and freedom—these are justified as well by simple goodness or happiness; but we should hardly call a people civilized if it produced no fruits of art or the mind. Writing is a prerequisite of civilization; and some form of education is indispensable. Civilization is an accumulation and treasure house of customs, institutions, techniques, records, memories, morals, manners, ideas, letters and arts; from this rich store the individual draws mental nourishment as the child draws milk from its mother's bottle.

Education is the conveyance and absorption, in part or substance, of this social heritage. No lifetime, however sleeplessly assiduous, could absorb it all; no mind, however learned or profound, could fully understand it, or be fit to judge its wisdom. If education should cease for a century, civilization would disappear; our grandchildren would be letterless, skill-less, lawless savages.

Art is a fragment of the cultural fragment of this racial lore; and yet art alone has a hundred varieties and a thousand styles. Men and women sing and dance, and play instruments, in the exuberance of their blood; they adorn their bodies with ointments and pigments and colorful robes; they labor to give beautiful form to buildings, images and sounds. This strange esthetic fever in man is a restless creator of civilized forms.

Science is older than civilization. It begins with the arithmetic of trade, grows with the geometry of measuring land, mounts with the astronomy of calculating seasons and crops by sun and moon, and guiding navigation by the stars. Astrology helped astronomy, as alchemy helped chemistry; and what were these men and women of so many races, who forged peace with the atomic bomb, except alchemists transmuting elements, and harnessing the energy of transmutation?

In like manner magic helped the noblest science of all—medicine. From medicine came hospitals, public sanitation, anesthesia, and that lowered death rate which, by permitting a lower birth rate, frees the individual from repetitious absorption in parentage. Through medicine came botany, physiology, anatomy, embryology and a hundred other sciences. Biology is the last great science that a civilization develops, for only in maturity do we dare to see life without mythology.

Philosophy need not develop formally in every civilization; but presumably in every civilization, and probably in barbarism and savagery, there have been philosophers—men who, like Dostoievski's Mitya, wanted "not millions, but an answer to their questions"; men who saw life in large perspective, and found everything forgivable when understood. Out of fear of the strange and unknown came curiosity and the zeal to understand; the grasp of this curiosity grew until it touched the stars; and philosophy presented the noble and at the same time ridiculous spectacle of a part trying to comprehend the whole. We shall always fail, and always try.

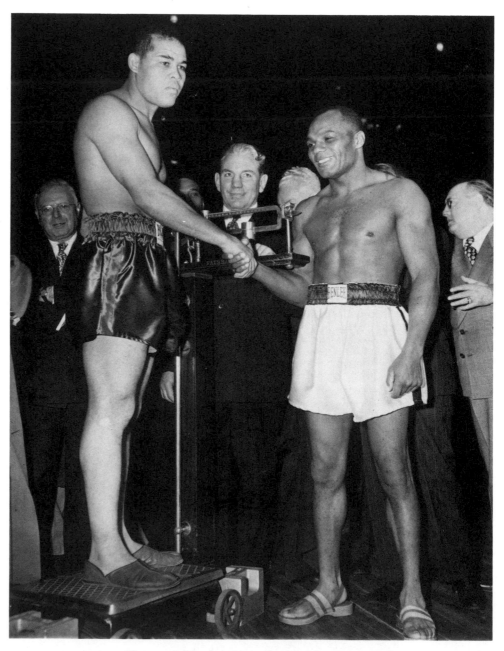

Heavyweight champion Joe Louis (on scales) shakes hands with challenger Jersey Joe Walcott as they weigh in for their bout on December 5, 1947.

PEACE AND ANOTHER WAR!

Walter Lippmann

It is often said that, in the nineteenth century, Great Britain regulated the peace of the world and managed the conditions of its prosperity, and that it is now the mission of America to play the part which Britain is no longer able to play. I have no doubt that this is true, provided we do not make the mistake of supposing that we are like a son who inherits from his father the assets, the good will and the going concern of a well-established business. For the international order which Britain regulated no longer exists.

During the century between the fall of Napoleon and the outbreak of the First World War, Britain, though the leading power, was only first in a community of fairly equal states. The powers were Britain, France, the Austro-Hungarian Empire, Germany and Russia. All of them, with the exception of France, were not only in form but in fact monarchies and empires. Their dynasties were related across the national frontiers by intermarriage. Their governing classes were bound together by many family and social connections. In the period of the Pax Britannica the masses of the people came awake and acquired more and more democratic power. But as late as 1914, international affairs, the conduct of diplomacy and the making of war and peace remained the special business of men who by inheritance or adoption were recognized members of the governing classes of Europe.

They were, moreover, all of them Europeans. The continent of Europe was in effect the center of government for the world. Though the powers of Europe were rivals and frequently at war, their rulers recognized one another as permanent members of one international society. Their wars—even their great wars—were limited and localized. There was no such thing as total war, no such thing as the extermination or deportation of masses of people, no idea that the object of diplomacy could be the destruction of a great power. Though there were national boundaries, national animosities and national ambitions, there remained, still strong from earlier days, a feeling that Europe, the center of the world, was itself a cosmopolitan community within the bonds of Christendom.

This was the world order which Britain, though never in fact an enormously powerful military state, was able to preside over and to regulate. It may well be the verdict of history that the Pax Britannica marks the last phase of the international system which ended with the rise of the masses of the people to political power. It was, perhaps, the Indian summer of the ancient aristocratic European regime. And we, I imagine, are living in the winter that has followed the decline and fall of that regime. The old order is dead. But the new, which is to come, is still only the seed in the ground.

The conference at Teheran in the autumn of 1943 might be said to have been the first occasion in history when the United States began to take a direct and leading part, as distinct from a regional and a subordinate part, in attempting to shape the order of the world.

American statesmen have not been trained to conduct a global policy. All of them were born and have spent most of their lives in a world where the great global decisions were made in Europe—in London, Paris, Berlin, Rome, Vienna, and in St. Petersburg or Moscow. Washington was not at the center of, nor closely in touch, nor much concerned with the conduct of, world affairs. Even Wilson and Roosevelt, though they were not isolationists when they were in the White House, had grown to maturity in the long epoch of American isolation. Today, though no one can doubt that the United States is a leading world power with global interests and responsibilities, there are as yet no Americans who have had more than a brief experience in world politics. So we are having to learn while we are acting.

If we are to shape the future, we must not forget the past. How has it come about, then, that as we enter upon the work of making peace, we find ourselves confronting the Soviet Union in all parts of the world, and engaged in a conflict of power and influence which many believe must, and all believe may, end in the most destructive war in the annals of mankind?

The present situation of the world is intelligible only if we remember that Germany and Japan were defeated decisively only by Russia and America. The Japanese have had to evacuate China. But China did not defeat Japan. China was helped enough to be able to avoid a defeat by Japan. The British, the Dutch and the French empires in Eastern Asia were conquered by Japan. The Japanese have had to give up their conquests. But these empires were not reconquered by the British, the Dutch and the French.

The Germans have had to evacuate the European countries which they conquered. But, though the underground resistance was an important factor in the defeat of Germany, though the part played by Britain in the war was enormous—and, in staving off a German victory, decisive—the fact remains that Europe was saved from Nazi domination by the two non-European Allies—by Russia and America.

That is why Russia and America are now

"Or do you like it better the way it was?"

the principal world powers in the postwar era. That also is why Russia and America confront each other directly in Europe, in the Middle East and in Eastern Asia. Until the two World Wars of our time Russia and America were separated by several great empires—the British, the French, the German, the Austrian and the Japanese. The international community consisted of at least seven or eight great powers. At the end of the Second World War there were in fact only two great powers.

As a result, the question in all men's minds is whether one of the two great survivors must eliminate the other, whether Russia and America must and will fight for the empire of the world, or whether there can and will come once again into being an international community of several relatively equal powers.

I maintain that the Second World War was not inevitable, that it could have been prevented, and that it need not have taken the course it did. Consider only our own part in it. Was it inevitable that we remained disarmed after Japan seized Manchuria and Hitler came into power in Germany? Was it inevitable that from 1931 to 1939 we should remain unarmed, neutral and isolationist? Was it inevitable that we did nothing while almost the whole European continent was conquered by the Germans, and all the ports of China by the Japanese? Was it predestined that when we were struck at Pearl Harbor in December, 1941, we should not be ready to fight back seriously until the end of 1943? If we were able to destroy the Japanese Empire in 1945, was it determined in advance that we could not have been powerful enough to check the Japanese Empire some years earlier?

If there were choices in the past, then there are choices in the future. Another war, though it is possible, is not inevitable. A peace, though it is not certain, is possible.

Between a possible war and a possible peace, what, then, are the probabilities? The best way to go about answering this question is to imagine how Russia and America would go about fighting a world war. The more that question is studied by the professional strategists of the Kremlin and of the Pentagon, the more surely, I contend, they will come to see that while two nations can fight, two nations cannot fight a world war. The reason is that there will be too many neutrals.

There is no way in which the great masses of mankind can be aligned into two opposing coalitions, the one under Russian leadership and the other under American. It requires strong governments to mobilize nations for war. The people have to be conscripted, regimented and commanded in order to fight a war. Now, as we have already seen, the greater part of the world, as a result of the two wars, is no longer firmly and strongly governed. The disorganization of the European continent and of most of Asia, the destruction of the old states and the liquidation of old empires makes it difficult to organize peace. It also makes it difficult to organize a world war. It makes it difficult to organize anything.

I do not say that Russia or America could not declare war, that the Red infantry could not begin to march, our bombers begin to bomb. But I do say that this could not become an organized conflict between Communist nations and anti-Communist nations, the reason being that only organized nations can fight wars.

There are few, if any, nations which could be organized by either Russia or America to fight this war. Between Russia and America there would be not their respective allies but an immense region containing many hundreds of millions of people engaged not in international war, but in a vast anarchy of many civil wars. Such a struggle could not be directed and controlled from the Kremlin and the Penta-

gon. It could not be ended by a military decision. Even to surrender, there must be a government capable of surrendering, and who could surrender to whom in a general condition of anarchy? Organized society—already so badly disorganized—would, as in the Dark Ages, dissolve among the guerrilla bands, and blood feuds, and uprisings, the war lords, local potentates, the usurpers and pretenders.

So, though I do not predict that a Russian-American war cannot happen, I do predict that it would end not in the victory of either, but in anarchy so general that it would be well-nigh universal. I am not, therefore, opposed to discussing a Russian-American war.

The more we talk about this war, and where it would be fought, and with what weapons, and by whom, and for what strategic objectives, the more we shall arouse, provoke, incite the peoples of Europe to bestir themselves, to unite, and to rise up again as principals and powers in an international community. If they cannot think of any better reason for ending the ancient divisions of Europe, then perhaps they will be moved by the terror and horror of becoming the battlefield of the two non-European powers.

I am in favor of discussing this Third World War continually and exhaustively. For the more it is talked about, the more surely shall we talk ourselves and the Russians out of it.

October 8, 1945.

The "big three"—Clement Attlee, Harry Truman and Joseph Stalin—relax at the Potsdam Conference after deciding the terms of Japan's unconditional surrender.

WHILE YOU ARE AWAY

Colette

"Did they tell you that while you're away I lead a lonely existence, unsociable and faithful, apparently waiting impatiently? . . . Don't believe it. I'm neither lonely nor faithful. And it's not you I'm waiting for.

"Don't get upset! Read this letter right through to the end. I enjoy taunting you when you're far away, when you can't do anything to me, only clench your fists and break a vase. . . . I enjoy taunting you without any risk, seeing you—separated by distance—quite small, angry and harmless, a watchdog and I'm a cat in a tree. . . .

"I'm not waiting for you. Did they say that I threw open my window at sunrise, longing for the day when you'd stride down the path, chasing your long shadow, before you came up to my balcony? They were lying. If I have left my bed, pale and still dazed by sleep, it's not the sound of your step that beckoned me. . . . How beautiful it is, the light, empty avenue! My gaze encounters no obstruction from dead branch or straw, and the blue stripe of your shadow no longer moves over the clear sand, patterned only by the birds' small claws.

"I was only awaiting . . . that moment, the start of the day, my own, the one I share with no one. I let you take hold there just long enough to welcome you, to seize your coolness, the dew of your path across the meadows, and close the shutters on us. . . . Now the dawn is mine alone, and I alone enjoy it, rosy and bedewed, like an untouched fruit despised by others. It's for that I abandon my sleep, and my dream that's now and then of you. . . . You see. Barely awake, I leave you in order to betray you. . . .

"Did they also tell you that around noon I went down, barefooted, to the sea? They were watching, weren't they? They've praised me to you for my sullen solitude and the still, aimless procession of my footsteps on the beach; they've pitied my bowed face, suddenly watchful, turned toward . . . toward what? Toward whom? Oh! If you could have only heard! I was laughing, laughing as you've never heard me laugh! It's because there, on the wave-smoothed beach, there's no longer the slightest trace of your games, your gamboling, your youthful violence, your cries no longer sound in the wind, and your swimmer's prowess no longer shatters the harmonious curve of the wave that rises, bends, rolls up like a transparent green leaf, and breaks at my feet. . . .

Colette

"Waiting for you, looking for you? Not here, where nothing remembers you. The sea rocks no boat, the gull that was fishing, clasping a wave and flapping its wings, has flown away. The reddish, lion-shaped rock stretches, violet, under the water attacking it. Is it possible that you once spurned that lion under your bare heel? The sand that crackles as it dries, like heated silk, did you ever trample it, forage in it, did it soak up odor and sea salt from you? I say all this to myself as I walk on the beach at noon and shake my head incredulously. But sometimes I turn around and look about me like children who frighten themselves with made-up stories—no, no, you're not there—I've been afraid. I suddenly thought I might find you there, looking as if you wanted to steal my thoughts . . . I was afraid.

"There's nothing—only the smooth beach that crackles as if under an invisible flame, only splinters of shells that pierce the sand, fly up to prick one's nose, fall down again and hem the seashore with a thousand broken, glinting stitches. . . . It's only midday. I haven't finished with you, absent one! I run toward the shadowy room where the blue daylight is reflected in the polished table, in the brown paunch of the cupboard; its coolness smells of the wine cellar and the fruit storeroom, thanks to the cider that froths in the jug and a handful of cherries in the fold of a cabbage-leaf. . . .

"Only one place is laid. The other side of the table, opposite me, glimmers like a pool. You know, I shan't put the rose there that you used to find every morning, limp on your plate. I'll pin it to my blouse, high up near the shoulder, so that I need only turn my head slightly to brush it with my lips. . . . How big the window is! You used to half-screen it from me and I never saw, till now, the mauve, almost white, underside of the drooping clematis flowers. . . .

"I hum quite quietly, quite quietly, just to myself. . . . The biggest strawberry, the blackest cherry, it's not in your mouth but in mine that they melt so deliciously. . . . You used to covet them so much that I gave them to you, not out of tenderness, but from sort of shocked good manners. . . .

"The whole afternoon lies before me like a sloping terrace, all radiant above and plunging down below into the indistinct, lake-colored evening. It's the time—perhaps they've told you—when I seclude myself. Faithful seclusion, eh? The sad, voluptuous meditation of a solitary sweetheart? . . . What do you know about it? Can you know the names I give the illusions I cherish, my thronging advisers, can you be sure that my dream bears your features? . . . Don't trust me! Don't trust me, you who've caught me unawares, crying and laughing, you whom I betray every moment, you whom I kiss saying, very softly, 'Stranger'. . . .

"Until the evening I betray you. But when it's night I'll rendezvous with you and the full moon will find me beneath the tree where the nightingale was so frenzied, so drunk from singing that he did not hear our footfalls or our sighs or our mingled words. . . . No single day of mine is like the day before, but a night of full moon is divinely like any other night of full moon. . . .

"Does your spirit fly through space, across sea and mountain, to the rendezvous I've made with you, under the tree? I'll be there as I've promised, unsteady as my head, thrown back, seeks vainly for the arm that once supported it. . . . I call you—because I know you won't come. Behind my closed eyelids I conjure with your image, soften the color of your glance, the sound of your voice, I shape your hair to my liking, refine your mouth, and I refashion you—discerning, playful, indulgent, tender—I change you, correct you. . . .

"I change you . . . gradually and completely, even to the name you bear. . . . And then I depart, furtive and embarrassed, on tiptoe, as if, having joined you under the tree's shadow, I left with a stranger. . . ."

CHRISTIAN DIOR

PLEATS, PLEATS—*black and brown chiffon
with a dervish whirl, thirty yards
around! Patent-leather belt shaping doll-
size waistline, narrow plunging neckline.
Velvet hat, canary-yellow diamond collar.*

COROT GREEN *changeable taffeta, wide circular skirt an inch
above the ankle. Waistline smaller than ever, belted in patent
leather, sloping shoulders, deep neckline with a cabbage rose.*

There is no doubt that fashion is
changing—and Christian Dior, brilliant
Paris designer, is in the forefront of that
change. The clothes on these pages selected
in Paris capture and dramatize that
change. They are beautiful clothes,
most as yet too extreme for general
American wear. But study them well—
they show the trends: skirts possibly
not so long as these, but growing
longer; waists small, if not miniature;
many wide, wide skirts; cossack and
princess coats; a romantic picture-
book look for evening. As a counter
note: long, slim, buttoned skirts
topped by brief and
bulky jackets.

BUTTONED *to the ankle, narrow at the
ankle, black velvet dinner gown with a
low fur-edged neckline, copper satin,
bow-twisted bra, long
brown gloves. Reminiscent of 1912.*

LONG NARROW *skirt with a bulky jacket,
newest look of all. This jacket is lined
with sealskin, collared and cuffed with sable.
Paris thinks two furs are better than one.*

SATIN AFTERNOON *dress in sea-green,
waist-deep V neckline managing marvelously to
be discreet. Belted with the ubiquitous patent
leather. Wearable, adorable.*

TIGHTLY BELTED *green herringbone
tweed suit with a bulky skirt, box-pleated,
narrow at the waistline, widening at the
hem. It carries its weight
gracefully, is enormously smart.*

TALKS WITH MOTHERS

Benjamin Spock, M.D.

"The thing that makes each child secure in the family is feeling that his parents love him and accept him for himself, whether boy or girl, smart or dull, handsome or homely."

Years ago the staff of the Sarah Lawrence College Nursery School, of which one of the authors was a member, were discussing a number of first-born children who had been very upset when the next younger sister or brother was born. Several of these children had changed at least temporarily from gay, friendly eager beavers to quiet, sad mopers. We on the staff were sympathizing with first children in general, because we had the impression that most of them found it tough to be displaced from the only-child position. Then one member of the staff went over the records of all the first children in that school, for several years back, to see how they actually added up. Much to our surprise, the informal statistics showed that for every one who had been distinctly upset at the arrival of the next

baby, there was another child who had taken the new arrival completely in his stride and had gone on being just as happy as before.

It may be that these children who breeze through the arrival of the second so successfully are able to do so because of a very special kind of security—just from being first.

Incidentally, a first child is rarely upset by the birth of a third. He or she has apparently experienced whatever jealousy he is capable of with the birth of the second and has been somehow purged in adjusting to it.

Though a child's position in the family is important, it's even more important what kind of family it is, in spirit, in attitude. If it's an easygoing family in which the parents just naturally take each child as he comes, then there is more chance that each child will feel comfortable in his particular spot, whichever it is.

Plenty of parents are reasonably casual with their first and some parents do their concentrating on a second or third child. This sometimes happens when they have been waiting impatiently for a girl after having had two or three boys. The girl who eventually appears may receive a greater amount of attention and end up with a character that is more like that of some first or only child.

In lots of families, to be the middle child looks like the most comfortable position of all. The parents have learned a lot of lessons the hard way with the first. They're now apt to be more sure of themselves, more relaxed. So many mothers have exclaimed to us, in almost the same words, "The second is so *easy!* I don't seem to worry about him. I don't even have to wonder what to do. I just find myself doing what's necessary and it usually turns out to be right. Why, I don't even have to stop to ask myself whether I should punish him or overlook his naughtiness. If I do punish him it always clears the air—I don't feel guilty about it and he cheers up soon afterward. Sometimes my husband and I wonder

if we're neglecting him—we fuss over him so little. But if it *is* neglect he seems to thrive on it. He keeps himself busy and happy most of the time. But when he does want a little company he's so appealing that no one can resist him, even strangers on the street. He enjoys being hugged, which is so different from the first."

Children who are second or later in the family are more apt than the first to learn early how to get along with other children —both positively and negatively. They catch the fun of rough and tumble when this comes naturally at one and two and three and four. (The first or only child, if he has few chances to be with other children in the early years, usually finds them pretty strange, thoughtless and violent compared with the polite grownups he's used to.) The second or later child in most families discovers how to defend himself without much delay. If he has an older brother who picks on him he may wince and cry at nine months or twelve months, but by eighteen months he will probably be able to hang onto his possessions like grim death and fight back like a tiger. It's amazing how often a younger child may eventually get the upper hand of one who is considerably older, bigger and stronger. Probably the main reason he can fight more boldly is that he doesn't feel the guilt which the older child has usually been taught to feel about meanness toward the baby.

But life can be tough for a second child too. A frequent source of tension may be a constant excessive striving of the second to keep up with the first: to *always* climb a tree if he climbs a tree; to stay up as late, to play with his brother's friends even if he has to neglect his own. This intense rivalry may or may not make the younger one miserable. More often he remains a cheerful person through all his striving, though it may keep him thin and high-strung, and it may irritate his older brother a lot. We've occasionally seen this kind of ambitiousness produce very strong leadership qualities in the second child among his own group, usually of a constructive type.

The second or later child in most families discovers how to defend himself without much delay.

Opposite: Illustration by Al Parker for THE WAYWARD PILGRIM *by Elizabeth Goudge.*

QUICK AND EASY'S
FOR TWO

Louella G. Shouer

Helen and Larry Fritz rent a charming apartment over a four-car garage on a private estate near Philadelphia. Because Helen works two days a week and commutes to New York those days, she's developed her own way of making dinner-getting quick and easy. You'll want to add some of her tricks to your own collection of in-a-hurry menus.

"In planning my dinner menus for the week," Helen confided, "I usually start with a roast. If we are going to have guests —either for the weekend, for Saturday dinner or for Sunday-night supper (when I will usually serve it sliced cold) —I buy a fairly large roast—five to six pounds, depending on the kind or cut. When we aren't having guests, I often have a roast chicken. In any case, the remains of the roast provide one or more different dishes during the week. If the leftover roast is lamb or pork, we will invariably have it curried over rice. If the roast is chicken, I use it in a casserole stretched with noodles."

So for Monday

Chicken-and-Noodle Casserole
Orange-and-Grapefruit Salad

A salad of cold sections of oranges and grapefruit is just the right tart accompaniment for the casserole.

Chicken-and-Noodle Casserole

Cut up 1½ cups cooked chicken. Leave it in fairly large pieces. Sauté 1 onion, chopped, 2 or 3 mushrooms, sliced, in 3 tablespoons butter or margarine. Push vegetables to side of pan and add 2 tablespoons flour and 1½ teaspoons curry powder. Blend smooth with the fat. Add 2 cups liquid gradually—½ cream and ½ chicken broth—or if you have a little chicken gravy left from the roast chicken, add that too. Cook, stirring constantly until thickened. Add chicken, salt and pepper to taste, and 2 tablespoons seedless raisins. If you like more curry, this is the time to add it. Cook 2 ounces (¼ package) noodles in boiling salted water until tender. Follow directions on package. Drain. Mix noodles and sauce together. Pour into a casserole and bake in moderately hot oven, 375° F., 20 minutes.

MONDAY MEMO. You will need to have cooked chicken on hand, of course, plus noodles, canned chicken broth, cream, mushrooms and nuts (optional), onion, curry powder, bread or rolls, milk, coffee or tea. One grapefruit and two oranges will make a salad for two, plus greens, French dressing and chutney.

Tuesday

Kidneys and Sausages—
Baked Potato Halves
Scalloped Tomatoes
Apple Compote

First off, put the potatoes in to bake. Scrub and cut them in half. They bake in half the time.

Kidneys and Sausages

Slice 1 veal kidney after removing the fat around it. With a pair of scissors, snip out the bit of membrane in the center of each slice. Cover with boiling water and simmer 5 minutes. Drain off the liquid and save. In the meantime fry ¼ pound link pork sausages (or ¼ pound bulk sausage meat). Drain off all fat but 2 tablespoons. Add 1 small onion, chopped, and if you have them, 4 mushrooms, sliced. Cook 5 minutes. Add kidneys. Sprinkle with 2 teaspoons flour. Stir well and add ½ cup of the strained liquid from the kidneys. Stir well until slightly thickened. Cover and simmer 10 minutes or until kidneys are tender.

Apple Compote

Peel, core and cut into eighths 1 quart tart apples (1½ pounds). Add 2 cups water, ¾ cup sugar, the juice of 2 lemons, and 1 lemon, sliced, and ½ stick cinnamon. Simmer until apples are tender. Add 2 tablespoons red cinnamon candies after removing from heat.

TUESDAY MEMO. You will need 1 veal kidney, pork sausages, 1 No. 2 can tomatoes, 1½–2 pounds tart apples, 3 lemons. Have on hand: onions, garlic, potatoes, mushrooms, brown sugar, sugar, stick cinnamon, red cinnamon candies (optional), salad greens—if you'd like a salad with this meal

—bread, butter or margarine, milk, tea or coffee.

Wednesday

Tomato or Onion Soup
Hamburgers—Green Salad
Ice Cream—
Apricot-Raspberry Sauce

Wednesday nights Helen doesn't get home much before 8 o'clock. Instead of a regular dinner, she and Larry like a soup-and-sandwich meal, topped off with ice cream, which she keeps in her refrigerator for quick desserts at all times. You may not have a schedule like Helen's, but there's always an evening when a hot soup, hamburgers and a salad hit the spot.

Apricot-Raspberry Sauce for Ice Cream

To ½ cup raspberry jam, add ½ cup puréed apricots. If you have stewed dried apricots cooked for breakfast, use those. Otherwise, you can use canned apricots.

WEDNESDAY MEMO. You will need ½–¾ pound ground beef, 1 pint ice cream, 4 hamburger buns. Have on hand also a favorite canned soup, greens for salad, dressing, raspberry jam, canned apricots or stewed dried apricots, butter or margarine, milk, coffee or tea.

Thursday

Ham-and-Broccoli Brûlée
Green Salad
Lemon Sponge

Make dessert first. Prepare the sauce for the main dish while the broccoli cooks and the ham is frying, then everything will be done together.

Ham-and-Broccoli Brûlée

Cook ½ bunch broccoli in boiling salted water until just tender. Meanwhile, cut a ½-to-¾-pound slice of smoked ham in half. Brown on both sides in hot skillet. Make the sauce as follows. Melt 2 tablespoons butter or margarine. Add 2 tablespoons flour and blend smooth. Add 1 cup milk and cook until thickened, stirring con-

Jack Tyrrell

stantly. Stir in ½ cup grated cheese and salt and pepper to taste. Lay ham in shallow baking dish. Drain broccoli and lay it on ham slices. Pour cheese sauce over the broccoli. When nearly ready to serve, place under broiler and broil about 4 minutes or until lightly browned.

Lemon Sponge

Mix together in the top of the double boiler 1 tablespoon cornstarch and ½ cup sugar. Add ¾ cup boiling water and cook, stirring constantly over direct heat until clear. Add 1 tablespoon butter or margarine, a pinch of salt and a little grated lemon rind. Put top of double boiler over hot water. Add 2 egg yolks, slightly beaten, and cook a few minutes until eggs thicken. Stir constantly. Remove from heat. Add ¼ cup lemon juice. Fold in 2 egg whites, beaten stiff but not dry. Cool and serve in sherbet glasses.

THURSDAY MEMO. You will need a ½–¾ pound slice smoked ham, 1 bunch broccoli (you will use half for another meal or cook and use in salad over weekend). Be sure you have on hand lemons, eggs, cornstarch, salad greens, dressing, cheese, butter or margarine, milk, tea or coffee.

Friday

Quick-Baked Fish Fillets
Boiled Potatoes—Peas

Hot Gingerbread
Honey Topping

For dinner tonight make gingerbread from a mix and serve it hot with a creamed honey topping. The fish fillets bake only 15 minutes at the same oven temperature as gingerbread.

Quick-Baked Fish Fillets

Spread a shallow baking dish with soft butter or margarine. Lay washed fish fillets on buttered dish; ⅔–¾ pound is enough for two. Sprinkle with salt and pepper, paprika and chopped parsley. Pour ¼ cup heavy cream over the fish. Dot with butter or margarine and bake 15 minutes in moderate oven—350° F.—just until the flesh of fish turns perfectly white. Serve with lemon.

Honey Topping

Cream ¼ cup butter or margarine, adding ¼ cup honey gradually. Then add 3 tablespoons cream bit by bit, creaming all the while. Serve a spoonful on top of hot gingerbread.

FRIDAY MEMO. You will need ⅔–¾ pound fish fillets—flounder, cod or haddock —1 package frozen peas, 1 package gingerbread mix. Check supplies for potatoes, parsley, cream, honey, butter or margarine, milk, tea or coffee.

THERE'S A MAN IN THE HOUSE

Harlan Miller

✧ ✧

Next to drumming up enough courage to ask the boss for a raise, what requires the most pluck for a modern father is to ask a modern son to sweep the driveway or wash the car. (Of course, it helps if you catch the lad in an amiable mood.)

✧ ✧

Among the smartest women in our little circle are the ones who sense the precise moment to remove the pressure on a husband, just one wink before he explodes. (When a man cries out "I won't be a henpecked husband!" it's probably too late.)

✧ ✧

We husbands are not so mysteriously hard to please as some female masterminds pretend. Some corned-beef hash, a favorite phonograph record and a kiss, and we're as happy as children.

✧ ✧

Maybe it's the influence of radio (heaven forbid), but I'm more than ever persuaded that no woman can be homely who has a charming voice. At least in the dark, or with my eyes shut.

If women understood how much religion dwells, for many men, in a woman's sweet and gentle face, they'd behave more like goddesses and less like bargain hunters.

✧ ✧

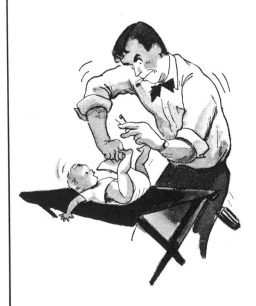

If males had been stuck with a baby, a diaper and two safety pins, they'd have hit on a more ingenious way to sheathe baby's derrière, long before they bothered about inventing an electric horse.

THE WORLD THROUGH THREE SENSES

Helen Keller

People often express surprise that I find life great and wonderful, when I have only three senses. From others' testimony I know that at the age of nineteen months I was exploring the world with five senses, playing, laughing and learning a few words. Then came the illness which deprived me of sight and hearing, and as a result of deafness I lost the ability to speak.

It was not possible for me to develop my remaining senses to a high degree without the stimuli that spring from speech and language, and that means that I was completely isolated. We use sight and hearing principally because from them we learn at once what goes on around us. Through the eye man acquires nine tenths of his experience. Through the spoken word and literature, hearing quickens his mental growth with information and ideas. In my case I was literally unworlded. Smell enabled me to find the fruit I especially loved—bananas; it directed me to the boxwood hedge out in my mother's garden. My nose could distinguish my clothes from those of the family when the laundry was brought home every week, and from imitation I put them away in the bureau. Wherever there was any cake or candy or ice cream I was sure to devour it. My mother wisely let me move about the house and the kitchen, and thus she preserved my health and appetite.

But, untaught, unstimulated, I acted and thought like a mere animal. I cannot convey verbally the state I was in—wrapped in a double silence, my own and that of others to me. I was not merely alone, I was a wild little creature.

The change which occurred after Anne Sullivan began my education still causes me to thrill and glow. It was not a child that confronted her, but an animal utterly ignorant of itself, its feelings and its place among human beings. For some time I was still devoid of a world—I had no sense of my own identity or time or unity or diversity, but Anne Sullivan did not let such details discourage her. She treated me exactly like a seeing, hearing child, substituting hand-spelling for the voice and the eye from which other children learn language. She encouraged me to observe all objects I could reach with my three senses, so that I could relate them bit by bit with the things which surrounded me and gain from them analogies with sight and hearing. She helped me to enrich my vocabulary through the flow of words from her fingers, through association and books to build a world in which color and sound took their place, even though I could not perceive them. That is how it happens that I am aware of sympathies with the seeing, hearing race.

Ideas constitute the world each of us lives in, and impressions are a wellspring of ideas. My outer world, wrought out of the

Helen Keller and friend.

sensations of touch, smell and taste, breathes and throbs because I have a thinking mind and a feeling soul. While others look and listen, I use my tactile faculty to secure information, entertainment and activity in which I have a share. In all I do and think I am conscious of a hand. People dependent upon their eyes and ears seldom realize how many things are tangible. Objects that can be touched are round or flat, broken or symmetrical, flexible or stiff, solid or liquid, and these qualities are modified ad infinitum.

Also I perceive the flow of straight and curved lines and their endless variety on all surfaces—regular or uneven, swelling, rough or smooth. In rocks full of grooves, jagged edges and lichens, in the queenliness of the rose and the velvet of a well-groomed horse's neck, the manifold shapes of young trees, bushes and grasses I find eloquent witness to the glory that once trickled into the seeing hand of the Greek, the Japanese and the South Sea Islander.

Again, with the skin of my face and nose I notice different atmospherical conditions according to the season, even at various hours of the same day and in different regions. For instance, in wintertime I recognize a cold sun, and the rain is chill and odorless. The rain of spring is warm, vital and fragrant. The air of midsummer is heavy and damp or dry and burning, and so the changes of weather go on.

Besides objects, surfaces and the weather, I perceive countless vibrations from which I learn much about everyday happenings. In the house I feel footsteps, noises of the broom, the hammer and the saw, the dishes as they are removed from the table, the excited bark of big Et Tu, my Alsatian, when

somebody comes to the door. Footsteps vary tactually according to the age, the sex and the manners of the walker. The child's patter is unlike the tread of a grown person. The springy step of youth differs from the sedate walk of the middle-aged and from the gait of the old man whose feet drag along the floor. In persons whom I know well I detect many moods and traits in their walk—energy or laziness, firmness or hesitation, weariness, impatience or distress. Thus I am aware to some extent of the actions of those about me.

Perhaps I am working at the desk. A sportive breeze blows some papers off, and I jump up to recapture them, guided by the direction from which their flutter on the rug reaches me. A flat thud warns me that a book has fallen. The ring of an electric bell on the desk informs me that I am wanted downstairs. Other vibrations past enumerating speak to my fingers: the wind or rain rattling against the windows as I open or close them; the ring of the telephone when I am close to it; the tic-tac of a clock I touch; the swallowed gurgle of the playing hose; the pop of a champagne bottle opened quite near to me.

There are other vibrations which do not reach me through skin-touch. They enter my nerves and bones loudly or softly. The beat and roll of drums pass through me from the chest to the shoulder blades. The rhythmic vibration of a well-made train over a smooth road is pleasing to my body. There is fascination for me in the echoing thunder and the tremendous booming of the ocean upon the shore. And the organ, whose harmony resembles the onrush and retreat of sea waves, swells my act of feeling to rapture. What I said in The World I Live In is still true: "If music could be seen, I could point where the organ notes go, as they rise and fall, climb up and up, rock and sway, now loud and deep, now high and stormy, anon soft and solemn."

On the other hand, I am annoyed by discords like scraping, the creaking of old floors, and foghorns. I have had contacts with bridges which were being built, and I felt the blows of giant hammers, the rattle of masses of stone and other materials, the rumble of engines and the dumping of dirt cars. I have visited factories and war plants and sensed the clangor and uproar of machines horrible and brutal. I have been shaken by the crash of giant trees as they were felled to earth, the concussion of huge logs sawed at lumber mills, explosions that follow blasting rocks in mines, the enormous clamor of switching freight trains and the roar of the airplane starting on its flight. At sea I have been pitched to and fro in a storm on a ship as it plowed foaming furrows through the water, and liquid mountains lashed its sides and tossed it aloft like a child's toy, it seemed to me, with devilish exultation. From all these vibrations I have gained my conception of war, earthquakes, tidal waves and raging forest fires.

When I work in my garden early mornings in spring and summer, my sensations are wide open to the "brightness, the spark and flame of the quick forge" of Nature's wonders. It is easy to trim by touch the grass down the driveway and around the trees, to remove stones that press upon the roots and to cut away vines that threaten to strangle other plants. I do not have to worry for fear my shears will murder the lusty pachysandra border, it is so unlike the slender blades of grass I cut. Having felt vines sprawling along the ground or seizing

bouquet of indescribable loveliness. I cannot hear the orchestra of bird voices that those who have ears observe, but the trees and flowers amaze me with their endless changes. The pines and spruces from which I pluck away dead herbage drop pitch upon my hand, and I take that as tidings that summer is near. These palpable phenomena awaken in me a train of happy memories, so that the seasons of each year mean more to me than those of the year before.

During the day I am absorbed by intense concentration on work at the desk and the sameness that ever-recurring demands for similar services create. It is to preserve my individuality and keep my three senses alert that I escape into the garden at dawn

primitive state, to philosophize as it is to speak. I happen to be among those who can think most effectively on their legs. Happy solutions of my perplexities have sprung up spontaneously on a stroll, after vain attempts to disentangle them indoors. Braille is none other than a brave blind man's philosophy put into practice of overcoming obstacles.

My brain and three senses, certainly, are needed to note every detail of interest in a ramble—whether the path is hilly or flat, grass or gravel, rocks or sand or soft soil. By the shade on my face I can tell when I come to a wood or a thicket. A rush of warm air indicates that I am in an open, sunny glade. Where the road is familiar to me, I hold out my hand to examine the

SPRING PLAY IN A T'ANG GARDEN. *Attributed to Hsuan Tsung of the Ming Dynasty. The Metropolitan Museum of Art.*

hold of any support with their tendrils, I do not mistake one of them for the foliage of a shrub. The tall, square-stemmed, coarse-leafed, rank weeds I pull up are not to be confused with ferns or delicate, feathery grasses through which the wind pipes tenderly.

The seasons always charm me as a succession of surprises. No matter how attentively I watch for their signs, they are never the same in odor or temperature. One day when I go out to clip grass it is frosty, and buds on tree and bush are still small and hard. A few days later I am at my outdoor work again, and lo, the maples are in leaf, the evergreens are beginning to put out soft new tips, the turf palpitates with promises of clover and dandelion. Soon the rosebushes and lilac trees are aflutter with fragrant little leaves that seem to my fingers cool distillations of dew and air. The time that passes varies before I discover one bush in flower, and, like wildfire, the blossoming spreads until the entire garden is a vast

or soon afterward. Just to have the sweet soil, the grass and dew between my fingers refreshes and clears my mind.

On my walk by the cedar railing at home I have noticed that the pine emits different scents—one wet with rain, one dry in midsummer. Mosses have a distinct olfactory character hard to define.

"But how can you take such pleasure in walking?" I hear someone who has all his faculties say. "We have all the colors of the landscape, the songs of birds, the ripple of streams, but you have only motion—placing one leg before the other, putting your feet on the ground in turn, lifting them again and stepping forward until intelligence revolts, and the motion ceases, as Rose Macaulay has written."

"Far from it!" I reply, amused.

The chief advantage of walking is the freedom of my mind to go on long excursions into philosophy. This is not a misfortune, I think, as several friends have said to me. It is as natural to man, even in a

bark and foliage of trees, or gather wild flowers or pick berries.

There is for me a wind-sweet, high resonance in the thin, narrow leaves of willows, agitation in the fussy motions of birches and poplars and a rich, musical depth in the foliage of oaks. Firs and spruces impart to me serenity in the thought that, though the winds from every direction bend them this way and that, yet the straining roots do not loose their hold upon the rock, and I lean against them sustained by their might, drawn from victorious combat.

In walking I also read the weather—and by the weather I mean the outdoors. I have a reasonably tough skin that welcomes most kinds of weather, and I am determined not to succumb to the allurements of a shielded old age. Often I fight a rough wind foot by foot as I struggle down the road, then it veers and pushes me forward like a leaf. Once I was caught in the terrifying clutches of a cyclone and only by bending very low I managed to follow my companion as we ran to a building nearby for shelter. Again a gentle breeze wavers on my cheek, quivers and shambles like the sea and drops into stillness lke a bird descending to its nest.

Without trouble I distinguish the hammering sleet and piercing wind from a still snowfall that has a scent of purity unlike any other element in the sky. Before a thunderstorm the fragrances from garden, field and wood swarm about me, then disappear as the rain falls. The climate of the mountains differs from that of the ocean,

Secrets

W. H. Auden

That we are always glad
When the Ugly Princess parting the bushes
To find out why the woodcutter's children are
    happy
Disturbs a hornet's nest, that we feel no pity
When the informer is trapped by the gang in a
    steam room,
That we howl with joy
When the shortsighted Professor of Icelandic
Pronounces the Greek inscription
A Runic riddle which he then translates,

Denouncing by proxy our commonest fault as our
    worst;
That, waiting in his room for a friend,
We start so soon to turn over his letters,
That with such assurance we repeat as our own
Another's story, that, dear me, how often
We kiss in order to tell,
Defines precisely what we mean by love:
To share a secret.

The joke, which we seldom see, is on us;
For only true hearts know how little it matters
What the secret is they keep:
An old, a new, a blue, a borrowed something,
Anything will do for children
Made in God's image and therefore
Not like the others, not like our dear dumb friends
Who, poor things, have nothing to hide,
Not, thank God, like our Father either
From Whom no secrets are hid.

which I identify by its salt dampness. In their turn these are utterly dissimilar to the breadth and sweep of the grain-scented, sunflower-flecked prairies on which I have walked during my journeyings out west. Always on my rambles it is a race for me to recognize a crowd of odors as they fleet by. Smell is fugitive and dependent upon the condition of the air on which it is borne. It is also subject to temperature. For instance, in cold weather there are few odors, while heat brings them forth abun-

dantly. From smell I gain a sense of distance, ubiquity and unlimited variety that suggests analogically what people mean by colors and their shades. I can imagine that blue differs from red as widely as an orange does in scent from an apple. The melon has a scent of its own, yet I can distinguish different kinds of melons, and I can understand that roses, while retaining the unmistakable rosaceous smell, have widely varied shades.

It has pleased me especially to learn that, from regarding smell as a sort of fallen angel, an unwelcome monitor of disagreeable objects or danger from fire or escaping gas, society is slowly accepting it as a priceless enrichment of experience. Not only is my olfactive joy in the earth's growth complete, I also recapture whole epochs of my life. Every time I smell daisies I am a radiantly happy little girl in the dew-drenched fields, walking with my teacher. A whiff from a meadow where hay has been cut transports me back to the big New England barn where my little friends and I used to play in a huge hay-mow. The days brimful of adventure, work and beauty I spent in California return to me whenever I catch the odor of a pepper tree, a eucalyptus or a citrus grove.

Never have I had a group of smell memories more delectable than those of Portofino, Italy, where Polly Thomson and I found rest on a mountaintop overlooking the Mediterranean last May. I reveled in the Italian sunshine and fragrances, which thronged upon me from all directions. The salt air streamed in a warm current, side by side with the boxwood hedges. The breath from the orange and lemon groves was an ecstasy, whether lingering lazily on a damp day or animated and strong in dry weather. There was a curious phenomenon which I observed at the lunch table: I could not easily distinguish the blossom of the orange from the fruit I was eating, or the strawberrylike smell in the honeysuckle from the wild berries on my tongue! In and out, all around, delicate grasses and leaves as unlike as the blossoms drifted among the floral odors, and formed an indescribable symphony of their own. The refreshment of mind and body which has invigorated me for my work I owe quite as much to those many well-defined, yet harmoniously blended fragrances as to the tranquillity of the weeks at San Sebastiano.

Last autumn I attended a gathering in Westport, Connecticut, where a professional perfumer talked most interestingly about the distillation of flower fragrances. He gave us all what he called the "blind test" to see how many floral perfumes we could identify. He presented to each of us eight fragrances on little blotters, or "whiff sachets"—rose, carnation, honeysuckle, lily of the valley, lilac, gardenia, jasmine and violet. Everyone complimented me on my ability to name correctly seven out of the eight flower fragrances. I found out that most women can identify only one or two. This is a sad comment indeed on their neglect of a faculty which would repay them a hundredfold for some patience in its development.

To my teacher's indefatigable vigilance that kept the fires of thought and observa-

tion burning in me I owe the wealth of experience I have gained through only three bodily faculties. This moves me to remind parents and teachers of their power to train children from the earliest years in the right use of their five senses. The surest hope of culture renewal is always the child. In order to attain his highest education he must be persistently encouraged to extract joy and constructive interest from sight, hearing, touch, smell and taste. Like all forms of education, the child's senses should be aroused by techniques suited to his individuality.

I am not a teacher or an educator, but I have always believed that infants should be taught as soon as possible, before they speak, to notice objects pretty or delightful or unusual. I have noticed the wholesome effect upon a baby of fixing his eyes upon a pleasing color or a delicately carved shell, listening to music that soothes or enchants him, touching a face he loves or smelling a flower at which he smiles. If the mother puts as much gentle art into this delicate fostering of all his physical powers as she does into the task of preserving his health, her reward will be past calculating. The child's five senses are the faithful fairies who, if cherished and heeded, will surrender to him their priceless tokens of royalty—the splendor at the rainbow's end, the seven-league boots of imagination, lovely dreams fulfilled. He will always be charmed or comforted by sky, earth and sea. Not only will he reach a well-ordered stewardship of his senses, he will also have the best chance of spiritual maturity. For there is, I am convinced, a correspondence between the powers of the body and those of the spirit, and when the five senses—or whatever of them there are—serve as entrances into an inner world, the individual attains his or her fullest capacity of pleasure as well as self-mastery. Every person, every group thus excellently equipped for living is the greatest possible contribution to humanity. That is why I like to celebrate the accomplishments of the handicapped whom necessity drives to use all the faculties that remain. They show what normal beings can and should do with a complete set of faculties. Once parents and teachers realize the tremendous potencies of good folded up in sense-life and set about developing them in children, they will confer upon the coming generation a blessing that will carry through untold ages its multiplying harvests of alertness, strength and beauty of life.

THE BARRETTS OF WIMPOLE STREET

Katharine Cornell (Mrs. Guthrie McClintic) and Brian Aherne in the first play McClintic produced under his wife's management. This photograph was taken fourteen years after the play's New York première, when the original American cast played for American troops in the mud of Italy, France and Holland.

JOURNAL ABOUT TOWN

First to use a typewriter.

Taylor Caldwell (THIS SIDE OF INNO-CENCE) wrote for thirty years without being able to sell a line. . . . Among the first advertisements in British papers were appeals by ladies wanting husbands. . . . **Mark Twain** was the first author to use a typewriter. . . . There are 7500 species of orchids. . . . The best hours of your nightly slumber are the first two. . . . At least 500,000 women are bald and more are getting that way, according to a Chicago wigmaker. After they've got their wigs, women are more reconciled to baldness than men, he said. . . . Definition of a fan club: a group of people who tell an

Olivier sets hearts aflutter.

actor that he's not alone in the way he feels about himself. . . . Much of **Van Johnson's** fan mail comes from older women with matchmaking tendencies who know "just the right girl" for him.

With more and more excellent British films in town here every month, the girls

James Mason—English star.

around the Workshop have practically all switched their favor from Hollywood heroes to the English stars like **Laurence Olivier, Rex Harrison, Ralph Richardson,** and—most of all—**James Mason,** in spite of the fact that in every picture of his we've seen he's tried his best to appear unattractive; never smiles; only scowls—which, as far as we can make out is why they like him. But as long as he's the rage, here's what he's like. Tall and dark, brown eyes; thirty-seven; 160 pounds; started to be an architect but soon found that too dull. He smokes cigars; doesn't exercise; likes **John Marquand** best of all modern authors—and has a wife, named **Pamela.**

Queen, and Queen-to-be, Elizabeth.

Hearing someone mention the approaching marriage of **Princess Elizabeth, Bruce Gould** remembered the time at Cliveden when **Lady Astor,** after a dessertless wartime lunch at which she was entertaining the Queen and the Princess, gave each of the Elizabeths, to their great joy, a great, green glistening American lollipop. "I am going to suck this all the way back to Windsor," said Her Majesty, delighted. Asked what she would like for her birthday, the Princess said she'd like to have dinner with **Tommy Handley,** who's the English equivalent of America's Jack Benny.

The reason **Hugh Kahler** was chuckling to himself the other day was because of a story **Booth Tarkington** had just told him about a farmer member of the Indiana legislature who was against a bill favored by many intellectuals. The opposition tried to reason with him, but after listening he told them, "You might's well quit where you be. You ain't got no chance to fool me. I'm too ignorant."

For some years back an old woman up in Northern Massachusetts had been selling to tourists the jellies and preserves which she put up during the summer. On the table where she displayed her wares, she used to stand some pictures she had painted, along with the plum jam and canned peaches. The pictures were "Sugaring-Off," "Covered Bridge," "Over the River," and other local scenes. If you inquired the price of a picture she'd ask what size you wanted. As a matter of fact, she was prouder of her preserves than of her paintings. That is the start of the story of **Anna Mary Robertson Moses.** It is told by Louis Bromfield in his introduction to GRANDMA MOSES, AMERICAN PRIMITIVE.

Grandma Moses

The best war play in town, and the biggest hit, is MISTER ROBERTS, starring **Henry Fonda.** Just one girl in the show—a nurse. And if the whole cast has a natural South Pacific tropical tan, without using make-up, it's because the director, **Joshua Logan,** has installed in the basement of the theater a battery of sun lamps under which everyone in the play must spend at least an hour a day.

There's a little hat story behind **Jessamyn West's** story called The Hat or at least a little story behind the painting that illustrates it; for, according to **Frank Eltonhead, Alex Ross,** the artist, designed the

The cast of "Mr. Roberts" gets its tan the easy way.

hat himself—fruit, flowers, veiling and all—got a milliner down the street in Wilton, Connecticut, to make it, and a neighbor's daughter to pose. Of course, by rights the model should now have the hat—but who has it instead? The model's mother.

She posed, but mom wore the hat.

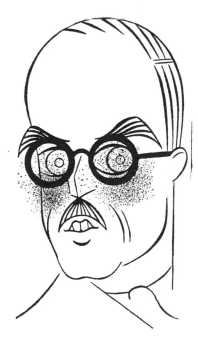

"The Hat" by Alex Ross.

Thornton Wilder

THE IDES OF MARCH is to our way of thinking not only **Thornton Wilder's** best novel but also the best picture of Caesar—and we're not forgetting Shakespeare or Shaw. Here is the Dictator, surrounded by enemies of whom he is eternally aware but unafraid, and by the masses of the people who adore him. He is the general become statesman.

Ingrid Bergman in "Joan of Lorraine."

In Maxwell Anderson's magnificent new version of the Joan of Arc legend, **Ingrid Bergman** plays Joan with such warmth and understanding that hard-boiled critics and theatergoers dusted off their superlatives, declared that Bergman had brought "an unaccustomed radiance into the theater of our day."

In the past decade New York City, which seems to get whatever it wants, has gradually wrested the honors away from Milan, Moscow, Paris and London to become the ballet center of the world; having now reached the point where, between the great ballet troupes and the finest modern dance groups, there are one or more major performances here practically every evening from the beginning of September to the end of May—not to mention matinees.

When Jean Arthur enters as Peter Pan, old hearts grow young.

Marquand's just completed JOURNAL serial, POINT OF NO RETURN; while also on the lists were THE SPRINGS, by *Anne Goodwin Winslow; Pearl Buck's* KINFOLK; *John Gunther's* DEATH BE NOT PROUD, and CHEAPER BY THE DOZEN, by the *Gilbreths*—all JOURNAL firsts. And leave it to *Hugh Kahler* to point out that no other women's magazine is represented by a single fiction feature on any list; further, that no other large-circulation magazine is represented by a single fiction feature on any list. Further bragging about how our JOURNAL material gets around: in the past 5 years, 65 LHJ features have been republished as books, of which 33 appeared on the best-seller lists

Ethel Waters

"Enchanting" is the word for Markova—she seems to float.

If there's a day here when there are dreamy-eyed expressions all around the Workshop and you keep catching the word "enchanting," the chances are **Markova** danced the night before at the ballet. In her Giselle this season she literally seems to float.

Following a request for the five works of fiction and the five nonfiction which they would recommend from the current crop, thirty-one literary . critics of the country's leading newspapers recently had their listings published in the Saturday Review of Literature. Twenty critics put down *John*

and 20 were chosen by book clubs; women's magazine coming nearest to this record had 25 books, 7 best sellers, 3 as book-club choices.

Peter Pan is a theater treat for all ages, played so winsomely, as it is now, by **Jean Arthur.** Maybe because it reminds us of our own childhood, maybe because it is all that we like most to believe about childhood. But in a world of dialectic materialism, all we can say is, "Thank God for James Barrie!"

Ethel Waters is an artist, and in her new book HIS EYE IS ON THE SPARROW her conquering of poverty, injustice and squalor is a great and heartening story. But so long as there are slums and injustice and squalor, there will be many who will not survive and triumph as she has done. "It's been such a hard, long road I traveled. I came up from so low down. Others who read what I've done may be encouraged. I want them to say 'If Ethel Waters, a colored woman, could do that, I can too.'"

Now that warm weather has set in, **Mary Martin** tells us she really looks forward to that shampoo she gives herself at eight performances a week in the smash hit, SOUTH PACIFIC, while singing I'm Gonna Wash That Man Right Outta My Hair. Furthermore, she feels that all the women who wonder what that daily drenching of soap and water must do to her hair should know her hair has never been nicer; back in her

dressing room, she just dries it and applies a little lanolin and, for what has by now become the most talked-about hair wash in history, she uses any ordinary shampoo. Something else her audiences don't know is that Miss Martin cuts her own hair, every two weeks, and every three weeks gives herself a permanent. But not on the stage. She does that at home.

Richard Rodgers, whose SOUTH PACIFIC music has become an obbligato to American life, has been asked why he doesn't write more songs. "If I wrote all the time" he says, "I suppose I *could* turn out a song every day, but what would I do with them? Who'd want them?"

A shampoo eight times a week.

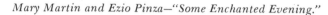

Mary Martin and Ezio Pinza—"Some Enchanted Evening."

Scene in that earlier Rodgers and Hammerstein milestone—OKLAHOMA! Remember "the surrey with the fringe on top"?

Richard Rodgers

251

DELIVERANCE

Rebecca West

One autumn evening a woman in her early forties walked along the platform of the Terminal Station in Rome and boarded a *wagon-lit* in the Paris Express. She sat down on the made-up bed in her compartment, took off her small, perfect, inconspicuous hat, and looked about her with an air of annoyance. It was a long time since she had traveled by rail, and she had been pushed to it against her will, because there had not been a seat free on any of the planes leaving Rome that day or the next. But this was the least of her worries, and she wasted no time on it, but set about arranging her passport and her tickets in order to have them ready when the *wagon-lit* attendant arrived. This required close scrutiny, for although she was a Frenchwoman named Madame Rémy, another impression was conveyed by her passport, her tickets and the labels on her luggage, and she had to remind herself what that impression was, for only a few hours before she had been yet a third person.

Such inconsistencies, however, never made her nervous. They were unlikely to be noticed because she herself was so unnoticeable. She was neither tall nor short, dark nor fair, handsome nor ugly. She left a pleasant impression on those she met in her quiet passage through the world, and then these people forgot her. She had no remarkable attributes except some which were without outward sign, such as a command of six languages and an unusually good memory.

When the door opened, Madame Rémy had not quite finished getting her papers out of a handbag which had more than the usual number of pockets and flaps in it, and some very intricate fastenings. Without raising her head, she asked the attendant to wait a moment, in her excellent Italian, which, just for verisimilitude, had a slight Florentine accent. Then, as he did not answer, she looked up sharply. She had only time to remark that he was wearing not the uniform of a *wagon-lit* attendant but a dark gray suit with a checked blue muffler, and that his pale face was shining with sweat. Then the door banged between them. She did not follow him, because she was as highly disciplined as any soldier, and she knew that her first concern must be with the tiny ball of paper which he had dropped in her lap.

When she had unrolled it she read a typewritten message: "A man is traveling on this train under orders to kill you." She rolled it up again and went into the corridor and stood there, looking out at the crowds on the ill-lit platform. It would

Rebecca West

have been unwise to leave the train. A clever man with a knife, she calculated, could do his work among the shadows and get away quite easily. Several times she had to step back into her compartment, to get out of the way of passengers who were coming aboard, and at these, if they were male, she looked with some interest. She was standing thus, looking up with a noncommittal glance, neither too blank nor too keenly interested, at a tall man in a tweed overcoat and wondering if he were so tall as to be specially memorable, and therefore ineligible as an assassin, when she heard shouts from the platform.

The tall man came to a halt, and she crushed past him and stood beside him, looking out through the wide corridor window at a scene still as a painted picture. Everybody was motionless, even the porters with their luggage barrows, while four men made their way back to the platform gates, at a quiet and steady pace, two in front, and two behind who were walking backward. Their faces were darkened by masks; and all held revolvers which they pointed at the crowd. The man beside Madame Rémy made a scandalized and bluff noise which told her that he was not an assassin, and at that moment the train began to move. He went on his way to his compartment and left Madame Rémy standing alone at the window, waiting to see what had happened at the end of the platform. But she saw nothing unusual till the train was leaving the station behind it and sliding out into the open evening. Then her eye was caught by the last iron pillar that held up the platform roof. A man was embracing it as if it were a beloved woman to whom he was bidding farewell. His suit was dark gray; and as he slid to the ground and toppled over and fell face upward, it could be seen that he was wearing a checked blue muffler.

Madame Rémy went back to her compartment and said a prayer for his soul. She looked at her hands with some distaste, because they were shaking, and took the little ball of paper out of her bag and read the message again. This was not because she feared she had forgotten it, or thought she had overlooked any of its implications, but because it interested her as a technician to see if there were any distinguishing marks in the type faces which recalled any typed letters that she had received before. Then she thought of all the things it would be sensible to do, such as ringing for the attendant and showing him the message, out in the corridor, in front of some open door, in the hearing of some other passenger, preferably a woman, and she decided to do none of them.

She said aloud, "I am a lucky woman." Leaning back her head against the cushions, she repeated, "How very lucky I am."

There had seemed no way out of the wretchedness that was all around her. She was under no illusion as to the reason why the doctor she had consulted in Rome concerning a slight but persistent symptom had begged her to go into hospital for an X-ray examination the next day and had urged her; when he found she was resolved to go back to Paris, not to let one day pass after she got there without seeking a surgeon. The thing was in her father's family, and she was familiar with its method of approach.

She was, moreover, in financial difficulties to which there could be no end. She had loved her dead husband very much, so much that she felt that she could deny nothing to the child of his first marriage. But Madeleine was sullen and unaffectionate, had early insisted on marrying a worthless young man and had three children already and might have more; and her only remarkable characteristic was a capacity for getting into debt without having anything to show for it in purchased goods. Madame Rémy really did not see how she could meet this last crop of bills without selling either the few jewels remaining to her, which were those she wore so constantly, except when she was on duty, that they seemed part of her body, or her little house in Passy, where she had spent all her married life. In either case it would be a joyless sacrifice, for Madeleine had nothing of her father in her.

Also, it was evident to Madame Rémy that her long-standing friendship with Claude was over. Just before she left Paris she had heard again the rumor that he was going to marry the Armenian heiress, and his denial had left her in no doubt that they were going to part before very long, perhaps even without tenderness. That would take from the last five years of her life the value which she had believed made them remarkable. She had always thought that she had taken up her peculiar work because she and a distinguished member of the French Foreign Office had fallen in love with each other, and that had made it a romantic adventure. But now she suspected that a member of the French Foreign Office had had a love affair with her because she had an aptitude for a certain peculiar kind of work; and though she recognized that even if this were so, Claude had formed some real affection for her, and that she owed him gratitude for much charming companionship, she knew that she would never be able to look back on their relations without a sense of humiliation. Even her work, in which she had hoped to find her main interest as her life went on, would now be darkened in her mind by association with a long pretense, and her own gullibility. There was nothing at the end of her journey except several sorts of pain, so if the journey had no end there was no reason for grief.

When she had worked it out to her final satisfaction she found that the *wagon-lit* attendant was standing in front of her, asking for her tickets and passport. She gave them to him slowly, feeling a certain sense of luxury, because his presence meant her last hope of life, and she was not taking it. They wished each other good night, and then she called him back, because it had occurred to her that it would be hardly fair if he had to go without his tip in the morning just because she was dead. Agents were trained never to make themselves memorable by giving more or less than the standard tip, and she acted according to habit, but regretted it, for surely the occasion called for a little lavishness. As she explained to him that she was giving him the tip in case they were rushed at the other end, she noted his casual air. He was evidently to be the second last man she was to see, not the last.

Once she was alone, she burned the message in her washbasin, and pulled up the window blind so that she could look at the bright villages and the dark countryside that raced by. She thought of the smell of anesthetics that hangs about the vestibules of clinics; and she thought of the last time she had met Madame Couthier in the Champs Élysées and how Madame Couthier had looked through her as if they had never been at school together, and how it had turned out that Madeleine had run up a huge bill with young Couthier, who was finding it hard to make his way as an interior decorator. She thought of an evening, just before she had heard the rumor about the Armenian heiress, when Claude had driven her back from dinner at Ville-d'Avray, and she had rested her head against his shoulder for a minute when the road was dark, and had kissed his sleeve. Claude and she were the same age, yet she felt hot with shame when she remembered this, as if she had been an old woman doting on a boy.

She pulled down the blind, and began to make very careful preparations for the night. Her large case was on the rack, and she did not care to ring for the attendant and ask him to move it for her, lest somebody else should come in his stead and the attack be precipitated before she was ready for it. But she was obliged to get it down, because she had packed in it her best nightgown, which was made of pleated white chiffon. For a reason she had never understood she had always liked to carry it with her when she went on a specially dangerous enterprise; and now she saw that it had been a sensible thing to do. It was very pleasant to put it on after she had undressed and washed very carefully, rubbing herself down with toilet water, as she could not have a bath. After she had made up her face again and recoiffed her hair, she lay down between the sheets. Then it occurred to her that she had not unpacked her bedroom slippers, and she made a move to get out of bed before she realized that she need not take the trouble.

She turned out the big light in the compartment ceiling, and left on only the little

---

Hope is a light diet, but very stimulating.   **BALZAC**

---

reading lamp at the head of her bed. She had not locked the door. Her careful toilette had made her tired; and indeed she had been working very hard for some days, preparing all the papers that were now safe in her embassy. She thought of Madeleine and Claude, and bleakly realized that she had no desire to see either of them ever again. She tried to remember something pleasant, and found that for that she had to go back to the days when her husband was alive. It had been delightful when he came back in the evenings from his office, particularly at this very time of year, in the autumn, when he brought her sweet-smelling bouquets of bronze and gold chrysanthemums, and after tea they did not light the lamps, and sat with the firelight playing on the Japanese gilt wallpaper. It had been delightful, too, when they went for holidays in Switzerland and skied in winter and climbed in summer, and he always was astounded and pleased by her courage. But dear Louis was not at the end of her journey. There was nothing waiting for her there but Madeleine and Claude, and the smell that hangs about the vestibules of clinics.

The train slowed down at a station. There were cries, lurchings and trampings in the corridors, long periods of silence and immobility, a thin blast on a trumpet; and the train jerked forward again. That happened a second time, and a third. But still the man who was traveling under orders did not come to carry them out.

Madame Rémy turned out the reading lamp and prayed to the darkness that he might hurry; and then for a little, retreating again from the thought of Madeleine and Claude to the memory of her husband, she passed into something nearly a dream. But she was fully awake as soon as someone tried the lock of the door with a wire. It was as if a bucket had been emptied over her, a bucket filled, not with water but with fear. There was not a part of her which was not drenched with terror. She disliked this emotion, which she had never felt before except in a slight degree, just as much as added to the zest of an enterprise. To escape from this shuddering abasement she reminded herself that she wanted to die, she had chosen to die, and she sat up and cried, *"Entrez! Entrate!"*

The door swung open, and softly closed again. There followed a silence, and, feeling fear coming on her again, she switched on the light. It was a relief to her that the man who was standing with his back to the door did not wear the uniform of a *wagon-lit* attendant, and that he was the sort of person who would be selected for such a mission. He was young and lean and spectacled, and wore a soft hat crushed down over his brows and a loose greatcoat with the collar turned up, in a way that she tenderly noted as amateurish. It would be very hard for him to get away from the scene of a crime without arousing suspicion. There was also a sign that he was the man for whom she was waiting, in the woodenness of his features and his posture. He knew quite well that what he was doing was wrong, and to persuade himself that it was right, he had had to stop the natural flow of not only his thoughts and feelings but his muscles.

Yet he made no move to commit the violent act for which this rigidity had been a preparation. Simply he stood there, staring at her. She thought, *Poor child, he is very young,* and remained quite still, fearing to do anything which might turn him from his resolution. But he went on staring at her. *Is he never going to do it?* she asked herself, wondering at the same time whether it was a cord or a knife that he was fingering in the pocket of his greatcoat. It occurred to her that with such a slow-moving assailant she had still a very good chance of making a fight for her life and saving it. But then there came to her the look of surgical instruments on a tray, the whine that came into Madeleine's voice when she spoke of the inevitability of debt, and the fluency, which now recalled to her a conjurer's patter, of Claude's love-making; and she was conscious of the immense distance that divided her from the only real happiness she had ever known. She flung open her arms in invitation to the assassin, smiling at him to assure him that she felt no ill will against him, that all she asked of him was to do his work quickly.

Suddenly he stepped backward, and she found herself looking at the door with a stare as fixed as his own. She had made an absurd mistake. This was simply a fellow passenger who had mistaken the number of his compartment, and all the signs she had read in his appearance were fictions of her own mind, excited by the typewritten message. It was a disappointment, but she did not allow it to depress her. When she thought of the man in the dark gray suit with the checked blue muffler, sliding down the pillar and turning over as he reached the ground, it was as a child might think of an adult who had made it a promise. She contemplated in sorrow and wonder the fact that a stranger had given up his life because he wished her well, and switched out the light and again said a prayer for him into the darkness. Then, although she had no reason to suppose that the man who was traveling under orders would come sooner or later to carry them out, she grew drowsy.

"What, not stay awake even to be assassinated?" she muttered to her pillow, and laughed, and was swallowed up by sleep, deep sleep, such as had often come on her at the end of a long day on the mountains.

The next morning a spectacled young man, wearing a soft hat and a loose greatcoat, who had made his way back to Rome while the sun came up, stood in a hotel room and gave a disappointing report to his superior.

train he must have warned her, this woman was not at all frightened. She had left her door unlocked, and when she saw me she showed no fear at all. Indeed," he said gloomily, "she was evidently a loose woman. Though she was in bed her face was painted, and her hair was done up as if she were going to a ball, and it was really quite extraordinary—she even stretched out her arms and smiled at me. I think," he asserted, blushing faintly, "that if I had cared to stay in her compartment I would have received quite a warm welcome."

His superior expressed an unfavorable opinion regarding the morals of all bourgeois women, but had his doubts, and made certain inquiries. As a result the spectacled young man was doomed not to realize what was at that time his dearest ambition, for

JENNIFER

"Maybe you want to grow up and get married—but, frankly, I'd rather get twenty-five cents every time I do the dishes!"

He said, "Madame Rémy was not on the train. It was all a mistake. There was one woman who answered to the description, and I went into her compartment, but I found she was quite a different sort of person. She was not at all haggard and worn; indeed, she looked much younger than the age you gave me, and she was very animated. And though we know that if Ferrero found Madame Rémy on the

he was never given another chance to commit a political assassination. He regretted this much less than he would have owned. Even then, standing in the golden sunshine of a Roman morning, he was not really disturbed because the night had been so innocent.

At that moment Madame Rémy was sitting in the restaurant car of the Paris Express, eating breakfast. She could have had

it brought to her in her compartment, but she had felt a desire to have it where the windows were wider and she could see more of the countryside. Her first pot of coffee had been so good that she had ordered a second, and she was spreading the butter on a roll, smiling a little, because it seemed so absurd that after such a night she should have awakened to find herself suddenly freed from the wretchedness that had hung about her for so long. Certainly she had lost none of her troubles; but they no longer appalled her. There came to mind the names of several among her friends who had survived serious operations. As for Madeleine's debts, if nobody paid them it might help the poor silly child to grow up; and the wisest thing, even the loyalest thing, for her stepmother to do was to keep the jewels and the house that Louis Rémy had given her and leave them intact to Madeleine's children. It might well be true that she could no longer support the desperate nature of her present work, but there was no need for her days to be idle, for the great dressmaker, Mariol, had always had a liking for her and had more than once offered her a post in his business. And there was no need for her to think of Claude. If she wanted to think of someone who was not there any more, she could remember Louis.

Some other names occurred to her: the names of people who had not survived operations. But they cast no darkness on her mind; she was conscious only of a certain grandeur, and they went from her. For all her interest was given to looking out the window at what she was seeing again only because of some inexplicable carelessness on the part of those who were usually careful.

Now the train was running toward the mountains, and was passing through a valley in the foothills. There were cliffs, steel-gray where the sun caught them, dark blue in the shadow, rising to heights patterned with the first snows, glistening sugar-white under the sharp blue sky. At the foot of the cliffs a line of poplars, golden with autumn, marked the course of a broad and shallow river racing over gray shingle; and between the river and the railway track was a field where a few corn shocks, like dried, gesticulating men, were still standing among some trailing morning mists. Across this field, through the mists, an old man in a dark blue shirt and light blue trousers was leading a red cart, drawn by two oxen the color of the coffee and milk in her cup. Deliberately the two beasts trod, so slowly that they seemed to sleep between paces, so dutifully that if they were dreaming it must be of industry. There was nothing very beautiful in the scene, yet it was wonderful, and it existed, it would go on being there when she was far away.

As the train met the mountains and passed into a tunnel, she closed her eyes so that she could go on seeing the cliffs and the snow and the poplars, the man and his cart and his oxen. Amazed by what the world looked like when one had thought it lost and had found it again, she sat quite still, in a trance of contentment, while the train carried her on to the end of her journey.

PICASSO'S CHILDREN: "Claude and Paloma."
From the Spanish-born "artist of the century," as the art world has begun to name Pablo Picasso, comes this newest, 1950, masterpiece, an oil portrait on metal of his two youngest. He has two other children—Paul and Maia.

THE BEST KINGS

Tsu Hsi, Empress of China,
brought educational, governmental reforms.

The Queen of Sheba—who
lived to become part of a religion.

Catherine the Great of Russia wrote a wise,
world-celebrated code of laws.

Maria Theresa, Empress of Austria,
combined devotion to duty and her
husband.

Queen Salote of Tonga. Her
South Sea kingdom is world's oldest
monarchy.

Juliana, university-educated mot
of four girls, is Netherlands quee

Cleopatra, Queen of the Nile,
worked for the union of Egypt
with Rome.

Isabella of Spain united her country,
subsidized discovery of the New World.

Anne of Austria saved the
throne of France for her son Louis XIV.

Queen Wilhelmina of the Netherlands
governed with wisdom and foresight.

Victoria, symbol of Great Britain's
Golden Age, virtue and romance.

Elizabeth I led Great Britain to its first
proud eminence on land and sea.

A new, young queen, lovely as eternal
hope, the living symbol that unites millions
of free subjects in one heart, belongs to
England, the British Commonwealth and
Empire. And because she also represents
mankind's loftiest vision of Ideal Woman,
Wife and Mother, she belongs also to all
the world.

"Famous have been the reigns of our
queens," Winston Churchill has noted.
"Some of the greatest periods in our history
have unfolded under their scepter." Nearly
four hundred years ago, the first Elizabeth

HAVE BEEN QUEENS

"Elizabeth Alexandra Mary is now . . . become Queen Elizabeth II, by the grace of God, Queen of this realm and all her other realms and territories, head of the Commonwealth, Defender of the Faith. . . ."

rhapsodic Irishman has described Elizabeth's eyes as "deep and blue as the sunny sea, large and lustrous and shining, but sometimes darkening with warning of a storm."

Elizabeth II must sacrifice to the Crown many of the normal pleasures of a young wife and mother, but she believes she can pamper her husband and children at no expense to duty. Adored and adoring Prince Consort Philip is always at her side. Bonnie Prince Charlie and Princess Anne will not be deprived of the usual romps with "mummy" and "papa."

"If I can't manage to look after my own family," Elizabeth reasons, "how will it ever be possible for me to see to the interests of a whole people?"

Her talent for organization and firsthand knowledge of people and their problems will help. Her simple grace and warmhearted charm stir all who meet her. "She instinctively does and says the right thing at the right time," one of her former ladies in waiting said of the new sovereign.

Elizabeth has learned to know her people by constant personal contact and plans to continue it. The most successful queens in history, she points out, did not rule from ivory towers. Coming to the throne at twenty-five, the same age as the first Queen Bess, she promises to be one of Britain's greatest queens. In her bright spirit she seems to bear the faith of a troubled world.

of England took over a kingdom riddled by political turmoil and military losses and brought it to the grandeur and genius of the Elizabethan Age. Not long ago, as royalty counts the years, another woman ruler—Victoria—wore the crown through turbulent times into an era of the greatest prosperity Britain has ever known.

Now, in a barren hour, to the delicately blond little princess, Lilibet, falls the task of leading her diverse and widely scattered subjects. For the difficult job ahead of her she has a firm will and steady gaze. A

"The other day I told her
a joke, and she actually
fell off the couch laughing."
ALEC GUINNESS *(The Swan)*

WHAT MAKES

"She's a refreshing change
from all these sexballs."
GARY COOPER *(High Noon)*

"She will probably go through
life being completely
misunderstood, because she usually
says completely what she thinks."
CARY GRANT *(To Catch a Thief)*

"She's really quite a sweet little girl
but I didn't fall in love with
her—I happen to be married to
quite a delicious girl myself."
STEWART GRANGER *(Green Fire)*

HOWELL CONANT

"How she can concentrate!"
WILLIAM HOLDEN *(The Bridges at Toko-Ri
and The Country Girl)*

"If she had married one of
these phony Hollywood characters,
I'd have formed a
committee of vigilantes."
JAMES STEWART *(Rear Window)*

"I knew her father before she was born,
and it still seems strange to me to hear an
Olympic rowing champion like Jack Kelly
identified as Grace Kelly's father."

PAUL DOUGLAS *(Fourteen Hours and Green Fire)*

GRACE KELLY DIFFERENT?

Margaret Parton

As she takes on her greatest role to date with a *real* prince for a leading man, the views of some of the men Grace Kelly leaves behind tell about the girl who caught the world's most eligible bachelor.

James Stewart, who played opposite Grace Kelly in "Rear Window":

"Hollywood just didn't know what to make of Grace. She didn't fit the pattern. You're supposed to be discovered behind some counter in a drugstore or a luncheonette, see? Then the producer brings you to Hollywood and says, 'I'll make you a star, but I'll have to pull your teeth out and put caps on them, and dye your hair and tell you where to stand and how to talk and what to do in your spare time.' So the little girl gets to be a star, but she's basically without confidence because she doesn't really know anything about acting. To cover up she does the hail-fellow-well-met act, slaps electricians on the back and plays jokes around the set. And the publicity people think this is fine, and put out all kinds of stories about the little cutie who doesn't know anything about acting but who's such a good egg. Grace wasn't like that at all. She didn't grow up in a garret. She wasn't discovered in a drugstore. She had a nice family in Philadelphia and she was given a good education. When she wanted to go on the stage they didn't throw up their hands in horror (the way families are supposed to do), but if you can imagine it, they helped her! She had training at the American Academy of Dramatic Arts in New York. Then she picked up more training and experience on the stage and in television. She kept on studying—she took ballet, she learned how to talk and walk and move beautifully.

"By the time she came to Hollywood she was a finished product. When she was called in front of the cameras, she knew her job. Then when she was finished she'd just go quietly away, and read or study.

"Nobody knew what to make of her. The publicity people didn't know what to write about her. Girls who just sit quietly aren't good copy—unless they get engaged to a prince, of course. So they had to hang this tag 'aloof' on her, for lack of anything else. Of course it was only a publicity tag! Grace, *cold?* Why, Grace is anything but cold. She has those big warm eyes—and . . . well, if you ever have played a love scene with her, you know she's not cold.

"She had it in her to become another Garbo, if she kept on the way she was going. Garbo played everything: tragedies like 'Camille,' comedies like 'Ninotchka,' romance like "Queen Christina." Grace

could have played all those roles too."

William Holden, who played opposite Grace Kelly in "The Bridges at Toko-Ri" and "The Country Girl":

"Popularity goes in eras, and depends on the mood of the world. In the late twenties and early thirties the grand movie stars like Norma Shearer and Joan Crawford provided the elegance and glamour that people wanted. Then came war, chaos, economic turmoil, religious insecurity—all those things. All this created a mood in which the emphasis was on bodily pleasures and excitements. For a long time our actresses were popular in proportion to the size of their breastworks. Phoniness didn't matter.

"But now I think the world wants something else. I hate to impose this responsibility on Grace—it just makes it harder for her in her new life—but I think she had become a symbol of dignity and all the good things that are in us all. I do think she has an honesty and a dignity, and I think the world has to get back to honesty and dignity, and *wants* to get back to honesty and dignity. Women like Grace Kelly and Audrey Hepburn help us to believe in the innate dignity of man—and today that is what we desperately need to believe in.

"Grace could do this because she had refinement and poise. She had good judgment, good taste and a tremendous ability to concentrate. She still has."

Cary Grant, who played opposite Grace Kelly in "To Catch a Thief":

"Grace never drenches anyone in unwelcome good will. You know what I mean? She doesn't force herself on you. Even now, she will probably go through life being completely misunderstood, since she usually says completely what she means.

"She owns a controlling interest in her own mind—and if you ever hear of her throwing herself away, I predict she'll be taking careful aim. . . . I wrote that about her in the days when she was still playing the field.

"I've made some trips around the country, giving speeches and answering questions from the audience. There was always sure to be someone—usually a woman—who asked me if Grace was really as cool as she seemed. And I always told them I didn't know what the word meant, except in relation to climate. Certainly I don't think it has anything to do with Grace.

"What they think of as coolness is really poise. Somebody asked me if this was because her family was wealthy. But poise

"I want an ordinary woman who will give me an extraordinary feeling." Prince Rainier III

doesn't come from wealth, it comes from inner security. And that comes from confidence, and confidence is based on knowledge and study.

"Grace is extremely vulnerable in being entirely herself, both off screen and on. But in all her roles Grace had to be herself, to look like herself.

"She surprises people because they are unaccustomed to reserve, just as they are unaccustomed to the truth. And Grace will not compromise with hypocrisy. She has the courage to be vulnerable. I believe all religions are good, and I believe Grace's religion has played a large part in her character, her integrity.

"Actresses have to work hard. They get up at dawn and rehearse scenes over and over again—and a lot of the young stars complain about it. 'So what?' I tell them. They've only got a million dollars and four swimming pools!

"But Grace never complained about anything. 'In Catch a Thief,' we had a scene where I had to grab her arms hard, while she was fighting me, and push her against a wall. We went through that scene eight or nine times, but Hitchcock still wanted it again. Grace went back alone behind the door where the scene started, and just by chance I happened to catch a glimpse of her massaging her wrists and grimacing in pain. But a moment later she came out and did the scene again—she never complained to me or to Hitch about how much her arms were hurting.

"She isn't one of those girls who waste time by being angry. She was always patient on the set, even when hairdressers and make-up men were fussing over her between takes of a difficult scene. If a dress didn't fit, well, it just didn't fit, and that was that, with no hysterics. So of course they got the dress fixed for her faster than they would have for a girl who was screaming about it. No wonder she was popular with the wardrobe and make-up people, even if she didn't go around slapping them on the back.

"Grace's acting looks slow. Good art always seems easy, and the slowness makes what she does seem easy. That's why she was a great champion.

"Also, she looks extremely well, talks well, and knows how to keep your attention on her. The great ones—Valentino and Garbo particularly—have always been able to do this, sometimes without doing anything more than moving their head slowly from right to left. Such people have no insecurities. Perhaps their inner security comes from a happy childhood, such as Grace had, or perhaps it has been trained in by years of hard work. Ingrid Bergman has that same quality of security and composure too. Such people have no temperament—temperament is insecurity.

"From the actor's point of view she was so easy to work with, it was a delight. From the producer's point of view she knew her business, she learned quickly if there was something new to learn, and she didn't slow things down by temper fits. She did her job well and she saved the studio money.

"No matter how technical the requirements were, Grace Kelly already understood all about them. I imagine the same thing will be true in Monaco."

Gary Cooper, who played with Grace Kelly in "High Noon":

"I first met her when I visited the set where 'Fourteen Hours' was being shot. She had a bit part in the picture, her first movie. I thought she looked pretty and different, and that maybe she'd be somebody. She looked educated, and as if she came from a nice family. She was certainly a refreshing change from all these sexballs we'd been seeing so much of.

"I'd like to use the word 'lady,' except it's been so overworked ever since 'Edie was a lady' and all that stuff.

"It was easy to work with her, even though her role was a thankless one. She seemed serious about her acting, keyed up, and she had good manners and a sense of humor.

"Once, when we were on location in

Sonoma, in Northern California, she was required to ride behind runaway horses in a rickety wagon. But she went through it all without turning a hair.

"Sometimes Grace and I and some of the others would drive through the mountains looking for a steak dinner—she loves steak. She was always fun to be with.

"You know, we Hollywood people are all on the defensive. We're different from the public idea of us, and the public makes it hard for us to keep on being ourselves. Really, it takes two things to make a good actor or actress: ability and humanity. Sometimes the public forgets about the humanity part.

"Grace is pretty and nice. She was a good actress and she deserves everything good she gets. I wish her luck."

Paul Douglas, who played with Grace Kelly in "Fourteen Hours" and "Green Fire":

"I've got a different angle on her because I knew her father before she was born. It still seems strange to me to hear an Olympic rowing champion like Jack Kelly identified as 'Grace Kelly's father.' I used to see her in New York sometimes after she'd grown up, around Sardi's or places like that. Then she had a bit part in 'Fourteen Hours.' She seemed like a nice girl, but she was always Jack Kelly's daughter to me.

"Now, of course, Grace is big stuff, and until the prince appeared the producers were all bidding for her. They wanted her because she had something we haven't seen since Irene Dunne came along. She was a young *lady*. She'd stayed that way, too, completely herself. She didn't go Hollywood, and I don't suppose she'll 'go Monaco,' if there is any such thing.

"There was bound to be a lot of gossip about Grace because she committed the unforgivable sin in Hollywood—she minded her own business. But for that very reason, the talk couldn't touch her.

"By the way, her brother's a rowing champion, too, you know, just like Jack Kelly."

Stewart Granger, who played with Grace Kelly in "Green Fire":

"Alas, Grace and I were together in 'Green Fire,' a picture I've been trying to forget ever since. I remember one time when we had to go out in a little motorboat during a storm. I was shaking like a leaf, I was so scared. But Grace stepped into the boat and said calmly, 'Well, if we have to, let's go.' I got in, too, but I remember thinking at the time, Most women would be screaming like mad if they had to do this.

"She has a mental attitude which says well, there's nothing she can do about a bad situation, she's perfectly calm. If there's something she *can* do about it, then she's not calm. It's a wonderful philosophy of life.

"Really, though, I know her very little. While we were in Colombia, three quarters of her mind was in France. She'd been promised 'To Catch a Thief' if she did this one first, and like the rest of us, she was just getting through a job which had to be done. I really think she was planning her Riviera wardrobe most of the time. But I

Never Underestimate the Power of a Woman!

do know she's a nice, quiet, co-operative and very lovely girl.

"Far from lacking emotion, she's very sensitive. As everyone knows, after you're a success, that's when you start getting clawed. After Grace became a success some of the press started clawing her—linking her name romantically with her leading men, and writing all sorts of nonsense about her. This was all before the prince, of course.

"One night when this was going on she came to dinner with my wife and me, and she started talking about all this. She was very sweet and naïve—she's not a tough dame at all. 'I don't understand why they're doing this to me,' she kept saying. 'I haven't done anything to hurt anyone.'

"She's really quite a sweet girl. But I didn't fall in love with her, because I happen to be married to quite a delicious girl myself."

Alec Guinness, who played with Grace Kelly in "The Swan":

"It's very difficult to say exactly what her quality is. I'm mad about her. She's enchanting! But I'm not sure why. She has a kind of balanced thing. She's not just sitting in a Beverly Hills mansion, dreaming about being an actress. She *is* an actress. That is, she was, and I hope always will be.

"She has great talent, great understanding, perfect timing. In 'The Swan' she played the part of an impoverished princess looking for a husband, and I was a prince, looking for a bride. Odd, isn't it? When we met she had to make a kind of gauche curtsy, and bring her head up on the point of my chin, almost knocking me out. She did it with perfection—it takes good acting to make gaucheness graceful, you know.

"Also, Grace has such spontaneity. I think she's very high-strung; her reactions are always spontaneous and warm. The

---

Definition of a gentleman: He has the will to put himself in the place of others; the horror of forcing others into positions from which he himself would recoil; the power to do what seems to him to be right, without considering what others may say or think.

—JOHN GALSWORTHY

---

other day I told her a joke while she was sitting on a couch, and she actually fell off the couch from laughing. No matter where she lives, Grace will never lose her quality of spontaneity.

"She doesn't talk about herself very much, and of course her reserve is part of her charm. Sometimes I saw her waiting on the set, just looking into space, and I asked her, 'Grace, are you feeling all right?' Then she came to, but always with a little start of surprise, as if she had been far away. Maybe with the real prince, now I come to think of it.

"Yes, she's reserved, and I think diffident.

Painting by Gladys Rockmore Davis for THE CLOAK *by Isak Dinesen.*

Sometimes I think she didn't quite stand up for her rights enough. In a way, this sort of thing makes a man feel protective—goodness knows why, because Grace can perfectly well take care of herself.

"Around her, one finds oneself being careful of language, and things like that. Not that she minds—once on the set I let loose a mild swear word, without thinking that she was present. Oh dear, I thought, and flicked her a glance. But it was all right —it's just that she'd never do it herself.

"She's a truly creative and cultured person; her friends are never phony—they're creative people. She's interested in art and literature as well as the theater, and she already knows Europe. She's a . . . well, she's a *balanced* person.

"Many people in our business are selfish —but Grace is different. But this isn't it, really, nor the fact that she's a good actress, nor that she's blond and pretty, nor that she's going to be a princess. It's just, oh . . . she's *special!*"

WHAT HUSBANDS DON'T KNOW ABOUT SEX

Abraham Stone, M.D.

The famous marriage counselor answers questions asked by readers:

Human behavior is generally influenced by two main factors: by nature and nurture, by heredity and environment. In sex behavior, environment plays a dominant role. What we learn from our parents, from the children in the neighborhood, from the stories we read, the pictures we see, the songs we sing affects us profoundly. These environmental influences can be instructive and constructive, or they can be destructive and handicap us for a long time in our sexual roles in marriage.

Although women are more likely to become inhibited and restricted in their sex behavior as a result of early training, men, too, in spite of the greater freedom given them, are apt to suffer from faulty parental teaching and attitudes. Many parents who readily encourage the general curiosity of their children, and are ever ready to dispense information on all kinds of topics, become reticent, embarrassed and even threatening when it comes to sex. The child then comes to regard any interest in sex or any sexual activity with the feeling that there is something vaguely wrong and shameful about it. Particularly harmful are threats of punishment for childhood sex curiosity or sex practices. The feelings engendered may persist into adult life and color the man's behavior for a long time. Even though he may later become intellectually free from these fears and anxieties, he may remain emotionally bound by them to the detriment of his sexual functioning.

Most of the early childhood training lies in the hands of the mother, and she, I would say, will probably have the greatest influence on the sex attitudes of the boy, as of the girl. Later on, however, the boy will identify himself more and more with the father and will endeavor to accept and adopt his viewpoints. If the father has himself failed to develop mature attitudes toward sex, he is likely to instill in the boy either a sense of its sinfulness and its dangers or else an attitude of flippancy and casualness, neither of which will help to foster sound viewpoints about the role of the husband as a sex partner in marriage. If the father, however, is intelligent and understanding and patient, he can help guide his son toward a mature love relationship.

There are some boys who fail to identify themselves with father and remain attached to "mamma." A boy who has been overprotected by a dominant mother, who has remained unduly bound to her emotionally, is likely to encounter difficulties in his growing up and especially in developing an adequate and sound sexual potential.

Satisfactory sex behavior does not come instinctively or automatically either to women or to men. It is a learned process which develops with understanding and experience.

The main reason husbands are supposed to be better informed about sex than their wives is the tacit acceptance in our society that most men will have had sexual experiences before marriage, and that they will therefore be able to teach and guide their young wives later on. In practice, however, this does not necessarily hold true. There are many young men who do not have premarital sex experiences, and even those who do may still know little of the sexual needs of their wives. I have seen any number of men who apparently had learned a good deal about physical techniques of the sex relation, yet had little understanding of the psychological and emotional implications of the sex act for the woman. The average young husband is therefore not necessarily an informed sexual guide for his wife. Husband and wife will have to learn together through practice and experimentation, and establish a good sexual relationship on the basis of their own mutual understanding and adjustment.

The experience which a man receives from a casual relation hardly prepares him for sex life with his young and presumably inexperienced wife. He is liable to waver, as Havelock Ellis once pointed out, between two equally mistaken courses of action. Either he will attempt to mold his wife much too rapidly into the sexual pattern he is most accustomed to, or he will treat her with too much concern and fail to arouse or to gratify her erotic needs.

In a casual premarital relation, a man usually approaches the woman primarily on a physical level, and hardly associates it with affection or a feeling of love. His young wife, on the other hand, is likely to regard her sex life with her husband as a part of the total love relationship, and she will look for tenderness, for affection, for consideration on his part.

The husband who has had casual experiences before marriage may fail to realize that it takes time for his bride to overcome the awkwardness and sometimes the discomfort of the first experiences, that it takes time for her to be freed from her accumulated inhibitions, and that she needs above all a "climate of love" for a satisfactory response.

In sexual activity, the male is generally the initiator. He takes the more aggressive role, while the female is the more passive and receptive. This passivity is, in our culture, reinforced by training, education and conventions. A wife's erotic desires, furthermore, may remain dormant at first, developing only after marital relations have been established for some time. Then again, a man can function sexually only when he is physically aroused, while a woman may be able to accept a man even though she has little desire. Hence the frequency of relations will normally be controlled largely by the needs of the husband. However, a wife should not always be passive and always wait for her husband to come to her. If by word or gesture she shows her desire for him, if she "invites" him at times, he will be deeply pleased, and his feelings for her will be greatly increased.

Statistical studies show a marked variation in the frequency of marital relations, ranging from once a month or less to once daily or more. Much depends upon the physical conditions, the emotional states and the ages of the couple, especially the age of the husband. On an average, men under 35 will have relations in marriage about two to three times a week. After 40 years of age, the frequency gradually diminishes to an average of one and a half times per week, and to about once a week after the age of 55. In any of these age groups, however, there are marked variations, and no couple should try to follow any particular "average."

Too frequent demands on the part of the husband may at times be a manifestation not of real sexual desire but of aggression, of a drive for conquest, of an attempt to escape from the frustrations of daily living. More often, however, a wife's complaint about her husband's too frequent advances is the result of her own inadequate sexual maturity, or else of the husband's failure to arouse her sufficiently to desire him more often. Normally, a sensitive man should be able to adjust his needs to those of his wife. A man and a woman who are emotionally compatible and have a deep affection for each other should have little difficulty in adjusting the frequency of their sexual relations to their mutual satisfaction.

Incidentally, with the removal of some of the inhibitions about sex, many women admit today that they have greater sexual drives than their husbands, and that they are, in fact, resentful of their husbands' infrequent desires. Here again, understanding, tolerance, acceptance and sometimes professional counsel may be needed.

She kissed him for luck,
for gratitude,
for good-by,
with a kind of
innocent passion.

Illustration by Joe de Mers for SCENT OF CLOVES *by Norah Lofts.*

Wives frequently complain that their husbands are too "perfunctory" and too "direct." Most women need a longer period and greater variety of play and physical stimulation before they are sufficiently aroused to want a sexual union. Tenderness, compliments, verbal love-making are very important in this period. One woman said to me, "A few kisses *before* bedtime make the sex relation so much more mutual and more meaningful for me later on."

If the wife is intelligent and mature enough, she might be the best source of information for her husband. She can make him aware of her wants and her reactions, of her need for preliminary rightness of mood, of the love play to which she is most responsive—in short, the kind of relation that is most satisfying to her. One of the major requirements for a good marriage is to keep the avenues of communication open, for each to be able to express to the other feelings and drives and wants. This helps to cement a good relationship and to bring a couple into much closer intimacy.

Though some men may be able to carry on the sex relation for a fairly long time, most of them will complete it within one to two minutes, unless they make a conscious effort to delay it. Often this effort is not easy for a man to sustain. As it takes the average wife a longer period to achieve a climax, this becomes a source of marital dissatisfaction and resentment. The husband ideally should employ in advance various forms of sex arousal and stimulate his wife to a degree where she, too, will attain a full response. With willingness, with practice, and with his wife's cooperation, this is usually possible to achieve.

I would like to stress, however, that even if a wife does not respond completely each time, it need not become a source of frustration to either. A woman may have sufficient satisfaction from being desired, and sufficient pleasure from the act itself, even without a climax, to make the love relationship gratifying for both.

Some men, it is true, do reach a climax much too rapidly; sometimes immediately upon, or even prior to, sex union. Patience and understanding on the part of the wife, and skilled professional care, may be required to correct such a condition.

In our culture, men are trained to repress their emotions, and they find it difficult to express verbally their feelings of affection. "I know he loves me," a wife will say, "but he never says so." It is necessary that men realize the importance of words of affection, of the "verbal caress."

One women recently expressed it this way: "A wife yearns to hear that she is desirable, that she is wanted; a spoken word can thaw out years of reserve, and help her to confident partnership in sex." What husband would not want to achieve this type of partnership with the wife he loves?

Husband and wife should be able to "talk" to each other; to communicate their needs and desires and feelings. Love may be deeper than speech, but often it needs to be spoken. It has to be continually strengthened by signs of affection and consideration, which, like the gentle rain, make it grow and flourish.

Suppose a child you loved came to you with the question, "Why was I born?" She wants to know what she is doing here on earth, what her purpose is in life.

A number of people were sounded out for their personal views: "In a world that sometimes seems full of horror and despair, what has been your reason for life?"

Here are the replies of some famous men and women:

Oscar Hammerstein II., the famous lyricist, replied, "Twenty-three years ago I wrote a song with Jerome Kern, and its title was 'Why Was I Born?' which is the very theme you have asked me to discuss. I must return to my song and quote the first four lines of the refrain: 'Why was I born? Why am I living? What do I get? What am I giving?' Here are four questions in a row. The third and the fourth question imply the answer to the first two. Why you are born and why you are living depend entirely on what you are getting out of the world, and what you are giving to it. I cannot prove that this is a balance of mathematical perfection, but my own observation of life leads me to the conclusion that there is a very real relationship, both quantitatively and qualitatively, between what you contribute and what you take out of this world while you are living in it, and that when you have spent your last day on earth, the history of what you have given and taken is the answer to the question, 'Why was I born?' "

Clare Boothe Luce wrote: "This question is the first question in every Christian catechism. And, the answer is always the same: 'You were born to know, love and serve God.' And so it is, and so I would answer a child, 'You were born, darling, to love and be loved. To love perfect Truth, perfect Mercy, perfect Love, and to be

loved by Him. And mamma and papa aren't perfect (as you will discover one day), but He who made you is. Seek Him. We will help you, child, as best we can, because this is what we are all born to do. And if we don't try to do it—together—it were better for us, and for you, that you had never been born.' "

Walt Disney, creator of world-beloved picture fables, answered, "The little girl who asked the question 'Why was I born?'

Clare Boothe Luce

WHY WAS I BORN?

What would you answer if a child asked you this?

reflects what nearly every parent in the world has been asked by his offspring from time immemorial. I came of a devotedly religious family. They told me everyone was sent here for a purpose, and the guidance I received from the Divine Spirit would direct me along the path intended for me to follow. The mission for which each of us is designated is accomplished sometimes through pain, strife, and again with a smoothness which sometimes amazes us as we reflect on our progress on earth. But always our objective must be attained through a spirit of contriteness and reflection and with a sincere belief that our Divine Guide knows what is best for us all. It's the anchor that helps us ride safely in port."

Albert Einstein, whose discoveries have reshaped our world, said: The question 'why' in the sense of 'to what purpose' has, in my opinion, meaning only in the domain of human activities. In this sense the life of a person has meaning if it enriches the lives of other people materially, intellectually and (or) morally."

Loretta Young, also wrote her answer as if it were addressed directly to a little girl: "You were born to know, to love and to serve God, in this world. And to be happy with Him, forever, in the next. I know this is true, dear, because the Creator of this world has told us so; through the teachings of His beloved Son, who was born nineteen hundred and fifty-two years ago for the purpose of showing us by His example —why all men are born."

Julian Huxley, the English philosopher and biologist, stated, "We are here to realize our possibilities to the fullest extent, and to help others, now and in the future, to realize theirs."

David Ben-Gurion, the Prime Minister of Israel, said, "Many an answer can of course be given to the question of the little girl: 'Why was I born?' It seems to me that we were born in order that humanity—and nature too—should always remain young in body and spirit, be able to see things as if for the first time, and act with new vigor—mental, moral and physical."

Joan Crawford wrote, "Personally, I am convinced that man is born to help others by means of whatever special talent he may be blessed with: whether it's the husband who brings happiness to his wife simply because she loves him, or the inventor who makes life easier for all, the physician who makes it healthier, the soldier who makes it safer, or the entertainer, the poet, the painter, the composer, whose talents bring joy to all of us. And certainly I feel that

Loretta Young

Walt Disney

all of us are born to learn that life in itself is beautiful. Men paint pictures, they compose music, they write books and they lead their lives, but the richest work of art of all is the beautiful life."

Rear Admiral Richard E. Byrd, famed Antarctic explorer, said, "Is it not likely that people are born to further the design of creation? The question then is, 'What is the design of creation?' To help that design.

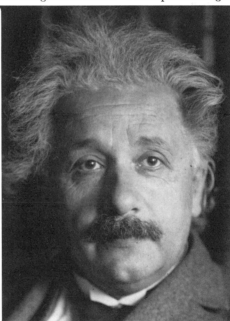

Albert Einstein

I think, the human race cannot go forward without liberty. If this be correct, then all people everywhere should strive for liberty. If they achieve liberty, they will get a chance to pursue happiness and perhaps will be able to develop toward the ultimate goal of creation."

Mary Roberts Rinehart, the best seller author, wrote: "If I were asked why I was born, I would probably say that I hope it is largely in preparation for a better and very interesting life hereafter. Also that I feel I have a real purpose while here on this earth; that is, to be helpful and useful, and perhaps to spread the thing in which Jesus Christ so thoroughly believed—loving-kindness and understanding."

HOW AMERICA LIVES:
NEWCOMERS TO ALASKA

Dorothy Cameron Disney

It rains a great deal in Juneau, Alaska. The weather ran true to form on July 14, 1949, the day that Phyllis and Bill Krasilovsky arrived from distant New York State determined to carve out a new kind of life for themselves. A gray, misty rain splashed around the craft in the harbor. Fog shrouded the towering, beautiful mountains that shut off and isolate Juneau's 7500 residents from the rest of the world.

Pretty city-born Phyllis was twenty-two years old, and so was her city-born lawyer husband. The Krasilovskys, who had grown up in the same Brooklyn neighborhood, attended the same Brooklyn high school and shared two college years of playhouse marriage in Ithaca, New York, were ending a journey of approximately 3200 miles. The last lap of the trip—they came up from Seattle by boat—took two and a half days.

The Krasilovskys had burned their bridges behind them. The adult life they had delayed until the head of the family could complete his professional education stretched before them. Their immediate assets were $250 in cash, a spanking-new diploma from Cornell Law School, and the courage of youth. In addition, Bill had a letter in his pocket. It was signed by one of Alaska's four Federal judges. Neither Bill nor Phyllis had ever laid eyes on the judge, but his name loomed large in their calculations. Several months earlier Bill had heard that the judge was without the services of a law clerk, and he had written from Cornell proposing himself for the job. To any but the young and the hopeful, the courteous but decidedly noncommittal reply Bill was treasuring in his pocket would have seemed a little discouraging. "You might come in sometime for a personal interview" was the gist of it.

Bill is an optimist from way back. On the strength of the judge's letter, he and Phyllis had raided their savings account, bade good-by to their friends in Ithaca and their families in Brooklyn, and headed for Juneau. When they got off the boat that day in the pouring rain, Bill escorted his wife to the town's second-best hotel—$4.50 a day and please use the bath down the hall —and hurried to the handsome Federal Building on Fourth Street to arrange for the "personal interview." There, an unpleasant shock awaited him. The judge was holding sessions in Ketchikan, a fishing community some 200 miles to the south, and would be away from Juneau for a period of weeks.

Phyllis and Bill conferred. Then they paid a visit to the Alaska Airlines office. They learned that the cost of a round-trip ticket between Juneau and Ketchikan was $70. They counted the Krasilovsky bank roll, already sadly attenuated by travel. Next day Bill took $70 from the $250 on hand and flew off to Ketchikan, leaving an anxious and homesick Phyllis behind. That same afternoon he had the promised interview. It lasted fifteen minutes. The results were inconclusive. The judge was impressed (and perhaps perturbed) by the distance the job applicant had traveled. He was favorably impressed by the applicant's record—William Krasilovsky placed seventh in his class at Cornell. But the matter must wait.

Two months later—or, it might be said, eight weeks of suspense and worry later— daring and ability paid off. Bill got the job he still holds today. In the worrisome interval while they sweated out the judge's decision, neither Phyllis nor Bill was idle. Phyllis took on the house-hunting assignment, while Bill scoured the town in search of temporary work. When nothing turned up in his own line, the fledgling lawyer put on overalls, applied at the U.S. Employment Office and got work as a day laborer. That job soon played out, but he landed another. This time he got temporary employment in the office of a busy Juneau lawyer ($250 a month) and started wearing his business suit again.

Overcrowded Juneau, bursting at the seams with Federal and territorial employees, Coast Guardsmen and the military, has a chronic housing shortage. When Phyllis applied at the new veterans' housing project, she discovered there were already hundreds of names on the list. Back in Ithaca she and Bill had lived in a "dreamy" seven-room house, which cost only $35 a month. Phyllis pounded the sidewalks, rang doorbells, climbed hills, explored alleys, asked questions of passers-by. She learned the names of landlords, sought them out personally, pleaded and cajoled. "Those landlords got awfully sick of seeing my mournful face," twenty-four-year-old Phyllis says today, "and sometimes I thought we would never be settled. Those first places I found were awful."

Agonies of homesickness tormented her during that period. She missed the gay life of Cornell, she missed the New York she knew so well, most of all she missed her family. Phyllis is unusually dependent on her mother and her two sisters; for weeks she cried "nearly every time we got the mail from home." At night she would dream of the familiar streets of Brooklyn, or of the carefree student establishment in Ithaca where unmarried classmates had dropped in every afternoon for "coffee and Cokes and plenty of good talk." Each day she would examine the shipping news in the Alaska Empire, steal time from the incessant house hunting, and rush to the pier whenever a boat left for the States. As she waved at the outgoing tourists, homeward bound, she would picture herself as stowing away and popping up back in Brooklyn "to surprise our relatives and friends." There were occasions when she wondered whether the Krasilovskys would ever manage to make friends in the strange new town which they had chosen. There were occasions when she was so dispirited she didn't much care.

In those first months, the newcomers had small chance to acquire any sense of permanence. Between July and September, Phyllis and Bill moved four times. For a while they shared the home of a young Federal worker whose wife was visiting in the States. The Krasilovskys next found refuge in a place which Phyllis describes as "a shack dug in the side of a mountain." Beautiful Juneau is almost entirely hemmed in by mountains; many of the town's houses and apartments perch on precipitous heights and can be reached only by breathless stretches of steep wooden steps. The Krasilovskys had 67 wooden steps to climb to reach their third temporary residence. This was "fine for the waistline but hard on the disposition, particularly when you forget you'd run out of bread."

In their fourth dwelling, a catastrophe befell them. The apartment was modern and pleasant and the first place the couple had lived that seemed like "a real home" to Phyllis. They had been in Juneau for barely six months when fire gutted the premises. Their furniture which had been shipped on from the East was destroyed, along with their cherished mementos of college and home.

Phyllis was in the early stages of her first pregnancy. Small Alexis was on the way. The combination of the fire and her pregnancy was almost too much for the homesick young woman to bear. For a time the whole Alaska venture teetered in the balance. Phyllis was tempted to persuade Bill to give up Alaska. But by then Bill was well established and happy in his job, and Phyllis loves her husband very much. She made up her mind to stick and she did.

complished the feat. A smartly cut raincoat is the mainstay of her wardrobe. A poncho, thrown over the buggy, keeps Alexis dry.

Twice a week the morning walk leads to the well-stocked supermarket on Franklin Street. Except for fresh vegetables, the shelves and bins display all the items to be found in a New York grocery. Phyllis saves both time and money by shopping in quantity, piling her loot in the buggy and wheeling it home. En route she usually drops by the library to exchange a book, and if Bill hasn't picked up the mail the afternoon before she stops at the post office. There are no home mail deliveries.

If it isn't a marketing day, Phyllis and Alexis are likely to call at the veterans' housing development and visit awhile. Mrs. Krasilovsky has friends there. She met them during the dreary months when she was trying to move in there herself. If the weather is fine, she is frequently able to organize an impromptu sketching party. Phyllis, who was interested in sketching back in Ithaca, has transplanted the interest and imbued others with her enthusiasm.

Phyllis' schedule, flexible but efficient, permits her a leisurely morning. Bill has an hour for lunch, and arrives home at twelveten on the dot. His working day is over at five. His Saturdays and Sundays are free, and he has six weeks' vacation a year.

Bill is lucky in his job, and knows it. Many of his classmates at Cornell who located along the Eastern Seaboard are still wondering anxiously how to acquire the experience necessary to attract clients, and simultaneously pay the grocery bill. Bill has solved this double dilemma. Each day at work he is gaining an invaluable knowledge of Alaskan law and laying a solid foundation that should ensure future success in private practice. In a highly competitive profession, he is making associations and is becoming acquainted with lawyers who live all over Alaska. His present income, what with the generous travel expenses allowed him when the court holds sessions outside Juneau, is approximately $6450. His base pay is $4800. He gets $11 expense money a day when his job takes him to Anchorage or Ketchikan.

If Bill held a similar job in the States, he wouldn't be traveling and his base pay would be less. Federal employees resident in Alaska receive a 25 per cent cost-of-living bonus designed to offset the higher prices generally prevalent throughout the territory. The isolation of Juneau, which added so much to Phyllis' initial feeling of strangeness and being cut off from the world, also adds to the cost of living there. The town has no railroads or through highways, and is wholly dependent on shipping and air for transportation. Prices are considerably higher farther north in Anchorage or Fairbanks, but Phyllis finds shopping in Juneau more expensive than in New York. Freight charges are necessarily included in the cost of every 12-cent ear of frozen corn or $2.50 bottle of cleaning fluid she buys. Her milk costs her 30 cents a quart. It costs her dairyman approximately $1.65 a day to feed each of his 80 cows on shipped-in fodder.

Thanks to Phyllis' shopping ability, the Krasilovskys' food bill is held to $20 a week.

Even as a boy Bill saw Alaska as his land of opportunity, planned his life and his work, law, toward that end.

The young Krasilovskys from Brooklyn are now nearing the end of their second year of residence in Alaska's capital city. They have solved their financial problems, located a place to live which "will do until we find something better," and almost won the battle of loneliness. When Phyllis goes on a shopping expedition these days, she counts on seeing at least half a dozen other young shopping wives of her acquaintance. She and Bill have made many new friends. Very small, very recent Alexis, who arrived in July of last year helps a great deal in the homesickness department. "You can't cry around a baby," says Phyllis, who is now able to smile at the wretched girl of a year ago. "I get too much competition from ours to make it worth while!"

Phyllis and Bill and the baby live in a modern gray shingled four room house, squeezed in between identical neighbors, on Willoughby Street. From their back door they look across the channel at forested mountains which have never felt a woodsman's ax. From their front door, they look across sidewalks and pavement at the neon lights of a fancy grocery store. They are only a few blocks from the bustling shopping and business district which is a boon to Phyllis, who retains her big-city appetite for the crowds and the people. Their rent, with the major furnishings provided by the landlord, is $75 a month. Juneau rents, if you're fortunate enough to find a place, aren't excessive.

The couple's daily routine is pretty much what it would be if Bill were practicing law back in a small town in New York. They usually rise at eight, unless, as is infrequent, Alexis chooses to wake at an earlier hour.

When the baby is cared for and quiet, Phyllis and Bill sit down and eat a substantial, unhurried meal. "Bill likes fancy breakfasts," says Bill's wife, and obligingly turns out waffles, French toast, omelets or the like. Often there is time for the two to share in the dishwashing. Bill isn't due at his office until nine, and is only a tenminute walk away. After his departure Phyllis whisks through the bedmaking and cleaning—efficient and quick, she has her home spotless in 45 minutes flat—bathes Alexis, pops her in the buggy, and the two of them go for a walk, rain or shine.

Phyllis, who thought she'd never get used to Juneau's ubiquitous rainfalls, has ac-

On occasion, Phyllis thinks, they spend as little as $15 or $18 a week. The smaller figure seems overoptimistic. Phyllis doesn't keep a budget, and freely confesses that she has a poor head for figures. In this connection, Bill tells a favorite family joke on her. Back in college, Phyllis promoted two student weddings by assuring the engaged couples, doubtful they could afford marriage, that the Krasilovskys got by on exactly $100 a month. After the marriages took place and puzzled questions from the brides rolled in, she consulted Bill and discovered with surprise that they were actually spending $140. "Both brides forgave me," unrepentant Phyllis will tell you with a giggle, "and both marriages are still going strong."

The family is saving $100 a month. Some of Phyllis and Bill's success in saving, they believe, is due not only to prudence and thrift, but to the way they go about it. The method might seem unorthodox, but it works for them. Bill's regular $159 check (taxes are withheld) is paid every two weeks. When he cashes the first monthly check, he keeps back $10 to cover his own incidentals and turns over $149 to Phyllis. She immediately pays the major bills—rent, oil, telephone, and so on—and has enough left in her purse to buy the food. With Bill's second check, the saving comes in. He deposits $100 in the bank, takes out his own $10 and hands Phyllis a meager $49. She is invariably obliged to call at the bank before the month is up, but those rising $100 figures in the book provide a fine checkrein against extravagance. "It's a kind of psychological trick," explains Phyllis. "I just hate to cash an unnecessary check."

This shouldn't be taken to mean that Phyllis and Bill stint themselves unduly, for they don't. They spent $250 to replace clothing lost in the fire; their families sent them many gifts at that time and two adoring grandmothers have presented Alexis with everything a well-dressed baby could possibly need. Oil, used for cooking and heat, costs them an average of $15 a month. Power is cheap; Phyllis and Bill don't bother much with turning off lights, but their electric bill runs around $1.60 a month. Cleaning and laundry in Juneau are expensive. Typical rates are $2.50 for cleaning a man's suit, $2.50 for cleaning a plain woolen bathrobe, $1.25 for pressing a woman's suit. In contrast, diaper service for Alexis at $2.50 a week seems modest, since the service includes the laundering of crib sheets, pads and the baby's small shirts. Phyllis does most of the household laundry in her electric washer, sending out only Bill's shirts at 35 cents apiece. She washes on Monday in exactly 45 minutes, and gives up an hour on Tuesday to ironing. "I don't believe in fooling around with jobs I don't like," she thinks is the secret of her speed.

Phyllis and Bill invest a surprising $1.40 a week in air-mail stamps; top-notch customers of the U.S. mails, they keep in touch with families and friends back East with an almost daily drumfire of correspondence. Like many of their neighbors, they find that magazine reading keeps them informed on world affairs and lessens the sense of remoteness of which even old residents complain. The Krasilovskys spend $27 annually on magazine subscriptions, buy other magazines at the newsstands, and they also take the Sunday edition of the New York Times, which reaches them by mail two weeks late.

Regularly every Sunday the two onetime New Yorkers make a ritual of opening their bulky out-of-date metropolitan newspaper —Phyllis pays close attention to the clothes advertised by Fifth Avenue—and a pleasant morning passes by while they catch up with the doings in the big town far away. In the afternoon, weather permitting, they may decide on a family picnic for three. In that case they pack up Alexis and her bottles, and sally forth to toast their wieners on one of the lovely, virtually unpopulated beaches outside town. If it's summer and the day is fine, they may telephone friends and a group of six or eight, babies and small fry included, will travel out for a view of awesome Mendenhall Glacier. Back in Ithaca the Krasilovskys were fond of bicycling, a sport which is impractical in Juneau. They have substituted mountain climbing, and several times have toiled up Mount Roberts to explore the mammoth shut-down gold mine that once showered the town with wealth. As yet, they haven't tried the fishing and hunting for which their part of the world is famous. "Those things take time," says Bill.

Alexis' arrival has curtailed her young parents' away-from-home recreation. But both love to dance and at least once a month they make it a point to escape from domesticity. The big evening out—they dine either at the popular Baranof Hotel or in one of the town's several night clubs —costs between $10 and $12. Phyllis and Bill depend on Alaska's friendliness to provide them with transportation. If they're headed for Mike's Place, located across the channel and several miles distant from their home, they start out gaily on foot and invariably are able to hitch a ride long before they reach the bridge. The elderly neighbor who sits with the baby on these occasions is further proof of Juneau's warmhearted ways. Mrs. Bayers lives in the Krasilovskys' block; Phyllis got to know her neighbor on her return from the hospital with Alexis; Mrs. Bayers called one afternoon with knitted bootees to ask whether "an old lady may make a present to a new baby." Alexis' sitter refuses to accept payment, and Phyllis returns her neighbor's kindness with small gifts.

Phyllis, who took a lively interest in social and political problems at Cornell, is an active member of the League of Women Voters, Juneau branch. Her membership in Juneau's Creative Writers Club, which meets one evening a week, also stems back to the Krasilovskys' college days. Phyllis started writing there. She has real talent in the field and plenty of stick-to-itiveness. Every afternoon, while Bill is at work and Alexis is napping, she gets in an hour at her typewriter. Last year she achieved her first published success with a charming child's book entitled The Man Who Didn't Wash His Dishes. This pleasing triumph gives Phyllis reason to hope that the day isn't too far distant when she can earn enough to pay for an annual trip back East. Most Juneauites who can afford it attempt to leave Alaska at least every two years.

Several times a month the Krasilovskys

Work as law clerk to one of Alaska's four Federal judges provides valuable experience and contacts for the future.

entertain their friends, many of whom are recent arrivals like themselves. They go in for buffet suppers, informal evening get-togethers, pretty much the same kind of fun they had back in Ithaca. They made their first friends in their new community through Bill. In a government town like Juneau, a job like his insures a certain number of introductions. Through his work Bill became acquainted with other young lawyers and Federal employees, and Phyllis became acquainted with their wives.

With nearly two years of residence behind them, it can be seen that the Krasilovskys have successfully become a part of their new community. They have made the adjustment and are happy. The move was Bill's idea. From boyhood he longed with a passion to live in Alaska. "I was determined to have a new kind of life, different from my family's life," is the way this recent Juneauite explains it. "I wanted to get away from the crowds and grow up in a country that was big and had room." As for Phyllis: "I always expected to live in New York, near my mother and sisters. The feel of New York—Fifth Avenue and Macy's, the subways and the theaters, the buildings and the people—means a lot to me. But I'm so much in love with my husband that if he suggested living on the moon on a nickel-and-dime budget I would try it."

Phyllis Manning and Bill Krasilovsky met at the age of sixteen when both were students at Brooklyn's James Madison High School (5200 students). They'd occasionally glimpsed each other in the crowded, clattering halls, but the formal introduction took place at a tryout for the high-school debating team. The adolescent contestants for debating laurels selected their own topics in the tryout. Bill's enthusiastic, optimistic speech dealt with the opportunities to be found in the land of Juneau, Skagway, Anchorage and Nome.

Both Phyllis and Bill made the debating team. They fell in love in the Brooklyn public library as they bent their heads over research books. For the next few years, sparkling-eyed and popular Phyllis Manning had plenty of chances to listen while her best beau expounded on his pet subject. The two had a longer-than-average courtship. After graduating from high school, Bill enlisted in the Navy but spent his service years in college classrooms rather than at sea. His career—law—was deliberately chosen with Alaska in mind. Reading had convinced him that professional men were needed in the territory. A goodly share of his service earnings went into a savings account earmarked: Alaska.

The Krasilovskys were married shortly after Bill finished his first year in law school. The bride, who was certain of her heart, was considerably less certain about life in the North. However, Phyllis did her best to maintain an open mind. During the two halcyon college years that preceded their arrival in Juneau, she buckled down to help Bill realize his ultimate ambition. His GI allowance barely covered their living expenses and simple, inexpensive fun; there was certainly nothing left over to swell the savings account. While Bill attended his law classes, Phyllis cheerfully pounded a typewriter. Most of her $35-a-week salary—she acted as secretary to a Cornell professor—went into the Alaska fund.

But when the time came to make the break, she still hoped that Bill might vote for New York. She had the vigorous backing of the elders in both families. Bill's father, who is a successful building contractor, thought his eldest son should practice in New York State, where he'd received his education and had connections. Phyllis' mother and father were separated when she was very young; Mrs. Manning, who brought up and supported all three of her daughters, wanted "my girl to settle near her family," and frankly said so. This situation hardly decreased Phyllis' homesickness during her first weeks in Juneau.

She adapted with difficulty. Less venturesome than Bill, Phyllis shrinks from the unfamiliar and the strange. Minor inconveniences disturb her. For instance, she still laments the lack of freshly picked corn on the cob, which is unavailable in Juneau, and isn't disposed to settle for freshly caught salmon instead. Bill is endowed with humor and is able to laugh at small troubles that strike his less-flexible wife as monumental.

Phyllis treasures friends, but the delicate business of making new friends in a new place was hard for her at first. Without knowing it, she occasionally blundered. She is sensitive and easily hurt herself, but it took her quite a while to realize that the new people she was meeting each day were also sensitive and very proud of the city which she and Bill had adopted. "I believe in being honest and direct," says Phyllis, who is young and sometimes fails to grasp that honest criticism of a town comes with more grace from old-timers. Accustomed to measure by the yardstick of New York, in the beginning she made thoughtless undiplomatic remarks that in turn made trouble for her: "My, but the roads up here are bumpy and rough." . . . "Why don't people up here patronize foreign movies?" . . . "Oh, I should think in a town this size there would be a good orchestra." This attitude, Phyllis now concedes, wasn't helpful in the painful process of adjustment. In a town of 7500 a single remark can travel with the speed of light.

Bill is a wise, understanding husband. Before the couple left New York, he had promised his wife a yearly trip back. He suggested that Phyllis collect on the promise in advance. Eight months after the Krasilovskys made their permanent move to Alaska, Phyllis returned to the Brooklyn of her girlhood.

The visit back home, both Phyllis and Bill now believe, represented the turning point. From the big city that she had yearned for, Phyllis got a better perspective on the small town she had left. She had the Empire State Building to look at, but she missed the mountains of Juneau. Among the friends of her childhood, she missed the new friends she had met in the north. Bill's career assumed in her mind the importance it deserves. The husbands of the girls she knew envied her husband his job and his flourishing prospects. Her visit lasted six weeks. She returned to Juneau in May.

On the Fourth of July, Phyllis and Bill and a group of other young Juneauites climbed Telephone Hill to watch the fireworks in the harbor below. Little Alexis, whom Phyllis calls "my first Alaska-born daughter," was born next day. From the tender inflections of her voice, you gather Alexis' mother came back to Alaska to stay.

When Bill finishes his present job he expects to go into private practice. The Krasilovskys may remain in Juneau, or they may decide to locate in booming Anchorage. They aren't quite sure. But one thing is sure—they will be somewhere in the territory. When Phyllis and Bill say, "Alaska is our home," they mean it.

"Bill likes fancy breakfasts." Phyllis obliges with waffles or an omelet while Bill mixes the baby's formula. To offset high prices, Federal employees in Alaska get 25% cost-of-living bonus.

GIVE US THIS DAY

Harriet Van Horne

I remember a quiet, firelit chat I once had with a woman whose outlook had been shaped by the rigors and graces of the Old World. We drank Russian tea in thick glasses with slices of lemon. We spoke of food, of the black bread and wild fruits of her youth. She told me then—though I was too shy to have asked—why her eight babies had been breast-fed. "They are infant creatures then," said her fond, tired voice, remembering the sons now past fifty. "And for the hungry infant there must always be a quiet place. Here"—the veined hand went to her lace collar—"it is warm and safe. They eat. Then they sleep, very good babies."

A mother who makes her dining table the warm, safe place her babes approach with joy is satisfying more than the immediate hungers of their stomachs. She is storing up goodness in their hearts. And peace and contentment that will one day light the table for *their* young.

As for her lord—her hunter home from the hill, her Oswald home from the office—in keeping a bower quiet for his dinner, she has bound him to her with hoops of steel.

How long since you've dined at a table where grace was said? How long since you've tasted bread with the grit of honest grain in it? Years, years that the locust hath eaten. How odd to think that there once was a day when a Christian quickly crossed himself if he dropped a bit of bread on the floor.

Our English word "lady," carried back to its Anglo-Saxon roots, has the literal meaning, "keeper of the loaf." The lady of the house, quite simply, had the sacred duty of making and guarding the bread. And what a satisfying labor it must have been, baking those warm, dark, crusty loaves! Something inside "the lady" must have risen up like the new bread itself when she beheld the stay and the staff of life, fresh from the oven, and all her own handiwork.

Since few households boast a cook and a waitress nowadays, simple meals ought to be the rule. Give the dinner table grace with flowers and candles. Yes, *candles,* and out with ceiling lights. By candlelight the family—or the guests—draw close, relax, and savor the juices of a good meal. And keep the meal you give them honest and simple.

Oatmeal Cornell Bread

Whole Wheat Bread

Unless it's a party, dinner at my house is often one great steaming casserole. A plain cut of meat, stewed in a pot with freshly minced herbs, and vegetables cooked lightly and lovingly in butter. With this stew, ragout, *pot-au-feu* or whatever, we have hot, hot bread, French or Italian, a cold bowl of celery, carrots and ripe olives, and a good, simple wine, often domestic.

For dessert, a chilled pear and a sliver of cheese. Sometimes a canned pear, a slice of melon or a small, perfect bunch of grapes. Hot black coffee in a lovely cup. And afterward, rich content—a very few dishes.

Whole Wheat Bread

Heat ½ cup each milk, brown sugar, shortening and 4 teaspoons salt in a saucepan. Stir constantly and remove from heat when shortening melts completely. Cool until tepid. Mix 1¾ cups lukewarm water and 2 teaspoons sugar. Sprinkle 2 envelopes quick dry yeast on top. Stir *once* and then let stand 7–10 minutes. Mix in warm milk.

Stir together 4 cups whole-wheat flour and 2 cups all-purpose flour. Make a "well" in the center of the flour and pour in the yeast mixture. Work the flour into the yeast a little at a time. Beat well. Turn out on a lightly floured board. Knead until smooth and elastic—at least 5 minutes. Place in a greased bowl. Brush top with melted shortening. Cover and let rise until double in bulk, about 1 hour and 10 minutes. Turn out on a lightly floured board. Knead 1–2 minutes. Divide in half. Shape into loaves. Place in greased bread pans 9" x 5" x 3". Brush tops lightly with melted butter. Cover and let rise until center of dough is slightly higher than edge of pan, about 45 minutes. Bake in a moderately hot oven, 375° F., for 40–50 minutes. The top should be brown and the bread should sound hollow when lightly tapped with the fingers. Remove from the pans immediately and cool on wire racks.

You may even find that a feast of one special, lovingly prepared dish affords more sensuous pleasure than a meal that begins with soup and proceeds, like a Victorian hunt breakfast, through course after course until the mind and body rebel.

Who's to say a tired "I'm-not-hungry" child can't make a fine supper of milk toast? Not ordinary, soggy milk toast. It must have body and flavor. I have made this dish for people who almost spat at me, crying "I loathe milk toast!" and they've eaten it like hungry bloodhounds.

Rich Milk Toast

First, you must have good, honest bread, preferably unsliced. The bread must be thick, the texture solid. I usually slice it too thick for the toaster. But it can be browned beautifully in the broiler, or on a small electric grill. When it's the proper desert gold, butter it generously. Then spread it—not too thickly—with a mixture of brown sugar and nutmeg. Put it in a soup plate (previously warmed in the oven) and pour over it two cups of hot milk. Eat it slowly—and all your sorrows will be solaced.

On Sunday nights we often have onion-soup dinners. The dish can be prepared in a few minutes. And it never, never fails.

Onion Soup

Heat 4 tablespoons butter in a heavy skillet and sauté 4 very thinly sliced onions until golden brown. Blend in 3 tablespoons flour. Then add two 10½-ounce cans beef consommé and simmer 5–10 minutes. Add 2 teaspoons lemon juice and transfer to a casserole or ovenproof tureen. Toast 8 slices French bread and spread with butter. Place on top of soup and sprinkle with ⅔ cup freshly grated Parmesan cheese. Place under broiler until cheese is lightly browned and serve immediately. Makes 4 servings.

Trust the French to make something elegant out of so plebeian a thing as a ham sandwich. These sandwiches take a few minutes of watchful, loving care. But served with something green, they make a fine repast.

French Ham Sandwiches

Thin slices of bread, as many as you'll need; Swiss cheese, grated; leftover ham; eggs, butter, a good skillet. Trim the crusts from the bread. Combine grated Swiss cheese with heavy cream to form a paste. Spread this on each piece of bread, dust it with pepper. Make sandwiches with a thin slice of ham in the middle. Now dip in 2 beaten eggs. Sauté in butter until they are a rich golden brown. (An iron skillet is best for this.) Prepare a cream sauce, blending 1 tablespoon butter with 1 teaspoon flour and 1 scant cup cream. Stir in a bit more grated cheese, freshly ground pepper, let it thicken and pour over the sandwiches.

Baked Flounder with Rice

Wash 6 fillets flounder in cold water and a little lemon juice. Drain well on paper toweling. Arrange in a shallow, well-buttered 2-quart casserole. Sprinkle with 3 tablespoons lemon juice, 1½ teaspoons salt, ¾ teaspoon nutmeg and a scant ½ teaspoon pepper. Drain two 3-ounce cans sliced mushrooms and scatter on top of fish. Dot surface with ¼ cup butter. Bake in a moderate oven, 350° F., 20–30 minutes or until the fish is just cooked. It should flake when touched with a fork. Baste occasionally. Meanwhile, make a cream sauce using 2 tablespoons butter, ¼ cup flour and 1 cup heavy cream. Cook and stir until thickened. When the fish is baked, carefully drain off as much liquid as possible. Add 1 cup fish liquid to the cream sauce and mix well. Pour the sauce over the fish and return to the oven for 5–10 minutes. If you like, dust the surface with paprika before serving. Serve with rice. Makes 6–8 servings.

RICE. Prepare 4 cups cooked rice. Season with ½ teaspoon salt and ⅛ to ¼ teaspoon pepper. Add 3 tablespoons butter. Mix well. Cover and let stand until butter melts. Just before serving, add ⅔ cup coarsely chopped walnuts and toss with the rice. Makes 6 servings.

If you must use garlic, use it subtly, deftly. Don't allow it to smother delicate flavors. Don't toss it indiscriminately into the broth, the beans, the chicken and the chocolate. Never use it unless the recipe commands. And to double-check the recipe, go to its nearest classic dish in a good French cookbook.

Beef Ragout

First of all dredge 2 pounds beef chuck, cut into 1″ cubes, in seasoned flour. Place in a 2-quart earthenware (baking) casserole. Add 1 strip bacon and 8 small white onions, peeled. Season with a *bouquet garni*—a whole carrot, a few celery leaves and 3 or 4 cloves stuck into one of the onions. Pour over all one 10½-ounce can condensed beef consommé. Place casserole in a moderate oven, 350° F., and cook, uncovered, for 2–2½ hours, until meat is tender (stir occasionally). Meanwhile, cook 6 carrots, sliced, and a sprig of fresh mint in a little water until tender. Drain. When meat is tender, remove the bacon strip and *bouquet garni*. Add the cooked carrots, 1 can sliced mushrooms, drained, 1 cup tomato purée, ½ cup finely diced celery, ¼ cup minced parsley and ¼ teaspoon basil. Mix well. Return to oven and cook a few minutes longer. Makes 5–6 servings.

Corn Spoon-bread Casserole

Cook 1 package frozen cut corn as package directions. Do not overcook. Drain well and cool. Heat 2 cups milk. Mix together 1 cup each yellow corn meal and milk. Add the hot milk. Mix well and return to the saucepan. Cook, stirring constantly, until thickened—about 15 minutes. Remove from heat. Add 2 tablespoons butter and 2 teaspoons salt. Mix well and allow to cool a little. Add 3 slightly beaten egg yolks, 1½ cups cooked corn and 1 teaspoon baking powder. Mix well. Beat 3 egg whites until very stiff (stand in peaks). Fold into corn-meal mixture. Be sure no flecks of white are visible. Pour into a greased 2-quart casserole. Bake in a moderately slow oven, 325° F., 40–50 minutes, or until golden on top. Makes 6–8 servings.

Baked Lemon Soufflé

Take five eggs and then separate the yolks from the whites. Beat yolks slightly. Gradually add ½ cup sugar, beating constantly. Add 5 tablespoons thawed frozen lemonade concentrate and 1 teaspoon grated lemon rind. Beat again 2–3 minutes. Beat the egg whites until very stiff (stand in peaks). Fold into the yolk mixture. Make sure no egg white is visible. Pour into an ungreased 1½-quart casserole. Place in a baking pan half full of warm water. Bake in a moderately slow oven, 325° F., for 50–60 minutes. Serve immediately or allow to cool, then chill for about 2 hours before serving.

NEW LINES
An overblouse silhouette in black jersey by Larry Aldrich.

271

WHAT DO YOU KNOW ABOUT FAMOUS LOVERS?

Eleanor Early

When Love comes knocking on the door, wisdom flies out the window and common sense goes straight into the ashcan.

QUESTIONS

1. Who was the handsome, virile lover who courted a famous little invalid (six years his senior), defied her tyrannical father and married the girl, carried her from her sickroom off to Italy, and loved her until she died?

2. What impassioned lover divorced the beautiful woman he adored in order to marry a stout, plain girl for whom he never cared?

3. What French novelist, famous for her numerous *affaires de coeur,* loved, successively, a famous writer and a distinguished musician, and drew freely upon her romances with them for use in her novels?

4. What Pre-Raphaelite painter placed in his dead wife's hands, and had buried in her coffin, a number of love poems which he had written to her, and, seven and a half years later, ordered her body exhumed and the verses published?

5. Who was the poor French milliner who became the adored mistress of an old king, was famed for her wild extravagances, and died beneath the guillotine?

6. Who was the nineteen-year-old poet, author of one of the greatest elegies in the English language, who advocated free love until his best friend made improper advances to his wife, after which he eloped with a brilliant sixteen-year-old girl, and was later drowned at sea?

7. Who was the maid of Astolat who died of unrequited love and left orders that her body be placed in a barge, with a lily in one of her hands, in the other a letter avowing her love? And who was the man who did not love her?

8. Who was the knight beloved by two beautiful women of the same name, one from Ireland and the other from Brittany, who married the Frenchwoman, and died for love of the woman from Ireland?

9. Who were the tragic lovers who gave each other up, to enter monasteries, after which they exchanged love letters that are models of tender passion, and when they died were buried in the same tomb?

10. Who was the poor English girl with a beautiful face and a more than questionable past who married a rich old nobleman and then fell in love with England's greatest hero, bore him a daughter and occasioned an international scandal?

11. What famous queen had romances with two invading generals, bore children to her lovers, and when her last lover died held him in her arms, and then killed herself?

12. Who was the English king, notorious for his amours, who, as he lay dying, asked his courtiers to provide for a girl who sold oranges in the theater and had become the favorite of the king?

13. Who was the girl who inspired Dante's poetry and what role does she play in his Divine Comedy?

14. Who were the unhappy lovers who could not bear to say good night?

15. What Italian poet and playwright wrote a play, a fabulous *succès de scandale,* about his youthful romance with a famous aging actress?

ANSWERS

1. The poet Robert Browning, who secretly married poetess Elizabeth Barrett.

2. Napoleon divorced Josephine for reasons of state and married Marie-Louise, daughter of the Emperor of Austria.

3. George Sand, whose most celebrated romances were with Alfred de Musset and Frédéric Chopin.

4. Dante Gabriel Rossetti, whose *Poems* (the ones that were buried with his wife, Elizabeth Siddal) brought him greater fame than his paintings. Christina Rossetti was his sister.

5. Du Barry, last mistress of Louis XV.

6. Percy Bysshe Shelley, famous romantic poet, deserted his wife and eloped with Mary Godwin, author of *Frankenstein.* When Keats died, Shelley wrote the beautiful poem called *Adonais.* The following year Shelley, who was only twenty-nine, was drowned in a storm at sea, and Mary remained forever faithful to his memory.

7. The Lily Maid was Elaine. The man was Lancelot, whom she loved "with that love which was her doom."

8. Tristram loved Isolde of Ireland. But he married Isolde of the White Hands. He was wounded by a poisoned spear and sent for his first love, who hurried to be with him. But Tristram's wife lied to him and said that his sweetheart would not come. Tristram died. "And when Isolde of Ireland came and saw him dead, for pain and dolour she died too."

9. Héloïse and Abélard. Héloïse is considered one of the three outstanding women of the Middle Ages. Abélard, a celebrated philosopher, was her tutor. They were married secretly after she gave birth to a son. Then she became a nun and Abélard became a monk.

10. Lady Hamilton, mistress of Horatio ("England expects that every man will do his duty") Nelson.

11. Cleopatra, Queen of Egypt, had a son by Caesar and twins by Antony. Antony died in her arms after he was wounded in battle and she killed herself with an asp.

12. Charles II said to his courtiers, "Let not poor Nell (Nell Gwyn) starve."

13. Dante's Beatrice was a young married woman of Florence who died when she was twenty-four. Dante made her his guide through Paradise, and is said to have paid her the greatest poetical homage ever paid to mortal woman.

14. Romeo and Juliet:

*"Good night, good night: parting is such
sweet sorrow,
That I shall say good night, till it be morrow."*

15. Gabriel D'Annunzio. His *Flame of Life* was the story of his romance with Eleonora Duse, who was at the end of her youth when she fell in love with him. Duse stimulated the unchivalrous genius, but was tormented by the realization that her great love had come too late and that she could not hope to hold him.

A romantic moment in FRENCHMAN'S CREEK, *the new novel by Daphne Du Maurier, her greatest since* REBECCA. *Illustration by Hy Rubin.*

Democratic nominee for President, Governor Adlai Stevenson, with his sister Mrs. Ernest Ives.

Presidential candidate **Adlai Stevenson's** reminiscing sister Elizabeth tells us: "At six he collected coins, tadpoles, cigarette-pack pictures, cats. It would be hard not to love so smiling, eager a little boy."

Mamie Eisenhower's friends called her "plumb crazy" to marry a second lieutenant whose pay was less than $150 a month! But it was love at first sight. And now she's First Lady.

BRUCE AND BEATRICE GOULD of the Journal sent us this picture of themselves, snapped with **Nehru** at a garden party at the Prime Minister's house in New Delhi, where they also renewed acquaintance with **Mme. Pandit**, the Prime Minister's sister. The Goulds admired Nehru greatly as a strong, intelligent, devoted leader, gradually unifying into a country the sprawling subcontinent only recently divided by bitter

In New Delhi, Beatrice and Bruce Gould with Prime Minister Nehru.

religious differences, its people speaking many different languages; feel he is rejecting communism in word and deed.

Looking for a director friend a while back on M-G-M's mammoth Culver City lot, we clambered over what seemed to us most of Paris being re-created; and that evening the director pointed out to us at Romanoff's a young and very beautiful little ballerina from France, who was just about to make her first movie in America. We saw the picture previewed, and all we

Ike and Mamie

Gene Kelly and Leslie Caron in "An American in Paris."

ABOUT TOWN

can say is, don't miss it. It's An American in Paris, flowing over with **Gershwin** music, **Gene Kelly**, Technicolor, and ballet backgrounds in the styles of Renoir, Toulouse-Lautrec, Rousseau, Utrillo and other celebrated painters. And the little ballerina from France, **Leslie Caron,** is so easy to look at, you never want to stop looking.

Over on Broadway the other evening, at one of Paramount's projection rooms, we sat with **George Stevens** watching the film he has directed so magnificently from **Theodore Dreiser's** An American Tragedy. Due this fall as A Place in the Sun—and worth waiting years to see. We spoke of the picture's close-ups—the closest ups we'd ever seen, of **Elizabeth Taylor** and **Montgomery Clift.** The picture will leave you limp.

Marlon Brando: "He's very young— he just needs a chance to grow up."

George Stevens prepares Elizabeth Taylor and Montgomery Clift for a close-up.

Kate Smith

Actor-producer **Eddie Dowling** recalls that **Kate Smith** played a bit part in one of his musicals in 1926. "She got $65 a week and was very well liked by the cast. One night she asked me if she could put a barber pole in front of her dressing room. It was the real thing and revolved just like the ones outside barbershops. Kate explained that 'When I was a kid, I was taught to be a lady barber.' She cut hair for almost everyone in the cast from then on and I guess she made almost as much money barbering as singing!"

"I do get a little weary of reading about **Marlon** as a strange schizophrenic, half genius, half moron," says his mother. "I went to New York to see him in A Streetcar Named Desire and I forgot it was

Marlon on stage. When your children can make you forget who they are, they're doing a good job."

Mrs. Marlon Brando looks almost, but not quite, like a Broadway casting office's conception of a "typical American mother." At home on her farm outside Libertyville, Illinois, she was warmly gracious.

"I think much of Marlon's unconventionality began when he discovered that all was not well with the world. He revolted, as many young people do. Some take socio-

logical jobs, others find outlets in the arts. Bud seems to show *his* rebellion through some of his attitudes, what he says—and even through his choice of clothes. He's very young and very talented. He just needs a chance to grow up some more."

Consuelo Vanderbilt had every privilege wealth can offer except the right to live her own life. The American girl who became a duchess (the Duchess of Marlborough) against her will now tells her memorable story in The Glitter and the Gold.

In the same kind of frilly white shirt front which **Dickens** wore when with sensational success he gave "readings" of his works in this country back in 1867, **Emlyn Williams,** the eminent English actor, has been marvelously impersonating the immortal novelist here in a one-man show.

"Dickens" à la Dickens.

Whoever has or hasn't seen KISS ME KATE on the stage will be wise to watch for the movie of this smash-hit musical. On the M-G-M set, we met the man who wrote the music, **Cole Porter,** absolutely spick-and-span, wearing his bow tie the new way. Told us in his unexpectedly thin voice he was a farm boy from Peru, Indiana. But what a farm! Born wealthy. Never knew hard luck until he fractured both legs at forty-five falling from a horse. Thirty-three operations. Walks with cane. Composes wherever he happens to be, but always between 11 A.M. and 5 P.M. First the title, then the melody, then the verse. Begins with last line and works backward. And when **Ann Miller,** in tights as Bianca, came over and sat on the arm of his chair, we never saw a man so nonchalant!

Danny Kaye as Hans Christian Andersen holds his "audience" spellbound—just as movie-goers are by the fantasy now showing.

Ray Bolger: "It's hard to be funny when no one's around to laugh."

Cole Porter (center) with Ann Miller and Bob Fosse, who take part in "Kiss Me Kate," adapted from "The Taming of the Shrew."

Millions of you who read MY COUSIN RACHEL in the JOURNAL, and still wonder whether she really did it or not, are going to have a good time reliving its exciting uncertainty all over again when you see the 20th Century–Fox movie. **Daphne du Maurier** devotees from the JOURNAL Work-

Richard Burton, as Philip, and Olivia de Havilland, as My Cousin Rachel, give movie-goers heart-throbs.

shop who covered the advance screening loved **Olivia de Havilland** and swooned for the young Englishman, **Richard Burton.**

Opposite: Yul Brynner and Gertrude Lawrence in the Rodgers and Hammerstein musical "The King and I." Charmed by the sparkling "Shall We Dance" number, her audience saw no hint of pain or worry in Gertrude's last performance three weeks before her death. "She never gave less than her best. . . ."

FOLK ART AT WILLIAMSBURG

The Abby Aldrich Rockefeller Folk Art Collection, containing these and many more delightful examples, is now on permanent public display at Williamsburg, Virginia. "It has been more than 25 years since my mother began to acquire these pictures and artifacts," says Winthrop Rockefeller, Chairman of the Board, Colonial Williamsburg, Inc., in expressing the hope "that everyone who visits the collection will enjoy it as my mother did."

Left: FRUIT IN BLUE COMPOTE. *Watercolor by an unknown American artist, probably living in New England. c. 1840.*

Below: VIEW OF HENRY Z. VAN REED'S FARM, PAPERMILL, AND SURROUNDINGS IN LOWER-HEIDELBERG-TOWNSHIP. *Oil painting by Charles C. Hofmann.*

VENUS DRAWN BY DOVES. *Watercolor and cut paper on silk,*
found in Quincy, Massachusetts, attributed to Betsy B. Lathrop.

The silver gleams in the candlelight, the big party
dish is a luscious beef, bean and sausage casserole.

DIARY OF DOMESTICITY

Gladys Hastings Taber

Especially Me likes the old stone wall where deer grass grows.

It is my daughter Connie's idea that we could keep a broom down by the pond, and keep sweeping the algae away. But it only folds itself right back and it is so hard to swim and wield a broom. I prefer to shut my eyes and strike out and assume the algae is full of minerals. I read somewhere that we might be eating it one day.

Now the truth seems to be that if you have a pond with fish and frogs and, alas, turtles, a pond edged with wild flags in spring and Queen Anne's lace and goldenrod in late summer, you have algae in the hot months. If we had a Hollywood swimming pool, cerulean-blue cement on the bottom, crystalline-clear sterile water pumped in and out, then we should have no trouble.

But we would not have the rushing brook purling over fallen logs and tumbled boulders. We would not have the forget-me-nots dipping blue lace into the water, fish leaping in the twilight stillness. The blue heron standing on one stilt at the shallow place where the minnows dart. I reflect, as I consider the algae, that dumping in stuff

to kill it would also change it from a wild-life home to just another swimming pool. It is a law of life that you can't have everything, so I swim happily around, feeling rather smug, if the truth be told, because our pond is sweet amber water. What's a little algae?

As we sit on the terrace sunning ourselves, and sipping cool drinks tangy with lemon, I pursue my thoughts. There are some people, I reflect, nipping up a cracker, who concentrate so hard on what is wrong with anything that they never get around to enjoying what is right. For instance, people who could watch Laurence Olivier's matchless portrayal of Richard III with the great beauty, amazing casting, deep understanding of Shakespeare, and say afterward, "Well, the battle scenes weren't very good."

It may well be that to be truly happy, one must have the ability to appreciate rather than depreciate. I dare say one can find fault in anything on this earth if one works at it. But how tiresome!

What a great gift water is! We could live longer without food than without water.

And how casually we turn the faucet and let it run. How easily we drive along the river roads and miss the beauty of riffles around the bend, willows bending over.

As for the ocean, it is to me the realization of infinity. When we go to the ocean for a weekend, I can sit and look at the water rolling in and feel the peace of God in every breaking wave. On the great beach, diminished to being of no more importance than a grain of sand, I feel eased, strengthened, as if I were in the hollow of God's hand.

As the hot days grow hotter, we change the rhythm of our life. Jill says the weeds keep the vegetables more moist and help the crop. Now we have read Ruth Stout's book on "How to Have a Green Thumb Without an Aching Back," we know this is so. Ruth Stout mulches and lets things alone. What a wonderful way to get bumper beans and tomatoes and lettuce and carrots. So Jill stops pulling weeds in the blazing sun (so they wilt faster) and sits with "The Last Hurrah" and reads!

We carry our trays to the coolest spot

and eat slowly. Decide the dogs all need baths, but we will wash them two a day, not all at once. Think we can put off painting the back kitchen until "a little later." Wonder if the beans will go another day without getting mature. (We freeze all vegetables when just young and butter tender.) Feel the gate will not fall off the hinges until next Tuesday.

Holly, the Irish, never loses a jot of her energy. Whatever a jot is, she does not lose it. She skims around, sits in the full sun tossing an empty can in the air and catching it. Zooms after swallows, which are always too high in the air and don't mind her anyway.

The cockers take the heat with dignity, they loll. Cats absorb the sun like a blotter, but they move languidly, stretch one paw, lick a few times, and stop. Their ears they treat in a desultory manner.

The Irish is a special breed. Holly can sit relaxed on a snowbank in a driving blizzard and it takes all our art to lure her in before she might catch pneumonia. And she will get so hot my hand burns when I stroke her. I think maybe the Irish have a special thermostat.

Cockers, on the contrary, dig deep holes under the lilacs, tossing out all the good dirt. Jonquil pillows her head in the cool shady spot where I always plant the violets. Sister tiptoes out and tiptoes back in, retires under my bed where the wide black oak floor boards are cool and nicely waxed.

My cooking ambition sizzles away and I feel like tossing things in the salad bowl.

But when Louella Shouer and her completely wonderful husband, George, take a weekend with us at the seashore, I am obliged to make Quiche Lorraine with clams. I have always wanted to make this, and never found the really right recipe. Louella did. And she says tidily, "You can use canned clams if you aren't digging your own. Very good," says Louella.

Line a 9″ pie plate with pastry (I let Louella make that). Add two 7½-ounce cans minced clams, well drained, and 6 slices bacon, fried and crumbled. Sprinkle with 3 tablespoons minced onions that have been cooked until golden in 2 tablespoons bacon drippings. Combine 4 eggs, 1 cup clam liquor, 1 cup milk, pepper, salt to taste. Beat until eggs are blended. Pour into pastry shell. Bake in moderate oven (375° F.) for 40 minutes or until knife inserted near center comes out clean.

Over the Quiche Lorraine and a crisp salad and hot coffee, the talk ranges high, wide and handsome. I think any good meal must be seasoned with warm conversation.

The most exhausting thing in life is to be insincere.
ANNE MORROW LINDBERGH

George is a gentle and quiet man, but with a rare wit and much wisdom. I suppose a crust of bread would taste quite delicious if George flavored it with his comments on everything from gardening to world politics.

And of course I like best the way in the midst of an analysis of the economic situation, he looks over the table at Louella and his face lights up as if to say, "My, isn't she wonderful?"

Holly adores her day bed. We call it that because she uses it only in the day when not curled up on my bed gently whacking the maple footboard with her tail as she dreams. This bed is aluminum and has a nylon top, and can be folded up. It is the only good dog bed, says Holly, for it gives with her weight, it is off the floor, it washes. It has everything. In fact, all the dogs love it, and when we have dinner guests who do not want dogs on their laps, we pop the bed in the back kitchen, and the dogs all arrange themselves on it, and are quite happy. With one hand, I can tip it back against the wall when not in use. Holly's bed will accommodate her, Jonquil, Sister and Especially Me, if they crowd. If I am showing it to some friend, they all stand on it, very proud. This bed will store in the car for travel, too, which is a fine thing.

On hot July evenings, I am apt to get out the game of Bali, which is a kind of combination of solitaire (but can be played by four) and all the word games there ever have been. I love word games. I began with anagrams, and progressed with all the variations.

Bali has an advantage, for you can build words as long as possible. Not just "cat" and "barn" and "prestige," but long, long words. Also, you can play it alone when you are too tired to work.

Jill loathes games and some of our friends are not what I would call game-minded. I like to play anything. I began with jackstraws and played my way through school with anybody who would play anything. Cicely says, after growing up as an unwilling but polite game player with me, that I am dreadful because I keep on helping my opponent as much as possible.

"Mamma," she says, "you have no competitive spirit."

Bridge I gave up years ago because I found so many people got so cross at bridge. I knew husbands and wives who nearly parted over a no-trump bid which didn't work out, and it made me nervous. So I gave that up, although it is a fascinating game.

I do think it would be fine if more families played a game—any game from croquet to gin rummy—once in a while. It is a sharing and a gay experience, and there are many games that the whole family can play, young and old. It gives a family experience, less passive than TV or listening to records—and reading aloud, alas, has gone out of style.

When the sun slopes down, the baking world draws a breath. "And little twilight winds that creep, Round twilight corners half asleep," as Rupert Brooke said, make the heat of the day forgotten.

The hills are deeply violet now and the moon is a pale silver disk. That silver never needs polishing, I reflect, as I look at the silver on the mantel.

Our little white house is like an island on the velvet sea of night. All the years—and the moon goes over, and the house stands secure.

"Tomorrow we better freeze beans," says Jill, looking up from the best and newest murder mystery.

Holly barks at the night. It is so exciting. She feels a summer night calls for barking in a very special tone!

Illustration by Paul Bransom

Opposite: Illustration by Joe de Mers for GIANT, *Edna Ferber's new novel set in Texas.*

CAN THIS MARRIAGE BE SAVED?

Paul Popenoe

SHE: *"I simply couldn't believe Dick could fall in love with another woman. He agreed to stop seeing her, but announced he intended to move out of our home."*

HE: *"There are times I get so hungry for warmth and comradeship, for somebody to really talk to, I feel a little batty."*

Andrea tells her side:

"My husband has seen the woman only four times in his life," thirty-eight-year-old Andrea said desolately. "I gather she has pretty legs, but Dick couldn't tell me the color of her eyes and he doesn't know her age. Clarice lives a thousand miles from here. Dick would like to walk out of an engineering job that seems to satisfy him perfectly and break up our home. When I asked him why, his story was that he and I have no common interests and can't communicate. We communicated well enough to have three fine boys and a lovely little girl. We have in common twenty years of marriage.

"Dick is a consulting engineer. Everybody says he is brilliant in his field—and I guess everybody also says he is married to a dumb bunny.

"Three weeks ago when Dick got back from the trip on which he met Clarice—he spent a month on some kind of inspection tour of Middle Western factories—I knew something had gone wrong the minute he walked in the front door. I saved my kisses for later when he might feel more affectionate. I just pecked his cheek. When I unpacked his bags, I wasn't surprised to discover he'd brought back nothing for the children. With the oldest two, it didn't matter. But Scott and Tommy had been looking forward to what daddy would bring. I produced a baseball and a catcher's mitt from a supply of toys I store in a closet for such emergencies. Dick grumbled that I'd raised Scott and Tommy—one is seven, the other six—to be materialistic and grasping.

"The notion of another woman didn't cross my mind. I suspected business troubles again. If Dick's work is criticized or he imagines he is being slighted, he boils inside, really boils.

"Once he invented a new method of installing heavy machinery which saved so much money for his employers he was invited to be a guest of honor at the annual banquet. The company president publicly congratulated Dick but mispronounced his last name. Next week, without a word—he was too proud to explain—Dick resigned

and accepted an unsatisfactory connection at a lower salary with another firm. Later on, he got the delusion I had suggested the change and fumed at me.

"Nearly always Dick comes back from an out-of-town assignment discouraged, angry, and tied in knots with nerves and tension. I do my best to help. I always try to welcome Dick from his trips so he will want to hurry back next time.

"The evening of his return I wore my new green dress—bright green is the color he prefers on me—and a new hairdo. Dick didn't comment on the dress, but he disliked the hairdo. I cooked his favorite dishes for supper. Our daughter—at fourteen Janet is already a real little woman—baked a perfect lemon-meringue pie. Dick ate crackers and milk.

"For Janet's sake I urged a tiny piece of pie on him. Dick shook his head and snapped that both she and I should skip pastries and improve our looks. I excused Janet from the table before she burst into tears and I joined her in the kitchen, ate two slices of her pie, and praised it to the skies. When she and I carried in the coffee a storm was brewing between Dick and our seventeen-year-old son. Ellis was planning to drive to the movies and Dick had ordered him to stay home and study. Ellis was standing up, stiff as a ramrod, in a humor to be ugly and defiant. I laid my hand on the boy's shoulder and got him to sit down again. In matters of discipline I stand with Dick, even when I don't agree with him.

"When we went to bed, it turned out we were in for a siege of Dick's insomnia. I'm scared to death of sleeping pills, but they are as common in our house as jelly beans. Dick took his usual number but couldn't close an eye. I rubbed his back and massaged the muscles of his neck. I brought him the heating pad, a pot of hot tea. He declined the pad, threw out the tea, and stamped off to the couch I bought for his dressing room. I put my head under the blankets so Dick couldn't hear and cried myself to sleep.

"Before that week was over, I was at my wits' end. Dick made the children's existence a misery—the four of them crept around like mice—and he made himself sick. He couldn't eat; he couldn't go to business. Finally I called the doctor. As usual, our doctor found nothing physically wrong and recommended a change of scenery.

"With our family a change of scenery means piling in the station wagon and driving to the mountains. We bought a cabin the summer our daughter was born.

In the old days, Dick was as big a kid about roughing it as any of my other children. But on the evening of our arrival I could see we might as well have stayed home.

"Neither Dick nor I have pleasant recollections of childhood. I have tried to build up pleasant traditions for our children. We have family jokes, family rules and regulations, family singing and reading aloud. Since Dick is away so much, I have tried to make the youngsters think him an important figure.

"Every year Dick is supposed to lay the first log fire of the family camping season. This time he forgot. I managed to smuggle the logs in from the woodpile. I laid the fire. I then slipped a box of matches into Dick's hand. His mind was a thousand miles away. He gave a jump, stared at me as though he were a stranger. Ellis lighted the fire. Our first meal of the season consists of baked ham, brown bread and beans. Scott and Tommy sharpened the knives—their task. But Dick didn't carve the ham. He asked me to slice it in the kitchen. After the meal, he was expected to lead us in a song while Janet played a guitar accompaniment. Janet brought her guitar to the table, but her daddy got up and walked out. Our dog hopped up and followed. Dick shoved Spot back inside and slammed the door.

"His manner was so peculiar I was badly scared. I took a lantern and went outside. In a few minutes I came on Dick. He sat on a fallen tree trunk, his chin buried in his hands. I went to put my arms around him."

Andrea's voice faltered.

"The whole story of Clarice came tumbling out. Dick was dreadfully upset, almost crying. I felt like someone in a bad dream. I simply couldn't believe Dick could fall in love with another woman on such a slight acquaintance. After a while he admitted sex had more to do with his feelings toward Clarice than tenderness. He agreed to stop seeing her, but announced he intended to move out of our home to a boardinghouse. For the next six months, it seems, he wants to be by himself so he can 'think things out.'

"Some of the things he said to me, there on the log, cut deeper than his infidelity. He told me I was uninteresting, that I did not inspire him, that he and I had always been unsuited, that we had never loved each other and should not have married.

"I guess I shouldn't speak for Dick, but the fact is he and I fell in love practically on sight. I was eighteen and a high-school senior, earning my keep as a mother's helper for a cousin. On Thanksgiving Day my cousin invited Dick to turkey dinner. I know he carries in his heart the memory of that Thanksgiving Day. Very soon he was begging me to be his wife. At twenty he was even more home-hungry than I was. I had a home until I was nine and my father deserted us. Dick was only two when his mother ran off and left him in the care of a crackpot father. Dick had joined the Navy at sixteen to get a start in engineering.

"Dick and I were the parents of two children before we saved the money to enable him to quit the Navy and put his full time on engineering studies. During those years I was always tired. I baked pies and cakes at home for a bakery chain. My days began at five A.M.

"Whatever Dick wanted I have always wanted too. Not once have I objected to his restless shifting from job to job. Maybe he should have married a woman who could have helped him climb higher and faster in his profession. But I doubt if Dick's conscience will give him any rest if he curses our children with a broken home. He remembers too well his own boyhood."

Dick tells his side:

"I suppose you've heard of Huckleberry Finn," Dick said. A handsome man of forty-one with deep nervous lines sketched around his mouth, he eyed the counselor with a mixture of wariness and suspicion. "Well, I grew up as haphazardly as Huck Finn. My father owned a construction business in the East when my mother ran out on him. In a matter of months he owned nothing except an old beat-up truck.

"The two of us took to the open road. My father was a great guy in some ways, in other ways an unregenerate bum. He blamed my mother for his comedown in the world, but I believe he thoroughly enjoyed our vagabond existence. Not me. I loathed it.

"When I was four or five, my father knocked together a sort of shack on two wagon wheels, and attached it to the truck. He fondly called this rattletrap a trailer. My passionate prayer was that our 'trailer' would fall to pieces, and that just once we would sleep in a clean, orderly house. It never happened. I don't recall that my father ever paid for a night's lodging. He refused to pay for anything he could scrounge. My father has been dead for years, but even now I have a recurrent nightmare which concerns an incident of my sixth year. He and I are in the truck speeding away from a filling station somewhere in Illinois and between us on the seat lies a monkey wrench he 'forgot' to hand back to the attendant. I wake up from this nightmare trembling, and drenched in sweat.

"My father wasn't a thief in the ordinary sense. But that wrench became a kind of symbol to me of his whole philosophy. He had a contempt for society, for law and order. Two great dreads of my fear-ridden childhood were the police, who might drag me off to jail, and social workers, who might drag me off to an orphanage.

"Perhaps once a month my father sloshed a bucket of water through the shack and called it a house cleaning. Ants and spiders ran about the greasy, crumb-strewn floor. I guess that background made me a fanatic about cleanliness. Sometimes now I hear myself yelling at Andrea because of a messy ash tray or because the youngsters have smeared the woodwork. I swear I have the same choked sensation I used to have in that shack.

"My father, incredible as it may seem, was a college graduate, and clever with his hands. He taught me to make boats, trains —small-scale accurate models—out of scraps. He read aloud to me from Dickens, Thackeray, Whitman. But I was eight before I learned to read and write; I was humiliated by my ignorance. One day I traced the word 'cigarette' from a magazine advertisement, and exhibited the tracing to my father as my 'handwriting.' This piece of deception alerted him to the fact that literacy is not inborn and he taught me my letters.

"Later we settled in a town long enough for me to enroll in school. There I made a friend. Bob owned a toy dump truck. It was out of kilter. I repaired the truck, and Bob invited me to his house for lunch. His mother took one look at my clothes and tactfully herded me and my small host out of the dining room into the kitchen. I choked down her food, but I can still remember my shame and anger. I never spoke to Bob again.

"I learned at a tender age to shy away from the well-scrubbed majority who would insult and patronize me. The habit sticks. Andrea says I'm too standoffish and suspicious. She is too naïve, too gentle-natured, to grasp the cruelty and evil in human beings, or to conceive of the close infighting waged all the time in the name of competition. At the rare social gatherings we attend with business associates, I hear her prattling on about my early struggles to rise from the muck. I shrivel inside and want to shout at her to be quiet.

"As a child, the only escape I could see— the doorway from the hobo jungle to the parlor of the gentry, so to speak—was through education. How I hurled myself at my books and studies when I had a chance! I did manage to get a high-school diploma before I went to sea. It's impossible for me to convey how much the Navy meant to me. I will never forget my joy at the antiseptic cleanliness of my first ship, or the shining beauty I found in the engine room.

"The big mistake I made was in marrying young." Dick's voice sagged. "I might have accomplished something worth while in my field instead of sinking into mediocrity. Andrea hasn't the faintest glimmering of the potentialities of my profession and drives me almost mad by praising my not-too-extraordinary achievements. She also sets my teeth on edge by referring to me as a great big kid.

"Most people would consider Andrea an ideal wife. She stood by me while I worked my way through the university. She is a conscientious housekeeper and an excellent mother, undemanding and unselfish. She puts my wishes and interests first. Indeed, in her determination to make me comfortable she often makes me feel like an A-one heel. Her undeviating good will is all too likely to bring out the worst in me. Sometimes when she runs and fetches my slippers I keep on my shoes out of sheer cussedness. For me to express a food preference is a prime hazard—one compliment on a lemon pie means lemon-meringue today, tomorrow and forever.

"I have the greatest respect for Andrea. Unfortunately, she offers me no mental stimulation. I sometimes think I may have married Andrea because at twenty I was seeking a mother. A man outgrows his need of a mother. I've got to the stage where I want a companion.

"For a while I thought I had found the companion. Clarice was exciting. She is a teacher, a talented musician and dancer as well. We had fun together. However, I guess we weren't in love.

"I am well aware that I am not easy to live with, and a poor father. I lose my temper over trifles. I can't help it any more than I can help my awkwardness with our youngsters. I am proud of the children, but I seem incapable of getting close to them.

"There are times I get so hungry for warmth and comradeship, for somebody to talk to, *really* talk to, I feel a little batty. I've worked like a slave since my earliest teens, and it seems to me I've wound up with nothing worth having. The truth is I am almost insanely bored with my marriage and my present existence. So bored that I am sick half the time from nerves and inner pressure. I believe I should clear out awhile for everybody's sake. Frankly, I think I'm near a crackup."

The marriage counselor says:

"Dick, dissatisfied with his life, was laying the blame on his marriage. Andrea wasn't responsible for Dick's bitter discontent, but he had convinced her, as he had convinced himself, that if she had offered him more mental stimulation he would have been happy. No wife could have solved Dick's thorny personality problem. The psychic wounds received in his early years were responsible for most of his difficulties as they also were, ironically enough, for his brilliant achievements in his profession. Former employers were almost unanimous in praise of his abilities; some regarded him as a straight-out genius.

"Dick was and is a perfectionist. Because he sets his standards so high, he seldom feels he has lived up to them. Dick had to believe the specific task on which he was engaged was of value to society, and unless his employers repeatedly told him that his services were of outstanding importance, he became hurt and angry. In one sense, Andrea wasn't too wrong in regarding her husband as a grown-up boy. Intelligent as Dick was, he was subconsciously determined to wipe out the memory of his vagabond father and the humiliations of the Huck Finn days. But as he shifted from job to job he may have been guided by one of his father's favorite maxims: 'If you don't like it where you are, quit and move on!'

"Often Dick's impulsive changes of employment did not turn out well and he would feel foolish. Early in his marriage he subconsciously hit upon a method of getting 'out from under' these uncomfortable feelings. He transferred the blame for his mistakes in judgment to Andrea. Uncomplaining as a door mat, she made the process easy. But a man of Dick's type usually fools himself in this fashion only at a price. A number of Dick's neurotic illnesses —his headaches, backaches, stomach upsets

—originated in work difficulties for which he unfairly held Andrea responsible.

"The pattern for Dick's illnesses, like the pattern for his loneliness and inability to communicate, was laid down in childhood. He then learned to use sickness as an escape. He decided that all people were ill-intentioned, and deliberately cut himself off from them. Not until after several interviews did Dick perceive a truth quite obvious to his loving wife—that to live alone in a bachelor apartment was hardly a sure cure for loneliness.

"He also agreed that he couldn't expect others to scale the walls he had constructed around himself. It wasn't likely, Dick acknowledged, that he would receive much affection from his sons and daughter so long as he snarled and victimized them with his moodiness. When Dick began to mind his temper and manners around his youngsters, relations speedily improved.

"Andrea, who is not the most intuitive of women, showed the benefits of her long study of Dick when she correctly judged that the affair with Clarice was of less consequence than his dissatisfaction with himself. When Dick met Clarice he was suffering from a bad case of what is often referred to as forty-year-old trouble. He had begun to wonder how many years were left in which he might find gaiety and fun. In his hard-working life, fun for fun's sake had played almost no part. All his creativeness —and Dick was a creative man—had been focused upon figures, facts and formulae.

"Andrea's youthful background, although less flamboyant than Dick's, was quite similar, but she did not grow up emotionally crippled. In Andrea's small-girl dreams she pictured herself as a self-effacing wife willing to forgo personal desires in order to maintain a successful marriage. When she married Dick, she found the frame for that picture waiting and she happily stepped into it.

"Andrea was much surprised when I suggested that, if anything, she had been too unselfish, that the time had come for her to develop her own individuality. She was leading too narrow a life, was too absorbed in domesticity. With a little encouragement, she broadened her horizons. Her first venture was to join a so-called 'charm course.' I soon noticed a marked improvement in Andrea's appearance. She lost eight pounds, then treated herself to a new wardrobe of smarter clothes in more becoming colors. I recall the day she proudly reported a compliment from Dick on a dress that was *not* bright green.

"Andrea selected more the sort of activity I had in mind when she joined the League of Women Voters. Neither she nor Dick had ever voted. Andrea didn't turn into a sparkling conversationalist overnight, but she did become interested in the issues of the day. A couple of months after joining the league Andrea surprised both her children and Dick by besting the head of the family in a dinner-table argument. She convinced Dick it was his duty to register and go to the polls.

"Shortly after this small triumph, something occurred that both Andrea and Dick consider a miracle. Dick discovered that painting was fun, and with the discovery burst through the walls of work and self-absorption that had so long imprisoned him. One of Andrea's league friends invited the couple to drop in on a class of amateur artists who hired a professional teacher. Andrea was interested in the class, Dick was fascinated. Three hours and one painting later, the first painting of Dick's life, the professional artist was their guest for dinner.

"Dick's illnesses are almost a thing of the past. Now if he feels inner pressures building, he paints. Paradoxically, as Andrea has grown more independent of her husband she has grown closer to him. Both he and she have developed within themselves. They have more to offer to each other and their children."

Could anyone look lovelier? A Vogue pattern gown in the palest blue satin accented with a bright green taffeta bustle with a pink rose nestled in the bow.

JOURNAL ABOUT TOWN

It's a measure of almost unmatchable fame that when the name "Bing" is mentioned, easily a billion people must know it's the man who forty-nine years ago in Tacoma was christened **Harry Lillis Crosby**. Even the name "Ike" doesn't so universally identify the President. So when we say we previewed Bing the other day in a new picture called Little Boy Lost, you know the man we mean. You even know what he was like in it. We think it's Bing's best picture so far. But it's not all his. A lot of it belongs to **Christian Fourcade**, a veteran of nine who's been a big hit in France since he was four, and who plays a little lost boy better than you ever saw one played before. It's a good story for a change. Get ready to laugh, and cry too. It'll be out any minute now.

Psychologists find that classrooms painted according to the principles of "color dynamics" improve grades and behavior of school children. A survey of three schools —one painted "psychologically," one painted conventionally, one left in need of paint—revealed that learning improvement between first and second grades was 34 per cent in the first school, 7 per cent in the second, only 3 per cent in the third. Boys seemed to respond to color more than girls. . . . The average American receives 80 pounds of mail per year. . . . Teachers find that most students study not from fear of ignorance or desire for knowledge—but from fear of failure.

We went twice to see A Star Is Born when it was downstairs here at the Music Hall in 1937. Which is why we'll be on hand when an altogether new production of that fine film appears any minute now, this time with **Judy Garland** in the part

Bing Crosby enjoying the puff that refreshes with Christian Fourcade, French child actor who nearly steals the show in "Little Boy Lost."

Ex-King Peter of Yugoslavia and Princess Alexandra exchanging New Year's greetings with the Duke and Duchess of Windsor. "The Duke's dancing," confessed Alexandra after accepting an invitation to sample it, "was even worse than mine."

Judy Garland

"Stars stay bright by exercising," **Dawn Norman** told us after talking to star **Roy Rogers** at his rodeo. "He's the only man I've met," said Dawn admiringly, "who can walk on his hands and converse charmingly at the same time." Exerciser Roy keeps in shape ranching on 136 acres, riding horses and bikes, playing pickaback with his

Roy Rogers with friends.

played before by an actress with the same initials—**Janet Gaynor**. There was a scene in which **Fredric March** proposed to Janet in a darkened movie theater, a scene that will have a sort of real-life twist now when **James Mason** proposes to Judy, because we recall Judy telling us a while ago that it was in a movie theater, back in the days of silent film, that her parents had met and fallen in love. Her father was the vocalist there, she said, her mother the pianist.

The American Kennel Club has just notified us that the flop-eared cocker spaniel has been nosed out as the most popular breed in this country by the beagle: 43,561 registered cockers to 45,398 registered beagles.

children. He has nine. Seven are adopted, including a Korean daughter, Debbie, and a Choctaw Indian daughter, Dodie, both 6. "Boys are harder to convince about exercise —afraid to be sissies," Roy told her. "That's why I tell *them* that children brought up in church are seldom brought up in court."

JACK KENNEDY:

DEMOCRATIC DYNAMO

Joan Younger

Tall, dark and handsome, Senator John Fitzgerald Kennedy of Massachusetts walked down the hall of the Senate Office Building, and all along the way people stopped to watch him pass.

"The uncrowned prince of politics," a reporter said. "The All-American boy grown to glory."

"He's very capable," said the congressman with him.

"I think he's just plain cute," said the teenage visitor. "Do you think he will give me his autograph?"

For almost four years now Kennedy has moved in this aura of wary excitement, approval and charmed delight. Ever since he was catapulted to national notice by the 1956 battle for the Democratic vice-presidential nomination, he has been heralded as the party's obvious choice for the presidency, and his good looks and pleasing personality have been treated as his major political assets. Fortunately for Jack Kennedy, however, behind that façade of easy victory lie other characteristics he can draw on now as the day of decision draws near—for, as well as being a charmer, he is a long-range planner, a thoughtful fighter, and a man whose drive and stamina are rooted in the simple declaration, "I love my work."

"He's never been taken in by his publicity," a politician said. "He cut himself a three-piece pattern to get the nomination some time ago, and he's never forgotten it. He's out to make a record in the Senate—get acquainted nationally—and win delegates politically. And he juggles all three at one time."

"He can put in a full day at the Senate, fly to Cleveland, say, make a speech, fly back, snatch a little sleep, hold a breakfast conference and then show up on the floor, fit as a fiddle and as well strung," one colleague said. Said his secretary: "I get in here before nine, and often he's already here—and I never plan to leave before seven-thirty." Said an old friend: "He's got the secret of youth. He loves politics, but he's not emotional about it. He's got a great ability to grasp both the big picture and the meaningful detail. And somehow he manages to separate his personal life from his political life. No matter how demanding his work has been, when he's

through with it, he relaxes with the same concentration with which he works." Said an aide: "He's not a man to look back. He's on to the next thing. It's deep waters run fast in his case." Said a newsman: "He's beautifully disciplined. Behind that generous smile is a cool, calculating machine that is constantly saying, 'What's in it for me?' "

Said his wife, Jacqueline: "Sometimes you have a man of ideas, sometimes a man of action; not often both in one, which is a kind of greatness. To me Jack's not boyish, as some people think, nor even very youthful. To me he's a mature man with an incredible mind who's enormously energetic."

Factually speaking, Jack Kennedy will be forty-three this May twenty-ninth, is six feet tall, and weighs 160 pounds. His hair is a dark chestnut with some gray in it; his eyes are blue with slanted lids, and, when he is not in motion, he likes to sit with his arms folded. He has a bachelor degree *cum laude,* and an honorary doctorate from Harvard, and sits on its board of overseers as an alumni representative. He has written two books of historical interest, one of which was a Pulitzer-prize winner, and more than twenty articles. Like many men of wealth, he rarely carries cash; and like many inveterate readers, he sometimes forgets he is talking to someone and picks up a paper which interests him. In college he played football, was on the swimming team, and he has sailed various kinds of boats since he was a freckle-faced boy. During the war he was a lieutenant in charge of a PT boat and was awarded the Navy and Marine Corps medal for "extremely heroic conduct." He likes to keep a golf club in his office to swing when he's tense, and on the wall facing the desk is a stunning sailfish almost ten feet long that he caught on his honeymoon at Acapulco. There are three pictures of his child and eleven of his wife, from girlhood on, around the room, and a lot of sharp cartoons about his political activities. His secretaries are allowed to keep a coffeepot going and take off their shoes if they want to, but are expected to work late whenever the need arises. The door to his office is always open, and he is readily available to his friends and to the press—if they can catch up with him.

With Jacqueline and daughter Caroline.

He was thirty-six when he married beautiful Jacqueline Bouvier on September 12, 1953.

FORGIVING

Shirley Hazzard

"Lucas," she said, crossing the lawn and sitting down on the grass beside him, "they will never forgive us for this."

He was smoking a cigarette, the other hand gripping his wrist around his bent knees. "What we have to say to each other," he said, "is more important than going to a dinner party." He spoiled the resounding effect of this by asking, "What did you tell them?"

"I said that you were sick and I had to stay with you." She sat sideways, and the folds of her skirt almost covered her bare feet. "I don't think they believed me—I'm not much of a liar." She thought she saw his eyes widen, and flushed. She tore up a few blades of grass and rolled them between her fingertips. "The grass is quite damp," she said. "Perhaps we should go inside?"

"No," he said. "It's pleasant here."

The house, although built inside a wood, was on a gradual slope, so that their view was framed but not obscured by trees. Below the wood, cultivated land—scarcely any of which was theirs—stretched across a little valley and up the opposite hill. The few lights already glowing in the warm evening came from farms or from other summer houses, or belonged to cars that passed along the road at the end of the valley. Their own house, at their backs, was unlit, sharply white in the fading sunshine—a small Greek-revival house just large enough for two people. For years Lucas had talked of adding a wing so that their occasional summer guests might be more comfortable, but in fact the house could only be extended at the sacrifice of its proportions. The wing had stayed unbuilt and the guests continued to sleep in the living room, able to return to town as soon as possible. Kate and Lucas had no children.

"Yes, it is lovely this evening," she agreed, enlarging his more moderate remark. She waited for him to speak again, but he only threw the end of his cigarette into the grass. "Should you do that?" she asked. "Is it safe?"

"You just said the grass was damp," he pointed out.

She thought, dejectedly, that a sudden conflagration would at least divert him from what he was about to say, but the moments passed with no delivering outbreak of flames, the cigarette having disobligingly fizzled out in a patch of clover. She wished she had brought a sweater for her bare shoulders, but did not like to go inside for one now. She changed her attitude and sat, like him, hugging her knees. "Let's hope they won't drive over to see how you are, and find us sitting out here."

Again he did not reply, and she was left to feel that her remarks were received as crude attempts at appeasement—which they were. She looked at him, and he lighted another cigarette, throwing the match away with a certain insistence. Then he said, "I just can't get used to it."

She said, cautiously, "I'm not quite sure what you feel."

"Well, I feel—all the classic symptoms, I suppose." He made a brief ironical movement with his shoulders. "Like the deceived husband in a play. I keep telling myself that after all it doesn't matter, you didn't mean it, it's only what I've done myself, but I still can't get used to it."

She curled her toes in apprehension. "From what you said this morning, I take it you don't intend to do anything about it?"

"*Do* anything? What should I do?"

"I mean," she said, knowing he had understood her, "that you don't intend to leave me."

"It doesn't seem on that scale, does it? From what you tell me. What was it you said it was—an aberration?"

"An incident."

Without turning to her, he suddenly burst out, "Ah, Kate, how could you?"

Twisting her fingers together around her knees, she said in a small, gruff voice, "You leave me alone too much."

"It's not *my* idea, for God's sake. What can I do, if they send me on these trips? It's the way I earn my living, after all." ("And yours" fitted neatly into a small pause.) "I don't choose it."

"You might be less enthusiastic about it. I mean, you could—*object* more."

"There wasn't anyone else who could do this last trip."

"You were away for two months," she said.

"Well, one doesn't go to Africa for the *day*, you know." He stopped, surprised to find himself in a defensive position.

She said, seeing this, "I'm not justifying myself."

"Hardly," he replied, ungenerously.

"Lucas," she said, not daring to touch him, but laying her hand on the grass between them, "you are right to mind. I would hate it if you didn't, and I'm terribly, terribly sorry. But it was just silly, that's all. It didn't *matter*. Please don't think it mattered."

"That seems, somehow, to make it worse." He drew on his cigarette. "Yes, I do mind. Of course I mind. I mind like hell."

"Don't," she said.

"What did you expect?"

"In the first place, I didn't think you'd —know," she said, barely hesitating to make the correction. "And then, I suppose I thought you would be more—philosophical about it."

"I can only say that you have a curious idea either of philosophy or of me."

She laid the side of her head against her knees. "Lucas—don't be so cold with me," she said. "Please don't be." The darkness was coming down quickly and she could hardly see him now: He was a black, self-contained shape, a ship exuding smoke and showing a single light. "We talk like a couple of stage Englishmen. I would really rather that you hit me."

"Don't be melodramatic—you know you'd have a fit if I hit you." He did agree, nevertheless, that his idea of acceptable behavior had left him no way of dealing with such a discovery.

A mosquito was biting her ankle; she felt that at this juncture she had no choice but to disregard it.

He went on. "It must make a difference."

"Everything makes a difference."

Annoyed by the solecism, he said, "Do you think I can ever be away from you again without thinking of this?"

She said, without spirit, "The other possibility would be not to go."

"You're unreasonable," he replied in a hard voice.

"In any case, it's not as though it had ever happened before. Or would again."

"I have no way of knowing that."

"Except that I tell you."

"Then why has it happened *now*? Kate, can you tell me why?"

The cars could be heard swishing along the main road. She put her cheek back on her knee and stroked her palms over the grass on either side of her. She said, apparently with total irrelevance, "It was my birthday."

"What?"

"I hadn't heard from you for weeks. And it was my birthday." She sighed. "That's all. I know it doesn't help."

"A form of celebration, I take it?"

She turned her face away.

After a moment he said, "The photograph you sent me, then—he took that?"

"What photograph?"

"A photograph taken up here. On your birthday, you said."

"Oh. Oh, yes. . . . I'm sorry. Yes."

"Kate," he said, aghast, "Don't you have any sensibilities at all?"

"Well," she said helplessly, "you kept asking for a photograph."

"I hardly imagined you would go to such lengths to obtain one. . . . How *could* you send that to me?"

She made an ineffectual gesture toward him. "It was the only one I've ever liked." Her voice, inexcusably, carried the suggestion of a smile.

"It didn't look a bit like you," he said crossly. They sat for a while without speaking. Presently he said, with an air of monumental acceptance, "Perhaps this is the customary thing. Perhaps one has no right to ask loyalty."

"Perhaps one has no right to *expect* it," she said. "But I think one must ask it."

He was silent again, making it clear that she had forfeited her right to adjudicate human behavior. He could tell, from the interruptions of her breathing, that she had begun to cry. He said unyieldingly, "Now Kate, pull yourself together," and added—as though tears were by nature frivolous, "this is serious."

"Yes, I'm sorry," she said, not raising her hands from the grass but rubbing her tears off on her skirt with motions of her head. "It's only because I'm tired. I couldn't sleep last night. In fact, I felt quite shaky all day."

He doubted this, but dared not say so. Once, years ago, he had expressed skepticism about an illness of hers, and she had promptly and irrefutably fainted, in a shop; since then she had been, in this respect, unchallengeable. Now, however, having dried her eyes, she began to cry all over again and with such a suppressed, pathetic sound that he could no longer ignore it. He said, in a milder tone, "Kate, please stop."

"I'm sorry," she said again, "but it's the way you speak to me."

"But, dear," he protested, with a sense of injustice, "I can't pretend this is nothing. I'm only trying to make you understand how much it matters to me."

She looked up at him in the darkness. "I can't help feeling," she said—and again he could hear her smile, "that you might have accomplished your object with a quarter of the exertion." She gave a sharp sniff. "I don't have a handkerchief."

"Nor do I. We'll go in, in a minute." He put his cigarette out carefully in the damp earth.

"Lucas," she began, "if it would help—I can tell you how it happened."

"Please don't," he said, his voice rising again. "I couldn't bear to know any details."

She was silent, and then said, "How strange—it's *so* what a woman *would* want to know. Isn't that interesting?"

"No," he said, but almost laughed. They were quiet for a while, and when he next turned his head he said, "Kate," sharply, as if she might have disappeared in the meantime. "Let us go in." He got up quickly and, feeling for her hand in the dark, helped her to her feet. He could not embrace her so soon without diminishing the significance of all he had said, and he let her go abruptly—thinking (mistakenly) that she would not have detected the passing of his anger. They stood for so long, however, facing each other, unseeing, that he was obliged either to speak or to take her in his arms, so he said into the darkness, "About the letters—I probably should write more."

She touched his hand lightly. *"Don't."*

"No, really, I think you have a point."

"Lucas," she said, "I'll cry again." He put his arm about her shoulders and they crossed the lawn awkwardly, holding each other and out of step. "Be careful," she said. "I left the watering can somewhere round here."

"What a dark night," he said, as they went up the path to the house. They stopped and stared at the sky. "Perhaps it'll rain. I'm glad we didn't go out to dinner."

They walked on. They had almost reached the door of the house when she stood still again, within his arm, and said, "Lucas—what did you mean when you said that it was only something that you'd done yourself?"

Illustration by
N. M. Bodecker for
PRETTY POLLY
a story by
Noel Coward

PARIS

A Little Incident on the Rue de L'Odéon

Katherine Anne Porter

Last summer in Paris I went back to the place where Sylvia Beach had lived, to the empty bookshop, Shakespeare and Company, and the flat above, where she brought together for sociable evenings the most miscellaneous lot of people I ever saw: persons you were surprised to find on the same planet together, much less under the same roof.

The bookshop at 12 Rue de l'Odéon has been closed ever since the German occupation, but her rooms have been kept piously intact by a faithful friend, more or less as she left them, except for a filmlike cobweb on the objects, a grayness in the air, for Sylvia is gone, and has taken her ghost with her. All sorts of things were there, her walls of books in every room, the bushels of papers, hundreds of photographs, portraits, odd bits of funny toys, even her flimsy scraps of underwear and stockings left to dry near the kitchen window; a coffee cup and a small coffeepot as she left them on the table; in her bedroom, her looking glass, her modest entirely incidental vanities, facepowder, beauty cream, lipstick. . . .

Oh, no. She was not there. And someone had taken away the tiger skin from her bed —narrow as an army cot. If it was not a tiger, then some large savage cat with good markings; real fur, I remember, spotted or streaked, a wild woodland touch shining out in the midst of the pure, spontaneous, persevering austerity of Sylvia's life: maybe a humorous hint of some hidden streak in Sylvia, this preacher's daughter of a Baltimore family, brought up in unexampled high-mindedness, gentle company and polite learning; this nervous, witty girl whose only expressed ambition in life was to have a bookshop of her own. Anywhere would do, but Paris for choice. God knows modesty could hardly take denser cover, and this she did at incredible expense of hard work and spare living and yet with the help of quite dozens of devoted souls one after the other; the financial and personal help of her two delightful sisters and the lifetime savings of her mother, a phoenix of a mother who consumed herself to ashes time and again in aid of her wild daughter.

For she *was* wild—a wild, free spirit if ever I saw one, fearless, untamed to the last, which is not the same as being reckless or prodigal, or wicked, or suicidal. She was not really afraid of anything human, a most awe-inspiring form of courage. She trusted her own tastes and instincts and went her own way; and almost everyone who came near her trusted her too.

James Joyce, his wife, his children, his fortunes, his diet, his eyesight, and his book *Ulysses* turned out to be the major project of her life; he was her unique darling, all his concerns were hers. One could want a rest cure after merely reading an account of her labors to get that book written in the first place, then printed and paid for and distributed even partially. Yet it was only one, if the most laborious and exhausting, of all her pastimes, concerned as she was solely with bringing artists together —writers preferred, any person with a degree of talent practicing or connected with the art of Literature, and in getting their work published and set before the eyes of the world. Painters and composers were a marginal interest. There was nothing diffused or shapeless in Sylvia's purpose: that bizarre assortment of creatures shared a common center—they were artists or were trying to be. Otherwise many of them had only Sylvia in common. She had introduced many of them to each other.

We know now from many published memoirs what Ford Madox Ford thought of Hemingway, what Hemingway thought of Ford and F. Scott Fitzgerald, how William Carlos Williams felt about Paris literary life, how Bryher felt herself a stranger to every one but Sylvia, and going back to an early book of Robert McAlmon's, *Being Geniuses Together,* what he thought of the whole lot. These recorded memories glitter with malice and hatred and jealousy, and one sees ten versions of the same incident in as many books: I have not seen one that spoke meanly of Sylvia. They seemed to be agreed about her, she was a touchstone.

She was a thin, twiggy sort of woman, quick-tongued, quick-minded and light on her feet. Her nerves were as tight as a tuned-up fiddle string and she had now and then attacks of migraine that stopped her in her tracks before she spun herself to death, just in the usual run of her days.

When I first saw her, in the early spring of 1932, her hair was still the color of roasted chestnut shells, her light golden brown eyes with greenish glints in them were marvelously benign, acutely attentive, and they sparkled upon one rather than beamed, as gentle eyes are supposed to do. She was not pretty, never had been, never had tried to be: she was attractive, a center of interest, a delightful presence not accountable to any of the familiar attributes of charm.

Sylvia loved her hundreds of friends, and they all loved her—many of whom loved almost no one else except perhaps himself —apparently without jealousy, each one sure of his special cell in the vast honeycomb of her heart; sure of his welcome in her shop with its exhilarating air of something pretty wonderful going on at top speed. Her genius was for friendship; her besetting virtue, generosity, an all-covering charity in its true sense; and courage that reassured even Hemingway, the distrustful, the wary, the unloving, who sized people up on sight, who couldn't be easy until he had somehow got the upper hand. Half an hour after he was first in her shop, Hemingway was sitting there with a sock and shoe laid aside, showing Sylvia the still-painful scars of his war wounds got in Italy. He told her the doctors thought he would die and he was baptized there in the hospital. Sylvia wrote in her memoirs, "Baptized or not—and I am going to say this whether Hemingway shoots me or not—I have always felt he was a deeply religious man."

Hemingway tried to educate her in boxing, wrestling, any kind of manly sport, but it seemed to remain to Sylvia mere reeling and writhing and fainting in coils: but Hemingway and Hadley his wife, and Bumby the Baby, and Sylvia and Adrienne Monnier, her good friend, all together at a boxing match must have been one of the sights of Paris. Sylvia tells it with her special sense of comedy, very acute, and with tenderness. Hemingway rather turns out to be the hero of her book, helping to bootleg copies of *Ulysses* into the United States, shooting German snipers off her roof on the day the American army entered Paris: being shown in fact as the man he wished and tried to be. . . .

As I say, Sylvia's friends did not always love each other even for her sake, nor could anyone but Sylvia expect them to: yet it is plain that she did. At parties specially, or in her shop, she had a way, figuratively, of taking two of her friends, strangers to each other, by the napes of their necks and cracking their heads together, saying in effect always, and at times in so many words, "My dears, you *must* love one another!"

Usually the strangers would give each other a straight, skeptical stare, exchange a few mumbling words under her expectant, fostering eyes; and the instant she went on to other greetings and exchanges, they faced about from each other and drifted away.

It was in Sylvia's shop that I saw Ernest Hemingway for the first and last time. If this sounds portentous now, it is only because of all that has happened since to make of him a tragic figure. Then he was still the *beau garçon* who loved blood

293

sports, the black-haired, sunburned muscle boy of American literature; the unalloyed male who had licked Style to a standstill. He had exactly the right attitude toward words like "glory" and so on. It was not particularly impressive: I preferred Joyce and Yeats and Henry James, and I had seen all the bullfights and done all the hunting I wanted in Mexico before I ever came to Paris. He seemed to me then to be the walking exemplar of the stylish literary attitudes of his time: he may have been, but I see now how very good he was; he paid heavily, as such men do, for their right to live on beyond the fashion they helped to make, to play out to the end not the role wished on them by their public but the destiny they cannot escape because there was a moment in their lives when they chose that destiny.

It was such a little incident, and so random and rather comic at the time, and Sylvia and I laughed over it again years later, the last time I saw her in New York.

I had dropped into Sylvia's shop looking for something to read, just at early dark on a cold, rainy winter evening, maybe in 1934, I am not sure. We were standing under the light at the big round table piled up with books, talking; and I was just saying good-bye when the door burst open, and Hemingway unmistakably Ernest stood before us, looking just like the snapshots of him then being everywhere published—tall, bulky, broadfaced (his season of boyish slenderness was short), cropped black moustache, watchful eyes, all reassuringly there.

THE WORLD'S RICHEST WOMEN ARE QUEENS

▶ Your mind is a sacred enclosure into which nothing harmful can enter except by your permission.
—ARNOLD BENNETT

He wore a streaming old raincoat and a drenched floppy rain hat pulled over his eyebrows. Sylvia ran to him calling like a bird, both arms out; they embraced in a manly sort of way, then Sylvia turned to me with that ominous apostolic sweetness in her eyes. Still holding one of Hemingway's hands, she reached at arm's length for mine. "Katherine Anne Porter," she said, pronouncing the names in full, "this is Ernest Hemingway. . . . Ernest, this is Katherine Anne, and I want the two best modern American writers to know each other!" Our hands were never joined.

"Modern" was a talismanic word then, but this time the magic failed. At that instant the telephone rang in the back room, Sylvia flew to answer, calling back to us merrily, merrily, "Now you two just get acquainted and I'll be right back." Hemingway and I stood and gazed unwinkingly at each other with poker faces for all of ten seconds, in silence. Hemingway then turned in one wide swing and hurled himself into the rainy darkness as he had hurled himself out of it, and that was all. I am sorry if you are disappointed. All personal lack of sympathy and attraction aside, and they were real in us both, it must have been galling to this most famous young man to have his name pronounced in the same breath as writer with someone he had never heard of, and a woman at that. I nearly felt sorry for him.

Sylvia seemed mystified that her hero had vanished. "Where did he go?" "I don't know." "What did he say?" she asked, still wondering. I had to tell her: "Nothing, not a word. Not even good-bye." She continued to think this very strange. I didn't, and don't.

Monarchy may be disappearing in Europe, but the Netherlands and Great Britain each retains a queen of vast popularity and equally vast personal wealth. Juliana, who here welcomes Elizabeth II to the Netherlands, is independently wealthy and also the daughter of possibly the richest woman in the world. Elizabeth is the wealthiest woman in her own kingdom; her jewelry collection alone is thought to be worth around $150,000,000. To their subjects, this is only as it should be. It takes money to keep royal traditions alive.

Opposite: MARILYN MONROE
In 1962 a coroner's report called the death of the actress on August 4 a "probable suicide." But few of her close friends believed it was suicide. To them it was a terrible accident.

FROM ENGLAND WITH LOVE

Nora O'Leary

With the breath-taking pace of a James Bond thriller, young British fashion designer Mary Quant has whizzed to fame and fortune on both sides of the Atlantic. Her uninhibited talent has admirably pepped up the British fashion scene and gathered together an international admiration society of Quant-girls who love to wear her clothes. On this page we show Butterick Patterns made from Mary Quant originals, all of them photographed on Candice Bergen, 19-year-old daughter of entertainer Edgar Bergen and Mrs. Bergen, former Powers model Frances Westerman.

Above: Wool plaid jumper with orange blouse and hat. Top right: The same blouse worn with a knee-skirting hip skirt. Right: Plaid jumper, this time without blouse, to wear as a dress up date dress. The slightly flared skirt allows plenty of dancing room for doing the Frog.

Left and in the background at right: Another sensational British export—whenever they can be spared at home—The Beatles.

HOW MOVIE AND T.V. VIOLENCE AFFECTS CHILDREN

Frederic Wertham, M.D.

In the course of many meetings with parents I have become increasingly aware of their concern over the amount of violence to which children are exposed nowadays through motion pictures shown on television and in movie theaters.

Before answering the questions parents most frequently ask of me about screen violence, let me first define two terms:

By "children" I mean young people from about the age of three, when many begin to be TV fans, up to about twelve, when it can be assumed that the average child has become better able to differentiate between the real and the unreal, the likely and the unlikely; more critical; his sensibilities and his standards of values better established.

By "violence" I mean people killing each other, hurting each other; I mean arson, torture, beating, knifing, lynching or any other physical action that would shock and frighten a normal child—or adult, for that matter—if he saw it happen in real life.

There is a lack of adventure in the lives of most children today. The world is full of dangers, but not of the kind that children can comprehend or come up against physically. So, adventure stories on television and in the movies can help to fill a need of children for their all-round development. Some violence or the threat of it, handled with respect for children's sensibilities, has always been an ingredient in good children's adventure stories. What has become so prevalent, and what parents are concerned about today, is the movie or TV show in which violence predominates—made more realistic and shocking because it is shown, in live action, rather than merely described.

In the course of its study NAFBRAT (National Association for Better Radio and Television) compiled the following list of violent acts taking place on various TV shows represented as being for children. Nearly all these were half-hour programs:

PROGRAM A: One murder, one robbery, one jailbreak.

PROGRAM B: One murder, three attempted murders, one robbery, one holdup.

PROGRAM C: Two attempted murders, one robbery.

PROGRAM D: Three attempted murders, one jailbreak, one arson.

PROGRAM E: Two attempted murders, one "justifiable" killing, one holdup, two attempted lynchings, two hangings prevented at the last moment, one mob violence, brutal fights.

PROGRAM F: Two murders, one attempted murder, one robbery, threats to kill, man tied up.

PROGRAM G: One attempted murder, one robbery, conspiracy to murder three people, one bomb explosion.

PROGRAM H: Two murders, one "justifiable" killing, one false murder charge, man dumped into well to die.

PROGRAM I: One "justifiable" killing, one attempted murder, one police car stolen.

PROGRAM J: One murder, three attempted murders, one "justifiable" killing, lots of shooting.

PROGRAM K: Three mass shootings, one holdup, one bank robbery, two attempted murders.

PROGRAM L: Four attempted murders of a twelve-year-old boy, one attempted murder, one fight with guns and fists.

These typical examples (1958) are from such allegedly wholesome programs for children as Wild Bill Hickok, Sergeant Preston, Robin Hood, The Lone Ranger, Steve Donovan, Superman, Sky King, Annie Oakley, Rin Tin Tin, Hawkeye.

NAFBRAT listed the toll of violence for one week in programs shown in Los Angeles before 9 P.M.: 161 murders, 60 so-called "justifiable" killings, 2 suicides, 192 attempted murders, 83 robberies, 15 kidnapings, 24 murder conspiracies, 21 jailbreaks, 7 attempted lynchings, 6 dynamitings, 11 extortions, 2 cases of arson, 2 cases of torture. What could not be counted were innumerable prolonged and brutal fights, threats of killing, sluggings, manhandling of women and children.

I know of no statistical measurement of violence in films shown in motion-picture houses, but the number of children under twelve who go to movies is infinitesimal compared with the number who watch TV, it should be remembered that many movies ultimately are shown on TV.

The (British) Association of Cinematograph and Allied Technicians, referring to American movies, had this to say in a resolution: "Beating up, gouging, knifing, flogging of women, and other forms of sadistic excess are too regular a feature of so-called motion-picture entertainment today." It added that in nine cases out of ten there was no artistic justification for the brutality. It made a clear distinction between films that respect human dignity and those that depict violent death as the natural order of things.

To the question "Children have survived plenty of violence in storybooks—is it so different on TV and movie screens?" I would say that the moving visual image on movie or TV screen, complete with sound, has a much greater impact on most children than the images they conceive in their own mind's eye from reading a story or having one read aloud to them. An eight-year-old boy, for example, gave me a most sensitive account of the movie The Grapes of Wrath, which much older youths could not give me from the book.

"Live action" on the screen, particularly when it is cruel or horrifying, works directly on the child without the—for some children—cumbersome detour of reading. The identification with a character in a motion picture may be almost overpowering. The very effort which even fair readers must make to read the abstract letters on the printed page is a barrier to merging completely with the story. The same exciting story on the screen can absorb a child immediately and entirely.

"Will watching violent TV shows and movies cause a child to become a criminal?"

Obviously no one can say exactly how any individual child will be affected without knowing a great deal about that child. But the connection between screen violence and the committing of crimes by young people has been pointed out by some distinguished jurists and criminologists.

Justice Curtis Bok, of the Supreme Court of Pennsylvania, has listed the primary causes of juvenile delinquency and crime; as one among only five groups of causes, he mentions crime and violence shows on TV and movie screens.

The director of the U.S. Bureau of Prisons, James V. Bennett, has noted that the modus operandi in an increasingly large number of crimes committed by young offenders closely parallels TV shows they have seen.

The British Report of the Departmental Committee on Children and the Cinema says that sadistic and brutal scenes have a bad effect on children and should not be seen by them.

Judge Frank J. Kronenberg, president of the New York State County Judges' Association, states that "television is an instrument of intense pressure that convinces the immature mind that violence is an accepted way of life. It is a subtle form of American brainwashing."

Parents reading of juvenile crimes, especially the mad, senseless stabbings that have become so prevalent in cities, ask, "Don't these young hoodlums have any *feelings?"* They certainly don't have much empathy—the capacity for feeling the pain of others and "hurting with them." There are many reasons for this callousness, but Dr. Walter C. Alvarez, formerly of the Mayo Clinic, has pointed out that violent movie and TV films may have something to do with it.

"Do we adults have any sense at all," he asks, "when daily we let people show our children pictures of murder, violence, shooting, hanging, kidnaping? . . . Today most children have become so hardened that they can look at these pictures of murder and sudden death without being upset."

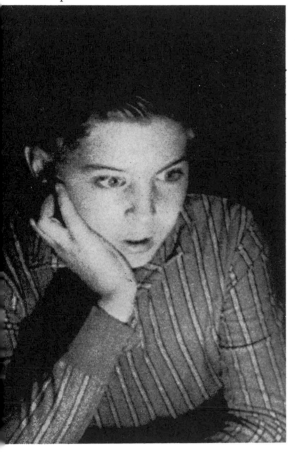

Commissioner Frieda B. Hennock, of the Federal Communications Commission, told a Senate subcommittee that television sets "are pouring an unending stream of crime, violence, outright murder, brutality, unnatural suspense and horror into the living rooms of America. The suggestions which have been made that there is no discernible relationship between these programs and the recent appalling increase in juvenile delinquency flout common sense and rudimentary sound judgment."

Well-authenticated observations indicate that delinquent children have been influenced—directly or indirectly—by the screen. Even the courts have taken official cognizance, in cases of robberies, of this "indirect incitement." Children have injured other children and adults with BB and other guns, re-enacting the shootings they had seen in screen Westerns. They have worn gloves when committing burglaries, imitating crime pictures, and used masks like that worn by Zorro.

In recent years I have had to examine a number of adolescents and postadolescents charged with homicide. Among them were cases which aroused national interest: the boy who killed a baby sitter and a baby in Massachusetts; the boy who shot the "model boy" on the streets of New York City; the high-school boy on Long Island who killed a fellow student with a shotgun in the school washroom; the Bible-carrying "model boy" who strangled a fifteen-year-old girl in New Jersey; the youth who shot a hotel employee during a robbery; the youth who was the leader of one group of young torturers and "thrill killers" in Brooklyn.

The circumstances, background, motivation and most other factors were very different in each case. But in each of them I found—and in several said so under oath—that the visual mass media (TV, movies and crime comic books), though not decisive or fundamental, played a contributing part in the final tragedy. They did not start the fire, but they did add fuel to it.

One boy who had beaten a girl told me he had had daydreams of doing this for a long time. When he saw a girl being beaten on the screen, the idea of actually carrying out his daydreams came to him for the first time.

I agree with Clifton Fadiman's statement that violent TV shows create in young people "a lust for violence."

I have often asked a special kind of expert in this field—the juvenile criminals themselves—what they think about the effect of violent screen fare on children. Nearly all have said the effect is bad. "They make you think you do something big," or "They show you how a man is killed," or "They make you want to try it out."

The screen may not only provide unhealthy suggestions, it may also lead to a subtle general conditioning. The child whose memory is filled with screen violence may have less psychological resistance to various evil influences.

The connection between violence and sex, as presented on the screen, is particularly apt to arouse fantasies and/or facilitate the transition from fantasy to action. Where the Western films stultify with violence, the horror shows titillate with sadism (sex combined with violence). I know of cases in which boys as young as eleven have been sexually excited by them. Sadistic daydreams, whether or not accompanied by masturbation, are certainly not good for children and may instill a liking for sadism that will cause serious trouble in later life.

"There is violence in real life; shouldn't children learn about it from watching violent TV shows and movies?" The fact is, many so-called children's TV programs, or movies available to children, portray in a half hour more violent excitement than the average person experiences in a lifetime. How many of us have seen a man shot down or knifed, pistol-whipped, deliberately run down by a car—in real life?

What children see on the screen is violence as an almost casual commonplace of daily living. Violence becomes the fundamental principle of society, the natural law of humanity. Killing is as common as taking a walk, a gun is more natural than an umbrella.

Sometimes very general questions will reveal how a child views the history offered him in Westerns. Witness this interview with an eight-year-old boy:

Q. Do you think it is good for children to watch television?

A. Yes. Yes, I do.

Q. Why?

A. They help you to understand real life.

Q. What do you mean, real life?

A. What it was like in the old days.

Q. From what you have seen on TV, what was it like in the old days?

A. Well, it was exciting.

Q. Fun?

A. Yeah.

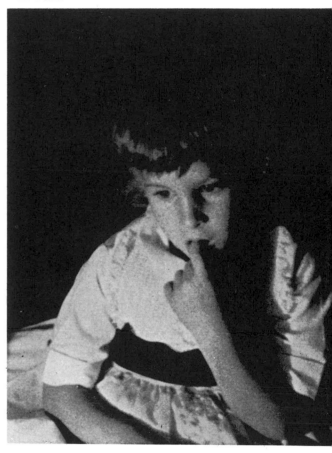

Q. What was the most fun they had?

A. Gun slinging, rounding them up and shooting them.

It would seem that these violent shows lead children to expect, and in some cases to crave, a kind of violence that they will not encounter in real life unless they stir it up themselves.

With the progress of civilization we have learned—slowly and painfully—that violence is not the best way to settle human differences. But we seem to be using the marvelous technical media of movies and television to teach children that it is the *only* way.

The late Arthur T. Vanderbilt, chief justice of the Supreme Court of New Jersey, wrote in the Washington University Law Quarterly: "Our greatest concern with the oncoming generation, I submit, relates to the perversion of young minds through the mass media of the movies and television. . . . The problem is only beginning to receive the serious consideration it calls for."

A NEW ROLE FOR BARBRA IN 1966

In a few months, Barbra Streisand plans to play the most important role of her spectacular young life. She's expecting a baby, of course, and having lots of fun while she waits. Barbra loves clothes (she's on the best dressed list!), so part of the joy of being pregnant for her was selecting a marvelous mother-to-be wardrobe. We picked some of our favorite maternity clothes, flew them to London, where Barbra was appearing in "Funny Girl." Here at Ennismore Gardens, she poses with schoolboys in a dress by Ma Mère.

WORDS MAKE THE BOOK

Rumer Godden

"The best. We want them to have the very best." How many young parents say that with determination and hope shining in their eyes? Most of us want something better for our children, and we make extraordinary sacrifices to achieve this end. It is this laudable determination, this hope and love, that makes us who are parents—and everyone who works with children—easy game for the deceptions of the commercial world.

With material things, things for the body, we are largely safeguarded; there are laws against food or drug adulteration, organizations that can often warn against dubious merchandise; but when it comes to things of the mind and spirit, a sham is far more difficult to recognize, so difficult that I think the perpetrators themselves often do not know what serious wrong they are doing.

"It's only a book for children. Why bother?" That is what many people say. "Does it matter much what children read as long as they are amused?" A child loves easy books or comics, we are told, and will ask for them over and over again. Of course! These are amusing, brightly colored, usually innocuous—but is that enough?

We all know that a baby kept too long on mushy food will not take to solids, and if we give children only this easy reading, accustom them to a "soft book" diet, with nothing to chew, as it were, nothing on which to exercise their intelligence and thought, very soon they will not be capable of reading or of having read to them anything on which they will have to use their minds, think about, reach up to. We would not give our children watered milk, stale eggs or meat substitute, but isn't what goes to feed the mind just as important? Surely it is even more important. This is not a fanciful analogy: Books are food for the mind, and a growing mind is just as hungry as a growing body—a child will often gobble up books. Then what a pity not to let these be the best, books that will satisfy for a long time, that a child will not grow *out* of, but grow up *with*.

We should remember that a child's mind is extraordinarily receptive; it is not like wax but like plaster of Paris that takes an impression and sets at once so that what goes into it goes in to stay, perhaps for a lifetime; but a good book can be a kind of widow's cruse, with a mysterious capacity for unfolding more meaning the more it is read, of yielding inexhaustible delight.

In the children's book world, books of this quality have always been compara-tively rare, considering the hundreds of titles published every year. To sift through even one season's output is rather like washing for gold; sieve after sieve is taken and yields nothing but dross, grit and sand, because it is a horrid fact that many books offered for children hide a poor text under a lavish jacket and illustrations. Only now and again is there a gleam of true metal. This rarity is understandable because, contrary to what most people think, writing for children is a difficult and disciplined art; not many authors succeed in it. But every generation does yield a few nuggets. The difficulty is to find them.

There used to be one almost infallible test: Just as gold has to be tested, so has literature, and for a children's book the best test has always been time; books that have endured, been read and loved by generations of children, are likely to be gold. This is not to say that only the old are good—that would be nonsense. Time moves more swiftly now, and a book that has managed to single itself out from the vast stream, not sunk out of sight but kept afloat for 30, 20, even 10 years, is sure to have grains of the authentic metal: books like Jean de Brunhoff's Babar books, the Orlando books, The Story of Ping, Ferdinand the Bull, Mary Norton's books, Arthur Ransome's, the Mary Poppins books, to name only a few published since the '20's. Every year adds one or two to these, perhaps even five or six, but probably not more; time will discover them.

One used to be able to rely on these time-tested books; they became, as it were, "brand names." The title or the author's name was a guarantee of their quality, but—and here is the big but—nowadays one has to make sure that it is the real book one is getting, not a spurious copy, a lopped and injured thing with the life blood taken out of it.

Once upon a time one could go into a bookshop and ask for, say, *Black Beauty* or *Treasure Island,* and be sold *Black Beauty* or *Treasure Island* as Anna Sewell or Robert Louis Stevenson wrote these stories, with all their gifts of drama, their variety of language. Nowadays, only too often, they are produced in a new edition, beguiling to the eye, but bearing somewhere the carefully inconspicuous phrase "retold," or "told to the children," or "reworded," or "re-edited"—meaning that these books are no longer what they purport to be.

A publisher has such famous classics "retold," reduced and simplified; often they are brought out in a "package" or a series in glossy format, with a name such as Famous Classics for Children, or Stories That Every Child Should Know. They are usually quite low-priced, but all the same questionable because, as I said, they are not what they seem but a prostitution in basic English.

This is counterfeit—no other term for it—and, to anyone who cares for literature, to anyone who wants the best for his or her children, it is a very grave matter indeed —yet it is really only a matter of words. It seems obvious to say that a book is made of words, but is it quite as obvious that it is the words that make a book? Yet this is true. It is in its words that the ultimate value of a book lies.

If books were Persian carpets and one wanted to assess their value, one would not look only at the outer side—the pattern and colorings—but one would turn them over and examine the stitch, because it is the stitch that makes a carpet wear, gives it its life and bloom, that expresses its design and color just as the ideas and philosophy of a book are expressed in its words. They should be woven in, "belong," bind together to make a whole, because, just as any valuable carpet has an individual pattern, through every well-written book there runs a rhythm that is its writer's style, an integral and unobtrusive rhythm that matches his ideas. Sometimes this rhythm is robust, sometimes so subtle that it is impossible for even another writer to say how it is done, but it is always a vital quality, and if it is interfered with, the whole style, the individuality, is immediately lost. Yet there is a growing and wicked tendency to rob children's books of their words, to limit these and simplify them, which results in real damage, as the words tend to regulate the ideas instead of the other way round.

Some books are limited to as few as 240 words; some bear a label saying they are Vocabulary Tested, which means the editors guarantee there are no words in them unfamiliar to the average child of the age groups concerned—and they take a very low average—no words which he can learn, savor and explore. Not only the classics suffer from this word limitation; one of the newest gimmicks is to get "names," well-known authors, whether they can write for children or not, to contribute to a modern series, using a limited vocabulary chosen by a panel of philologists; the name "philologist" impresses parents, and it is good advertisement. I have been approached by one of these firms, and the size of the financial bait offered for one short story showed what big business this combination of word limitation and children's books has become.

It has been explained to me that one reason for this business drive is that publishers have become aware of a vast market opening up in the developing countries of Asia and Africa; the peoples there are "book-starved," especially for children's and school books. This is very heartening, but it is the reverse of heartening if the same book is being made to do for a Swahili or Bengali boy struggling with English—a foreign language to him—and an English or American child reading his mother tongue. Naturally, the little Swahili or Bengali needs few and basic words—but English and American children are born with the richest inheritance of words in the world; there are over 414,825 in the Oxford Dictionary, over 450,000 in the latest Webster's. Then isn't it a cheat to accustom a child to use only 240 of them? It is like forbidding him to walk or run because others are learning to take their first steps.

One thinks with apprehension of the future. Not only are classic books being damaged but new ones as well; the young and coming writer is often pressured into writing in this limited vocabulary—he has, after all, to earn his living, and today it is very difficult for new authors to get started. Besides, it all sounds so harmless, even desirable. The philologists, editors assure the young writer, can tell him what words appeal to children. He will reach, he is told, more and more children—always a beguiling prospect—and the financial bait, as I said, is usually handsome; but the effect on his writing is crippling. To understand just how crippling it is, one needs to explore a little into the writer's craft, especially that difficult branch of it (which can be an art) of writing for children. Again it is a matter of words.

Children's books are made with fewer words than books for adults, so that this already imposes a discipline on the writer, as each word becomes more important. Added to this, such books are usually meant to be read aloud, so the rhythm is doubly integral. No panel of philologists, however learned, can know what words the writer will need. He needs not the narrowest but the widest range of English from which to choose.

The restricted-vocabulary experts act on the principle that children reject polysyllable words, but they do not. Far from it. A friend of mine was acting librarian when one day into the library came a small girl wearing a new and far too large hat. She had lacquered it with shiny black dye so that it smelled like stove-pipe varnish and it was topped by an enormous rose. She was so obviously proud of it that my friend said, "What a wonderful hat!" The child beamed and replied, "Yes, and it reflects the rays of the sun with more than oriental splendor." How pleased Kipling would have been to know his Parsee's hat had made such an impression, but would it if it had been flattened out to something like "his hat shone brightly in the sun," as the advocates of word restriction would want it? They would *never* have passed "reflects," let alone the magnificence of "oriental splendor." Even a little child feels their

freshness—*unconsciously* because, as I have said, if the reader is conscious of the writing, it is overdone. It is the writer who must be conscious of every word, weighing and feeling each one.

Words not only have meanings; they have shades and shades of meanings. This is not fanciful thinking; words were originally chosen to fit the things they describe, to give the essence of them, often to sound like them. Think of the word "shadow" with the harder first syllable, the open *a* rising to the *d*, then falling away with the soft *ow* with its longer sound. It gives the feeling of a shadow, as does the French word *ombre*, again with the falling away of the soft *bre*. The expressive beauty of certain words runs through all languages. One akin to "shadow" is "twilight"; twilight, crepuscule, *crepuscolo,* and finally *Dämmerung,* which seems to glimmer.

Illustration by Roy McKie for Rumer Godden's poem "Saint Jerome and the Lion."

None of this sensitivity is wasted, because children, as I said, given the chance, glory in words; new words, long words, euphonious phrases that can make a storehouse in the mind, even the minds of the very young. Three-year-olds often chant phrases they have picked up: I remember one who could not sleep, stamping up and down the corridor repeating a phrase from *The Tailor of Gloucester* by Beatrix Potter: "No more twist . . . no more

twist," which soothed him as a lullaby would have done. I remember, after one of my poetry readings, given in a poor London district, meeting some of the seven- and eight-year-olds on their way home; in the drab street, that chill November day, they were chanting a refrain from W. J. Turner's poem *Romance:* "Shining Popocatepetl! Shining Popocatepetl!" There is a treasure-house of words, of books waiting for children to explore. Keats's "realms of gold" is no exaggeration.

But even made aware of their value, no rules can be given for this exploration. Books are such unpredictable things that they are always breaking rules. For instance, one might advise, "Always buy whole books, not condensed ones," a good general rule, but there *are* books, some of the Victorian classics, for example, so wordy that they are better pruned—but pruned, *not* simplified. There are no absolute rules to guide anyone, but there are a few wise tips:

First of all, spend as much money, not as little, as possible on books for children, and spend it, whenever possible, *in a real bookshop;* a bookshop can give a child a taste of the great world of literature, and the best books are sold seriously, not as sidelines.

As with all commodities, it is wise to be suspicious of the cheap, the "packaged" books, the bargain. The best writers for children do not have to be presented as bargains: Their books sell too well, for years.

One could say "avoid all cheap books," but this, though generally wise, is not infallible. There are good paperbacks for children and very good reprints, but one should see that it is a true reprint—not "retold," which usually means simplified. I, myself, would avoid all "told to children" versions of adult classics; though there are good ones, such as Barbara Leonie Picard's *Iliad* and *Odyssey,* it seems a pity to give these to children, because the time to read them will come later and to have a simplified version now is to rob a future pleasure.

I avoid "series" books too: They are seldom as good as those published individually because the best authors do not, and will not, write in a series—unless it is entirely their own, as with Laura Ingalls Wilder's enchanting Little House books or the famous Anne of Green Gables. And, always, everywhere, everyone should watch for that limited vocabulary and instantly reject it.

Perhaps, above all, one should take the trouble to ask advice, and the best place for this is the local library: Children's librarians are some of the most dedicated, least self-seeking people in the world, and they love to help a child to books. For parents who really care, there is *The Horn Book,* a bimonthly magazine, published in Boston, devoted entirely to literature for children—and when I say "literature," I mean it.

A children's book, in its small compass, can be true literature with all its gifts of thought, drama, beauty and words. Then let each book we give to a child be one of this true metal; only a little book for children, it is true, but one a writer is proud to write, a publisher to publish, in fact, the best.

What is the special magic that some books hold for some children? Why is Pooh beloved by one child, while another thrills to the adventures of Tarzan? And what are the books that they will remember long after they are grown up and have children of their own?

"What was *your* favorite book as a child?" The *Journal* put this question to a number of distinguished people, and got some fascinating answers. Here they are—for parents who believe, as we do, that books belong under the Christmas tree along with dolls, tricycles and electric trains.

Truman Capote
(Author)

"The first books I remember reading were The Rover Boys and The Hardy Boys series; and I remember these with much affection, particularly because they were lent to me by my nearest neighbors and greatest childhood friends, Harper Lee and her brother, Edwin. This was in a small Alabama town, and we three children used to while away the endless summer afternoons reading aloud from these very innocent adventure books, then acting out the various stories—a pastime that usually ended in tears, for one or the other of us was always falling out of a tree or otherwise damaging ourselves. But the book that made the greatest impression on me was Poe's *Tales of Mystery and Imagination*. To this day I can recite *The Tell-Tale Heart* virtually word for word."

Mrs. Lyndon B. Johnson
(First Lady)

"When I think back over my own life, books seem always to have been with me, throwing open windows to the wondrous world outside. My mother and my Aunt Effie first took me through the magic of Grimm's Fairy Tales and Greek and Teutonic myths. Then I delighted in my own reading of *The Child's Garden of Verses* and *Huckleberry Finn* and *Tom Sawyer*, and I delighted still more to discover—as my daughters grew up—that these fine old works had a quality which did not grow stale."

Robert F. Kennedy
(U.S. Senator)

"I recall with pleasure a series of books called *Billy Whiskers, The Autobiography of a Goat*, by Frances Trego Montgomery. My mother urged me to read the books when I was young, advising me they would become favorite books, and that my older brothers had loved the stories. I began reading the series, and found them fascinating, mainly because Billy Whiskers was an adventuresome goat who traveled a great deal and told many things about different parts of the world."

Art Buchwald
(Columnist)

"I imagine that my favorite book as a kid was *Penrod*. The first one I read was probably *Penrod and Sam*. There was a great deal of identification between the hero and myself in those days. I have been surprised that the Penrod books haven't held up with the kids today. I'd love to see a resurgence of Penrod fans. *Tom Swift* came back; perhaps *Penrod* will, too."

Marianne Moore
(Poet)

"My two favorite childhood books: A heavy-paper Caldecott picture-book with colored illustrations, containing *John Gilpin's Ride* by Oliver Goldsmith—a gay, sad book with *brio*. Also *The Merry Adventures of Robin Hood*, by Howard Pyle (illustrated by him)."

John Lindsay
(Mayor of New York)

"As a boy I enjoyed all the adventure stories I could put my hands on, particularly *Treasure Island*, which took me to faraway places (and that is something I still enjoy). I was excited by some of John Buchan's books, and especially *Prester John* and *The 39 Steps*. Then I enjoyed many of the series books like *The Boy Allies, Tarzan*, the Oz books and *Dr. Dolittle*. I also liked the funnies, and still do."

John Lindsay

Woody Allen
(Comedian)

"The book I remember most fondly from childhood was *The Little Prince*, by Antoine de St. Exupéry. For one thing, it was the only clean book I read as a child. But, more important, it was imaginative and presupposed a little intelligence on the part of its readers. The usual claptrap about giants and fairies and/or beanstalks left me cold, and seriously in doubt about

Marianne Moore

my parents' sanity. I always hoped to find a book where the ugly troll scored heavily at the expense of the miller's son. Anyhow *Le Petit Prince* was a hip, amusing and bright piece of work."

Woody Allen

PAUL NEWMAN, *idol of millions, claims that he hates to see his electric blue eyes in the mirror. "On my tombstone it's going to say, 'He was a terrific actor until one day his eyes turned brown.'"*

SOPHIA LOREN *could have married Cary Grant; Frank Sinatra thought she was "the most." So did Peter Sellers, William Holden, and Mastroianni, Gable, Chaplin. "But," says Sophia, "neither before nor since I met Carlo Ponti have I belonged to any other man."*

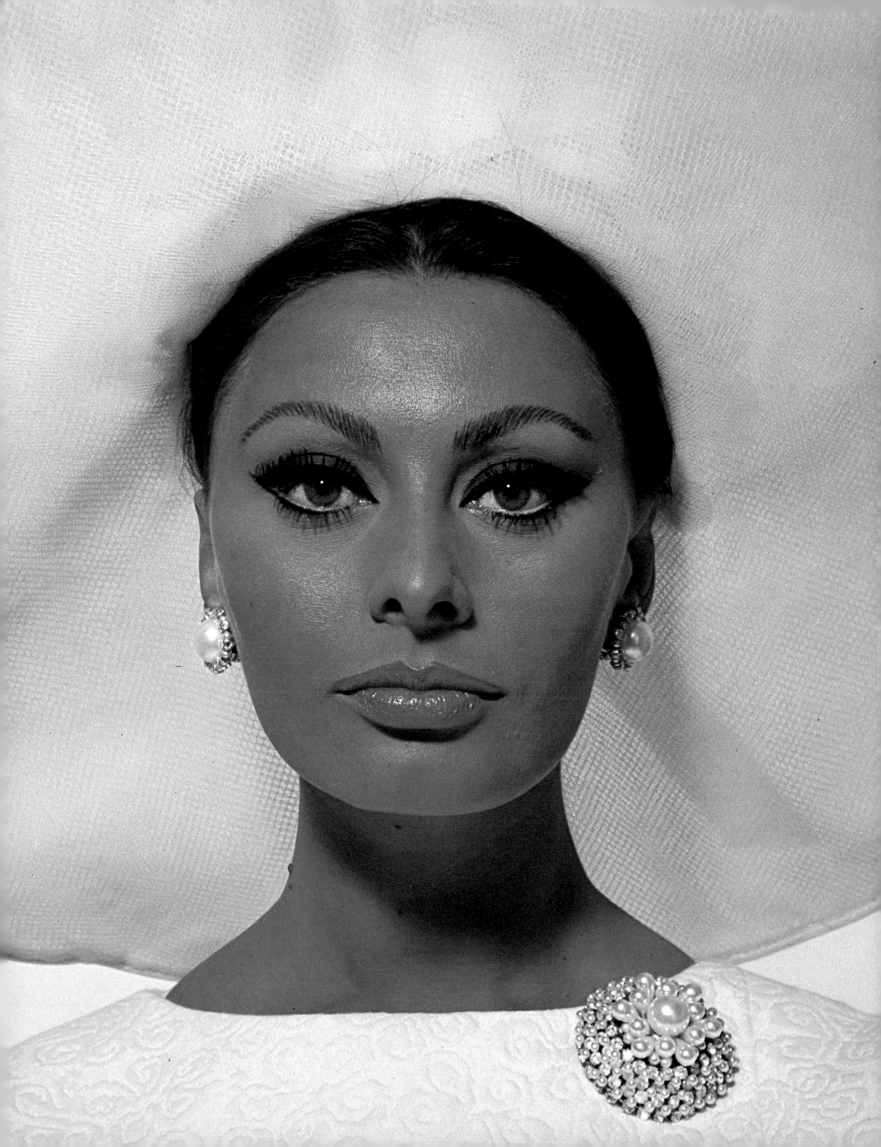

MY FAIR LADY

At Warner Brothers Studios, final touches are being applied to the film version of almost everyone's favorite musical—"My Fair Lady"—featuring Rex Harrison, Audrey Hepburn, and the costumes and sets of Britain's jack-of-all-artistic-trades, Cecil Beaton. Even the reluctant Professor Higgins admits, "Eliza, you're magnificent." At right, dressed for one of her final scenes, Eliza (Audrey) wears an enchanting, delicate pastille-mauve muslin gown. For the opening scene, Beaton designed from museum sources fabulous jeweled and feathered cocoonlike cloaks as photographed at left. As Professor Higgins, Rex Harrison (below) repeats the role he played in the stage version of Lerner and Loewe's musical adaptation of Shaw's "Pygmalion."

AN IRISH LEGEND

Whoever's born on Christmas
  Is favored from the start;
Has laughter and good fortune
  And a contented heart;
Is loved by noble company,
  Has all that should suffice.

But he that dies on Christmas
  Goes straight to Paradise.

THE LEGEND OF THE CAT

At midnight's stroke,
On the first Christmas, half the world awoke.
Then out of nest and lair
Came thronging to Bethlehem the wordless folk;
Hurried the beasts of the forest, the birds of the air,
To pay the Lord their homage and His due.
And Cat came, too,
Mincing on delicate feet to see the Child.
But being shy and wild,
Approached no nearer than the hearth; lay dumb
And dazzled there.
While the rest knelt in praise,
The Cat by too much glory overcome
Could not withdraw her gaze
From the Nativity; could only stare
Through slitted eyes at things of fur and feather
(The deer beside the lion, the pheasant, the hare
Safe in the fox's paws) bent down together.
Although their anthems lifted all around,
She, in her throat, made only a trembling sound
And could not bow her head.
Yet as the morning dawned
And one by one the other creatures fled
Each to his habitat—
The eagle to his crag and to his pond
The otter—only Cat
Remained beside the dying fire, unable
To quit the place that was both Crib and Stable.
Then Mary spoke aloud.
"Dear Cat," she said, "dear, stiff-necked, proud
And obstinate beast, I bless you. From this hour
Leave wilderness behind you.
Because you stayed, though none shall have the power
To call you servant, yet the hearth shall bind you
Forever to itself. Both fond and free,
Wherever Man is, you shall also be.
And many a family
Will smile to hear you singing, where you settle,
Household hosannahs like a pulsing kettle."

Some winter night
Observe Cat now. Her eyes will suddenly gleam
Yellow against the light,
Her body shudder in a jungle dream,
Her claws unsheath their sharpness. She remembers
Old times, old barbarous customs, old Decembers
Before she called the tribes of Man her friends.
But the dream ends.
Then, reassured, she curls herself along
The floor and hums her cool, domestic song.

THE NIGHT

On the night that Christ was born
The rivers, one hears, ran fine
And sweetly between their banks,
Filled not with water but wine.

And any man who drank
Of that beneficent tide
(Though he had stooped in anger
To drink), grew pacified,
Loving even his foeman
As dearly as his bride;

Wholly at peace with himself,
The world and everything.
While the trees in the forest blossomed
As if the winter were spring.

Paintings by Gervaslo Gallardo.

POEMS
By
Phyllis McGinley

STORY FOR AN EDUCATED CHILD

It used to be, when the world was young,
Animals spoke a Christian tongue,
    Articulating clearly.
And still do those of peaceable bent
Practice the kind accomplishment
    On Christmas evening, yearly.
With human wit, in a human voice,
The beasts of the barnyard all rejoice
    From Vespertime to Matin,
Recounting tales of the little God
Over and over. But isn't it odd?
    The speech they speak is Latin.
The strident Cock lifts up his crest,
Stuttering, "*Christus natus est!*"
    Till midnight splits asunder.
Laborious from his stable box,
"*Ubi? Ubi?*" lows the Ox,
    Bemused with sleep and wonder.
The somnolent Sheep, adrift from dreams,
Bleats "*Bethlehem!*" and her quaver seems
    Half question and half promise.
Then Ass that wears by an old decree
A cross on his back for prophecy,
    Brays forth his loud "*Eamus!*"
And there they gossip while night grows gray
And curious stars have slipped away
    From shimmering thrones they sat in.
So many a child might brave the cold
To hear them talking. But I am told
He mustn't be more than six years old.
    And who at six knows Latin?

DEAR ABBY: I WANT TO GET MARRIED UNDERWATER

Abigail Van Buren

In the dozen years that I have been Dear Abby, I have received almost every conceivable kind of question about marriage. Many come from members of the wedding who have an itch to hitch with a novel touch, and want someone to confirm the propriety of it.

For example, one prospective bride wrote to ask if it would be all right to have *What Kind of Fool Am I?* sung at her wedding. "It's kind of our theme song," she explained. "We fell in love to it."

Feeling as I do that weddings are a personal affair, I publicly (and perhaps foolishly) OK'd *What Kind of Fool Am I?* Irate readers promptly evidenced their disapproval. Like this one:

"Dear Abby,
The bride who wanted *What Kind of Fool Am I?* sung at her wedding showed what kind of fool *she* was. And Abby, you showed your ignorance, too. Popular love songs are out of place in church. Any qualified organist can assist the bride in selecting appropriate wedding music, and there is no excuse for all the trash that's being played at weddings these days.
IRATE ORGANIST"

This letter inspired still another:

"Dear Abby,
I was pleased to see that somebody finally spoke up to protest the improper music one hears at weddings lately. In the Protestant Episcopal Church, secular music is not permitted in the marriage liturgy, as marriage is a religious rite. I personally have dissuaded couples from using *Lohengrin's Processional,* because it's from an opera involving a heathen musician, and that marriage ended in failure. The other, *The Recessional,* is also unacceptable because it's from *A Midsummer Night's Dream*—a Shakespearean fantasy in which a lovely young maiden is wedded to an assheaded individual. No publicity, please, as I am a clergyman.
NAMELESS"

I escaped all controversy, though, when a bride who signed her letter "Bonnie from Duluth" wrote to ask if it would be proper to walk down the aisle to *Second Time Around.* "It's the second time around for both of us," she explained. Bonnie requested a personal reply, but she failed to include her last name and address, thus taking me off the hook.

Another second-time-arounder, a lady signed Myrtle, wrote to ask for clearance on a different aspect of wedding protocol:

"Dear Abby,
I am approaching my second marriage. My father is dead, and I have no brothers, uncles or close relatives, so my ex-husband has offered to give me away. Would this be proper? He said nothing would give him greater pleasure.
MYRTLE"

I advised Myrtle to hunt up a *distant* relative.

Then there was the rather lively controversy about what an "official" wedding cake ought to be. One bride asked if she couldn't have a *chocolate* wedding cake. ("Jack won't eat any cake but chocolate, and it's my favorite, too," she wrote.) I saw no good reason why a wedding cake couldn't be chocolate, and told her so.

This reply initiated still more questions about cakes: "How about the *shape* of the wedding cake?" a reader asked. "I'd like to have a square one because it's more economical and easier to cut."

I OK'd that, too, although I admitted I had never *seen* a square wedding cake. I soon learned that wedding cakes of varying shapes had been around for years. The best of the "cake letters" came from a true Texan:

"Dear Abby,
If you have never seen a square wedding cake, you should get around a little more. Wedding cakes don't have to be round. They can be any shape. My sister had her wedding cake made in the shape of Texas. It was beautiful. Unfortunately, not many of the guests saw it because my brother-in-law got potted and fell in it right about El Paso, and he broke it off clear to Galveston."

And then there was a boots-and-saddle bride with her own bizarre wedding plan:

"Dear Abby,
My future husband and I were making plans the other night and want to know what you think. We are both horse crazy, and so are most of our friends. We can't afford a big church wedding, so what do you think about getting married on horseback? We could have Western music.
My fiancé said as much as he likes the horseback idea, he kind of wanted to have me married in a gown, but you can't very well combine the two, can you?
HORSE CRAZY"

I replied: "Dear Crazy: If you can find a galloping clergyman with a stable mind, go ahead and have your Western wedding—and good luck."

Letters from people like "Horse Crazy" invariably set off a chain reaction (mostly encouraging) from readers of Dear Abby. This suggests to me that, far from being scorned, the unconventional wedding is applauded by more people than one might have guessed.

Here are a few responses to "Horse Crazy's" letter:

"Dear Abby,
Our daughter got married on horseback. The minister who performed the ceremony was on horseback, too. The bride and groom were dressed exactly alike, white shirts and black trousers. The wedding took place at a rodeo, and there were about 1,500 people present, and about 1,200 horses.
ALSO HORSE CRAZY"

There were a few grumps who complained that horseback weddings were not religious enough for their taste, and that all weddings ought to take place in church. I do not quarrel with these people about their religious views, of course, but isn't it a little narrow-minded—and a little irreligious—to feel that God's presence is confined to church or temple, and is not to be found on horseback under the great, arching sky? And what about the joy content? Isn't that an important part of the wedding ceremony, wherever the ceremony takes place?

"Horse Crazy's" letter not only inspired an initial response from the horsey set, but created a secondary wave as well. It began with this letter:

"Dear Abby,
I was tickled to note that a girl inquired about the possibility of being married on horseback. My ambition is also out of the ordinary. I would like to be married underwater.
My boyfriend and I belong to a skindiving club, and we think it would be fun to have an underwater wedding. Has it ever been done? So far everyone we have mentioned this to (except the members of our club) thinks we're crazy.
But, Abby, you have no idea how pure and spiritual you feel underwater. After all, isn't water a very important part of the baptismal ceremony?
SKIN DIVER"

I replied, "Dear Skin Diver: I have never heard of an underwater wedding, so don't order the seaweed until you find a water-repellent clergyman who shares your enthusiasm."

But if I was doubtful, my readers were not. They blessed the proceedings in loving detail, with letters like these:

"Dear Abby,
Approximately 25 years ago, as a United Press reporter, I covered (from the surface) a wedding in which all participants were clad in diving suits of the bulky, weighty type, with helmets and air hoses to the surface.

The words of the ritual, along with the bubbles, came to the surface over a loudspeaker.

I never did hear whether the marriage remained solid—or dissolved.
WILFRED BROWN"

"Dear Abby,
On March 8, 1954, Bob Smith married Mary Beth Sanger at the Aquarena in San Marcos, Texas. I am sure this was the first underwater wedding on record. The bride's flowers, gown and veil had been waterproofed, and so had the groom's tuxedo. They had bridesmaids and ushers, just like a dry-land wedding, The only difficult part was that they all had to have 25-pound weights in their shoes.   READ ABOUT IT"

I asked one kid if he believed in Santa Claus and he said, "I dunno . . . what channel is he on?"
—BOB HOPE

My bafflement about submarine weddings was nothing compared with the reaction of another reader, who signed her letter "Puzzled."

"Puzzled" wrote a bemused account of a wedding uniting a couple of sunworshipers near Delray Beach, Florida. The bride wore a fingertip veil and high-heeled shoes. Nothing else. The groom outstripped her by simply wearing nothing. Three naked musicians provided the music, as 200 naked guests looked on.

"I know this is a free country, Abby," said the letter from "Puzzled," "but doesn't an affair of this sort really puzzle you?"

Fresh from my dip in the lore of underwater wedding ceremonies, I was not prepared to be puzzled about much. I said, in a somewhat abbreviated reply, "Dear Puzzled: Yes. I wonder where the best man kept the ring."

The spread of public nudity, at least from the navel north, has been finding its inevitable way into the marriage happening. In Corpus Christi, Texas, a 19-year-old go-go dancer who bounces topless for the customers was married between acts—still topless. Her maid of honor, another topless go-go girl, stood up for her. The justice of the peace who performed the ceremony was not at all shook. "I don't pay any attention to what the people wear," he said. "My job is to get them married."

POOR WOMAN'S ALMANAC

BY BERYL PFIZER

Did anyone ever think of the right thing to say on a postcard?

All mothers have the attitude that the only reason single daughters aren't married yet is they're not trying hard enough.

Even when I'm going ten miles under the speed limit, I slow up when I see a police car.

Everyone is entitled to his own opinion—except *after* the new living room draperies are hung.

Most boutiques make me feel like a frump.

If they don't play "Good Night, Ladies" or "Stardust" at the end of the dance anymore, how do you know when it's over?

I'm all thumbs—and none of them is green.

It used to be a fool and his money were soon parted. Now, with checks, credit and withholding, they never even get together!

Most kiddie show hosts on television aren't talking to any of the children *I* know.

How come every silver lining has to have a cloud around it?

It makes me mad when everyone else is using a new word before I even know what it means! *e.g.*, psychedelic.

If you didn't have something you wanted to get away from, and had to get back to—how would you know what a good time you were having on weekends?

No one wants to be called a tourist anymore.

The biggest break mothers get is, they aren't the parent who's supposed to know how to fly a kite.

Where are the Grannies of yesteryear?

Does anyone ever use those clever souvenir salt-and-pepper shakers for salt and pepper?

I still can't count above XX in Roman numerals without having to stop and figure them out.

WAYS WITH CHICKEN

CHICKEN AND VEGETABLES IN MILK GRAVY

An old-fashioned fricassee; subtly delicious gravy. Bake crisp-crust biscuits to do it justice.

1 roasting chicken (4–5 lbs.) quartered
½ cup flour
½ teaspoon salt
⅛ teaspoon pepper
¼ cup butter or margarine
2 cups chicken broth
2 tablespoons chopped parsley
12 peeled small white onions
6 carrots, scraped and cut into chunks
2 cups milk
¼ teaspoon nutmeg

Wash chicken and pat dry. Dust with flour and sprinkle with ½ teaspoon salt and ⅛ teaspoon pepper. Brown slowly in butter in a heavy casserole. Pour in chicken broth and add parsley. Cover and bake in a moderate oven, 350° F., 1 hour, basting chicken occasionally. Meanwhile, parboil onions and carrots for about 15 minutes. Drain and arrange around chicken. Cover, return to oven and continue baking until chicken and vegetables are done, about 30 minutes. Remove to serving dish and turn broth into a saucepan. Skim if necessary. Make a thin paste of ½ cup flour and ⅔ cup cold water. Add to broth, stirring constantly. Then add milk and simmer until thickened. When sauce has reached boiling point, add

"Don't be ridiculous—if I were trying to poison you it would taste delicious!"

remaining seasonings and pour over chicken and vegetables. Serve over split hot biscuits. Makes 6 servings.

CRISP-CRUST BISCUITS

2 cups sifted flour
1 tablespoon baking powder
1 teaspoon salt
7 tablespoons shortening
¾ cup milk
1 tablespoon dried parsley (optional)
Pinch thyme, marjoran (optional)

Sift together dry ingredients. Cut in shortening so mixture looks like coarse meal. Make a well in the center and stir in milk all at once. Stir with a fork until a soft dough is formed, about 18 strokes. Turn out onto a well-floured board. With floured hands, pat dough out ½" thick. Cut with 2" biscuit cutter. Bake on an ungreased baking sheet until golden, in a very hot oven, 450° F., 12–14 minutes. Makes 12 biscuits or 6 larger 3" biscuits.

For variation, add parsley and herbs to dry ingredients.

TARRAGON-BAKED CHICKEN

Try this for a touch of adventure! Its gravy, unthickened, is pungent with the flavor of herbs and vinegar.

2 (3½-lb.) frying chickens, cut up
¼ cup melted butter or margarine
2 teaspoons salt
1 teaspoon tarragon
¼ teaspoon garlic powder
⅛ teaspoon pepper
2 tablespoons chopped parsley
½ cup cider vinegar
2 tablespoons tarragon vinegar
½ cup chicken broth

Wash the chicken parts and pat them dry. Arrange skin side up in roasting pan. Brush with butter. Mix seasonings. Sprinkle over the chicken parts, adding parsley. Cover and bake in a moderate oven, 350° F., for ½ hour. Uncover, add vinegars, and continue baking in a very hot oven, 400° F., until chicken is golden brown and tender. Baste often. When chicken is done, arrange on platter and keep warm. Drain off any extra fat but leave pan-browned juice. Stir in broth, heat until bubbling. Pour over chicken. Makes 6 servings.

COUNTRY CHICKEN BAKED IN MILK

Don't forget to serve this succulent cas-

serole with soft-crumb biscuits.

1 (3–3½-lb.) frying chicken, cut up
¼ cup flour
½ teaspoon dry mustard
½ teaspoon paprika
1½ teaspoons salt
⅛ teaspoon pepper
¼ cup melted butter or margarine
1½ cups milk

Wash chicken and pat dry. Mix flour and seasonings. Roll chicken in mixture and shake off excess flour. Melt the butter in a large skillet. Fry the chicken slowly until golden on all sides. Then transfer it to a shallow baking pan or dish. Add milk to the skillet. Heat and stir until all brown bits in pan are loosened. Pour over chicken. Bake, uncovered, in a moderate oven, 350° F., until tender, about 45 minutes. Makes 4 servings.

SOFT-CRUMB BISCUITS

2 cups sifted flour
1 tablespoon baking powder
1 teaspoon salt
5 tablespoons shortening
⅔–¾ cup milk
3 tablespoons finely chopped parsley (optional)

Sift dry ingredients into a bowl. Cut in shortening until mixture looks like coarse meal. Make a well and add milk all at once. Stir with a fork until a soft dough is formed, about 18 strokes. You might need a little more milk. Dough should be soft and light, but not sticky. Turn out onto lightly floured board; knead lightly about 20 times until smooth. Roll lightly ¾" thick. Cut out with a 2" biscuit cutter, or roll into an oblong and cut into diamonds by making diagonal cuts with a long, thin knife. Bake for 12–15 minutes in a very hot oven, 450° F., until golden. For variation add finely chopped parsley with the milk. Makes 12–14 biscuits.

CHICKEN IN ORANGE SAUCE WITH MUSHROOMS

Orange dominates the deep glaze on this chicken. Have buttered green beans, split toasted biscuits.

2 (2-lb.) broiling chickens, quartered
2 teaspoons salt
⅛ teaspoon pepper
½ cup butter or margarine
½ pound mushrooms
¼ cup finely chopped onion
2 cups orange juice

Chicken and vegetables in milk gravy.

1 tablespoon sugar
¼ cup beef consommé

Wash chicken and pat dry. Sprinkle with salt and pepper. Brown in butter in a large skillet. Remove chicken to paper toweling. Wipe, trim and quarter mushrooms. Add to skillet and cook until golden. Remove and set aside for use later. Stir onion into remaining drippings in skillet and cook a few minutes. Add orange juice and sugar and cook over high heat until mixture is reduced by half. Lower heat and stir in consommé. Arrange browned chicken in sauce. Cover and cook over very low heat until tender, about 1 hour. Add mushrooms during last 10 minutes of cooking. Makes 4 servings.

Moroccan Chicken

1 (3–3½-lb.) frying chicken, cut up
½ cup flour
1 teaspoon salt
⅛ teaspoon pepper
½ teaspoon paprika
¼ teaspoon powdered turmeric
½ teaspoon rubbed thyme
1 egg, slightly beaten
Shortening

Wash and dry chicken. In a paper bag mix flour and all seasonings. Shake chicken in seasoned flour. Dip into egg and then into seasoned flour again. Heat enough shortening to cover the bottom of a large skillet. Fry the chicken until crisp and golden all over, turning the pieces often. Drain each piece on paper toweling. Serve with saffron rice pilaf; garnish the platter with clusters of white grapes. Makes 4 servings.

Saffron Rice Pilaf

¾ teaspoon saffron
1 can (13¾-oz) chicken broth
3 tablespoons butter or margarine
1 cup long-grain rice
2 tablespoons finely minced onion
2–3 tablespoons slivered, toasted almonds

Soak saffron in ¼ cup chicken broth for 1 hour. Strain and reserve saffron liquid. Heat butter or margarine in a heavy 2-quart ovenproof kettle. Add rice and onion and sauté, stirring constantly, until rice becomes straw-colored. Do not allow to overbrown. Stir in 1 cup chicken broth and saffron liquid. Cover kettle, transfer to a moderately hot oven, 400° F., and bake for 20 minutes or until rice has absorbed all liquid. Stir once with a fork. Heat remaining chicken broth and add to rice. Cover, reduce heat to 200° F., and bake 10–15 minutes more. Remove cover, add almonds, toss lightly with a fork. Leave in oven (uncovered) for 4–5 minutes. Makes 4 servings.

Human nature is the same all over the world; but its operations are so varied by education and habit, that one must see it in all its dresses.
—LORD CHESTERFIELD

Princess Lee Radziwill

Princess Lee Radziwill

I think a person's true manners are revealed immediately by his way of meeting people. This social ritual can be performed so gracefully and easily, but many people ignore its importance, and create an unfortunate first impression by a careless and indifferent greeting. True, the formula of handshake and "How do you do?" is a rigid one, as fixed as a military salute, but you can and should make it meaningful. Say the words with sincerity instead of indifference, and look the person in the eye as you shake hands with him or her.

It is hard, if you're at a large party or in a receiving line, to repeat parrotlike, "How do you do?" but no substitute has been invented and the problem is the same in all languages. One should make an effort to smile, to really look at the person one is greeting, and to speak with warmth and expression.

Famous or distinguished people? How would I greet them? The same way—with a firm handshake and a tone of respect. The person who has truly good manners doesn't have a special set for celebrities and another set for humbler people.

I think one should stand up to be introduced, especially when one is meeting a distinguished or elderly person. Young people and children should always rise when elders enter a room.

Once you have met a person, the problem begins of what to talk about. A universal approach to conversation, and especially to conversation with new acquaintances, is to ask people questions—not personal questions—about themselves

A CONVERSATION ON MANNERS

and to be a good and patient listener to their answers. I like to talk with one person about things which are meaningful to me or to him. General conversation I find more difficult; but when you are giving a party, it is often easier and more pleasant to bring everyone into the conversation, especially at the beginning.

General conversation is a good ice-breaker. Finding a subject to talk about is not difficult—so much happens these days, we are all held together by the same problems. One can begin with the latest world crisis, a play, a movie, the current best seller, a favorite TV program. No one should be left out—a hostess should be ready to draw in someone who seems excluded with a "What do you think?"

There are other problems too. It seems that almost everything is controversial today—politics, foreign policy, national issues, religion. Even a play or a painting that most people are enthusiastic about may have a hostile critic in the company. A good hostess must be careful that discussion does not lead to too loud or unpleasant an argument; she learns to change a subject tactfully before enemies are made and feelings are hurt, and how to ease a tense atmosphere, perhaps by offering to refill glasses, or by suggesting a move into another room.

This brings us to the question of what constitutes bad manners in conversation. The laws of good taste and charity rule out malicious gossip. You can be sure that those who say damaging things about others to you will say derogatory things about you to others, too, and I think the best thing to do is to stay a little away from these people.

It is also impolite as well as boring to try to monopolize a conversation, to proclaim opinions and convictions too often or too loudly, especially ones you know are different from those held by others in the room, and therefore possibly very irritating to some in the company.

Direct personal questions, like "How old are you?" . . . "Is your husband with you?" are bad manners because they can be embarrassing. And don't discuss your health and physical condition, operations you have had or are going to have, financial or domestic worries. Why? Because it is boring to other people, who have to live with similar problems of their own.

Common sense and a little ordinary thoughtfulness will keep you from making conversational blunders. In fact, I think that with this approach you can handle any social situation successfully.

Parties? The first thing I'd say is: do your worrying before the party begins. The nervous hostess who spends her time in the kitchen and looks around the room with a worried face while she talks to her guests makes them feel ill at ease. Start working the day before. Clean your house or apart-

ment; organize the silver, china, napkins you are going to use; check on cigarettes, guest towels in the bathroom, the flowers you will have. I go through my house like a hotel manager or a mechanic, inspecting all the rooms in which guests may find themselves.

There should be no last-minute discoveries of something you've forgotten to make you feel rushed and rattled just as people arrive. I always allow myself time to rest and to dress without having to hurry. There are so many details in giving a party, but it should be enjoyable rather than hard work. You should never plan anything that you are not sure of really being able to handle.

ABRAHAM LINCOLN SAYS:

We should be too big to take offense and too noble to give it.

It has been my experience that folks who have no vices have very few virtues.

Tact is the ability to describe others as they see themselves.

He has the right to criticize who has the heart to help.

A government had better go to the extreme of toleration than do aught that could be construed into an interference with the common rights of the citizen.

The good party begins with your guest list. Naturally you will invite only people who are congenial and who will interest one another. There should be a nucleus of people who know one another, who are friends, so that conversation will be easy and there won't be that great strain of having to introduce *everyone* to everyone else. If you live in a large city, as I do, you should allow a fair interval between the time for which you invited your guests and the time you actually sit down to eat. It is nice to have time for drinks before you are rushed to the table because the soufflé will fall or the soup will be cold. With today's unpredictable traffic conditions many people who set out in time and mean to be prompt get held up and arrive late. Allow a good half hour.

Other rules I've put down for myself (I'm talking now about seated dinner parties): have the plates hot; keep flowers in the center of the table low so the guests can see one another; play music softly (if at all) so as not to drown out conversation.

When it is time for coffee in the next

room, don't break a conversation or a general good mood by leaving the table too abruptly; wait until there is a pause and the guests are ready to move. I'm rather nervous at every party I give unless I know the people well, and afraid that everything will go wrong. I don't know of anyone who isn't.

Another facet of good manners I would like to talk about is writing notes. I think it's almost a neglected art today. My sister and I were brought up to write thank-you notes and I think they are very important. Of course you should always write a note after receiving a present, or spending a weekend as a house guest. but I think there are many other times when a thank-you note is appreciated—after a dinner party, for example. I myself have always been in the habit of writing my host and hostess and I am always pleased when people are considerate enough to thank me in this way.

It is not necessary to write a note after a cocktail party or a small informal dinner (but I think it is nice to thank the hosts by telephone the next day). It's amazing how pleased people are when you let them know that you appreciate their efforts. In a note, it's not the length that counts—three or four lines are enough. You can keep them from sounding insincere by mentioning some special thing—perhaps what you most enjoyed about the weekend, or how much you liked meeting So-and-so at the party, or when you first used your new present.

Children should be started as early as possible on proper manners, so that they will soon become a habit with them. Learning by example is not enough; you must teach them to do the right thing.

Bringing up children is a continual round of do this and do that. You must teach them to say "Please" and "Thank you," to bow or curtsy to grownups, and say "How do you do?" nicely—not "Hi" to adults—to write thank-you notes, to be well behaved in other people's houses and when their parents have guests.

Children should not be allowed to show off in front of visitors, to make a lot of noise and demand attention. I find the best way to discourage this is simply to leave them alone. Adults often bother them with banal questions, not realizing that a child's world is sometimes of a greater horizon than their own and that their imagination is tremendous.

As children we were made to learn the Golden Rule. I think that's a whole philosophy of manners by itself, rolled into a single sentence: "Do unto others as you would have them do unto you." After all, what are "manners" but simply a way of treating people the way you would like them to treat you? If more of us remembered and tried to live by the Golden Rule, bad manners would cease to exist.

AMY VANDERBILT

Answers Some Questions on Etiquette

Using the Telephone

Q: What can I do about discouraging long telephone conversations without hurting the caller's feelings?

A: Telephone conversations can usually be shortened if you make your replies brief and thus don't give the impression that you have all the time in the world to talk. If this doesn't work, wait for a pause in the conversation and then make a plausible excuse, such as, "I'd love to talk more now, but I have to get the children off to school. I'll try to call you back. When would be a good time?" Of course, you should make sure, first, that there is no urgent information that needs to be imparted.

It is a good idea for anybody making a purely social call to say to the other person, especially if you know her to be a busy mother or a busy career woman, "Is this a good time for you to talk?" If she says it isn't, arrange to call back or say quickly whatever is necessary.

Twin Beds

Q: My mother insists that when I get married my husband and I should have twin beds; she says that this is "American" and modern. Is she right?

A: My research indicates that twin beds do seem to have originated in America, in the days of the Hays Code (1930), which prohibited showing a couple on the movie screen in a double bed. This gave the United States—and the world looking at American movies—the idea that twin beds were "nicer" than what was always known as the marital bed. Today, according to the world's largest and oldest mattress manufacturers (Simmons), the most popular size bed is the queen size, followed by the double bed, and then the king size (third on the list because it is so expensive, as are the linens for it). Today twin beds are used mainly for children. Most couples who have twin beds now have a double headboard. "Togetherness" is in.

College Roommates

Q: My daughter shares her dormitory room with her boyfriend and expects the same arrangement when she brings him home for the weekend. We realize that her friends are relaxed about these things, but we have younger children and different mores. What should we do?

A: In your own home you have every right to insist that your daughter follow your rules. Put her boy friend in a separate room.

Making the Bed

Q: My wife makes a trim bed that leaves no room for my big feet. I have to kick the bed covers clear before I can sleep. Please explain how she can make the bed to avoid this irritation.

A: Tell your wife to put her forearm under the top sheet and then under the blankets as she tucks them in, holding the corner high enough to accommodate your feet before she tucks the covers in. Have a look at the foot of the bed before you get in to be sure it is right for you.

Birth Announcements

Q: I am expecting our first baby soon and would like to know to whom we should send birth announcements. Most of our relatives live in a distant state and we don't see them anymore. I don't want the announcement to seem like a request for a baby gift.

A: Sending a birth announcement is not asking for a gift; it is a lovely way of letting friends and relatives know the new baby has arrived. Send announcements to any close friends and relatives you feel would be interested no matter how far away they are.

Exchanging Wedding Gifts

Q: Is it a social error to ask a member of the family to exchange a wedding gift when the bride has received more than one of the same thing? I did this, and the relative was so offended she refused to exchange the gift.

A: You should have exchanged the gift yourself. Many brides exchange gifts, and usually do so without notifying the donor.

Continental Style

Q: If a person is right-handed, he cuts his food with the knife in his right hand, and holds the fork in his left. Is it proper to then put food into the mouth with the fork still in the left hand?

A: Yes, if you are eating in the Continental style, as many Americans now do. In this method, both knife and fork are used at the same time, and the knife is not put back on the plate after each use.

FARAWAY.

By Andrew Wyeth.

NEW VISTAS FOR AN OLD HOUSE

With glass, wood, stone and color, a bold architect, Taylor Hardwick, transformed a forty year old house with a spectacular view into a modern airy dwelling that embraces all outdoors. In the end, it cost less, he said, than building a new one.

The twenty foot square room viewed from the balcony. The foundation walls, made of New England stone brought to Jacksonville in the nineteenth century as ship's ballast, enforce the continuity of interior and exterior, provide display space, bench support and mantelpiece. Furnishings, too, were chosen for their overhead eye appeal. The blue George Nelson coconut chair, the black Eames swivel, the blue Colby lounger, the yellow Saarinen design and the Japanese parasol tables all create a fascinating pattern on the centrally placed Oriental rug—again an attractive blend of old and new.

Photo: Alexandre Georges.

RETURN

OF

THE FEMME FATALE

It's love against the world for history's beautiful, fatal women who refuse to be ruled by conventional morality. They say, "I cannot help myself," and rush toward a fate beyond their control. But how many of them find fulfillment?

There isn't anything in the Elizabeth Taylor story itself which hasn't been warmed over by the principals with wearisome repetition. What the world has been watching, with attitudes ranging from compassionate sympathy to shocked outrage and from absorption to bored indifference, is the urgencies of a tortured triangle hot on and off the marital griddle. But amidst the daily spate of headlines, something has been lost, and I think it is something important.

It is perspective that has been lost. Except in some of its outward aspects, it is not the new things in the Elizabeth Taylor story that are most worth attention, but the old elements of it that link it with other women and other men and other times, with people in the past who walked the same perilous path of the grand passion, and stumbled and often got bloodied in the process.

For there is a long history of love in the Western world. I don't mean the love of men and women, humble or distinguished, who kept their private lives private, but the love of the famous and infamous, whose private passions were blazoned all over the public world. All through the history of Eros, from the Greek hetaerae to the latest publicized front-page affairs, are examples of the *femme fatale* who seeks release from feeling caught within the body of herself and the narrow world of her womanly pursuits, into something she feels is larger than herself and her world. In all her friendships and marriages, Miss Taylor has sought this sense of being transported out of herself into a grand passion. She has never achieved it. Will she ever? How many women do you know who have achieved it, or are likely to?

I cannot pretend to any special knowledge of the interior of Miss Taylor's mind and heart. But as it happens I spent some time with her, over a period of several months, working with her on what was to have been a chapter of her autobiography. It is my own unverifiable hunch that she sees herself as a *femme fatale*, one of those beautiful, historic, fateful ladies who draw men irresistibly toward them, and who are therefore to be judged not by standards of conventional morality, but by more spacious standards applied over centuries to the grand passion.

—MAX LERNER

Miss Taylor as Cleopatra in the new film, soon to be released. Photograph by Roddy McDowall.

I read with interest the autobiography of Elizabeth Taylor in the *Ladies' Home Journal*. But I was disappointed no end to note that she had not mentioned the important role I played in her life.

The first time I met Elizabeth Taylor was when we were both street urchins in London. I remember her saying to me, "Arthur, when we grow up, will you marry me?"

I patted her on the shoulder and said, "Elizabeth, my family wants me to go to Sandhurst and then on to Oxford. You'd only be in my way."

The years passed, and one day I was driving down a street in Paris when I saw this lovely flower girl. I stopped the car and told the chauffeur to wait. I said to her, "Your face looks familiar."

"It should, Arthur," she said, smiling. "I'm little Elizabeth Taylor who used to play with you in the streets of London."

"So you are," I said. "How much are you selling the flowers for?"

"One franc for the bunch."

"I'll give you a half franc. They seem quite wilted."

"Thank you, Arthur. You were always a kind person."

"Keep well, Elizabeth," I warned. "It's quite damp this time of year." And then I got into my car and drove off. The flowers died in a couple of days.

As you all know, I joined the Royal Air Force and shot down 54 German planes. But in the last hunt I was wounded. They brought me to a hospital in Sussex. One day I saw this Red Cross girl distributing cigarettes to the patients.

"Could your name be Elizabeth?" I asked.

"Yes, Arthur, it's me. I joined the Red Cross to forget."

"Forget what?"

"You," she said, as tears welled up in her eyes.

Tears started to well up in mine. "You know I have a bad leg," I said.

"It doesn't matter, Arthur," she said, sobbing.

"Well, it should," I said. "I think I ought to get two cartons of cigarettes instead of one."

After the war was over, I went into the banking business with my father, and one day I had to fly out to California. While there, I decided to go for a swim in the Pacific above Malibu. But I got a cramp in my bad leg. I shouted for help and suddenly, swimming out to me, I saw Elizabeth.

"Hold on, Arthur, I'm coming." She brought me in to shore.

"Thank you, Elizabeth. I swallowed a little water, but I don't imagine that was your fault."

"I don't know what I would have done," she said, "if you had drowned."

"It would have been hard to explain to the authorities," I admitted. "Tell me, what are you doing now?"

"I'm a movie actress, Arthur."

"Is that so? I imagine you make quite a bit of money."

"A million dollars a picture. But money doesn't mean anything to me, Arthur."

"It should, Elizabeth. Why don't you open an account with my bank? We pay four percent and there are no charges for writing checks."

I went back to London the next week and forgot all about Elizabeth until one day when I happened to be strolling down the Via Veneto in Rome. There was Elizabeth, gorgeous as ever and, as usual, glad to see me.

"I'm making *Cleopatra*," she said excitedly. "Arthur, have you ever married?"

"No," I said. "There is only one girl I ever wanted to marry."

Elizabeth started weeping. "Who was that?"

"Baby Jane Holzer. But she married somebody else."

Then Elizabeth said a funny thing. She said, "I'm going to marry Richard Burton, Arthur."

"Why him?"

"Because I couldn't wait for you any longer, Arthur. Don't you understand?"

"Yeh, I guess so. Well, lots of happiness. And if you want to open a joint bank account, let me know."

That was the last time I saw Elizabeth Taylor. But occasionally I hear that people say, even to this day, when they see her, "Isn't that the girl who had the unhappy love affair with Art Buchwald?"

THE VANISHING ART OF SWEET TALK

Russell Baker

To make love, in any man's language, all a woman needs is the knack—of sounding as adorable as she looks.

At a party I met a woman of unutterable beauty. Before a word was spoken you wanted to be in love with her. Then she opened her mouth and destroyed the evening.

"How many children do you have?" she asked.

Nothing less than full confession was possible with this woman. Yes, I have children. Yes, they brush their little teeth three times a day. No, my wife is not employed. I work for Consolidated Dynamics. No, I have no stock in A. T. & T., and yes, you are quite right, I am merely a drab husband and nothing, nothing is ever possible between us, thank God, because you aren't a woman. You're just another of those census takers who have been murdering evenings for me all my life.

It was unjust, of course, to detest this woman. What she desperately needed were sympathy and help. For, like millions of American women today, she suffered from that most tragic of all feminine disabilities—conversational inadequacy. Years of repression, inhibition and taboos had created fears in her subconscious that made it impossible for her either to gain fulfillment or to satisfy her partner in the conversational act.

To such women, conversation often seems a nasty, unnatural activity forced upon them by a male-dominated society. And so, out of terror and hostility, they deny themselves the joy of one of nature's noblest pleasures by retaliating against their partners with such conversation wreckers as, "How many children do you have?" "You've been drinking again," and "How do I know you really love me?"

Can these women be helped? Of course they can, if they will only put aside fear and ignorance and recognize that conversation is a perfectly normal and healthy pastime. Indeed, smooth and conversational technique is absolutely essential to any successful transaction between man and woman, be it marriage, romance, light flirtation or lunch at the drugstore counter.

First of all, the woman must understand something of the rich diversity of the female conversational organs. These include not only such physiological marvels as the larynx, the glottis, the palate and the lips, but also the volume modulator, the whine suppressor and the screech muffler.

The untutored woman who flings herself into conversation with nasal brayings, keens that can slice cheese or a voice that sounds like walnut shells going through a meat grinder will repel her partner and render him incapable of engaging even in low-level foretalk. This is because the male ear is exquisitely sensitive to feminine pitch. A little-understood mechanism linking the male ear to the male terror glands cuts in the instant it detects a feminine voice that sounds like Adolf Hitler and fills the male impulse cavity with overpowering urges to run.

If, for some reason, running is out of the question, as in marriage for example, the male will seek release in screams or low groans. If the condition is not corrected, he may start seeking casual conversational adventures with women who have taken the trouble to master their screech mufflers.

Along with shattering voice, the most common cause of female conversational failure is poor taste. The successful feminine conversationalist realizes that the male is a creature of exceedingly delicate aesthetic sensibilities. It is the nature of woman to inject conversation with utterances so coarse and gross to the male sensibility that he loses all zest for continuing the discussion.

No wife, for example, should expect a satisfying conversational experience with a husband if she greets him on his arrival home with the question: "What is that red stuff on your collar?" Any woman who would utter such a question at the start of conversation doesn't deserve a good conversation. The woman who has mastered her art knows that, instead of making some offensive remark about her husband's collar, she should say, "Darling, slip out of that dirty old shirt right away so I can wash it while you're telling me all you've done today for the children and me."

Here is a brief, and by no means all-inclusive, list of similarly offensive utterances to be avoided, no matter how great the temptation:

1. "Have you ever thought of elevator heels?"
2. "But you're old enough to be my father!"
3. "Mother's coming for a three-week visit."
4. "The termite inspector was here today, and guess what!"
5. "So you finally decided to come home!"

Women need not be ashamed of their natural desire to make such utterances, for they are the signs of a wholesome and healthy femininity. They must, however, learn to suppress this desire if they expect conversation to be entirely satisfying. No woman who thinks selfishly only of her own conversational satisfaction can hope for a meaningful exchange if she ignores her partner's taste in discussion topics. Remember, as the Hindus said centuries ago, it takes two to talk.

For each of the odious conversation lines listed above, there are perfectly good substitute strokes that will arouse and thrill

Illustration by Hillary Knight.

the male instead of disgusting him. For example:

1. "Why are shorter men always so much more virile?"
2. "I'm so tired of silly immature boys with no gray in their hair."
3. "Surprise, darling! I've been saving coins in the cookie jar, and we're going to Jamaica for three weeks!"
4. "The termite inspector was next door at the Dombeys' today, and it couldn't have been funnier."
5. "Why don't you make us both a little drink?"

From all this it should be obvious that the female role in conversation is that of the active partner, the aggressor. This does not mean that the woman should be an inquisitor or a district attorney. Quite the contrary. The sophisticated conversational partner senses the mood of the male and artfully guides him to talk the role of debonair and charming man-of-the-world, long-suffering father, unappreciated em-

ustration by Isa Barnett for Isak Dinesen's new story, THE SECRET OF ROSENBAD.

ployee or dynamic romantic, depending upon his mood at the time conversation begins.

Being the active partner does not mean that the woman should force conversation day and evening without cease. The male conversational appetites are quite different from the woman's. Some women have been known capable of talking without pause for days on end. The male is quite another creature. After a particularly satisfying evening of mutual dilation upon his many excellences, he may not desire conversation again for two or three days.

In determining whether the male is ready for conversation, the woman should not hesitate to employ the delicate techniques of foretalk. She might, for example, open with some tentative little remark such as, "Gosh, I was lucky to have married you." If the husband shows no sign of ego tumescence, or if he responds by saying, "I'm going to watch football today," the wife should find some housework to do.

The most common feminine error during the period of foretalk is to subject her partner to withering cross-examination. It is, again, a perfectly normal feminine urge. Meeting a man for the first time, she wants to know immediately what possible future they may have together.

Is he employed? Where? How much does he earn? Is he already married? Is it an indissoluble case? How many children does he have?

This leads to the tragedy of all those unutterable beauties, glimpsed longingly at parties, who, on first opening their mouths, murder conversation with, "How many children do you have?"

The joyful feminine conversationalist never makes such mistakes. She knows that the strange man with the provocative glance is also interested in future possibilities, but not—at that moment anyhow—in the same future possibilities that interest her. She knows that a skillful act of conversation can often lead him to ponder the future that does interest her, and she knows that clumsy, inept foretalk can only foreclose the possibility of any future whatsoever.

Thus, instead of opening with "How many children do you have?" she murmurs, "Let us walk together in the garden and watch the moon rise through the leaves of the chestnut trees." *That* is foretalk.

Though conversation, as it progresses, may disclose that their only possible future is a mutual conversational escape from the host's tedium through the dessert course, the evening will not have been destroyed for either.

The man will have had the chance to feel poignant about all the women who can never enjoy the power of his charm. The woman will have had the gratification of making an impossible man feel the sweet languor of post-conversational *tristesse*.

It is one of the ironies of American society that the millions of marriage manuals flooding the mails and bookshops virtually ignore the subject of conversation and its techniques. In these manuals love is usually reduced to an industrial process that suggests a mechanic's guide to auto maintenance.

A successful relationship with a man takes more than that. It is all very well to know about rotating the tires every 10,000 miles and putting anti-rust in the cooling system, but the manuals should frankly tell women that the amount of time they will spend at the mechanics of love is negligible compared to the time they will have to spend just talking to the men in their lives.

Why should women be ashamed to try mastering the pleasures possible in these continual encounters?

After all, as the sage Vatsyana wrote long ago, "Sex isn't everything."

Carol Burnett

In the Autumn of 1958, a young actress named Carol Burnett was collecting unemployment compensation between jobs. She isn't working regularly today, either, but with a difference. Until she left the **Garry Moore Show,** she appeared every Tuesday night for three years in 24,000,000 living rooms, and entranced audiences with her songs and kookie skits. Today she is at the top by all the hard-boiled standards of her profession: box office, ratings, fan mail and just plain money. But hard-boiled standards never quite describe the phenomenon of capturing the affections of the American public. It seems more important to say that Carol Burnett has now become one of the handful of truly beloved figures in the entertainment world.

Opposite: Not light years away, but right now, this summer, 1969, a chance to soar off into a new fashion orbit wearing clothes that make you feel as free and weightless as a space-walker: a sleeveless white skimmer of dacron and cotton knit by Ingeborg for Jane Irwill, and, far right: op-checked culottes of double woven cotton by Regina Porter.

A DINNER FOR JULIA CHILD

A toast to the guest of honor—Julia Child.

Taking a tip from a dinner party we helped plan for Julia Child, here are a few ideas that will make you the toast of your own gourmet party—whether it's a cooperative venture with a few friends or a go-it-alone enterprise. What makes it all so possible today is the simple fact that so much of the cooking can be done well ahead of the party and stashed away in the freezer. And if you have any hostess qualms about how dishes are going to turn out, this is the perfect system to use—no need for doubt when you draw from the freezer, since everything has been pre-tasted and preserved in its perfect state.

CONSOMMÉ MADRILÈNE, MELBA TOAST
VEAL PRINCE ORLOFF
ENDIVES BRAISÉES AU MADÈRE
GLACÉ AUX ANANAS AUX ORANGES GLACÉES

CONSOMMÉ MADRILÈNE

4 (10-oz) cans beef consommé

5 large ripe tomatoes
Boiling water
Salt and pepper to taste
¼ to ⅓ cup dry Port wine
⅓ cup finely minced fresh parsley

Bring 4 (10-oz.) cans beef consommé to simmer in saucepan. Drop 5 large ripe tomatoes in boiling water for 10 seconds. Remove and take off stem and skin. Add stem and skin to simmering consommé.

Cut tomatoes in half and gently squeeze seeds and juice into consommé. Simmer 5 more minutes. Strain consommé into another saucepan. Mince tomato pulp very fine and add to consommé.

Just before serving, heat to below simmer for 3 to 4 minutes to cook tomatoes. Season carefully with salt and pepper, then stir in ¼ to ⅓ cup dry Port wine and ⅓ cup finely minced fresh parsley.

Ed. Note: If you wish to freeze the consommé, add the Port wine and parsley after defrosting.

VEAL PRINCE ORLOFF

⅓ cup oil
2 (3½-lb.) boneless veal roasts
1 cup sliced carrots (about 3 carrots)
1 cup sliced onions (about 2 medium onions)
¼ cup butter
1 tsp. salt
1 tsp. thyme
2 bay leaves
2 strips fresh pork fat

Dry veal thoroughly in paper towels. In a large skillet, heat ⅓ cup oil. When oil is almost smoking, brown 2 (3½-lb.) boneless veal roasts, one at a time, on all sides.

Sauté 1 cup sliced carrots (about 3) and 1 cup sliced onions (about 2) in ¼ cup butter until carrots are tender.

Sprinkle veal with 1 teaspoon salt and place in large casserole (with a cover) with carrots, onions, 1 teaspoon thyme and 2 bay leaves. Cover each veal roast with a strip of fresh pork fat. Tuck aluminum foil over meat and cover casserole.

Place casserole on lowest rack in 325° oven. Bake 1 hour.

Remove cover and insert a meat thermometer through foil into center of one roast. Continue baking for 20 minutes or until meat thermometer reads 175°. (When juices run clear yellow, meat is done.) Remove meat and let rest 20 minutes. Strain pan juices and cool. Skim fat from surface. Set aside for sauce. Prepare Sauce and Stuffing (see recipes).

Carve veal into slices ³⁄₁₆-inch thick, piling neatly. Grease 1 fireproof serving platter (12 inches long and 1½ inches deep). Place last slice of veal at one end, spread with spoonful of stuffing. Overlap the first slice on the next. Spread with stuffing. Continue to fill platter. Spread any extra stuffing over veal. Spoon Mornay Sauce (see recipe) over veal. Sprinkle remaining grated cheese over sauce.

Place platter of veal on highest rack in 375° oven for about 30 minutes or until sauce bubbles and is nicely browned. Serves 12.

If you want to freeze it, let cool uncovered, then wrap airtight and freeze.

RICE, ONION AND MUSHROOM STUFFING FOR VEAL PRINCE ORLOFF

½ cup plain, raw, white rice
3 quarts boiling water
1½ Tb. salt
6 cups thinly sliced yellow onions
½ cup melted butter
3 cups finely diced fresh mushrooms

3 Tb. butter
Salt and pepper to taste

Combine ½ cup plain, raw, white rice with 3 quarts boiling water and 1½ tablespoons salt. Bring to a boil and cook 5 minutes. Drain immediately.

Combine 6 cups thinly sliced yellow onions with ½ cup melted butter in a casserole, stirring to coat onions. Stir in drained rice.

Cover casserole and bake in 325° oven for about 1 hour or until rice is tender. Remove from oven and set aside.

Meanwhile, a handful at a time, twist the 3 cups finely diced mushrooms in the corner of a towel to squeeze out as much vegetable water as possible. Sauté mushrooms in 3 tablespoons butter until pieces begin to separate and to brown lightly. Season to taste with salt and pepper. Set aside.

Rice and onions, and mushrooms, are now to be combined with part of the sauce (see recipe) to complete the stuffing.

Sauce for Veal Prince Orloff

½ cup butter
⅔ cup flour (measure by scooping dry-measure cups into flour and sweeping off excess)
6 cups liquid (the reserved, strained veal juices plus 3 to 4 cups milk)
Additional milk if needed
Salt and pepper to taste
Pinch of nutmeg
½ cup heavy cream
3 cups reserved onion-rice stuffing
1 cup reserved sautéed mushrooms
½ to ¾ cup heavy cream
1 cup grated Swiss cheese

Melt the ½ cup butter in a heavy-bottomed 2½- to 3-quart saucepan. Blend in the ⅔ cup flour and stir over moderate heat until flour and butter foam together for 2 minutes without coloring. Remove from heat and let cool 1 minute. Meanwhile bring the 6 cups combined veal juices and milk to a simmer in a separate pan, then pour all at once into the cooked butter and flour, beating vigorously with a wire whip to blend thoroughly. Bring to the boil, stirring, and thinning out if necessary with tablespoons of milk to make a very thick sauce like a heavy mayonnaise. Season carefully to taste with salt, pepper and a pinch of nutmeg. Remove from heat. Part of sauce is to be combined with stuffing, rest is turned into Sauce Mornay covering.

For the stuffing, combine 3 cups onion-rice mixture with 1¼ cups sauce and ½ cup heavy cream. Purée through a food mill or whir in a blender. Stir in 1 cup sautéed mushrooms. Stuffing must be thick enough to spread over meat and to stay in place for final baking. Stir in a spoonful or so more sauce if too thick.

To remaining sauce, add ½ cup heavy cream and simmer 5 minutes, stirring. Sauce must be thick enough to coat the meat, so must coat a spoon quite heavily. Thin out with spoonfuls of cream if necessary. Correct seasoning again, and stir in ⅔ cup of the grated Swiss cheese. Remove from heat. Clean off sides of pan with a rubber spatula and float a tablespoon or 2 of cream on surface to prevent skin from forming while you are stuffing meat.

When meat is stuffed, spoon the sauce over it and sprinkle top with remaining ⅓ cup grated Swiss cheese.

Endives Braisées au Madère

36 endives, trimmed and washed
1½ cups water
¾ cup butter
3 Tb. lemon juice
½ tsp. salt
½ cup finely diced boiled ham
½ cup finely diced carrots
½ cup finely diced onions
3 Tb. butter
2 cups beef bouillon
¾ cup Madeira wine

Arrange the endives in a flameproof casserole that has a cover. They will cook more evenly if they are in 1 layer, but you may use 2 if necessary. Add 1½ cups water, ¾ cup butter, 3 tablespoons lemon juice and ½ teaspoon salt. Spread waxed paper over, to keep the endives moist and to prevent them from burning in the oven. Cover the casserole and boil slowly on top of the stove for about 20 minutes, or until endives are tender.

Combine ½ cup each boiled ham, carrots and onions, all finely diced, and 3 tablespoons butter. Cook slowly until the vegetables are tender (about 5 minutes). Add 2 cups beef bouillon and ¾ cup Madeira wine. Boil until liquid is reduced by half. Remove waxed paper and spoon sauce and vegetables over endives. Cover baking dish. Bake at 325° for 30 minutes. Garnish with parsley sprigs. Serves 12.

Glacé aux Ananas aux Oranges Glacées

Pack 2 quarts pineapple sherbet into a stainless steel bowl, or mold. Cover with plastic wrap and freeze for 3 hours. Unmold by dipping into very hot water for 2 seconds and place on a serving platter. Cover sherbet again with plastic wrap and freeze.

Cut off orange part of peel of 12 large firm navel oranges with a vegetable peeler, taking with it as little as possible of the white part. Cut peel into matchstick strips about 2 inches long and 1/16 inch wide.

Combine peel with 1 quart water, and simmer 10 minutes or until peel is tender. Drain thoroughly.

Dissolve 2 cups sugar completely in ⅔ cup water over high heat. Cover and boil 5 minutes. Uncover and boil to soft ball stage, 238°. (Dip metal spoon into syrup and pour a few drops into cup of cold water. If you can form a ball with your fingers, it is ready.)

Put drained orange peel into syrup. Boil 2 minutes. Cool.

Cut off white peel from oranges and remove sections. Cover and chill. Just before serving, remove sherbet from freezer and arrange orange sections around it. Spoon peel and syrup over oranges. Serves 12. You can keep the sherbet frozen in its mold for several weeks, but do not freeze peel or orange segments. Peel can be refrigerated for several weeks in a covered jar; orange segments must be fresh.

Christmas Is Love
By Joan Walsh Anglund

Christmas is Snow...
Christmas is Night...

Christmas is Home,
and candles, bright...

Christmas is Prayer,
and one Star, above...

Christmas
is Children...

Christmas is Love.

WHAT'S HAPPENING

Gene Shalit

If you're interested in *people,* see the gorgeous film A MAN AND A WOMAN, **Claude Lelouch's** masterpiece. It is above all concerned with beauty, with love. And you may never again behold such photography.

That haunting musical, BRIGADOON, is set for TV. . . . CAMELOT is being filmed in Hollywood by Warner Bros. at stupefying cost. . . . MY FAIR LADY is still playing all over the world . . . and now **Alan Jay Lerner,** the author of them all, is preparing a new musical, COCO. "It's about Mademoiselle Chanel," he says, "really the most extraordinary woman I've ever met. She has something to say about everything. Usually bad. And usually accurate. She's designed the clothes for the emancipated woman. She's changed the way everybody looks. She invented suits. Short skirts. Bobbed hair. Slacks. She's eighty-four . . . but you're not aware of that when you're with her. Picasso says she's the most intelligent woman in Europe."

I ask Lerner if he has a favorite lyric. He says yes: two. (Pause. Think of his shows. His songs. Try to guess. OK, time's up.)

"*Gigi.* I like that better than anything else I've written. I set out to do something, and I did it better than I thought I would. Besides, I forget I wrote it when I hear it. My other favorite is *Accustomed to Her Face.*"

Is there a song he's written that he doesn't like? "I think *I Could Have Danced All Night* is boring. I hate the middle part— *I'll never know, what made it so, ex-ci-ting* —those were just dummy words. I wrote them quickly, to have some idea of the rhyme scheme. I was so unhappy that when we opened on the road—even though the song was stopping the show—I made up my mind to rewrite it. But it's terribly easy to convince anybody to be lazy—so I never did. I do think the song expresses the feeling of Eliza Doolittle at that moment, but I wish I could have surprised myself a little, that's all."

A jumping up and down rave: **Warren Beatty's** new film, BONNIE AND CLYDE, is a work of cinematic art. Beatty *is* Clyde, **Faye Dunaway** is fine as Bonnie. **Arthur Penn** is perfect as the director. The screen is strewn with violence, but, in a departure from Hollywood's current vogue of shock for shock, the violence is meaningful, vital to an understanding of these real people. (Clyde Barrow and Bonnie Parker actually lived and murdered their way through the Depression.) **Estelle Parsons** is brilliant, **Gene Hackman** convincing and **Michael Pollard** could not be improved upon. Many of the others are amateurs picked up on location. Penn's evocation of the early 1930's—tin lizzies, moneyless banks, hopelessness on every face—is unforgettable. Homage to all.

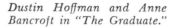

Dustin Hoffman and Anne Bancroft in "The Graduate."

Julie Andrews' SOUND OF MUSIC RCA album is the biggest seller ever (8 million), but she's competing with herself at the gift counters: Her new record with **Andre Previn,** *A Christmas Treasure,* is luscious. . . .

After his hit DON'T DRINK THE WATER **Woody Allen** is already set with his next show. Woody must have been traumatized by the Bogart-Bergman film CASABLANCA, because he's going to call it PLAY IT AGAIN, SAM. Up we loped to Woody's swell apartment. He greeted us in chinos that didn't reach his ankles, dirty white sneakers, and surely a shirt of some sort. "I'm doing this new play for Merrick with me in it," he said with excessive seriousness. "I know from my experience that I've got to get it right *before* we try it out of town, because I won't have time to rewrite: I'll still be doing TV while I'm on Broadway. Doing the same thing night after night, I suspect it's going to be a bad, unpleasant, disastrous feeling. But I'm doing it because I have a terrific idea for a comedy and it's got a *great* part for *me*. It just happens to." Woody will write roles for five beautiful girls: "I have a rule that there should be plenty of girls in any enterprise in which I'm involved." If you have to have rules, you may as well have good ones.

Clark Gable was the first star to say *damn* on screen (in GONE WITH THE WIND —and he probably said it again, off screen, when he didn't win the Academy Award for his performance). Coming soon: a TV special about the Gable years, with an analysis of his grip on the people. His popularity was easy to understand. I mean, can anyone with a mustache be *all* bad? . . . **Bill Cosby** will eye spy Philadelphia, his hometown, on a new TV tour, and **Grace Kelly,** who also grew up in Philadelphia, is ready with a razzle tour of her Princessipality. Title: *Monte Carlo . . . C'est la Rose.* Joining her: **Terry-Thomas, Françoise Hardy, Gilbert Becaud.** To honor the grand prix, Princess Grace promises to zip through Monaco in a sports car.

Mike Nichols' THE GRADUATE is a class picture. Rarely will you see a film with finer acting in every role, or observe the work of a director whose eye and ear are so exquisitely keyed to the nuances of his time. **Anne Bancroft** is wickedly perfect as **Dustin Hoffman's** alma mater. Hoffman— his portrayal is extraordinary—ultimately graduates to her daughter, **Katharine Ross.** One of Nichols' devices is that the film does not end, it just stops.

Hal Roach's THE CRAZY WORLD OF LAUREL AND HARDY is a cheek-aching series of takes and double takes clipped from their funniest films. No one was ever nuttier with doors and derbies. Although cinema is today's most expressive art form, there's very little visual comedy. Now it's sex, slaying or slice of life. Suggestion to Hollywood: What Roach has done for **Laurel and Hardy** someone should do for **Jerry Lewis.** There is hardly a Lewis movie that an intelligent adult can sit through, but most of his movies have a scene or a sequence that is memorably funny. If these could be spliced together into a 100-minute anthology, he would have a hit, and the world a treasury of comic insanity.

Julie Andrews in "The Sound of Music."

Warren Beatty and Faye Dunaway in "Bonnie and Clyde."

And eighty cheers for United Artists for re-releasing **Mike Todd's** extravagant Academy Award–winning version of Jules Verne's AROUND THE WORLD IN 80 DAYS. Remember? **David Niven, Shirley MacLaine, Noel Coward, Frank Sinatra, Marlene Dietrich, Trevor Howard, Red Skelton, Beatrice Lillie,** even **Edward R. Murrow**—more than 40 stars. One reason for the smash: a script by **S. J.** (for Superb Jocularity) **Perelman.** Be sure your children take their parents.

Jerry Lewis

WHAT PEOPLE ARE REALLY SAYING

Robert F. Kennedy

Not since the founding of the Republic —when Thomas Jefferson wrote the Declaration of Independence at 33, Henry Knox built an artillery corps at 26, Alexander Hamilton joined the independence fight at 19, and Rutledge and Lynch signed the Declaration for South Carolina at 27— has there been a younger generation of Americans brighter, better educated, more highly motivated than this one. In the Peace Corps, in the Northern Student Movement, in Appalachia, this generation of young people has shown an idealism and a devotion to country matched in few nations, and excelled in none.

We have shown our admiration for them in the sincere flattery of imitation, in ways large and small. Café society and country clubbers follow their fashions in slang and skirt lengths, listen to their music, and dance their dances. Detroit styles its cars and designs its engines on the model of those built by teen-age "hot-rodders" of a few years ago. The sit-in movement, which energized the Negro of the South and resulted in the Civil Rights Act of 1964, began with a few college students. And it was a small group of Northern students, in the Mississippi Summer Project, who taught thousands of adults how to make personal witness for civil rights in conditions of difficulty and danger.

Yet for all the inspiration, all the freshness and imagination our young people have given us in the last few years, we are now profoundly troubled by them; and so we should be. For the gap between generations, always present in the past, is suddenly widening; the old bridges that span it are falling; we see all around us a terrible alienation of the best and bravest of our young; the very shape of a generation seems turned on its head overnight. Stokely Carmichael, Rap Brown—and beyond them, others—offer dark visions of an apocalyptic future. Peace Corps recruiting is not so easy as it was; and we read less of tutoring programs in the ghetto than of "trips" and drugs with strange new names. There are youth riots in our cities and at dozens of colleges; hundreds of young men dodge the draft in Canada, and unknown numbers effectively do the same in years of graduate study; the suicide rate among young people is rising, and so is the rate of juvenile delinquency.

Bob Dylan, the troubador of their generation, who once sang of the changes that were "Blowin' in the Wind," now dismisses our pronouncements as "propaganda, all is phony."

This rejection we see most clearly in the growth of a youthful "underground" culture. Its essence seems to be that participation in public affairs is a "hangup"; that all power corrupts absolutely; and that salvation is to be found in a wholly new life style, sparked by drug-induced fantasies and preoccupation with self.

This small minority not only preaches total estrangement; it lives it. In new communities that have sprung up from New York's East Village to Haight-Ashbury in San Francisco, this "underground" community preaches the message of total alienation: "turn on, tune in, drop out." Their life style is in every way a repudiation of modern American life.

These "underground" communities are small, but many more young people are sympathetic to their message of estrangement and disillusionment even as they reject total alienation. The premises of the underground are, I am afraid, shared by far too many responsible young people on whom we depend to commit themselves personally to public change. Time and again I have heard these young leaders—whether college editors or community-action organizers—express their dissatisfaction with the direction of American society.

They seek change, but with an increasing sense of futility; theirs is not the estrangement that leads to complete alienation, but a despair that leads to indifference. Even those young people who are anxious to alter conditions they deplore, retreat in the face of inflexible institutions with overwhelming power, and become no different from the majority of their generation. They, too, "drop out"—but by becoming part of the "system" they deplore. They join the corporation, or the multiversity, or the law firm, not because they think they can contribute to those institutions, but out of resignation, out of the conviction that commitment to anything broader than their private welfare is fruitless.

Thus, more and more of our children are estranged and alienated, almost unreachable by the familiar arguments of our adult world. The task of leadership is not to condemn or castigate or deplore; it is to search out the reason for this disillusionment and alienation, this protest and dissent—perhaps, indeed, to learn from it. And we may find that we learn most of all from those political and social dissenters whose differences with us are most grave; for among the young, as among adults, the sharpest criticism often goes hand in hand with the deepest idealism and love of country.

What estranges these young people? What are they dissenting from, and what do they tell us about ourselves?

They begin, of course, with the war in Vietnam. Let me emphasize that I am not talking about all our young people. After all, Vietnam is a young man's war; the men who fight and die there, with bravery and endurance equal to any in our history, are young. Others, as I have seen on many campuses, are in favor of escalation through increased bombing of the North—though many who favor escalation also favor continuation of the student deferment, their seeming slogan being "Escalation Without Participation," or, at any rate, "Escalation Without Me." But when a hundred student-body presidents and editors of college newspapers, hundreds of former Peace Corps volunteers, and dozens of present Rhodes Scholars question the basic premises of the war, they should not and cannot be ignored. If called upon most will serve with courage and responsibility. Still their basic loyalty and devotion cannot obscure the fact of dissent.

These students oppose the war for the same reason that many Americans do: they recoil from the brutality and the horror of all wars, and from the particular terror of this one. But to our young people, I suspect, Vietnam is a shock as it cannot be to us. They did not know World War II, or even Korea. This is a war surrounded by rhetoric they do not understand or accept. These are the children not of the Cold War, but of the Thaw. Their memories of Communism are not of Stalin's purges and death camps or the terrible revelations of the Twentieth Party Congress, or the streets of Hungary. They see the world as one in which Communist states can be each other's deadliest enemies, or even close to the West; in which Communism is no better, but perhaps no worse, than many other evil dictatorships with which we conclude alliances.

Even as the declared foreign policy of our government is to "build bridges" to this new Communist world, youth sees us, in the name of anti-Communism, devastating the land of those we call our friends—the people of Vietnam. However the war may seem to us, they see it as one in which the largest and most powerful nation on earth is killing children (they do not care if accidentally) in a remote and insignificant land. We speak of past commitments, of the burden of past mistakes. They ask why they should now atone for mistakes made before many of them were born, be-

Opposite: The Reverend Martin Luther King, Jr., leader of the Civil Rights Movement in America. Photograph: Alfred Eisenstaedt.

331

fore almost any could vote. They see us spend billions on armaments while poverty and ignorance continue at home; they see us willing to fight a war for freedom in Vietnam, but unwilling to fight with one-hundredth the money or force or effort to secure freedom in Mississippi or Alabama or the ghettos of the North. And they see, perhaps most disturbing of all, that they themselves do not share in the power of choice on great questions that shape their lives. These, at any rate, are some of the sources of their dissent from the war. It is not difficult to understand them.

It would be tempting, but wrong, to trace all the problems of our disaffected youth to Vietnam. Nor can this problem be traced to any individual, or to any administration, or to a political party; the challenge is deeper and broader.

Consider, for example, our economy: the wondrous production machine that has made us richer, as we count, than any other people in history. It is a business economy. Indeed, Coolidge was accurate, if not notably edifying, when he said that "the business of America is business."

Yet in a recent survey only 12 percent of all college seniors hoped for a career in business, or thought such a career would be worthwhile and satisfying.

Part of the reason, surely, is that the great corporations, which are so large a part of American life, play so small a role in the solution of its vital problems—civil rights, poverty, unemployment, health, education. Of course, it may well be argued that the business of business is to make a profit, that to attempt more is to do less than its stock-holders deserve. But does such an argument have relevance, ask the young, when the annual profits of a single company, like General Motors, are greater than the gross national product of any one of 70 nations in the world?

Even more distasteful to the young, as it has been to moralists for thousands of years, is the ethic that judges all things by their profit. They have seen high officers of the nation's largest corporations engage in con-spiracies to fix prices, gathering in shabby secret meetings to steal pennies from mil-lions of Americans. They have seen us send people to jail for the possession of mari-juana, while refusing to limit the sale or advertising of cigarettes, which kill thou-sands of Americans each year. They have seen us hesitate to impose the weakest of safety standards on automobiles or require that a "respectable" store or lending com-pany tell the simple truth about the interest rate it is charging on loans. They have sensed that organized crime, an empire of corruption, venal greed and extortion, con-tinues to flourish, not only tolerated but often in alliance with significant elements in labor, business and government. It is perhaps for these reasons that many of them echo the words: "the rich He hath sent empty away."

For it is more than these abuses of the profit motive that young people reject; often it is the very materialism in our society, and what it has brought us. The suburbs are "little boxes on a hillside all made out of ticky-tacky, and they all look just the same." "Money can't buy me love," they sing. In their eyes, we too often mea-sure the worth of a man by the size of his salary or the number of his possessions. In short, they think their elders have sur-rendered community and personal values in exchange for the tailfins and trinkets that Westbrook Pegler once called "a variety of dingbats for the immature."

Nor—painful as it may be for liberals to acknowledge—are these young people en-chanted with liberal institutions. When most Americans over the age of 30 think of unions, they remember organized labor's 50-year struggle to make the workingman something more than an industrial serf. But youth looks with other eyes, and their view is very different. They see labor grown sleek and bureaucratic with power, sometimes frankly discriminatory, occasionally even corrupt and exploitative, a force not for change but for the status quo, unwilling or unable to organize new members, in-different to the men who once worked the coal mines of Appalachia, a latecomer to the struggles of the grape pickers of Cali-fornia or the farm laborers of the Missis-sippi Delta. This is a one-sided picture, without the dimensions of 50 years of struggle, and the undramatic yet vital work of labor in many parts of the nation today. But there is enough truth in some of it for us to be concerned about our children's view, and not to ignore the need for change.

Senator Robert F. Kennedy.

We have treasured our educational system as a firm pillar of the liberal community. This faith, however, is not unanimously shared. One critic has said: "Education [is] by its very nature an individual matter not geared to mass production. It does not produce people who instinctively go the same way [yet] our millions learn the same lessons and spend hours before television sets looking at exactly the same thing at exactly the same time. For one reason or another we are more and more ignoring differences, if not trying to obliterate them. We seem headed toward a standardization of the mind, what Goethe called 'the deadly commonplace that fetters us all.'" This critic was not addressing a Berkeley protest rally; it was Edith Hamilton, one of our greatest classicists.

We hear much the same from our young people—as in this comment from a student representative, speaking to a meeting of the Board of Regents of the University of California: "We have asked to be heard. You have refused. We have asked for justice. You have called it anarchy. We have asked for freedom. You have called it license. Rather than face the fear and hopelessness you have created, you have called it Communistic. You have accused us of failing to use legitimate channels. But you have closed those channels to us. You, and not us, have built a university based on distrust and dishonesty."

It is impossible to mistake the anguish of that voice, to ignore the protest of individuality against the university as corporate bureaucracy, against the dull sameness Miss Hamilton also saw. For in bureaucracy and sameness lies the denial of individuality, and the denial that human beings matter; if everyone is the same, why listen to what anyone says? If we are not prepared to listen, then men are merely numbers in statistical collections, a part of the gross national product like so many coffee cups or carpet sweepers.

The suppression of individuality—the sense that no one is listening—is even more pronounced in our politics. Television, newspapers, magazines, are a cascade of words, official statements, policies, explanations and declarations. All flow from the height of government down to the passive citizen: Who can shout up against a waterfall?

More important, the language of politics is too often insincerity, which we have perhaps too easily accepted but which to the young is particularly offensive. George Orwell wrote a generation ago: "In our time, political speech and writing are largely the defense of the indefensible. Things like the continuation of British rule in India, the Russian purges and deportations, the dropping of the atom bombs on Japan, can indeed be defended, but only by arguments which are too brutal for most people to face, and which do not square with the professed aims of political parties. Thus political language has to consist largely of euphemism, question-begging and sheer cloudy vagueness. Defenseless villages are bombarded from the air, the inhabitants driven out into the countryside, the cattle machine-gunned, the huts set on fire with incendiary bullets: this is called *pacification*. Millions of peasants are robbed of their farms and sent trudging along the roads with no more than they can carry: this is called *transfer of population* or *rectification of frontiers*. People are imprisoned for years without trial, or shot in the back of the neck or sent to die of scurvy in Arctic lumber camps: this is called *elimination of unreliable elements*. The inflated style is itself a kind of euphemism. A mass of Latin words falls upon the facts like soft snow, blurring the outlines and covering up all the details."

In this respect, politics has not changed since Orwell wrote that. And if we add to the insincerity, and the absence of dialogue, the absurdity of a politics in which elected officials find sport in joking about children bitten by rats, we can understand why so many of our young people have turned from engagement to disengagement, from politics to passivity, from hope to nihilism, from SDS to LSD.

Some adults, while admitting the disillusion of youth, discount its importance. There has always been generational conflict, they say, and it has always been resolved as the flaming youth of 20 matures into the parent, breadwinner, and community pillar of 30.

This view, in my judgment, is as wrong as it is seemingly comforting. At the most simple and direct level, the contributions of young people are sorely needed by the nation. Their work in the Peace Corps is our greatest asset in dozens of nations. Their willingness to work in VISTA, or other volunteer efforts, is critical to the solution of our domestic problems. And if young men do not run the country, they are needed to fight its battles.

More significantly, the protest of the young both reflects and worsens their elders' own lack of self-confidence. Societies confident of their wisdom and purpose are not afflicted with rebellions of the young. But if young people question our involvement in Vietnam, surely this in part reflects their elders' own uncertainty. If the young reject a life of corporate bureaucracy and suburban sameness, surely this reflects their parents' dissatisfaction with their own lives, the realization at 40 or 50 that money and status have not brought happiness or pride along with them. If the young scorn conventional politics and mock our ideals, surely this mirrors our own sense that these ideals have too often and too easily been abandoned for the sake of comfort and convenience. We have fought great wars, made great sacrifices at home and abroad, made prodigious efforts to achieve personal and national wealth, yet we are uncertain of what we have achieved—and whether we like it.

It seems that the young no longer want to exchange their innocence for responsibility; instead, many adults seek to recapture childish things. Thus when we confront the question of our disaffecting young, we confront also our own dissatisfactions and problems, as individuals and as a society.

The gap between generations will never be completely closed. But it must be spanned. The bridge across the generations is essential to the nation in the present; and more, it is the bridge to our own future—and thus in a central sense, to the very meaning of our lives. Whatever their differences with us, whatever the depth of their dissent, it is vital—for us as well as for them—that our young people feel that change is possible, that they will be heard, that the follies and cruelties of the world will yield, however grudgingly, to the sacrifices they are prepared to make. They must feel that there is a sense of possibility.

Possibility must begin with dialogue, and dialogue is more than the freedom to speak. It is the willingness to listen, and to act. To the extent that the young only mirror the dissatisfactions of their elders, they are raising matters that should concern us in any case. To the extent that they demand the observance of long-proclaimed ideals, they perform for us the ancient service of the prophets. And as they ask for opportunities to contribute to mankind and shape their own fate, they lend greater urgency to a concern that all of us share: that our lives should make a difference to ourselves and our fellow men.

To achieve the vital sense of possibility, to take up the challenge our young pose to us, we must remember that idealism and morality—in politics, and in the conduct of our lives—is not just a hope for the future, and must not be a thing of the past. Even though they seem totally estranged, many of our youth do propose to improve our society, and not abandon it. In their "free universities" in the United States, they are trying to offer exciting alternatives to conventional education. In the Netherlands the bizarre young "Provos" have elected one of their leaders to the Amsterdam city council, and have offered serious, if unorthodox, proposals to solve some of the city's dilemmas, such as air pollution and traffic congestion. We can help link the practical idealism of such youths with our tradition of moral dissent; and we should remember how difficult it must be for the young dissenters of today to have before them only the example of the beat and silent generation of the 1950's.

We may find some of their ideas impractical, some of their views overdrawn. Still, there is no question of their energy, of their ability, and above all of their honest commitment to a better and more decent world for all of us. It is for us now to make the effort, to take their causes as our causes, and to enlist them in our own, to lend to their vision and daring the insight and wisdom of our experience.

Every generation has its central concern, whether to end war, erase racial injustice, or improve the condition of the working man. Today's young people appear to have chosen for their concern the dignity of the individual human being. They demand a limitation upon excessive power. They demand a political system that preserves the sense of community among men. They demand a government that speaks directly and honestly to its citizens. We can win their commitment only by demonstrating that these goals are possible through personal effort. The possibilities are too great, the stakes too high, to bequeath to the coming generation only the prophetic lament of Tennyson:

Ah, what shall I be at fifty,
should nature keep me alive,
If I find the world so bitter
When I am but twenty-five?

HOROSCOPE FOR SLEEPERS

Do the stars influence your sleep? According to most astrologers, the planetary forces that shape your days are equally busy at night. Your dreams, sleeping habits, and the troubles that keep you tossing in bed are charted by your stars.

Here is a breakdown of how sleepers born under the various astrological signs spend their nights.

Capricorn (Dec. 22-Jan. 20): Capricornians are worriers. They spend hours in bed brooding over their troubles. They often mumble in their sleep. Some sleepwalk. Their dreams are frequently troubled and may involve money worries or being lost in a strange landscape. In a happy dream, they may find a fortune, but even here they become anxious that someone will appear to steal it away. President Nixon is a Capricorn. So are Elvis Presley and Loretta Young.

Aquarius (Jan. 21-Feb. 19): These are amiable, good-natured people. They dream a lot and like to talk about their dreams, which are often pleasantly romantic. They prefer dreams that are not openly sexual. Sex troubles them. They have a tendency to suffer from twitchy legs at night and should take a late-evening stroll before retiring. They often snore. Zsa Zsa Gabor, Vanessa Redgrave and Mia Farrow are Aquarius people.

Pisces (Feb. 20-March 20): Pisceans have superior minds and a very imaginative dream life. Sleeping is pleasurable, and they enjoy lying in bed at night and in the morning. At the same time, they are often troubled by nightmares. Ferocious animals or dangerous people pursue them in their sleep. Part of the problem may be that Pisceans have a tendency to eat and drink too much—especially when they are emotionally troubled—and this can cause indigestion and bad dreams. Elizabeth Taylor, Peter Fonda and Liza Minnelli were born under this sign.

Aries (March 21-April 20): Arians are highly imaginative and frequently become artists and inventors. Sometimes they get their best ideas while asleep. They dream incredible adventures, filled with smells and colors. They sometimes laugh in their sleep. Arians are hyperactive and often sexually demanding, which can be exhausting for the mate who may need more sleep. Omar Sharif was born under the sign of Aries as were David Frost and Steve McQueen.

Taurus (April 21-May 21): These are sensual, theatrical people. Their dreams are imaginative and dramatic, expressing many of the things they don't express when they are awake. They enjoy the dreams where they are applauded, dread the ones in which people hiss and boo them. Taurus people delight in good food and tend to be overweight. They should use firm mattresses to avoid back trouble. Barbra Streisand is a Taurean as are Carol Burnett and Albert Finney.

Gemini (May 22-June 21): These are restless people who frequently toss about in bed at night. As youngsters, they suffer from nightmares. As adults, they are afflicted with insomnia, often the result of too many pills or stimulants or resentment over what they feel is "wasted" time in bed. Gemini people include Bob Dylan, Paul McCartney, Joe Namath and Peggy Lee.

Cancer (June 22-July 23): Cancerians are attached to their family and frequently dream about their parents or the old family house. They are often shy and won't talk about their dreams unless someone draws them out. They tend to store up grievances from the day, and this produces troubled sleep. When insomnia hits, they raid the refrigerator. Happy Cancerians dream about inheriting a fortune so they won't have to go off to work in the morning. Unhappy ones have nightmares of their home being invaded by criminals or eaten by termites. Ringo Starr is a Cancer. So are Lena Horne and Bill Cosby.

Leo (July 24-August 23): They have fantastic dreams and love to talk about them. But their hectic daytime life can sometimes lead to a troubled sleep. A typical Leo nightmare—being locked outside the house or apartment without any clothing on. Jackie Onassis, Mae West, and Dustin Hoffman are Leos.

Virgo (August 24-Sept. 23): These are the computer minds. They like to go to bed at the same time every night, rise at the same hour every morning. The only dreams they remember are the ones in which someone criticizes them or they forget to pay a bill. A crossword puzzle or perusing the closing stock market quotations can relax them for the evening. Lyndon Johnson is a Virgo as are Sophia Loren and Lauren Bacall.

Libra (Sept. 24-Oct. 23): Libra people seem to be easy-going, but there is a lot of tension beneath that pleasant manner. Librans tend to have complex dreams aswarm with Freudian symbols. They often dream about family members or office associates as if they were father figures. They enjoy sleeping a lot and like to lie in bed in the morning. Brigitte Bardot and Julie Andrews are Librans.

Scorpio (Oct. 24-Nov. 23): It's sex, sex, sex with Scorpio people. Sex fills their dreams. They often dream of flying and soaring. They also have dreams in which they are jealous or envious of others. Spiro Agnew was born under this sign. So were Richard Burton and Burt Lancaster.

Sagittarius (Nov. 24-Dec. 23): These are healthy, well-balanced people. They dream about things like sports or traveling. They laugh a lot in their sleep, too. High living sometimes cuts down on their sleep time, but they seem to manage on less sleep than most. Jane Fonda and Frank Sinatra are Sagittarians.

BY BOB GAINES

WHAT I HAVE LEARNED FROM CRISIS AND DEFEAT

Richard M. Nixon

The number of crises a man has been through is relatively unimportant; what counts is what he learns from them and how he applies what he has learned in one to the next crisis.

The major crises of John F. Kennedy's administration are a case in point. During the Bay of Pigs disaster, the new President learned about the dependence of expert advice, the need to exercise enough power to guarantee success, and the requirement of leadership to assume responsibility for failure.

At the next major crisis, the Cuban missile confrontation with Khrushchev, the lessons of the Bay of Pigs served him in good stead. The President's ability to understand the proper use of power learned tragically at the start of his term led to what was undoubtedly his finest hour in turning back an unacceptable threat to our security.

The crises of the Eisenhower years, and of the Kennedy administration, were on the whole short-term moments of tension; they were resolved one way or another with national leadership strengthened.

But with the Johnson-Humphrey administration, the nature of crisis changed. The remarkable characteristic of the crises of today is their continuity—they have moved in, it seems, to stay. Let us examine some of them:

1. The continuing crisis in Vietnam. The decision to rise to this crisis was, in my view, the right decision; the method of meeting it was wrong. We frittered away our power through piecemeal escalation that locked us in a long land war in Asia; we had no global strategy to induce the Soviet Union to stop making it possible for the war to go on. And so that crisis has dragged on for years.

2. The crisis of the American city. A welfare philosophy tuned to the 'Thirties that overlooks the need for human dignity, combined with the frustration of unfulfilled promises, has led to riots and sustained civil disorder. The two-day crisis of a riot led to the summer-long crises of 1966 and 1967 and to the year-round crisis of today.

3. The crisis of the American dollar. A policy of heavy government spending has led to a worldwide loss of confidence in the American dollar—endangering jobs and hurting most those on fixed incomes. And this crisis is not being resolved, as the cost of living rises at an ever-faster rate.

4. The crisis of crime. As the forces of

Richard M. Nixon

justice were hampered by court decisions that put the scales of individual liberty and public protection out of balance, crime in America has increased by 55 percent—and this crisis is getting worse every day.

Add to these the growing crises of housing, of pollution, of inadequate education, and a picture emerges of government by

⌖⌖⌖⌖⌖⌖⌖⌖⌖⌖⌖⌖⌖⌖⌖⌖⌖⌖⌖⌖⌖⌖⌖⌖

GLOSSARY OF NURSERY TERMS
By Suzanne Douglass

Crib: *A rocking conveyance that travels by caster*
And bumps into walls and gouges out plaster.

Blanket: *A satin-bound cover that warms the spot*
At the foot of the bed where the baby is not.

Scale: *Where baby wiggles and screams with alarm*
And mother will wind up by weighing her arm.

Playpen: *The most useful item beyond any doubt;*
To relax, just climb in it and shut baby out.

⌖⌖⌖⌖⌖⌖⌖⌖⌖⌖⌖⌖⌖⌖⌖⌖⌖⌖⌖⌖⌖⌖⌖⌖

crisis, of "crash programs" that only lead to crashing hopes.

The new President cannot be expected to lead an administration of serenity and calm, of no crisis. Too many events press in upon us from abroad to hope for that; the momentum and ferment of change at home clearly means that the "revolution of rising expectations" will cause crises for us at home as well.

But something can be done to alleviate the *continuity* of crisis, the atmosphere of crisis, that pervades American life today.

We need not wait for explosions in our cities to begin realistic programs that restore self-respect to the poor and open up opportunity for the jobless man who wants to work. We need not wait for infiltration and invasion abroad to practice the kind of preventive diplomacy that averts crisis rather than responds to crisis; we need not wait until inflation backs us to the wall to start to get our economic house in order.

Some crisis is unavoidable, and proves a test for leadership; some crisis is healthy, when it snaps us out of our lethargy; but crisis cannot be allowed to become the American way of life. A national crisis is a shock to the body politic. Too many shocks, especially long-sustained shocks, drain a nation of its energy; it can cause a national punchiness, and, even worse, cause a rebellion against creative change and progress.

There are more than enough "natural shocks that flesh is heir to"—crises that cannot be avoided—for us to add to them by lack of foresight or a willingness to act in time. This may disappoint those who are attracted by the excitement of high drama, but the best way to meet a crisis is to anticipate it and avoid it. Those who ignore impending crisis are condemned to live through it. The reader will judge for himself how the writer met unavoidable crises in the past, how they affected him and what he learned from them. My own attitude toward crisis is best expressed in the way the word "crisis" is written in the Chinese language. Two characters are combined to form the word: one brush stroke stands for "danger" and the other character stands for "opportunity."

All too often we concentrate only on the danger presented by a crisis. The fears of mankind go with those who recognize the danger; but the hopes of mankind go with those who seize the opportunity.

THE FORDS

Candice Bergen

In August 1974 America was ready for an affair. The lucky guy was Gerald Ford. In fact, so ready and willing were we to hail our new chief that when we learned that he made his own breakfast, we were delirious. Never before had so much been made over an English muffin. So eager were we at that time that anyone, short of Attila the Hun, would have seemed like Mr. Wonderful. But Gerald Ford won our affections not by default, but because the new President seemed to be just the sort of man we should

"I know all about the birds and bees, Dad. What I really want to know is how do I get to be a corporation president?"

be getting involved with after a disastrous last marriage: sincere and sensible, simple and straight-shooting.

In the first rush of romance, America was acting like a gay divorcee. Even the press reported the reaction in romantic terms, calling Ford's first few weeks in the White House a "honeymoon." We were fairly giddy with the prospects. Till President Ford's pardon of Richard M. Nixon. Then, suddenly, the honeymoon was over.

Perhaps not. People are saying the pardon may be reviewed differently in the future, and despite unpopular energy proposals, a recession economy and severe budgets, President Ford seems to be regaining our reluctant affection.

My knowledge of Washington has largely been based on participation in Democratic Party and anti-war functions. Most of Republican Gerald Ford's Congressional votes were consistently cast against all forms of liberal legislation. On the issues, we're at odds. Yet, through the media, I found Gerald Ford and his family personable and sympathetic. If this seems unprincipled, call me spineless. Life no longer seems to me a question of good guys and bad guys. It's just not that simple.

I wanted to meet Gerald Ford and I wanted to meet his wife, Betty. Like most of us, I had never met a First Family, and like some of us, I had never been inside the White House. Thanks to the Fords, now I have.

My escort around the White House was 28-year-old David Kennerly, the President's Official Photographer, who showed me into the Oval Office and introduced me to the President so quickly that I was in shock. I couldn't believe being in the White House, much less the Oval Office, not to mention meeting the President and his golden retriever, Liberty. A few photographs later and we were gone—on our way upstairs to see the First Lady.

I don't care who you are—the White House is overwhelming. Secret Service men are at each and every entry, planted firm like thick potted palms, and you find yourself saluting posts and pillars, saying "Yessir, Your Lordship" to floor lamps. I expected it would all look familiar from film and photographs or simply from being inscribed on my cultural subconscious, but I was stunned by how beautiful I found it to be. It is a breathtaking and surprisingly personal place, warm and welcome, streaming with sunlight, filled with flowers, redolent of the past.

We happen upon Mrs. Ford crouching in front of the television set in the West Sitting Hall, wearing a ruffled, pastel robe. In one hand she holds a bottle of astringent; in the other a piece of cotton. Intently watching the big tennis match between Rod Laver and Jimmy Connors on TV, she looks up, surprised and smiling, and explains that she was cleaning her face but got waylaid by the tennis on her way in to get dressed.

She emerges later, trim and tailored in a camel knit dress.

I ask if it's true that she sees the President more now than she did when he was in Congress.

"His nature is to work incessantly," she says, "but now, with the Oval Office so close by, I do see him more—and he doesn't travel like when he was in Congress or when he was Vice President. Sometimes I stand here at this window because it looks directly onto his office. Only I wish that tree weren't in the way."

When she learns this is my first time in the White House, she offers me a personal tour.

"I'm trying to learn as much about the history of the White House as I can. I have learned a little but there's so much to know. There's a story behind every piece. It's fascinating learning, but it's hard to find the time. If I take people around it helps me to remember."

I remark that I can't imagine living in the White House—the hugeness, the splendor of it all.

Mrs. Ford nods wryly. "Um hum," she says. "We left an eight-room house with a pool for a three-room apartment."

I hadn't thought of it that way, but it's true. Except for the First Family's corner living area on the second floor and Susan Ford's bedroom and the guest bedrooms on the third, the White House is open for tours six days a week. There is never any privacy.

The next day Mr. Ford flew to Atlanta for one night. I was allowed to accompany the Presidential party. We landed in a rainstorm. At the bottom of the steps, the President was greeted by a welcome committee that included Miss Georgia, whose laminated pageboy wouldn't wilt, even as she stood in the pouring rain.

The route into the city and to the Regency Hyatt Hotel was cleared of traffic and the Presidential motorcade included five motorcycle police, two police cars, a helicopter, the Presidential limousine (which had been flown down ahead of time), a Secret Service car, a control car and a trail of others. The President held a press conference, then had a working dinner with a group of Southern governors.

Gerald Ford has been described by satirist Gore Vidal as the man in horror movies who comes running up shouting that the monster is attacking. Comedian Mort Sahl characterized him as the man at Safeway who okays your check.

"He'll charm you," a newspaperman warned me. And the President did.

The overwhelming impression one gets from Gerald Ford is that he is a decent man doing what he believes is right. Whether his beliefs are good for America remains to be seen. But we're hardly suffering from a surplus of decent men these days. I found the Fords nice, easy, honest people. And for now, maybe that's enough.

The President of the United States and the First Lady.

*Right: Country airs in Giorgio di Sant'An-
gelo's easy-moving sashed shirtdress awash
with field flowers and blue horizons. In
jersey of Qiana nylon.*

*Left: Adrift in the lily pads on a wistful
afternoon wearing Leo Narducci's nostalgic posy print. Cape-sleeved dress has a
fitted bodice and a skirt cut softly on the
bias. A bright-red poppy is pinned at the
neckline. In Qiana georgette by Gianni
Cereda.*

The Dresses
That Flower Year Round

SPENDING YOUR MONEY

Sylvia Porter

Q: We have invested quite heavily in common stocks on the theory that stock prices have been rising faster than the cost of living and that stocks, therefore, are a good "hedge against inflation." But with the inflation we have now, how much of a hedge *are* stocks today?

A: Obviously, there are no guarantees for the stock market. But if "what is past is prologue," the pace of the rise in common stocks prices should, *over the long range,* outrun the rate of rise in the cost of living. A major survey of stock prices and the cost of living over the past 94 years shows that living costs have risen in 62 percent of the 10-year periods and in 77 percent of the 20-year periods. Stock prices have matched or bettered increases in the cost of living in 69 percent of all 10-year periods since 1871, and in 89 percent of all 20-year periods.

Dividends, too, have kept well ahead of inflation over the long haul, increasing in fully 73 percent of the one-year inflation periods since 1871; in 94 percent of the 10-year periods, and in all of the 20- and 30-year spans.

However, you must abide by the following fundamental guidelines: select investments wisely; watch them carefully; and be able and willing to hold them through the difficult times.

Assuming you obey these basic rules, your stocks should give you a hedge against inflation in the long run.

Q: My brother-in-law has just announced his intention to divorce my sister. Emotional considerations aside, I think he doesn't realize how much a divorce will cost him. Is there any rule of thumb on the financial cost of this decision to him?

A: The divorce will cost him at least twice as much as he thinks. He should be prepared to cut his standard of living in half.

Q: Our daughter and son-in-law, now in their late twenties, are agonizing over the question of whether to buy their first home now and pay an interest rate of more than 9½ percent on a mortgage, or whether to wait until the interest rate drops. What's your advice?

A: My advice would depend on how fast the prices of homes in the area in which they want to live are rising. If the prices of houses are rising rapidly, a drop of ½ or even 1 percent in the mortgage interest rate in the next year or so easily might be canceled out.

Specifically, a price rise of 3 percent on the house would just about erase the savings from a ½ percent drop in the interest on a 20-year mortgage. A price rise of 5

percent would just about cancel out an interest-rate drop of a full one percent. And these points are clear: the long-term trend of housing prices is up; there is little probability of a return to the "old" mortgage rates of 4–5 percent in the foreseeable future.

Q: Is it true that an illegitimate child cannot get Social Security benefits if the child's parent becomes disabled?

A: Not long ago the U.S. Supreme Court

declared unconstitutional such a provision of the Social Security law—a clause which denied benefits to a wage earner's illegitimate children who were born after the onset of the disability. The grounds for the decision were that refusal of benefits constituted a denial of equal protection under the law.

Q: I'm wondering how my father, who is due to retire next year, will manage on just 60 percent of his present income. Have you

any suggestions we can pass on to him?

A: Your father might want to consider taking a part-time job. Remind him that under the new Social Security amendments he is allowed to collect full benefits, provided he does not earn more than $1,500 a year. He can cut housing expenses by reducing his mortgage, thus saving on interest costs; by closing off extra rooms to save on fuel bills; and by renting part of his house, if it's large enough. He can save on food by pooling his money with other retired people to buy in bulk. He can cut his clothing costs by shopping during clearances and choosing clothes that combine with his present wardrobe. And if he needs a car, he should buy a small one to save on gas. In short, he must learn how to make a nickel do a dime's work.

Q: How can a working mother be sure that her savings are inherited by her children if she should die before her husband does?

A: She can—and should—draw up her own will, stating her wishes on how her own money should be distributed. Your family lawyer is your best guide on how to go about this.

Q: My husband just lost his job because of a company merger. He is only 55 years old, but he is finding it awfully hard to get another job anywhere near the status of his old one. Employers tell him that because of his age it would not be economical for them to invest in retraining.

A: The fact is, Labor Department studies show, that the average 55-year-old stays on a new job longer than a 25-year-old, that absenteeism is considerably lower in the older age group, and that productivity is at least equal in each age bracket. These facts should be brought to the attention of any employer who insists on outright discrimination on the basis of your husband's age.

Opposite:
THE GREAT GATSBY: It's a novel, it's a movie, it's a look—it's our recurring and incurable fascination with a romantic madcap world that perhaps never quite was and never again will be. On the screen, Mia Farrow and Robert Redford play Daisy and Jay, the ill-starred lovers who lived in F. Scott Fitzgerald's fairy-tale Twenties before the Great Crash.

> To do for the world more than the world does for you—that is success.
> **HENRY FORD**

A CHRISTMAS MEMORY

Truman Capote

Imagine a morning in late November. A coming of winter morning more than twenty years ago. Consider the kitchen of a spreading old house in a country town. A great black stove is its main feature; but there is also a big round table and a fireplace with two rocking chairs placed in front of it. Just today the fireplace commenced its seasonal roar.

A woman with shorn white hair is standing at the kitchen window. She is wearing tennis shoes and a shapeless gray sweater over a summery calico dress. She is small and sprightly, like a bantam hen, but, due to a long youthful illness, her shoulders are pitifully hunched. Her face is remarkable—not unlike Lincoln's, craggy like that, and tinted by sun and wind; but it is delicate too, finely boned, and her eyes are sherry-colored and timid. "Oh my," she exclaims, her breath smoking the windowpane, "it's fruitcake weather!"

The person to whom she is speaking is myself. I am seven; she is sixty-something. We are cousins, very distant ones, and we have lived together—well, as long as I can remember. Other people inhabit the house, relatives; and though they have power over us, and frequently make us cry, we are not, on the whole, too much aware of them. We are each other's best friend. She calls me Buddy, in memory of a boy who was formerly her best friend. The other Buddy died in the 1880's, when she was still a child. She is still a child.

"I knew it before I got out of bed," she says, turning away from the window with a purposeful excitement in her eyes. "The courthouse bell sounded so cold and clear. And there were no birds singing; they've gone to warmer country, yes indeed. Oh, Buddy, stop stuffing biscuit and fetch our buggy. Help me find my hat. We've thirty cakes to bake."

It's always the same: a morning arrives in November, and my friend, as though officially inaugurating the Christmas time of year that exhilarates her imagination and fuels the blaze of her heart, announces: "It's fruitcake weather! Fetch our buggy. Help me find my hat."

The hat is found, a straw cartwheel corsaged with velvet roses out-of-doors has faded: it once belonged to a more fashionable relative. Together, we guide our buggy, a dilapidated baby carriage, out to the garden and into a grove of pecan trees. The buggy is mine; that is, it was bought for me when I was born. It is made of wicker, rather unraveled, and the wheels wobble like a drunkard's legs. But it is a faithful object; springtimes, we take it to the woods and fill it with flowers, herbs, wild fern for our porch pots; in the summer, we pile it with picnic paraphernalia and sugar-cane fishing poles and roll it down to the edge of a creek; it has its winter uses, too: as a truck for hauling firewood from the yard to the kitchen, as a warm bed for Queenie, our tough little orange and white rat terrier who has survived distemper and two rattlesnake bites. Queenie is trotting beside it now.

Three hours later we are back in the kitchen hulling a heaping buggyload of windfall pecans. Our backs hurt from gathering them: how hard they were to find (the main crop having been shaken off the trees and sold by the orchard's owners, who are not us) among the concealing leaves, the frosted, deceiving grass. Caarackle! A cheery crunch, scraps of miniature thunder sound as the shells collapse and the golden mound of sweet oily ivory meat mounts in the milk-glass bowl. Queenie begs to taste, and now and again my friend sneaks her a mite, though insisting we deprive ourselves. "We mustn't, Buddy. If we start, we won't stop. And there's scarcely enough as there is. For thirty cakes." The kitchen is growing dark. Dusk turns the window into a mirror: our reflections mingle with the rising moon as we work by the fireside in the firelight. At last, when the moon is quite high, we toss the final hull into the fire and, with joined sighs, watch it catch flame. The buggy is empty, the bowl is brimful.

We eat our supper (cold biscuits, bacon, blackberry jam) and discuss tomorrow. Tomorrow the kind of work I like best begins: buying. Cherries and citron, ginger and vanilla and canned Hawaiian pineapple, rinds and raisins and walnuts and whiskey and oh, so much flour, butter, so many eggs, spices, flavorings: why, we'll need a pony to pull the buggy home.

But before these purchases can be made, there is the question of money. Neither of us has any. Except for skinflint sums persons in the house occasionally provide (a dime is considered very big money); or what we earn ourselves from various activities: holding rummage sales, selling buckets of handpicked blackberries, jars of homemade jam and apple jelly and peach preserves, rounding up flowers for funerals and weddings. Once we won seventy-ninth prize, five dollars, in a national football contest. Not that we know a fool thing about football. It's just that we enter any contest we hear about: at the moment our hopes are centered on the fifty-thousand-dollar Grand Prize being offered to name a new brand of coffee (we suggested "A.M."; and, after some hesitation, for my friend thought it perhaps sacrilegious, the slogan "A.M.! Amen!"). To tell the truth, our only *really* profitable enterprise was the Fun and Freak Museum we conducted in a back-yard woodshed two summers ago. The Fun was a stereopticon with slide views of Washington and New York lent us by a relative who had been to those places (she was furious when she discovered why we'd borrowed it); the Freak was a three-legged biddy chicken hatched by one of our own hens. Everybody hereabouts wanted to see that biddy: we charged grown-ups a nickel, kids two cents. And took in a good twenty dollars before the museum shut down due to the decease of the main attraction.

But one way and another we do each year accumulate Christmas savings, a Fruitcake Fund. These moneys we keep hidden in an ancient bead purse under a loose board under the floor under a chamber pot under my friend's bed. The purse is seldom removed from this safe location except to make a deposit, or, as happens every Saturday, a withdrawal; for on Saturdays I am allowed ten cents to go to the picture show. My friend has never been to a picture show, nor does she intend to: "I'd rather hear you tell the story, Buddy. That way I can imagine it more. Besides, a person my age shouldn't squander their eyes. When the Lord comes, let me see him clear." In addition to never having seen a movie, she has never: eaten in a restaurant, traveled more than five miles from home, received or sent a telegram, read anything except funny papers and the Bible, worn cosmetics, cursed, wished someone harm, told a lie on purpose, let a hungry dog go hungry. Here are a few things she has done, does do: killed with a hoe the biggest rattlesnake ever seen in this county (sixteen rattles), dip snuff (secretly), tame hummingbirds (just try it) till they balance on her finger, tell ghost stories (we both believe in ghosts) so tingling they chill you in July, talk to herself, take walks in the rain, grow the prettiest japonicas in town, know the recipe for every sort of old-time Indian cure, including a magical wart-remover.

Now, with supper finished, we retire to the room in a faraway part of the house where my friend sleeps in a scrap-quilt-covered iron bed painted rose pink, her favorite color. Silently, wallowing in the pleasures of conspiracy, we take the bead purse from its secret place and spill its contents on the scrap quilt. Dollar bills, tightly rolled and green as May buds. Somber fifty-cent pieces, heavy enough to weight a dead

Rudolf Nureyev in The Royal Ballet spectacular "Romeo and Juliet."

man's eyes. Lovely dimes, the liveliest coin, the one that really jingles. Nickels and quarters, worn smooth as creek pebbles. But mostly a hateful heap of bitter-odored pennies. Last summer others in the house contracted to pay us a penny for every twenty-five flies we killed. Oh, the carnage of August: the flies that flew to heaven! Yet it was not work in which we took pride. And, as we sit counting pennies, it is as though we were back tabulating dead flies. Neither of us has a head for figures; we count slowly, lose track, start again. According to her calculations, we have $12.73. According to mine, exactly $13. "I do hope you're wrong, Buddy. We can't mess around with thirteen. The cakes will fall. Or put somebody in the cemetery. Why, I wouldn't dream of getting out of bed on the thirteenth." This is true: she always spends thirteenths in bed. So, to be on the safe side, we subtract a penny and toss it out the window.

Of the ingredients that go into our fruitcakes, whiskey is the most expensive, as well as the hardest to obtain: State laws forbid its sale. But everybody knows you can buy a bottle from Mr. Haha Jones. And the next day, having completed our more prosaic shopping, we set out for Mr. Haha's business address, a "sinful" (to quote public opinion) fish-fry and dancing café down by the river. We've been there before, and on the same errand; but in previous years our dealings have been with Haha's wife, an iodine-dark Indian woman with brassy peroxided hair and a dead-tired disposition. Actually, we've never laid eyes on her husband, though we've heard that he's an Indian too. A giant with razor scars across his cheeks. They call him Haha because he's so gloomy, a man who never laughs. As we approach his café (a large log cabin festooned inside and out with chains of garish-gay naked lightbulbs and standing by the river's muddy edge under the shade of river trees where moss drifts through the branches like gray mist) our steps slow down. Even Queenie stops prancing and sticks close by. People have been murdered in Haha's café. Cut to pieces. Hit on the head. There's a case coming up in court next month. Naturally these goings-on happen at night when the colored lights cast crazy patterns and the victrola wails. In the daytime Haha's is shabby and deserted. I knock at the door, Queenie barks, my friend calls: "Mrs. Haha, ma'am? Anyone to home?"

Footsteps. The door opens. Our hearts overturn. It's Mr. Haha Jones himself! And he *is* a giant; he *does* have scars; he *doesn't* smile. No, he glowers at us through Satan-tilted eyes and demands to know: "What you want with Haha?"

For a moment we are too paralyzed to tell. Presently my friend half-finds her voice, a whispery voice at best: "If you please, Mr. Haha, we'd like a quart of your finest whiskey."

His eyes tilt more. Would you believe it? Haha is smiling! Laughing, too. "Which one of you is a drinkin' man?"

"It's for making fruitcakes, Mr. Haha. Cooking."

This sobers him. He frowns. "That's no way to waste good whiskey." Nevertheless, he retreats into the shadowed café and

seconds later appears carrying a bottle of daisy yellow unlabeled liquor. He demonstrates its sparkle in the sunlight and says: "Two dollars."

We pay him with nickels and dimes and pennies. Suddenly, jangling the coins in his hand like a fistful of dice, his face softens. "Tell you what," he proposes, pouring the money back into our bead purse, "just send me one of them fruitcakes instead."

"Well," my friend remarks on our way home, "there's a lovely man. We'll put an extra cup of raisins in *his* cake."

The black stove, stoked with coal and firewood, glows like a lighted pumpkin. Eggbeaters whirl, spoons spin round in bowls of butter and sugar, vanilla sweetens the air, ginger spices it: melting, nose-tingling odors saturate the kitchen, suffuse the house, drift out to the world on puffs of chimney smoke. In four days our work is done. Thirty-one cakes, dampened with whiskey, bask on windowsills and shelves.

Who are they for?

Friends. Not necessarily neighbor friends: indeed, the larger share are intended for persons we've met maybe once, perhaps not at all. People who've struck our fancy. Like President Roosevelt. Like the Reverend and Mrs. J. C. Lucey, Baptist missionaries to Borneo who lectured here last winter. Or the little knife grinder who comes through town twice a year. Or Abner Packer, the driver of the six o'clock bus from Mobile, who exchanges waves with us every day as he passes in a dust-cloud whoosh. Or the young Wistons, a California couple whose car one afternoon broke down outside the house and who spent a pleasant hour chatting with us on the porch (young Mr. Wiston snapped our picture, the only one we've ever had taken). Is it because my friend is shy with everyone *except* strangers that these strangers, and merest acquaintances, seem to us our truest friends? I think yes. Also, the scrapbooks we keep of thank-you's on White House stationery, time-to-time communications from California and Borneo, the knife grinder's penny postcards, make us feel connected to eventful worlds beyond the kitchen with its view of a sky that stops.

Now a nude December fig branch grates against the window. The kitchen is empty, the cakes are gone; yesterday we carted the last of them to the post office, where the cost of stamps turned our purse inside out. We're broke. That rather depresses me, but my friend insists on celebrating—with two inches of whiskey left in Haha's bottle. Queenie has a spoonful in a bowl of coffee (she likes her coffee chicory-flavored and strong). The rest we divide between a pair of jelly glasses. We're both quite awed at the prospect of drinking straight whiskey; the taste of it brings screwed-up expressions and sour shudders. But by and by we begin to sing, the two of us singing different songs simultaneously. I don't know the words to mine, just: *Come on along, come on along, to the darktown strutters' ball.* But I can dance: that's what I mean to be, a tap dancer in the movies. My dancing shadow rollicks on the walls; our voices rock the chinaware; we giggle: as if unseen hands were tickling us. Queenie rolls on her back, her paws plow the air, something like a

grin stretches her black lips. Inside myself, I feel warm and sparky as those crumbling logs, carefree as the wind in the chimney. My friend waltzes round the stove, the hem of her poor calico skirt pinched between her fingers as though it were a party dress: *Show me the way to go home,* she sings, her tennis shoes squeaking on the floor. *Show me the way to go home.*

Enter: two relatives. Very angry. Potent with eyes that scold, tongues that scald. Listen to what they have to say, the words tumbling together into a wrathful tune: "A child of seven! whiskey on his breath! are you out of your mind? feeding a child of seven! must be loony! road to ruination! remember Cousin Kate? Uncle Charlie? Uncle Charlie's brother-in-law? shame! scandal! humiliation! kneel, pray, beg the Lord!"

Queenie sneaks under the stove. My friend gazes at her shoes, her chin quivers, she lifts her skirt and blows her nose and runs to her room. Long after the town has gone to sleep and the house is silent except for the chimings of clocks and the sputter of fading fires, she is weeping into a pillow already as wet as a widow's handkerchief.

"Don't cry," I say, sitting at the bottom of her bed and shivering despite my flannel nightgown that smells of last winter's cough syrup, "don't cry," I beg, teasing her toes, tickling her feet, "you're too old for that."

"It's because," she hiccups, "I *am* too old. Old and funny."

"Not funny. Fun. More fun than anybody. Listen. If you don't stop crying you'll be so tired tomorrow we can't go cut a tree."

She straightens up. Queenie jumps on the bed (where Queenie is not allowed) to lick her cheeks. "I know where we'll find pretty trees, Buddy. And holly, too. With berries big as your eyes. It's way off in the woods. Farther than we've ever been. Papa used to bring us Christmas trees from there: carry them on his shoulder. That's fifty years ago. Well, now: I can't wait for morning."

Morning. Frozen rime lusters the grass; the sun, round as an orange and orange as hot-weather moons, balances on the horizon, burnishes the silvered winter woods. A wild turkey calls. A renegade hog grunts in the undergrowth. Soon, by the edge of knee-deep, rapid-running water, we have to abandon the buggy. Queenie wades the stream first, paddles across barking complaints at the swiftness of the current, the pneumonia-making coldness of it. We follow, holding our shoes and equipment (a hatchet, a burlap sack) above our heads. A mile more: of chastising thorns, burs and briers that catch at our clothes; of rusty pine needles brilliant with gaudy fungus and molted feathers. Here, there, a flash, a flutter, an ecstasy of shrillings remind us that not all the birds have flown south. Always, the path unwinds through lemony sun pools and pitch vine tunnels. Another creek to cross: a disturbed armada of speckled trout froths the water round us, and frogs the size of plates practice belly flops; beaver workmen are building a dam. On the farther shore, Queenie shakes herself and trembles. My friend shivers, too: not with cold but with enthusiasm. One of her hat's ragged roses sheds a petal as she lifts her head and inhales the pine-heavy air. "We're almost there; can you smell it, Buddy?" she says, as though we were approaching an ocean.

And, indeed, it is a kind of ocean. Scented acres of holiday trees, prickly-leafed holly. Red berries shiny as Chinese bells: black crows swoop upon them screaming. Having stuffed our burlap sacks with enough greenery and crimson to garland a dozen windows, we set about choosing a tree. "It should be," muses my friend, "twice as tall as a boy. So a boy can't steal the star." The one we pick is twice as tall as me. A brave handsome brute that survives thirty hatchet strokes before it keels with a creaking rending cry. Lugging it like a kill, we commence the long trek out. Every few yards we abandon the struggle, sit down and pant. But we have the strength of triumphant huntsmen; that and the tree's virile, icy perfume revive us, goad us on. Many compliments accompany our sunset return along the red clay road to town; but my friend is sly and noncommittal when passers-by praise the treasure perched on our buggy: what a fine tree and where did it come from? "Yonder ways," she murmurs vaguely. Once a car stops and the rich mill owner's lazy wife leans out and whines: "Giveya two-bits cash for that ol tree." Ordinarily my friend is afraid of saying no; but on this occasion she promptly shakes her head: "We wouldn't take a dollar." The mill owner's wife persists. "A dollar, my foot! Fifty cents. That's my last offer. Goodness, woman, you can get another one." In answer, my friend gently reflects: "I doubt it. There's never two of anything."

Home: Queenie slumps by the fire and sleeps till tomorrow, snoring loud as a human.

A trunk in the attic contains: a shoebox of ermine tails (off the opera cape of a curious lady who once rented a room in the house), coils of frazzled tinsel gone gold with age, one silver star, a brief rope of dilapidated, undoubtedly dangerous candy-like light bulbs. Excellent decorations, as far as they go, which isn't far enough: my friend wants our tree to blaze "like a Baptist window," droop with weighty snows of ornament. But we can't afford the made-in-Japan splendors at the five-and-dime. So we do what we've always done: sit for days at the kitchen table with scissors and crayons and stacks of colored paper. I make sketches and my friend cuts them out: lots of cats, fish too (because they're easy to draw), some apples, some watermelons, a few winged angels devised from saved-up sheets of Hershey-bar tin foil. We use safety pins to attach these creations to the tree; as a final touch, we sprinkle the branches with shredded cotton (picked in August for this purpose). My friend, surveying the effect, clasps her hands together. "Now honest, Buddy. Doesn't it look good enough to eat?" Queenie tries to eat an angel.

After weaving and ribboning holly wreaths for all the front windows, our next project is the fashioning of family gifts. Tie-dye scarves for the ladies, for the men a home-brewed lemon and licorice and aspirin syrup to be taken "at the first Symptoms of a Cold and after Hunting." But when it comes time for making each other's

gift, my friend and I separate to work secretly. I would like to buy her a pearl-handled knife, a radio, a whole pound of chocolate-covered cherries (we tasted some once, and she always swears: "I could live on them, Buddy, Lord yes I could—and that's not taking His name in vain"). Instead, I am building her a kite. She would like to give me a bicycle (she's said so on several million occasions: "If only I could, Buddy. It's bad enough in life to do without something you want; but confound it, what gets my goat is not being able to give somebody something you want them to have. Only one of these days I will, Buddy. Locate you a bike. Don't ask how. Steal it, maybe"). Instead, I'm fairly certain that she is building me a kite—the same as last year, and the year before: the year before that we exchanged slingshots. All of which is fine by me. For we are champion kite-

fliers who study the wind like sailors; my friend, more accomplished than I, can get a kite aloft when there isn't enough breeze to carry clouds.

Christmas Eve afternoon we scrape together a nickel and go to the butcher's to buy Queenie's traditional gift, a good gnaw-able beef bone. The bone, wrapped in funny paper, is placed high in the tree near the silver star. Queenie knows it's there. She squats at the foot of the tree staring up in a trance of greed: when bedtime arrives she refuses to budge. Her excitement is equaled by my own. I kick the covers and turn my pillow as though it were a scorching summer's night. Somewhere a rooster crows: falsely, for the sun is still on the other side of the world.

"Buddy, are you awake?" It is my friend, calling from her room, which is next to mine; and an instant later she is sitting on my bed holding a candle. "Well, I can't sleep a hoot," she declares. "My mind's jumping like a jack rabbit. Buddy, do you think Mrs. Roosevelt will serve our cake at dinner?" We huddle in the bed, and she squeezes my hand I-love-you. "Seems like your hand used to be so much smaller. I guess I hate to see you grow up. When you're grown up, will we still be friends?"

I say always. "But I feel so bad, Buddy. I wanted so bad to give you a bike. I tried to sell my cameo Papa gave me, Buddy"—she hesitates, as though embarrassed—"I made you another kite." Then I confess that I made her one, too; and we laugh. The candle burns too short to hold. Out it goes, exposing the starlight, the stars spinning at the window like a visible caroling that slowly, slowly daybreak silences. Possibly we doze; but the beginnings of dawn splash us like cold water: we're up, wide-eyed and wandering while we wait for others to waken. Quite deliberately my friend drops a kettle on the kitchen floor. I tap-dance in front of closed doors. One by one the household emerges, looking as though they'd like to kill us both; but it's Christmas, so they can't. First, a gorgeous breakfast: just everything you can imagine —from flapjacks and fried squirrel to

'Operator, could you trace this call and tell me where I am?'

hominy grits and honey-in-the-comb. Which puts everyone in a good humor except my friend and I. Frankly, we're so impatient to get at the presents we can't eat a mouthful.

Well, I'm disappointed. Who wouldn't be? With socks, a Sunday school shirt, some handkerchiefs, a hand-me-down sweater and a year's subscription to a religious magazine for children. The Little Shepherd. It makes me boil. It really does.

My friend has a better haul. A sack of Satsumas, that's her best present. She is proudest, however, of a white wool shawl knitted by her married sister. But she says her favorite gift is the kite I built her. And it is very beautiful; though not as beautiful as the one she made me, which is blue and scattered with gold and green Good Conduct stars; moreover, my name is painted on it, "Buddy."

"Buddy, the wind is blowing."

The wind is blowing, and nothing will do till we've run to a pasture below the house where Queenie has scooted to bury her bone (and where, a winter hence, Queenie will be buried, too). There, plunging through the healthy waist-high grass, we unreel our kites, feel them twitching at the string like sky fish as they swim into the

CHRISTMAS FROM THE KITCHEN

Here are a whole battery of thoroughly unlikely personages, places and other amusing creations made from the most ordinary kitchen equipment. Fishes that are spoon holders, a perfectly charming castle made from tin cups and cans, a wreath of plastic spoons pretending to be holly. To make these zany decorations you'll need a collection of dispensable objects, glue, paint and a family with a sense of humor.

The funnel couple. Cover two funnels, add paper cut-out ears, painted eyes and smiles.

Wood garden. A painted pot of flowers made with wooden cooking spoons with paper petals and leaves.

Bright blooms. Plastic-flatware wreath mixed with real holly and tied, appropriately, with dish cloth.

Santa's mug. His cap is a child's sock. Add tassel. Paint the face.

A rare bird. Two butter melters with painted wings, straws for crest.

Fish story. Two spoon holders with painted scales and tails.

Candlesticks. Funnels and bottles to stripe with colored tape, decorate with a mosaic of glued beans, paint, fill with tinted water.

Canned castle. Built from foil cups and cans with funnel turrets. Doors and windows are paper cut-outs. Painted details.

Drawings by Murray Tinkelman

wind. Satisfied, sun-warmed, we sprawl in the grass and peel Satsumas and watch our kites cavort. Soon I forget the socks and hand-me-down sweater. I'm as happy as if we'd already won the fifty-thousand-dollar Grand Prize in that coffee-naming contest.

"My, how foolish I am!" my friend cries, suddenly alert, like a woman remembering too late she has biscuits in the oven. "You know what I've always thought?" she asks in a tone of discovery, and not smiling at me but a point beyond. "I've always thought a body would have to be sick and dying before they saw the Lord. And I imagined that when He came it would be like looking at the Baptist window: pretty as colored glass with the sun pouring through, such a shine you don't know it's getting dark. And it's been a comfort: to think of that shine taking away all the spooky feeling. But I'll wager it never happens. I'll wager at the very end a body realizes the Lord has already shown Himself. That things as they are"—her hand

circles in a gesture that gathers clouds and kites and grass and Queenie pawing earth over her bone—"just what they've always seen, was seeing Him. As for me, I could leave the world with today in my eyes."

This is our last Christmas together.

Life separates us. Those who Know Best decide that I belong in a military school. And so follows a miserable succession of bugle-blowing prisons, grim reveille-ridden summer camps. I have a new home too. But it doesn't count. Home is where my friend is, and there I never go.

And there she remains, puttering around the kitchen. Alone with Queenie. Then alone. ("Buddy dear," she writes in her wild hard-to-read script, "yesterday Jim Macy's horse kicked Queenie bad. Be thankful she didn't feel much. I wrapped her in a Fine Linen sheet and rode her in the buggy down to Simpson's pasture where she can be with all her Bones . . ."). For a few Novembers she continues to bake her fruitcakes single-handed; not as many, but

some: and, of course, she always sends me "the best of the batch." Also, in every letter she encloses a dime wadded in toilet paper: "See a picture show and write me the story."

But gradually in her letters she tends to confuse me with her other friend, the Buddy who died in the 1880's; more and more thirteenths are not the only days she stays in bed: a morning arrives in November, a leafless, birdless coming of winter morning, when she cannot rouse herself to exclaim: "Oh my, it's fruitcake weather!"

And when that happens, I know it. A message saying so merely confirms a piece of news some secret vein had already received, severing from me an irreplaceable part of myself, letting it loose like a kite on a broken string. That is why, walking across a school campus on this particular December morning, I keep searching the sky. As if I expected to see, rather like hearts, a lost pair of kites hurrying toward heaven.

At the "Women of the Year, 1976" NBC-TV celebrations (front row, left to right) : Rita Moreno, Cicely Tyson, Bettye Caldwell*, Florence LaRue Gordon, Kate Smith, Betty Ford*, Barbara Walters, Valerie Harper, Annie Dodge Wauneka*, Petula Clark; (second row, left to right) : Betty Furness*, Sylvia Porter, Lamonte McLemore, Sheila Young, Lenore Hershey, Jill Ruckelshaus, Cindy Nelson, Micki King*, Maya Angelou*, Billie Jean King.

* In addition to those whose names are starred, the other "Women of the Year," not pictured here, are: Ella T. Grasso, Shirley Hufstedler, Margaret Mead, and Beverly Sills.

ACKNOWLEDGMENTS

The editor wishes to thank the management and staff of the *Ladies' Home Journal* for their trust and enthusiastic support of this project from beginning to end, particularly Lenore Hershey, Joyce Kuh, Phyllis Levy, and Ed Morehouse. Sincere thanks are also due to all my publishing colleagues who in various ways have been of the utmost help: Olga Zaferatos, Lewis P. Lewis, Gael Dillon, Jay Holme, Christopher Holme, Peter Grant, Mary Velthoven, Carol Sue Judy, and David Bell.

PICTURE CREDITS

INDEX